W9-CTC-031

GEORGE V

BY THE SAME AUTHOR

The Letters of Edwin Lutyens (co-editor with Clayre Percy)
Fox Hunting: A History
The Letters of Arthur Balfour and Lady Elcho
(co-editor with Clayre Percy)
The Young Disraeli
The Architect and his Wife: A Life of Edwin Lutyens
Bertie: A Life of Edward VII
Victoria: Queen, Matriarch, Empress (Penguin Monarchs)

GEORGE V

Never a Dull Moment

JANE RIDLEY

Chatto & Windus

LONDON

1 3 5 7 9 10 8 6 4 2

Chatto & Windus, an imprint of Vintage, is part of the Penguin Random House group
of companies whose addresses can be found at global.penguinrandomhouse.com

Penguin
Random House
UK

Copyright © Jane Ridley 2021

Jane Ridley has asserted her right to be identified as the author of this
Work in accordance with the Copyright, Designs and Patents Act 1988

First published by Chatto & Windus in 2021

penguin.co.uk/vintage

A CIP catalogue record for this book is available from the British Library

ISBN 9780701188702

Lines from 'Ballade Tragique à Double Refrain' by Max Beerbohm (p. 189)
are reproduced by permission of Berlin Associates on behalf of the
Max Beerbohm Estate; lines from 'Death of George V' by John Betjeman
(p. 419) are reproduced by permission of Hodder & Stoughton.

Typeset in 10.5/12.5pt Sabon LT Std by Jouve (UK), Milton Keynes
Printed and bound in Great Britain by Clays Ltd, Elcograf S.p.A.

The authorised representative in the EEA is Penguin Random House Ireland,
Morrison Chambers, 32 Nassau Street, Dublin D02 YH68

Penguin Random House is committed to a sustainable future
for our business, our readers and our planet. This book is made
from Forest Stewardship Council® certified paper.

MIX
Paper from
responsible sources
FSC
www.fsc.org   FSC® C018179

For Toby and Humphrey

Contents

GEORGE V

Never a Dull Moment

In Search of George

The reign of King George V spans more than twenty-five of the most tumultuous and eventful years faced by any twentieth-century British sovereign. How George V managed to steer the monarchy through the perils of a constitutional crisis, the First World War, the Russian Revolution, the collapse of dynastic Europe, Irish Home Rule, strikes, Bolshevism, the rise of the Labour Party and the Great Depression – only to be out-manoeuvred by an American divorcee – is a great story and the central theme of this book. A key player in national politics, he guided his country through political crises, acting as conciliator over Home Rule and skilfully facilitating the appointment of four prime ministers at a time of party realignment. Most remarkable of all, perhaps, he nurtured the Labour Party through its rise, actively promoting the first Labour governments.

Yet this statesmanlike sovereign has been undervalued by posterity. He has been dismissed as dull and limited, a martinet overly concerned with petty details of dress and protocol. 'He *was* dull, beyond dispute,' wrote Alan (Tommy) Lascelles, 'but my God, his *reign* (politically and internationally) never had a dull moment.'[1] Having spent seven years working on George V, I disagree about the dullness. As for the reign, Lascelles was absolutely right.

In 1948 Lascelles, who was private secretary to King George VI, commissioned Harold Nicolson to write the official biography of George V. He told Nicolson: 'You will be writing a biography on the subject of a myth and will have to be mythological.'[2] Nicolson was given unrestricted access to the king's papers. He was not expected to write anything that was not true; but he was ordered to leave out anything discreditable. Silences, then, but not lies.

Nicolson wrote a magisterial biography which succeeded in its purpose of promoting the monarchy and placing it at the centre of the nation's political life. Sometimes, especially when dealing with the post-war period, he seemed to conflate the king's life with the story of British politics. But Nicolson, who was a fine biographer, had no illusions about the book. 'I have created a pure tailor's dummy,' he wrote, 'and have not tried to make him live at all, since if I did so he would appear as a stupid old bore.'[3]

Nicolson framed the king as 'the simple man with a categorical sense of duty'.[4] For seventeen years before his accession to the throne, however,

George 'did nothing at all but kill animals and stick in stamps'.[5] This was a problem for Nicolson as it undermined his careful construction of the dutiful prince. These missing years seemed to show George to be lazy and selfish, neglecting to prepare himself for kingship.

Nicolson began the research for his book by talking to the surviving members of George's household and others who had known him. 'Being "in search of George" will be fun,' he wrote.[6] The old courtiers talked very freely about the late king. The royal household was still reeling from the Abdication in 1936, and the great enigma was Queen Mary. Some said she managed her husband, others claimed that she was terrified of him and failed to confront him. Words used to describe the king were: stupid, ignorant, horrible, garrulous, simple, unimaginative; but also: loyal, modest, funny and acute.

None of this went into Nicolson's book, but he recorded the conversations in his diary. Reading Nicolson's unpublished diary and his letters to his wife Vita Sackville-West, I glimpsed for the first time the reality behind the myth of King George the Dull. 'We must not let in daylight upon magic,' warned Walter Bagehot, the Victorian constitutionalist, speaking of royalty. In the case of George V, however, letting in the daylight reveals the magic which was concealed behind the humdrum exterior.

King George V wrote his diary nearly every night of his life, slowly and laboriously forming the letters in his schoolboy handwriting, using a gold-nibbed fountain pen.[7] He recorded the time he got up, the times he ate breakfast and dinner and the time he went to bed (usually 11.30). The weather and the direction of the wind are noted, and so are his engagements and the names of the people he met. There is a lot of counting: miles walked, birds shot, cartridges fired, hands shaken, medals pinned. There are few comments, and no descriptions; no confessional nor any evidence of an inner life.

Sitting high up in the Royal Archives in the Round Tower at Windsor, I have spent many months reading and transcribing the diary. When he wanted to be, George V was a surprisingly good letter writer – succinct, entertaining and often affectionate. No one could describe the diary as a lively or enjoyable read, however. But to criticise the diary as mundane is to fail to see the point of it. King George's diary is similar to the one his father kept – a narrative of names and engagements: a royal exercise in social accounting. For the biographer the diary is indispensable; it gives a detailed chronology almost hour by hour of the king's life. And there are nuggets of humour and flashes of insight as well as invaluable detail.

When John Gore was commissioned to write a personal memoir of

George V in 1938, the royal librarian Owen Morshead made the diary available to him. The king had been dead for only two years, and Queen Mary objected that 'she never meant the diary of George V to see the light for years, if ever', though she changed her mind and co-operated when she saw Gore's manuscript.[8] He used the diaries to construct an image of the king as a saintly paragon: 'frank, simple, honest and good' – too good perhaps to be interesting.[9]

George was a second son. Eddy, Duke of Clarence, the elder brother, died suddenly when George was twenty-six, leaving George the unexpected heir. If Eddy hadn't died, George would have grown up to become a minor prince, quietly pursuing a career in the navy, making an arranged marriage to a suitable princess and ending by serving in an office such as governor-general of Canada, as his uncle the Duke of Connaught was to do. Instead, he found himself plunged into the role of heir for which he was totally unprepared.

George's reputation has suffered by comparison with that of his flamboyant, charismatic father, Edward VII. The contrast between the hedonistic, playboy father with his glamorous court and the uxorious, domestic son could hardly be greater. The son spoke languages badly if at all, thought abroad was a bloody place and never dined out if he could help it. The father was cosmopolitan, fluent in French and German and acted as an ambassador for his country. He was a philanderer with a string of affairs who kept an official mistress when he was king. The son declared: 'I'm not interested in any wife except my own.'[10] The father was a big man with a 48-inch waist. Except when he was ill, the son's weight never varied from ten stone five pounds.[11]

The relationship between father and son was neither easy nor straightforward. When King Edward died in 1910 George wrote: 'I have lost my best friend & the best of fathers, I never had a word with him in my life.'[12] There is no reason to doubt this. But it's probably also true, as George declared in later life, that he was 'terrified' of his father.[13]

The Hanoverians were notorious for quarrelling with their heirs. Queen Victoria bullied Bertie as a boy mercilessly. Bertie, in turn, bullied Eddy; a slow, dawdling child and chronically unpunctual, Eddy drove his father mad. Little Georgie was Bertie's favourite – bright, quick and affectionate. After Eddy's death, Bertie went out of his way to build his relationship with George, and treated him with great sensitivity. He wrote letters to him asking him to consider him as his brother. There can be no doubt that he adored George. And each morning when George was in London he walked round to consult with his father.

But Bertie's relationship with George was not one of equals, nor did the king become a brother to his son. George was a late developer, and he worshipped his father, deferring to him on the smallest of matters. One of his first cousins (who disliked King Edward) considered that Bertie's affection for Prince George 'was due mainly to the fact that the latter was prepared to be his complete slave'.[14] George's letters to Bertie are stilted and conventional, written in the same costive style as the diary. But his letters to his mother, whom he adored, are lively and entertaining; to her he could speak his mind.

George was in awe of his father, yet Bertie's death liberated him, and when George became king aged forty-four he grew up at last. This book tells the story of how the unpromising prince developed into a statesman king and the founder of the modern monarchy.

The most recent full biography of George V was written by Kenneth Rose in 1983. Rose succeeded in bringing the king to life: gruff, Tory, bad-tempered and kind-hearted. He interviewed people still living who had known George, and there are many references in his sources to 'private information' and letters to the author. The book is a fount of anecdotes, and is especially strong on the 1920s and 1930s. Rose used published memoirs and a wide range of manuscripts, but he rarely climbed the eighty-nine steps of the Round Tower at Windsor to the reading room. Instead, he used the transcripts from the Royal Archives made by Harold Nicolson and lent to him by Nigel Nicolson, Harold's son.[15]

Unlike previous biographers of George V, Rose didn't have George VI and Queen Mary 'breathing down his neck'. His diary records, however, that he had several interviews with Queen Elizabeth the Queen Mother, whom he found 'a mine of information'.[16] Note taking upset her, so he trusted to memory and 'rushed to the loo to write it all down'.[17] But he was more than an interviewer; for many years he had been a regular guest and companion of hers. Perhaps this intimacy with the Queen Mother hobbled him. He wrote little about sensitive topics such as George V's relations with his eldest son.

Queen Mary features only obliquely in Rose's biography. He describes her as living in 'dignified slavery' as George's consort, which hardly suggests that her life was interesting or significant in itself.[18] She is almost invisible in Harold Nicolson's life, and receives only eight entries in the index.

I have tried to put Queen Mary at the centre of my book. George V was an intensely domestic man, and no portrait of him is complete unless he is seen in the context of his marriage. Queen Mary is an important figure in her own right – founder and curator of the Royal Collection, collector, royal historian, charity organiser and *grande dame*. She played a pivotal role in George's reign, exercising far more influence than historians have suggested. This was a true partnership and a strong marriage.

Anyone writing about Queen Mary finds themselves in sparkling company. James Pope-Hennessy's life is a masterpiece and a delight to read. The surprising thing is that it was published as long ago as 1959. Even harder to credit, it was an authorised royal biography, and so was presumably expected to play by the Lascelles rules.

When Pope-Hennessy was commissioned to write the book in 1955, Queen Mary had been dead for only two years. The first thing her biographer needed to do was deconstruct the image of the formidable Victorian matriarch with her toque hats, ankle-length skirts, ramrod-straight back and ample bosom armoured with diamonds. The opening sentence of the book reads as if it was the start of a fairy tale: 'One late April day in the year 1867 a letter from England reached Schloss Reinthal, the turreted, ochre-coloured castle of the von Hügel family, hidden in the fir woods of the Styrian hills, within an easy distance of Graz.'[19]

Pope-Hennessy circumvented the restrictions on royal biography by lavishing space on the early life of Queen Mary. In a book of 622 pages, he took 420 pages to reach the accession, and devoted only 120 to the twenty-five tumultuous years of the reign. To the charge that Queen Mary failed to stand up to her husband, he claimed that she was consumed by a passion for the mystique of monarchy which rendered her unable to contradict George after he became king. This is not a view that I share. Queen Mary's career as queen consort has been underestimated, and I have tried to redress that in this book. At times I thought of writing a joint biography, but the book is framed round the narrative of George's reign.

Pope-Hennessy knew much more about Queen Mary than he admitted in the biography. His papers contain transcripts of many thousands of documents, which I have used for this book. As Harold Nicolson had done earlier, he interviewed people who had been members of the royal household or who were related to Queen Mary. He worked up these essays for publication, but he considered that the material was so confidential that they could not appear for fifty years. Hugo Vickers published the interviews in *The Quest for Queen Mary* in 2018, and the interviews – some screamingly funny, others wickedly indiscreet, some settling old scores – give a picture of the queen which is far more lifelike than the biography and at times cruel.

Working on this book has taken me on a very different journey from my earlier book on Edward VII. In Bertie's case there was a sense that, in spite of all the scandals and the mistresses and the family quarrels, the monarchy was unshakeable. The challenge for George was existential – how to adapt an essentially Victorian institution to the industrial warfare and democracy of the twentieth century. During his reign thirteen European monarchies fell. Not only did the British monarchy survive, but it emerged from the convulsions stronger than ever. One American publisher writing in 1940 put his finger on the conundrum posed for George's biographers: 'How was it that one apparently so ill-equipped by education and natural endowment for the task that awaited him should have been able in the end to succeed so decidedly?'[20]

London
February 2021

PART ONE

SECOND SON

1865–1892

CHAPTER 1

'My Darling Little Georgie'
1865–1879

On Friday 2 June 1865 the Prince and Princess of Wales hosted a grand dinner party of twenty-six guests, including three dukes and the leader of the Conservative Party. Alexandra, who was pregnant, had complained all day of feeling unwell and did not come down. While Bertie entertained his guests to the music of the Scots Fusiliers, upstairs Alix's pains became acute. The doctors were called as she went into labour at around midnight, and shortly after 1 a.m. on Saturday 3 June a healthy prince was born. Bertie was present at the birth. This baby being third in line to the throne, the Home Secretary arrived immediately afterwards.[1]

The birth of this second child was sudden and premature, but this time the doctors were not caught napping, as they had been by the birth of the princess's first son, Albert Victor, also known as Eddy, who arrived two months early. This was an eight-months baby, about two pounds heavier than Albert Victor, who had weighed three-and-a-half pounds.[2] Alix had intended to nurse this baby herself, in defiance of Queen Victoria, who strongly disapproved of royal mothers breastfeeding, but a wet nurse was engaged.[3]

At 3.30 a.m., Queen Victoria, who was at Balmoral, was 'quite startled' by two telegrams being brought to her bedroom 'which they said I must have'.[4] These were from Bertie, announcing the birth. They confirmed the Queen's fears that Alix would again be prematurely confined in this second pregnancy, the prematurity explaining why 'we get such terribly small children wh. wd have annoyed dearest Papa so much'.[5] 'Dearest Papa' was Prince Albert, who had died four years previously. The report from Dr Farre the obstetrician fuelled her forebodings. According to Farre, the rapidity of the labour was 'not good & may really make it vy dangerous in future. Only 2 hours really ill, & only ¼ of hour's bearing pains! Pleasant for dear Alix but not good for her health or for the Child.'[6] When Victoria saw the two-week-old baby, she found him very small and not as pretty as the first child. 'It is sad that the race shd become smaller & smaller,' she remarked – sad indeed, as she herself measured no more than four 4 feet eleven inches.[7]

The christening was clouded by a spat over the child's name. When

Bertie told his mother that he proposed to name the little boy George Frederick Ernest, the Queen replied that she had hoped for a 'fine old name', unlike George, which 'only came over with the Hanoverian family'.[8] Bertie added Albert to the list, to please his mother, but wrote an 'objectionable' letter refusing to change the other names.[9] The Queen observed, however, that the baby was 'certainly like all our Children wh poor little Albert Victor is not. He is not at all robust and looks so pale & puny.'[10] George, by contrast, was by now growing into 'a much more satisfactory child' – a sturdy little Saxe-Coburg-Gotha.[11]

These two women – George's stout, strong-minded, blunt-speaking grandmother Victoria and his pretty, defenceless Danish mother – shaped his early childhood. Since the birth of Eddy, the Queen had claimed 'a strong right . . . to interfere in the management and education of the child or children'. Bertie must understand that 'it was my duty to do so . . . he should never do anything about the child without consulting me.'[12]

George's parents drew up no grand plan for their children's education, as Victoria and Albert had done. Bertie was determined not to replicate the misery of his own childhood – regimented, timetabled, reported and spied upon by nurses and tutors. The nursery was Alix's sphere: as Bertie wrote, 'her whole life is wrapt up in her children'.[13] She was a 'capital nurse', never happier than wearing a flannel apron in the nursery and tucking up her sleeves to bathe her baby.[14] Her ideas about her children were simple but strongly held. She wanted to have her children with her all the time, and she wanted to give them the freedom that she had enjoyed as a child of the informal Danish royal family. When George was only fifteen months old she boasted to her sister that he and his brother were 'already now just as wild as we were, and are climbing about on everything'.[15]

But Alix was torn. The devoted mother was an adoring wife who clung to Bertie and his hectic social life. As Victoria later wrote, he 'never left her quiet a moment and she was dragged about everywhere'.[16] In February 1867, when George was twenty months old, Alix became suddenly and frighteningly ill, allegedly with rheumatic fever. 'I always feared they were wearing themselves out – & that some day a great crash would come! – And I fear it has come,' wrote the unsympathetic mother-in-law.[17] For three months Alix was confined to bed, and the illness left her with a permanently stiff right knee. Her semi-invalid state was worsened by her frequent pregnancies. Louise, born four weeks prematurely when Alix was ill (20 February 1867), was followed by two normal pregnancies – Victoria (6 July 1868) and Maud (26 November 1869): three births in under three years. Illness and recuperation brought long separations from her small children. Her deafness, which was inherited but made worse by her illness, meant that even when she was with them she was hard to converse with.

To Victoria, who had given birth to nine healthy children, Alix was a pathetic reproductive failure, producing 'miserable, puny little children ... I can't tell you how these poor, frail little fairies distress me for the honour of the family and the country.'[18] None of Alix's children were to enjoy the vigorous health and long lives of Victoria's brood. The Queen blamed Alix for insisting that her children stayed with her in unhealthy London, and counselled Bertie to 'try and do as we did in former days', and take the children to the country, especially in the summer when the London air was 'poisonous', polluted by effluent which had caused the Great Stink of 1858.[19] But, as Bertie explained, the widow Queen's refusal to come to London meant that he and Alix were forced to live there:

> I think it is rather hard to say that we keep the children with us here for our own pleasure instead of looking after their health, which we in fact neglect. It would doubtless be far pleasanter to live much more in the country, but as you know we have certain duties to fulfil here – and your absence from London renders it more necessary that we should do all we can for society, trade and public matters.[20]

The children had become entangled in the quarrel between the prince and his mother.

The conflict was always worse when Alix wanted to take the children to visit her family in Denmark. George first went to Denmark when he was three. The Queen insisted that the little boys could only travel if the doctors agreed. 'They are the children of the country & I should be blamed for allowing any risk to be run.'[21] Bertie intervened on his wife's behalf: 'I think a child is always best looked after under the mother's eye – and the children are so <u>very</u> much with us,' he pleaded.[22] When their parents embarked on a journey to the Nile via Berlin, the children were sent home to Victoria at Osborne on the Isle of Wight, and they stayed with their grandmother for three-and-a-half months. She thought them 'most wretched' with perpetual colds, 'excepting Georgie, who is always merry and rosie'.[23] From the Nile, Bertie worried that his mother ruled the nursery with a rod of iron. 'We certainly do not wish that they should be spoilt ... but if children that age are too strictly or perhaps severely treated, they get shy & fear only those whom they ought to love, & we should naturally wish them to be very fond of you, as they were in Denmark of Alix's parents.'[24] It was a conflict between two very different ideas of child rearing. A generation later, when George's children stayed for months with *their* grandparents, George was to complain that they were spoilt.

When George was five or six his grandmother's interference increased. She was horrified by reports that Alix was in the habit of having all five children together in the room, 'even when the youngest could hardly walk – without any nurse – writing herself – and not hearing! It is so very dangerous.'[25] 'They are such ill-bred, ill-trained children, I cannot fancy them at all,' grumbled the Queen.[26] Not only were they spoilt and rough, but they had no regular governess.[27] The Queen set about finding the boys a tutor. The man she stumbled upon was the curate to the vicar of Whippingham on the Isle of Wight, where she heard him preach: the Reverend John Neale Dalton.[28]

There were two people who wrote letters addressed to 'My darling little Georgie'. One was his mother. The other was his tutor, Mr Dalton.

Dalton arrived when George was nearly six and Eddy was seven. He was a 32-year-old bachelor with a deep, sepulchral voice, thinning hair and gold-rimmed spectacles. Instructed by the Prince of Wales to avoid the cramming which had ruined his childhood, Dalton devised a timetable for the boys at Sandringham which imposed a fixed daily routine and plenty of outdoor exercise but only four hours of lessons.

The process of Dalton's appointment remains a mystery. Prince Albert had taken great care in selecting tutors for his sons. George's father Bertie, on the other hand, allowed his mother to choose a tutor and made no attempt to appoint one for his sons himself.

Bertie's tutor, Mr Gibbs, had come on the recommendation of Sir James Stephen, whose ward he was. This began a tradition of picking royal tutors from the Victorian intellectual aristocracy, many of whom by a curious twist were related to Virginia Woolf.* Dalton, the son of a vicar of Milton Keynes, was not a member of this elite, but was descended from a well-established family of Cambridge-educated clergymen. No doubt he owed his appointment to the Queen's recommendation, as most biographers suggest. There may have been another influence too. Dalton was a friend of Edward Carpenter, a Cambridge high-flyer and fellow of Trinity. Carpenter later claimed that he had been offered the post of tutor and turned it down, and it's possible that he recommended

---

*Sir James Stephen was her grandfather and Herbert Fisher, Bertie's tutor at Oxford, married Woolf's aunt, while James (Jim) Stephen, who later became tutor to Eddy, was her first cousin.

Dalton in his stead.[29] When Carpenter resigned his fellowship to preach socialism and live openly as a homosexual, Dalton remained friends with him. The gay campaigner seems an unlikely role model for the royal tutor, but Dalton claimed that Carpenter left 'an enduring influence' on his moral and mental outlook.[30]

Dalton swiftly earned the approval of the Queen. She found him 'a very good, sensible man', and her acid comments on the little boys turned to butter. 'They really are very dear children,' she wrote, 'so quick & observant, so friendly, honest & truthful & without any pretension.'[31] Dalton disciplined the boys and taught them not to behave as 'great princes'. As Victoria observed, 'it is . . . so difficult to prevent little Princes from becoming spoiled as everybody does what they wish'.[32] Eddy and George had the 'immense advantage not to have been "born under the purple"' as their father had been, but, like Victoria herself, brought up privately and at one remove from the court.[33]

Dalton was less successful in educating the princes. He complained that his lessons were constantly interrupted by George's parents and their restless way of life, but he showed little understanding of the education of princes as it had evolved since Renaissance times. When George was nine a temporary tutor reported that he and Eddy 'knew nothing' and could 'neither speak nor understand French which is a serious drawback for a Prince'.[34] French and German were essential in an age of dynastic diplomacy, yet George grew up speaking neither language well. Queen Mary considered it 'disgraceful' that Dalton 'never tried really to educate the princes'.[35] George was taught no history. Not until he was king did he discover his own family's story. 'Did you know that George III was *not* a son of George II?' he would innocently inquire.[36]

In spite of his poor teaching, Dalton was (according to George's biographers) the most important person in George's early life.[37] The discipline, the routine and the tidiness instilled by Dalton spoke to a psychological need in George. Order made him feel safe and in control of his own little world at an age when his father was often absent and his mother affectionate but unpredictable. Dalton's weekly reports criticise the eleven-year-old George for his 'self-approbation' which was 'enormously strong, becoming almost the only motive power'.[38] But George's bumptiousness was a measure of the tutor's success in gaining his confidence.

Tidy-minded George later kept his letters in white linen bags. There were more letters in Dalton's bag than anyone else's, and they stretched over fifty years. Beginning in 1873 'My darling little Georgie', they end in 1921. 'I do not care for Dalton,' wrote Harold Nicolson, 'but his affection for George was very real.'[39] As was George's for him – aged twelve George signed off his letters to Dalton 'with very much love and many kisses'.[40]

Dalton was widely disliked. In the first draft of his biography, Nicolson described the tutor as 'a man of character, precision, tenacity and profound religious convictions. He was not a born courtier.' Owen Morshead, the royal librarian, who read the proofs, crossed most of this out. Dalton, he told Nicolson, was 'about as oily as a courtier could be; nor did he believe in the fundamental verities of the Christian religion. He was a horrible man.'[41] Nicolson's published version reads: 'he was a man of character, precision and tenacity'.

After Dalton died in 1931 his son the Labour politician Hugh Dalton sorted through his papers. He found them full of letters from men, some very affectionate. 'A strong homosexual strain is very clear. Men fifty and sixty years younger than he called him "John".'[42] No one has hinted, however, at a dark or abusive side to Dalton's relationship with 'my darling little Georgie'.

Less is known about the family life of the children of Edward VII than about that of any other royal children. At Sandringham they were secluded and shielded from the public gaze. In later life George himself said almost nothing about his childhood.

The official biographer John Gore, who in 1941 wrote what is still the fullest account of George's childhood, considered that the upbringing of the Wales children, divided between London and Norfolk, 'differed in no vital detail' from that of the children of the upper class. But Gore also observed that Alexandra's 'loyalty to the ideals of family affection' retarded the boys' development'. From George's earliest days, 'the banner over him was love'. He was nurtured in family affection, and this childhood idyll was, according to Gore, the formative influence on his character. Nothing could ever equal the happiness of his childhood, but it infantilised him too.[43] His quick-tempered father was frequently absent – a frightening but distant figure.

The family life that Alix created was not English but Danish. A house that swarmed with children, sitting down to vast family meals, days filled with energetic outdoor games and rooms crowded with relatives whose incessant chatter made it impossible to write a letter: this was the atmosphere of Alix's Danish home. 'Dear old Sandringham', as Alix and George lovingly referred to it, was the house where Alix replicated Danish family life. In fact it wasn't old at all – the large rambling brick villa (Nikolaus Pevsner described it as 'frenetic Jacobean') had only been

built in 1870, replacing an earlier Georgian house.* Calling people and
places 'dear little' or 'poor little' was the special way of speaking of the
Wales children – 'as though life would have been very wonderful and
everything very beautiful, if it had not been so sad'.[44]

The shining beacon of 'dear old Sandringham' was 'Motherdear'.†
Her letters – a stream of speech, picked up and put down at random like
the knitting which her handwriting resembled – give glimpses of her
relationship with 'my darling little Georgie'. He was 'a naughty little
fellow' whom she tucked up in bed each night – 'do you remember how
often we were surprised by Mr Dalton in the midst of our . . . little chat,
as you call it.'[45] Alix had an affinity with small children – some said that
'she remained a schoolgirl all her life' – but there was something else
about her magic: her extraordinary beauty.[46] George's cousin Missy of
Edinburgh, later Marie, Queen of Romania, remembered Aunt Alix as
a dazzling vision wearing a ruby-red velvet gown, but this beautiful
creature was no proud lady: she enchanted small children because she
genuinely enjoyed coming to the nursery and seeing them in the bath.[47]
George remembered her in her youth as 'one of the most beautiful
women he had ever seen'.[48]

George's constant companion was his brother Eddy. Photographs
show a hauntingly beautiful, waif-like little boy with long hair and large,
soulful eyes. Eddy was different from the others. He was quiet and apathetic where George was 'a jolly little pickle' and his sisters were loud
and boisterous.[49] Whether Eddy was quite right was an anxiety that
hung over the family. Victoria observed him aged five, and was reassured
to find him 'not wanting but merely languid and listless from want of
vigour'.[50] His first cousin the Grand Duchess Xenia of Russia recalled
that once at Fredensborg, the summer palace of the Danish royal family,
she was in a boat with Eddy on the lake when he suddenly threw his
sisters' little dog into the water. His Danish grandfather then pushed
Eddy in.

> He didn't seem at all surprised and just said, 'I'm very wet.' 'Of course
> you're very wet,' said my grandfather, 'you've been in the lake.' 'Why
> did you do that to me?' Eddy asked. 'Because you did it to the little
> dog' . . . He was like that, the Duke of Clarence [Eddy]. He never
> *minded* anything.[51]

---

*Alix wrote of 'dear old Sandringham' as early as 1877 (RA GV/PRIV/AA28/5, Alix to
G, 2 May 1877).
†Alix referred to herself thus as early as 1875, when George was ten (RA GV/PRIV/
AA28/3, Alix to G, 6 December 1875).

George's three sisters – Louise, Victoria and Maud – were very close in age, born (as we have seen) within a span of less than three years, and they were brought up together. The girls ran wild at Sandringham and enjoyed boisterous games, but they also suffered from poor health, constantly complaining of fever, neuralgia, cysts, colds and flu. Motherdear was a constant presence in their childhood; at least George's naval training removed him from her stifling emotionalism. The sisters were not allowed to make friends, and some said they lived in a mutual admiration society within their own exclusive world, with their schoolgirl nicknames – Louise was known as 'Toots', Victoria was 'Gawks' and Maud 'Snipey'. Little attention was given to their education, which remained in Alix's hands. They were well taught in music, and there was a German governess and a French one, but that was about all – no maths or English or history. In spite of this, however, Maud became an accomplished linguist, fluent in Russian, and also a talented chess player. Their lack of schooling seems astonishing; as the Cabinet minister W. H. Smith later pointed out, Louise stood next in line to the throne if her brothers should drown at sea.[52]

Bertie's determination to avoid inflicting the misery of his own school days on his sons shaped the next stage in their education. In February 1877 he saw the Queen and told her (as she wrote in her journal) that 'for the boys' education, proper discipline & undisturbed studies, they must leave home'. She continued: 'After much discussion, he had finally come to the conclusion that it would be best for them to go on board the *Britannia* training ship. Eddy would naturally not <u>enter</u> the Navy & Georgie only if he liked it.'[53]

Over in Berlin, Bertie's sister Vicky, the German Crown Princess, envied his freedom to educate his sons as he pleased, untrammelled by 'absurd and injurious rules and customs about the education of ... Princes'; but the decision to send the two boys to *Britannia*, the hulk moored in the river Dart where naval cadets served a two-year apprenticeship, needs some explaining.[54] As Dalton admitted in the memorandum he wrote for the Queen, the attempt to educate the boys at home had failed.

The very position which the two Princes occupy and the constant change of residence and surroundings they are liable to and the quite unavoidable and natural excitement continually caused thereby ... interfered so much with anything like steady application to work as to render it impossible to obtain any really satisfactory result.[55]

Public school was ruled out because it would result in the boys being separated. This, in Dalton's view, would be a disaster. Not only did Eddy require 'the stimulus of George's company to induce him to work at all'; but for George, now eleven, Eddy was a 'wholesome ... check against that tendency to self-conceit which is apt at times to show itself in him. Away from his brother, there would be a great risk of his being made too much of and treated as a general favourite.'[56]

The princes, in Dalton's view, were co-dependent. Eddy, who took almost no interest in his lessons, could not function without George. Yet Eddy was to be forced, aged thirteen, to train for the navy, which he was definitely not going to join and in which he showed little interest. What Eddy thought is not recorded, but the arrangement was hardly calculated to incentivise him to work. George was at least destined for a naval career, though 'only if he liked it'. But he was tied to his brother as a sort of whipping boy. He was to take the punishment for Eddy's backwardness. And Eddy's role was to bash George into submission. On *Britannia* the boys' examination results were not to be made public. Most important but least discussed, Dalton was to accompany them. The oily courtier had engineered a plan that rendered it essential that he should remain in charge.

Victoria strongly objected to the *Britannia* idea. She thought the princes should be educated in seclusion from other boys at Wellington, a school with strong royal connections – since 1864 Bertie had been president of the board of governors, an office which his father had held before him. Dalton was sent to Osborne and he managed to persuade her of his plan. 'What a fearless, honest man he is,' said the Queen.[57]

The sharpest comment about *Britannia* was Victoria's. She observed that a naval education would make Eddy think his own country was superior to any other, as George III and William IV had done. Britain's greatest rulers in her opinion were William III and her own Prince Consort, and both were foreigners: 'this gave them a freedom from all national prejudices which is very important in Princes'.[58] Cosmopolitanism was certainly crucial to the dynastic realm over which Victoria later presided as Grandmother of Europe in consequence of the dynastic marriages of her children. What she could hardly have foreseen was that in the war-torn Europe where George was to reign, believing one's own country to be better than any other was essential to a monarch's survival.

Britannia was an experiment. It avoided the things the Prince of Wales worried about. The boys were not be educated at home, as he had been. Nor were they to attend a school, exposing Eddy's backwardness. The navy was the preferred career choice for a second son and, as such,

Britannia suited George. He flourished, but for Eddy, the heir to the throne, the experiment achieved nothing.

The entrance examinations for *Britannia* took place at the Royal Naval College at Greenwich in May 1877. Dalton worried that the boys would fail, and from Athens Alix wrote anxiously urging George to work extra hard: 'Remember that your efforts to do well now will have an influence for the rest of your lives.'[59] George passed, but – contrary to the announcement in *The Times* – it seems likely that Eddy failed.[60] Why he was made to sit the examinations when he was evidently poorly prepared was not explained.

It was not a good summer for Eddy. In July he and George watched Alix lay the foundation stone for a dramatically designed water tower at Sandringham. Bertie's narrow escape from dying of typhoid in 1871 had prompted investigation of the water supply at Sandringham, and it had been found to be contaminated. A spring of pure water was identified but in July the supply was temporarily interrupted and water was drawn from the old, poisoned source. Within days of the laying of the foundation stone, Eddy was struck down with typhoid.[61] Alix nursed him devotedly day and night, but the illness changed him. He grew very tall for his age – the top of his head now came up to Alix's eyes – and he became 'as thin as a stick'.[62] Perhaps it was then that he developed a piercing, high-pitched voice. His arms and neck grew abnormally long, and his attempts to disguise them in special collars and cuffs earned him nothing but ridicule. It was also apparent that he had inherited Alix's deafness.[63]

Delayed by Eddy's illness, the princes entered *Britannia* in October. Alix took a masochistic pleasure in protracted, painful partings – for her a long, tearful goodbye was an index of love – and this departure was gratifyingly emotional: 'poor little boys they cried so bitterly'.[64] Smartly dressed in their new uniforms as naval cadets, the gawky Herring and his small brother Sprat, a diminutive of W(h)ales, travelled with their father to Dartmouth, where they were rowed across the harbour to *Britannia* by twelve cadets dressed in white uniforms.[65]

On board the old wooden sailing ship the princes shared a cabin in the poop but otherwise they were treated no differently from the other 200 cadets. After a life spent in palaces, the princes found the *Britannia* horribly cold and draughty.[66] The day began at 6.30 with a bugle call, then baths – bathing from the shore twice a week – drill at 7.15 followed by lessons in maths, navigation, steam ships and seamanship. It was a narrow, practical curriculum which effectively knocked out any inclination to independence or originality. No Latin or Greek was taught, no languages except for French, no history or music. Obedience to orders was enforced by brutal discipline.[67] Almost every senior naval officer endured the *Britannia* battery farm, and most remembered it as the worst experience of their lives. George was no exception; but this didn't stop him from putting his own sons through the same experience.

The princes were unexpectedly behind in their studies when they joined, and Alix wrote urging Dalton to impress upon them that 'they are doing discredit both to themselves and to us'.[68] George heeded this advice, Eddy did not. Dalton's report to the Queen claimed: 'There is no fear of the elder Prince working too hard, or overtaxing his powers, as Your Majesty seems to fear: in fact he might work harder than he does without any risk of detriment.'[69] If Dalton had possessed a sense of humour, this would have been a joke. Eddy's reports were consistently bad. Bertie told Victoria: 'Unfortunately Eddy is backward in his studies – as he is lethargic & will not concentrate his attention on his work.' George, on the other hand, was 'doing remarkably well & has not received one bad report since last term'.[70] The reality was that George told the seamanship instructors 'not to bother about his brother, who was not going to sea, but to devote their attention to him'.[71] When George scrubbed the deck he did it carefully and took trouble to learn how to do it properly.[72] Eddy, who was still convalescent, was left to his own devices. One can but admire Eddy's independence of mind. Surely no other cadet managed to defy the martinets of *Britannia* so successfully.

Bullying of a 'gross nature' was rife and, in spite of a public scandal the previous year, the officers did nothing to check it.[73] Half a century later George recalled that being a prince did him no good:

> The other boys made a point of taking it out of us on the grounds that they'd never be able to do it later on . . . They used to make me go up and challenge the bigger boys – I was awfully small then – and I'd get a hiding time and again. But one day I was landed a blow on the nose which made my nose bleed badly. It was the best blow I ever took for the Doctor forbad my fighting any more.[74]

This sounds like a speech from *Tom Brown's Schooldays*. Significantly, George doesn't mention Eddy in this account of the fighting. The cadet whose duty it was to sit between the princes at meals reported that George joined in the pranks but Eddy took no notice.[75]

If Dalton knew of the bullying, he did nothing to stop it. Though he was disliked by the staff as a 'supernumerary', he enjoyed the status that came from acting *in loco parentis* for the Prince of Wales. He gave sermons to the cadets which were published in a book that (as one historian wrote) 'would cast a gloom over anyone's day in the British Library'.[76]

After a year on *Britannia*, Lord Ramsay, the commander, wrote to Bertie advising him to remove Eddy from the course. His progress was 'very, very unsatisfactory', and he was learning nothing. 'The experiment has failed.' George, by contrast, 'is not only doing capitally but is doing better and better every day.'[77] Ramsay's letter caused distress to Alix: removing Eddy, she thought, would be 'a great mistake'; 'nothing could be worse for him in every way than to be *educated at home alone* this time without even his brother!'[78] In the passing-out exam at the end of the *Britannia* course in April 1879 Eddy failed in all subjects, while George scored high marks.[79]

Failing was not in itself disastrous. George's son Bertie came bottom in his exams at Osborne naval college, and went on to become a naval officer. Princes did not need to try like other boys, as George's father had discovered. It had been clearly understood from the start that *Britannia* was an experiment for Eddy. In the seamanship examination in July – naval education was heavily exam-based – both Eddy and George took a first class, and 'Eddy stood higher in the list than Georgy'.[80]

Dalton, however, insisted that Eddy had a mental problem. The 'abnormally dormant condition' of his mind meant that he was unable to 'fix his attention to any given subject for more than a few seconds consecutively'.[81] Dalton 'evidently did not like Albert Victor at all', and because he was unable to teach him he concluded that the boy was abnormal.[82] It never seems to have occurred to Dalton that the fault lay with him. And Bertie accepted Dalton's advice and solicited no other opinions.

Because Eddy, now fifteen, was so backward, school was out of the question, if only because it would expose his stupidity. Dalton's solution was to continue the *Britannia* arrangement: Eddy should accompany George on the next stage of his naval training, serving as a midshipman on an extended world cruise. The officers in the ship would be hand-picked to protect the young princes from evil influences; and while George advanced his naval skills, Eddy would study with tutors in seclusion. The Prince of Wales embraced this startling proposal. Victoria did not like it at all. But her objections were overcome by a visit from the silver-tongued Mr Dalton. When the Cabinet interfered, raising objections to the plan of sending the two heirs to the throne round the world in a perilous sailing ship, Victoria became a staunch supporter. Once again, George was the solution to the Eddy problem. And, as before, Dalton had made himself indispensable to the scheme.

CHAPTER 2

A Disgraceful Education
1879–1886

The scene now shifted to HMS *Bacchante*, the ironclad corvette or small warship with 450 men on board which was chosen for the princes' voyage around the world. If George had been a person in a play, there would have been only five other characters: Alix, his idealised but neglectful mother; Bertie, his distant and frightening father; Eddy; Dalton; and Fuller, his personal servant.

Fuller was the nursery footman who arrived a fortnight after Eddy was born, and he looked after the princes on board *Bacchante*. The affection between George and his valet was very real. George later claimed that he was 'devoted' to Fuller, and when the two were separated Fuller wrote to the eighteen-year-old George: 'You cannot think how I miss your dear face, the place don't look like the same. I used to look at the vacant bed in your room ... I scarcely knew what I was doing.'[1] The linen bag in which George kept letters from friends contained far more from Fuller than from anyone else, and very few from boys of George's age.

Making friends with other children was actively discouraged in the royal family. 'Never make friendships,' Victoria exhorted her Hesse granddaughters: 'girls' friendships and intimacies are very bad & often lead to great mischief.'[2] The Queen was especially concerned that Eddy and George should be kept apart from 'the society of fashionable & fast people'.[3] She insisted on the 'absolute necessity' of the boys 'not mixing' with Bertie's friends, by which she meant the social clique known as the Marlborough House Set.[4]

Lacking a job description as Prince of Wales, Bertie had established himself as the leader of fashionable, 'fast' society. The Marlborough House Set were notorious for their philistinism, louche morals, late nights, party-going, gambling and corridor-creeping. Mistresses and adultery were openly accepted, but the rule was never divorce – not for reasons of morality, but because divorce cases risked inviting damaging public exposure. Famed for his glamorous mistresses such the American Jennie Churchill, Winston's mother, or the professional beauty Lily Langtry, Bertie lurched from one scandal to another – from the Mordaunt divorce case, when he was summoned to appear in court as a witness, to the Aylesford scandal, when Lord Randolph Churchill tried to blackmail him over love letters he had written. Living far beyond his means, the Prince of Wales depended on loans from his plutocratic friends such as the Rothschilds to finance his extravagant lifestyle. Addicted to pleasure, the prince bankrupted several members of his set by forcing them to entertain him. His elaborate social life revolved around annual fixtures such as Goodwood races, Cowes week and yachting in Cannes – all in a desperate effort to keep the restless prince amused.

'Our greatest wish,' Bertie told his mother, 'is to keep [the children] simple, pure, and childlike as long as it is possible.'[5] Both Bertie and Victoria were Hanoverian extroverts who had been brought up in seclusion, and both had railed against their solitary state. George was no extrovert, and he didn't complain. He had Eddy. Perhaps the most important part in the process of becoming George was played by Eddy.

The two princes embarked on 17 September 1879 for their first voyage in *Bacchante*, a trial six months at sea. They shared a cabin, which was joined to Dalton's quarters by a connecting door. Bertie ordered that in all other respects they were to be treated exactly like other naval cadets.[6] This is not what happened. Though they messed in the gunroom, the princes' shipmates had been carefully picked by Dalton.

The captain, Lord Charles Scott, was a son of the Duke of Buccleuch, and Lord Charles's nephew John Scott, the future 7th Duke of Buccleuch, was a naval cadet. The princes were instructed in seamanship by the First Lieutenant Assheton Curzon-Howe, a son of Earl Howe and future commander-in-chief of the Mediterranean Fleet. Their fellow cadets included R. E. (Rosy) Wemyss, a future admiral of the fleet, who was befriended by the princes with Dalton's approval. Another of Dalton's protégés was Lieutenant Hugh Evan-Thomas, a slightly older boy whom Dalton encouraged because of the 'good influence' he had on the princes.[7]

There was no danger of bullying in *Bacchante*. Even in their relations with this head-hunted crew of aristocrats and prigs, the boys were closely chaperoned by Dalton. He didn't allow them to consort with their peers, and he wrote letters complaining of the naval officers. The senior midshipman E. L. Munro was removed because Dalton objected to his 'almost feminine ways' and 'silly over-deference' to the princes.[8] Paranoid in his fear of evil associations, Dalton was desperate to ensure that the boys 'should be exposed to no influence other than his own'.[9] He was always there. Each night the boys wrote up their diaries under his supervision. Dalton messed with the captain, and in the wardroom he was regarded as an 'incubus', but in spite of his unpopularity with the officers he never lost the affection of the princes, or at least of George.[10]

The first *Bacchante* cruise, to the Mediterranean and the West Indies, was uneventful. In Barbados the princes sniffed a lily in the botanical gardens, and when a reporter spotted the pollen on their faces he wired home that their noses had been tattooed. Alix's reaction to the news was as amused as it was restrained: 'Now you stupid Georgie how could you have your little impudent snout tattooed. What an <u>object</u> you must look and won't everyone stare at the ridiculous boy with an <u>anchor</u> on his nose! Why on earth not have put it somewhere else!'[11]

The princes passed their midshipman's exams in January 1880, but Dalton's reports on Eddy made depressing reading. Eddy, said the tutor, 'sits listless and vacant . . . This weakness of brain, this feebleness and lack of power to grasp almost anything put before him, is manifested . . . also in his hours of recreation and social intercourse. It is a fault of nature.'[12]

When George arrived home in May 1880 he was four feet ten inches tall and weighed just over six stone. On his fourteenth birthday the previous June his mother had written: 'Victoria [sister] says "so old and so small"!! oh my! You will have to make haste to grow, or I shall have the sad disgrace of being the mother of a <u>dwarf</u>!!!'[13] He was knock-kneed, as can be clearly seen in photographs of him wearing plus fours. All his sons except the eldest were knock-kneed too, and his sensitivity about his legs can be gauged from his insistence on their wearing painful splints.

Harold Nicolson thought George's tender and affectionate letters to 'My darling Motherdear' were 'the best in the whole collection'. He added: 'He simply worshipped her.'[14] George's letters to Alix brim with emotion and affection which would have been judged unmanly by the standards of late-Victorian public schoolboys. His letters to his father, by contrast, are stilted and repressed.[15] According to Alix's biographer, her relationship with George became 'unusually close' at around this time.[16] Without Alix's letters to Eddy (which were allegedly destroyed), it's hard to be sure, but disappointment over Eddy's seemingly incurable lethargy appears to have shifted the dynamic in Alix's relationship with her sons. Reliable, conscientious little Georgie, who obeyed her constant exhortations to work hard, who reciprocated her loving letters and who read to her while her hair was being done in the morning, had now become the favourite.[17]

At 10 a.m. on 14 September 1880, Eddy and George, smartly dressed in midshipmen's uniforms, departed on their most testing voyage so far in *Bacchante* – a two-year world cruise. Alix and the three sisters assembled in the painted hall of Marlborough House to say goodbye. Painful partings were, as we have seen, a feature of Wales family life, but this one was heart-wrenching even by Alix's standards. George's eyes streamed with tears.[18] Bertie, who was to accompany his sons, was late. 'It made it much worse,' wrote George, 'having to wait till dear Papa came, because none of us could speak we were all so crying so much.'[19]

The special train bearing the tearful princes and their father reached Portsmouth at 12.35. It was blowing a gale, with torrential rain, and after George and Eddy had boarded ship *Bacchante* attempted to weigh anchor – only to find herself tangled up with another ship. At length the anchor was freed, and in gushing rain and thunder the *Bacchante* steamed with the Prince of Wales beside them in the *Osborne* to Cowes, where the royal yacht signalled farewell.[20] Here the sea was so rough that *Bacchante* anchored for the night. Next day the gale was still blowing, and a homesick and seasick George wrote a sad little letter to his mother: 'I miss you so very much & felt so sorry when I had to say goodbye to you and sisters & it was dreadfully hard saying goodbye to dear Papa ... So goodbye once more my darling Motherdear.'[21]

The voyage of *Bacchante* was chronicled in two very fat volumes totalling 1,478 pages which were published by Macmillan in 1886. The book appeared under the names of Prince Albert Victor and Prince George of Wales with additions by John N. Dalton. In the preface Dalton claimed that it was compiled from the diaries and letters written by the princes, and his own additions were marked off in square brackets.[22] This was misleading. The dull, long-winded accounts of the places where they went ashore, and the quotes from Latin authors and the verses from Browning which adorn the text, did not come from the princes' pens.

'I did not like the way Dalton had lied about the *Bacchante* book,' Harold Nicolson told Queen Mary in 1949.[23] The book was intended as royal propaganda. 'It would appear in the Princes' names and would redound to their credit and to that of Your Royal Highness, I hope,' Dalton told Bertie.[24] Nicolson remarked drily that those who believed they were reading the princes' actual words 'must have been horrified to discover what insufferable midshipmen the two princes were'.[25] Even George conceded that it was 'one of the dullest books ever written'.[26] *The Times*, however, applauded the princes' industry and discipline: 'If they continue to be as earnest, as painstaking, as true to duty ... it will be fortunate for themselves and the Empire.'[27]

It is unclear who is actually narrating. Most of the time, Dalton writes as 'we', meaning the two princes. He occasionally uses the first person singular, but it is never clear which prince 'I' is. The princes have become conflated and dissolved into a composite person.

The book succeeds in obliterating their characters and silencing their voices altogether.

Here is George writing to his mother: 'At about 11 o'clock William Fairlie AB fell off the topsail yard on to the forecastle and was killed. In the afternoon at ½ past 5 we buried him after evening quarters just before sunset.'[28] These two sentences were inflated by Dalton into a long prosy account of death at sea. George's letter home went on to describe another casualty the following day: 'A sad thing happened this morning at about 9 o'clock a man fell overboard from the "Inconstant" she was then quite close to us, I was on the deck at the time & saw him swimming to the life buoy but just as he got a few yards from it he sank, & when the boat came they could not find him.'[29] For the fifteen-year-old George this second death – thought to be by sharks – was traumatic because he witnessed it, but Dalton dismisses it in a mere two lines.[30]

George's day in *Bacchante* began at 6.00 with drill. After breakfast at 8.00, he and Eddy had lessons with Mr Lawless, their mathematics teacher, from 9.30 until 11.45, then dinner at 12.00 followed by French – a total of three hours' teaching. From 1.45 George did midshipmen's exercises such as shifting topsail, rifle and cutlass drill or gymnastics. Tea was at 6.30 and if he wasn't keeping watch he would spend the evening reading before bed at 9.30.

As part of a detached or flying squadron which cruised the world for training purposes, *Bacchante* sailed to most of the parts of the British Empire except for India. After the squadron had crossed the Atlantic to the Falkland Islands, the plan to round Cape Horn and make for the Galapagos Islands was interrupted by news of the outbreak of the First Boer War in South Africa, when the Boers of the Transvaal rebelled against British rule (the Transvaal had been annexed in 1877). The *Bacchante* was ordered to the Cape – a move which prompted a spat between Bertie, who hoped that his sons might witness the fighting, and Queen Victoria, who objected to the second in line to the throne being mixed up in a civil war. After six weeks at anchor off the Cape, the *Bacchante* set sail for Australia, where the princes spent nearly three months, returning via Japan, Hong Kong, Shanghai, Singapore, Ceylon and the Suez Canal. There followed a journey down the Nile, a tour of the Holy Land and a visit to their cousins in Greece.

Harold Nicolson considered that the years on *Britannia* and the *Bacchante* 'formed and moulded' George's character. It was then that George developed the 'categorical sense of duty' which became the 'fly-wheel of his life'.[31] The naval education which George received, however, was ill-suited to modern warfare. As a training ship, *Bacchante* was under orders to use sail rather than steam wherever possible. Though

George excelled in seamanship, the skills that he learnt were no longer relevant to naval warfare.[32]

Queen Mary thought that the period aboard *Bacchante* was 'pure stupidity' because it meant that the princes were not properly educated. 'It was disgraceful', she thought, 'that "the King" had not been taught more.'[33] Even the places for which George was prepped by Dalton made little impression. In the Holy Land, where the princes followed the itinerary their father had undertaken in 1862, George showed a sad lack of intellectual curiosity. 'All the places,' he wrote, 'are only said to be the places.'[34] Climbing a mountain near the Mount of Olives reminded him of hill walking with his mother in 'dear old Scotland except that I got very hot & that there was no heather about'. He was far more excited about getting tattooed – 'by the same old man that tattooed Papa & the same thing too the 5 crosses, you ask Papa to show his arm'.[35]

Sailing around the rim of the world, George knew very little of Europe. Queen Victoria summed up the deficiencies of Eddy's education in words that apply no less to George:

> He has been dosed with [the Colonies] and he has been . . . nowhere but to Denmark in Europe. He is only able to speak French badly and German equally so. He has never, like every other Prince been in contact with any other court but Berlin or seen fine works of art. Italy, Spain, Austria, Hungary, Germany, Holland even Russia, all these he ought to see and know and not merely go to young colonies, with no history, no art and nothing but middle class English speaking people.[36]

In spite of his ignorance of European courts, however, George was very much aware of the dynastic network, and he was close to Alix's sister, his aunt Minny, and her husband Tsarevich Sacha, the future Alexander III.

Alix, who took a ghoulish delight in blood and gore and liked nothing better than a good death, spared none of the lurid details in her letters to George describing the assassination of Tsar Alexander II in 1881. Driving home from a parade in St Petersburg, the Tsar was hit by a bomb which exploded between his legs: 'he was frightfully injured, both legs hanging by the flesh, one of them shattered right up to the thigh . . . his face also badly wounded and one of his eyes forced from its socket, too frightful!'[37] Minny saw him at the Winter Palace:

> There he was lying on his bed, apparently dead though he still breathed, half naked, all his clothes having been blown off him, with the blood streaming out of his poor mangled legs. The room was filled

with the soldiers who had carried him up, and who were . . . wounded themselves and covered with blood – one poor man's eye was completely gone & the blood streaming over his face.[38]

For Alix the lesson was plain:

> Only think of poor Sacha and Minny's despair and what a future for them! And I do not think they are any of them safe while those dreadful nihilists and secret societies are in existence as their whole aim is to destroy Monarchy no matter who the individual is. It makes me tremble for my beloved sister and Sacha.[39]

The following year the danger came closer to home when Queen Victoria was fired at in her carriage at Windsor. 'Was it not awful that poor Grandmama was shot at but thank God she is all right,' wrote Alix to George.[40] Victoria's would-be assassin was a madman not a terrorist, but the incident underlined the point: however secluded or well guarded they were, monarchs could never be safe.

George's scanty education was topped off with six months in Lausanne, where he and Eddy were sent to learn French, from October 1882 to May 1883. They stayed with Dalton at the luxurious Beau Rivage Hotel, but in spite of exhortations from his parents, both of whom were fluent linguists, George learnt very little French.

George grew up to consider French an effeminate language, and when he read a menu in French he would deliberately mispronounce the words.[41]* But his inability to learn French does raise questions about his intelligence. The tutor, Gabriel Hua, was a black-bearded Frenchman whose voice was even deeper than Dalton's. He became a master at Eton, and George liked him so much that he appointed him French tutor to his own sons (with equal lack of success). Hua reported that George had 'a remarkable spontaneous intelligence – quickly grasping some explanation or principle – but also sometimes the faults which go with the same qualities – and a momentary discouragement at meeting the first difficulty.'[42] After Hua's death George periodically visited his grave in Kensal Green.

---

*Perhaps this brought him closer to his people. As George Orwell wrote in 1941, 'nearly every Englishman of working-class origin considers it effeminate to pronounce a foreign word correctly'. (George Orwell, 'The Lion and the Unicorn' in *Essays* (Everyman's Library, 2002), p. 301).

'It was not a lively time,' wrote Harold Nicolson.[43] The two boys relieved the tedium by playing games with English visitors to the hotel. Dalton reported that Eddy had 'relapsed into his old habits of indolence and inattention'.[44] Eddy was bored and depressed, and his relations with the ever-critical Dalton soured. The two princes squabbled too. Alix urged George to 'be as nice as you can to your brother or you will surely be sorry for it afterwards when you are separated'.[45]

The fractious triangle of Eddy, George and Dalton broke up soon afterwards. In June 1883 George embarked on HMS *Canada* for a year with the North American Squadron. For the first time in his life he was entirely alone – no Eddy, no Dalton, no Fuller even. Left behind, Fuller 'cried all day' and was too unhappy to appear at meals.[46] Never before had George slept without Eddy in the bed next to him. 'So we are at last separated for the first time; and I can't tell you <u>how</u> strange it seems to be without you and <u>how</u> I miss you in everything <u>all day</u> long,' wrote Eddy.[47] '[I] can hardly realise yet that you are not there and I miss you more when I go to bed more than at any other time.'[48]

Eddy and Dalton kept George supplied with cigarettes while he was with the *Canada*. George had started smoking early – as a boy Fuller used to beg him not to smoke too much on the grounds that it would stunt his growth.[49] Little did anyone realise that the habit was to cause his premature death.

For Dalton too the separation from George was a wrench. He was now engaged to Kitty Evan-Thomas, sister of Hugh Evan-Thomas, the young midshipman whom he had befriended on the *Bacchante*. Kitty was half Dalton's age, and he had proposed within three days of meeting her. But the *Bacchante* cruise had been the happiest time of his life, in sole charge of the princes, and now he reverted to being a mere tutor. 'How often I do long to be at sea with you again,' Dalton wrote to George from Sandringham. 'It is frightfully dull here. I never felt so dull in my life, and shall be awfully glad when our time is up. We miss your voice so at meals: they all sit round the table and eat and eat and never say a syllable: I never knew such a lot.'[50] This letter was addressed to 'My darling little Georgy'. When King George VI read Nicolson's proofs he pencilled a note: 'The date of this letter must have been much earlier. He was then 18 yrs old. Please omit.'[51] Nicolson commented in his diary: 'They think, it seems, that these endearments may indicate either undue familiarity on the part of Dalton or arrested development on the part of Prince George.'[52]

George's first biographer, John Gore, claimed that 'there was not the least doubt' that the prince was emotionally retarded by his mother's overwhelming love and his father's power of inspiring fear.[53] Reading of his early life, Nicolson was struck by George's persistent homesickness, which he considered a sign of 'protracted adolescence'.[54] For the late-twentieth-century psychiatrist Dennis Friedman, on the other hand, homesickness represented George's continuing need for a home that had failed to provide adequate parenting.[55] George had a detached and intimidating father and, although his mother undoubtedly loved him, she not only sent him away from home but often failed to write for months at a time. She was 'either overwhelmingly loving or completely absent'. George survived by finding alternative 'mothers'. He and Eddy both played mother to one another. Dalton and Fuller acted as surrogate parents. Dalton's role as authority figure was complemented by Fuller's motherly fussing over George's clothes and his health.[56] Now George was separated from the substitute family that he had so carefully constructed.

At 12.30 a.m. on 13 June 1883, the day George departed for HMS *Canada*, Alix wrote him a farewell letter:

> My own darling little Georgie, I have only just left you going to bed after having given you my last kiss & having heard you say yr prayers. I need hardly say what I feel – and what we both feel at this sad hour of parting. It will be harder for you this time to have to go quite by yourself – without Eddy, Mr Dalton or Fuller – but remember darling that when all others are far away God is always there . . . I need hardly say my darling little Georgie <u>how</u> much I shall always miss you – now we have been so much together & you were such a dear little boy not at all spoilt & so nice & affectionate to old Motherdear. Remain just as you are but strive to get on in all that is good – & keep out of temptation as much as you can – don't let anyone lead you astray – remember to take the Sacrament about every quarter, which will give you fresh strength to do what is right – & also never forget either yr morning or evening prayer.[57]

Alix was perhaps concerned more with her own anguish at parting than with consoling George. Her six commandments were so impossible that (in Friedman's view) George must either have rebelled, as Eddy did, or have internalised her imperatives and used them to command those beneath him – both in the navy and later with his own children.[58] On any reading, Alix's attempt – unconscious though it was – to control her son by infantilising him seems hard to deny. In her defence, we should note that extravagant endearment was a habit of the Danish royal family.[59]

Very few letters survive from George as a midshipman. We can picture him standing ramrod straight on the deck of HMS *Canada* during the night watch somewhere in the Atlantic Ocean. Back in Britain, meanwhile, Prince Eddy stumbled into the way of life which – unfairly perhaps – would earn him a reputation as a libertine.

Eddy was installed in the Bachelors' Cottage at Sandringham to cram for Cambridge with a tutor, the 24-year-old James (Jim) Stephen. According to the author of *Prince Eddy and the Homosexual Underworld*, the woman-hating Stephen, a member of the elite intellectual group of Cambridge Apostles, 'could hardly have been a more unfortunate choice' as mentor for the malleable, sexually equivocal Eddy.[60] There was nothing surprising about the appointment, though. A son of Sir James Fitzjames Stephen, Jim was a talented member of the Victorian intellectual aristocracy from whom, as we have seen, the royals picked their tutors.

Eddy found him 'not a bad fellow on the whole though I thought him rather a curious chap at first. He is rather lazy in his movements but I think he is clever in some things, and I get on very well with him on the whole.' Far from being star-struck, Eddy considered the fifteen-stone Stephen a clumsy clown. 'They sent down a cob for him to ride, which he half killed one day as he rode 13 miles to a place and then back the same evening. He is not bad at tennis and I often have a game with him. He is most stupid in finding his way about here and he has lost himself several times.'[61]

Unlike Dalton, Stephen liked Eddy, whom he thought 'a good-natured unaffected youth'.[62] Where Dalton had diagnosed sinister mental problems, Stephen noticed nothing more serious than an inability to concentrate.

Eddy stayed at Balmoral. On the first day Grandmama gave him the Garter. 'There was no ceremony or anything of that sort; as I went to her room and she gave it to me there. I wore it every evening at dinner while I was there and the Garter round my leg.'[63]* Contrary to the legend of the languid, effete prince which later developed, Eddy went out stalking every day and shot fourteen stags, averaging two each time. 'He is an amiable, good boy, free from all evil propensities,' was the Queen's oddly guarded verdict on her grandson and heir.[64]

Eddy went up to Trinity College, Cambridge, in October 1883. He

---

*The Garter is the senior order of knighthood, in the sole gift of the sovereign. Giving the Garter to Eddy in this way is typical of Queen Victoria's relaxed attitude towards court ceremonial. The blue Garter ribbon is always worn over the left shoulder; the star is pinned to the left breast.

had rooms in college, which he thought 'a very drafty [*sic*] cold place, quite as cold as the Britannia'. 'I found it very strange here at first but begin to get more used to it now,' he wrote. 'I found it very difficult at first getting about, as one college is so much like another.'[65] Jim Stephen, who (as we have just seen) ironically had found it hard to find *his* way about at Sandringham, accompanied Eddy along with Dalton. Eddy's biographer Theo Aronson has suggested that Stephen initiated Eddy into the Cambridge world of Greek love. *Punch* caricatured the prince as an effeminate youth with scented hair. Through Stephen, Eddy became friends with the Apostle Henry (Harry) Wilson, and he was introduced to homosexuals such as A. C. Benson and Lord Ronald Gower, said to be the original for Lord Henry Wotton in Oscar Wilde's *Picture of Dorian Gray* (1891).[66]

Most of Eddy's papers were destroyed, but his letters to 'My dear Boy' as he called George survived, and there is little here to confirm the construct of the limp-wristed prince.[67] 'I know several very nice fellows now two of which [*sic*] are Bearing [*sic*] and Cust,' Eddy told George.[68] John Baring, later Lord Revelstoke and head of Barings Bank, was a Trinity oarsman who left the university without a degree and became one of George's closest friends. Lionel Cust was a cousin of George's friend Charles Cust, a Trinity man and later surveyor of the King's pictures. Though he neither rowed nor played cricket, Eddy was not an indoors hothouse plant: 'I have had several good rides lately and have just come in from the drag [hunt] which is rather fun as you get a very good ride and plenty of jumping.'[69] As for Aronson's speculation that Eddy's first sexual encounter took place at Cambridge and that it was likely to have been homosexual, this must be set against Eddy's remark to George: 'Have you had any fun with anybody yet; because I have not?'[70] By 'anybody' he had in mind 'pretty girls'.[71] As Andrew Cook, Eddy's 2008 biographer, suggests, the hard evidence seems to point to heterosexuality.[72]

The stories told about the 'Pragger', contemporary slang for 'prince', stress his simplicity. When the master of Trinity, Dr William Hepworth Thompson, showed him a portrait of himself by Hubert Herkomer, Eddy innocently – or perhaps wittily – responded: 'Another old master, I suppose?'[73] Eddy attended an evening party held by Oscar Browning, an Eton master sacked for indecency, in his rooms at King's. Browning proudly showed off his new bathroom to the prince, whereupon a wag locked the two men inside. The Pragger 'took the prank in good part'.[74] Locking people in the WC was Eddy's idea of wit – he had played the joke on his father's court fool Christopher Sykes the previous year: 'He went to sleep in there some time and was rather annoyed when we let him out.'[75]

* * *

George returned from the West Indies and left the *Canada* in July 1884. He spent the next eighteen months in Britain, attending the Royal Naval College in Greenwich and training in Portsmouth in gunnery, interspersed with long holidays at Abergeldie and Sandringham.

Julie Stonor was four years older than George, an English rose with a tip-tilted nose. Her mother, a daughter of Sir Robert Peel, was Alexandra's woman of the bedchamber, and when she died with Alix at her side ('I cannot get her last minutes out of my head – those poor heartbroken children kneeling round her bed & sobbing their hearts out') Alix vowed to take care of the orphan Julie and her brother Harry.[76] Julie and George became close. From reading George's diary, it was clear to Harold Nicolson that 'at the age of eighteen he fell very much in love with Julie Stonor. It is all rather pathetic.'[77] Matters seem to have reached a climax at Christmas 1885 when Julie was at Sandringham.

There was talk of an engagement, but marriage was out of the question.[78] Julie was not only a commoner, but a devout Roman Catholic of the purest and bluest recusant blood and was thus excluded from the throne by the 1701 Act of Settlement. George's relationship with Julie brought him very close to Alix that winter. 'We seem to have grown so much nearer to each other,' she told George, '& I feel I have all yr confidence as well as yr affection. You cannot think what pleasure it gives me that there is <u>nothing</u> my little Georgie does not tell his Mother dear who you know is always yr best & truest friend.'[79] Mother and son had 'little talks' late at night or after tea in the hall at Sandringham, and George assured Alix that he had 'resisted all temptation so far'.[80] 'It is the greatest proof you could possibly give', she wrote, 'of how much you wish to please me, that you should have done it for my sake, & the promise you gave me of yr <u>own</u> accord a few days before you left.'[81]

Alix acted as Julie's confidante too. She saw her often, and she managed to persuade both George and Julie that their relationship must end, though they continued to write and to see one another for two years or more. 'She & I as she will have told you had long talked about you & it all, but there it is & alas! Rather a sad case I think for you both, my <u>two</u> poor children! <u>I</u> only wish you could marry & be happy but alas I fear that cannot be! Yet she is such a dear good sweet girl & always the same & comes to me old mother dear for everything'.[82]*

George was tender-hearted and cried easily, as Eddy observed.[83] He

---

*In 1891 Julie Stonor married the Marquis d'Hautpoul. She didn't go out of George's life: he continued to pay her visits, and he was loyal to her as he was to his old tutors and servants. This was tolerated by Queen Mary, although both Pope-Hennessy and Nicolson held

idolised his mother. 'Sat up till 2 talking . . . with darling Mother-dear,' he wrote in his diary.[84] His letters to her read more like those of a lover than a son's. 'My own darling sweet little beloved Motherdear,' he begins. 'Of course I forgive you my darling for not having written for so long . . . You say your letter is stupid. It is not. Darling Motherdear, it is dear & charming & you write just as if you were talking, although I have no doubt the banging on the piano did not help you.'[85]

The letters to Motherdear contradict the bluff and manly character that later became George's public image. John Gore considered that George wrote to his mother using the verbal 'fancy dress' that she had taught him, and the letters belie the real George.[86] The correspondence, as Alix's biographer observed, is more Edwardian than Victorian.[87] At the time of Bertie's 'Fall' in 1861, when he was discovered to have slept with the prostitute Nellie Clifden, his father wrote him an angry, emotional letter, and his mother was brutally unforgiving. The contrast with Alix's gentle handling of the Julie Stonor affair, transforming it into something beautiful while skilfully defusing it, could hardly be greater. But if the mothers were very different, so were the sons. Alix created a Peter Pan world of whimsy and perpetual childhood. It is not the boy who refuses to grow up, however, but the mother who won't let him. 'May you ever remain the same dear unspoilt boy as you are now. This indeed is my greatest wish,' wrote Alix to George on his twenty-first birthday.[88]

George's favourite novel was a romance entitled *Olga; or, Wrong on Both Sides*.[89] 'Such a lovely book, I always cry over it,' he wrote.[90] Written in the 'revolting' style of Little Lord Fauntleroy, the book is snobbish and mawkish and Harold Nicolson was right to say that it has 'no literary merit whatsoever'. It is 'interesting psychologically', however.[91] The hero is a hot-tempered young viscount with whom George could identify, and the book tells of his quarrel with his father, a harsh old earl, who loves him deeply underneath. The boy becomes close to a beautiful older woman and her young daughter whom he loves, but in a violent ending he unintentionally causes her death when her horse is frightened by a threshing machine. This pulp melodrama with its echoes of his love for Julie Stonor delineates George's emotional landscape.

---

back from writing about Julie for fear of offending the Queen. (Nicolson Diary, 12 August 1949. Pope 194/3, JPH Note of Interview with Lady Shaftesbury, October 1956.)

CHAPTER 3

Naval Lieutenant
1885–1891

George spent six months at Portsmouth in 1885 in HMS *Excellent* working for his lieutenant's exams. He took a first class in torpedo, gunnery and seamanship. To his disappointment he narrowly missed a first in pilotage. His father wrote: 'It would of course have been better if you <u>had</u> obtained it, but being only within 20 marks is very satisfactory, and shows also that there is no favouritism in your case.'[1] The next stage had already been decided by Bertie, who micromanaged his son's career: George was to serve under Captain Harry Stephenson in his ship *Thunderer* in the Mediterranean station.

Stephenson was a royal favourite. He was an equerry to the Prince of Wales and, rather like a naval version of Flashman, he had served in every adventure since the 1850s, from the China war to the Indian Mutiny, as well as on the 1875–6 Arctic expedition. He was a big man, with the drooping eyelids of a bloodhound and a walrus moustache. Alix considered him one of her best friends, 'charming kind sensible & trustworthy'. She told George: 'In him you have the best companion possible & one who reminds you of home too … & to whom you can talk openly!'[2] George wrote to Stephenson to say 'how delighted I am that Papa and Mama have chosen you to be my next Captain … I would sooner serve under you than with any other Captain, because I have known you ever since I can remember anybody and we have always been such good friends.'[3]

Bertie gave Stephenson strict instructions about his son. 'Don't <u>spoil</u> him <u>please</u>! … He is sharp and quick and I think likes the Service, but he must be kept up to his work.'[4] To George he wrote: 'I hope that you will set an example to all the officers, in quickness, smartness & intelligence.'[5]

Contrary to the Prince of Wales's instructions, Stephenson did not treat George in exactly the same way as he did the other officers. On his way out to join his ship, George wrote to his father: 'Although now I am separated from all I love & from all my friends I still have one left in Captain Stephenson.'[6] Later he told Alix that Stephenson 'used to come & sit in my cabin & we had such nice talks'.[7] John Gore thought Stephenson one of the two great influences in George's early life (the other being John Dalton).[8] Rather than friends of his own age, George was drawn to older men, authority figures and substitutes for his absent father.

With the Mediterranean Fleet, George found himself a member of 'the greatest display team in the world'.[9] It was here that the Royal Navy paraded in all its glory of complex evolutions of fleet formation, scrubbed decks, sparkling paint and crisp white uniforms. George spent two years in the Mediterranean and for over half that time he was at Malta. This infuriated his father, who wrote repeatedly to Stephenson deploring George's long stays on the island. 'It is a waste of time and there is nothing but gossip and tittle tattle and what I call "coffee housing".'[10] Fever was endemic, and as typhoid was the 'family failing', the royal doctors considered George to be at high risk – though 'Malta fever' in fact turned out to be brucellosis, not typhoid.[11]

Malta was a gap-year paradise of regattas, balls and polo. The part of Prospero on this island of pleasure was played by George's uncle Alfred, Duke of Edinburgh and commander-in-chief of the Mediterranean Fleet. Then at the height of his career, with 'a deep tanned face in which his eyes shone extraordinarily, fascinatingly blue', the duke held court at San Antonio, a romantic seventeenth-century castle where he brought his children and his Russian wife Marie, the sister of Tsar Alexander III.[12] 'I am devoted to Aunt Marie,' George assured his mother, '& I am sure you could not find a better friend, she is so honest & straightforward & always says exactly what she means.'[13] At San Antonio, Marie gave parties where they danced the cotillion until 3 a.m. and George was stalked by socially ambitious young naval officers. Lieutenant Bryan Godfrey-Faussett, who spent his time drinking in the Union Club in the Strada Reale, playing polo and recovering from hangovers, carefully noted in his diary his sightings of the prince, who comes across as a lonely, remote figure.[14]

We tend to think of the Victorian navy effortlessly ruling the waves during the long years of the Pax Britannica, but in the Mediterranean Fleet George encountered a navy which had seen no action since Nelson's day eighty years before, a peacetime force which had forgotten how to fight. 'Bull' (super-shiny shoe polishing), discipline, unquestioning obedience to orders, deference to seniority and rank and meticulous attention to order, cleanliness and uniform were rewarded with promotion. There was no place for the lateral-thinking rat-catcher warrior. The higher ranks of the navy were clogged with blinkered martinets in superbly tailored uniforms. The historian of the Victorian navy has described these conformist officers as 'authoritarians'.[15]

One way or another, 'authoritarian' is a word which keeps cropping up in accounts of George's early life. For the psychobiographer Dennis Friedman, George's strained relationship with his father and his deference to surrogate fathers such as Stephenson left him with 'an unhealthy respect for authority and, by extension, authoritarianism'.[16] George's exposure to the navy reinforced his respect for hierarchy and his willingness to obey orders. Contrary to Harold Nicolson's view that the main framework of the prince's character was already fixed by the time he became a serving officer in 1883, the navy changed George.[17] Unlike Eddy, he did not rebel. He conformed to the culture of obedience and anti-intellectualism. The navy validated and rewarded traits such as neatness, punctuality and a need for order. Correctness in dress was for him almost a religion.

Influenced by his uncle Alfred, George took up stamp collecting, a pastime for the more painstaking individual. Godfrey-Faussett gives a glimpse of him at Malta on afternoon watch: 'He took us into his cabin, showed us his collection of foreign stamps, about 3 or 4000. Also gave us each some photos of himself, some of which were very good.'[18]

George grew a beard. Even this followed the rules, laid down by Queen Victoria when she authorised beards for sailors in 1869: a full beard was required, including moustache (one without the other was forbidden by the Queen, and in any case missed the point, which was to remove the need to shave), and it was to be kept short and very clean.[19] George was to wear his beard in this style for the rest of his life. He sent photos home. 'You look so fierce,' commented Alix.[20] The bristling beard hedged around the 'pretty red lips' made 'My darling little Georgie' appear boyish.[21] Eddy was not impressed:

> Oh yes, I got your photos all right and I think them very good, but I would have preferred you without a beard. I daresay it is more comfortable than shaving, which I now do nearly every day, but it makes you look much older and I think you might take it off before you return home, if you feel inclined to.[22]

As Alix explained, Eddy was jealous as he showed no sign of a beard, 'tho' he fiddles about at his little wee moustache in a most ferocious way thinking that will make it grow ... But what I cannot understand is why you little mite should have so much hair about you when the biggest has none of it!'[23]

The bearded stare masked an unhappy prince. His father wrote in August 1887: 'I was sorry to hear from hints that you dropped that you were not as keen about the Navy as formerly.'[24] When Stephenson left the Mediterranean Fleet in December 1887, George was heartbroken.

'I can't tell you how I miss you dear Capt. Stephenson,' he wrote, 'everything seems a blank without you, and now I have nobody to talk to or to ask advice from which is horrid.'[25] 'Dear old Stephenson,' wrote Eddy, 'I can well understand your being fond of a man like him.'[26] Spending Christmas with 'the darling cousins' on Malta, George was homesick for Sandringham, 'the dear place I love better than anywhere in the world'. He told Alix:

> I can picture you there at different times all through the day; now you are all sitting in the hall having tea, or perhaps now you are playing the piano with darling Toria. Oh! Why am I not there too, it seems cruel that I should be separated from you in this way.[27]

From England Alix wrote to say how much she missed 'yr bright little face with its turned up snout'.[28]

George's wails were not ignored. Back at Sandringham, Stephenson had long talks with Bertie and Alix. George received permission to spend the early weeks of 1888 at Athens (the Greek Christmas fell on 7 January) with his uncle Willy, Alix's brother King George of Greece, and Aunt Olga. 'Humorous, gifted and affectionate,' the Russian queen provided 'my little Sunbeam', as she called George, with a female royal environment that reminded him of Sandringham.[29] As Queen Mary later remarked, she was a second mother to him.[30] 'I am writing this in darling aunt Olga's room,' George told Alix, 'she is such an Angel, she is also writing at another table & every now & then we stop & talk & we have been talking such a lot about you.'[31] When Queen Victoria objected to him spending time at Athens, George complained to Alix: 'Why on earth should I not? Why may I not go & see uncle Willy, if you & Papa wish me to, it is the greatest bosh I ever heard, I am very angry.'[32]

In 1888 George joined the *Alexandra*, the admiral's flagship. His biographer John Gore dates a new note of confidence from this time.[33] The prince's letters home are frank, breezy and philistine. After visiting 'some old ruins' discovered by Dr Schliemann (that is, Mycenae), he reported: 'They are no doubt very fine but I am afraid I don't take much interest in old stones.'[34] He addressed Stephenson no longer as a father figure but as an equerry and factotum, briskly asking him to do errands or write letters. For the first time in his life, George had a friend of his own age – Charles Cust, a fellow lieutenant. 'That brute Charles Cust is sitting on the deck of my cabin behind me because I have not got another chair, abusing me and my cabin so I can't write any more.'[35] Cust was to become one of George's few intimates and their friendship would prove to be lifelong.

By now George had lost his virginity – not just a rite of passage, but a muted rebellion when we remember the promises he had made to Alix to resist all temptation at the time of his infatuation with Julie Stonor two years before. When he was back in England on leave in 1888, his diary records that he had a girl he slept with at Southsea, and another in St John's Wood whom he shared with Eddy. 'She is a ripper,' he wrote.[36] The fact that Eddy shared a girl with his brother is hardly consistent with the theory that he was gay.

George was given his first command – of a torpedo boat – in July 1889, and in August he took part in the annual manoeuvres off the west coast of Ireland on the side of the 'enemy'. He had to rescue and tow to safety another broken-down torpedo boat in stormy weather – a difficult feat of seamanship, though modestly he made no mention of it in letters home.[37] The year before, Admiral Sir George Tryon had commanded the 'enemy' and captured Liverpool, sensationally demonstrating the navy's shortcomings as a fighting force. 'I congratulate myself that I was well out of those manoeuvres,' George declared.[38]

Tryon was a reformer, intent on breaking up the navy's dependence on the signal book – the system of hoisting flags to issue instructions which enabled an admiral to exercise tight top-down control over his fleet but prevented officers from acting on their own initiative. Signals allowed the fleet to execute parade-ground evolutions in harbour but crippled it as a fighting machine. Of Tryon's radical thinking George was probably unaware. The senior officers he was close to were traditionalists. At Malta his uncle Alfred was famed for his skill in handling the acrobatic routines of the fleet – the peacetime drill which Tryon considered a waste of time. Captain Stephenson was another 'tramline authoritarian', devoted to hierarchy and the signal book.[39]

Bertie believed that 'no finer profession for an Englishman exists in the world' than the navy, and 'some members of our family ought always to be actively employed in it'.[40] As already noted, the navy was the preferred career for a second son, which the Duke of Edinburgh himself had been. 'I want you to keep up the reputation of being the smartest officer in the squadron,' Bertie told George.[41]

But the royal connection was not altogether a good thing. Not only did the navy shape George, as we have seen, stunting his emotional growth and impoverishing him intellectually, but royal influence had a baleful effect on the navy. Royal favour was a passport to promotion, but the officers connected to the court were usually traditionalists, fanatics for drill and discipline. Royal yachts were the worst of all: 'the innermost temple of formality, ceremonial and cleanliness; nowhere in the Navy afloat was further from the mentality and practices of war'.[42]

'Every morning now I wake with a jump & a start & expect to see you standing before me with your poor dear tear stained little face.'[43] Thus the Princess of Wales wrote to her 25-year-old son when he sailed for Bermuda in command of the gunboat *Thrush*. George replied: 'That horrible morning shall I ever forget it, when I said goodbye to you darling when you were still in bed.'[44] George spent fifteen months with the West Indian and North American Squadron. He sailed from Bermuda to Jamaica, and on to Trinidad and Barbados, and wherever he went, pootling around this backwater of empire, he was received with the ceremonial and hospitality due to a minor royal. Accompanied by Admiral Watson, the commander-in-chief, on each island he stayed at Government House, where he was entertained with tennis and dances. 'I danced 17 times,' he wrote in his diary at Trinidad. 'Miss Robinson dances quite beautifully, I danced 5 times with her. Best ball I have been to for some time.'[45] He bought stamps from a telegraph clerk in Trinidad named Mr Galbraith, and he played the piano with Miss Daisy, the admiral's daughter.[46]

From Bermuda, George wrote to his first cousin Marie (Missy) of Edinburgh: 'Darling Missy, you are constantly in my thoughts.'[47] George's affection for Missy dated back to his time in Malta. Ten years younger than him, Missy was the eldest and prettiest of the 'dear three' Edinburgh princesses, a wilful horse-mad tomboy with whom George had enjoyed wild romping rides and picnics on his cob Real Jam. He was Missy's 'beloved chum', and in her autobiography she recalled 'what a delicious relief' it was after a scolding 'to lay my humiliated head upon his shoulder, and to weep my heart out, my face hidden in the mass of my "yellow" hair. "Poor dear little Missy," said Cousin George, "poor dear little Miss," and Missy learned at that hour how very sweet the big grown-up cousin could be!'[48]

This was the closest that Queen Marie of Romania (as Missy was to become) got to revealing her relationship with her grown-up cousin, and when it was published in 1934 even this coy and guarded account was enough to earn the displeasure of George, who disapproved of people writing their memoirs. But George had undoubtedly been smitten, in 1888 writing to the twelve-year-old girl: 'I am so longing to see you my darling Missy. I never show your letters to anybody, & I hope you don't show mine.'[49]

In March 1890 George accompanied his father on a state visit to

Berlin. Alix, who never lost an opportunity of abusing the young Kaiser William II – 'Oh he is mad & a conceited ass' – teased 'my Georgie boy' for becoming 'a real live filthy blue coated Pickelhaube [spiked helmet] German soldier!!'[50] George then travelled to Coburg, where the Edinburghs now lived (Alfred was in line to succeed his uncle Ernest as grand duke).* A photo of a family group shows George with his arms folded and a spikey waxed moustache standing behind the blonde, round-faced Missy, a very grown-up fourteen-year-old. 'What fun we had when we danced,' he wrote.[51]

And that was all. The pair exchanged letters, but mostly George (as Queen Victoria wrote) was 'waiting & waiting'.[52] Being at sea, there was little else he could do. But he thought he had done enough to fish Missy out of the dynastic pool of eligible first cousins.

Meanwhile, news reached George of Eddy's romance with the Roman Catholic Hélène of Orléans (see pages 46–8), and Queen Victoria wrote urging George that he too should marry. This grandmotherly matchmaking was not welcome, and George turned to his mother for support: 'I always feel I can confide anything in you sweet Motherdear & you always give me such good advice'.[53] Months later he added: 'I am in no hurry at all & I told [Grandmama] that I thought it was very bad for men to marry too young, don't you agree with me.'[54] Alix, who knew of George's feelings for Missy, replied: 'So Grandmama thinks the best thing to be done is for you to be married & get an heir!!! But I quite agree with you it certainly wld be too soon in every way!! Particularly as the bride elect is not in long petticoats yet!!!'[55] As well as her age, Alix had other objections to Missy. She thought it 'a pity those children shd be entirely brought up as Germans', speaking English with a strong German accent.[56] This upbringing was understandable perhaps given the Coburg succession, but in Alix's view it was not desirable in an English princess.

'Well & now about yr Matrimonial prospects!!! ha ha ha,' wrote Alix.

You are quite right to think Grandmama has gone mad on the subject – & it is too ridiculous & it wd be a very bad plan both for you in yr profession & the girl being a perfect baby yet – altho Aunt Marie begging her pardon does all she can to make her old before her time, which I think the greatest mistake.[57]

---

*The childless Duke Ernest was Prince Albert's elder brother and a notorious womaniser. Missy remembered him as 'an old beau, squeezed into a frock coat too tight for his bulk' with 'the jaw of a bulldog, the lower teeth protruding far beyond the upper with a pair of bloodshot eyes alive with uncanny, almost brutal intelligence' (Marie, Queen of Romania, *The Story of My Life* (Cassell, 1934), vol. 1, p. 166).

Treating George's relations with Missy as a joke was Alix's way of discouraging her son. If anyone could prevent Queen Victoria from rushing George into matrimony it was Alix.

Unlike Bertie, whose relations with his mother were notoriously strained, Alix knew how to handle the old Queen. The two women shared a sense of the ridiculous, and Alix could make Victoria laugh in a way that none of her children dared. Here is Alix describing to George a royal drawing room at which the Queen, feeling hot, asked the Duchess of Buccleuch, the mistress of the robes, to remove her shawl:

> The latter being rather fidgety & fussy and over-anxious poor thing caught it in the veil at the same time as Grandmama turned her head leftwards . . . lo & behold the whole head edifice veil cap crown & all were flying off in a jiffy – & there stood poor little Grandmama with her bare head & nothing on but her little twisted pig tail as big as a shilling at the back of her head. I thought I should have died – but thank goodness I behaved beautifully & never laughed till Grandmama roared till the tears raced down her cheeks. We clapped it on as quickly as we cld after having recovered from the first shock – I in an awful fright at having put it on the wrong way up. In the meantime ladies were waiting to be presented & cd not make out what all this shuffling was about, & when at last they were let loose with a rush – Grandmama was in fits of laughter in their faces!![58]

'George is devoted to Missy, & I think she is to him,' wrote Queen Victoria in June 1891.[59] Some have questioned Missy's feelings for George.[60] And George's 'devotion' to Missy could be seen as a psychological stratagem. Choosing a child bride and then waiting and waiting was a way of evading a meaningful relationship. Missy's youth put her out of bounds (she was below the age of consent in Britain, which had been raised from thirteen to sixteen in 1885). In much the same fashion Julie Stonor's Catholicism had ruled out marriage. Adoring the teenage Missy unrequitedly from the other side of the world was a fairy tale that suited George well.

George sailed home in *Thrush* in July 1891. Shortly after his return he was promoted to commander. This was an accelerated elevation: George had served only six years as lieutenant, and most Victorian officers had to wait at least twelve years before advancing to commander. To contemporaries, however, the question was not whether George had been overpromoted but why he hadn't received the third gold ring on his cuffs earlier. Princes were expected to follow a different career path from ordinary officers. Alfred, Duke of Edinburgh skipped the ranks of sub-lieutenant and commander, becoming a captain at twenty-two and an admiral at thirty-four. He retired aged forty-seven, having snaffled up all the ranks and commands available. Delaying George's promotion would protect him against early retirement in his prime: it was seen as a clear signal that he was destined by his father to serve in the navy for life.[61] His next job was expected to be the command of a flagship in the Channel Squadron starting in May 1892.[62] In the meantime, he was on leave.

Days after he had left *Thrush*, George crossed to Denmark. Not since he joined *Britannia* aged twelve had he spent a family holiday at Fredensborg with his Danish grandparents. He was reunited with his Russian cousins, including Nicky, the Tsarevich, whom Alix had described as 'a charming boy [who] reminds me of my Georgie & is your height too'.[63]

The friendship between Nicky and Georgie dates from this Danish visit. As well as looking almost identical, the two cousins had been brought up by adoring Danish mothers who smothered them. They were both small men overwhelmed by their fathers, who were big men, physically and in personality. The two cousins were anti-intellectual, conscientious, dutiful and not at all political. Both the prince and the Tsarevich existed within the extended dynastic family and looked to their relations for their friends and their wives.[64] But George was just a second son. No one could have predicted the historical significance of this friendship. Nor could anyone have predicted the tragedy that was about to transform George's life.

CHAPTER 4

Eddy

1891–1892

In November 1891 George fell ill. The royal physicians diagnosed typhoid fever, and for nearly six weeks he never moved from his bed at Marlborough House. He was attended by two doctors and two nurses, and allowed to see no one but his parents. It was a 'sharp attack' but (according to the very well-informed Queen Victoria) he progressed 'quite satisfactorily': though he felt very weak, his fever rose no higher than 103.4 degrees.[1] Alix, who was staying with her sister in the Crimea, rushed home, travelling the entire journey by train, in order to nurse her son.[2]

George was strong enough to be with his family for New Year at Sandringham, and here he slowly recuperated, walking on the arm of an equerry. The tail end of the deadly Russian flu – the world's first lethal influenza pandemic – swept the country, and several people in the house fell ill. On 7 January Eddy walked home early from a shoot complaining of feeling unwell. George took his temperature, which was over 101 degrees, and sent him to bed.[3]

The next day, Friday, was Eddy's twenty-eighth birthday. George came down to dinner for the first time in two months, but Eddy was too ill to appear.[4] On Saturday Eddy was worse, with a temperature of 104 degrees and inflammation of the lung. The physicians who had treated George – Francis Laking and William Broadbent – were summoned, and the nurse who had barely ceased caring for George was hired to tend his brother.[5]

At first the doctors were cautiously optimistic that Eddy's condition was satisfactory and the pneumonia was following its normal course.[6] By Tuesday 12 January the inflammation of the lungs had almost cleared but, contrary to expectations, the patient was in a worse state. After a dreadful night, never sleeping more than fifteen minutes, he was delirious and exhausted, and his fingers and lips were blue.[7] This greatly worried the doctors, as it showed that 'the fever and other symptoms were not due to the inflammation of the lungs, but were caused by the poison of Influenza present in the blood' – in other words, sepsis.[8] In Broadbent's opinion, Eddy's extremely rapid breathing was the result of influenza acting on the brain and nervous system. Eddy's case was hopeless. As Bertie put it, 'the poison of that horrible Influenza had got into the dear boy's brain & lungs & baffled all science'.[9]*

On Wednesday George wrote in his diary: 'Poor darling Eddy is much worse & has had a very bad night, he is delirious & has been talking at the top of his voice all night.'[10] Eddy shouted without ceasing from 1 a.m. until 10 p.m., raving about the prime minister, the Marquess of Salisbury, and his Liberal opponent, William Gladstone, in a way which showed (too late) that he had formed independent judgements, and repeatedly claiming: 'I'm devoted to Gran'ma.'[11] The delirium was ominous, the doctors believed: it was more violent and more active than the raving characteristic of pneumonia. By now the normally stoical George had broken down. 'I am in utter despair, the darling boy ... We are so anxious & sad, one can't do anything ... After lunch went for a sad walk by myself & "Fluffy". I am longing to see the dear boy but I may not.'[12]

That evening Eddy became calmer, and the doctors allowed themselves to hope for a miracle. By 2 a.m., however, he was unconscious and plainly dying – his face was livid and bruised, and his chin jerked forward with every laboured breath.[13] Bertie woke George, who woke his sisters, and the family gathered for a ghastly vigil round Eddy's bed. Alix held his hand and bathed his forehead throughout. George, who knelt beside the bed, wrote in his diary: 'At 9.35 my beloved darling Eddy passed away quite quietly & peacefully. Oh! how shall I ever forget that dreadful scene all of us sobbing round him as if our hearts would break.'[14]

Later that day they arranged flowers on the bed and, the prince's sister Maud wrote, Eddy 'looked so beautiful with a most heavenly expression on his beloved face, just as if he was asleep with his dear hands folded in front of him, like a saint or some knight of old ... Quite like a beautiful marble statue.'[15] Three days after the funeral, Bertie commissioned the sculptor Alfred Gilbert to create a monument in the Albert Chapel at Windsor. Working from photographs and a watercolour of the corpse, Gilbert designed a full-size effigy of the Duke of Clarence, as Eddy had become in 1890, wearing the uniform of the 10th Royal Hussars executed in bronze, with marble head and hands: 'a noble young knight at rest, after the cruel battle with death'.[16]†

*

*Queen Victoria later reported that according to Laking 'the whole illness was abnormal like blood poisoning, & that they now knew darling Eddy had felt unwell more or less for 3 weeks' (Pope 203/6, QV to Vicky, 27 January 1892).
†This enlightened royal commission did not go smoothly. The twelve figures of saints surrounding the sarcophagus were still unfinished in 1903, to the fury of King Edward

Messages and telegrams of condolence flooded in – in the first four days George counted 2,419 telegrams and more than 9,000 letters.[17]* In London the streets were almost deserted, the omnibuses carried black bows and black flags and shops shuttered their windows.[18] West End theatres closed their doors and hunts cancelled meets as a mark of respect. But little was known about this young prince whose sudden death had caused such an outpouring of public grief.

A legend formed around the blank slate that was Eddy. Eddy was special because he was royal, but he was a special sort of royal because he was ordinary. Much was made of his parents' efforts to give him a normal upbringing. At sea, it was claimed, he was treated like any other midshipman, and at Cambridge he enjoyed no special privileges but mixed with other undergraduates, shunning the fast set and preferring quiet and clever men.[19] Modest and highly strung, he conscientiously performed his royal duties – though they made him so nervous that he once said that he would chuck it all up for £5,000 a year. Some saw him as a saint – a prince of a 'singularly pure, delicate and guileless nature'.[20] In his authorised memoir, the *Times* journalist J. E. Vincent evoked a lost king whose simple, affectionate and faithful character was a tribute to his parents' inspired training.[21]

But there was an alternative view. Some thought that Eddy's very ordinariness disqualified him for the role of monarch. The *Pall Mall Gazette* described him as 'an amiable young man, whose not over-keenness of mind was outwardly manifested in a somewhat phlegmatic exterior'.[22] The republican *Reynolds's Newspaper* condemned him as 'an insignificant, utterly unintellectual young man' who had never done anything noteworthy. 'Weak physically, not strong mentally, having, seemingly, no interest whatever in life', Eddy exemplified the futility of Britain's doomed monarchy. 'It may end with the Queen or her possible successor.'[23]

A darker side to Eddy's story began to emerge sixty years after his death. Lord Goddard, the lord chief justice, told Harold Nicolson that Eddy had been involved in the Cleveland Street scandal, 'a most unsavoury case' concerning a male brothel. 'It is one of God's mercies

---

VII. The King was even crosser when he discovered that Gilbert had removed two of the ivory and bronze statues and sold them to a dealer, replacing them with all-bronze figures – even though the King had already paid him for the originals (Richard Dorment, *Alfred Gilbert* (Yale University Press, 1985), pp. 148–75, 199–202. Richard Dorment, 'Gilbert, Sir Alfred (1954–1934)', *Oxford Dictionary of National Biography* (2004)).

*Jim Stephen, who had meanwhile been committed to St Andrew's mental asylum in Northampton after a brain injury, refused to eat when he heard the news of Eddy's death, and died twenty days later.

to us that that horrible young man died,' said the judge.[24] Eddy became a foil to his brother George, whose virtues shone by comparison with Eddy's debauchery. 'Yes it was a good thing that the Duke of Clarence died,' concluded Nicolson in his diary.[25]

In the 1970s the reinvention of Eddy lost all contact with reality when his name was linked with the Jack the Ripper murders of East End prostitutes in 1888. Dr Thomas Stowell published an article implying that Eddy himself had been the Ripper. Stowell claimed to possess evidence that Eddy had contracted syphilis in the West Indies on the *Bacchante* tour, and he alleged that the prince murdered prostitutes during fits of syphilitic insanity.[26]

Fantastical though the Ripper stories are, they suggest a picture of Eddy which is at odds with the simple, saintly prince: a sinister, cloaked figure prowling the London streets by night. As in Robert Louis Stevenson's story *The Strange Case of Dr Jekyll and Mr Hyde* (1886), there are two Eddys. 'Dear Eddy', the innocent, guileless prince, has a depraved doppelgänger, just as the good Dr Jekyll's other self was the hideous Edward Hyde. In reality, too, there are hints that Eddy led a double life.

After Cambridge, Eddy joined the 10th Royal Hussars. Stationed in York, he did a lot of hunting – his passion for the sport contradicts the picture of him as an effeminate, listless youth. 'Just a silly young army officer he was,' thought Nicolson.[27] But Eddy's medical history suggests a more depraved side to his life. Aged twenty-one he suffered from gleet or discharge, a symptom of advanced gonorrhoea. A doctor prescribed capsules, and advised him to cut down on food and alcohol.[28] At twenty-four he was diagnosed with gout, which caused a painfully swollen big toe. 'It sounds as if one was talking of an old man,' said George.[29]

The first woman Eddy wanted to marry was his cousin Alicky of Hesse, to whom Queen Victoria had recently introduced him. Urged on by his matchmaking grandmother, he arrived at Balmoral in September 1889 ready to declare his love, only to meet with a firm rejection before he was able to propose.[30] In October he departed on a six-month tour of India, leaving London just as the Cleveland Street scandal broke. Whether or not Eddy had patronised the male brothel has never been firmly established.

Eddy returned from India in May 1890 looking 'dreadfully yellow & thin' and 'pale & drawn'.[31] Alicky, who had never cared for him – she had her eye on Nicky of Russia – wrote finally refusing him. Though he claimed to be broken-hearted, Eddy immediately began a romance with Princess Hélène, the Roman Catholic daughter of the Comte de Paris, the Orléanist pretender to the French throne.

Later that summer Eddy had a sharpish attack of 'fever', and he left his regiment to recuperate with his family in Scotland. The exact nature of his malady is not clear. Alexandra wrote in October: 'Thank God he is nearly right now & looks ever so much better.'[32] Much later, in 1905, she reflected that Eddy 'never got right again after India'.[33] Alfred Fripp, the young doctor who treated him in Scotland, was instructed by Sir Dighton Probyn, one of Bertie's equerries, to effect 'a thorough and permanent restoration to health, no mere tinkering up for a few years, but a lasting cure. The gout and <u>every other ailment must be completely eradicated</u> from his system.'[34] Among Fripp's papers there is a prescription which suggests that Eddy was suffering from a gonorrhoeal infection.

Eddy's illness did not prevent him from proposing to Hélène, who happened to be staying with his sister Louise, Duchess of Fife, at Mar Lodge in Aberdeenshire. Hélène accepted him, regardless of the fact that she was a Roman Catholic and therefore excluded from the throne by the Act of Settlement – as Eddy himself would be if he married her. This marriage could therefore never take place – in spite of the support of Queen Victoria and Eddy's parents – unless Hélène changed her religion, which, as a member of the Catholic Orléans dynasty, she was unable to do.

Forbidden to meet, the lovers wrote. Eddy's letters, which have survived, are affectionate and self-deprecatory. 'To think that a darling like you should really love so much this unworthy creature, which I know and feel I am, is too lovely for words,' he declared.[35] There is much more in the same vein. They exchanged tokens – a ring, a pin – and photos: Eddy took a narcissistic pleasure in getting himself 'done'. His letters show him to be fluent and empathetic, and more articulate than his brother George. But there is no urgency or passion about them, nor any impatience with the lovers' predicament. Hélène tried to break the deadlock by seeking an interview with the Pope (which made matters worse, as he predictably refused to assent to her request to change her faith), but Eddy seemed content to wait for ever. With his gold nib he effortlessly covered page after page saying nothing at all: no plans, no conversation, just tender endearments. Perhaps this passivity was due to his apathetic nature. Or perhaps it suited him to be 'in love', as he described it – in a state of permanent limbo.

Eddy's favourite photographs of himself were taken by 'a certain Mrs Fairfax', who lived near York (her daughter Eve Fairfax would one day become Rodin's mistress). 'I often used to drive over and see her,' he told Hélène. 'She has quite a mania for photography and is always wanting to do me when I go to see her . . . I am sure you would like her, for there is no nonsense about her, and she is quite natural and very nice.'[36] It's unlikely that Hélène picked up the hint, but Mrs Fairfax supplied more than photos. She introduced Eddy to Lady Sybil St Clair-Erskine, the beautiful twenty-year-old half-sister of his father's mistress Daisy, Countess of Warwick.[37]

When Eddy received Hélène's letter breaking off the engagement at the end of May, he was at first 'violent, then in despair'.[38] A few days later, however, Sir Henry Ponsonby, Queen Victoria's private secretary, was surprised to find that 'he did not appear depressed but talked away in a most lively manner'.[39] Soon he was writing long, flirtatious letters to Lady Sybil. What did he mean when he wrote: 'I thought it was impossible a short time ago to——more than one person at the same time, and I believe according to things in general it should be so, but exceptions will happen at times.'[40] Dodging his father, who spent adulterous afternoons at Sybil's Curzon Street home with Lady Warwick, Eddy asked Sybil: 'I wonder if you really love me a little? I ought not to ask such a question I suppose, but still I should be very pleased if you did just a little bit.'[41]

Eddy's freedom was short-lived. In August 1891 his parents, despairing of his army career and unable to think of any alternative, decided that Eddy should marry. The wife they chose was Princess May of Teck. This was a cynical arranged marriage. As Francis Knollys, the Prince of Wales's private secretary, wrote:

> I don't imagine that Prince Eddy is anxious to marry Pss May; on the contrary I fancy he would much rather not do so. But I feel convinced that with a little kindness and a good deal of firmness he will act in accordance with his parents' wishes in the matter.[42]

The royal advisers set about arranging for Princess May, who, as we shall see, had hitherto been marginalised as a poor relation, to make the all-important visit to Queen Victoria at Balmoral.

Meanwhile, reports appeared in the newspapers of the suicide of Lydia Miller, also known as Lydia Manton, a chorus girl at the fashionable Gaiety Theatre in the Strand. Like many Gaiety girls, for whom the theatre functioned as a marriage agency into the peerage, she was the kept mistress of a rich man, and she lived in style in a flat in Burlington Mansions, Cork Street. According to the official story, she swallowed a bottle of carbolic acid and died in agony when her lover Lord Charles Montagu was late for lunch one day. This was evidently a cover-up. The facts of the case were suppressed at the inquest, which was attended by George Lewis, the royal solicitor who specialised in shutting down Society scandals. Lord Charles Montagu was not rich.

He was screening someone else, and that someone, according to the press, was Prince Eddy. Lydia died wearing precious diamonds given 'as a mark of princely favour', and she killed herself, so they said, because of his coldness.[43]

The Lydia Manton story fits with another piece of evidence which suggests that Eddy was trying to disentangle himself from chorus girls and other women in preparation for his marriage. Two letters which have come to light from the prince to George Lewis reveal that Eddy was blackmailed by another Gaiety girl, Maud Richardson, who at the time of his engagement demanded money for his letters.[44] Little wonder that Eddy wrote anxiously to Lady Sybil, urging her to keep his letters in a secret place and cut off the crest and signature. 'You can't be too careful what you do in these days, when hardly anybody is to be trusted.'[45]

Eddy's chief occupation, it seems, was sex. Perhaps it was rumours such as these that Queen Victoria had in mind when she complained in December 1891 that he led 'a dissipated life'.[46]

Four days before he proposed to Princess May, Eddy wrote a last letter to Sybil:

Don't be surprised if you hear before long that I am engaged ... for I expect it will come off soon. But it will be a very different thing to what it might have been once, and which I told you about this summer, but it still can't be helped and I must make the best of a bad job.[47]

On his deathbed, however, he raved in French, and some said he shouted for Hélène.[48] His sisters wrote to the Orléanist princess telling her about his last hours, and assuring her that 'he was fond of M. [*sic*], but you are the one he loved'.[49] In his coffin they placed the coin which Hélène had given him, and which he always wore round his neck.

Among the papers of James Pope-Hennessy is a note about a story told to him by the royal librarian Owen Morshead that Prince Eddy had syphilis, and that in later life Queen Mary learnt of this.[50] In 1958 Pope-Hennessy spent a weekend with George's third son, Prince Henry, Duke of Gloucester, and he recorded how, in one of their late-night conversations, Prince Henry 'edged towards the subject on which he really wanted to pump me: The Duke of Clarence'.

'Well now I want to ask you – did Uncle Eddie *have ziph*?' (Pronounced *sic*)
　'So I believe, Sir.'
　'But you haven't found anything about it?'
　'It's not the sort of thing people keep evidence of, Sir.'

'Well I know when we were children the first time we ever *heard* of ziph was when we were told Uncle Eddie had it. Who told us, God knows. So I always wondered. Funny chap, Uncle Eddie.'[51]

Later, writing the chapter of his book about Eddy, Pope-Hennessy confessed:

I am become ... so dreadfully sorry for him ... All that thinness and yellowness of course was syphilis; I suspect QV knew of it, when she writes about him not being well enough for a long time to marry. The cure by mercury was very langsam [slow] in those days.

When Pope-Hennessy reached the pathetic story of Eddy's death, he 'howled'.[52]

Eddy's death left George second in line to the throne. He was not a public figure. On the contrary, he was an obscure and sickly royal about whom very little was known. He had not yet made a public speech.[53] As he was still convalescent from typhoid, some doubted whether he would live to succeed his father.[54] If George died without an heir, the throne would pass to his sister Louise, Duchess of Fife, and the press clamoured for him to marry at once.[55]

George could hardly have been less prepared for the new position which was thrust upon him. In his diaries he made no mention of politics. Nor, after Eddy's death, did he reflect at all on the fact that he would be king – though his diaries carefully conceal his feelings. To his cousin Louis Battenberg he confided his panic at being totally unfit for his new role. '"George, you're wrong," Prince Louis allegedly replied. "There is no more fitting preparation for a King than to have been trained in the Navy."'[56]

Barely recovered from his illness, he had lost over a stone in weight, reduced to nine stone three pounds, and he was suffering from sleeplessness and nightmares. In letters he described himself as 'utterly crushed & heartbroken ... I am entirely stunned ... I cannot realise yet that I shall never see that darling beloved face again.'[57] For the rest of his life he wrote with Eddy's gold-nibbed pen. The shock of his brother's sudden death coming on top of his own typhoid left George a lifelong hypochondriac, nervous of minor symptoms, fussy about colds and mollycoddled by doctors.[58] People around him worried too. As the Prince of Wales's only surviving son, George was 'a terrible anxiety', his aunt Vicky wrote, 'and one is always trembling lest anything should happen'.[59]

With his family he retreated into mourning. They stayed first at the Duke of Devonshire's Compton Place in Eastbourne, and then on the French Riviera in Menton and Cannes. George's diary records an idle round of engagements, which some thought 'did his character more harm than good'.[60] He read novels to pass the time – Hardy's *Tess of the d'Urbervilles* and Thackeray's *Pendennis*.[61]

Back in England in May 1892, George was established in his new position. 'Today Grandmama has made me Duke of York, Earl of Inverness & Baron Killarney,' he wrote in his diary.[62] Not that the Queen herself approved. 'I am glad you like the title Duke of York,' she wrote tartly. 'I am afraid I do not & wish you had remained as you are.'[63]* Not only did she consider a prince superior to a duke, but the last Duke of York, her uncle, had resigned in disgrace as commander-in-chief.[64] One naval contemporary who called on him found George 'very glad to see me; just as cheery as ever tho' a little older looking & he pointed out to me that he had got lines under his eyes. He took me into his bedroom & showed me the bed he'd lain in for 42 days with typhoid.'[65]

Arrangements were made for George to move into the houses once destined for Eddy: the newly built cottage at Sandringham and a suite at St James's Palace. His first household was appointed. He had no private secretary, but his comptroller was Sir Francis de Winton, a bald, bearded retired army officer and old Africa hand whom he had inherited from Eddy. His friend Charles Cust became his equerry. 'He [Cust] is a very lucky fellow I think, I wish I was in his shoes,' wrote Bryan Godfrey-Faussett.[66] Cust was joined by Derek Keppel, another man who was to spend his life in George's service.

The next thing was to find George a wife. As we have seen, George's first choice was his young first cousin Missy, daughter of his uncle Alfred, Duke of Edinburgh and his aunt Marie. The match was supported by Queen Victoria, and in February George noted: 'Motherdear & I concocted a letter to aunt Marie.'[67] This tentative proposal was refused outright. George then wrote himself to Missy, but she rejected him in a letter which appears to have been dictated by her mother.[68] It seems that the Edinburghs didn't consider this to be final, but when George received Missy's refusal, Bertie in a rage 'cut it [the relationship] off at once', without giving George an opportunity to speak to her.[69] Missy's parents were hurt and upset but, as Queen Victoria pointed out to George, the change in his position altered things: 'I know how much

---

*Much later, George liked to reflect that he and Henry VIII were the only two men who had been Duke of York, Prince of Wales and King (Wigram Papers, Clive to Nora, 14 August 1930). This is still the case.

you <u>did</u> wish to marry her some day, & [Alfred and Marie] say you declared that you wld never marry anyone else! But <u>then</u> you did <u>not</u> <u>know</u> that she did not care to <u>marry</u> you, nor that you wd be placed in a totally different position – which may oblige you to marry earlier, when she would be almost too young.'[70]

In June the sixteen-year-old Missy became engaged to Ferdinand, Crown Prince of Romania, sending shock waves through the dynastic networks. Why she should have turned down 'the greatest position there is' in favour of marriage to the adopted heir to an obscure country which (said Queen Victoria) 'is vy insecure & the Society – dreadful' has baffled historians.[71] Missy's father burst into tears when he heard of her engagement to Ferdinand – her marriage to George had been the dream of his life.[72] Aunt Marie pretended to be disappointed too, and she complained vigorously about Bertie's angry letter – 'What <u>did</u> <u>hurt</u> her dreadfully', the Queen asserted, 'was <u>a</u> letter that was written wh <u>ought</u> <u>not</u> to have been.'[73]

Marie succeeded in hoodwinking Queen Victoria, but it was she who had blocked her daughter's marriage to George. The match with Ferdinand was her doing: she had intrigued for Missy to take part in a beauty contest of princesses arranged for Ferdinand and then pushed her daughter into his arms.[74] Her concern was less to ensure her daughter's happiness than to spite her English relations. Snubbed by her mother-in-law, Queen Victoria, who refused to give her the precedence which she considered her due as an emperor's daughter, she took her revenge by marrying her own daughter off to a German princeling who was heir to a German client state in the Balkans.

'Disgusted to see the announcement,' wrote Lady Geraldine Somerset, lady-in-waiting to the old Duchess of Cambridge, who kept a deliciously waspish diary. 'It does seem too cruel a shame to cart that nice pretty girl off to semi-barbaric Romania and a man to the knowledge of all Europe desperately in love with another woman' – that is, with Elena Văcărescu, a lady of the Romanian court to whom marriage was out of the question.[75]

As it turned out, however, Aunt Marie had saved George from a wife only fractionally less disastrous than Alicky of Hesse would have been for Eddy. The Queen of Romania, as Missy became, developed into 'a very theatrical personage . . . as neurotic and self-satisfied as her cousin Kaiser Wilhelm II, whose character hers, indeed, slightly resembled'.[76] As Dorothy Parker put it: 'Oh, life is a glorious cycle of song, / A melody of extemporanea; / And love is a thing that can never go wrong; / And I am Marie of Romania.'

George was 'not bitter', neither was he heartbroken.[77] As for Missy, when George saw her in June, she 'seemed to know nothing at all about that tiresome & for us all most disagreeable business', as Alix wrote: 'Evidently she never cared one bit really about you or she would not now be so happy with <u>her Ferdinand</u>.'[78] George no longer cared. For one thing, he had found another young first cousin to admire: Xenia, a sister of Nicky of Russia.

This was a Fredensborg flirtation. George had first met her when he stayed with the Danish royal family in 1891. 'Talked to Xenia in her room' or 'Played the piano with Xenia' appear often in his diary.[79] In 1957 Pope-Hennessy interviewed Xenia, then an old lady of eighty-two, living in exile in a grace-and-favour house at Hampton Court. Her face was 'a synthesis . . . of all the Danish Family's faces, with large, slightly protuberant eyes, and the narrow heart-shape of Queen Alexandra'. Still apparent were 'the charm and high spirits which had bewitched Prince George in Copenhagen in 1891'.[80]

Ten years younger than George and very like his mother: did Xenia bewitch him? In the margin of his diary for 17 April 1892 is written in another hand: 'My 17 birthday Xenia'. 'Wrote to Xenia' appears three or four times in George's diary for 1892. He visited Copenhagen again that summer, and Xenia was there too. Above the diary entry for 4 June is written, in the same hand as the annotation to the 17 April entry: '"Beastly old hound" never touch me in the morning!!'[81] No doubt it was Xenia who made Alix worry that George's 'head was a little turned & you were not quite the same old affectionate Georgie boy towards yr old Motherdear'.[82]

Marriage to a Romanov would have been an even greater dynastic disaster – given the events of 1917 – than to the headstrong Missy. But Xenia secured George's lifelong loyalty. In 1919 he sent a warship to rescue her from the Black Sea, and he gave her a home at Frogmore Cottage.

Queen Victoria, however, who loathed the Russians, had other plans for George.

First, George must play out his navy career. He was given command of a major warship named *Melampus* for the summer manoeuvres. Eddy's death had brought him closer to Dalton, and he wrote asking the creepy canon to come as his guest: 'Perhaps this will be the <u>last</u> ship I shall ever serve in.'[83] The wardroom of *Melampus* was 'a hatchery of courtiers'.[84] Dalton's brother-in-law Hugh Evan-Thomas, a royal favourite, was first lieutenant, and the lieutenants included Charles Cust and Bryan Godfrey-Faussett. 'What good fortune. I am glad,' wrote Godfrey (as he was known) when he got the news – his hopes of serving with Prince George on his next ship had been dashed by Eddy's death as he had expected George to leave the navy, and this appointment signalled the longed-for royal approval.[85]

The manoeuvres were a blur of seasickness and foul weather. 'Hate the whole thing,' wrote George.[86] Some claimed that *Melampus* was let off lightly because of the prince, but this was unfair.[87] True, there was fresh food at the captain's table while the wardroom lunched on salt horse, but for five nights George hardly slept, lying down in the chart room as the ship rolled. 'Everything damp & beastly,' he wrote. On Wednesday 10 August he noted: 'I am so tired have not taken my clothes off to sleep since Friday.'[88] When the news came that the manoeuvres were ended, recorded Godfrey, 'His Royal Highness who has been knocked up a bit the last few days thro' the constant strain of being on the Bridge so much cheered up like anything.'[89]

George left the navy without regret. Unlike his father, who hankered after the army career that was denied him, he never chafed at his inability to remain at sea. But what exactly he was supposed to do as second in line to the throne seemed remarkably unclear.

He was sent to Heidelberg in September to learn German. For the writer Somerset Maugham, who had studied at the university the previous year, Heidelberg was a sexual and cultural awakening. Not so for George, who arrived at the villa of his tutor, the white-haired, bespectacled Professor Ihne, bringing luggage bulging with German uniforms and assorted medals, including the Garter.[90] 'It certainly is beastly dull here,' he wrote.[91] He heartily disliked the professor, and he made little progress in his daily lessons in what Alix described as 'that old Sauerkraut German language'.[92] His sole English companion was the nineteen-year-old Maurice Baring, who returned to England when his mother died. 'How little did we think that this terrible blow was going to fall,' wrote George to his new friend, who was to become a distinguished writer, 'when we were sitting round this table only a fortnight ago; your place opposite me is now vacant, & I can only say that I have missed you very much, my dear Maurice, ever since you left.'[93] In spite of learning little German, George couldn't wait to get home. 'I really can't remain here much longer than two months & miss all my hunting & shooting in England, as I had none last year at all.'[94]

Once back at Sandringham, George settled into a routine of idling with his sisters and dining to the music of Gottlieb's German Band, alternating with the massacre of obscene numbers of pheasants. 'I killed 92 at the last stand . . . we got about 2264 head.'[95] 'We were only 8 guns & got 2207 head before luncheon.'[96]

His future was firmly taken charge of by Grandmama. Victoria had been genuinely fond of Eddy, whom she had loved 'as her own child' and considered her favourite grandson (though in competition with Kaiser William II it wasn't hard to shine), and she lost no time in building a relationship with Eddy's successor as second in line to the throne.[97] As she told George, 'dear Eddy told me <u>all</u> about himself & showed me great confidence & I am sure you wd do the same. It is moreover <u>necessary</u> that I shd know the exact state of the case so that I can be able to help you' – and by this she meant promote his marriage plans.[98]

Victoria purred approval of the new heir: 'Dear Georgie is so nice, sensible & truly rightminded, & so anxious to improve himself.'[99] She pushed him to work on developing his mind. 'I hope you are practising your French? For French & German is really a <u>necessity</u> for <u>you</u>? & I hope you read?'[100] George soon became her favourite, as he recalled many years later, and it was said he could 'do more or less what he liked with Grandmama', often acting as an intermediary between her and Bertie. Once she summoned him to Osborne, and he found in his room a sealed letter from the Queen asking him to change his name to Albert. George consulted her private secretary Sir Henry Ponsonby, who laughed heartily. Defying Ponsonby's advice to write in reply, George went to see the Queen, though 'this was never done', and told her he would never change his name. 'The Q was charming and said she quite understood.' Evidently she wanted to satisfy her conscience that she had done all she could to make Albert one of the names of future sovereigns.[101]

Victoria, as we have seen, was already 'mad' on the subject of George marrying when Eddy was alive.[102] Now she became positively frantic. George was summoned to Balmoral alone and cross-questioned – 'I hope you were careful in what you said!' wrote Alix.[103] In August George visited Osborne and 'had a long talk with Grandmamma who was most kind & said a great deal about dear May'.[104] Bertie saw her later and found her 'in a terrible state about your marrying'.[105] In December at Windsor George wrote in his diary: 'Had long talk with Grandmama about M.'[106]

PART TWO

DUKE OF YORK

1893–1901

CHAPTER 5

May of Teck

When Princess Victoria Mary Augusta Louise Olga Pauline Claudine Agnes, known informally as May of Teck, became engaged to Prince Eddy in December 1891, she was twenty-four and staring spinsterhood in the face. She was not photogenic, which makes it hard for us to judge her looks, but few considered her striking. As one of her friends remarked, 'I suppose she really was very pretty, but one somehow never thought of her as so'.[1] Less charitably, others thought that as a young woman she was 'German-looking and frumpish'.[2] She wore an artificial fringe over her forehead and her abundant gold/light-brown hair was tightly scraped up high at the sides. Some thought this hairstyle disfiguring, but May had no illusions about her appearance. 'I am afraid I am too much like Queen Charlotte ever to be good-looking,' she once remarked.[3] The reference to Charlotte, the heavy-jawed Mecklenburg princess, the wife of George III and May's great-grandmother, tells us as much about May's sense of self as it does about her looks. Legitimacy and royal status mattered more to her than the narrative of romantic love.

May positioned herself firmly in the 'old' English royal family. Her mother, Princess Mary Adelaide of Cambridge, was a first cousin of Queen Victoria, and May was a second cousin once removed of Eddy and George.* But May had few prospects. Her parents were notoriously short of money, and she seemed destined to live as an unmarried and obscure princess on the fringes of the 'royal mob', as Queen Victoria liked to call the extended royal family.

Eight years before, the sixteen-year-old May had endured the shame and humiliation of her parents' near-bankruptcy and exile from the British court to live in Italy. This disgrace was the culmination of her parents' pathological inability to live within their income, and it left lasting psychological scars.

May's parents were an ill-matched couple. Princess Mary Adelaide was hugely fat. Even in her twenties she was reckoned to weigh

---

*George's grandmother Queen Victoria was a first cousin of May's mother, the Duchess of Teck, which makes them second cousins once removed. George was related to May on his mother's side as well. Alexandra's mother, Queen Louise of Denmark, was a grandchild of Prince Frederick of Hesse-Cassel (1747–1837). The Duchess of Teck's mother, the Duchess of Cambridge, was a daughter of Prince Frederick, making George and May second cousins once removed twice over.

seventeen-and-a-half stone. She was an exuberant extrovert – gushing, warm-hearted and boisterous – and 'would have been beautiful if she hadn't been so gigantic'.[4] Her popularity in London society, where she upstaged the tight-laced Queen and Prince Consort, meant that Victoria looked upon her stout cousin with a jaundiced eye.

By the time she was thirty-three Fat Mary was still unmarried. A husband was found for her. Franz Teck was four years younger, a handsome, penniless German princeling. He would have been heir to the King of Württemberg had his father not married for love a Hungarian countess rather than a royal princess (the countess was trampled to death by Austrian cavalry when Franz was four). The tainted blood caused by his father's morganatic marriage – that is, to a non-royal whose children were unable to inherit – was the dominating fact of Franz Teck's life. It meant that he was obsessed with protocol and rank. Franz allowed himself to be dragged into an arranged marriage to Fat Mary, and then bitterly complained that the settlements from his wife's family were too small. That he might do something to improve matters himself seems never to have occurred to him. A life spent begging for royal handouts had robbed him of agency and left him a victim of dynastic dependency culture. His daughter May inherited a sense of inferiority. She never felt properly royal, and in later life she compensated for this by behaving as though she was more royal than the royals.

The newly wed Tecks were installed in a chain of ground-floor rooms at Kensington Palace. May was born on 26 May 1867 in the same room as Queen Victoria, who was struck by the coincidence that May 'shld be born so near my birthday [24 May], in the same House, & bear my name'.[5]

Franz Teck – created Duke of Teck by the King of Württemberg in 1871 – had an urge for arranging rooms (which his daughter inherited), and he and Princess Mary Adelaide spent lavishly on decorating and entertaining. Princess Mary persuaded the Queen to lend her, in addition to the Kensington Palace apartment, White Lodge in Richmond Park, a country retreat where the duke could indulge his passion for gardening. With two establishments, the Tecks spent more than double their income of £7,000 (£850,000 in today's values), and their finances soon tipped into crisis. Tradesmen threatened to take legal action for unpaid bills, and bankruptcy and scandal loomed. Princess Mary's mother, the old Duchess of Cambridge, 'a large, stately German lady with a heavy rather coarse face and thick black eyebrows', had already paid £60,000 towards her daughter's debts.[6] She refused to pay more unless the Tecks went abroad and economised. Queen Victoria became involved, and eventually the Tecks agreed to surrender Kensington Palace, shut up White Lodge and live in Florence.

In July 1883 the Tecks were forced to sell the contents of their home at Kensington Palace at auction. May said little about her youth in later life, and what she felt at the sale of such treasures as the gilt carved sedan chairs which had belonged to Queen Charlotte or the portrait of George IV can only be imagined.[7] But the compulsion that she developed for collecting objects belonging to the 'family' surely had its origin in the traumatic loss of these treasures.

On her seventeenth birthday she listed precisely the presents she had received. 'Mama gave me her carbuncle diamond star earrings, 2 little bracelets with pearl clasps, & a plain pair of earrings.'[8] Her biographer comments that 'she would have made an admirable and efficient museum curator'.[9] But May's passion for collecting and cataloguing filled a deep psychological need. Family jewels validated her identity as an English princess. At her confirmation (August 1885) she listed the jewellery she was given, especially the gift from Uncle George, Duke of Cambridge: 'a clasp . . . with George III & Queen Charlotte's hair in it, which I greatly value'.[10] When she was twenty-one she received more jewellery. Most prized was her grandmother's gift: 'a beautiful bracelet with Gd Papa's cameo set in pearls & diamonds'.[11] Aged eighty, rereading her diary entry for 27 February 1892, which would have been her wedding day had Eddy lived, she 'felt compelled to add that the kind "Uncle Wales" and "Motherdear" gave me a beautiful *rivière* of diamonds which they had destined for me as a wedding present'.[12] What stuck in her mind was not her grief for Eddy but the gift of jewels, which was important not just for its own sake but because it signified the approval of her putative in-laws. For May diamonds thus spoke louder than words.

In Florence the Duke of Teck suffered a severe stroke aged only forty-seven. He had always been spoilt and 'childish' with a terrible temper.[13] May remembered when she was very young seeing him hurl a plate at her mother across the dining-room table.[14] Now his rages were pathologised, and he had attacks 'when his brain feels as though loose and moving in his head'.[15] May was frightened by her father's tantrums, and to protect herself from violent, raw emotion she developed a carapace of icy self-control.

May was frightened of her mother too. With her ungovernable appetite and her passion for 'rrrich crrream', as she pronounced it (rolling her *rrrs* but without a German accent), the duchess was larger than life – so much so that she took up not one but two of the gold chairs where mothers sat watching their daughters at Taglioni's dancing class.[16] May, 'a big, pink and white, gawky girl', was overwhelmed by her mother, whose exuberance and impulsive charm made her feel inadequate.[17] The duchess's habit of referring in front of other people to her daughter's shyness only made her more self-conscious.[18]

The Tecks returned to White Lodge in May 1885. The house had been built as a shooting lodge for George II; a dramatic classical box, it was approached by a fine avenue through Richmond Park down which George II's daughter Princess Amelia, the ranger of the park, would gallop at full tilt. White Lodge was smaller but grander and more royal than Sandringham. In the palatial hall, the furniture-arranging Duke of Teck did his best to smother the classical proportions with palms and heavy furniture in the fashion of 1890. It was relatively remote from London, even more so in the days before telephones when the nearest telegraph office was in Richmond. Some thought that because Queen Victoria was jealous of the duchess's popularity she 'rather liked her to be "isolated"'.[19]

The duchess was incurably, magnificently unpunctual. May spent hours sitting in the hall waiting for her mother. Her family joked that she had ploughed through the whole of Motley's three-volume *Dutch Republic* while waiting.[20] The duchess would drive up to London for the day and arrive back late for dinner 'to find the Duke fuming', then wander upstairs to spend three-quarters of an hour changing 'till he was almost *mad* with rage'.[21] May, by contrast, was obsessively punctual, once observing: 'I simply can't understand unpunctuality. Why should anybody be late? I know exactly how long it takes me to dress.'[22]

When May turned eighteen she was belatedly confirmed, this being the essential prerequisite for a young woman to go to balls or be presented at court. But May never really 'came out' with a full London Season. Instead for six years she worked as her mother's 'secretary and lady-in-waiting combined'.[23]

Reckoned by historians to be the hardest-working member of the Victorian royal family, the duchess devoted herself to charities such as Dr Barnardo's and the NSPCC.[24] Fat Mary, as she was affectionately known in the East End, was the queen of the bazaars, galvanising the dreary, earnest ladies of the guilds with her charisma and energy, but she was chaotically disorganised. She didn't answer letters and her rooms were cluttered with piles of papers. May, by contrast, was well organised and tidy-minded. She ordered and answered her mother's correspondence. May was an avid reader and the duchess, while she rarely opened a book herself, interrogated her daughter about her reading and then impressed clever men by talking brilliantly about the latest authors. 'Now I have read the book,' said May, 'but I can't talk about it.'[25] Wearing an apron with a pair of scissors hanging on a string from her waist, she spent days sorting, listing and labelling the parcels of clothing made by middle-class women for the poor which flooded into the London Needlework Guild.

Some said that May remained unmarried because, as a morganatic princess and a mere serene highness, she was not eligible for the hand of even the most obscure German prince, while her parents' shortage of money ruled out marriage to all but the richest of British aristocrats. She was 'too Royal to marry an ordinary English gentleman and not Royal enough to marry a Royalty'.[26] More pressing was the co-dependence between the mother and her dutiful, unselfish daughter. 'I am not my own mistress', declared May aged twenty-four, unable to fix an appointment because 'I am sure to choose a date when my parents want me'.[27] When she became engaged to Eddy, Queen Victoria wrote: 'What Mary will do without May, I cannot think, for she is her right hand.'[28] May admitted: 'Poor Mama, she keeps up her spirits fairly well but I fear she will miss me terribly.'[29]

May had three brothers, and she enjoyed male company. She wrote from a visit to France with her parents in 1892: 'I am longing for one of the boys, I must say I do like men & here I see nothing but women, women, women, except Papa & he don't count to talk to.'[30] Nor did she lack admirers. Later, among her ladies-in-waiting rumours circulated about her romances. Some whispered that the man she adored – 'the love of her life' – was Lord Hopetoun (later Marquess of Linlithgow). The Teck family stayed at Hopetoun for months at a time, and Princess May, who was remembered by the Hope family as a high-spirited and mischievous teenager, may well have nursed a crush on the rich and virtuous future governor-general of Australia.[31] His sister recalled that the Hope family always thought that 'if one of the royalties failed [Princess May] might marry my brother'.[32] He died at the early age of forty-seven, and Princess May wrote to her aunt: 'We feel very unhappy today as our dear friend Hopie died yesterday ... I had known him for 28 years & he was so nice & always the same kind friend.'[33] 'Friend', perhaps, is the operative word here – not a love affair, nor an *amitié amoureuse*, but a lifelong friendship between two good people.

Another story was that May fell in love with Prince Henry of Battenberg, the dashing, flirtatious husband of Princess Beatrice. He apparently reciprocated, but 'they agreed to behave well and stop seeing each other'.[34]

May was not above sliding down the staircase on a tea tray but she was no socialite. She loathed the dawdling and 'flying about' of the London Season. 'Rushing about does not suit me,' she wrote, 'though Mama & Papa thrive on it.'[35] She preferred what she called a quiet life. With her governess Mademoiselle Bricka she learnt French and German on four mornings a week. Bricka was stout and warm-hearted, with 'a terrible complexion, short-sighted eyes and false hair'. She has been credited with educating May, broadening her reading and instilling a social conscience, but her real importance was to act as May's confidante, providing an ally against the domestic tyranny of her parents.[36] Living so much at home, it was noticeable that May had 'not had many friends of her own'.[37]

Into this dutiful life of George Eliot's novels and good works there burst a bombshell in late October 1891: an invitation to Balmoral.[38]

In August 1890 Arthur Balfour, the minister in attendance at Balmoral, had a conversation with Queen Victoria about Prince Eddy and the royal marriage market. According to Balfour, the Queen observed that

> there are but three marriageable Protestant princesses at this moment in Europe, besides the Teck girl and the Hesse girl. The Teck girl they won't have, because they hate Teck & because the vision of Pcss May haunting Marlborough House makes the Prince of Wales ill. The Hesse girl wont [sic] have him. There remain a Mecklenburg and two Anhalt Princesses (I am not sure that I have the names right). According to Her Majesty they are all three ugly, unhealthy, and idiotic . . .[39]

The shortage of Protestant princesses partly explains why Eddy, having been rejected by Alicky of Hesse, proposed to the Catholic Princess Hélène. Significantly, May was already on the Queen's list. When the Hélène project failed, the only princess remaining – apart from the ugly Germans – was May. By August 1891 Eddy's marriage had become a matter of urgency. The Prince of Wales swallowed his objections to the Teck princess and set about persuading his mother to agree to the marriage. Hence the invitation to Balmoral. No one doubted that May would say yes.

May's Balmoral trial was a success. She survived the ordeals of freezing carriage drives and tea time tête-à-têtes with the Queen, who decided: 'May is a particularly nice girl so quiet & yet cheerful & so vy carefully brought up & so sensible.'[40] As for May, she considered that she and the Queen had 'made the greatest friends'.[41]

Some questioned the Queen's sincerity. 'I wonder why Grandmama is so charmed with May? She used not to be,' asked one princess.[42] The acid-tongued Lady Geraldine Somerset gnashed her teeth: 'The Queen . . . thinks her well brought up! so amusing (the very last thing in the world I should say she is!!)'[43] The German Empress grumbled that 'there was not much in May – that she was a little "oberflächlich" [shallow]'. But, as Victoria replied, 'she is the reverse of oberflächlich. She has no frivolous tastes.'⁴⁴

Once Victoria had given her approval, the royal marriage machine ground into action. Eddy, as we have seen, broke off with his Gaiety Girl and with Lady Sybil and braced himself to 'make the best of a bad job'.⁴⁵ On 29 November he wrote his last letter to Lady Sybil. The next day May recorded that 'he began to pay me marked attentions'.⁴⁶ On Wednesday 2 December Eddy and May were both guests of the Danish minister, Christian de Falbe, at a large house party at Luton Hoo. On Thursday the 3rd there was a ball, and May wrote in her diary: 'To my great surprise Eddy proposed to me during the evening in Mme de Falbe's boudoir – Of course I said yes – We are both very happy.'⁴⁷

May admitted that she had 'for some time thought that this might happen one day', but Eddy's whirlwind courtship was completely unexpected.⁴⁸ The other girls staying at Luton related how May amazed them all by picking up her skirts and waltzing round the room when she announced her engagement.⁴⁹ Even Lady Geraldine's stony heart melted when May rushed into her arms, 'so radiantly happy one could not but be glad'.⁵⁰

The papers hailed it as a love match – writing 'columns of rot' according to Lady Geraldine, 'twaddling and asinine'.⁵¹ For May, however, it 'felt as if the whole thing was a dream'.⁵² In the space of four days she had leapt from the outer fringes to the pinnacle of royalty. When she received visitors at White Lodge she would conduct them down the long corridor hung with portraits of her great-uncles – the sons of George III – and explain their history. 'She has a wonderful memory for these details.'⁵³ For this ancestor-worshipping princess, royalty came close to religion, and engagement to the son of the heir apparent was her wildest dream come true. Little wonder that she announced: 'I am very happy I may say radiant.'⁵⁴

The wedding was fixed for 27 February 1892, and May busied herself arranging her bridal wardrobe or trousseau and answering the showers of telegrams which arrived at White Lodge. Standing arm in arm, Eddy and May posed for the photographers, two young people staring straight ahead, remarkable for their distorted bodies – Eddy's abnormally long neck clothed in an absurdly high collar and Mary's large bust and tiny waist emphasised by her tight, shiny bodice.

As her days filled with family celebrations, and cheering crowds greeted her in the street, May's euphoria turned to panic. She very rarely spoke about this engagement, but half a century later, in the privacy of a motor car – this most clam-like of royals would speak frankly only inside a car – Queen Mary had a conversation with her woman of the bedchamber, Miss Maggie Wyndham. When Miss Wyndham suggested that the death of the Duke of Clarence had been providential, and the marriage would have been 'uphill work', Queen Mary replied, placing her hand on Miss Wyndham's knee:

> My dear, how right you are. I even realised it at the time I got engaged. My father-in-law was always saying to me 'See that Eddie does this, May' or 'Make sure Eddie does that, May' so that I got so worried I went to my mother and said: 'Do you *really* think I can take this on?' 'Of course you can,' she replied.[55]

Nevertheless, the Duchess of Teck confided in a friend: 'Our darling May is bright and happy though at times her heart misgives her, lest she may not be able fully to release all the expectations centred in her.'[56]

May and her parents joined Eddy and the Wales family at Sandringham early in the new year. In her diary May describes how after lunch with the shooters she walked home with Eddy, who was feeling unwell, and sat with him when he went to bed.[57] Her matter-of-fact notes about his influenza give way to horror two days later when pneumonia was diagnosed. 'Poor darling Eddy . . . very ill indeed, most anxious. I saw him one minute.'[58]

On 14 January she was called at 3.30 a.m. and joined the family vigil, waiting for six hours in her fiancé's sitting room next to his bedroom. Towards the end, the delirious Eddy cried out 'Hélène', and (according to Lady Geraldine) May had to be kept out of his room 'as they did not wish her to hear what he said!!'[59] If May knew of this deathbed snub she made no mention of it. In her diary she wrote: 'The suspense was awful & I shall never forget this awful night.'[60]

After the prince's death the Duchess of Teck wrote of her daughter's 'dazed misery', but May didn't give way to maddened grief.[61] There are no accounts of her weeping. Nor did she endure the sleepless nights that tormented Alix, who told May that 'I expect the Dear One to come in, or to hear his dear voice calling me – and then I realise with sharpest pain that he is gone for ever'.[62] May, by contrast, barely mentioned Eddy's name. Despite being engaged to marry him, she never put her own loss first. She seemed always outside the story, a detached observer. The closest she came to expressing her feelings was to mention 'the agony of those three dreadful days of anxiety'.[63] She confessed to finding letters difficult – 'I simply cannot write for it is dreadful to have to open the wound afresh.'[64] Her family marvelled at her composure and found May 'wonderful in her calmness'.[65] But, as Queen Victoria remarked, 'you know May never was in love with dear Eddy'.[66]

The poet Alfred Austin rushed to compose a dirge depicting May as a tragic figure:

> Alas for Her! the graced, the good,
> For ever doomed to wear
> The mockery of widowhood
> About her maiden hair.
> Scarce had she time to reach and clasp
> The gifts of Love, but they were ashes in her grasp.[67]

Austin's reading of May's story could hardly have been more wrong. May was not broken-hearted. If she was traumatised, she didn't show it. She was mortified, however, as her aunt Augusta perceived, having come so close to the crown and been 'taken up so high, for the bright prospect of such a future position before her, her affections being engaged as well, only to be thrust down, after a short 6 weeks into this misery'.[68] As May wrote in her diary on the day of Eddy's funeral at Windsor, 'it was too sad for words to think that our [sic] darling's coffin lay close to the altar at which we were to have been married on February 27th'.[69] Her family worried about the cost of the trousseau, which the cash-strapped Tecks could ill afford: 'It is hard enough to lose poor Eddy but to be still more ruined, cannot be expected!'[70]

Weeks after Eddy lay in his coffin at the altar in Windsor, a second engagement was projected for May. On 9 February Lady Geraldine wrote in her diary: 'I hear <u>all</u> from the Queen downwards are resolved P. George shall marry May! All except P. Geo.!'[71] George, as we have seen, wanted to marry the sixteen-year-old Princess Marie of Edinburgh. When Missy rejected George, the Queen fell back on May – as she had done in the case of Eddy. The Duchess of Teck spoke openly about the project of George marrying May. Even more significantly, she seemed not to worry about paying for the Clarence trousseau – proof positive in Lady Geraldine's view that it was to be recycled for a second engagement.[72]

If May knew of this project – and it seems likely that she did – she was careful not to mention it. She had some choice in the matter. She could have given way to hysterical mourning, which would have allowed her to retreat into the life of sad seclusion suggested by Alfred Austin. But she didn't break down. On the contrary, she courted Queen Victoria, requesting the privilege of addressing her as Grandmama, as she would have done had she married Eddy. 'Please let me always call you that in remembrance of what might have been,' wrote May, signing off, 'Your broken-hearted little granddaughter.'[73]* After a visit to Osborne, Victoria wrote approvingly: 'Poor dear May looks thin, & sad & <u>crushed</u>, but is so nice & reasonable & resigned & likes to talk of it all.'[74]

The Wales family embraced May too. 'They have quite adopted her as their daughter & she calls Alix "Motherdear",' wrote the duchess.[75] May reciprocated. 'Their kindness to me is beyond words & I adore them,' she told a friend: 'nothing cld have brought us nearer together than this common grief, & I cling very much to them all.'[76] Motherdear invited May to stay at Eastbourne, where the family had withdrawn to mourn, for the day on 27 February. May wrote in her diary: 'This day is a very sad one for me for it was to have been our wedding day.'[77] This flat, closed little sentence hardly suggests a woman devastated by grief.

Wearing deepest mourning the Tecks departed in early March for Cannes, where the duchess had persuaded her rich patron Lady Wolverton to take a villa. Here amid blue skies and flowers, May's spirits revived; she could laugh once more and her face lost the 'sad, weary look' it had worn since Eddy's death.[78] However, as she confided to Bricka, 'when I am alone I feel the loneliness, some vague dream of something pleasant having passed out of one's life for ever', and she confessed that 'I am getting more reserved than ever'. She resented resuming her old role as dutiful daughter: 'My hands are full, my father pulls me one way, my mother the other, it is good not to become selfish but sometimes I grumble at my life, at the waste of time, at the <u>petitesse</u> de la vie when one feels capable of greater things.'[79]

A glimpse of greater things occurred a few days later when George and his father, who were staying further up the coast at Cap Martin, arrived on a visit to Cannes. To judge from the circumspect record of lunches, dinners, drives and yachting expeditions in intense heat that both of them kept in their diaries, the feelings of neither George nor May were engaged. In Cannes May was a public figure, mobbed in the streets by sympathisers, and observers noted that George spent much of his time in May's company. This was enough for the gossip columns, which confidently predicted an engagement.[80] Lady Geraldine reported

---

*Hitherto Queen Victoria had ended her letters to May 'Your devoted Aunt', when actually she was first cousin once removed (Pope 203/6, QV to M, 14 January 1892). This suggests that with Victoria forms of address such as aunt signified intimacy and shared suffering as well as degrees of kinship. Hélène too was invited to address Victoria as Grandmama after Eddy's death (Prince Michael of Greece, *Eddy and Hélène: ... An Impossible Match* (Rosvall Royal Books, 2013), p. 88).

that 'it is all settled about P. George!! ... to my mind too disgusting.'[81] More telling, Queen Victoria, keeping an eye on her grandson from Hyères, where she was staying, wrote to George: 'Have you seen May & have you thought more abt that possibility or <u>found</u> <u>out</u> what her feelings might be?'[82]

'Take leave of the dear Wales [sic],' wrote May in her diary on 23 April. 'So sorry they have gone.'[83] While George travelled on to Copenhagen, where he was united with his Romanov cousins Nicky and the lively Xenia, the Tecks headed for Württemberg. They stayed in the vast, decaying baroque Schloss Ludwigsburg, driving out for meals with the King and Queen of Württemberg at Marienwahl, a villa some distance away, and as the duchess was always late the arrangements were fraught. 'I certainly do <u>not</u> like Germany,' wrote May. 'I think Wurttemburg [sic] a primitive place, they have no idea of comfort & are so narrow minded.'[84] She told Bricka: 'My feelings at this moment are these "Thank God I am English".'[85]

The nine-year-old Princess Alice of Albany (later to become May's sister-in-law) was also staying in the schloss with her family. She remembered May as 'full of fun' and 'not at all buttoned up', taking the children into the woods 'to get away from the Germans, who we all hated, and Queen Mary particularly. She couldn't bear'em.'[86] Almost as bad as the Germans were May's parents. They never ceased talking about her engagement to George. 'They told her it had to happen.' This made her intensely uncomfortable. Marrying her dead fiancé's brother was 'almost a scandal' (marriage to a deceased wife's sister was prohibited in the UK until 1907).[87] Little wonder that May confessed: 'I have become <u>extremely</u> silent & quiet & cannot talk to people'.[88]

George and May by now exchanged friendly letters. May complained: 'I cannot stand Germany for long ... we do nothing & go nowhere – I never knew such people for wasting time as they do here.'[89] By contrast with George, who, as we have seen, gained little from his stay at Heidelberg, May worked at her German and after six weeks she was able to speak quite fluently. 'I felt I was a <u>succès</u> & was delighted,' she wrote.[90] On a visit to the archives at Stuttgart she was fascinated to read letters from her German grandfather.[91] Excursions such as these help to explain how it was that, as a widowed queen, Mary alone of the British royal family understood the intricacies of the Windsors' German genealogy.

Back at White Lodge in July, the Tecks regarded themselves as 'shut up for a year' until the anniversary of Eddy's death released them from mourning.[92] All May had to do was wait for the pieces to fall into place. She noted in her diary without comment the engagement of her rival

Missy 'who is only sixteen and a half to the Crown Prince of Romania'.[93] Summoned to Sandringham to commemorate the anniversary of May's engagement to Eddy in December, the duchess found it 'embarrassing, but we have to do it'.[94] Afterwards May showed Queen Victoria the rivière of diamonds intended for her wedding present which Bertie and Alix had given her. 'It made me very sad to look at them,' wrote the Queen. 'I said I hoped much happiness might still be in store for her.'[95]

May's biographer James Pope-Hennessy considered that 'this book, <u>to be done at all</u>, has to be like a novel. The actual existing heroine is, for <u>many</u>, <u>many</u> years <u>intractable</u> and <u>non-existent</u>: <u>therefore</u> I have hastened up her development, and probably exaggerated reactions <u>she did not have</u>.'[96]

As a shy, reserved young woman May was not remarkable. 'I should not call her a brilliant girl, but she is perfectly charming ... You seldom hear her say much,' was the best that 'One Who Knows the Princess Well' could write about her.[97] But during the Interregnum (as Pope-Hennessy called it) between Eddy's death and her engagement to George, May showed a steeliness of character that was astounding for a woman of her time and class. Brought up in a generation where daughters counted for nothing unless they married, and overwhelmed and outshone by her larger-than-life mother, May emerged from the wreckage of Eddy's death poised to marry his brother. Lady Geraldine gleefully reported that Aunt Augusta was now of the opinion that 'May never cared a bit for P. Eddy!' and considered 'what bosh all the romance of the desperate love affair was! and how entirely arranged the whole matter was!!' Augusta (continued Lady Geraldine) was 'quite satisfied May has never been in love & is <u>most</u> unlikely ever to be so'.[98] This was the nub of the matter. Ambitious May most certainly was, but whether she was capable of feeling was a question that baffled her associates. As the Countess of Shaftesbury, one of her ladies, tactfully remarked many years later, Queen Mary was '"luckily" – not of a passionate nature, nor emotional'.[99]

CHAPTER 6

George and May

1893–1894

On 14 January 1893, the anniversary of Prince Eddy's death, George and his parents laid two crosses of lilies on the coffin in the Memorial Chapel at Windsor, and then travelled to Sandringham. After tea the Wales family all entered 'darling Eddy's room', the *Sterbezimmer* or death chamber, where fresh flowers were strewn daily on the bed and his soap and hairbrushes remained as on the day he died.[1]* 'All those terrible hours of weary watching & of hopes & fears came back to me most vividly,' wrote George, '& I could almost hear His dear voice.'[2]

The end of the year of mourning meant that George and May were released from limbo. Pushed by his autocrat grandmama the Queen-Empress into an arranged marriage to a second cousin once removed whom he didn't love, George felt trapped and anxious. He saw little of May, 'only a passing glimpse every now & then', and their relations were friendly, but the idea of marriage terrified him.[3] He confided in Alix, who wrote a diplomatic letter to Grandmama. 'I told her,' Alix informed George, 'that I thought you required a complete change & rest before settling down in life – & that I intended & proposed to take you with me on the Yacht for a short time – & you wld come back fresh & less worried & ready to settle yr own affairs.' She added: 'I too am worried to death about it – & can so well enter into all yr poor feelings!'[4]

George's aunt Vicky, the German empress dowager, was not encouraging. She told her daughters that May was perfectly dressed in her black mourning but 'a little stiff & cold . . . I do not think she has much charm or is very fascinating!'[5] May's position, conceded Vicky, was

> most difficult and embarrassing . . . the newspapers are constantly writing about her becoming engaged to Georgie, and the whole of the public seem to wish it ardently. Of course not a word has been

---

*Eddy's room was kept as he left it until George V and Queen Mary moved into the big house at Sandringham, and the room was given to Prince Henry. 'I cleared it all out,' the prince recalled. 'It was horrible.' He saw Eddy's collars: '"They were so high" (holding his hands ten inches apart) "I always say a bloody good thing he died when he did."' (Pope 196/19, Interview with Duke of Gloucester, 24/26 May 1957, pp. 41, 52).

mentioned in the family, but there is a universal feeling among them all that it is almost sure to take place sooner or later.[6]

Vicky doubted whether May was the right wife for George: 'many think her rather dull – & superficial – I feel there is not much *geistiges Leben* [intellectual life]'.[7]

With his mother and sisters, George cruised round Italy in the *Osborne*. Lacking both education and intellectual curiosity, he was unable to appreciate the treasures he saw. Of the Uffizi he wrote 'saw some of the finest pictures & statues in the world'; that was all.[8] How different from May, whose idea of fun was to spend an afternoon in a museum: 'How much one learns & picks up,' she wrote, '& how much nicer than going out to tea & gossip.'[9]*

George stayed a week in Athens, visiting his uncle the King of Greece and his aunt Olga. Each day he sat and talked for hours with 'Darling Tootsums', as he called his aunt. She noticed how troubled her 'darling little Sunbeam' was about the future: 'I trust when the great step is taken you will feel more calm & peaceful, than you have done for a long time.'[10] Princess Sophie, Vicky's daughter who was married to Olga's eldest son, the Duke of Sparta, reported to her mother that George's likely engagement was 'dreadful' for his sisters: 'They avoid speaking about it, & don't like the idea! ... It seems so hard that he should in a way have to sacrifice himself for his country because they say there is no one else for him to marry!'[11]

George wrote dutifully to May, but his letters were hardly passionate. 'You are often in my thoughts dearest May & I trust when I come home we shall be able to see more of each other than we have lately' was not the sort of thing to set the pulses racing.[12] He worried about boring her with dreary accounts of his travels but couldn't bring himself to write about his feelings. 'Now you must be sick of reading this very stupid long epistle, & I have got a great mind to tear it up only that I think it might be useful to light your fire with.'[13]

Feeling more like a condemned man than a lover, George left his family in Greece and travelled home to propose to May. The letter his mother penned from Athens after his departure was more of a threat than a comfort:

---

*The Wales sisters were so uneducated that 'when they went abroad in the yacht and stopped e.g. at Naples, they looked at no sights, and only bought tourist knick-knacks' (James Pope-Hennessy, *The Quest for Queen Mary*, ed. Hugo Vickers (Zuleika, 2018), p. 133).

Indeed it is <u>sad</u> to think that we shall never be able to be together . . . in the same way – but yet there is a bond of love between us – that of Mother & child – which <u>nothing</u> <u>can</u> ever <u>diminish</u> or render less binding – & <u>nothing</u> & <u>nobody</u> can or shall ever come between me & my darling Georgie boy.[14]

Only four days after returning home, George did the deed. He arranged to stay with his sister Louise at East Sheen Lodge, a brisk mile away from the Tecks at White Lodge. On 3 May, his diary records, May came to tea with Louise at Sheen at 5 p.m. 'Afterwards we two walked in the garden here, & I proposed to her & the darling girl consented to be my wife, I am so happy.'[15] May's diary is even more discreet: 'Went to tea with Louise at Sheen. Found Georgie there. We walked together afterwards in the garden & he proposed to me, & I accepted him.'[16] Evidently she was certain that George's parents and grandmother would approve.

After telling the Duke and Duchess of Teck, George telegraphed Queen Victoria. He received her reply at 8 p.m.: 'Most gladly give my consent,' and he scribbled an excited note to May.[17] From White Lodge, May wrote George a worried letter: 'I could not say to you today all that I felt, I only hope you did not think me unfeeling & cold. Thank you a thousand times for all the happiness I am sure you will bring into my life, which just lately has been rather a sad one.'[18]

The Queen's consent was the signal for the Duchess of Teck to spread the news and, overjoyed, she was still hard at it sending telegrams at 10.30 that night. As for Victoria, she was thankful that the succession at last was settled. But the letter that Alix wrote Georgie was not ecstatic: 'With <u>what</u> mixed feelings I read yr telegram . . . I am longing to hear details about it all – and <u>how</u> you made up your mind so quickly after yr return.'[19] The German relations were not thrilled either. 'Over all,' wrote Vicky, 'there is a mist of sadness & melancholy.'[20] As her daughter Victoria observed, 'there is nothing sympathetic about her . . . poor Georgie – he is such a loving nature himself & her cold reserved way, must strike him.'[21]*

Presents poured in, many of them paid for by public subscription. The City of London voted £2,500, and all over the country town and county

---

*Victoria, the third Victoria in this paragraph, was Vicky's second daughter. She survived a traumatic love affair with the dashing Prince Alexander of Battenberg, sometime Prince of Bulgaria, and in 1890 married the boorish Prince Adolf of Schaumburg-Lippe, whom Sir Alan Lascelles considered 'the most physically repulsive man he had ever seen' (Pope 194/3).

councils opened subscriptions and instituted books for subscribers to write their names in. Schoolgirls throughout the land gave their pennies to buy gifts for Princess May. George counted 14,000 presents. The republican *Reynolds's Newspaper* condemned the public's gifts as a gigantic exercise in royal cadging, a forced levy to subsidise the penniless Tecks.[22] At Northampton socialists passed a resolution declaring that no more notice should be taken of the wedding, and in Bristol the mayor was hooted at for starting a subscription.[23] William Gladstone's Liberal government refused to declare the wedding day a bank holiday on the grounds that 'the working-classes are decidedly opposed to it'.[24] But the subscriptions were not orchestrated by the royals – this was a genuine demonstration of loyalty, especially to Princess May. No chance was lost of turning the presents to advantage: they were put on display at the Imperial Institute in South Kensington, where the public paid to see them and the proceeds went to the Victoria Fund.

George and May spent their engagement struggling to keep pace with the avalanche of presents, making lists and writing letters. No doubt exhaustion accounts for the somewhat high-handed thank you letter that May penned to the Bishop of Rochester, Randall Davidson:

> I hope you will forgive me for telling you that I already possess "Jane Austen's" works and should be so pleased if you could exchange them for something else. I have not yet got any of Sir Walter Scott's novels. Pray let me know if I may return the books to Bumpus.[25]

Assembling May's second trousseau was a full-time occupation in itself. The idea of reusing the trousseau acquired for her marriage to Eddy was quietly dropped. It was the bridal equivalent of stepping into a dead man's shoes, and the duchess commissioned a new and more splendid collection for this second engagement. The forty outdoor dresses, fifteen ballgowns and five tea gowns described by the *Ladies' Pictorial* represented only a fraction of the roomfuls of garments. Philanthropic as ever, the Duchess of Teck determined to use the wedding to help England's struggling weavers and lace makers, and on her instructions every item was made at home by English dressmakers of cloth manufactured in Britain. Not even the lingerie came from Paris.[26] The duchess didn't pay for all of this. Her sister Augusta contributed £1,000, and May told her mother that she had received a wedding present of £500 from Baroness Burdett-Coutts, who 'did not say it was for charities, so I handed it over . . . for trousseau purposes in order not to cripple you.'[27]

When May wasn't having sweaty fittings with dressmakers she was sitting for portraits by Heinrich von Angeli and Luke Fildes, both commissioned by others. George thought it 'a great shame making you sit to all these artists, just at this time too'.[28]

Tempers were not eased by a report which first appeared in the *Star* claiming that in Malta George had secretly married the daughter of a naval officer, by whom he had several children. 'I say, May, we can't get married after all,' he joked. 'I hear I have got a wife and three children.'[29] The story was baseless, but the allegation of a bigamous marriage created a furore, and the Archbishop of Canterbury felt obliged to deny it, which only added fuel to the flames.[30] Fearing that an official denial of the story would merely boost publicity, the royal advisers chose to ignore it, a decision which George came to regret.[31] The story was to haunt George for twenty years, which was particularly unfair, as Alexandra pointedly remarked, thinking no doubt of her philandering husband: 'It is hard on the best people like you, who really have steered so straight in your life, to be accused of such base things . . . & many bad people who really are known to lead the worst of lives are never mentioned or attacked ever.'[32]

The summer of 1893 was freakishly hot, and as temperatures climbed into the eighties the couple became fractious and irritable. George exploded at White Lodge when the duchess – he called her by her pet name, Maria – allowed them no time alone. May agreed: 'I was so angry with her, I felt like a little devil.'[33] But when they *were* alone they were 'cold & distant to each other', and they worried about being shy in each other's company.[34] No doubt it was hard for the cousins to adjust to the shift in their relationship: as George put it, 'we have known each so well for so many years that we hardly yet realise that we are engaged'.[35]

'This is simply a <u>horrid</u> time we are going through,' wrote May. 'It is so stupid to be so stiff together & really there is nothing in the world I would not tell you, except that I <u>love</u> you more than anybody in the world, & this I cannot tell you myself so I write it to relieve my feelings!'[36] May's anxiety about her inability to show emotion made her even more inhibited when she was with George. As she explained, 'the more I feel the less I say, I am so sorry but I can't help it, I often wish I could be less reserved'.[37] But perhaps it was not May's self-restraint that was to blame, buttoned up though she was, but her inability to simulate feelings that she didn't have. According to Lady Geraldine Somerset, 'there is not even any pretence at love-making. May is radiant at her position and abundantly satisfied, but placid and cold as always, the Duke of York apparently nonchalant and indifferent.'[38]

George was distracted, anxious about the naval disaster off the coast of Lebanon on 22 June when HMS *Camperdown* rammed HMS

Victoria, which 'sank bottom up in 15 mins: Poor Adml Sir G. Tryon & 400 officers & men lost'.[39] Complaining of neuralgia and toothache he escaped to Sandringham, feeling 'wretched' and 'very seedy'.[40] The dentist arrived and stopped his tooth, and he immediately recovered.

This second engagement of May's 'seemed ambitious, and in a way it was', a woman of the bedchamber later suggested: she was not in love with George.[41] But, as another of her ladies reflected, the engagement appeared natural to her because May 'put the Throne above everything else and all personal feelings'.[42] As *Reynolds's Newspaper* cruelly observed, she was 'in love with the Crown, irrespective of whose head may wear it'.[43]

Three days before the wedding George wrote to May: 'It is just two months today that we were engaged, how quick the time goes, I loved you then very much, now I adore you.'[44] This sounds like a man hoping that if he says something often enough it will come true. The reality was, as George told May a year later, 'when I asked you to marry me, I was very fond of you but not very much in love'.[45] In her widowhood Queen Mary reflected: 'My husband was not in love with me when we married. But he fell in love with me later.'[46]

The marriage of George and May was a classic exercise in dynastic matchmaking on the part of Queen Victoria. But the union of these two level-headed second cousins, lacking any aspiration for a romantic marriage and accepting of their fate, turned out to be stronger and more successful that anyone could have predicted in 1893.

The wedding itself was an old-fashioned dynastic affair. The date of 6 July was not fixed until six weeks before.[47] Some called for it to be held in St Paul's Cathedral, but this was a break with royal tradition and Queen Victoria refused to attend a wedding there. To please the Queen it was held in the tiny Chapel Royal in St James's Palace, where Victoria herself had been married.[48] By removing pews, room was made for 300 people to cram into a space that usually seated 150.[49]

For George the most important wedding guest was 'dear Nicky, who arrived from Russia looking so well' on 30 June.[50] Nicky was given a cosy room upstairs at Marlborough House between George and his sisters; he grumbled at having to share a bathroom with the prince.[51] The two cousins were photographed standing in the garden at Marlborough House: two young men of five feet six or seven inches, trim and dapper, both smoking cigarettes and looking almost identical with their neat beards, small heads and boyish features.[52] Twenty years before, their double-dressing mothers, who were equally hard to tell apart, had teased London Society by wearing identical dresses. George and Nicky were less amused at being mistaken for one another. When someone asked George whether he had come over especially for the Duke of York's wedding, he joked: 'I am the Duke of York, and I suppose I should attend my own wedding.'[53]

On the wedding morning the Queen drove in her new glass state coach from Buckingham Palace with the Duchess of Teck. This was Princess Mary Adelaide's apotheosis. Bowing extravagantly right and left to the roaring crowds, she quite eclipsed the tiny Queen, who fluttered a small hand.[54] By some oversight the Queen's carriage was the first to arrive at the Chapel Royal (etiquette dictates that the monarch should be the last to enter). The duchess beckoned to her cousin to wait in a side room while she swept magnificently up the aisle. There came a tug on a skirt and a voice from behind saying 'I am going first', and the Queen – an unsteady bundle on sticks – scuttled past Princess Mary Adelaide and took her seat near the altar.[55] Unperturbed by the lapse, Victoria was glad to see all the processions arrive, and as each of the royalties entered, they bowed or curtseyed, which 'was <u>extremely</u> pretty to see'.[56] Lady Geraldine, critical as ever, observed that May was 'not veiled <u>at all</u>!!' and as she walked up the aisle she 'looked right and left and slightly bowed to her acquaintance! a great mistake'.[57]

The grand dynastic painting which the Danish artist Laurits Tuxen made of the sunlit wedding scene in the Chapel Royal is dominated by the two matriarchs. Victoria, small but controlling, is the focal point in direct line with May. The Prince and Princess of Wales fade into the background – which is perhaps just as well as Alix, though outshining the bride, looked pale and sad. The Duchess of Teck, wearing a glorious sapphire-blue velvet gown, is seated in the foreground, 'quite recognisable altho' not flattered!' she wrote after sitting to the artist. 'What a pity, as I am to be such a prominent figure in the picture there can only be a <u>back</u> or <u>side</u> view of my lovely person!'[58]

After the wedding breakfast at Buckingham Palace – an unseemly crush of famished wedding guests and angry ambassadors demanding to eat with the Queen – George and May were photographed. Old William Downey, a dignified gentleman in his sixties, who never 'took' anyone lower than royalty nowadays, shot the official photograph. George, wearing the uniform of a naval captain which, unlike most royals, he had earned, stands modestly to one side, displaying his bride as if she were a mare at a horse show. May thought the photos were 'fairly good on the whole', but Downey's image of her was hardly flattering.[59] Her wedding dress of silver and white brocade embroidered with shamrocks, roses and thistles shows off her tightly laced small waist, exaggerating her overlarge bust. Dwarfing the diminutive George, she looks (in the words of a later critic) 'positively anthropoid – low forehead, scowl and large jaw. Not the face of a happy woman … No radiance for poor old P.M.' No doubt her shoes, which were unnaturally narrow, caused her tortures (unless she had 'very aristo feet'). The gold-embroidered white poplin going-away dress, into which she changed after the photographs, was even more disastrous. 'Anything hotter and more uncomfortable to wear on a broiling July day it would be hard to imagine', not least because it fastened along one shoulder and down the side under the same arm. Getting into it involved an awkward manoeuvre – 'head through, both arms into the leg of mutton sleeves (making neck appear short, & adding to P.M.'s height), & then wriggling the arms straight'.[60]

Promptly at 4.30, George and Mary said goodbye and drove away in an open carriage through enthusiastically cheering crowds. The Duke of Teck sobbed bitterly and the Duchess undressed alone.

After the wedding George and May travelled by special train to Wolferton in Norfolk. People lined the route cheering all the way. The couple drove from the station in intense heat at foot pace with the dust rising in clouds under the horses' hooves, and when they reached Sandringham George's black frock coat was white and May's white going-away dress had turned black.[61]

York Cottage, where George brought his bride, had been given to him after Eddy died. Built by Bertie as the bachelors' annexe, it stood on the edge of the lake across from the main house, a gloomy villa surrounded by laurels and rhododendrons. Of all royal residences, York Cottage has been ridiculed and vilified the most. Pope-Hennessy, visiting in 1956, described it as 'grotesquely ugly, unarchitected'; like something designed by a child, it was 'all gables, and beams, and little balconies, and hexagonal turrets'.[62] Harold Nicolson, writing in 1949, likened it to a 'glum little villa' in Surbiton. 'It is almost incredible that the heir to so vast a heritage lived in this horrible little house for thirty-three years.'[63]

Mocking the philistinism of the royal family was a twentieth-century intellectual sport, and the criticism of York Cottage reeks of snobbery. Frances Donaldson, one of the more thoughtful of royal biographers, observed that York Cottage was 'too large and too full of footmen to be unremarkable in Surbiton', and considered that it should be read as 'a monument to the eccentricity of the family who lived there'.[64] The sharpest comment was made by the Duke of Windsor, as Edward VIII became after the Abdication, who told Nicolson: 'Until you have seen York Cottage you will never understand my father.'[65]

York Cottage was George's creation. He furnished and decorated it, spending many hours with 'Maple's man' choosing patterns for carpets and wallpapers.[66] (Maples was a fashionable furniture emporium on Tottenham Court Road.) The rooms were small and dark. George's study faced north, and laurels pressed against the windows shutting out the light. The walls were covered with the red cloth used for making the trousers of French private soldiers, and were hung with reproductions of Royal Academy pictures – no one could have guessed that George was heir to one of the world's greatest art collections.[67]

If George imagined that arranging the house would please his wife, he was mistaken. May was 'furious' at finding the house fully furnished, and 'furnished from Maples at that'.[68] They spent their honeymoon arranging furniture and hanging pictures, negotiating an uneasy truce. May established herself as the one in control of the organisation of the domestic space, and George gave way. 'I won't touch anything darling till you come,' he wrote in October 1893, 'and then you can arrange the room as you like.'[69]

George was devoted to the cottage. Perhaps, as some have suggested, the small rooms reminded him of a ship, making him feel safe.[70] No doubt for George, who disliked Society, it helped that formal entertaining was impossible at York Cottage. But his need for domesticity ran very deep. Like Mr Pooter, the hero of lower-middle-class London suburbia in *The Diary of a Nobody* (1892), George was a man who liked to be at home. 'What's the good of a home if you are never in it?' declares Mr Pooter. 'I am always in of an evening . . . Carrie [Mrs Pooter] and I can manage to pass our evenings together without friends.'[71] By contrast with Mr Pooter's life at The Laurels, however, the secluded domesticity of the Duke of York was no more than make-believe. In York Cottage he was always surrounded by servants and footmen. An equerry and a lady-in-waiting were present in the dining room at every meal. The fact is that he and May were never really alone.

The remarkable thing is that the retired private life of the second in line to the throne was never questioned or criticised by a prurient or hostile press. The Prince of Wales's Children Act, which made public provision for George and his siblings, had provoked heated parliamentary debate in 1889. As the only surviving son of the heir apparent, George received the lion's share of the annual payment of £36,000 which Parliament had voted to the Prince of Wales for the purpose of maintaining his children.[72]* But no one considered that the Yorks were

---

*The Prince of Wales suggested in 1889 that his eldest son should receive a payment of £25,000 upon his marriage.

accountable, nor did radicals murmur that the public was receiving poor value for money by paying for the duke and duchess to live a life of domestic retirement at York Cottage.

Two days into the honeymoon the hot weather broke, and George found himself in the cottage in the pouring rain with only his wife for company. He wrote cautiously to his mother-in-law about his growing love for May. 'I was at first very shy, but now it is all right.'[73] This was perhaps more hope than reality and so were the breezy letters May wrote to her friends: 'Georgie is a dear & we get on beautifully, he adores me which is touching.'[74] In fact the honeymoon was clouded by rows and sulks. The couple barely knew each other, and there were frequent misunderstandings.[75] May was different from George's mother and sisters, the only other women he knew well. She did not shower him with endearments and bathe him with uncritical affection as they did. On the contrary, she was reserved and often silent.

They were alone for only twelve days. Then the Wales family descended, and George and May dined at the big house almost every night and Motherdear and sisters popped round most afternoons for tea. This didn't help the newly-weds. May later reflected: 'I sometimes think that just after we married we were not left alone enough & had not the opportunity of learning to understand each other as quickly as we might otherwise have done, & this led to so many little rubs which might have been avoided'.[76]

George's sisters had seemed friendly with May to her face (though not behind her back, as we have seen), but after the marriage the Waleses 'made a set against her', and (according to her sister-in-law Princess Alice) she 'had a horrid time when she first married, simply horrid'.[77] Trapped in the cottage on the other side of the lake, she couldn't escape. Some thought the sisters were jealous of May's popularity and the cheering crowds who turned up wherever she went. For Motherdear it was painful to see Georgie boy's obvious affection for his wife, and in her letters 'sweet May' soon became 'poor May'. (When Princess Louise was annoyed with her sister-in-law she would say: 'Poor May! poor May! with her Württemberg hands!'[78]) The most spiteful of the Wales sisters was Princess Victoria. Manipulative and emotionally needy, she stayed very close to George and intrigued against May. She was once overheard saying to a guest at Windsor: 'Now do try to talk to May at dinner, though one knows she is deadly dull.'[79]

May never complained to George about her treatment by his sisters. She remained resolutely serious-minded, however, telling Bricka: 'I hope

I may prove worthy of that admirable education – I must always keep up my goal very high.'[80] Not that she envied university-educated women. When she visited Newnham College, Cambridge she wrote: 'The hideousness of the students horrified me.'[81] Staying at Osborne with Queen Victoria she found the 'eternal waiting about & dawdling which runs away with half the time' intolerable.[82] But she was acutely aware of the change in her status. At dinner she was placed next to Kaiser William,

> who made himself most agreeable ... Fancy me, little me, sitting next to William, the place of honour!!! It seems so strange, & all the Aunts push me on & make such a fuss about me while I laugh in my sleeve & say to myself 'Dear me how times have changed'.[83]

George wrote his first real love letter to May three months after their marriage, when she went to stay with her parents at White Lodge. Alone at York Cottage, George told May:

> I thought of you the whole time in the train coming here; I had no idea that I could miss you so much ... I have said lots of nasty, stupid & rude things to you I know, half in anger & half in chaff, but I didn't mean them really, & I ask you to forgive me for having said them, I was always furious with myself the moment after I had said them ... I wanted to say it to you often, but I couldn't but I feel I must write it to you. I also want to tell you how happy how very happy I am with you now my own darling, at first I don't think we were, but we did not understand each other properly, but I assure you I am indeed intensely happy & I hate you to be out of my sight; I love you my darling with all my heart & soul, I can't say more than that.[84]

Pouring out this flood of pent-up feeling must have come as a relief. In his letters to May, George repeatedly apologised for his fits of temper and his selfishness, but when they were together he couldn't bring himself to say it. The pattern continued throughout his life. He assured May that 'you are not shy with me, that has quite passed', and she agreed that 'now that I am at last able to talk to you without feeling shy everything will be easier'.[85] But it wasn't. May was still reserved – 'my visible but silent presence' was how she described herself – and George still found it impossible to say how he felt.[86] 'I wish,' said May, 'you would tell me yourself when you feel in the wrong instead of writing it, it would be so much easier.'[87] For George, a man of few friends who knew no equal relationships but only the adoration of his mother and sisters and the domination of authority figures such as his father and John

Dalton, this was hard to do. His letters, which are direct and self-deprecatory, make it easy to forget that, as a royal, he was conscious of belonging to a race apart. As someone once remarked, 'he was a very modest man personally but believed in the divine right of Kings'.[88]

At York House, the slice of St James's Palace where George and May lived in London, the family geography of Sandringham was replicated. With seventy-five rooms, it was gloomy, north-facing and furnished by Maples. The Duke of Windsor, who lived there after the First World War, described it as a rabbit warren, 'with passages interrupted by unexpected flights of steps leading to unsymmetrical rooms full of ugly Victorian furniture, brass beds and discarded portraits of former Monarchs'.[89] Across the road lived the Waleses at Marlborough House, and when George was in London he walked over to visit his parents each morning as he did at Sandringham. As his diary shows, his days in London revolved around his family, an undemanding round of afternoon calls and teas, of dinners and trips to the opera or theatre. Emotionally as well as physically, George had not yet left home.

He complained vigorously, however, about his mother-in-law's intrusion on his family space. York House had been the home of May's grandmother, the old Duchess of Cambridge, and the Duchess of Teck was accustomed to spending time there and running in and out. George did his best to circumvent his mother-in-law. According to Lady Geraldine, the Duke of York 'has taken pains so to arrange his house that it shall be impossible for her to sleep at St James's!! and announces he will not have her to dine with him "as he likes to dine punctually"'.[90] Whenever the duchess appeared George was furious. 'It used to make me so angry,' he told May, 'that when we were alone at dinner or afterwards I used to be sulky & wouldn't talk to you, which I was dying to do all the time.'[91] At White Lodge, where the couple spent six weeks when their first child was born, the duchess drove George frantic. 'I wanted so much to be with you alone, & whenever we began to have a talk or anything she used to come in & disturb us & then her unpunctuality used to annoy me too dreadfully.'[92]

May by contrast never complained about *her* mother-in-law, putting up with Motherdear rearranging the furniture, popping round on a daily basis and being just as unpunctual as Maria. May even surrendered Heather, the collie dog which had been given to her as a wedding present. 'I really think you might give him to me,' wrote George. 'I don't think you care about him as much as I do, if he was mine I should never let him go to the kennels, he would always sleep in my dressing room . . . I should like to have him more than anything I know.'[93] As his son Henry, Duke of Gloucester later remarked, 'my father stole it, of course'.[94]

As if to assert himself over his taller wife, George wore heels. 'May, he says, won't change hers, but he wears much higher ones,' reported his cousin Alicky. 'At first they had been uncomfortable, now he did not mind it any more.' Alicky's husband-to-be Nicky was also shorter than her, but he rejected George's advice to wear heels.[95]*

George's first significant separation from his wife came in November 1894 with the death of his uncle, Tsar Alexander III. To his dismay, George was summoned to Russia by his father: 'I should think you should certainly come out of respect for poor dear Uncle Sacha's memory,' wrote Bertie. However, 'it would not do to bring May'.[96] George owned himself 'perfectly miserable at leaving the darlings', by which he meant not just May but also his grieving sisters, especially Victoria – 'that girl is an Angel of goodness & unselfishness'.[97] To May he wrote: 'I simply loathe the idea of being separated from you my sweet Tootsums darling.'[98] Lord Carrington, the lord chamberlain, who accompanied him on the journey, found George 'very low at leaving his wife'.[99]

In St Petersburg George attended daily services and kissed the holy picture in the hand of his uncle Sacha in his open coffin – 'it gave me a shock when I saw his dear face so close to mine'.[100] The face of the emperor, who had by now been dead for a fortnight, was a terrible colour, but George was unmoved by this ritual. Nor did the fabulous wealth and ceremonial of the Romanovs make much impression. He saw the Hermitage, noting that it 'contained everything which belonged to different emperors since Peter the Great', apparently unaware that Catherine the Great had bought the Walpole collection from Houghton, the great house near Sandringham.[101] For George this was essentially a family occasion, and he dutifully listed the members of this dynastic realm in his letters home. Above all there was Nicky, at twenty-six the new tsar, whom George talked to in his room late at night: 'He is a charming boy so natural & simple & the views he has on different subjects are so broad & sympathetic.'[102]

The marriage of Nicky and Alicky, which had been postponed on account of the tsar's death, took place a week after the funeral. 'I never saw two people more in love with each other,' George told May. 'I told them both that I could not wish them more than that they should be as happy as you & I were [sic] together. Was that right?'[103]

---

*According to Kenneth Rose, George spurned the raised heels worn by his father; presumably he changed his mind on the matter (Kenneth Rose, *King George V* (Phoenix Press, 2000), p. 78).

Alicky and Nicky wrote to one another in English and, like George and May, they found it easier to express their feelings on paper. But the Romanovs' letters differ markedly from those of George and May. They write of their overwhelming longing for each other, they kiss each other's photographs. There is much about praying and religion in the Russians' letters, subjects rarely discussed by George and May. The dynamic is different too. Alicky is the dominant partner, mixing assurances of her undying love with hectoring exhortations to Nicky to assert his autocratic powers. May, by contrast, never discusses politics in her letters, and neither does she presume to tell George what to do.

The 'Tootsums' letters are not erotic. Tootsums, the name they both used in their letters, seems to have been a family term of endearment – George also used it with his aunt Olga, Queen of Greece. George and May rarely burn and they are too well mannered and too English to write about sex. The closest they come to a kiss is when, after a visit to St Moritz, May tells George to 'meet me at the station – you can always get into the railway carriage & embrace me there instead of before the crowd!'[104] George's return after the weeks away in Russia was (said May) 'divine'. 'I am very much in love with you,' he wrote, 'like people are before they are married.'[105] But the constant rows, which were 'generally about nothing at all', continued. May wrote sadly about a letter from George which had upset her, 'though I think you were quite right to write like that as then I know your feelings on the subject'. She went on:

> Anyhow Tootsums dear you must know by this time that I adore you & that it grieves me terribly to think we cannot get on as well as we ought to – I will try now to be more amiable & not as grumpy & please please try yrself not to be depressed which always worries me so & disarms me as I never know what to do or say when you have the 'blight'.[106]

Merry little Georgie was only one side of the story. George suffered from mood swings. 'You are sometimes "angel Georgie", sometimes "d—l Georgie",' May told him.[107] Their letters refer often to the 'blight', which was the name they gave his depression. 'I am looking forward to this next winter in our dear little cottage where I hope we may often be quite alone together which is what I like best when my Georgie dear has not got the "blight",' wrote May.[108] 'I will promise not to have the blight at all,' George assured her. But it wasn't within his control. The trauma of Eddy's death had perhaps left deep psychological scars, and his succession to a position he had never wanted made him painfully anxious.

After the death of Alexander III, the Duchess of Teck found George

'terribly low & [we] had in consequence a very silent & depressing dinner'.[109] Life with a depressive who believed in the divine right of kings
can't have been easy.

Their first child was born within a year of the wedding, on 23 June
1894. The birth was planned to take place at Buckingham Palace, which
meant that Queen Victoria would probably have attended – witnessing
the births of her great-grandchildren was one of her favourite diver-
sions. Fortunately perhaps for May, the hot weather ruled out the Palace
as unhealthy, and May, who 'was so anxious' to be at White Lodge, got
her way.[110] According to the story told by the Duke of Windsor, keen
perhaps to show his father's indifference from the start, George was in
the library, pretending to read *The Pilgrim's Progress* when the baby
was born.[111] In his diary, however, George gives another version. May's
pains began at 1.45 a.m., and at 7.30 p.m. they became much worse.
The doctor gave her chloroform, and 'I held her hand the whole time'.[112]
'My darling May was not conscious of pain during those last 2½ terrible hours,' George told Victoria.[113] After a 22-hour labour, 'a sweet
little boy was born'.[114] Motherdear and May's parents were the only
other people in the room. H. H. Asquith, the home secretary, appeared
later. The child was christened Edward Albert Christian George Andrew
Patrick David.

It was a difficult birth and, according to a close friend of the Duchess
of Teck, it had 'given cause for anxiety, although the public did not
know'.[115] May's pregnancy had shown very little, but she had felt very
ill, a fact that was later concealed from her children, who imagined that
'we came out like a litter of puppies'. When her son the Duke of Gloucester learnt this from James Pope-Hennessy, he remarked: 'I hope you put
that in, I think that is very important, put in every bloody thing you
can.'[116] As the duke implied, May's sufferings in pregnancy perhaps
helped to explain her indifference towards her babies.

CHAPTER 7

The Wasted Years
1894–1897

For George, wrote his biographer John Gore, 'life was an idyll in the nineties'.[1] He spent as little time as he could in London and as much as possible at Sandringham. Few public duties were expected of him, and his functions were scheduled to take place outside the shooting season. For seventeen years, in Harold Nicolson's famous phrase, 'he did nothing at all but kill animals and stick in stamps'.[2]

It was not the cruelty nor the ecological impact of shooting that concerned Nicolson, though that might be our worry today. On the contrary, the thing that Nicolson found hard to forgive was the prince's idleness and selfishness. 'The moment he marries and settles down at York Cottage all the basic stupidity of his character becomes apparent.'[3] George knew he was uneducated yet he neglected to prepare himself for becoming king. 'All the famous "sense of duty" becomes rather thin when one realises that during those idle years he made no real attempt to read history or to familiarise himself with the great events or the leading figures of his epoch. Just partridges and grouse all the time.'[4]

To be fair, George did make some effort to improve his education. In 1894 J. R. Tanner, a Cambridge professor, was engaged to teach him about the constitution. Much has been made of George's study of Walter Bagehot's *The English Constitution* (1867) – a choice which did not amuse Queen Victoria, who was 'displeased' that he should be studying such a radical writer.[5] Historians have argued that George's reading of Bagehot provided him with an understanding of the fundamental precepts of constitutional monarchy.[6]

Bagehot drew a distinction between the 'efficient' parts of the constitution, which exercised power, and the 'dignified' parts, which attracted and preserved the loyalty of the people. 'The use of the Queen, in a dignified capacity, is incalculable,' he wrote. 'A *family* on the throne is an interesting idea.' Royalty must be revered. 'Its mystery is its life. We must not let in daylight upon magic. We must not bring the Queen into the combat of politics.'[7] Bagehot argued for a constitutional monarch above and outside party politics, without executive power. This was not a job description that Queen Victoria would have recognised. On the contrary, in the last decades of her reign she endeavoured to block the emergence of modern constitutional monarchy, and she remained fiercely partisan. This was perhaps why she objected to Bagehot.

But Bagehot's analysis was right, and George was the first heir to the throne to read him – all his successors have done so since. He read the book after dinner, on one occasion aloud with May.[8] No doubt he absorbed Bagehot's dictum that the sovereign possessed three rights: the right to be consulted, the right to encourage and the right to warn. It is doubtful, however, whether George learnt much from his studies. 'Mr Tanner came & I read & talked with him about the English Constitution,' he wrote, and he noted Tanner coming on a couple of other occasions.[9] Eddy Hamilton, a Treasury mandarin, was asked by the then prime minister, the Earl of Rosebery, to teach George about the machinery of government. He recorded that George

> was reading Bagehot's book on the Constitution with a professor; but he found it difficult to follow and hardly gave him the information he wanted. I found him very easy to talk to because he asked so many questions . . . He confessed that he had read very little and knew very little. He could not remember what he read and he had no power of assisting his memory with notes.[10]

George didn't give up altogether. He ploughed through Erskine May's *Constitutional History* – 'parts of it were very interesting but others distinctly dull'.[11] One evening in 1898, he noted, 'May dictated to me the names of all the books I have read since 1890 which I wrote in a new book'.[12] He kept that book to the end of his life. But reading wasn't enough to fill the gaps in his knowledge. Nor did it occupy his time.

'If you left the navy what would you do?' Bertie once asked George. 'Would you lead an idle life?'[13] George had left the navy, but it was far from clear what the second in line to the throne should do instead, apart from marry and beget an heir. His public duties were few. Shooting saved him from an idle life, providing structure, discipline and exercise. Perhaps too it helped protect him from the 'blight'.

During almost five months, from August, when grouse shooting began, until the end of January, George spent most days slaughtering gamebirds. The 12th of August invariably found him on a grouse moor, often in Yorkshire, staying at Bolton Abbey with the Duke of Devonshire. After shooting grouse for over a week, George travelled north, often to Tulchan, near Perth, where he shot more grouse while staying with the fabulously rich Sassoon family. From there he proceeded to Balmoral, where he spent a month deer stalking, returning to Sandringham for partridge shooting in October. The season climaxed with the big pheasant days in December, when well over a thousand birds were regularly shot. The only interruption to this iron routine came with the death of a relative. The cancellation of his sport was no doubt one reason for George's depression when he heard of the death of Tsar Alexander III. The season of 1896/7 was free of deaths, and George notched up ninety days' shooting.[14]

In the last years of George's reign, his apologists made a virtue of his shooting, claiming that 'the King who steered this country through the most epochal moments of its history ... was at heart a country squire'.[15] The author of *King George V as a Sportsman* pictured the grizzled sovereign, worn out by long days spent in the service of his country, a solitary figure on a cold January evening on the north Norfolk marshes, expertly pulling flighting duck from the air. 'George the Fifth of England, for one brief and precious hour the plain Squire of Sandringham.'[16]

George's sporting life must be set in context. As Alan (Tommy) Lascelles, royal private secretary and diarist, pointed out, 'in that late Victorian/Edwardian country house world ... there were dozens of English gentlemen exactly like KG V [*sic*] ... Nobody, in those days, thought such a life in any way eccentric.'[17] But George was not really a country squire. At Sandringham he didn't run the estate; his father did that. George was given a small farm to manage, and in consultation with Jackson, the head keeper, he organised the shooting.

Spending fifteen years in the navy meant that George was slow to develop as a marksman. Not until he was twenty-seven or so was he recognised as a crack shot. Staying in a shooting party in 1895 Lord Carrington noted that 'the best of all is the Duke of York who promises to be the best shot in England'.[18] He never became the number one, but by 1900 he was reckoned by some to be the sixth best shot in the country, and he was certainly one of the top ten.[19] As Duke of York, he was always given the best stand where the most birds flew, but he was nevertheless one of the elite of so-called Big Shots, the aristocratic marksmen who dominated the pre-1914 golden age of battue shooting. This was a world where he excelled on his own merits.

England's top shot was usually agreed to be Lord de Grey (later Marquess of Ripon), with whom George sometimes stayed to shoot grouse at Studley Royal in Yorkshire. Famed for killing twenty-eight pheasants in sixty seconds at Sandringham, de Grey liked to pretend that his excellence was effortless. He was annoyed to be discovered in the library of a country house before breakfast, practising changing guns with his loader. A somewhat humourless character, he was the improbable husband of Gladys de Grey, a glamorous member of the Marlborough

House Set and friend of Queen Alexandra. De Grey's rival was Lord Walsingham, a Norfolk landowner who killed a record 1,070 grouse by himself one day in 1888. To put this in perspective, in the season of 1896/7 George shot a total of 1,116 grouse over twenty days.[20]

Battue shooting – the industrial slaughter of thousands of reared pheasants – was the court sport of Edward VII. Predictable, controllable and exclusive, this was a closed spectator sport where the protagonists competed against each other. It had little to do with the countryman's skill of hunting; the crack shots were effectively professional marksmen.[21] George belonged to a generation of princes who excelled at this type of shooting. King Carlos of Portugal, who was assassinated in 1908, was a very fat man who liked to shoot alternately from both shoulders, and who killed low-flying pheasants by holding his shotgun outstretched in front of him like a pistol rather than mounted on his shoulder. Archduke Franz Ferdinand was a talented shot; he specialised in shooting deer and he was alleged to have killed half a million beasts before he too was assassinated aged fifty-one.

George was fiercely competitive. He counted everything. At Sandringham an equerry asked each gun how many birds he had killed at the end of the drive, and the totals were read out at lunch. George wore a pedometer, and noted that he walked between nine and twelve miles on a shooting day. He counted all the birds he shot, and all the cartridges he fired. He noted the bag on every day's shooting. At Panshanger in Hertfordshire in 1896 at one stand he recorded 'the highest pheasants I have ever seen, I got 126 there; there were over 100 people as spectators, it was a lovely day, we got over 1800 pheasants, which has beaten the record here by 600 birds'.[22] At Holkham, the mecca of battue shooting, ruled by the Earl of Leicester, a heavily bearded patriarch, George witnessed 'the best day's [partridge] driving I have ever seen. I was third with 141 birds ... Lord Leicester walked with us all day & looked after the beaters.'[23] At the end of the shooting season he pasted into his diary a card headed 'Game Killed by Me During Season 1896–97'. He calculated that he had shot a total of 11,006 head, including 2,509 partridges and 5,993 pheasants.

At a single stand one day at Holkham in December 1898 George shot 282 pheasants.[24] Surrounded by heaps of dead birds piled high he felt no twinge of guilt about the cruelty of the sport. Self-contained and single-minded, he glides silently through the social memoirs of the time. Few stories are told about him. His diary gives little away. Apart from having a shaky hand after shooting, the physical toll of firing thousands of cartridges day after day is barely mentioned.

* * *

George spent nine days shooting at Bolton Abbey with the Duke of Devonshire in August 1896. 'Had 6 drives, 8 guns, killed 350 brace of grouse, splendid lot of birds, I got 115 birds,' was a typical diary entry.[25] He said nothing about his eccentric host or his German wife Louise, the Double Duchess (her first husband was the Duke of Manchester), nor the long days spent on the moor in this sporting paradise which swarmed with birds. Nor did he mention the letters he received from May, who never accompanied him on grouse-shooting expeditions: that summer she was in St Moritz on an Alpine holiday with her mother. On 16 August George wrote to May:

What an infernal bore that nothing has happened yet . . . it is certainly very bad luck & not at all what we want just now, we are both quite agreed on that subject. And I thought everything was so safe & going so well . . . I was looking forward to spending such a happy winter with my sweet little Angel wife when all our functions &ct [sic] were over & we could enjoy ourselves & you strong & well & come out shooting with me & now all our hopes are dashed to the ground by this!!![26]

May's second child Albert (Bertie) had been born on 14 December 1895, and she was appalled to discover herself pregnant once more eight months later. 'I really do not feel up to having another just yet, & look forward with horror to the next 10 months!'[27] She told George: 'I had been so hoping for a nice winter & going out shooting with you & now I shall have to revert to those deadly dull daily drives which I have learnt to dread.'[28] George was so upset by May's news that he came down with the 'blight' and one day he felt too low even to go shooting. In St Moritz, meanwhile, the rain poured unceasingly and a little French girl staying in the same hotel remembered the German-looking princess – 'she was of the heavy German type' – being 'very very cross' about the rain. ' "Hang the weather!" she would impatiently exclaim.'[29]

The 'accident' brought them closer. On subjects such as this, George found it easier to write than talk – 'I just pick up my pen & write what comes in my head as if I was talking to you, perhaps I can almost write more than I can say.'[30] Revealing another side of himself from the wooden automaton of the diaries, he penned affectionate, sympathetic letters which gave May comfort. 'I am so pleased you wrote to me like that, you so seldom talk to me of such things,' she told him.[31] By the end of the six weeks apart they were desperate to see each other. George had by now reached Birkhall on Loch Muick, the house on the Balmoral estate lent to the Yorks by Queen Victoria, whitewash outside and dark pitch pine and Landseer prints within.[32] He eagerly awaited May's arrival at Ballater: 'You will find me D.v. [*Deo volente* – God willing] waiting on the platform of the station, ready to kiss you, you mustn't be shy. We will have a better kiss when we are alone in the house.'[33]

At Balmoral, George's routine was interrupted by the visit of his cousins Nicholas and Alicky. On his father's instructions, George received Nicky at Ballater station wearing 'full Highland dress and claymore of course with ribbon and star of St Andrew'.[34] On a deer drive in pouring rain George killed five stags, including one weighing over seventeen stone, and Nicky shot nothing. 'My uncles,' wrote the Tsar, 'seem to consider it necessary to take me shooting every day along with the gentlemen. The weather is awful, rain and wind every day, and on top of it all no luck at all – I haven't killed a stag yet.'[35] George had a talk with 'dear Nicky' and found him, in spite of being emperor, 'just the same dear boy as he always was'.[36] The security was tight. One reason for inviting Nicholas to Balmoral was that the Russians feared an anarchist attack in London. Sir Matthew White Ridley, the home secretary, reassured the Queen's private secretary Sir Arthur Bigge: 'None of our information points in the direction of an attempt on the Tsar or Balmoral. Quite the contrary. This, however, has in no degree affected our action in taking every possible precaution for his safety.'[37] Out shooting Nicky was accompanied by an escort consisting of Detective Inspector Melville, the superintendent of Scotland Yard's Special Branch, as well as an armed guard and a member of Russia's Special Service Police.

May had good reason to dread another pregnancy.* Bertie was born after only four hours of labour, and May recovered more quickly from this second birth than she did from David's.[38] But the pregnancy had been difficult. At eight months May still suffered from morning sickness and nausea. She told George:

> You really need not be anxious about me for I am sure that my often feeling uncomfortable & sick are merely due to my state & cannot in any way be stopped – Of course it is a great bore for me & requires a great deal of patience to bear it, but this is alas the penalty of being a woman![39]

---

*Queen Mary had six children: Edward, Prince of Wales, known as David, born 23 June 1894; Albert (Bertie), born 14 December 1895; Mary, born 25 April 1897; Henry, known as Harry, born 31 March 1900; George, born 20 December 1902; John, born 12 July 1905.

As her third pregnancy advanced, May showed little sign of her condition. At six months the Empress Vicky remarked that 'there is absolutely nothing to be seen' of the baby. 'She is not at all pleased at having another & does not wish it remarked or mentioned. She does not seem to have the passionate tenderness for her little ones wh seems so natural to me.'[40] The Empress was an obsessive worshipper of babies, but May's apparent lack of maternal feeling was remarkable even by the standards of motherhood that prevailed among aristocratic women at the time. Vicky thought her 'strangely cold and indifferent with her children'.[41] Showing one of her babies in its cot to Lady Juliet Duff, May remarked: 'I wonder what it's thinking? Nothing at all of course, stupid little thing.'[42]

Biographers have pronounced a harsh verdict on May as a mother. Frances Donaldson considered that the little princes suffered from 'their almost total estrangement from their mother, the coldness with which she rejected them'.

> Queen Mary's exceptionally reserved and undemonstrative temperament made it impossible for her to give her children the love and affection which is taken for granted in happier homes. From the first she disliked the period of pregnancy and the physical aspects of childbirth and held herself aloof from the demonstrations of intimacy and affection these were apt to provoke.[43]

The evidence is mixed, however, and the truth more nuanced than this sweeping judgement suggests. There seems to be no mention of May breastfeeding her babies, and when David was just six weeks old she departed on a trip to St Moritz with the Duchess of Teck. Leaving home made her miserable, however. She told George: 'I don't think I quite realized when I said I would go abroad what it wld cost me to leave you & our darling little baby.'[44] A nanny called Mrs Peters was engaged when David was one month old. She was 'an elderly Scotch nurse – a plain homely woman', and she claimed to have reared twenty-eight babies (and only lost one) on a regime of sterilised, boiled cow's milk (no solid food until nine months) and plenty of fresh air.[45] Peters's cows milk diet did not agree with Prince Bertie, who developed chronic stomach trouble, made worse, it was said, by her habit of giving him his afternoon bottle in a coach called a C-spring victoria, 'a process not dissimilar from a rough channel crossing'.[46]

In his memoirs, the Duke of Windsor told a story about Peters. He claimed that when she brought him down as a baby to the drawing room at tea time she would pinch him and twist his arm so that he bawled and sobbed. Embarrassed, puzzled and annoyed, the parents hastily returned the screaming infant to the nanny, who removed him from the room.[47] The evidence shows that behind the swing door at the end of the first-floor passage which led to the York Cottage nursery, Peters ruled supreme. No one except Peters was allowed to do anything for David. When David was eighteen months his mother pathetically wrote: 'I really believe he begins to like me at last, he is most civil to me,' a remark which some have read as proof of May's lack of feeling, but what it really shows is that May had become a stranger to her own child.[48]

The Princess of Wales adored baby David, a small, pretty child; she claimed – ominously perhaps – that he reminded her of Eddy.[49] When the children stayed with her she made Peters bring David downstairs. She was 'very firm' if he cried and soon he was happy to remain with her. 'Poor Nana herself was so delighted about this change & with tears in her eyes she said if only the Duke & Duchess could see him now.'[50] Alix's success no doubt undermined May's fragile confidence even more, but it was short-lived. Soon the little princes were not allowed to see their grandmother for more than five minutes, after which they were dragged away by Peters and a doctor, who between them 'seem to think the children ought not to be looked at by anyone except themselves'.[51] By now even George was concerned about the little princes, grumbling that 'this confounded Dr & nurses think they are made of sugar & are different to anybody else's children'.[52] David was unsettled and nervous, and May worried that he was not normal. She wrote anxiously: 'David was "jumpy" yesterday morning, however he got quieter after being out, what a curious child he is.'[53]

Peters had achieved total ascendancy over David. 'She put all sorts of things in Davies's [sic] head against his Parents,' wrote the Duke of Teck.[54] York Cottage was not a happy place. 'I was quite sorry all this winter,' Alix told George, 'to see how uncomfortable it all was & how estranged the children got from you & how little pleasure you had from them.'[55]

In March 1897, when May was eight months pregnant, Peters left. It turned out – to the surprise of the parents – that she had never taken a day off since she came, and her nerves were 'quite unstrung'. She felt the parting 'most terribly', wrote George, '& it distressed me very much to see her grief . . . Poor May was quite upset when she said goodbye to her and cried.'[56] Peters, who was evidently suffering from a breakdown, departed for a nursing home in Eastbourne.

The remarkable thing about the Peters saga is not that May didn't realise what was going on – she certainly did – but how long she took to do something about it. Spending long periods of time away from the children forced her to depend upon Peters more than she might have wished. But the real problem was that May feared confrontation and avoided it.

The tyrannical Peters was replaced by a nanny named Parker, 'a very nice sensible little woman' (according to George).[57] For the time being at least, peace ruled in the nursery. May told George that she found the children 'too delightful just now ... I shall miss them terribly as I have been so much with them lately – I am more delighted than ever with Parker, she is so sensible & so pleased when the children are a good deal with me.'[58] These were hardly the words of the cold, indifferent mother of royal myth. David was apparently 'quite a different child, he is full of fun, quite good humoured, full of wit, likes to drive with his Mama only in the Carriage'.[59] But Parker turned out to be no good either, and she was replaced by the under-nurse, Charlotte Bill, known as Lala, who at last brought stability and good sense to the royal nursery. When Pope-Hennessy met her, he thought her a delightful, simple woman who, fifty years on, 'talked of them all with real affection and amusement and not in the least tainted by the royal atmosphere'.[60]

Children who fail to form a strong emotional bond with a parent figure in the first years of life are more likely to suffer from aggression, defiance and hyperactivity and less likely to succeed in later life. In the 1890s no one expected an aristocratic woman to look after her own children, but the nanny's role was crucial and so was a good relationship between the nanny and the mother. It is not altogether fanciful to suggest that the road to the Abdication began in the troubled nursery at York Cottage in Nurse Peters's day – a tragedy of good people held back by good behaviour from doing the right thing.

May's third child – a girl named Mary – was born at York Cottage after a twelve-hour labour on 25 April 1897. At White Lodge on the same day the Duchess of Teck was seized with sudden, excruciating pain, and the doctors advised her that they must operate at once to save her life. The Duchess was diagnosed with a strangulated hernia, a medical emergency which carries a risk of death from septicaemia even today, and was all the more hazardous in the 1890s when gastric surgery was in its infancy.[61]

The 63-year-old duchess was already in poor health, massively overweight and exhausted by unceasing work for her numerous charities. Her legs and ankles were dangerously swollen, which made standing for any length of time impossible, and her doctors forbade her from attending the Queen's drawing rooms. (It never seems to have occurred to Queen Victoria to suggest that her cousin might be permitted to sit in her presence.) The duchess suffered from frightening fainting fits, and her physician warned her that her heart was weak. 'I don't want to die yet,' she sobbed, 'I cannot leave my children – my sons want me still.'[62] Bricka, her devoted attendant, despaired of her life. 'What will England be without her? I feel too sad for words,' she wrote.[63] As for May, knowing that her mother could never say no to a public function, she wrote stern letters imploring people not to invite her.

The duchess agreed at once to the operation, which took place in her bedroom at White Lodge. She displayed characteristic courage, smiling at the people in the room as she inhaled the ether. Defying the risks, she made a rapid recovery. She boasted to May of her 'wonderful progress . . . Taking roast lamb & mint sauce, boiled mutton, roast chicken, asparagus, spinach etc – beside invalid turtle soup brought by kind Ly Mayoress . . .'[64]

May recuperated more quickly from this third birth than she had from the previous ones, but her confinement kept her at York Cottage with her daughter,

> a dear little child & quite good looking for so small a baby, she does not cry much so I can have her here in my room where she sleeps placidly in her cradle, I am so pleased that I have got a daughter & Georgie is quite enchanted with her as he wanted a girl.[65]

It was George who visited the duchess at White Lodge, finding her in buoyant spirits, describing every detail of the operation for him 'in a most amusing way' and looking ten years younger with no swelling in her ankles or legs.[66]

The duchess's recovery seemed complete. With George and May she attended the Diamond Jubilee, marking the sixtieth anniversary of Victoria's accession, her 'dear smiling face . . . bowing acknowledgement to the roar of cheers that greeted her approach'.[67] When May stayed at White Lodge in August, the duchess annoyed her as much as ever, insisting on going to an exhibition – 'such a bore as you know I hate fuss & of course Mama will have to go in a bath chair with an admiring crowd following!'[68] The meals at White Lodge got later and later. 'Really the hours here are getting quite impossible,' grumbled May after dining at 9.40 one night, 'no idea of time & one loses no end of time waiting.'[69] If there was any cause for worry at White Lodge, it concerned the duke, who forgot everything and couldn't find his words. He had always been irascible, but this was something different.

*   *   *

Early in October George's valet, Mr Algar, wanted to commit suicide but ended up firing two shots from a gun into the ceiling of his room at York Cottage. He 'funked it' and ran away to Peterborough.[70] Algar, who had been with George for fourteen years, had apparently got into the hands of a bad woman. George was sympathetic but angry. 'It is very sad, & I was fond of him,' he wrote, 'but he has treated me abominably after all my kindness & I hope I shall never see him again, but I should like to know what has become of him & get him sent back to his wife.'[71] It was particularly upsetting because Algar had charge of all George's things, which made it difficult to find anything. George hastily departed for three days' shooting at Houghton with Lord Grey de Wilton where they killed record-breaking numbers. 'My hand shakes so much after shooting I can hardly write,' he told May.[72]

Later that month George stayed for a shooting party at Elveden in Essex with the Earl and Countess of Iveagh, and the bombardment was so terrific that one gun had to 'lie down for three quarters of an hour under a hedge to recover, so as to be able to go on shooting again'.[73] Before shooting on 27 October George was stunned to receive a telegram: 'My darling mama passed peacefully away at three a.m. Am heartbroken come as soon as you can May.'[74] He left at once, remarking as he stepped into the motor car, 'It is very hard on me: as it knocks all my shooting on the head'.[75]

The duchess's death was shockingly sudden. May happened to be at White Lodge, spending a week as she usually did helping her mother unpack the parcels of clothes for her guilds. On Monday 25 October the duchess stayed in bed with a chill. The rest of the party went up to London for a play, and May remained behind with her mother, thankful 'to get out of the drive there & back'; they had a nice long talk after dinner.[76] The next day the duchess was worse. The doctor reported that it was the same thing as before and a second operation might be needed. 'I am so awfully upset that I can hardly write ... I feel in an agony of fright,' wrote May.[77] At about 8 p.m. the duchess was gripped with acute pain, and the surgeon was summoned from London. He was delayed by fog, and when he arrived around midnight decided to operate at once. The operation seemed successful, but the duchess died from heart failure at 3 a.m. with May sitting at her side. The duchess had been living on borrowed time. A recurrence of the strangulated hernia had always been likely, and a second operation of this sort was 'nearly always fatal'.[78]

'Darling my whole heart goes out to you & I long to be with you,' wrote Lady Eva Dugdale, May's lady-in-waiting.[79] This was the second death that May had witnessed in five years, and it affected her more deeply than Eddy's. People commented on how calm and controlled she was. She had to be. The duke had collapsed into a pathetic wreck. He wept bitterly, laughed, talked incoherently and declared himself helpless without his wife, who had always done everything for him. Upstairs the duchess was laid out on her bed, looking peaceful as if asleep, and the duke kept talking to her 'in the most piteous way'.[80] He cried repeatedly, 'It is not true, it cannot be true! She does not look dead!'[81] The only person who had any influence over poor, mad Teck in this state was May.[82]

George stayed at White Lodge for four weeks. It was not a cheerful time. 'A dark gloomy cold day,' he wrote on 4 November, 'feel awfully depressed & have got the blight.'[83] Day after day his diary records sorting and destroying the duchess's letters. At least this activity gave him something to count. By the time he left he had torn up more than sixty boxes of letters.[84] When he escaped for two days' shooting his mood lifted – indeed his depression seems not unrelated to cancelling the shooting he had arranged that month. From Newmarket he wrote to May:

> I am afraid I have been selfish & not half as nice to you during these last three weeks . . . as I ought to have been . . . but darling I have felt out of sorts & disappointed & have had the blight etct [sic] & have been selfish & am selfish I suppose . . . if anything it has made me love you more than I did before if that is possible; & I feel now that your darling Mama has been taken away from you, I must do more for you & try to be more to you now that you have lost her sacred love & confidence . . . [85]

It was some comfort that he had the self-knowledge to write this; but his letter hardly suggests that he made May's grieving for her mother in the chaotic household at White Lodge any easier.

'What is to happen with poor Teck?' wrote May's aunt Augusta, the Grand Duchess of Mecklenburg-Strelitz. 'Poor May will have to think & act for them all.'[86] After a month at White Lodge with her demented father even May could bear it no longer and she retreated exhausted to Sandringham – 'it is all too too painful,' she told Queen Victoria. A 'brain doctor' was consulted, and he 'thought very badly' of the duke, both mentally and physically, and insisted that he should be cared for by a medical attendant.[87] The duke became psychotic and paranoid. George visited one day and found him 'howling & shrieking like a maniac' about his shirt collar, and complaining that 'he was miserable, he was a prisoner, arrested by the Queen & <u>deserted</u> by his family'.[88]

The duchess left no will, and there was not enough money for the duke – who was incapable of managing his own affairs – to remain at White Lodge in the lavish style to which he was accustomed. He was packed off to stay with his cousin the King of Württemberg at Stuttgart. Predictably perhaps, this arrangement was a disaster. Alone and confused, the duke made violent scenes which brought on a stroke.[89] He was sent back to England, and returned in a far worse state than before, with his mouth drawn up on one side, twitching and incoherent. The doctors arranged to have him certified, and he was classed as insane. Thankfully he grew calmer, and this meant that he could be kept at home at White Lodge, more cheaply than before, rather than in an asylum, which, as May wrote, 'will cause less bother & publicity'.[90]

Mad Teck lingered on alone at White Lodge with four keepers – two at night and two in the day – and a doctor. His children were not allowed to visit because they made him excited. The last time May saw her father was in October 1898. He had a white beard and he went around in bare feet and a nightshirt. The expression on his face was 'quite happy & contented' though he still believed that all his things were poisoned. 'He knew me at once & was so pleased to see me, kissed me & took my hands in his . . . then after a minute he said "You better go" & left the room.'[91] The visit made him agitated and she was asked not to go again. For the last year of his life he was an imbecile. He died of a stroke in January 1900.

CHAPTER 8

'I Find Life in General Very Dull'

1898–1901

In March 1898, travelling incognito as Lady Killarney, Princess May journeyed to Menton to stay with her aunt Augusta, the Grand Duchess of Mecklenburg-Strelitz. Worn out by caring for her mad father and grieving for her mother, May had need of a rest. But there was another reason for her trip.

For the past few months the German courts had buzzed with rumours about an unmentionable scandal at Strelitz. 'All Berlin knows and talks of it,' the Empress Vicky told her daughter, and Vicky herself did 'much harm in writing to all the Courts'.[1] Queen Victoria was beside herself with curiosity when Vicky refused to tell her the story, and when she learnt what had happened she was horrified. 'Can it <u>really</u> be true?' she asked.[2]

Aunt Augusta's granddaughter, the nineteen-year-old Marie of Mecklenburg-Strelitz, was brought up with her sister in strict seclusion in her parents' palace in Strelitz by a governess. In the autumn of 1897 her mother discovered that Marie was eight months pregnant. Neglected by her parents, Marie was an innocent who apparently knew nothing of the facts of life, and somehow or other – the charitable explanation was that she had been hypnotised or drugged – she had become pregnant. Her seducer was the footman who lit the lamps in the palace, a married man whose name was Hecht.

Having allowed this to happen under their royal noses, the parents miserably mishandled it. Hecht was dismissed, rather than being paid off to keep silent: he went to a lawyer and the story appeared in the radical press. Marie was packed off to Paris for the birth, and her parents refused to have anything to do with her, forbidding her name from being mentioned. The baby was removed to an orphanage. 'It is too awful, & shameful & almost sinful to send the poor Baby away,' wrote Queen Victoria.[3]

Aunt Augusta intervened and took charge of her granddaughter Marie. Under pressure from her son, she tried to cover up the scandal and pretended that Marie was ill – a lie which Queen Victoria thought 'very wrong'.[4]

When May learnt the story from Queen Victoria she was 'greatly shaken'.[5] This grotesque scandal was (as one courtier wrote) 'an incident worthy of Russia in the seventeenth century'; but it mattered to the British royal family because the Grand Duchess was a first cousin of Queen Victoria.[6]

Aunt Augusta was a sharp-tongued, cantankerous old lady of seventy-seven, eleven years older than her sister the Duchess of Teck. Short, plump and birdlike, she was locked by her marriage to the blind and dull Grand Duke of Mecklenburg-Strelitz into a small obscure German court, but she continued to take a passionate interest in her British royal relations. Shabbily dressed and notoriously tight-fisted, Aunt Augusta clung to the famous Cambridge sapphires and believed in the divine right of kings.

At Menton, where they shared a small house adjoining the hotel, May and her aunt talked late into the night. For Augusta the secrecy imposed by her son was unbearable because it cut her off from her English family, and May saw that 'it is a great relief to her to talk of it to me'.[7] Marie, who accompanied Augusta, was in 'an apathetic state' and (wrote May) 'oh! so badly dressed, so very German which is scarcely a pretty fashion'.[8] May had some sympathy for Marie, whom she described as an innocent victim, but her prime concern was to repair the damage to her aunt.

That spring Queen Victoria was staying along the coast at Cimiez on her annual migration to the Riviera, and May persuaded Augusta to pay her a visit. The Queen was 'most kind' and listened 'most attentively' to Augusta, who told her 'the whole ghastly truth'.[9] Victoria signalled her approval by asking to see Marie, whose visit was duly reported in the Court Circular, thus sending a coded snub to Marie's parents.[10]

Marie remained a difficult, damaged young woman. In June 1899 she married Count Georges Jametel, the elaborately moustachioed son of a French banker. All her German family attended the wedding, which took place at Kew, and her father, who was doubtless relieved at getting his disgraced daughter off his hands, gave her a generous settlement. Jametel turned out to be a villain. Not only was he unfaithful, but he bullied Marie, who was '<u>so</u> weak'; he took control of her money, attempted to cut her off from her grandmother and, horror of horrors, tried to make her give up her title.[11] In 1908 Marie divorced him.

Among the James Pope-Hennessy papers in the Getty Research Institute in Los Angeles can be found two flimsy typewritten letters written in 1960 from an address in LA. The writer, whose name was Cyril von Sellheim, revealed that he was the illegitimate son of Duchess Marie of

Mecklenburg-Strelitz, whose story he had been startled to read in Pope-Hennessy's book. He related how, after his birth in Paris (which was verified by his birth certificate), he had been placed in the Bethel bei Bielefeld Orphanage in Germany, 300 miles from Strelitz. At the age of two and a half he was removed from the orphanage, and adopted by a German doctor and his wife, who lived in St Petersburg. This was arranged by Marie's cousin Princess Helene of Saxe-Altenburg, who had a palace in the Russian capital. As a child Cyril was sent to play in the garden of the palace in order that Princess Helene could observe him through the window.

His dying adoptive mother told him about his birth mother when he was in his teens. But then the Russian Revolution scattered the family; he joined the Russian Imperial Navy, was taken prisoner by the Japanese and eventually reached America. He never made contact with his mother.[12] By a strange twist Sellheim's letters ended up in the same archival file as transcripts of his great-grandmother Augusta's correspondence.

For May Menton was an epiphany. In those long evenings closeted with her aunt she discovered an emotional connection which she had lost when her mother died. She wrote to Augusta afterwards:

> I cannot tell you how much good it did me to have those long delightful talks together & to feel that you understood & sympathised with me. For now alas that my darling Mama is no more I have really no one to talk to in the way I could always talk to her, and it was such a relief to me to be able to speak openly to you on subjects which were near to both our hearts.[13]

For Aunt Augusta, May had become 'like a Daughter and I love her <u>so</u>'.[14] She later wrote that only in 1898 did she

> get to know her real character, a real Angel of mercy at that terribly sad and trying time for me, then only did I find in her ... the warm heart, the clear, good and quiet judgement in all things, her gentle reserve and yet coming forward, when it was right, I ... by degrees felt more & more, that she would some day fill her place and be a real Queen.[15]

May shared with her aunt a passionate interest in the history, genealogy and possessions of the wider royal family which was almost obsessive. Augusta filled the role which every queen consort needs: she acted as mentor, tutoring her niece in the job, providing shrewd advice and common sense of a sort which Princess Alexandra could never have given her daughter-in-law.

May's need for someone to whom she could speak openly reveals much about her marriage to George. The biographer searches George's writings in vain for an inner life. He spent the month of March, when May stayed in Menton, at Abergeldie near Balmoral, salmon fishing with his friend and equerry Charles Cust as sole companion. This was a new sport; it had the advantage of not clashing with the shooting season, thus extending the sacred time when he was out of London and not available for functions. For a month George fished every day except Sunday in finger-numbing snow and hard frost. After flogging the icy river Dee with a heavy cane rod for a week he caught his first salmon.

Before May left for Menton their relations had been strained. When George fell silent, May worried that 'something had happened & that you had changed'; but she was too insecure to have it out with him.[16] Not until George wrote explaining that 'simply I didn't feel inclined to talk, that's all, you mustn't think that I have quarrelled or changed because I am silent' could May relax. 'I am much relieved to find I am mistaken,' she wrote.[17] But this wasn't a misunderstanding about nothing. As George told May, 'you ... are almost shy with me sometimes now which makes me the same & frightens me & chokes me off rather'.[18] George could not perceive what May perhaps did not admit even to herself. Not only was she grieving for her mother – and suppressing her grief made her depressed. But she was beginning to realise that her marriage to George might never meet her need for emotional or intellectual companionship.

As usual they worried about being 'so dreadfully stiff & cold together without meaning it'.[19] But the letters they wrote about resolving the problem only revealed how far apart they had grown and how little they had in common. From Menton May wrote suggesting that George should meet her in Paris where they could spend a few days together.[20] George refused. 'I must say I don't care about going abroad, I never did,' he growled.[21] May gave in but not without firing a parting shot: 'I quite understand about yr not wishing to come to Paris & am not angry, I only thought it wd be nice for a change as I find life in general very dull – unless one has a change sometimes.'[22] So much for the view that May was a doormat princess, overcome and silenced by George's royal status.

The charge of dullness stung. George next suggested that they should spend Easter at York Cottage alone with the children without ladies or equerries. 'I don't think you would be very much bored with me alone, would you Tootsums, I will try & be very very nice to you & do every-thing you wish, walk with you, drive with you &ct [*sic*].'²³ May jumped at the suggestion. 'It will be so nice being together again & if you will really walk & drive with me as we used to do, I am sure we will be quite happy.'²⁴ Not since August 1895 had they spent time alone together, when they had ten days at York Cottage.²⁵

Lady-in-waiting Eva Dugdale and equerry Derek Keppel were duly sent home, but the royal couple's few days of solitude at York Cottage were far from blissful. Most days George's diary records: 'Tearing up letters with May all the morning.'²⁶ Destroying the papers of the Duch-ess of Teck was hardly a joyful occupation, though at last they managed to finish it. George complained about May's rest, which she took in the evening in the sitting room before dinner: 'You lie on a sofa, one side of the room & I sit at the other, that is a mistake, we ought to sit together, but it is difficult for me to sit on the sofa on which you are lying.'²⁷

This picture of life in the cramped sitting room of York Cottage made May shout with laughter; but she begged George to show affection to her before other people. 'It wld please me very much as I always think Louise & Macduff & Maud & Charles are so charming together.'²⁸*

May's concern with how their marriage appeared to outsiders wasn't just a matter of adjusting the terms of their relationship. She under-stood, perhaps in a way that George did not, that projecting a public image of marital harmony would strengthen her position as consort. When May told George that 'if only you wd help me to be more affec-tionate it would be a great thing both for yr own happiness & for mine', she was thinking not only of their relationship but of how it was per-ceived.²⁹ She was thrilled when Queen Victoria told her that 'she was so glad we got on so well together as in these days it was such an example to others!'³⁰ Recognition of the happiness of their marriage would release both of them to spend more time apart.

They bickered about the children. When May joked that an eight-pound salmon that George caught was 'about the weight of my babies at birth', he ticked her off for saying '<u>my</u>' when she ought to have said '<u>our</u>' children.³¹ To which she responded: 'My joke about "my" children was the fact of the weight I had to carry which did not affect you, that's why I put "my", otherwise you know <u>I</u> generally say "our" tho' <u>you</u> don't you know!'³²

In the summer of 1898 George spent eight weeks commanding a cruiser named the *Crescent*, first on a short cruise and then teaming up

---

*Macduff was Princess Louise's husband, the Duke of Fife. Maud's husband was Prince Charles of Denmark, later King Haakon of Norway.

with the Channel Squadron in Orkney for manoeuvres.[33] May joined him for three days in July, and they stayed in a borrowed house at Weymouth. 'I was <u>so happy</u> with you there,' wrote George, 'I think you were nicer to me than you have ever been before.'[34] He wrote passionate letters telling her that life without her was a blank and he hated being parted for a single day, though perhaps what he really hated was being at sea, which reawakened old memories: 'I did feel so lonely when I walked down to the boat alone & nearly cried, & I could hardly trust myself to say goodbye to you Sweetie for fear of breaking down.'[35]

George's uxorious emotionalism at parting from his wife contrasts sharply with his reaction to a disaster which occurred a few weeks earlier, when May launched a battleship named the *Albion* on the Thames at Blackwall. She made three attempts to smash the bottle on the bows but failed each time; the cord was too short and the ship moving too fast. The ship entered the water at such speed that it caused an enormous wave. Nothing could be seen from the royal box or heard above the cheering, and not until they returned to London did George and May hear of the disaster. As George wrote: 'I regret to say that as the ship was launched, the backwave washed away a staging on which about 200 people were standing & they were thrown into the water, I am afraid over 30 were drowned. Got home at 4.15.'[36] The indifference of that last short sentence is chilling. George sent a telegram expressing his 'profound regret', and he and the officers of his ship gave £6 5s to the disaster fund.[37] This was not the caring king that he was to become after 1914.

In March 1899 May departed for Nice to stay with Queen Victoria at Cimiez, travelling out on the special train, sustained by Irish stew which was made at Windsor and kept tepid by being wrapped in red flannel cushions. At Cimiez, the court ran on English hours which meant that no one went outside until 4 p.m. and most of the day was lost. Victoria's children descended in droves to discuss the pressing dynastic question of the moment: the Coburg succession.

'Little Alfred', the only son of George's uncle Alfred, now Duke of Coburg, had died the previous month aged twenty-four. That the cause of death was syphilis seems evident from a letter which Alix wrote to George: 'That <u>poor poor</u> boy! Actually dying <u>like that</u>! & from <u>such</u> a terrible horrible illness & disease too! Poor poor thing! I am so sorry for him! His young life blighted & wasted ... how I pity those miserable unfortunate parents.'[38] According to a Dr Bemkart, who was with him when he died, 'the end was paralysis of the larynx caused by the state of the brain', which was due to the 'fast' life he had lived in Berlin in the fastest Prussian regiment. 'How strange Royalties are,' reflected Marie Mallet, Queen Victoria's strong-minded woman of the bedchamber, 'their children seem to lack the ordinary care bestowed on our own humblest middle class.' Such a thing, she thought, could not have happened to middle-class boys, whose parents would never have neglected their sons as the Edinburghs did Alfred.[39]*

No one wanted Coburg. It brought an income of £300,000 a year, but it meant becoming German. The Duke of Connaught, who was next in line, refused it, and so did his son. Eventually the succession devolved on Charles Edward, Duke of Albany, fourteen-year-old son of Prince Leopold, himself the Prince of Wales's youngest brother. He turned out to be a weak man placed in an impossible position by two world wars, and his later espousal of Nazism was to be a lasting embarrassment to the British royal family. Cracks were already appearing in the dynastic edifice. Marie Mallet thought the Princess of Wales's restlessness was 'alarming'; 'her one idea is to be constantly travelling'. As for her daughter Maud, her dyed canary-coloured hair 'makes her look quite improper and more like a little milliner than ever'. Princess May, by contrast, was 'most sensible and reliable, my admiration for her increases and if only she could shake off her shyness she will make a model Queen'.[40]

Harold Nicolson noted with dismay that 'George V never mentioned in his diary the outbreak of the South African War. It is all about pheasants.'[41] The Boer republics declared war on 11 October 1899, successfully invading British territory before the British army could arrive. All three of May's brothers served in South Africa, but to judge from his diary George seemed remarkably detached from the war. In the winter of 1899/1900 he pursued his campaign against the driven pheasant as relentlessly as ever. During Black Week in December, when the British army reeled from repeated defeats at the hands of the Boers, George was shooting with the Earl of Leicester at Holkham. He wrote in his diary: 'We had a capital day's partridge driving & got over 700 birds. And so end 4 splendid days' driving, in which we have killed over 1500 brace, which is wonderful considering it is the middle of Dec: & not a very good year.'[42] On 16 December he observed that the disastrous defeat of General Buller at the Battle of Colenso 'makes one very

---

*The Times reported that the cause of death was 'chronic cerebral affection' (7 February 1899). George had a long talk with Dr Bemkart about Alfred's death (RA GV/PRIV/GVD/18 February 1899).

anxious'.[43] This was his only reference to Black Week. George's reaction contrasts sharply with that of his father, who wrote: 'The news from S Africa is no better and I own I am very despondent and can think of nothing else.'[44]

Perhaps George's shooting addiction represented a psychological compensation for his lack of real power, or possibly it was a displacement activity which justified him in ignoring realities and failing to prepare for becoming king. It meant that George and May spent considerable time apart. In October 1898 George calculated that he and May had been separated for three months already that year.[45] Pope-Hennessy was right when he noted that by 1900 May and George 'appear to have come to an agreement about acting independently – she seems to have evolved a technique for avoiding shooting parties'.[46]

York Cottage for May was becoming a prison. In February 1900, while George occupied himself shooting duck (the pheasant season was over), she wrote to her brother Adolphus, known as Dolly: 'It is so dull here & I feel very low & depressed tho' I am pretty well on the whole.'[47] At the time she was heavily pregnant with her fourth child. Another boy, named Henry, was duly born on 31 March. May told Aunt Augusta:

> I confess I am just a little bit proud of myself for having produced another boy which was greatly wished as alas we have so few Princes in our family & now I think I have done my duty & may now <u>stop</u>, as having babies is highly distasteful to me tho' once they are there they are very nice![48]

Royalty was under threat. After the assassination of the Empress Elisabeth of Austria in September 1898, the Empress Vicky for the first time in her life travelled with a detective.[49] In April 1900 an attempt was made on the lives of the Prince and Princess of Wales by a teenage anarchist named Sipido in Brussels, after which Bertie was always accompanied by a detective on his journeys abroad.

In August 1900 the Duke of Coburg died, and George travelled to the funeral in Coburg with his father, attended by 'the celebrated detective' William Melville, the Special Branch superintendent, who was responsible for royal security.[50] 'I must say I think it is quite right in these days, when there are so many anarchists about,' wrote George; the Shah of Persia had been attacked in Paris by an Italian anarchist who tried to stab him, and King Ferdinand of Bulgaria, who was also in Coburg for the funeral, had received death threats.[51] 'It is really most alarming,' wrote George, 'as nobody is safe any more.'[52] As their train passed through Holland, armed gendarmes with loaded pistols faced the crowd: 'one thought [it] very theatrical, but Melville heard that 100 Dutch burghers had landed today from the Transvaal, so perhaps it was just as well'.[53] The Boer War was acutely unpopular in the Netherlands, where the Dutch sympathised with their compatriots the Afrikaners – in October Queen Wilhelmina sent a ship to evacuate the Boer government – and this was a dangerous time for a British prince to travel there.

On Saturday 19 January 1901, a day of pouring rain and high winds, George was out shooting at Sandringham when a note was brought from his mother, telling him that Queen Victoria was critically ill at Osborne and she was leaving immediately to join his father, who was already there.[54] The 81-year-old Queen had suffered another stroke following the one she had had two days before, since when George had feared the worst. As he told May, who was in London, 'I miss you dreadfully & wish you were here, I feel miserable & upset by all this'.[55] From Sandringham George hastened to London, reaching York House at 9 p.m., where he found a telegram from his father telling him to remain there, as 'symptoms rather more favourable ... Am in despair about it all, fear there is very little hope,' wrote George.[56]

'You can imagine the state of our feelings at getting such an alarming report of the dear Queen's health yesterday,' May told Aunt Augusta, writing from London on the Sunday. 'So here we are, miserable, all our plans upset & one dreads the future, fancy England without the Queen, it is almost impossible to contemplate such a thing.'[57] That evening, George accompanied his father to meet Kaiser William II at Charing Cross station. The news from Osborne was worse, and George with Bertie and William left early in the morning of 21 January for the Isle of Wight. George went to Victoria's bedroom: 'she looked just the same, not altered at all ... she looked so nice lying there, she had her eyes closed & was almost asleep, I kissed her dear hand, which was quite warm.' He had several talks with William, whom he (unlike others of his family) found 'most amiable'.[58]

The next morning it was evident that Victoria might die at any time. George sent for May, who arrived at 5.30 p.m. Victoria died an hour later. 'I shall never forget that scene in her room,' wrote George, 'with all of us sobbing & heartbroken round her bed.'[59] For May, 'it all brought back so vividly the death of darling Mama & I was fearfully upset & cried a great deal – I cannot tell you how miserable I am at the dear Queen's death as she was always so kind to me & ever a great friend & counsellor'.[60]

The Yorks were marginalised after Victoria's death. Though George succeeded his father as Duke of Cornwall, he was not created Prince of Wales. 'The King does not wish it for some reason or other (which I think is a great mistake),' wrote May, who bitterly resented the snub. 'I believe it is the first time that the Heir Apparent has not been created Prince of Wales! I dislike departing from traditions.'[61]

Then, still on the Isle of Wight, George succumbed to German measles. This prevented him and May from attending Queen Victoria's funeral, which was to be held in St George's Chapel, Windsor. As Harold Nicolson remarked, George 'has a bad habit of being ridiculous . . . It is quite impossible to deal with that without becoming comic. I shall just have to leave it out.'[62] He did.

Stuck at Osborne and unable to leave George's sickbed, May walked down to the pier to watch the procession of yachts crossing the Solent with the queen's coffin, 'one of the saddest finest things I have ever seen – a mixture of great splendour & great simplicity . . . It is so dull & quiet here,' she wrote. 'It is very depressing to be left behind & we both feel it much.'[63]

PART THREE

PRINCE OF WALES

1901–1910

CHAPTER 9

The Heir Apparent

1901–1902

'We have only heard yesterday that our visit to Australia is to come off after all,' wrote May on 8 February 1901.[1] Sending the Yorks to open the first federal parliament of Australia had been resisted by Queen Victoria, on the grounds that the only son of the Prince of Wales could not be spared from his duties at home. Victoria eventually relented, but the new king was even more reluctant to let go of his heir apparent, and agreed only when the prime minister, Lord Salisbury, via his nephew Arthur Balfour, virtually ordered him to comply. 'I think it is right! we should go,' wrote May, 'especially after the fine way Australia has come forward during the [Boer] war.'[2]

The displays of lachrymosity over the departure of George and May on their voyage on *Orphir* were exceptional even by royal standards. When the King proposed their health at a farewell dinner on 16 March he broke down altogether, and 'only suppressed sobs were heard'. Aunt Augusta remarked: 'I would not have believed he could have been so very low & upset'.[3] George was so affected that he 'could hardly speak' in reply.[4]

The next day *Orphir* steamed out of Portsmouth, passing the King and Queen as they waved from the royal yacht. After this poignant moment, wrote George, 'May & I came down to our cabins & had a good cry & tried to comfort each other'.[5] Aunt Augusta paid Alix a visit soon afterwards, 'when she told me all about it, crying all the time'.[6] As for May, she confessed that 'those dreadful farewells nearly killed me, & I was obliged to take to my bed & do nothing but rest', staying there until Gibraltar.[7] 'The pent up emotions of the last days had much upset me, particularly having to keep one's feelings under control, so no wonder I collapsed.'[8]

George did his best to ensure that *Orphir* was as comfortable as modern science and the decorators S. J. Waring & Sons could make her. On George's insistence, the royal couple shared a bed, rather than sleeping in two beds side by side; 'I certainly prefer one bed,' George had earlier told May, 'I thought you did so too.'[9] But nothing could save May from seasickness. 'I <u>detest</u> the sea,' she wrote.[10] 'Even when not really sick, I always feel so,' she complained: 'my head always feels so odd & empty at sea, & everything is a frightful exertion.'[11]

The Indian Ocean was calmer and, after entertaining the elite of Aden ('the ladies are the funniest part, & their conversation too idiotic, to which I have to listen deeply interested, while internally I giggle'), May lay on deck all day, dressed in the thinnest white clothes, reading books about Australia.[12] This, as her son Henry, Duke of Gloucester later remarked, was typical: 'she was always swotting things up before she went anywhere'. When Henry himself visited Australia thirty years later and read none of the books she gave him, she was 'FURIOUS'.[13]

Unlike May, George loathed the heat. His hand was so sweaty that he could barely write, '& I am always wet as if I was in a bath which is quite beastly'.[14] At stopping points such as Malta, Colombo and Singapore, George was presented with rare stamps, which he arranged at sea, 'between blotting paper to prevent them sticking together'.[15]

Lengthy accounts of royal tours can be wearisome, but the *Orphir* cruise is interesting because of the changes it brought about in both George and May. John Gore considered the tour to be a turning point for the Yorks, and especially for George. 'Of the two the Duke had the more to learn, the greater need to make calls on his reserves of patience and discipline,' wrote Gore in a sentence loaded with understatement.[16] Harold Nicolson considered that it was on the Australian tour, his first independent mission, that George acquired 'self-realisation', meaning a sense of public duty.[17] The man who enabled this change to happen was George's new private secretary, who accompanied him on the cruise: Sir Arthur Bigge.

Now fifty-one, Bigge had spent twenty-two years working in Queen Victoria's private secretary's office, starting as assistant to Henry Ponsonby. Unlike Ponsonby, Bigge was not an aristocrat nor a member of one of the dynasties of court servants. His father was the vicar of Stamfordham in Northumberland; he had served in the Zulu War in 1879, and his report on the death in Zululand of the Prince Imperial Louis-Napoleon brought him to the attention of Queen Victoria. In 1895 he succeeded Ponsonby as private secretary.

Later, Bigge was in the habit of grumbling that Queen Victoria had been the only sovereign who understood how constitutional monarchy worked. During his time as her private secretary, however, the old queen's behaviour was far from constitutional. By now almost blind, Victoria was unable to read the documents in her red boxes. She had no trust in Bigge, and insisted that her letters be read aloud to her by her daughter Princess Beatrice, who knew little of politics, and by her Indian servant Abdul Karim, who knew even less. 'Many things that are important do not go through Bigge's hands,' wrote a colleague in 1898, 'and the result is that he is in total ignorance of what the Queen hears or is told.' Government business was no longer sent to the private secretary, as it had been in Ponsonby's time; the papers went directly to the Queen, or rather to Beatrice and the Munshi, and 'the inevitable result is that the Queen is looked upon more and more as a figurehead and not even consulted'.[18]

Balfour, running the Foreign Office on Lord Salisbury's behalf, was quick to take advantage, keeping the monarch in the dark even on matters of the royal prerogative such as declaring war. Henry Ponsonby's son Fritz, Bigge's assistant, noted:

> The Duke of York was here the other day and was given by HM the latest telegrams about China ... he is very sharp and he found that Balfour had issued ... what might have resulted in a declaration of war and the Queen had not even been told of it.[19]

Rarely before had George been described as very sharp. Bigge's appointment as George's private secretary represented a demotion; he resented being passed over for the top job of private secretary to the new monarch, which went to Bertie's long-established servant Francis Knollys. But, for the businesslike Bigge, working for an orderly, obedient prince must surely have come as a relief and an opportunity after his years spent dodging the capricious old queen and her camarilla of unpolitical daughters and the Munshi. No doubt it was Bigge who recommended George's reading matter on *Orphir*: Theodore Martin's five-volume life of his grandfather the Prince Consort, a work which George (unlike most readers) found 'very interesting'.[20]

'I find Bigge as I knew I should quite invaluable,' said George, '& he is of the greatest help to me, & writes the answers to the addresses so well.'[21] On board *Orphir*, George and Bigge settled the itineraries for the Australian and New Zealand visits. Their careful preparations formed a stark contrast with the last royal visit to Australia (apart from George's visit with Eddy on *Bacchante*), made by the 23-year-old Duke of Edinburgh in 1867. Prince Alfred had received an unexpectedly hearty welcome, but he was haughty and insolent, and the tour disintegrated into drunkenness, gambling and brothel scandals. Planning and security were non-existent, and an Irish gunman took a pot shot and wounded the prince.[22]

The Duke and Duchess of Cornwall, as they had now become,

landed at Melbourne on 6 May 1901 to be met by a wall of cheering crowds.* 'Our reception,' wrote May, 'was simply splendid, the streets beautifully decorated & crammed with people from all parts of Australia.' For May this was a crash course in modern monarchy: 'We have large dinners each night when many ladies & gentlemen must be talked to, I am getting quite adept at this job with its endless banalities!'[23]

After the formal opening of the federal parliament, George and May spent almost three months touring Australia and New Zealand. George read replies to addresses drafted by Bigge, and shook hands at official receptions. Someone with a clicker counted the hands he shook, just as at home his valet counted the birds he shot and the shots he fired. At one levee in Melbourne, he greeted almost 4,000 people, which left him with a sore arm; 'the Australian handshake or grip is not a thing to be winked at'.[24]

For May, being constantly on show, 'knowing that every word & look is being criticised' and always having 'to beam & smile', was a 'terrible life'.[25] But she was unexpectedly good at it. She was gratified to see from the local papers that she had found great favour with the Australians; 'rather different to at home, where they always find fault with what I do or do not do'.[26] In spite of wearing a black mourning dress, it was May, not George, who electrified the Australians.

In New Zealand their schedule was even more packed. 'I certainly never had such hard work for 17 consecutive days before,' wrote George to his mother, 'but strange to say neither May or I were any the worse . . . It is all very well for you & Papa to say we mustn't do so much but it is impossible to help it.'[27]

George's health held up until Adelaide, when he was afflicted by a painful abscess. After he had shaken 2,100 hands at a levee, a dentist was summoned to pull out the tooth. May carried on with the functions, taking George's role, and (according to Bryan Godfrey-Faussett) 'she did it splendidly – & looked ripping as usual – so queenly, dignified & gracious'.[28] As her lady-in-waiting Lady Mary Lygon observed, 'she took the whole of Australia and New Zealand by storm; and every state has successively fallen in love with her looks, her smile and her great charm of manner'.[29]

The tour continued to the other dominions – three more months of punishing schedules with diminishing interest in the British press. After Mauritius and South Africa, where their visit was overshadowed by the

---

*Their correct title was now the Duke and Duchess of Cornwall and York, but as Cornwall was the older title this was the one that they used.

continuing war, they sailed to Montreal for a further thirty-five days of being on show.* 'People seem to think George & I are like machines & can go on for ever without any rest!' wrote May.[30] They crossed Canada on the Canadian Pacific railway, travelling in comfort on a special train fitted with bedrooms and baths; 'the only tiresome bit is having to get out at the various towns for the usual receptions'.[31]

At Calgary they were greeted by two or three thousand indigenous tribesmen. They drove between lines of them, 'mounted on painted horses, dressed in the weirdest of costumes, feathers and many colours ... picturesque & Fennimore Coopery', wrote George's aide-de-camp. In spite of the bitter cold, some were almost naked, with their skin painted yellow.

> They took little or no notice of the Duchess, all their eyes being for the Duke who was dressed in his [scarlet] Royal Fusilier uniform. The Chiefs came up one at a time ... some of them seemed contented, but others were full of growls & dissatisfaction with their lot. The principal cry was more food & one of the Blackfeet chiefs said that having once owned the whole country practically now they were given a small 'reserve' of land ... the white man was very often in the habit of encroaching on it. Another growled at the white man having destroyed all the buffalo.[32]

This unreal encounter in the snow with the vanishing world of the indigenous chiefs made little impression on George. On his return home he gave a speech at Guildhall in which he spoke of the loyalty to the Crown and 'attachment to the old country' that he found among the white settlers in the dominions.[33] Nothing was said about the plight of the indigenous people.

A week after the return of *Orphir*, on 9 November 1901, the King created the 36-year-old George Prince of Wales and Earl of Chester, in recognition of his services in the dominions. 'This annoys me,' wrote May; as we have seen, she thought (as did Bigge) that George deserved the title as of right, as heir apparent.[34] George wrote to May:

---

*Though Mauritius had been British since 1810, French was still the language of the island, and the ladies 'hurled' themselves at May, 'asking all at once & the same moment, "Comment trouvez vous notre Ile?" which I thought rude considering it belongs to us!' (RA QM/PRIV/CC23/3, M to Augusta, 11 August 1901).

Somehow I can't tell you, so I take the first opportunity of writing to say how deeply I am indebted to you darling Tootsums for the splendid way in which you supported & helped me during our long Tour, it was you who made it a success everybody lost their hearts to you & said how wonderfully you did it all.[35]

The grammar was clumsy, using the comma splice as he (and May) habitually did to bolt together two independent sentences (he was almost a stranger to the semi-colon), but George's letter was a generous one. May's popularity didn't make him jealous. There was no doubt in his mind, however, that her role was to help and support him; she was his consort, and she had succeeded in that contract. May understood this. 'I hope my darling that as long as you & I live you will ever rely on me to do what I can to help you, now more than ever in yr new & very responsible position.' A strong marriage was essential to being a successful consort. 'After what you told me the other day of the sad lives of both Missy & Ducky' – the Queen of Romania and her sister the Grand Duchess of Hesse, both of whom had been forced into unhappy arranged marriages – 'we should be even more grateful to feel that such sympathy exists between us 2.'[36]

George was now a rich man. The Duchy of Cornwall brought an income of over £60,000. Additionally, under the financial settlement for the new reign, fixed by the Treasury civil servant Eddy Hamilton, George received a parliamentary vote of £40,000. (The total of £100,000 represents over £12 million in today's values.) At Hamilton's suggestion, he agreed to contribute £10,000 a year to the upkeep of Balmoral and £10,000 towards Sandringham, 'considering that he lived in the place rent free and had all the enjoyment of the shooting and gardens' – thus ensuring that the King did not need to ask for a potentially unpopular increase in the Civil List.[37]

George appointed a household. In addition to Charles Cust and Derek Keppel, he asked two of his aides-de-camp from *Orphir* to become equerries: Godfrey-Faussett, his old navy friend, and Lord Crichton, heir to the Earl of Erne, a major in the Royal Horse Guards and, according to Bigge, 'a splendid-looking chap'.[38] Aunt Augusta noted disapprovingly that 'all but Cust are Whigs [Liberals]! Or perhaps now [Liberal] Unionists . . . not a Tory among those gazetted'.[39]

As the Wales household expanded and the family grew, York Cottage became increasingly squashed, and many people, including Bigge, considered it an unworthy residence for the heir apparent. There was talk of renting Houghton, ten miles from Sandringham. Alix went round the house and thought it 'a very fine old place which might be made beautiful', but advised her son: 'Do not be in a <u>hurry</u>.' She implored him: 'Let us be <u>near each</u> other this winter.'[40] George was only too willing to oblige, having no intention of taking Houghton or any other place. 'I don't think there will be any difficulty in spending my money which they tell me I have got so much of; I expect I shall want all I can get.'[41]

Unlike his father, George was careful with money and tried to avoid extravagance and live within his income. Parsimony was not, however, the reason why he stayed at York Cottage. As we have seen, the cottage was too squashed for house parties and this suited George, who liked to be in bed at 11.30; but the parties in the big house across the lake kept him in contact with his father's court. Staying at York Cottage pleased his demanding and manipulative mother. Above all, there was the shooting.

Bertie, who now inherited Windsor, Buckingham Palace and Balmoral in addition to Sandringham, offered Osborne to George. 'I cannot live in and maintain five palaces!' said the King.[42] As the sailor prince, a father of young children and a yachtsman, George seemed the perfect fit for Osborne; and he could easily afford it. Bertie wrote: 'It will cost you between £20 and £30,000 a year to keep up, but you are much better off than I was as Prince of Wales, & beyond your town house have no other to keep up, as I can hardly look upon the Cottage as a country house.'[43] George turned it down. Osborne was given to the nation and became a naval college and hospital for officers.

Bertie lent Frogmore House, close to Windsor, to May and George – 'really a charming little house,' he called it. 'Would you and May like to occupy it whenever you want to get out of town?'[44] The Waleses gladly accepted the offer of the *trianon* modernised by James Wyatt for Queen Charlotte, and the pattern of the King occupying the palace and the Prince of Wales staying in the smaller house nearby was replicated in all the royal residences: at Sandringham; at Balmoral, where George occupied Abergeldie; and in London, where George moved into Marlborough House. This arrangement of the Prince of Wales following the court as a sort of satellite worked with the King and his son, but it imposed a considerable strain on May, who was obliged to suffer the humiliation of being constantly upstaged and snubbed by her mother-in-law.

As Prince of Wales, George spent as much time shooting as he had done as Duke of York, if anything slightly more. In the seasons of 1902/3 and 1903/4 he counted up 'What I shot': a total of more than 12,300 head of game each year. This was higher than the tally of 'Game Killed by Me' in 1896/7: 11,000 head.[45] But in the months that he was in London, he was far busier than he had been as Duke of York. His diary filled with meetings of the Duchy of Cornwall, with speeches and 'functions' such as lunch with the lord mayor of London at the Mansion House, admission as a fellow of the Royal Society or visiting hospitals such as St George's, where he became president.

The partnership with Bigge was central to the prince's work. For the former the *Orphir* had been a trial. 'It is exactly 20 weeks since we came on board this good ship,' he wrote; 'please God in 13 weeks we shall be home again.'[46] By the end of the voyage, however, he had won George's trust. Without Bigge writing the addresses George couldn't have managed, as he freely admitted. 'I feel that I can always rely on you to tell me the truth, however disagreeable & that you are entirely in my confidence,' wrote George. 'To a person in my position it is of an enormous help.'[47]

In the last years of Victoria's reign Bigge had modernised the private secretary's office at Buckingham Palace, which was better organised than Bertie's Marlborough House, where Sir Francis Knollys still wrote every letter out by hand. Typewriters, shorthand secretaries and efficient filing systems were now installed in the office of the Prince of Wales. When George was away from May he now rang her every evening for 'a talk through the telephone'.[48] Press cuttings were pasted into volumes bound in blue leather and stamped with gold, signifying a modern awareness of public opinion.

The *Orphir* voyage changed George. Eddy Hamilton met him in 1902 and found him much improved. 'He has lost that silly laugh and has broadened out enormously. He takes an intelligent interest in what is going on and a sensible view of things. His journey round the world turned him into a man, and Bigge has been a great god-send to him as he himself recognises.'[49]

Underpinning and perhaps controlling George as Prince of Wales was a strong relationship with his father. Exceptionally for the Hanoverian dynasty, where quarrels between the monarch and the heir were normal practice, King Edward was an affectionate father to George. 'I have always tried to look upon you far more as a brother than a son,' he repeatedly told George.[50] When Bertie became king he asked George to share the work: 'I know I can always count on your support & assistance in the heavy duties & responsible position I now occupy.'[51]

Bertie's years as Prince of Wales had been shadowed by his mother's bullying, and he was careful to avoid a Hanoverian feud with his own heir. As Harold Nicolson commented, 'evidently they were very fond of each other. Something more than just royal gush.'[52] At Frogmore, where the King stayed with George in 1901 (Windsor was being refurbished), George had a writing table next to his father's. 'Fancy that being possible in dear Grandmama's time,' said he. 'Anyway it shows that Papa & I are on good terms.'[53]

In spite of the affection, this was not an easy or equal relationship. George remained in awe of his father. According to one courtier, George consulted his father about everything, 'even as to whether his footmen are to wear black or red liveries at dinner'.[54] He visited the King most mornings in London after his 9 a.m. ride. Lord Esher, a close adviser of Edward VII and a sharp observer, noticed that George was 'shy' with the King. He also remarked that George was 'a chip of his grandmamma'.[55] The letters that George wrote to Bertie continued to be stilted and formulaic, lacking the spontaneity of his correspondence with May or Alix. He was frightened of his father; he also disapproved of him. He was openly critical of the King's mistress, Mrs George Keppel (sister-in-law of Derek Keppel), and he disliked the plutocrats of the Edwardian court. 'The Crown will certainly not fall off Prince George's head,' wrote Eddy Hamilton. 'It might be a dull Court, but it will certainly be a respectable one.'[56]

On 14 June 1902, twelve days before the coronation was due to take place, George accompanied the King to a military review at Aldershot. Bertie complained of a pain in his side, and in the evening he suffered agonies. George sent for Francis Laking, who arrived at 5 a.m. and gave the King a large dose of castor oil, which relieved the pain. In this crisis, George was 'beyond all praise, good, helpful & quiet', according to his sister Princess Victoria. 'He managed everything.'[57]

But the King was not cured. On 24 June the coronation was cancelled, and the surgeon Frederick Treves performed an emergency operation at Buckingham Palace. That morning he told the Prince of Wales that 'it was quite possible the King might die on the table'.[58] When Bertie came to after the operation, his first words were: 'Where's George?'[59]

The surgeon had found an enormous abscess, and a pint of fluid was drained. 'If the operation had not been performed,' wrote George, 'he must have died.'[60] As he later told his father, this was a 'terribly anxious time & especially for me being so devoted to you which I think you know.'[61] The unspoken meaning is plain: George was in no hurry to become king. His loyalty was beyond reproach. Each day he visited his father. Treves noticed that the King was 'always glad to see the Prince of Wales, with whom he discussed all public matters'. His favourite visitor, however, was neither George nor the Queen, who tired him with her deafness, but Princess Victoria, 'to whom he was devoted'.[62]

During his father's convalescence, George took the King's place in reviewing troops and meeting politicians. He apologised afterwards to May for being 'rather disagreeable, but I have been so busy & worried & anxious that I am sure you will forgive me'.[63] These weeks tested George's fitness for becoming king. He made a success of it. As May wrote, 'you must have the satisfaction of knowing that everybody thinks you did most extraordinarily well under most trying & exceptional circumstances & that you were a great help & standby at Buck Palace during this time'.[64]

'The Prince & Princess of Wales' domestic quiet & happy life is appealing very much to the people of England,' wrote Lord Lincolnshire in 1901. 'He has a capital household: my brother Bill* and Bigge serve him really well: His speeches are carefully prepared, and have already made a very good impression – but I fancy there is a certain amount of friction and jealousy between the young and the old court, particularly between the Queen and the Princess of Wales. The latter has very difficult cards to play.'[65] It was a shrewd assessment.

As Princess of Wales, May too had a larger household. Her first lady-in-waiting, Lady Eva Greville, a sister of the Earl of Warwick, known as 'Little Bird' and a favourite of the Duchess of Teck, was perhaps May's closest friend. When Eva married Frank Dugdale in 1895, May appointed a second lady-in-waiting, Lady Mary Lygon, sister of Earl Beauchamp, whom she had known before her marriage. In 1901 Frank Dugdale joined May's household as equerry ('an innovation on my part as I wish to have someone of my own when I travel alone') and May recruited two ladies of the bedchamber, the Countess of Bradford and the Countess of Airlie.[66]†

Mabell Airlie, a childhood friend of May's, was a young widow whose husband had been killed in the Boer War; she wore her prematurely grey hair in the pompadour style and seemed made to be sketched by Sargent. At first she rejected the offer to become lady-in-waiting, so May wrote herself, explaining the duties.

I propose having four ladies who will each do duty for three months in the year, say a month at a time, and I propose that the ladies should

---

*Sir William Carington (with one r) was comptroller of George's household.
†As the daughters but not the wives of peers, Lady Eva Dugdale and Lady Mary Lygon were women (not ladies) of the bedchamber (Pope 195/15, M to Augusta, 30 November 1901).

arrange the dates of their waiting among themselves. The principal part of the writing will be done by my private secretary, the ladies only doing my private charities & so forth ...[67]*

Overcome by May's personal appeal, Lady Airlie relented.

When Mabell arrived for her first waiting May greeted her coldly and formally, but as soon as they were alone together 'she put her arms round me and kissed me on both cheeks'. Only then did Mabell realise the change in her old friend: 'her shyness had become so crystalized [sic] that only in such moments of intimacy could she be herself. The hard crust of inhibition which gradually closed over her, hiding the warmth and tenderness of her own personality, was already starting to form.'[68]

Mabell blamed Queen Alexandra, who, in spite of outward friendliness, had succeeded through her unspoken criticisms in undermining her daughter-in-law. In letters to Aunt Augusta, May made no secret of her criticisms of her mother-in-law. When Alix refused to move into Buckingham Palace on the grounds that the accommodation for her lady-in-waiting Charlotte Knollys, sister of the King's private secretary, Francis Knollys, was inadequate, May dismissed her anxieties as 'too ridiculous, she [Charlotte] has <u>great</u> influence'.[69] Nor was May impressed by Alix's dedication to her role as queen consort:

> Alas when she once gets <u>stuck</u> at Sandringham, it is difficult to move her, I had so hoped that in her new position as Queen all this would have improved, & I do feel that one should take a lively interest in Art or in anything connected with the good of one's country ... it does not look well either for her so constantly to leave him alone as she does.[70]

For May, Alix provided a lesson in how not to be queen.

There were rows about the children too. When George and May were away on the *Orphir*, they entrusted the children to their indulgent grandparents. The King and Queen took their grandchildren to Sandringham for two weeks, and the governess Bricka was left behind in London. This provoked such an 'explosion' from Bricka that May did something she had never done before in her life and complained to her mother-in-law about neglecting David's French lessons with the governess. Alix's response was to attack May where she knew she was weak, on the subject of child rearing:

---

*May's private secretary during her time as Princess of Wales was Alexander Hood.

The reason we did not take [Bricka] there was that Laking particularly asked that [David] might be left more with his brothers & sister – for a little while – as we all noticed how precautious [*sic*] & old-fashioned he was getting – & quite the ways of 'a single child'! which wld make him ultimately a 'tiresome child' – laying down the law & thinking himself far superior to the younger ones – It did him a great deal of good – to be treated the same as Bertie – who is after all very little younger than he . . .[71]

The *Orphir* voyage had given May new confidence, but back home she was as thin-skinned, vulnerable and isolated as ever. Soon she found herself pregnant with her fifth child, and for many months she was 'wretched'.[72]* She dreaded being at York Cottage, where she feared she would be 'horribly bored'.[73] Abergeldie, where she and her children stayed for August and September, was worse. 'Je suis très depressed,' she told Bricka.[74] 'I cannot get out & it is so gloomy & depressing for me I am in despair.'[75] Alix wrote to George when May was in labour: 'I only wish I could be with you . . . but I quite understand dear May does not want me – altho' she need not mind old me particularly as I was with her the first time.'[76]

May retreated into her own world. She liked nothing better than spending an afternoon in the British Museum, improving her mind – 'dear me, what wonderful things are there, one gets quite bewildered'.[77] She wrote in her diary: 'We had a good look at the Syrian & Egyptian Antiquities, the glass & china, the Waddesdon Cinque Cento things, the gold room . . .'[78] On a visit to Copenhagen, where 'the 6.30 dinner is our despair' and the endless evenings standing with *cercle* 'a bore',† May found diversion in the Rosenborg Castle museum of Danish kings with English queens, and she enjoyed long discussions on the subject of genealogies with an elderly Danish prince.[79]

Genealogies were a passion. When she asked Alix for genealogies of her family, and the answers were predictably slow to come, May contacted Charlotte Knollys, which produced a furious outburst from Alix. She complained to George: 'Oh by the by tell dear May that I am rather hurt in my feelings that she evidently thinks I forget everything . . . I now find that she has been asking Charlotte to get her the names or genealogies of my ancestors.'[80] One of the duties of May's ladies was to

---

*Prince George was born on 20 December 1902.

†At the court *cercle* guests standing in a circle were led up to the monarch and presented while the others watched.

act as her research assistants. Here is Lady Mary Lygon describing a week in waiting at York Cottage with the heavily pregnant princess:

> I read aloud daily to Her Royal Highness for at least two hours – take the two eldest boys for an hour's lessons, in the absence of the tutor – play the organ for an hour before breakfast – work at genealogies or at Henry VIII for an hour, drive with Her Royal Highness for two hours in the afternoon, and write heaps of letters – yesterday it was twenty – so as you see I have not much time for meditating on the want of picturesque in the Norfolk scenery.[81]

Lord Esher, who found her charming 'when alone', considered that May had the force of character and sound sense of Queen Caroline, wife of George II. 'In fact she reminds me of Queen Charlotte, only much handsomer.'[82] Like those eighteenth-century German princesses, May was a clever woman – and that was not an easy thing for a princess to be, as Empress Vicky had discovered to her cost.

CHAPTER 10

Family Life

1902–1905

As Prince of Wales, George succeeded his father at Marlborough House, the imposing brick mansion on The Mall where he was born. May wrote in her diary on 20 April 1902: 'At 11 we went all over Marl. House which the King and Queen left on the 27th March. It is an enormous house, & I think will do up well.'[1] Bertie and Alix had taken over a year to move into Buckingham Palace. In spite of his lavish refurbishment of the Palace, the King was annoyed when May insisted that Marlborough House must be done up. May was firm. 'Surely he must know we really cannot go into a filthy dirty house,' she wrote.[2]

May took charge of the redecoration herself. 'How right you are to superintend it in person!' wrote Aunt Augusta.[3] Unlike his father, who insisted on controlling all the work on his palaces, George's role was merely to approve the estimates. He held strong views on the subject of gold leaf, however. 'There seems to be too much money spent on gilding, I hate gilding.'[4]

May claimed to have inherited her father's love of arranging rooms, but Marlborough House was a daunting project. All the floors were taken up in order to install drains, bells and electric light. The dark, crowded rooms which Alix had filled with pot plants and painted in 'ugly green and pink' were opened up and painted white.[5] May 'worked like a slave' arranging the rooms and organising furniture, and in April 1903, a year after the King and Queen moved out, May and George were installed.[6] George wrote to his father: 'Here we are in dear old Marlborough House at last ... This is the first letter I have written in this house, in your old room and on your writing paper which you so kindly gave me, I find there is enough to last for years.'[7] They gave a family dinner, and to May's relief (as Aunt Augusta wrote) Alix approved of the decorations, though not without letting fall some 'semi-sarcastical words'.[8]

In Bertie's day, Marlborough House had given its name to the fast and fashionable set that revolved around him. Not a breath of scandal tarnished the new tenants. Some said they were dull. May disliked the 'surfeit of gold plate and orchids' of the plutocratic Edwardian court and preferred a life of quiet domesticity.[9] She considered that her dancing days were over, as 'I do so dislike sitting up late'.[10] At a ball at

Windsor, May's brother Dolly was dancing with Princess Victoria, George's sister, when 'his spurs caught in Mrs George Keppel's long gown, & he & Victoria fell heavily on their backs'.[11] The spectacle of the King's mistress with her flowing fashionable chiffon gown tripping Dolly and Victoria, the virtuous royals of the younger generation, epitomised the tensions at the Edwardian court.

The wreckage of the Teck fortunes had undermined the status of May and her brothers. When May and George returned from the *Orphir* cruise, the King didn't invite May's brothers to welcome them at Portsmouth. May was upset by this snub, which she thought 'very rude'.[12] By establishing her brothers as members of the inner ring of the new Wales court, she sought to restore the Teck connection and buttress her own standing.

Dolly (Adolphus), the eldest of the three brothers, succeeded his father as Duke of Teck. Back in 1894 he had married Lady Margaret (Meg) Grosvenor, a daughter of the super-rich Duke of Westminster, owner of Mayfair. 'It is a vy good connection,' wrote Queen Victoria, '& she will doubtless be well off.'[13] May was delighted. 'I am so excited about it I hardly know what to do,' she wrote.[14] Most importantly, Dolly managed to hit it off with George. 'I never met a nicer fellow, I think him quite charming,' wrote George, 'he has got such excellent manners & is so quiet & nice, he really shoots very well.'[15] Coming from George this was high praise indeed. A last-minute hitch occurred when George hurt the feelings of the Grosvenors by threatening not to attend Dolly's wedding because it clashed with his shooting; but, tactfully steered by May, he did turn up, giving his approval to the marriage and ensuring that this valuable income stream was not jeopardised.

Meg's father had written generous cheques for Princess Mary Adelaide when she was in trouble. Now the Grosvenor connection dominated George's court, cropping up like ground elder in the household. Equerry Lord Crichton married Lady Mary Grosvenor, one of Meg's sisters. Lord Wenlock, one of the lords of the bedchamber, was the son of Lady Elizabeth Grosvenor, a sister of the duke. Lord Chesham, also a bedchamber lord, married Lady Beatrice Grosvenor, another daughter of the duke. These marriage alliances brought Grosvenor dowries, enabling courtiers to live on the equerry's salary of £400 a year, about £50,000 today, as it had been in 1901.[16]

Alge (his nickname was a conflation of the first two letters of Alexander and George) was the youngest of the three Teck brothers. Seven years May's junior, he was dutiful and competent and she had always 'bemothered' him.[17] He accompanied May and George on the *Orphir* cruise and lived in their house on their return. Alge had served in the Boer War, along with his two brothers, and he was awarded the DSO, as was Dolly. When his regiment ordered him to South Africa in 1903 Alge summoned up the courage to propose to 'nice little Alice Albany', the daughter of Queen Victoria's son Prince Leopold, Duke of Albany, with whom he had been 'much taken for some time'. Encouraged by May, who was 'in a great state of excitement over it all', and also by Alice's mother Helen, Duchess of Albany, the couple gained the King's approval – 'the King is delighted so that's all right,' wrote a relieved May.[18] They married in February 1904: 'It was a most cheerful wedding, no crying & A[un]t Helen behaved like a brick,' wrote May. 'The King and Queen were charming & kind & so civil to all so I think they must have been pleased.'[19] The King's smiles were crucial: he gave the couple a grace-and-favour home in the Henry III Tower at Windsor and, with a joint income of £4,000, Alge and Alice were comfortably installed in the style of minor royals.

Frank, the middle brother and the cleverest, was not so pliable. He inherited his father's black-haired good looks and his mother's charm and extravagance. Like her he knew no boundaries. As a schoolboy at Wellington he was alleged to have thrown the headmaster over a hedge, and he grew up to become a dashing horseman, a dandy and *flâneur*. Princess Maud wanted to marry him, but Frank didn't bother to answer her letters, thus throwing away the chance of a match with a daughter of the ruling house, a prize which royal matchmakers considered beyond the wildest dreams of any mere Teck serene highness prince. He was, said his sister-in-law Alice, 'perfectly <u>outrageous</u> – he was terribly funny but outrageous. And he did some very naughty things too. We were all very cross with him.'[20]

In 1895 as a young officer in Ireland Frank lost £10,000 on a bet at Punchestown races. May and George bailed him out, the scandal was hushed up and Frank was packed off to India with the army. May was not amused. 'Today I heard from Frank, a long letter from Mahabaleshwar, written in his very flippant style which honestly I cannot understand.'[21] May had earlier been close to Frank, who wrote her funny, confiding letters, but this was the beginning of a falling-out between the siblings. 'We were so very intimate in the old days until alas the "rift" came,' she wrote in 1910.[22]

Frank served in the Boer War but unlike his brothers he didn't win a DSO and, to May's dismay, he returned home ahead of his regiment: 'too foolish of him & looks so bad – I fear he will leave the Army which will be a great misfortune as he has nothing to do & next to nothing to live on, Dolly & I feel quite worried about his future.'[23] He did leave the army, but worse was to come. In a letter to May in January 1902 Aunt Augusta related how George had stayed with her at Strelitz and told her 'Frank's story'. 'I am truly grieved,' she wrote.[24]

Frank's story was this. He had departed for Ireland, where he began an affair with a woman twelve years older than him, Nellie, Countess of Kilmorey. A friend and perhaps an old flame of Edward VII, Nellie was an heiress. Born Ellen Baldock, she inherited a fortune from her grandfather, the antique dealer Edward Baldock, and married the Earl of Kilmorey, a cash-strapped peer sixteen years her senior. Frank's devotion to his *chère amie* ruled out marriage to a suitable rich woman and left him with neither income nor home. May's letters to her Aunt Augusta are peppered with disapproving remarks. October 1902: 'Dolly tells me [Frank] has got rooms in Welbeck St. & intends settling there, a nice expense, living in London I should think, doing nothing. The flirtation is going on as much as ever.'[25] A few months later: 'Frank is still in Ireland, giving no *signe de vie*.'[26] A year after that: 'Frank still has no occupation which is a great pity.'[27] Then: 'Frank is still travelling about'.[28]

In January 1902 Frank drafted a will in which he bequeathed all his jewels to Lady Kilmorey.[29] These jewels, which had belonged to his mother, included the magnificent emeralds which had been acquired in unroyal fashion by the Duke of Cambridge in 1808: he won them in a lottery in Hanover. The Duchess of Teck, who inherited the emeralds, died leaving no will, and at some point the gems were given to Frank. May, who had a photographic memory for family jewels, must have known that Frank had the precious emeralds. In 1906 when she was sharing out some family gold plate from Aunt Augusta between her brothers she wrote her aunt a rather curious note: 'Frank: Small teapot with no history (he not being worthy of plate with a history) I don't mean this unkindly, only you understand.'[30] If feckless Frank was not worthy of a family teapot with an interesting provenance, he was hardly worthy of the Cambridge emeralds.

The Grand Duchess of Mecklenburg-Strelitz's unloved husband died in 1904, and May rushed to comfort her aunt. She couldn't help noticing 'what a lot of family things Aunt Augusta has, I am going to help her make a catalogue'.[31] Rumbling in an old-fashioned carriage over Strelitz's bumpy roads – 'Dear Aunt Augusta won't have india rubber tyres (too luxurious)' – and shouting to make themselves heard, May and her aunt travelled to inspect the family silver held in the Mecklenburg-Strelitz palaces. The holy of holies was Aunt Augusta's hoard of jewels. The previous year May had persuaded her aunt to alter her will and leave her some bracelets which had been given by William IV and Queen Adelaide to

Augusta, who had intended to leave them as heirlooms to the house of Strelitz. The old lady sat up late to write a codicil to her will, for fear that 'I might have been called away on that night'.[32] On this second occasion, however, May was less successful. To her disappointment she discovered that none of Augusta's jewels apart from the bracelets were bequeathed to the English family; all were to stay in the house of Strelitz, 'only a fine set of sapphires to me for my life! This one can scarcely accept. There are some glorious emerald brooches which I would give anything to have – Such a waste of jewels for this tiny place.'[33]*

A state visit to Austria in 1904 offered more opportunities for May's dynastic ambitions. She was thrilled to find herself at the court where her father had spent his youth as an officer in the Austrian army. She found 'the Emperor', Franz Joseph, 'charming'.[34] Breaking all her habits of early beds, she danced until 4 a.m. 'She is much better looking than any of the Archduchesses,' wrote Lady Mary Lygon, 'and better dressed – also they are very stiff – so everyone raved over the ease and charm of the princess's manners.'[35] George was less amused by the Hofburg palace. 'My goodness this court is stiff,' he wrote, 'and they are all frightened of the Emperor.'[36] Archduke Franz Ferdinand, nephew and heir of the Emperor and a fellow fanatical marksman, entertained George with a nocturnal sporting expedition. Leaving Vienna at 10 p.m. in a special train, they slept until 1.30 a.m., reaching the hunting lodge in time for George to shoot four capercaillie in five shots by 4.45 and return to Vienna at 9 a.m. for a full day of court visits.[37]

George wrote in his diary on 14 January 1904: 'I heard today from Tilleard that yesterday at a sale in London he bought an unused 2d blue "Post Office" Mauritius stamp for £1450. About the rarest stamp in the world & this is a record price.'[38] John Tilleard was George's philatelic adviser, a golf-playing City solicitor who lived in Hampstead and wrote in a tiny neat hand; he gave up his own stamp collection in order to work for the prince, and it was through him that George was elected a member of the Philatelic Society, of which Tilleard was honorary secretary. Tilleard's connection with George began in 1893 and, as Harold Nicolson wrote, the visits of Mr Tilleard to York House were more frequent than those of Mr Tanner, his tutor on the constitution.[39] But it

---

*When Aunt Augusta died, May inherited the Cambridge sapphires. These lustrous blue jewels had been given to Augusta as a wedding present by her mother, the Duchess of Cambridge (*Manchester Guardian*, Obituary of Grand Duchess of Mecklenburg-Strelitz, 6 December 1916).

was only after George became Prince of Wales that he could afford to pay the record price of £1,450 – £160,000 in today's prices – for a rare stamp.

The story of the Blue Mauritius is a fairy tale of stamp collecting. When George and May had visited the island of Mauritius on the *Orphir* tour, May commented that 'though Mauritius has belonged to us for over a century it was the most unEnglish place we have yet come across, the old French families being in great predominance & French still being the language of the island which is a grave mistake.'[40] Back in 1847 the British governor had caused offence by ordering that English should replace French as the language of the courts and, presumably as part of the same policy of modernisation, in that same year the first Mauritius stamps were printed – the first colonial stamps ever issued. Five hundred orange penny and five hundred blue twopenny stamps were made, engraved with a crude image of the Queen's head and inscribed 'Post Office', signifying that the postage had been paid by the sender and the recipient would not be charged, as hitherto. These so-called Post Office stamps were unique – subsequent issues were inscribed 'Post Paid'.

The stamp which George bought was a perfect, unused Post Office stamp – the finest of the four surviving unused Mauritius blues in the world. It had turned up in an album of stamps collected by a Scottish schoolboy in the 1860s. George attempted to buy it privately, but his offer was rejected and the stamp was sold at auction. Although *The Times* reported a rumour that the Prince of Wales was the buyer, George was secretive about the purchase, warning his stamp-collecting equerry Godfrey-Faussett: 'Don't say anything about it to anyone.'[41] He liked to tell a story about it against himself. An equerry had asked him: 'Did you happen to see in the newspapers that some damned fool had given as much as £1,400 for one stamp?' George replied: 'I was the damned fool.'[42]

A small, crude deep-blue stamp mounted in the centre of a page of one of 132 bound volumes containing George's collection, the Blue Mauritius is today worth between £2 million and £3 million. With this purchase George entered the top league of stamp collectors. In 1906 he ceased to collect foreign stamps, concentrating on Britain and its empire. He told Tilleard in 1908: 'Remember I wish to have the best collection & not one of the best collections in England.'[43]

It is tempting to dismiss stamp collecting as a schoolboy hobby. For George, however, the two or three afternoons he spent each week on his stamps when he was in London were work. Nor was philately lacking in intellectual substance. When Lord Balcarres succeeded his philatelist father in 1913 as 27th Earl of Crawford he confessed to despising his father's obsession. When he came to look at the collection, however, he was 'amazed at the patience and research shown on the one hand, and the courage in buying displayed on the other'.[44] The 26th Earl had been the greatest philatelist of his day, remarkable not just for the stamps he bought, but also for his pioneering analysis and documentation. This was the sort of collection that George aspired to build with Tilleard's aid – indeed he later bought parts of the Crawford collection. For George, however, stamp collecting was also a dynastic project. By specialising in stamps which bore the head of his grandmother, of his father and later of himself, he made philately the equivalent of May's jewel collecting.

'Mama as I have always said is one of the most selfish people I know,' wrote George in 1903.[45] Alix still clung, writing to her 39-year-old son: 'You do not know what happiness it is to your old Mother dear to have her Georgie boy near her.' George could escape: his sisters were not so lucky. Victoria and Maud in their twenties were semi-invalids. Toria complained of sciatica, and (according to Queen Victoria) 'is terribly thin & she comes out vy little indeed as she can hardly digest anything – but she can now walk – she never comes to dinner.'[46] The Queen reported the same symptoms in Maud, who was 'much out of health, vy thin & suffering like Victoria fm indigestion'.[47] Laking, the royal physician, prescribed a rest cure for Victoria, who was confined to bed for five weeks and allowed to see no one for the first week, when she was put on a diet of nothing but milk.[48] Looking at photos of the two princesses with their pale, strained faces, dark-rimmed, heavy-lidded eyes and painfully thin waists, it seems likely that – even allowing for corsets – a modern diagnosis might be anorexia.

People wondered why Alix didn't encourage her daughters to marry, and criticised her for keeping them at home. Perhaps the reality was more complex. Suffocated by their mother's emotionalism, tormented by the intrusions of the press, desperate to avoid being always on show, the princesses retreated into ill health and eating disorders. This in turn made marriage impossible, at least for Victoria. 'She will never marry I am sure,' Queen Victoria confidently predicted, 'she is not strong enough.'[49]

Maud married Prince Charles of Denmark when she was twenty-six. Her first and only child, Alexander (later Olav), was born six years later in 1902. A Norwegian biographer has speculated that her son was conceived by artificial insemination administered by Laking, and suggested that the sperm donor was the doctor's son Guy Laking, who happened to be May's artistic adviser.[50]

The delicate constitutions of the two princesses made them natural patients for the vogue for minor operations. In 1905 Sir Frederick Treves, the celebrity surgeon who had saved the life of Edward VII, operated on Victoria at Buckingham Palace to remove her appendix. This was then a dangerous procedure, especially for someone like her who suffered from 'nerves'. 'I am afraid all this will have agitated & worried her again,' wrote George, 'just what the Drs didn't wish. I trust Mama will not always be running in & out of her room, it will not be good for her.'[51] A week later, Treves performed a painful operation on Maud's nose, removing an abscess from the inside, laying her out on the same table as Victoria at Buckingham Palace.[52]

The eldest sister, Louise, Duchess of Fife, who was created Princess Royal in 1905, also suffered from poor health. Her illness was sometimes described as neuritis; it seems to have been nervous in origin.[53] In 1908 George reported that Louise 'looks awfully ill & suffers very much again; it seems a hopeless case & she gets worse every year & I fear there is nothing whatever to be done, it is really very sad'.[54] Louise was pathologically shy and some considered her to be 'idiotic'.[55] Alge went to see her one day and she jumped up and stood on top of her desk when she saw him come in.[56] Another time May spotted her in the next box at the opera, and Louise hid behind a curtain in order to avoid meeting May's companions.[57]

By contrast with his sisters, George now enjoyed robust good health. There were no more complaints of the 'blight'. He wrote to Bigge from Balmoral in September 1904: 'I have now killed 18 stags & never felt better or more fit, I can walk on the hill all day without feeling tired.'[58] Even he did not escape the surgeon's knife, however. In April 1905 he was circumcised by Treves. The operation took place under anaesthetic at Marlborough House with Laking in attendance. In his diary George described how sick and miserable the anaesthetic made him, though he was in no pain. Treves visited once or twice a day, helping the prince to remove the dressings, which he did by sitting in a hip bath, 'not very painful but disagreeable'.[59] After twelve days in bed, the wound was healed.

George gives no reason for the decision to undergo this painful and disruptive procedure in his fortieth year. Nor did he keep it secret. He was visited by the King on the day of the operation, May sat with him much of the time; Bigge and Godfrey-Faussett came to his room, while his mother wrote congratulating him on the success of the procedure.

The story reached the ears of Lord Lincolnshire, who noted in his diary that the prince had had a slight operation, 'the same as is performed on a Jewish baby. Poor thing, he must feel very sore.'[60]*

The fashion for circumcising British upper-class boys began in the 1890s. As an assertion of manliness and a symbol of true masculinity, circumcision no doubt appealed to the virile prince. Circumcision was also advised on health grounds for men working in hot humid climates such as India, and it seems likely that George's operation was recommended by his doctors in preparation for his visit to India later in the year.[61]

From Bertie onwards, all George's sons were circumcised at birth. Only David escaped, but when he was seven and his parents were on the *Orphir* cruise, the operation was performed on him by Treves, who (wrote Alix) 'found it most necessary'. It was done under chloroform, and for David it was more confusing than painful, as no one seems to have explained what was happening. Alix related:

> He screamed loud when he came to & kept on hollering he knew he had been mad & did not know how he had got into that room ... Laking gave him the chloroform to sniff telling him it would cure the hay fever so poor little boy told me he had had no breakfast as they are going to do something to my nose.

However, he was pleased with the result: '"My top's gone", as he said, "now Lala [nanny] need not wash it any more" which hurt him.'[62] George approved. 'I always knew it was necessary & now all the boys have no "tops" & they look alike.'[63]

A photograph taken in about 1902 shows George with his four eldest children, all wearing sailor suits, dressed for walking at Sandringham. 'I shall soon have a regiment, not a family,' the prince declared, and he taught his children to follow 'march discipline' on their walks around the estate.[64] On parade and dragooned, the children's peaky faces stare anxiously out of the picture – a little 'walled-in family'. As David recalled, 'we had a buttoned-up childhood, in every sense of the word'.[65]

When the children were babies, George was perhaps more tactile than May and he found it easier to show affection. He enjoyed bathing

---

The Times printed a statement from Treves and Laking: 'Owing to a slight operation performed this morning HRH the Prince of Wales will be confined to his room for a few days. As HRH's condition gives rise to no uneasiness, no bulletins will be issued' (4 April 1905).

his babies. 'I undressed, washed, dried & put to bed David all by myself, I think it rather amused him. Peters said I did it really very well.'[66] This was behaviour unimaginable in George's father Bertie, but the prince's visits to the nursery at bedtime were rare. As the children grew older he became a figure of fear, in the habit of mercilessly 'chaffing' or teasing them.

Today George's chaffing would be seen as bullying. His banter embarrassed and silenced his children; as one biographer wrote, 'he had a way of asking what they had been doing and then supplying chaffing answers before the little boys could find their own words'.[67] This was especially damaging to his second son, Bertie, who developed a severe stammer at the age of eight. 'Get it out!' his father would shout, as Bertie struggled to say a word.[68] George's favourite was his daughter Mary, the third child; his jokes at her expense made her blush but she was rarely scolded.[69]

George was a martinet, especially so where dress was concerned. 'I hope your kilts fit well,' he wrote to nine-year-old David at Balmoral. 'Wear the Balmoral kilt and grey jacket on weekdays and green kilt and black jacket on Sundays. Do not wear the red kilt till I come.'[70] A dirk or sporran out of place would be greeted with an outburst worthy of the quarterdeck. Lala the nanny was ordered to sew up the pockets of the little boys' sailor suits to prevent them from slouching with their hands in their pockets.

Not that George saw much of his sons. 'The children all arrived at 3.0 from Sandringham looking wonderfully well,' wrote George in April 1905. 'I had not seen them for nearly 3 months.'[71] From February until Easter and again from October until Christmas, the children stayed behind at York Cottage while their parents were in London. In the summer when Marlborough House became too hot the children decamped to Frogmore. The boys took their lessons in the grandeur of Queen Charlotte's Green Pavilion, and romped in Windsor Great Park, but there was nothing luxurious about the house; the royal family installed a single bathroom on the ground floor, and there was no electricity.[72]

When George became Prince of Wales he made arrangements for the education of his two elder sons. Though aware of how badly educated he was himself, George insisted that his sons' schooling should replicate his own as far as possible. They had lessons at home with a tutor until they were old enough to join the navy as cadets. George's education had required the approval of the monarch, and Queen Victoria had frequently interfered, but Edward VII seems to have played no part in his grandsons' schooling.

The tutor arrived in the spring of 1902. David remembered the ominous tread of his father stamping heavily up the stairs. '"This is Mr Hansell," my father said coldly, "your new tutor," and with that he walked out of the room.'[73] Six feet four-and-a-half inches tall and an Oxford graduate, Henry Hansell was a pipe-smoking bachelor in plus-fours who believed in Muscular Christianity. A crack shot with a rifle and a talented golfer, he was a companion for George, an indifferent golfer whom Hansell partnered, as he did his sons. Hansell has been criticised for the 'disastrous' effect he had on his pupils' intellectual development.[74] True, Hansell was neither clever nor imaginative. But nor was he manipulative and controlling, as John Dalton had been – though such was George's faith in his old tutor that he employed him to teach his sons religion.

Being a conventional character, Hansell strongly believed that the princes ought to be sent to prep school. As this was out of the question, he organised the schoolroom to resemble a prep school, furnishing it with desks, a globe and a blackboard. He introduced a strict timetable, starting with prep each morning at 7.30. May sat in on Hansell's history lessons and was impressed. 'I must say Hansell teaches it well & they really answer the questions very nicely, taking a real interest in what he tells them. This pleases me immensely.'[75]

The boys suffered from lack of contact with other boys of their age. Hansell warned George of his sons' poor progress, but he took no notice. In retrospect, David was 'appalled' at how little he had learnt from five years with Hansell. Ineffectual and suffering from 'mental claustrophobia' or perhaps depression in the crowded household of York Cottage, each morning after breakfast Hansell would walk to exactly the same spot and smoke his pipe for fifteen minutes, looking out over the flat Norfolk plough.[76]

In *A King's Story*, his autobiography written with the help of the American journalist Charles Murphy, David gave the most vivid, detailed account of a prince's boyhood ever written by a royal. In David's narrative Sandringham was an Eden: a boyhood idyll of days spent cycling along the woodland trails of the enchanted forest of the great estate. For the children open sesame was the Big House across the lake, which would light up in advance of their grandparents' arrival – a thrilling glimpse of a rich and glamorous world far removed from the strict discipline of York Cottage.

A King's Story is the autobiography of an exile. For the purposes of his story David and/or Murphy needed to show his childhood as a prelapsarian paradise from which he was ejected. The form of the book imposed distortions. David once told Murphy that 'growing up for me was a prolonged misery'.[77]

Perhaps most memorable is the portrait of George – a gothic figure who shadows the children's Eden. Heavy-footed, with the loud voice which was a legacy of his navy days, George was fanatically punctual. Each morning and evening he compulsively tapped the barometer. How the boys dreaded the summons to the study where their father would scold them. 'He literally pounded good manners into us, hammering home ... the rules of courtesy.'[78] However, as one biographer points out, David's account of what actually happened in the interviews in the study comes as an anti-climax.[79] There was no shouting or caning; perhaps the most striking thing was the violent language used by David to describe his father.

The children saw their mother for an hour in the evening before dinner as she rested on a sofa in her boudoir, as was now her habit. For David, 'her soft voice, her cultivated mind, the cosy room overflowing with personal treasures were all inseparable ingredients of the happiness associated with this last hour of a child's day'.[80] Not only did May's gentleness provide an antidote to their father's stern, stamping masculinity, but according to David she never failed to take the children's side when she considered George was too harsh. Lady Airlie was probably right to say that George and May were 'more conscientious and more truly devoted to their children' than most Edwardian upper-class parents.[81] But George's harsh discipline and excruciating teasing frightened his sons. As for May, she was excluded from contact with her boys when they were handed over to the care of men – to Hansell and Finch, the boys' valet who arrived when David was eight. The boudoir hour was her only chance to spend time with her sons, and that, as Lady Airlie observed, was not enough – the less so as she was often away from her children for five or six months a year.[82]

In January 1905 May found herself pregnant again. 'Such a surprise, so unexpected,' wrote Aunt Augusta on hearing the news.[83] The pregnancy was easier than previous ones – 'I feel far less tired & exhausted,' wrote May.[84] The baby was born on 12 July after only three-and-a-half hours' labour. George was not pleased. 'I am very disappointed it wasn't a girl as now we have got 5 boys,' he wrote in his diary.[85] When the King learnt that George proposed to call his new son John Charles Francis he wrote: 'I wish you would call him by the 2nd name and put it first, as I confess that I think John an ugly name and unknown in our history, excepting the wicked king.'[86]

CHAPTER 11

George's Progress

1905–1910

'And so my poor Georgie boy has lost his May who has fled to London town to look in her glass!!' wrote the Queen in September 1905. 'What a bore & a nuisance, but I cannot understand why she should have gone so soon! as the dresses for India cannot take quite such a long time to do!'[1] Alix was being mischievous. George and May were due to sail for India in October, and May needed at least a week to try on her dresses. She declared herself 'much pleased with all my new clothes' which, by her special decree, were made only of British cloth.[2] The packing was an ordeal. May calculated that she would need at least twenty-five boxes, and George required even more.[3] George was annoyed to read in the newspapers detailed descriptions of May's outfits inserted by their creators. 'They had no business to do it without asking, of course they have done it for the advertisement,' he grumbled.[4] Among the self-promoting couturiers was Mr Phillips of Sloane Street, who was particularly proud of his dress in a green and brown leaf pattern to be worn on tiger-shooting expeditions.[5]

The Indian tour had long been planned for the Prince of Wales to complete the circuit of the empire begun with the *Orphir* cruise. The chief of staff and organiser of the tour was Sir Walter Lawrence, a member of the Indian civil service who had served as private secretary to the viceroy Lord Curzon. During his many interviews with the prince, Lawrence noted: 'He had the keenest memory that I had ever met in any man.'[6] As for May, Lawrence observed that she eagerly devoured the small library of books on India which he had assembled.

Curzon, the supreme imperialist impresario, who had staged the grandest Indian durbar ever in 1903 to celebrate the coronation of Edward VII, threw himself into the planning of the tour. But in August 1905 he unexpectedly resigned, and the Prince of Wales's tour was caught up in the quarrel between Curzon and Lord Kitchener, commander-in-chief in India.

As a sop to Curzon's injured pride, the King suggested that he should receive the Prince of Wales on his arrival at Bombay and then hand over to the incoming viceroy, the Earl of Minto, a week later. This arrangement did not go smoothly. George and May arrived at Bombay on 9 November on board the battleship *Renown* to find that the sheets had barely been changed on their beds at Government House, and the viceroy's train, which Curzon had used only four days before, had not been prepared for the royal tour.[7] For whatever reason, Curzon failed to give Minto the official welcome traditionally afforded to the new viceroy, and rumours spread that this was a deliberate snub. These reached the ears of George, who reported them back to his father. 'It is simply inconceivable that Lord Curzon should have shown such bad manners,' wrote the King.[8]

Kitchener did his best to win George's sympathy. The Prince 'likes Kitchener very much', wrote Godfrey-Faussett after a lavish dinner at Fort William in Calcutta.[9] George told his father: 'I have gained a lot of most interesting information since I have been in Calcutta with regard to the controversy between Lord C and Lord K. I fear the latter has been grossly misrepresented.'[10] George had not yet learnt the lesson that where political quarrels were concerned his role was to listen to both sides without revealing his sympathy for either.

The prince and princess criss-crossed the Indian subcontinent in the viceroy's train, carrying out each and every one of the engagements in the packed schedule planned by Lawrence. George always insisted on making his entry in an open carriage so that he could see the crowds and, defying the security officers, he tried to mix with the people and dispense with a police cordon.[11]

George's biographers claim that this Indian trip confirmed his belief in 'some sort of mystical association between the Sovereign and the common people'.[12] The tour itself was hardly mystical, however. Even Lawrence admitted the 'considerable monotony' of the endless receptions and banquets.[13] May, who yearned for the magic of India, regretted the 'tedious, tiresome European functions' they were compelled to attend 'while our hearts were so much more interested in the Natives & their life & religions'.[14]

The viceroy's private secretary, an official named James Dunlop Smith, noticed that there were two sides to the Prince of Wales. One was the 'cheery talkative young sailor' who was 'just a little bit too out-spoken'. The other George he discovered was a man of 'distinct ability, great shrewdness and a wonderful memory'.[15] George's phenomenal memory was much remarked upon. It was a trait he shared with Queen Victoria. Bigge, the private secretary, confessed that he 'almost trembled' at the likeness between George and the old queen.[16]

Out of loyalty to the memory of his grandmother, George paid a visit to her Indian servant Abdul Karim, now living at Agra. 'Please remember to see Grandmama's Munshi don't forget,' Alix had reminded him.

'She wd have been so pleased and he has behaved so well & quietly since he left – no one ever hears a word against him.'[17] Abdul Karim had been a divisive, disruptive figure at Victoria's court, but in India George found him subdued. 'He has not grown more beautiful & is getting fat. I must say he was most civil & humble & really pleased to see us.'[18]

George was naturally an imperialist, but not an unthinking one. In India he spoke briefly with Gopal Krishna Gokhale, the moderate leader of the Indian National Congress. George, who claimed to understand 'the look in the eye of the Indians', asked Gokhale if the people would be happier if he, Gokhale, ran the country. Gokhale replied that they would have more self-respect. 'That may be,' said George, 'but I cannot see how there can be real self-respect while the Indians treat their women as they do now.' To this unexpectedly thoughtful reply, Gokhale could only respond, 'Yes, that is the great blot.'[19] Though George opposed Indian self-government, he considered that the Europeans were 'unsympathetic' in their relations with the 'natives'. In the speech he made at Guildhall on his return, he appealed for 'wider sympathy' on the part of the British rulers.[20] This coded criticism of the racism of the British earned him the support of John Morley, the Liberal secretary of state for India, who claimed to be 'enchanted' by George's letters to him from the subcontinent.[21]

For May the trip was not without annoyances. The death in January 1906 of George's grandfather King Christian of Denmark meant that she was obliged to wear mourning white, 'and all the coloured clothes upon which I had to pay hundreds have had to be put away. Such a waste!'[22] The packed schedule was exhausting, the great heat of ninety degrees in South India was trying, and she suffered from acute indigestion. She was plagued by mosquitoes, and 'I have to smoke in self-defence'.[23] Little wonder May lost her temper now and then. Harold Nicolson's brother Arthur, the future Lord Carnock, then a sub-lieutenant on the royal ship *Renown*, recalled that they arrived an hour late at Rangoon. He was 'standing at attention at the head of the gangplank, when the [princess], fuming & gathering up her skirts, shoved her parasol into his hand, remarking, "hold that, you idiot!"'[24]

Private secretary Dunlop Smith had to sit next to May at every meal on her visit to Barrackpore. 'She is a handsome woman. When she is animated her face lights up.' He found her 'not what one could describe as light as a feather' to waltz with, but he was impressed by her deep knowledge of India.[25] When George departed to shoot tigers with the Maharajah of Gwalior, May spent time sightseeing at Lucknow, 'doing as I liked, no functions, no fuss, oh! such a blessing after weeks of nothing else'.[26] On a motoring tour at Dehra Dun she wrote: 'It is sad to think how soon we shall be leaving India to which I have become deeply attached.'[27]

May's lady-in-waiting Lady Shaftesbury, who accompanied her on the tour, recalled that 'she adored India and was quite different there'.[28]* This was not, as some have suggested, a throwback to the divine right of kings. On the contrary, May was captivated by the romance of the east. As she later explained: 'I simply revel in the sunshine, the colours, the complete contrast to our Western civilisation, the whole thing has a fascination of its own.'[29] Her 'beloved' India invigorated her. Back in London Godfrey-Faussett found her 'looking wonderfully well, thinner than when she left England'.[30]

When George and May returned from India in May 1906, so one of May's ladies later related, they sat on a sofa with the ten-month-old Prince John between them and, 'looking at each other, said "But *can* this be *our* Child?"'[31] The baby had been separated from May aged four months and she was a stranger to him. He wasn't a backward child. At ten months, he spoke his first word – 'Lala', the name of his nanny. In her baby book, May recorded that he crawled aged one, and at sixteen months took his first step.[32] She told her aunt that he was 'a huge child & very good tempered & amiable'.[33] On his third birthday she reported: 'He is very big for his age & rather a pickle.'[34] But there are hints that May's fifth son was different from the others. He was naughtier. George told his mother that 'Johnnie is most impertinent & pulled Papa's hair at lunch today. I don't think he quite liked it but one couldn't stop him.'[35] The disciplinarian George would surely not have tolerated his three-year-old son pulling the monarch's thinning hair unless there was an underlying worry about the child.

David, on the other hand, made his parents proud. Now thirteen, he took the entrance examination for Osborne early in 1907, and he excelled in the viva before a committee of the Admiralty. George wrote in his diary: 'I am glad to say he did remarkably well, they said he was the best boy they had examined, which is very gratifying.'[36] There followed three tough days of examinations in a public hall in London along with 100 other boys. The record is silent about the result; it transpired later that David failed by a few marks to pass the qualifying exam, scoring 291 out of 600.[37] He found the maths especially challenging, and for this he blamed his unfortunate tutor Hansell.

Neither David nor his father seem to have been aware that the prince had failed the written papers.[38] His marks were just good enough for

---

*Lady Shaftesbury, who was a lady of the bedchamber on and off from 1905 to 1953, was another member of the Grosvenor family, the sister of Bendor, 2nd Duke of Westminster.

him to be offered a place, however, and in May he travelled down to the naval college at Osborne with George. Repeating what *his* father had said to him, George told David: 'Always remember that I am your best friend.'[39] But George was hardly that. A frightening figure who summoned his son for interviews about his end-of-term report in the red-cloth-covered study, he instilled such an overpowering sense of failure in David that on one occasion the boy burst into tears before his father even spoke.[40]

David did well at Osborne. He worked hard and survived the bullying. He was not near the top of his class as George had been, but this was partly because he couldn't do maths. May's confidence in her son seemed well placed. She enjoyed David's company: 'It is nice having him alone with me as he is quite amusing to talk to & comes out with his thoughts & makes most sensible remarks.'[41] She found his interest in her collection of family miniatures particularly pleasing. 'I do so hope our children will turn out commonsense people which is so important in this world,' she wrote. 'We have taken no end of trouble about their education.'[42]

Christmas 1908 at Sandringham was like any other Christmas and seemingly followed time-honoured custom. In reality the tradition was invented – a confection of Dickens, Fabergé and Saxe-Coburg which had been devised by Bertie and Alix. For many weeks before, May was occupied with Christmas presents, choosing, buying and arranging them, 'always a terrific and fatiguing operation', as gifts had to be bought not just for immediate family and members of the household but also for the extended dynastic network.[43] The royal exchange of gifts could never be shirked. At the height of the 1905 Russian Revolution Nicholas and Alexandra took care to send their Christmas gifts, consisting chiefly of Fabergé novelties, which arrived at Sandringham 'in spite of all by a messenger', a sign interpreted by Alix to mean that the Tsar was still in business and 'things are much exaggerated in our English papers'.[44]

At 3 p.m. on Christmas Eve George took the children to the coach house, where long tables covered with white tablecloths groaned with joints of beef. The room stank of raw meat. All the estate workers – about 300 people – waited outside, and each family received a joint: George calculated that one-and-a-half tons of beef were distributed among the 1,420 people living on the estate.[45]

In German fashion, the present giving took place on Christmas Eve. At 5.30 the Wales family piled into an omnibus and rode the short distance to the Big House. They were greeted by the King and Queen and, to the children's delight, one of the servants dressed as Santa Claus, who led them into the ballroom. A Christmas tree almost as high as the ceiling stood in the centre of the room, which was lined with trestle tables, divided into sections piled with presents for each person. For the household, who assembled in the corridor outside and were called in one by one to receive their gifts, it was 'rather a trying experience' with the King on one side and the Queen on the other trying to explain their presents.[46] Fritz Ponsonby, the King's assistant private secretary, was overcome by the number of things he received – watercolours, silver cigarette cases, a silver inkstand, pins and studs. For the children, made to wait until the end, the suspense was thrilling; and even when the presents had been opened, they had to be left on display in the ballroom until New Year's Day.

George and May and the children were back at York Cottage at 7.30. Then George wrote letters. On Christmas Day as well he wrote many letters.[47] The year before he had written forty letters over Christmas, including one to Bigge, thanking him for all he had done. 'I am a bad hand at saying what I feel, but I thank God I have a friend like you, in whom I have the fullest confidence.' As in his letters to May, George apologised: 'I fear sometimes I have lost my temper with you & often been very rude, but I am sure you know me well enough by now to know that I did not mean it.'[48]

These were generous sentiments, but Christmas at York Cottage was a joyless occasion by contrast with the feasting and festivities at the Big House. On Christmas Day May and George spent the entire afternoon arranging and giving presents to servants and dispatching parcels to poor people. 'Very nice to be able to do it but so fatiguing to body & mind,' wrote May.[49] George and May tell us nothing about food or drink or Christmas cheer: even at Christmas it seems George was his abstemious self and 'drank very little, smoked very little, and ate very little'.[50]

Christmas Day 1908 was still and dry but this was the calm before wintry storms, and one can picture George striding through the hall at York Cottage and tapping the barometer in anticipation of the next day's shooting.[51] In Europe, the outlook for monarchy was stormy too.

The Russian Revolution of 1905 was sparked by Bloody Sunday at the start of the year, when the Imperial Guard in St Petersburg opened fire on workers seeking to deliver a petition to the Tsar. Hundreds were killed or wounded, and strikes and demonstrations spread throughout the tsarist empire. Nicholas II survived the disturbances, but he was obliged to soften the tsarist autocracy and introduce a democratic legislative assembly, the Duma. 'The horrors of Russia are indeed appalling,' wrote May.

She felt sorry for Nicky, who she thought was never told the truth by his entourage. But she considered that 'to meet an unarmed crowd, headed by a priest, by firing on them, seems incredible in these times & they have made a severe blunder'.[52]

Nicky's cousin the Prince of Wales was soon to witness the revolutionary threat elsewhere. George was ordered by his father to represent him at the wedding in May 1906 of King Alfonso of Spain and Princess Ena, the daughter of George's aunt Beatrice. May asked permission to accompany him – 'I was a help to you at Vienna, wasn't I, & my goodness that was stiff.'[53] The King consented, and May wrote to Bricka asking her to 'write out some notes for me on Madrid & Spanish History'.[54]

Ena had been forced to become a Roman Catholic in order to marry the Spanish king, and both George and May tut-tutted at her changing her religion so easily.[55] But mild disapproval turned to horror at the wedding, when a bomb was thrown by an anarchist at the state carriage of Alfonso and Ena, causing carnage among the bobbing plumes of the procession. Twenty were killed, but Alfonso and Ena were unhurt. 'We can only thank God that the anarchist didn't get into the church in which case we must all have been blown up!' wrote May.[56]

'The Spanish police and detectives are about the worst in the world,' wrote George. 'No precautions whatever had been taken.'[57] Security could protect the sovereign, but it could not save the Spanish monarchy. The anarchist bomb was symptomatic of turbulence and discontent which the monarchy was incapable of containing. Ena's dress was splattered with blood, a grotesque premonition of the haemophilia that she was to bring to the Spanish royal family. Herself a carrier of the gene, two of her sons were bleeders, which ultimately caused her husband to reject her.

Terrorism came closer in 1908 with the assassination of King Carlos of Portugal and his son the Crown Prince, both killed with rifle bullets as they drove into Lisbon. Like the heroine of an opera, Queen Amelie shielded her dead husband, brandishing her bouquet of camellias and violets at the assassin who was clinging to the carriage.[58] Carlos's grandfather King Ferdinand was a Saxe-Coburg and a first cousin of Queen Victoria. When the couple visited Windsor in 1904, May had noted that 'Amelie has grown very stout . . . but she has kept her charming face & lively eyes & is most natural & nice, he is quite nice & easy to get on with but awfully fat'.[59] The regicide horrified the British royals. 'We can think & talk of little else,' said May. 'I feel so upset about it all I can scarcely write.'[60] She found it 'incredible' that Carlos had been allowed to drive in an open carriage, refusing all security.[61]

This could not be dismissed as an isolated attack by a lone anarchist. Portugal, as George observed, had been in 'a disturbed state' for some time.[62] It was a failed state on the verge of a republican revolution, and King Carlos had lost all support. Most chilling, as May noted, was 'the indifference displayed by the Portuguese at the death of the King and Prince'.[63] No longer could monarchy be taken for granted, in southern Europe at least.

In northern Europe, monarchy was changing too. In June 1906 George and May had represented the King at the coronation of Maud and Haakon, as Charles now became as king of the newly independent Norway (its union with Sweden had been dissolved the year before). For Aunt Augusta the idea of an English princess sitting on a 'Revolutionary Throne' was 'too horrible'.[64] Haakon was the elected king of a new country: aware of strongly republican feelings among the Norwegian people, he had made his acceptance of the crown dependent on a referendum. As Augusta wrote, with her unerring eye for the rules of old monarchy, 'he is making speeches, poor fellow, thanking the revolutionary Norwegians for having <u>elected</u> him! No really, it is all too odd!'[65]

Haakon was to become the architect of a new model of social democratic monarchy. In June 1906, however, the coronation at Trondheim seemed very second-rate by comparison with British pomp. Because there were no grand houses in Trondheim, George and May were obliged to live (admittedly in great comfort) on board the royal yacht. The procession was plain and pared down – the contrast with the baroque swagger of the Spanish ceremony could hardly be greater. George and May arrived at the landing stage by boat, a perilous procedure because (as May explained) 'it turned cold & we had much wind & rain which was unpleasant for landing from the yacht in evening dress when the boat jumps up and down'.[66] Maud's legs were too weak for her to walk in procession to the cathedral, but the ceremony, said George, was simple and fine: 'Both Maud & Charles went through their parts very well & they both looked very nice & impressive.'[67] It lasted just two hours and the Waleses were back on the royal yacht in time for lunch. The Norwegian ladies admired May's elegant pale embroidered gown and tiara, but 'frankly they . . . all thought her rather stiff'.[68]*

For Christmas 1908 George gave May some boxes and enamels which had once belonged to her uncle the Duke of Cambridge. Much of the

---

*George found consolation with a fishing trip in the fjords: he caught a 28-pound salmon. In the absence of a boat, his sisters Maud and Louise fished sitting on the shoulders of members of the Norwegian household. In spite of her coronation, the new Queen Maud found time to go fishing.

Cambridge family silver had been bought at auction by Lady Armstrong, who, according to May, 'was obliged to sell privately as Lord A has lost his money stupid man'.[69]* The Waleses bought back more and more – four handsome silver candelabra and then four very fine silver sauce boats – and May busied herself checking that the inventories were correct and seeing 'that everything is entered as far as possible with its history'. These items formed a family collection and, said May, 'it is rather wonderful what we have managed to collect & get together since we married'. In 1909 she added a further twenty pieces to the collection. 'I hope you won't laugh at me,' May told Aunt Augusta. She claimed that she had 'induced George to get almost as keen about Family Things' as she was.[70] But though George wrote the cheques, he didn't share her collector's obsession.

May devoted time and money to her collecting in the same way as George did to his stamps; probably rather more. She found compiling inventories intensely soothing. It gave her the sense of control and tidiness that George found with his stamps.

Her collecting went along with a passion for family history. Staying at Darmstadt with Ernie, Grand Duke Ernest of Hesse, she was 'thrilled' to discover a painting of her great-great-grandparents the rulers of Nassau-Usingen. 'Ernie was delighted at my keenness,' she told her aunt, and said 'I was "splendid" in my knowledge of History!!! You will laugh at me & think my head is being turned in my old age of nearly 41, but as I feel about 25 I don't mind.'[71] In discovering her German ancestors, May reconnected with the family history of the Hanoverians which had been ruptured by Prince Albert the Saxe-Coburg interloper, thus restoring the legitimacy of the old English royal family and especially her own Cambridge line.

Jewels and precious things reinforced this dynastic identity. When May saw the Kaiser wearing the 'beautiful' Garter and badge which had formerly belonged to her uncle George, Duke of Cambridge, she observed: 'Really they are so fine they ought to belong to our Crown jewels.'[72] They do now. In 1949 she sent Owen Morshead to Doorn to search for them after William had died, and they were bought back by George VI. Then there was the fine collection of china made by George III's fifth daughter, Princess Sophia, which had seemingly vanished after her death. What had become of that? May knew about it from the Duchess of Teck: 'Mama was so correct in her statements that she cannot surely be wrong.'[73]

---

*Lord Armstrong had a lot to lose. He inherited a fortune from his great-uncle, Lord Armstrong of Cragside, the armaments manufacturer, who left £1.5 million on his death in 1900.

May kept a beady eye out for royal souvenirs hanging on the walls of tumbledown country houses. As a house-party guest, she exhausted her hosts with her sightseeing itinerary. At West Dean in West Sussex, on a visit to the socialite Mrs Willie James, while George went shooting May enjoyed a packed schedule of motor expeditions, including one to Uppark where she was thrilled to discover 'two charming pictures of George III and Queen Charlotte by Dance given to the family by George IV'.[74] On another outing she saw the catalogue of the paintings and plate belonging to Charles I which had been sold by Cromwell: 'too interesting as it shows what beautiful things he had. The plate alas was given to the mint for coining, what a sin! & so were the jewels . . . It makes my blood boil that all these historical souvenirs have disappeared.'[75]

When May and George made a holiday visit to Paris in April 1908, the princess plunged into an orgy of sightseeing. They were guided round Versailles and Chantilly by the directors, 'which made the visits far more interesting as they showed us things no one sees'.[76] But George was bored. For him, complained May, 'all these things are a sealed book, such a pity & so deplorable in his position!'[77] She told Lord Esher that George 'suffered from not knowing French and German'.[78] But the truth was that, in spite of growing up surrounded by the treasures of the Royal Collection, George possessed the aesthetic sense of a schoolboy. At the Paris Salon, George told his mother, 'we saw one or two nice pictures & any amount of horrors, mostly naked women'.[79]

Attending the annual Royal Academy dinner was a duty which George took over when he became Prince of Wales, and it was one of the functions he most disliked. In 1908, at his request, the traditional after-dinner speeches – including the reply to the toasts by the Prince of Wales – were dropped. The result, wrote Esher, was 'dull', and generally admitted to be a mistake, and some said George was shirking his speech. 'The Prince of Wales is bound to have to yield on this subject.'[80] He did. The next year, George noted, 'alas we had speeches again'.[81]

Domestic politics were beginning to intrude into the life of the very Tory Prince of Wales. The general election of January 1906 had brought a radical Liberal government into Downing Street. Back in 1886 the Liberal Party had split over Gladstone's proposal to give Home Rule (or self-government) to Ireland, with those Liberals in favour of the Union defecting to form the Liberal Unionist Party. In alliance with the Conservatives the new party held office from 1895, under the prime ministership of the Tories Lord Salisbury and A. J. Balfour, during which time the two parties were together known as Unionists. The coalition came to an end in December 1905, when Balfour resigned as prime minister. By then the Unionists were themselves split over tariff reform – that is, the proposal to abandon free trade and raise revenue through tariffs while giving preferential tariffs to trade with the colonies. At the election the following month, boosted by these divisions among their opponents and fired by their own adoption of progressive New Liberalism, the Liberal Party led by Henry Campbell-Bannerman won 397 seats. Balfour was humiliatingly defeated in his own constituency, and the Unionists shrank to 156 MPs.

During the 1906 election George in India was kept informed by Reuter telegrams of Campbell-Bannerman's landslide victory. 'It is dreadful to contemplate,' wrote May, '& we feel much distressed.'[82] In February she wrote: 'What a terribly radical speech the King had to make at the opening of Parlt, how he must have hated it.'[83]

In April 1908 ill health forced Campbell-Bannerman's resignation, and Asquith succeeded him in Number 10 and as leader of the Liberal Party. The following spring the new chancellor of the Exchequer, David Lloyd George, introduced his radical Budget – the so-called People's Budget, which sought to fund social welfare reforms by hitting the rich, by means, for example, of land taxes and a supertax on higher incomes.

The People's Budget was not popular at Marlborough House. May thought land taxes spelt ruin for everyone: 'It is wicked the way the Govt has started Old Age Pensions & wild schemes of the kind without having the least idea how the money is to be raised.'[84] The Prince of Wales held similar Tory views, and no one at this time questioned his right to hold political opinions.[85] But he was expected to keep his views private, and George seemed worryingly indiscreet, not helped by his having an exceptionally loud voice.

When a feud broke out between the first sea lord, Admiral Fisher, and Admiral Lord Charles Beresford, George openly supported the latter, an old navy friend. In attacking Fisher, George opposed the line taken by his father, who was one of Fisher's supporters. George's behaviour earned him a rebuke from Lord Esher, the enforcer of the Edwardian court, who warned him of the risks to his reputation if it became publicly known that the Prince of Wales was trying to bring down a man in high office who was a friend of the King.[86]

George made his most damaging gaffe when Asquith succeeded Campbell-Bannerman. The prince told Winston Churchill, a member of the government, that the new prime minister was not a gentleman; and Churchill of course repeated it. Esher, who had become close to May, received an urgent summons to lunch at Marlborough House. He found George in an agitated state, worried that he had 'put his foot in it'. As he explained what had happened, May interrupted: 'You said it, George, at the top of your voice. Everyone heard you.'[87]

George was echoing the private opinion of the King, who considered that Asquith was 'deplorably common and very vulgar'.[88] As it happened, the prince liked Asquith but not Churchill, agreeing with his father that the latter was 'almost more of [a] cad in office than he was in opposition'.[89] Later that month when Churchill was defeated in an important by-election at Manchester North West, George noted in his diary: 'We were all very excited when we heard that Winston Churchill . . . has been beaten.'[90] But, as we shall see, George's unfortunate indiscretion about Asquith was to cost him dear when he became king.

George celebrated his forty-fourth birthday in June 1909, and three days later May wrote to Aunt Augusta:

> I should like you to know, entre nous, that he has come on enormously the last year, taking much more interest in things generally, talking & discussing matters with men of all views & positions, this I think good & a great help for the future & as he gets more known people appreciate him and his good qualities more & more. His views are so sound on most points & he is so thorough in what he takes up, taking infinite trouble to master details, that all this must help him in the long run, besides the serious view he takes of his responsibilities, so different from the frivolous view of life which so many people alas have in these terribly restless days when no one can be still an instant.[91]

That May felt impelled to report on her husband's progress betrays an anxiety that he might not be up to the job of being king, and it's significant that she made no mention of his distressing habit of putting his foot in it. These were not the words of a woman who, as some have suggested, was cowed by her husband. She kept a sharp watch on their marriage too, ticking George off for 'drifting' when he spent less time sitting with her before dinner.[92] George replied: 'I have so much to do that it is often impossible.'[93] A year later he told her: 'You know in spite of occasional drifting, how devoted I am to you & how really deeply I love my beloved little wife.'[94] If there was a threat to their marriage, it came from George's work, which took up more and more of his time. As John Gore noticed, after about 1909 the prince's diary is increasingly concerned with politics, which elbow out the more trivial things he had previously recorded.[95]

Balfour, the leader of the Unionist opposition, who was re-elected in a safe seat almost immediately after his defeat in the 1906 election, admired the Prince of Wales, remarking that 'except the German Emperor, he is the only royal prince to whom I find I can talk as a man ... He is really clever.'[96] For 'clever' perhaps we should read 'Tory' here. Certainly the Asquiths were not impressed. Margot Asquith, the voluble, socialite wife of the prime minister, wrote in her diary that George was a 'dunderhead' and much inferior to his father.[97]

In August 1909 Tsar Nicholas and his family made an official visit to Britain to cement the Anglo-Russian entente of 1907 which had settled the two countries' rivalries in central Asia, ending the long-lasting enmity between them. For security reasons, the imperial family barely set foot on dry land, in spite of the detectives and police provided by the British. The King and his family boarded the Russian yacht in the Solent, where they were received by the imperial family, and then the imperial family boarded the British royal yacht, the *Victoria and Albert*, to return the salutations. The navy laid on a review of the fleet at Spithead, an exhibition of naval might which the Russian empire could never emulate. Wearing full uniform, George and 'dear Nicky' steamed down through the lines of the fleet, the crew of each ship cheering as they passed.[98]

This was the first meeting of the two first cousins for nearly thirteen years, and it was a family reunion as well as a show of British strength. Nicky made George an admiral of the Russian fleet. Alicky gave May the Order of St Catherine, 'which for years I had wanted to have!!!!!!'[99] George slept on the royal yacht at Cowes, but May preferred to remain on land, and installed herself in comfort at Barton Manor in the grounds of Osborne House. Here the 'charming little Russian children' came one day to pick up shells on the beach.[100] Nicky and Alicky landed only once, to make a visit by motor car to Osborne, followed by tea with May and George at Barton out of doors with their five 'delightful' children.[101]

By contrast with the Romanovs, who were the prisoners of their security police, the British monarchy seemed confident and secure. The King won the Derby in the summer of 1909: 'You have no idea what a scene of wild excitement & joy this caused among the people, high & low, I have never seen anything like it,' wrote May, 'really too touching, & it was delightful seeing the King leading his horse into the paddock & he was so pleased.'[102] Aunt Augusta, the guardian of the rules of royalty, was quick to comment on the significance for the monarchy: 'What a thing this was to happen in this era of Democracy! In no other Country this could have been! How right and fine of the King leading his horse himself! That is also "unique"!'[103]

In the autumn of 1909 the People's Budget, now embodied in the Finance Bill, moved to the House of Lords, and there the struggle intensified. The House, whose members were of course all hereditary peers, was overwhelmingly Unionist, and since 1906 the Unionist opposition had been mobilising that majority to defeat measures introduced by the elected Liberal government, exploiting the peers' so-called veto power. Balfour declared: 'The Unionist party shall still control, whether in power or whether in opposition, the destinies of this great nation.'[104] The Liberal programme of social reform was therefore targeted by the upper chamber, which prompted Lloyd George to dub it 'Mr Balfour's Poodle'. With the People's Budget, the Liberals had declared war not only on poverty but also on the House of Lords and the very rich. The Tories claimed that the government was using financial legislation such as the supertax and land taxes as a weapon of class politics, and clamoured for the Finance Bill's rejection. This unprecedented move was strongly opposed by King Edward, who anticipated that it would exacerbate the crisis. Behind the scenes he tried to dissuade the Unionist leaders from throwing out the bill, but without success. On 30 November 1909 the House of Lords defeated the People's Budget by a vote of 350 in favour and 75 against.

Rejection of the Budget made an immediate election necessary, and in December Parliament was dissolved. The Liberals now claimed that the behaviour of the peers justified them in calling for legislation to restrict the veto power of the House of Lords.

The January 1910 election resulted in a hung parliament – 274 Liberals and 272 Unionists. In order to stay in office and pass the Budget the Liberals needed to make a deal with the Irish nationalists, who held eighty-two seats in the Commons. The House of Lords had thrown out the second Home Rule Bill in 1893; and it was evident that, in order for a third Home Rule Bill to pass, the power of the peers had to be clipped. In exchange for the Irish nationalists voting for the Budget, Asquith introduced resolutions for a curb on the veto power of the House of Lords. To gain a mandate for this very significant constitutional reform – later embodied in the Parliament Bill – the government needed to call a second election. Intensifying the pressure on the King, Asquith proposed in April 1910 to ask him to give guarantees that if the Liberals won he would create more Liberal peers, to ensure the passing of the bill in the

Lords – that is, the King was being asked for guarantees contingent on the Liberals winning that election.

On 13 April Asquith duly wrote to the King warning that, when the Lords rejected the veto bill, the Cabinet would immediately ask him for contingent guarantees.[105] The next day in the Commons Asquith rashly pledged not to call a second election until he had obtained these guarantees. But the King had not agreed to give them, and he was very reluctant to do so. Not only would this involve the Crown in party politics, placing it on the Liberal side, but by giving contingent guarantees to create peers after a second election, the Crown was being asked to hand over control of the royal prerogative of peer creation to the government.[106]

Rejection of the Budget by the Lords thus created a fiendishly complex political situation. In this drama of high politics it was easy to overlook the steady growth of the Labour Party. At the January 1910 election the number of Labour MPs had increased from twenty-nine to forty – an underlying trend that was shortly to reconfigure the political landscape. Labour also demanded the curbing of the Lords' veto as a condition of their support for the Liberal government.

King Edward was thus at the centre of the battle over the Parliament Bill. He held the trump card, the power to create a 'swamping' majority of peers, and because of his standing with the public he was seen by many as a mediator – a non-partisan, neutral figure who could break the deadlock.

Early in March 1910 the King departed for Biarritz, where he was reunited with Mrs Keppel. In France he became very ill with a bronchial attack, but seemed to recover. Alexandra, who had been prepared to go to Biarritz at any moment, wrote to George: 'Thank God dear Papa is really all right again now <u>such</u> a relief!! I confess I was really dreadfully anxious.'[107]

George wasn't privy to his father's thinking on the constitutional crisis. From Biarritz the King wrote to his son: 'As regards politics at home I think I had best keep my views to myself.'[108] Apart from a few angry remarks about the Liberals, this was what he did, with unfortunate consequences for George.

The King returned home on 27 April and George, who met him at Victoria station and drove with him to Buckingham Palace, thought him 'looking very well'.[109] On 3 May he visited his father, who was suffering from another cold ('too unlucky').[110] The next day Laking called to see George, who was the only member of the immediate family in London, and 'gave a bad account' of the King, who now had bronchitis. When George saw his father 'his colour was bad & his breathing fast'.[111] George wrote to his mother and sister Victoria, who were returning from a trip to Corfu: 'Thank God you are coming home to look after him.'[112] To his diary he confided: 'Wish they were here now.'[113]

On 5 May the King was worse. 'What gives the greatest anxiety is the strain on his heart,' wrote George.[114] The next day, the 6th, was a 'terrible day', and George hardly left his father's bedside.[115] In spite of repeated heart attacks, the King was conscious until 4.30 p.m. With the family gathered kneeling in prayer round his bed, he died at 11.45 that evening.

At 12.17 a.m. George and May drove out of Buckingham Palace. The crowds waiting at the gates noticed that May was weeping.[116] 'I am quite stunned by this awful blow,' wrote George. 'Bed at 1.10.'[117]

PART FOUR

PRE-WAR

1910–1914

CHAPTER 12

King

1910

Tired and distressed by the death of his father the night before, George drove at 4 p.m. on 7 May in a closed carriage from Marlborough House to St James's Palace to meet the Privy Council in the gilt and crimson splendour of the banqueting hall. Wearing an admiral's uniform, he underwent what he described as 'the most trying ordeal I have ever had to go through': addressing the peers and grandees assembled in the Accession Council.[1] He had written the brief speech himself that morning, basing it on the entry in his diary made the night before, shortly after the King's death, and sending the pencil draft for approval to the Archbishop of Canterbury, Randall Davidson.[2] Reading in a 'strong and musical' voice, the new king now declared: 'I have lost not only a father's love but the affectionate and intimate relations of a dear friend and adviser.'[3] His audience praised his simple dignity and depth of feeling, but Sir Almeric FitzRoy, the clerk of the Privy Council, considered that this was not as striking as Edward VII's Accession Council had been, marking as it did the end of an epoch.[4]

That morning a baggy-eyed George had summoned his two eldest sons to his study at Marlborough House. According to David, he wept as he told them that their grandfather had died. David remarked that Bertie and he had already noticed from their bedroom window that the royal standard was flying at half-mast over Buckingham Palace and they understood what this meant. '"But that's all wrong," muttered George. "The King is dead, long live the King!"' An equerry was summoned, and soon the royal standard fluttered from the roof of Marlborough House.[5]* Downstairs in the dining room the equerries struggled to answer the thousands of telegrams – over 12,000 – that flooded in. When Cust and Godfrey-Faussett kissed the new king's hand, they broke down, but George himself was 'calm and collected'.[6]

---

*Archbishop Davidson was amused to note the sailor king's obsession with flags, 'when and how exactly they were to be hoisted and lowered, e.g. a flag on the Victoria Tower to be hoisted at the instant the flag on Buckingham Palace was lowered – which of them were to be at half-mast and when' (Davidson Papers, 'Deathbed', pp. 17–18, 15 August 1910).

King Edward's death had long been predicted by his doctors, but the end when it came was shockingly sudden. On 4 May, 'dear Papa' had a bad attack of bronchitis; two days later, after a series of heart attacks, he was dead. Archbishop Davidson was struck by the 'self-possessed dignity, along with the greatest affection and anxiety for the King', which George displayed during the crisis. 'Nothing could have been better or more natural than the behaviour of the Prince of Wales.'[7] George was met by his staff in the hall at Marlborough House when he returned from the Palace, and they found him calm.[8] The diary entry which George made on the night his father died was written in his usual firm schoolboy script and not, as one biographer claimed, 'in a hand which betrays deep agitation'.[9]

'The whole thing came as such a shock to us all I can scarcely realise it yet,' wrote May. 'Everything seems to be slipping away, such an uncomfortable feeling.'[10] George acceded in the midst of the constitutional crisis described in Chapter 11, at a time when the public regarded his father as the saviour of the country. How could George ever equal his father who, as May wrote, was 'so wonderful & so much beloved?'[11]

The public knew little of George, but *The Times* predicted that in the same way as his father had been an unexpectedly successful king, so George would reveal 'unknown talents of a more solid and sterling character'. His chief merit as Prince of Wales was considered to be his relationship with the King, who had 'trained the Prince to be a statesman'.[12] The politicians were not so optimistic. Lord Balcarres, the Tory chief whip, considered that George was 'not so well able to control his emotions' as his father, and gave vent to opinions 'which he should have kept to himself'.[13] Liberals found him 'weak and talkative'. His remark to the permanent secretary of the Treasury that 'I can't think how you can go on serving that d—n fellow Lloyd George' did not inspire confidence.[14]

George's great advantage was his wife. In his speech to the Privy Council he declared that 'my dear wife ... will be a constant helpmate in every endeavour for our People's good'.[15] May was deeply touched when she read this. 'Thank God George & I are such good friends,' she wrote.[16] She had been frightened of Edward VII, who 'froze her up', and now she could play a bigger part.[17] On George's insistence, she took the name Mary as queen – 'curious to be rechristened at the age of 43', she wrote.[18] George's inclusion of his wife implied a very different style of monarchy from his father's: a domestic sovereign and a strong marriage. People trusted that her 'shrewdness and common sense' would keep her husband straight.[19] For six months after Edward's death May never left George for a single day. Being in mourning, each night they dined together at Marlborough House. 'I can't imagine how I could have got on at all without you,' wrote George. 'I shall never forget it.'[20]

On 18 May George gave an audience to the prime minister. Asquith had been 'deeply moved' by George's 'modesty and good sense' in an interview the previous week.[21] Now in the course of a long talk he 'said he would endeavour to come to some understanding with the opposition to prevent a general election'.[22]

Asquith was still under pressure from the Irish nationalists to ask for a second election in order to give the government a mandate for the Parliament Bill and also for Irish Home Rule.* King Edward had died at a critical moment, and he left no directions to his son, nor had he discussed the crisis with him. Asquith was struck by 'the contrast between the worldly experience of King Edward and the unsophisticated mind and tastes of his son'.[23] To protect the inexperienced monarch, Asquith persuaded Balfour, the Unionist leader, to agree to a Constitutional Conference, a ceasefire in the party hostilities while the leaders attempted to negotiate a settlement. But Asquith had been bruised by George's disparaging remarks of the previous year, and he felt little good will towards the monarch, whom he distrusted as a Tory. Nor did George respect the champagne-drinking, bridge-playing prime minister, about whom Belloc's lines 'On a General Election' (1923) might well have been written: 'The accursed power which stands on privilege / (And goes with women and champagne and bridge) / Broke – and democracy resumed her reign / (Which goes with bridge and women and champagne).'

Becoming king was an exhausting and stressful business. Today the death of the sovereign and the accession of a successor is choreographed and timetabled almost to the minute in plans known as Operation London Bridge which are constantly updated.[24] In 1910 no such plans existed. All the decisions were referred to the King. 'It has been endless,' wrote May, 'so many questions, so much to arrange, so many boxes, quite overwhelming.'[25] The strain of becoming king almost killed Edward VII, whose stress-induced overeating caused a life-threatening abscess. George, by contrast, was calm, clear-headed and businesslike and, said May, 'sees the various people who want to ask things, & this is a great help'.[26] But he slept badly, waking each morning at five and making lists.[27]

---

*The Parliament Bill removed the veto of the House of Lords and replaced it with the power to delay a bill by two years.

The decision that King Edward should lie in state in Westminster Hall was made at Marlborough House the day after he died.[28] Some claimed that it was George's idea; he certainly supported it, and he attended the daily planning meetings at Marlborough House. On his insistence the lying-in-state was made 'as democratic as possible – admission open to all – no privileged persons to take part in it'.[29] This very first action of the reign reveals George's understanding of the role of monarchy in a democracy. For the simple dignity and solemnity of the ceremony on 17 May, when the late king's coffin was moved to Westminster Hall, George deserves much of the credit.

Schomberg (Pom) McDonnell, who as secretary of the Office of Works was responsible for making the funeral arrangements, found the new king alert and quiet and admired the way that he wrote his own notes at meetings. The Duke of Norfolk, whose hereditary duty as earl marshal it was to arrange the state funeral service, exasperated the King by his incompetence. When he published the ceremonial in a form littered with errors, George exploded.

What is the use of my taking all this trouble and labouring at it as I have done if these stupid men are to upset everything? I love the Duke: he is a charming, honourable, straightforward little Gentleman: no better in the world. But as a man of business he is absolutely impossible. I ask you Pom . . . is it not hard on me?[30]

The funeral procession on 20 May conveying King Edward's remains from Westminster Hall to Paddington through dense crowds took three hours – 'an awful ordeal', said May.[31] 'The most striking thing was the absolute silence.'[32] The funeral at St George's Chapel, Windsor was (wrote George) 'beautiful but terribly painful & affecting'.[33] Afterwards George sent Kaiser William a photograph of the nine sovereigns who had ridden in the procession. By 1918 only four – Denmark, Belgium, Norway and George himself – were still on their thrones; Germany, Greece, Portugal, Spain and Bulgaria had all fallen.[34]

At the funeral George walked behind the king's coffin with his mother on his arm, and May followed on the arm of the Kaiser. Alix alone knelt in prayer at the foot of the coffin as it was lowered into the vault. This 'displeased' Aunt Augusta and May's ladies, who felt that the new queen was not 'in her right place'; she should have walked on George's arm and ahead of her mother-in-law.[35] For this public snub to May, Aunt Augusta blamed the 'pernicious influence' of Alix's sister Minny, Dowager Empress of Russia, who had rushed to the side of her grieving sister and stayed for three months.[36] Not only did Minny prevent Alix from seeing her children. She also encouraged Alix to play the part of widow queen as she did in Russia, taking precedence over her daughter-in-law and refusing to relinquish the Crown Jewels.

'Now . . . come all the disagreeables,' wrote May to her aunt after the funeral.[37] Next on the list was the move to Buckingham Palace, but Alix showed no inclination to pack up and return to Marlborough House. May was careful in her letters not to mention Alix by name, but her frustration is plain. 'It is difficult to get a certain person to see things in the right light,' she lamented. 'Everything at this moment appears to me to be chaos, & with my methodical mind I suffer in proportion.'[38]

Not that May disliked Alix. She perceived how utterly broken she was by Bertie's death. Her letters leave no doubt about her sympathy with Alix's deafness. She saw her mother-in-law as a sad and pathetic figure. But Alix's procrastination drove her wild. 'We seem to be at a standstill,' she wrote, 'not able to get on, not able to decide much which ought to be done, & this indecisiveness is far worse than hard work.'[39] As she told her aunt, 'the odd part of it all is that the person causing the delay & trouble remains supremely unconscious as to the inconvenience it is causing, such a funny state of things & everyone seems afraid to speak'.[40]

May was not helped by George, who (wrote Lord Esher) 'is afraid of hurting his mother's feelings and does not insist upon his wife's rights'.[41] Without George's backing, May was powerless against her mother-in-law; but George defected. His sympathy for his mother in her grief was heartfelt, and mother and son became closer than before. He wrote to her:

> You know darling Motherdear how devoted I am to you & I have always told you everything since I was a little child, we have never had any secrets. My greatest object now is to try & help & comfort you in any way I can & make your life easier & your sorrow lighter to bear.[42]

*   *   *

That autumn George cancelled his annual grouse-shooting tour at Bolton Abbey and points north, granting a royal reprieve to thousands of birds, and headed to Balmoral in early August. The royal family travelled in the largest and heaviest special train ever known; it was pulled by two new engines, the *George V* and the *Queen Mary*. Painted on the outside in the colours of the London and North-Western Railway, ivory and chocolate, and emblazoned with the royal arms, the twelve coaches included King Edward's saloon, decorated in the manner of the royal yacht, with polished brass and white enamel paint, as well the Queen's new saloon, draped with soft pink and furnished with inlaid satinwood. Hand signalling by porters stationed all along the line from Euston to Ballater for the journey of twelve hours fifty-five minutes ensured that the 'train passed through a continuous avenue of green lamps'.[43]

May, who usually complained about Deeside holidays, found the life at Balmoral agreeable. She often drove and walked alone with Lord Esher, who had worked hard to gain her confidence. 'I sat next to her at dinner,' he wrote, 'and she talked more intimately than ever.'[44] Balmoral under George, noted Esher, was very different from the previous reign. Gone was 'the curious electric element' which pervaded the surroundings of King Edward.[45] No bridge was played. The Queen knitted after dinner, while the King sat on a sofa talking until bedtime.

May's brother Frank came to stay. Attired even in the heather like a Savile Row tailor's dummy, Frank was recovering from a minor operation at the back of the nose. May watched with mounting alarm as he developed first a chill and a fever, and then pleurisy – the result, she wrote, of 'the nasal operation which has affected the lungs'.[46] He returned to London miserably ill from 'the poisoning effect of the fluid from the pleurisy', and an emergency operation to drain the lungs was performed the same evening.[47]

Back in London, as Frank's illness worsened, May gave orders that she was to be woken if the doctors telephoned in the night. At 4 a.m. on 22 October Godfrey-Faussett knocked on her bedroom door with a message that Frank was dying. The Queen turned to the King beside her in the bed and said: '"Shall I go up with Godfrey or do you wish to come?" The King replied: "Of course I shall go with you to the nursing home."'[48] Frank died later that morning with both May and George by his bed. 'Darling May was most brave but felt it terribly,' wrote George in his diary that night.[49]

'[Frank] never should have died,' said his sister-in-law Princess Alice.[50] Aged forty, he was a casualty of the royal vogue for minor operations where the risks of lethal infection far outweighed the benefits. An unrepentant gambler who expected other people to settle his debts, he had redeemed himself by his work as a governor of Middlesex Hospital, raising large sums to pay off the hospital's deficit.

May was genuinely saddened by Frank's death, and George was little help. As he wrote, 'I fear that I have not properly shown you how deeply I have felt for you in your great sorrow.'[51] At Frank's funeral at St George's Chapel, Windsor, May openly wept.[52]

Presumably May was not yet aware that in his will Frank had left the Cambridge emeralds – the prized Teck family jewels – to his *chère amie* Nellie Kilmorey. When she did discover she set about getting them back.

May's two other brothers were Frank's executors, and in February 1911 probate was granted by order of the president of the Probate Division of the High Court without annexing a copy of the will. As the historian of royal wills has observed, this was a radically new departure. It meant that Frank's will was 'closed'. Ever since Queen Victoria closed the will of Prince Albert, royal wills had been sealed. The wills of Victoria and Edward VII remain closed. But Frank was not a royal, he was a mere serene highness. Presumably Frank's will was sealed because there was something to hide – the story of Nellie Kilmorey and her jewels, or perhaps his secret life. On whose authority the president of the Probate Division was acting when he sealed the will remains something of a mystery.

Documents discovered in Lady Kilmorey's papers reveal that she received the jewellery from the executors in accordance with Frank's will. With her agreement the emeralds were then sold to the Queen in July 1911 for £10,000 – over £1 million in today's values. Not only did Queen Mary believe that the Cambridge emeralds should remain with the family;* but, as we shall see, she planned to wear the emeralds on her state visit to India later that year.[53]

George was at York Cottage for the shooting on Friday 11 November 1910 when the political crisis exploded beneath his feet. At 6.30 p.m. Asquith arrived from London to inform the King that the Constitutional Conference had failed to reach agreement, and the Cabinet demanded an immediate election. Asquith's political survival was on the line and he was 'in a very bullying mood'.[54] He asked the King to dissolve Parliament, and the King agreed. However, the prime minister did not ask for guarantees to create Liberal peers if the Unionist peers in the House of Lords rejected the Parliament Bill. In his notes on the meeting, Bigge underlined this sentence: 'He did not come to ask for anything from the King: no promises, no guarantees during this parliament.'[55] This was a mistake on Asquith's part; it meant that the King assumed, reasonably enough, that he would not be asked to commit himself until after the election.[56] They then moved on to dinner – after which, wrote George, 'Mr Asquith made himself most agreeable'.[57]

---

*In October 1921 Nora, wife of assistant private secretary Clive Wigram, saw the Queen wearing 'white satin with her wonderful emeralds. The splendid cabochon brooch she has told me belonged to Prince Francis of Teck – and at his death she bought it from his estate' – the Queen was careful not to mention Nellie Kilmorey (Wigram Papers, Nora to parents, 16 October 1921).

Asquith returned to London in the morning. Over the weekend George talked at length with his advisers. When he became king, he had kept on the faithful Bigge as private secretary. In addition, he retained Lord Knollys, his father's private secretary, who was given the senior role of communicating with the government. Knollys was more aware than anyone of King Edward's views on the constitutional crisis: the late king had often told him that if Asquith asked for a guarantee to create peers, 'I should certainly decline'.[58] Knollys himself considered that the request for guarantees was 'the greatest outrage on the King which has ever been committed since England became a Constitutional Monarchy' – an outrage because it implied that the government was planning to take control of the sovereign's prerogative of creating peers.[59]

On Monday morning (14 November) Knollys travelled to London and drove straight from the station to 10 Downing Street, where he spent one-and-a-half hours with the prime minister. Asquith's views had hardened over the weekend. He now demanded that George 'should give guarantees at once for the next Parliament'.[60]

This demand for contingent guarantees to create peers plunged the novice monarch into the gravest constitutional dilemma of his reign. By agreeing, wrote Bigge, 'he becomes a Partisan' – a puppet in the hands of the Liberals. Asquith was being urged by his Irish allies and by the radical wing of his own party to redeem the pledge he had made in the Commons on 14 April to obtain guarantees before an election. King Edward had not agreed to give Asquith these guarantees before his death, and this placed Asquith in an awkward position. But, as Bigge wrote, 'it is not His Majesty's duty to save the Prime Minister from the mistake of his incautious words on the 14th of April'.[61]

On the other hand, if the King refused the request, the government would resign, an election would follow and the King would be blamed. As the Liberal chief whip warned, this would stoke unrest in the country, encourage the socialists and 'drag the King into the vortex of our political controversies'.[62]

Something happened to Knollys at Downing Street on 14 November. As Bigge wrote, 'in less than 48 hours Lord Knollys's mind has been entirely changed'.[63] Not only did he write to the King to advise that 'you can safely and constitutionally accept what the Cabinet propose', namely contingent guarantees, the request which only a few months earlier he had condemned as the greatest outrage ever.[64] But he deceived the King by withholding a crucial piece of information. The government's power to threaten the King depended on the assumption that the Tory opposition was unable to form a government. In fact Knollys had been present at a meeting at Lambeth Palace in April 1910 with Lord Esher, the Archbishop of Canterbury and Balfour, when the latter had indicated that he was prepared to take office if Asquith resigned.

At Sandringham on 15 November the rain poured all day; it was so wet that the pheasants refused to fly, and George went home from the shoot at lunch time. He confessed himself 'much worried by the political crisis, they are trying to put the whole responsibility on my shoulders'.[65] After dinner he received letters from Asquith and Knollys which made it necessary for him to go to London.

George and Bigge travelled up by the 9.35 a.m. train on 16 November. They reached Buckingham Palace at 1.00 and George had a meeting with Knollys. At 3.30 he received the prime minister and the Earl of Crewe, the secretary of state for India. Stammering, sensible and clear-headed, Crewe was a personal friend of the King. In his diary George wrote:

> After a long talk I agreed most reluctantly to give the Cabinet a secret understanding that in the event of the Government being returned with a majority at the General Election, I should use my Perrogative [sic] to make Peers if asked for. I disliked having to do this very much, but agreed that this was the only alternative to the Cabinet resigning, which at this moment would be disastrous.[66]

Asquith reported that he 'had never seen the King to better advantage. He argued well and showed no obstinacy.'[67] But George's misspelling of the crucial word 'prerogative' gives a clue to his state of mind. Later he claimed that he had been bullied. At first Asquith did the talking, warning that if George refused to give the guarantees he would immediately resign and fight an election on the cry of King and Peers against the People. When George walked away in disgust to the fireplace, he overheard Asquith say to Crewe: 'I can do nothing with him – you have a go.'[68]

What George especially minded about Asquith was 'his having brought Crewe with him'.[69] Lord Crewe in the opinion of King Edward was 'the only member of the cabinet who possesses [gentlemanlike] feelings'.[70] On this occasion those feelings were not in evidence. Crewe behaved as 'disgracefully' as Asquith did. They talked about the danger to the Crown, dragging in the bogey of the instability of foreign thrones – King Manuel of Portugal had abdicated the previous month. When the King said, 'I have been forced into this, and I should like the country to know it,' they refused to allow this and insisted that the guarantees must be kept secret.[71]

*   *   *

'Francis [Knollys] strongly advised me to take this course,' wrote George, 'and I think his advice is generally very sound. I only trust & pray he is right this time.'[72] The private secretaries were divided, however. Bigge believed that Knollys had given the King the wrong advice, and he wrote a memo, placing on record his opposition: 'I solemnly believe that a grave mistake has been made resulting from a dread . . . of danger to the Crown; whereas the real danger is to the position of the P.M.'[73]

There can be little doubt that Knollys betrayed his master. Reading through the file on the Parliament Bill at Windsor, Harold Nicolson wrote in his diary: 'It is quite evident that Knollys behaved very badly on that occasion and misled the King for his own party purposes.'[74] Knollys was a Liberal, and in this crisis he allowed his personal opinions to override his duty as private secretary to remain politically neutral.[75]

In 1910 Knollys was seventy-three; he had spent almost fifty years in the service of King Edward, and some thought that he had lost his nerve. The letter that Asquith's private secretary Vaughan Nash wrote, thanking Knollys for 'the incomparable services that you have rendered King and Country', makes plain that he had crossed the line of political neutrality: 'Mr Asquith is not an emotional man, but he spoke today after the cabinet with a degree of feeling which he rarely shows when he was dwelling on all that you had done.'[76] What Knollys had done was save Asquith's political skin.

George's biographers have argued that the only course available to him was to accept Asquith's advice. Kenneth Rose contended that to this end Knollys was justified in deceiving the King by concealing the information that Balfour was prepared to form a government. In his view, Knollys emerges from these tangled events as having shown 'more wisdom, more caution' than Bigge, whose advice to refuse the government's request would have triggered a political crisis.[77] As Esher wrote:

> There was only one possible and prudent course for a young monarch i.e. to abide strictly within the Constitution & to take the official advice of his responsible ministers. It was fortunate for him that F. Knollys was near him and that he had the good sense to take his advice.[78]

The knot that lies at the heart of this controversy concerns Asquith's advice to the King – whether or not the prime minister acted constitutionally in demanding hypothetical guarantees. Current thinking suggests that Asquith's request was dodgy. Vernon Bogdanor, a leading authority on the monarchy and the constitution, has argued that George was not obliged to give conditional guarantees. The King was entitled to refuse to commit himself in advance of an election and without yet knowing the form of the Parliament Bill.[79] By giving a hypothetical pledge to create peers *if* the government won the election and *if* the Lords threw out the Parliament Bill, George wrote a blank cheque which compromised his political neutrality. In other words, it was Bigge, not Knollys, who was right. In retrospect, Harold Nicolson considered that the whole episode was pointless. 'What was the point of extracting pledges from the King in advance of the election and then keeping them secret,' he asked. 'I simply do not understand it.'[80]

Those five days in November were the defining crisis of George's reign. For the rest of his life he considered that Asquith's treatment of him on 16 November was 'the dirtiest thing ever done'.[81] But at first George persuaded himself that he had acted correctly on that day. He told Godfrey-Faussett that 'he had made up his mind as to what was the right thing to do constitutionally & the best for the country & that he was going to stick to it'.[82] Buyer's remorse soon set in. In 1913, when he was given documents proving that Balfour had after all been willing to take office, he wrote a note for the file saying that these papers 'would undoubtedly have had an important bearing and influence upon my decisions with regard to Mr Asquith's request for guarantees on Nov 16th 1910'.[83] He told Archbishop Davidson in 1914 that if he had known about this, 'it would have changed the whole situation, for he would not have felt so helpless as he did when, against his will, he was forced by Asquith and Crewe to make the secret promise on which so much turned'.[84]

Twenty years after the event, in an interview with Crewe, the King reflected that what he ought to have said was: '"All right Mr Asquith – put everything on paper and I will give you my answer by 12 noon tomorrow."'[85] He added that 'if he had known as much about constitutional practice then as he had learned later, he would never have agreed'.[86]

There was a deeper lesson too. As Frank Mort has observed, the constitutional crisis was a catalyst for George's new style of monarchy. The moral of the crisis was that the King should never again allow himself to become involved with party politics. His private sympathies were robustly Tory, but so long as he did not allow his private opinions to influence his public duty this was not an issue. His role as monarch must be above party – to act as an arbitrator and to broker agreements. Asquith's attempt to trap him over the guarantees threatened to compromise his neutrality.[87] George especially resented the demand for secrecy. As he told Esher, 'I have never in my life done anything that I was ashamed to confess – and I have never been accustomed to conceal things'.[88] Being a decent, honourable man was essential to his style of monarchy. So was discretion, and the King tried to bite his tongue, not always with success. 'The King has improved very much in self-restraint,' noted Esher. 'He still talks a great deal, but with far more caution.'[89]

'Politics are so depressing I scarcely speak of them,' wrote May. 'George is much worried & anxious about it all, but scarcely mentions the subject to me, so I say nothing.'[90] The secret of the guarantees placed a strain on their relations. So did George's workload. He was so busy that May complained: 'I see him but little except at meals.'[91] He spent long hours at his desk; 'the work is very fatiguing for George, who being extremely conscientious & anxious to be au fait of everything, reads all that is sent him'.[92]

'Thank goodness the Civil List is settled, some of the speeches were most uncivil,' wrote May in August 1910.* 'The position [of monarch] is no bed of roses, & if one is not even allowed to keep up the position where would one be.'[93] In spite of the uncivil speeches, George was given a generous settlement. His income from the Civil List was fixed at £470,000. Of this, £110,000 went to the Privy Purse, the private expenditure of the King and Queen. The rest was earmarked for household salaries (£125,800), household expenses (£193,000), maintenance of Buckingham Palace (£20,000) and charity (£13,200). Various other payments such as the upkeep of other palaces and royal yachts brought the total received by the King from the state to £800,000 (£96 million in today's money), while £146,000 was paid in annuities to other royals.

Unlike King Edward, who had been asked to pay taxes, much to his annoyance, George did not pay tax on the Civil List. King Edward had paid £18,000 in tax; the new supertax, imposed by the Liberals in the People's Budget on very high incomes, would have pushed George's tax demand up to £25,000. When King Edward died, Francis Knollys had moved fast to strike a deal which ensured that the new king was not ensnared into paying tax as his father had been. A Treasury memo dated 8 May exempted the Civil List from tax in exchange for the king paying the costs of visiting heads of state.[94]

The surprising thing is that Chancellor of the Exchequer Lloyd George, the architect of the People's Budget and the scourge of the dukes, agreed the deal. In the House of Commons he argued that paying

---

*The Civil List was the money paid from public funds to support the monarch's position as head of state.

tax was a 'voluntary undertaking' on the part of the sovereign; but though this had been true of Queen Victoria, it was certainly not the case with Edward VII. Shortly after George became king, Lloyd George saw him and 'promised to do all he could to help H.M.'.[95] By lifting the hated income tax, Lloyd George perhaps hoped to win the King's support in the constitutional crisis.

Exempting the Civil List from tax ensured that the monarchy grew richer relative to its wealthy subjects, escaping scot-free from the high taxes of the First World War and after. Moreover, as Sir George Murray of the Treasury wrote, the King was 'a very careful person in money matters', and he ran a tight ship at court. This enabled him to make savings on the Civil List. Averaging £22,000 a year, this money was regularly transferred to the Privy Purse, forming the beginning of the monarch's private fortune.[96]

It helped that the royals seemed so normal. When Lloyd George stayed at Balmoral in 1910, he found the King 'a very jolly chap but thank God there's not much in his head. They're simple, very, very ordinary people.'[97] Asquith privately considered the King 'a nice little man with a good heart [who] tries to be just and open-minded'.[98] George was no celebrity. One day in October 1910 he walked for one-and-a-half miles in Hyde Park. He was recognised and people took off their hats, but no one followed or bothered him in any way.[99]

George's reputation for ordinariness was threatened by two rumours that circulated at the time of his accession. One story claimed that he drank. This slur on the abstemious monarch, who carefully controlled his alcohol intake, bore no relation to fact; it seems to have been inspired by his red shooter's face. Sir George Armstrong's newspaper the *People* offered £1,000 to anyone who could prove the King had ever been drunk.[100]

A more outlandish rumour alleged that George was a bigamist, married to an earlier wife by whom he had three children. In 1910 a republican paper called the *Liberator* which was published in Paris carried an article by an anarchist named Edward Mylius entitled 'Sanctified Bigamy'. This revived the tired old story that had first emerged when George became engaged to May – namely, that George had legally married the daughter of Admiral Sir Michael Culme-Seymour, also named May, while serving in Malta in 1890. (See above, page 75.)[101] A copy of the paper was sent to every MP.

George told his mother in 1911 that when the 'odious lie' had started twenty years before, 'I fully made up my mind that if I ever did get the opportunity I would have it officially & publicly disproved. Therefore when the wretched creature Mylius put himself in the position to be arrested, I urged his arrest.'[102] The government law officers supported him, and the home secretary, Winston Churchill, entered enthusiastically into the case, preparing the 'legal tackle' for Mylius's prosecution.[103] Mylius was arrested on a charge of criminal libel. At the trial in February 1911 Culme-Seymour testified that he had not been posted to Malta until 1893, and his daughter claimed not to have met George between 1879, when she was eight, and 1898. Mylius insisted on defending himself, and demanded unsuccessfully – and unconstitutionally – that the King should appear in the witness box. He was sentenced to twelve months' imprisonment; and George issued a statement confirming that he had only ever been married to Queen Mary.

In prosecuting Mylius the government was on shaky ground. Sir John Simon, the solicitor general, wrote: 'If Mylius, instead of justifying, had pleaded guilty, and explained that he was only reporting what thousands of respectable people had said for years without being prosecuted for it, we could never have established the falsity of the lie so effectively.'[104] One recent legal commentator has argued that the legal process in the case was constructed to secure a particular outcome and vindicate the King, and that it arguably subverted the interests of justice. There was no filtering process, no preliminary hearing before the case was heard by the lord chief justice. 'As an exercise of the Attorney General's powers, it was arguably a prosecution that focussed inappropriately on the settling of a personal dispute between the monarch and one of his subjects.'[105] The trial was ignored in legal reports of the time. Mylius himself was determined to be prosecuted and become a martyr for the republican cause. As for the King, he got what he wanted: a fast-track process to vindicate his honour.

The bigamist rumour had been scotched, and no one now questioned George's fidelity to his wife. To fashionable London the verdict in the Mylius case came as a disappointment. It proved that the King was dull.[106]

Nor was the new king a confident performer. The opening of Parliament on 6 February 1911 was for George 'the most terrible ordeal I have ever been through'. He told his mother: 'I was horribly nervous besides feeling so sad thinking of the many times we had seen you & beloved Papa do it that I nearly broke down. The House of Lords was crammed with people & so many I knew which made it worse.'[107]

CHAPTER 13

Constitutional Monarch

1911

Coronation Day, 22 June 1911, was overcast and cloudy, noted George, with 'slight showers & a strongish cool breeze'.[1] The weather suited his mood. At 10.30, looking 'a little pale', he left Buckingham Palace with May, riding in the uncomfortable coronation coach drawn by eight cream horses.[2] They jolted in procession past the Victoria Memorial, which had been unveiled only a few weeks earlier. The ceremonial route projected by King Edward and designed by Aston Webb, which led down The Mall and through the newly built Admiralty Arch, had been finished in the nick of time.[3]

Eight thousand people had been waiting in Westminster Abbey since 7.30 that morning. George's coronation was considered superior in pageantry and ceremonial to his father's in 1902, though it lacked the emotional drama and there was less sense of this marking the end of an era as Queen Victoria's death had done.[4] One significant innovation went unnoticed: the veteran photographer Sir Benjamin Stone MP, by permission of the King, took photographs of the ceremony, though not of the religious parts. On the insistence of the Archbishop of Canterbury, Randall Davidson, he was placed in the abbey in 'a position absolutely concealed'.[5]

Which crown the King should be crowned with was a question upon which the archbishop had strong views. St Edward's Crown, which weighed five pounds, was the proper crown; it had been used in every coronation except that of 1902, when Edward VII rejected it in favour of a lighter model. George complied with Davidson's advice.[6] *The Times* noted that after the crowning George 'wore a very serious expression and looked somewhat tired'.[7] Before he emerged from the abbey, he had changed out of his coronation robes in the retiring room behind the altar, donning an immense purple velvet train trimmed with ermine and, in accordance with tradition, he exchanged St Edward's Crown for the Imperial State Crown.

George's account of the day was, in Harold Nicolson's phrase, 'disconcertingly restrained', but he did admit that 'Darling May looked lovely & it was indeed a comfort to me to have her by my side, as she has been ever to me during these last 18 years'.[8] May allowed her feelings to show.[9] As she told Aunt Augusta afterwards, 'for me, who love tradition & the past, and who am English from top to toe [*sic*], the service was a very real solemn thing & appealed to my feelings more than I can express'.[10] When her crown was placed upon her head, she seemed 'much moved, and she was evidently engaged in silent prayer'.[11]

At the moment the Queen was crowned, as Vita Sackville-West recounted in *The Edwardians*, the peeresses put on their coronets 'in a single gesture of exquisite beauty, their white arms rising with a sound like the rushing of birds' wings and a proud arching like the arching of the neck of a swan'. Then out came the mirrors as the ladies furtively adjusted their headgear, and the dowagers looking down from the galleries above tut-tutted. 'In their day, they said, ladies were not in the habit of producing mirrors in public. It was easy to see, they said, that the reign of Edward the Seventh was over and the days of decent behaviour ended.'[12]

The royal children travelled in a coach in the procession with no adult in charge. On their return from the abbey in the coach, to the delight of the crowds, a stand-up fight broke out between the two kilted princes, Henry (aged eleven) and George (eight), the future Duke of Kent. 'The efforts of [the fourteen-year-old] Princess Mary to mollify the combatants were sincere but ineffectual,' wrote Lord Balcarres, the Conservative chief whip, 'and during the strife she nearly had her sweet coronet knocked off!'[13]

George and May returned to Buckingham Palace in the state coach at twelve minutes to three. At three minutes to three the King and Queen appeared on the balcony – two miniature figures, the white of their ermine robes standing out against the ugly, soot-blackened east front of Buckingham Palace. This was the climax, the moment when (said *The Times*) 'popular emotion was most deeply stirred'.[14] A great roar of loyalty and affection burst from the crowd gathered outside; the empire troops lining the railings waved their rifles and the officers brandished their swords. The magic lasted a mere three minutes. As Big Ben struck three, the royal couple retired. That was the end of the balcony appearance. George and May were photographed in their robes and crowns by the royal photographer Downey and, after lunch, George 'worked all the afternoon with Bigge & others answering telegrams & letters of which I have had hundreds'.[15]

As Princess of Wales, May's style of dress and taste in jewels had been unformed and uninspired. She followed her glamorous, fashion-conscious mother-in-law, wearing pale, tailored dresses and pale jewels. An eleven-strand pearl choker linked with diamonds enclosed the princess's neck, and on ceremonial occasions she wore a pearl and diamond tiara.[16] Unlike Alix, May was no creature of fashion, but she clearly understood the need to project an image of majesty. By 1911 she had evolved her own style: imperial, grandiose, unchanging. No one else dressed like Queen Mary. There exists a list in her own hand of the fifty dresses which she ordered for the coronation summer. It was worse than getting married. 'My tiresome trousseau of clothes ... has meant endless trying on,' she complained.[17] Chief dressmaker to the Queen was Miss Rossiter of Reville & Rossiter, the holders of the royal warrant. Most of the Queen's Rossiter gowns were in pastel colours – pink, yellow, mauve and white. As her niece Princess Arthur of Connaught remarked, 'she had *no eye* for colour; always liked pale colours as she hated anything gloomy'.[18]*

The Queen's waist on her Coronation gown measured twenty-seven inches.[19] This was achieved with the help of stays; she was statuesque rather than thin. She took little exercise. When she complained that Buckingham Palace was 'so straggly, such distances to go & so fatiguing', George sharply replied: 'It is good exercise for you as you never walk a yard in London.'[20] Frightened of becoming fat like her mother, May ate very little.[21] She was tall, probably about five feet nine inches, and her back was ramrod straight.† The slender waist accentuated her substantial bust, making her body shape distinctly top-heavy.[22] Often cut with a low, square neck, the Queen's gowns were designed to display the magnificent jewels which she wore on her capacious bosom. Wits dubbed her 'Soutien George', a pun on the French for bra (*soutiengorge*) and her support for her husband.

Since becoming queen, May had added considerably to her collection of bling. She acquired all the Crown jewellery, once Alix had been persuaded to part with it. George 'kindly' gave her the Garter on his birthday in 1910, and on official occasions she was rarely seen without the blue ribbon and diamond star.[23] After the opening of Parliament in 1911, she wrote: 'What I liked best was wearing Grandmama's Crown, and the ribbon, star & badge of the Garter.'[24]

---

*Queen Mary's spending on dresses for the coronation season totalled £1,333, which equates to over £150,000 at today's prices.

†This was the opinion of Mrs Hunt, who knew her when she was young. She recalled: 'I am 5ft 10½, and I could wear her dresses, but the bodices had to be taken in' (Pope 202/3, note by Pope-Hennessy re Mrs Hunt, n.d.). Queen Mary's dresses also fitted Maggie Wyndham perfectly, 'except of course for taking them in at the chest and waist', and she was five feet six or seven inches; but this was towards the end of the Queen's life, when she perhaps had lost height (James Pope-Hennessy, *The Quest for Queen Mary*, ed. Hugo Vickers (Zuleika, 2018), p. 119). According to Kenneth Rose, Queen Mary was five feet six inches (*King George V*, p. 79).

She inherited from Edward VII a 94.8-carat diamond known as Cullinan III. This was the third of the stones cut from the Cullinan diamond, the largest rough diamond ever known. Weighing one pound six ounces (3,106 carats), it was found in the Cullinan mine and presented to Edward VII in 1907 by the Transvaal government. The two largest stones cut from the rough gem, Cullinan I and II, were known as the Stars of Africa and became part of the Crown Jewels. On 28 June 1910 the South African high commissioner, Sir Richard Solomon, presented May with 'some beautiful diamonds in the name of the Gov & people of S. Africa in memory of the inauguration of the Union'.[25]* These were the rest of the Cullinan stones, six large brilliants and ninety-six smaller diamonds. Known today as 'Granny's chips', the diamond brooches were so heavy that May needed to have her gowns reinforced with buckram.

When full mourning for Edward VII ended in May 1911, Queen Mary began to keep a book entitled 'The Gowns and Jewels Worn by Her Majesty at Important Functions'. In this leather-bound volume stamped with ostrich feathers one of her ladies itemised Her Majesty's toilette on formal occasions. The book forms an audit of royal dressing, cataloguing her self-fashioning as queen. The jewels and orders that she wore are recorded precisely and in greater detail than the gowns. This was a queen who measured her self-worth in diamonds, for whom the semiotics and dynastic narrative of jewellery mattered far more than the ephemeral, sexualised world of fashion.

For her coronation the Queen wore:

> White satin gown, hand embrd [*sic*] in gold with design of rose shamrock & thistle, border embrd with the lotus flowers & Star of India in centre front at bottom of skirt.
>
> Robe of purple velvet lined ermine & embrd national emblematic design, with M & Crown at end of train, deep cape of ermine finished with gold.[26]

The satin gown was made by Miss Rossiter and cost £25. The gold embroidery of national symbols – English rose, Irish shamrock, Scottish thistle (where were the Welsh?) – costing £200 was executed by Princess Louise's Ladies' Work Society, her charity for middle-class women who had fallen on hard times.[27]

---

*In the wake of the Boer War, the four British and Dutch colonies were brought together in the Union of South Africa in 1910, becoming a self-governing dominion. The inauguration took place on 31 May.

Here are the jewels which Queen Mary wore that day:

Collar formed of rows of diamonds with large row under.
    Diamond Cockade arranged with drops to form stomacher, with four diamond bow brooches under the pearl drops.*
    South African pendant brooches on sleeves of gown.
    Diamond bracelets with blue enamel clasps, with VA in diamonds on clasps.[28]

Encased in diamonds and ermine, wearing some of the most valuable diamonds in the world pinned to her sleeves, Queen Mary was a living icon of empire.

George's attempts to control his image were less happy. The Philatelist King had 'looked forward to producing a Stamp that would rank as one of the finest in Europe' in time for the coronation.[29] On his instructions, the head was a three-quarter-face photograph by Downey. None of the designs for the frame of the stamp produced by the Post Office pleased the King, and at his request the Australian sculptor Bertram Mackennal was commissioned to do the work.[30] Mackennal had designed the King's head on the coinage for the new reign, but he had never designed a stamp. His drawing needed so many alterations that the King was 'quite in despair' about the stamps.[31] To make matters worse, the production was botched. De La Rue, who had printed British stamps for over fifty years, lost their contract, and the new stamps were produced by the Royal Mint, who had neither expertise nor experience. The result was a truly 'dreadful' set of stamps.[32] *The Times* complained that the diminutive portrait of the King was 'poor and unflattering and lacks the fine execution which the public has been led to expect'.[33]
    George was mortified. He wrote formally through Ponsonby to rebuke the postmaster general, Herbert Samuel.

It was a great disappointment to him that the new stamps have been such a failure ... and a stamp totally unworthy of this country has been produced ... [which] has been received with loud abuse in the United Kingdom and judging by the letters addressed to His Majesty with contempt abroad.[34]

---

*A stomacher is a triangular panel that fills the front opening of a woman's gown. The Diamond Cockade was originally a clasp for a cloak, which was altered by Queen Alexandra to form a very large brooch; she wore it at her coronation.

In private George complained that the stamps made him look like 'a stuffed monkey'.[35]

George himself was partly to blame for the fiasco. The 'Downey Head', as it came to be known, was not a flattering likeness, showing the King with bulging eyes and thinning, short-cropped hair. George's constant meddling, and his insistence on a three-quarter head which was hard to reproduce, did harm. Not until the Downey Head was replaced by the 'Profile Head', produced by Mackennal from a statue in 1913, did George produce a stamp that did him justice.

The coronation was followed by brief state visits to Ireland, Wales and Scotland. At Carnarvon Castle, David, now seventeen, was invested as Prince of Wales. This was an invented tradition, suggested by Lloyd George as a gesture to please the Welsh. Neither George nor his father had been invested as Prince of Wales; not for 300 years had the ceremony taken place. At first David rebelled at wearing the 'preposterous rig' of purple velvet robe edged with ermine and white satin breeches. A 'family blow-up' took place.[36] On the day, David 'played his part to perfection' according to May, who thought he 'looked so nice in his purple & miniver robe & gold coronet'.[37] He knelt before his father, and George placed a mantle on his shoulders, a coronet on his head, a ring on his finger and a gold rod in his hand, raised him up and kissed him on both cheeks.

Lord Esher thought David was 'backward but sweet', a 'darling boy' with angelic good looks who was always anxious to please.[38] Since 1909 David had been at Dartmouth naval college, where he was about to be joined by Bertie.* David left without completing the course in order to prepare for the coronation summer. On his arrival at Buckingham Palace, George took him for a walk round the garden and warned him that henceforth all eyes would be upon him.[39] 'He has come on capitally lately, which is a great pleasure to us,' wrote May.[40] At the coronation, George 'nearly broke down' when David did homage to him: 'it reminded me so much of when I did the same thing to beloved Papa, he did it so well'.[41] The relationship between father and son seemed set to follow that of George and *his* father, between whom (said May) 'no cross word had <u>ever</u> passed'.[42]

Early in 1911 a particularly virulent epidemic of measles had broken out at Dartmouth, and more than eighty boys were infected. David and

---

*In spite of coming 68th out of 68 in the entrance exam, Prince Bertie had earlier been awarded a place at junior college at Osborne.

Bertie were kept in isolation in the captain's house, but they too came out in spots. According to David, writing his autobiography later, this was their second attack of what he called 'measles and mumps'.[43] Mumps may have caused David to be infertile. People who knew him believed he 'had something wrong with his gland', which 'went wrong' on reaching puberty.[44] Some have speculated that this was one of the reasons for David's later rebellion and estrangement from his family. For now, however, he won golden opinions. 'What a dear David is, everyone likes him so much,' his aunt Maud, Queen of Norway, wrote to May from Appleton, her house on the Sandringham estate. 'He has such good manners too, all the ladies were talking about it here, & I thought I must tell you.'[45]

Johnnie, now five and a half, was a worry. Aged four, he had been diagnosed with epilepsy. In 1911 the fits became more frequent, and the royal doctors were consulted. Laking and Treves attributed the little boy's deterioration to a change of medication – the doctors had ceased to prescribe the anti-epileptic drug bromide. They begged May not to become despondent, assuring her that he would grow out of his illness and be quite well by the time he was seven. May was not convinced. 'I feel he has got so much worse during the last 3 months that the prospect is not very encouraging,' she wrote. 'It certainly is very sad.'[46] His illness was intermittent. He seems to have suffered from autism as well as epilepsy, and he talked very little, especially when he had attacks. In August 1911 May reported that he 'was looking so well, talked more & up till 2 days ago had not had an attack for 7 weeks. He had 2 slight attacks Wedy & 1 yesterday but Treves told me we could not expect him to lose them all at once.'[47] That summer at Balmoral Johnnie stayed with Lala at Altnaguisach, one of Queen Victoria's secret hideaways, where he could be 'alone & quiet'; this was thought to be better for him than a house full of people.[48]

Some have claimed that Johnnie was kept out of public view because his parents refused to admit any imperfection in the royal blood. He spent his childhood in seclusion at York Cottage, but so did the other royal children. When he was well he often played with Prince Olav, the future king of Norway, his first cousin, staying at Appleton.[49] Johnnie's illness was a cause of distress. 'It is very sad for the little boy & makes me very unhappy,' wrote George.[50] But it wasn't a source of shame, and no one whispered about madness in the family.

George returned from Holyrood, the last stage of his royal tour, on 21 July to find London sweltering in a heatwave and a political storm building over the Parliament Bill. The bill had passed the House of

Commons in May, and in July the Lords made wrecking amendments, altering its whole nature. The Cabinet therefore warned the King that the time had come for him to create Liberal peers to order to break the deadlock and ensure the passing of the bill, in accordance with the November pledges. Here is George's account of 22 July, the day after he returned from Scotland, when the temperature was ninety-three degrees in the shade:

> Spent a very harassing & strenuous day on account of the political crisis. Directly after breakfast had a long talk with Francis [Knollys] & Bigge about the situation. At 11.30 I received the Prime Minister & I only promised to allow him to create a sufficient number of Peers, in event of House of Lords throwing out Parlt Bill, to pass the bill & no more. All this worries me very much & I fear the Unionists will be sore, but I have only acted constitutionally as General Election at the present moment is out of the question. I spent an hour with the dentist.[51]

A creation of peers, especially a 'swamping' creation of 350 or more, was the thing above all that George was determined to avoid.* As he later made clear, 'if he had had to create 400 new peers, he would never have held up his head again'.[52] He worried that the Unionists would see the guarantees as a stab in the back – a betrayal of the aristocracy by the monarch in league with the Liberals.

George's first move was to inform the opposition leaders of the guarantees. On 19 July Knollys, with Asquith's consent, told Balfour of the King's promise to create peers. The secret had been extraordinarily well kept, and the news came as a bombshell to the Unionist leaders. The Marquess of Lansdowne, the Unionist leader in the Lords, held a meeting and advised the Unionist peers to abstain, thus giving the Liberal peers a free run and allowing the bill to pass. The so-called Diehards, led by the octogenarian Earl of Halsbury and the Earl of Selborne, rebelled and urged resistance to the bitter end. From this point on the fight was an internal one within the Unionist bloc between Diehards, or 'ditchers', and 'hedgers'.

The political arithmetic in the House of Lords was stark. The eighty or so Liberal peers were hugely outnumbered by the growing band of Diehard rebels. The only way to save the King's face and prevent the creation of peers was to persuade some Unionist lords to vote for the government and not just abstain. This was what George and Bigge – newly created

---

*Asquith had already drawn up a list of 249 Liberal nominees who he proposed should be made peers.

Lord Stamfordham in the Coronation Honours – now endeavoured to do. It was a risky business. As Lord Curzon warned, pressure brought by the King personally on peers would 'raise the cry of unfair Court influence' – a cry that had not been heard since the Hanoverians.[53]

'The King has at present a rage for seeing people about the crisis,' Knollys told Asquith on 23 July.[54] Archbishop Davidson spent an hour and a half with the King that afternoon. Davidson was a worldly prelate who had been close to both Queen Victoria and Edward VII, and he boasted of being in George's 'personal confidence'.[55] He found George 'much distraught ... over-strained, and even excited ... He evidently felt very deeply the criticism which is rife about his action in promising to create peers.' Davidson thought the King was 'rather out of his depth'.[56] He was 'exceedingly strong' on the mischief made by the Halsbury group, and he hoped that enough Unionist peers would vote with the government rather than force a creation. It was clear to Davidson that the King wanted him to act as his emissary in this project.

Over the next few days, Stamfordham was in constant communication with Davidson. On behalf of the King, he urged the archbishop to see Lord Lansdowne and ask him to vote for the Parliament Bill. Though Lansdowne demurred, he admitted that he would be 'very glad' if some Unionists voted with the government.[57] At dinner at Lambeth Palace, Stamfordham asked Davidson if he could induce the twenty-six bishops with seats in the House of Lords to vote for the bill.

George was not alone in canvassing Unionist peers to vote with the government. The leader of the pro-bill 'hedger' peers was Lord Curzon. Convinced that a House of Lords with reduced powers was preferable to a flooding creation, Curzon campaigned to defeat the Diehards. The King sent a message of approval.[58] Stamfordham wrote to Lord Minto, ex-viceroy of India, begging him to come down from Scotland and vote for the bill 'much as we all hate it' to prevent the 'disastrous' creation of peers.[59] The King saw Lord St Aldwyn and noted: 'He is going to help me all he can to prevent these peers being made.'[60]

Lord Rosebery, the former Liberal prime minister who had drifted away from his party, was asked to lunch alone with the King and Queen at Buckingham Palace on 26 July. The King reminded Rosebery of the promise he had once made to render any service in his power.

'What can I do?' asked Rosebery. 'You must speak and vote for the bill.' Rosebery threw up his hands and said 'I cannot do that. I should be stultified.' The King said not another word and passed to other topics ... Next day he had a short note from Rosebery to say he would do what the King wished.[61]

Having made his preparations, George departed for Cowes on 29 July. He was conspicuously absent from London, visiting his mother at Sandringham, on 9 August, the first day of the crucial House of Lords debate, when the temperature in London reached a record-breaking 100 degrees.

In the final debate on 10 August the result was uncertain right up until the division took place. The House of Lords was as hot as an oven, and Lord Midleton, one of the leaders of the pro-bill peers, watched Curzon's 'usually immaculate collar gradually dissolving into a shapeless mass'.[62] Archbishop Davidson was undecided at dinner time, but after speaking to Stamfordham and spending ten minutes' quiet in his room, he declared his support for the bill.[63] His speech 'raised the temperature' according to *The Times*, and persuaded twelve bishops to follow him into the government lobby.[64] At 7 p.m. Rosebery told Davidson that he wouldn't vote against the bill – 'it would be crucifixion to do so'.[65] At dinner he was still undecided. He then disappeared. He was discovered in a club and dragged off to the Lords where he made a short speech which was reckoned to have persuaded twenty Unionist peers to follow him in voting for the bill.[66]

The bill passed by 131 to 114. Eighty-one Liberal peers joined thirteen bishops and thirty-seven Unionist 'rats' to give the government a majority of seventeen. As David Gilmour wrote, 'without the work of Curzon, Midleton and (through Stamfordham) the King, there would not have been enough of them to win'.[67]

On the night of the vote, the King and Queen dined alone at Buckingham Palace. George was 'very anxious', and elaborate arrangements had been made to ensure that he received the result of the division within minutes. In the House of Lords, Stamfordham waited outside the chamber near the telephone room ready to phone through the result. At the Palace a footman was primed to pass on the message. After the vote Godfrey-Faussett happened to hear a footman remarking that the bill had passed, and when he went to see the King about something, he said: 'I am so thankful, Sir.' 'What for?' asked George. It turned out that somehow Stamfordham's message had still not reached the King, and Godfrey was the first to bring the news. 'The Queen jumped off the sofa' and the King's 'relief was immense'.[68] He wrote in his diary that night: 'I am spared any further humiliation by a creation of peers. Rosebery saved the situation by voting for the Govt & 20 Unionist peers joined him ... Bigge & Francis have indeed worked hard for this result.'[69]

The Parliament Bill crisis split the Unionists, destroyed Balfour's leadership, blasted Curzon's political career and compromised Lansdowne's leadership of the Unionist peers, but it left the monarchy stronger. The 'rats' were excoriated and Curzon was vilified, but nothing was said of the role of the King in swinging the vote, which remained a closely guarded secret. Only now, with the discovery of Archbishop Davidson's detailed narrative of events, can the full picture of George's involvement be revealed. Far from being a cipher sovereign, George emerges as a smart political player, prepared to take risks and make political interventions without informing or consulting the prime minister. But George's intervention in high politics was an exercise in damage limitation, a one-off made necessary by the November pledges. Never again did the King use his influence in Parliament in this fashion.

The day after the vote, George travelled north to shoot grouse at Studley Royal with the de Greys and then on to Bolton Abbey as a guest of the Duke of Devonshire. He shot with exceptional accuracy. Over seven days he averaged 207 birds a day, and once he killed nineteen birds out of one pack with twenty-three cartridges.[70] This was a man invigorated by success.

He wrote to May expressing his 'everlasting gratitude':

The strain of the last few months has been very great with this ghastly political crisis hanging over my head, the relief that the bill has passed is intense & that the odious necessity of the creation of Peers is over. If they had been made I should never have been the same again, the humiliation would have been so great.[71]

'I am glad you wrote as you did,' May replied, 'because I was afraid we were beginning to drift.'[72] Released from the burden of secrecy over the guarantees, George assured May of his wish to tell her everything: 'Sometimes I am so tired after having talked to people all day that I have no time or forget to tell you things, but it is not because I don't want to.'[73] May depended entirely on George for access to inside information about politics, and when he was away or too busy to talk she felt 'out of it all' and vulnerable.[74] At Balmoral that autumn, Esher talked politics with the Queen. 'She knows much more about our current politics than she did. I think the King is less reserved with her than he was.'[75]

May later considered that becoming queen had made her lose her shyness. Annotating John Gore's life of George V in proof, she wrote 'Untrue' beside a passage about her shyness: 'I used to be rather shy but after the King succeeded and when one shared the central figure with the King this feeling vanished.'[76] The phrase about sharing the central figure is revealing. Lady Airlie, May's oldest and not uncritical friend, observed a change in May after she became queen. She was proud and more self-confident; but 'she could never forget that her husband was now the Sovereign; her devotion to the monarchy demanded the sacrifice of much of her personal happiness'.[77] That sublimation to monarchy was reinforced, in Lady Airlie's view, by May's unassertive, early Victorian attitude towards her husband, whom she never contradicted or defied, even in matters of dress.

George swore that he would never forgive the government for all the worry and anxiety that they had caused him. But a few days later, when a railway strike threatened to cause a national emergency, and troops were moved to London and Parliament was summoned, George gave ministers all the support he could. He swallowed his personal opinions and volunteered to act in a public role. Kept fully informed by Winston Churchill, he telegraphed the prime minister offering to come to London (this was refused). From Bolton Abbey he wrote to May: 'Ever since church I have been sending off telegrams to Lloyd George, Churchill & [Sydney] Buxton [president of the Board of Trade] to congratulate them on the happy termination of what was fast becoming a terrible calamity.' He told her: 'I have indeed been terribly worried & most anxious & have been receiving telegrams & messages all day & well into the night. I did not at all feel happy shooting while this serious state of affairs existed.'[78]

When Lloyd George stayed at Balmoral as minister in attendance in September, he declared himself disgusted by the King's private views. 'The whole atmosphere reeks with Toryism,' he wrote. 'The King is hostile to the bone to all who are working to lift the workmen out of the mire. So is the Queen.'[79] Not surprisingly, Lloyd George made a less good impression than he had the previous year. When Churchill took his place in the minister's room, he found that Lloyd George had 'electrified' Their Majesties by declaring that it would be a pity if war didn't come immediately. Churchill, whom George had heartily disliked before he became king, was now on cordial terms with the sovereign. 'The King talks much to me about affairs,' he wrote. 'Everyone is most civil & friendly & life is vy quiet & easy . . . There is very little formality & much comfort.'[80]

In July 1911 the German government sent a gunboat named the *Panther* to the Moroccan port of Agadir, posing a threat to French interests in Morocco and triggering a diplomatic crisis. By making a show of strength over Morocco, the Germans hoped to intimidate the French and drive a wedge between France and Britain, who had been allies since the formation of the *entente cordiale* in 1904. George was kept informed throughout, and he worried that the negotiations between France and Germany over Morocco would fail, in which case 'we shall probably propose a conference which however may be refused by Germany, then there would be nothing more to be done'. He told May: 'It is a distinctly anxious time, & we must be prepared for every emergency, but a European war coming at a time like this would indeed be a ghastly catastrophe. Of course you must consider all this as absolutely secret.'[81]

As George's letter shows, Europe seemed on the brink of war. In the end, the Germans backed down and recognised French interests in Morocco in exchange for compensation in the French Congo. The Agadir crisis revealed a Europe divided into two armed camps – on the one hand, the Central Powers of Germany and Austria-Hungary, led by the loose cannon William II, and on the other the Triple Entente of Britain, France and Russia.

The unstable European situation threatened to jeopardise King George's next plan: a state visit to India. The Queen was not enthusiastic about the tour. She worried about leaving home when the Agadir crisis threatened war. 'I wish we were not going just now (tho' I do not say so),' she wrote to her aunt, 'when the world is in such a state of unrest, it gives me a feeling of being so unsafe.'[82]

On 11 November 1911 George and May, accompanied by their suites and by three cows from Windsor, embarked on a voyage to India. They sailed in a new, luxurious P&O liner named the *Medina*. The spacious cabins of the King and Queen were superbly fitted up, but unfortunately they were towards the front of the ship. When a high gale blew in the Bay of Biscay, May was horribly seasick and so was George, though he hadn't been ill for years. As the ship pitched and rolled, the 'poor Queen' was carried on a stretcher to her rough-weather cabin amidships where the motion was less violent.[83] Once they reached calm seas George spent the days reading on deck and listening to the band which played morning and afternoon, enjoying 'the first real rest I have had for 1½ years'.[84]

The state visit to India was George's idea. Back in August 1910 he had tried to work out what he aimed to achieve during his reign. He told Esher that 'he meant to do for the Empire what King Edward did for the peace of Europe'.[85] He proposed to attend the 1911 Coronation Durbar and crown himself at Delhi. He insisted that going to Delhi was no use unless he could make an important announcement. The boon that he intended to bestow upon his Indian subjects was sensational: he proposed to announce the cancellation of Curzon's unpopular 1905 partition of Bengal. This had divided Bengal into a predominantly Muslim East Bengal and a Hindu West Bengal, thus reducing the power of the British-educated middle-class Hindu Bengalis, the dominant force in the province before partition. It led to riots, boycotts of British goods and terrorism. Reversing the partition was a concession to the Hindus, and to balance this it was proposed to transfer the capital of India from Calcutta to Delhi. Delhi was the ancient capital of the Muslim Moghul emperors, and the move of the capital was intended to appease the Muslims, compensating them for the loss of East Bengal.

Lord Hardinge, the viceroy, is usually credited with the decision to move the capital to Delhi. He certainly approved and enabled it. George claimed, however, that he had suggested the idea to Hardinge in October 1910. Hardinge's initial reaction was negative, but in July 1911 he composed a dispatch proposing the scheme. 'It therefore appears,' wrote Esher, 'that the policy was really the King's.'[86]

The Cabinet were 'very uneasy' about the Indian trip.[87] They grumbled about the King spending so long out of the country. They grumbled even more about the decision to move the capital. The creation of a new city involved significant expense and implied a commitment to the permanence of British rule which many Liberals resisted. The decision, taken in secret by the viceroy, the India secretary, Lord Crewe, and the monarch, was 'undemocratic', as Esher observed. 'There was not much deliberation or consultation, and not much chance given to hear what men with much experience and knowledge had to say.'[88] The Cabinet was not informed until the day that the King sailed for India.

Evie, Duchess of Devonshire, mistress of the robes, accompanied the royals on the *Medina*. Sitting with the Queen all day on deck, she got to know her very well and found her 'a great dear'. 'She never lets herself go before more than one person, which is what makes people think her so formal.'[89] The duchess thought the King neglected his consort: 'I can't help feeling that in his efforts to have a strong and independent character [George] has not been quite so nice to her since he became King. I hope I am wrong but she strikes me as rather lonely sometimes.'[90] The duchess noted that the journey brought the royals together: 'She occasionally lets herself be a little bit demonstrative with him – not quite sure whether he will like it or not. I think he really does only he is afraid to show it.'[91]

George and May made their state entry into Delhi on 7 December. They were met by chilly, unfriendly crowds. John Fortescue, the royal

Eddy in a basket, left, and George as a baby on the right: 'the children of the country.' Alexandra holds the pony.

Left: 'My darling little Georgie boy,' here aged about ten.

Right: The Wales children. The three sisters are, from left to right, Louise (b. 1867), Maud (b. 1869) and Victoria (b. 1868). Queen Victoria called them 'poor little fairies,' but others thought them a rough, 'knock-about family.'

The Waleses. Standing are Eddy, Louise (who married the Duke of Fife), Alexandra, Maud (who married the King of Norway) and Bertie. Victoria (who never married) sits next to George. Alexandra looks younger than her daughters.

Prince George became a naval lieutenant with two gold rings on his cuffs in 1885 aged twenty. He grew a beard, the bristles hedging round his 'pretty red lips.'

Left: Eddy in 'collars and cuffs,' wearing the exaggerated trimmings for which he was notorious.

Right: Engagement photo of Eddy and May of Teck. This was an arranged marriage, and May accepted Eddy's proposal at once, but she soon had second thoughts about taking him on. His death six weeks later would put an end to the engagement.

The Duchess of Teck and her children. Frank (b. 1870) stands behind Adolphus (Dolly, b. 1868). Alexander George (Alge, b. 1874), the youngest, has his arm around his mother. May sits upright and detached.

The wedding of George and May in the Chapel Royal, St James's Palace by the Danish artist Tuxen. The Duchess of Teck, seated front right, wearing a blue velvet gown, complained that there was 'only a back or side view of my lovely person!'

Wedding-day photo. 'My husband was not in love with me when we married,' Queen Mary later said. This too was an arranged marriage, but it worked.

George at Sandringham with his children in 1902. 'I shall soon have a regiment not a family,' he joked. Left to right: Albert (Bertie), Mary, Edward (David), and Henry (Harry).

Arthur Bigge, later Lord Stamfordham, served George as private secretary from 1901 until his death aged eighty-one in 1931. He taught George how to be king.

York Cottage, Sandringham, where George lived for thirty-three years. 'Until you have seen York Cottage you will never understand my father,' said the Duke of Windsor.

King George shooting grouse. Note his straight left arm: George was reckoned to be the sixth best shot in the country, and he always mounted his gun in this unorthodox fashion. His loader can just be seen, hiding from the grouse.

'Dearest Nicky' arm in arm with cousin Georgie in 1893. Which is which?

The last meeting of the cousins George and Nicky in Berlin, 1913. George wears the white uniform of the Prussian regiment of which his cousin William had made him colonel-in-chief.

Left: Four generations: Edward, George and Queen Victoria with newest great-grandson David. Not such a secure succession as they might have imagined.

Right: Father and son. George's relationship with his father was conflicted. He admired him, but he was frightened of him.

Shooting party at Sandringham. Left to right: Queen Alexandra, King Edward VII, Prince Harry, Princess Mary, David, May (Princess of Wales), Prince Albert (Bertie) and George (Prince of Wales).

librarian, who accompanied the suite as historian of the tour, claimed that the crowds were silent because they couldn't see the King.[92] George chose to ride a horse instead of the traditional elephant because he thought it would make him more visible. This was a mistake. The crowds expected the King-Emperor to process seated in an elephant howdah, and they failed to spot the small figure in field marshal's uniform riding an insignificant horse and wearing a white helmet which concealed his face. The Queen followed him in an open landau with a gorgeous golden fan and a crimson and gold umbrella held over her, and she was instantly recognisable as an empress. Many thought that she had left the King behind. May was in her element. 'It is marvellous to me being in India again,' she wrote later that day. 'I am so glad I came.'[93]

At the Delhi Durbar on 12 December, George didn't crown himself, as this posed complicated questions about undergoing a second coronation in a non-Christian country. Instead he wore a crown. It was a new crown, specially created, as the Imperial State Crown was prohibited by law from leaving Britain. Manufactured by Garrard, the Imperial Crown of India sparkled with 6,000 diamonds and cost £60,000 (£6.7 million in today's money), paid for by the government of India. It was worn only once.

May left the Crown Jewels behind, as they too were not allowed to be taken out of the realm. Instead, she brought her emeralds. Her dress book lists the jewellery that she wore: 'Emerald & diamond diadem, diamond collar, emerald & diamond necklace under with new India necklace of emeralds between, large carved emerald brooch'.[94] The new Indian necklace of emeralds and the large carved emerald brooch had been given to the Queen by the ladies of India. The emerald and diamond necklace which she wore included the Cambridge emeralds, which had been retrieved from Frank's mistress Nellie Kilmorey in the nick of time. 'Mama's Emeralds appearing there amused & pleased me,' wrote Aunt Augusta. 'What would she have said to her Grandchild's Imperial glory? In which I so rejoice.'[95]

The Indian princes, resplendent in their gorgeous silks and glittering with priceless gems, advanced one by one to pay feudal homage to the King-Emperor. If George and May noticed the Gaekwar of Baroda, second greatest of the Indian princes, rip off his jewels, bow to the King and then turn his back and walk angrily away – an insult which can be clearly seen in surviving footage – they made no mention of it. George's announcement of the change of capital came at the end of the ceremony. The secret had been well kept, and it was received with cheers. Old India hands had worried that the silence of the crowds at the entry into

Delhi showed that the royal visit had been a mistake, but the King and Queen were now greeted with rapturous enthusiasm.[96]

Duchess Evie, who believed herself to be one of the few people who dared argue with her sovereign, considered that the announcement should not have been made by the King, as the changes were not within his gift and they needed to be ratified by Parliament. She noticed his acute sensitivity to criticism:

> How I do wish that he had a bigger mind and more reasoning power – one sees more and more how absolutely he depends on the opinion of those around him – and how he is swayed by most shallow arguments – yet he is so straight and so desperately anxious to do what is right.[97]

'Rather tired after wearing the Crown for 3½ hours, it hurt my head as it is pretty heavy,' was George's comment after the durbar.[98] Next day at the Red Fort George and May stood on Shah Jehan's balcony dressed in their robes and crowns and showed themselves to the people as the Moghul emperors had done 300 years before. 'A wonderful sight to see them all gazing up,' wrote May. 'I believe our suite were so delighted they were almost reduced to tears.'[99]

Three days later, George having invested May with the Order of the Star of India – that the King decorated her himself in a special ceremony 'gave her intense pleasure' – the royal couple parted company.[100] George departed on a shooting expedition to Nepal. Firing from the back of an elephant ('the more I see of elephants the more I admire them, they are so patient, so intelligent') he killed twelve tigers in four days, and triumphantly shot two rhinos with a right and left.[101]

'My party is sworn to secrecy over your bag,' wrote May to George, who was presumably worried that his slaughter would be reported in the newspapers. She embarked on a grand tour by train and motor of the princely states via Agra, Rajputana, Jaipur, Bundi and Kotah. For her the maharajahs were the real India, almost an extension of the British aristocracy, though she complained: 'It is all very tiring for one has always to bow & smile & talk to people & one has absolutely no rest.'[102]

At Calcutta they were reunited. For May the capital of British officialdom was dreary: 'too European for my taste & not really India as the other places I have visited have been. We have nothing really interesting to do here only the unreal functions such as garden party, large dinner, drawing room, levee etc.'[103] But the crowds were more enthusiastic and demonstrative every day.

Reading his farewell address at Bombay, George broke down. 'I simply couldn't help it.'[104] The five-week tour had been a triumph. He wrote to May after the Delhi Durbar: 'It was one of the moments in one's life (there have been several others in the last year and a half) when one must really play up & do one's utmost to create a good impression.' He was the first emperor to visit India, and May the first empress consort, and 'I feel that our coming here . . . has certainly proved itself to be what I always predicted, a great success, & one that will have far-reaching effects'.[105]

On the voyage home, the King, who always left the door of his sitting room open, could be heard discussing confidential matters in a loud voice which boomed down the passages, and Duchess Evie worried that the footmen overheard everything he said.[106]

Whether or not the decision to move the capital of British India to Delhi originated with George, it was, as he wrote,

> entirely my own idea to hold the Coronation Durbar at Delhi in person & at first I met with much opposition, but the result has I hope been more than satisfactory & has surpassed all expectations. I am vain enough to think that our visit will have done good in India.[107]

With the Delhi Durbar he positioned the monarchy at the apex of the empire. Monarchy was elevated into the great unifying force; all hierarchies of empire culminated in allegiance to the King-Emperor. This was George's insight. He perceived that the ceremonial monarchy which King Edward had established in Britain could be transplanted to India.[108]

George, in his homely fashion, linked the success of the tour to the strength of his marriage. 'I thank God every day that he should have brought us together,' he told May, 'especially under the tragic circumstances of Eddy's death & people only said that I married you out of pity or sympathy. That shows how little the world knows what it is talking about.'[109] They had been married for eighteen years, and this was one of the very few occasions when he mentioned the name of the brother whose death had made possible his marriage to May as well his succession as sovereign.

CHAPTER 14

'The King is Duller Than the Queen'

1912–1913

The homecoming of the King and Queen from India in February 1912 was spoilt by mourning. George's brother-in-law the Duke of Fife had died from pleurisy in Egypt after the P&O liner in which he was travelling with his family was wrecked. The royal party arrived at Victoria to an 'icy red-carpeted platform – everyone looking very pinched & rednosed – in hastily improvised mourning'.[1] Deaths were so frequent in the extended royal family that a black dress was an essential item in the luggage of a lady-in-waiting: one complained in 1913 of being 'sunk in crape as usual (I've never yet been in a waiting out of black clothes)'.[2]

At Buckingham Palace with 'its apparently innumerable narrow passage-ways, its vast sombre throne room, its ballroom, its various dining-rooms, its great picture galleries alternating with nests of small sitting-rooms and bedrooms, its landings and staircases, and its acres of red carpeting', George and May had been established since February 1911.[3] The renovations made by Edward VII meant that few changes were needed in the state rooms, but in the private apartments May worked fiendishly hard decorating and arranging the rooms; her sitting room was hung with blue silk, and the bedrooms were given 'white moiré [rippled] paper with roses & pink silk curtains, sofa etc'.[4]

The evening courts which Edward VII had introduced continued in the new reign. In Queen Victoria's time, drawing rooms were held at three o'clock in the afternoon, and ladies were expected to wear full evening dress, with bare shoulders, feathers and veils. Under George, the evening courts were not the 'brilliant functions' they had been in his father's reign.[5] George noted in his diary that the court began at 9 or 9.30 (King Edward's courts began at 10 p.m.) and was over by 11.00.[6] One can imagine him looking at his watch; for this king the courts were a dreary chore. 'Thank goodness!' wrote George after a state ball of 2,000 people. 'The last Court function this year!'[7] At one court, Prime Minister Asquith's daughter Violet thought he 'looked rather amusingly bored towards the end – two hours of frumps & freaks having defiled past him'.[8] King and Queen sat on their thrones on the dais in the ballroom. For the first court of 1912 May wore a gown of rich black satin trimmed with jet, a diamond tiara, diamond collar and diamond stomacher.[9] She complained to her aunt that the court was 'so dull & such awful people, heaven only knows where they come from. In spite of injunctions the clothes are all too weird.'[10]

The posts in the Queen's household had changed little in the two centuries since Queen Anne.[11] At the head of the household came the mistress of the robes, Evie, Duchess of Devonshire, wife of the 9th Duke. She held the post from 1910 to 1953 with a break between 1916 and 1921 when her husband served as governor-general of Canada. As we have seen, she was on close terms with the Queen. The duchess's papers at Chatsworth give a vivid snapshot of her role as mistress of the robes. She organised the Queen's gowns for ceremonial occasions such as the opening of Parliament, and arranged meetings between the Queen and the royal dressmaker, Miss Rossiter. 'One thing my dresser is anxious you should impress on Miss Rossiter,' wrote the Queen to the duchess, 'is that it is better for me to have gowns made of good material (not flimsy stuff) & not a great deal of embroidery as this is unnecessary with jewels. In fact well cut gowns of handsome material rather securely made suit me best I think.'[12] After a successful interview with the Queen, Miss Rossiter reported back to the duchess: 'I was able to persuade Her Majesty to have some corsets.'[13]

It was the duchess's job to organise the ladies' rota of waitings. She passed on instructions from the Queen to the ladies regarding matters such as dress. 'Her Majesty objects to short walking skirts being worn in the house at Windsor and wishes day gowns indoors to be worn on the ground but of course not necessarily very long.'[14] At the coronation and at the opening of Parliament, the mistress of the robes had an important role, holding the end of the queen's train. 'You have to stick to your Queen, like a leech, all the time,' wrote the Duchess of Buccleuch, Duchess Evie's predecessor in the post.[15]

Next came the ladies of the bedchamber, who were all the wives of peers. In addition to Lady Airlie and Lady Shaftesbury (referred to by the Queen as 'My Woman, Shaftesbury'), who had joined May's household when she was Princess of Wales, May appointed three more ladies.[16] Lady Ampthill, said May, was 'a great success, charming manners & most helpful'; others found her dull.[17]* The same could not be said of the witty socialite Ettie, Lady Desborough, a leader of the cultured aristocratic clique known as the Souls, who owed her appointment to her

---

*Asquith dismissed her as 'Beauchamp's sister, of whom there is not much to be said' (H. H. Asquith, *Letters to Venetia Stanley*, ed. Michael and Eleanor Brock (Oxford University Press, 1982), p. 46). Both her brother Beauchamp and her son, the Hon. John Russell, were at the centre of scandals which rocked the post-war court: see below, pages 376–9, 341.

'knack for entertaining George V'.[18] Lady Minto, the third new lady, was the wife of an Indian viceroy and a court insider – she was the daughter of Queen Victoria's private secretary General Sir Charles Grey. The work of a lady-in-waiting was not arduous:

> The Ladies will be on duty one fortnight in every two months but, as a rule, the Queen will only want them when the Court is at Windsor or Buckingham Palace & only at Windsor will they be in residence, &, in London, they will always be told beforehand when they are wanted.[19]

After the ladies came the women of the bedchamber. The daughters or granddaughters of peers, they were of a lower social rank than the ladies. The difference between them and the ladies-in-waiting was explained by one of the latter thus: 'The Women of the Bedchamber did all the work, poor dears, and the Ladies were, well, more there for ornamental purposes.'[20]* In addition to her two trusty women, Lady Eva Dugdale (née Greville) and Lady Mary Trefusis (née Lygon), who had been with her since she was Duchess of York, May appointed Lady Bertha Dawkins, a widow who was 'awfully poor', whom she had 'known & liked in the old days'.[21] According to the Duke of Gloucester, Bertha was the nicest of women, loved by the royal children, but one of the ugliest: 'The King loathed sitting next to her because she was so ugly, and used to try to avoid it.' (She disliked sitting next to him too.)[22] The ladies were summoned for important occasions, but there was always a bedchamber woman present. The rota system on which they worked had been introduced by the Queen in order to prevent one woman from gaining an ascendancy over her, as Charlotte Knollys had done over Queen Alexandra.[23]

Ladies-in-waiting and bedchamber women were paid the same salary of £300 a year (roughly £35,000 today).[24] In Queen Anne's day, the bedchamber women had done the work of the queen's personal maid, but that had long since become the job of the dresser. May's dresser, Tatry, had been her maid before she married, and treated her as though she was still a little girl and 'made endless trouble always'.[25] She was gravely short-sighted with a screwed-up yellow face, and May pensioned her off

---

*After the bedchamber women came the maids of honour. May appointed four in 1911: Mabel Gye, Sybil Brodrick, Venetia Baring and Katherine Villiers. 'Being young and mostly attractive they were generally removed from the Household by marriage before very long', and the Queen was expected to provide a dowry (Mabell, Countess of Airlie, *Thatched with Gold: The Memoirs of Mabell, Countess of Airlie*, ed. Jennifer Ellis (Hutchinson, 1962), p. 127). Queen Mary abolished the post after 1918 as an economy.

in 1912 with rooms in Kensington Palace next to Queen Victoria's dresser, Mrs Tuck, 'and in this way the two can live together'.[26]* The bedchamber women acted as the Queen's PAs or secretaries, organising her charity work and dealing with her correspondence.

This was a Tory court. Lady Airlie was described by her niece Clementine Churchill as being 'sunk in the most stagnant bog of Toryism'.[27]† By contrast with the court of Edward VII, the new court was neither glamorous nor racy. No stories of royal corridor-creeping enlivened the household. The King famously declared: 'I am not interested in any wife except my own.'[28] Nor were Edward VII's Jewish friends in evidence. Max Beerbohm made a caricature of Lord Burnham, Sir Ernest Cassel, Alfred and Leopold de Rothschild and Arthur Sassoon walking along a corridor at Buckingham Palace, captioned: 'Are we as welcome as ever?'[29] The answer in most cases was no. Some claimed the court was dreary. Certainly, it was domestic, sober and unfashionable. Beerbohm composed a ballad about an exchange between a lady-in-waiting and a lord-in-waiting at Windsor:

> HE:
> Last evening
> I found him with a rural dean
> Talking of district visiting . . .
> The King is duller than the Queen.

> SHE:
> At any rate he doesn't sew!
> You don't see him embellishing
> Yard after yard of calico . . .
> The Queen is duller than the King.[30]

* * *

'We are now in a great state of mind over the threatened coal strike on March 1st which means dislocation of all trades & ruination to millions,' May told her aunt in February 1912.[31] The government failed to

---

*Tatry's successors were no better: all the Queen's dressers were 'idle and disagreeable' and unpleasant to other people's servants, according to the Duchess of Devonshire (James Pope-Hennessy, *The Quest for Queen Mary*, ed. Hugo Vickers (Zuleika, 2018), p. 82).
†None of Queen Mary's ladies were married to Liberal peers. The Duke of Devonshire and Lord Minto were Liberal Unionists, and Lords Ampthill and Desborough had switched from Liberal to Conservative. However, as already noted, George's household in 1901 as Prince of Wales was criticised by Aunt Augusta as being all Whigs, with only one Tory (Charles Cust) among them.

avert the catastrophe, and a million miners came out on the first national coal strike, protesting against low pay and calling for a minimum wage. The Cabinet advised the King to postpone his proposed visit to Europe that year. 'Really with our country in the state she is in we feel we cannot make any plans & must remain here in London for the present,' reported May.[32] But there was nothing they could do. 'If one could only act,' she added a week later, 'but like this one feels so impotent & all this time our blessed & beloved country is in a state of stagnation & misery.'[33]

One person who heaved a sigh of relief at the King's decision to cancel his plans was Captain Evan-Thomas, a royal favourite, picked by Dalton to sail on the *Bacchante*, and now commander of the Royal Naval College at Dartmouth, where Prince Albert was still a cadet. The King had presented the college with a handsome statue of himself, which he intended to inspect in March, but pranksters threatened to paint it red. Captain Evan-Thomas was rescued from a potentially disastrous embarrassment by the coal strike, which forced the King to scratch the visit.

Six months earlier, after the August 1911 railway strike, George had written to the prime minister, proposing the introduction of legislation to stop strikes spreading. Asquith was irritated by the King's political meddling and he had no desire to introduce anti-trade union laws. He buried the proposal. In his letter, George had warned of a renewal of strikes which 'might lead to political elements being introduced into the conflict which might perhaps affect, not the existence, but the position of the Crown'.[34]

The threat to the crown was the nub of the matter. Of course, the King and Queen were horrified by the plight of the miners. But, as one historian has pointed out, their response to the strikes was political, not altruistic.[35] For George, socialism was synonymous with republicanism. Both he and May agreed that the Liberal government was to blame for the strikes in 'encouraging Socialism all these years & in pandering to the Labour party'.[36]*

What or who prompted George's decision to visit the mining districts in the summer of 1912 is not clear. The idea that the King should go out among the poor has Esher's fingers all over it. Another influence was Cosmo Gordon Lang, the Archbishop of York. Staying at Balmoral, he urged the importance of the King's coming into contact with the masses,

---

*Under the 1903 Lib–Lab pact, Herbert Gladstone of the Liberal Party and Ramsay MacDonald of Labour agreed that the two parties would not stand against each other in thirty constituencies. As a result Labour won twenty-nine seats in the 1906 election.

arguing that 'it was not enough that they should assemble in the streets on ceremonial occasions to see him, but that he might, so to say, go to see them – move about with as little ceremony as possible through their own towns, villages and workshops'.[37]

George and May visited south Wales in June. This was a new type of royal tour. By royal standards, it was informal. An open motor car, no escort or guard of honour. 'No tall hats and black coats,' just 'ordinary country clothes'.[38] They came to see and learn as much as to be seen. They visited black-faced miners at work in the pits of the Rhondda Valley, and May drank a cup of tea in a miner's cottage. *The Times* hailed the new style as 'a revival of the monarchical idea, which re-establishes the vanishing conception of the King and his people, and helps the popular imagination to rid itself of the oppressive weight of the intervening apparatus of government'.[39] This was a new concept of democratic monarchy, calling for a direct relationship of mutual dependence between king and people.[40]

The constant bowing and the noise of the cheering was 'very fatiguing', said May, but she and George were assured that 'we had done the best day's work in all our lives!' Their triumph was the sweeter because the Rhondda was 'right in the heart of Keir Hardie's constituency who will not have liked it!'[41] 'That beast' Keir Hardie, as George called him, leader of the Labour Party until 1908, had written an open letter denouncing the royal visit as a ruse to whitewash the employers.[42] A keen republican, he had caused a sensation at the time of David's birth, back in 1894, when he presciently declared:

> From his childhood onward this boy will be brought up by sycophants and flatterers by the score, and will be taught to believe himself as of a superior creation. A line will be drawn between him and the people whom he is to be called upon some day to reign over. In due course following the precedent that has already been set, he will be sent on a tour round the world, and probably rumours of a morganatic alliance will follow – and the end of it all will be that the country will be called upon to pay the bill.[43]

With his visits to the people the King sought to undermine Keir Hardie's powerbase. As Cosmo Lang wrote, 'I feel sure that these tours did much to create and sustain [the people's] sense that he belonged to them and they to him in a very human and personal way'.[44]

A few days later (8–12 July) the royals visited Lord Fitzwilliam at Wentworth Woodhouse, his palace in the heart of the South Yorkshire coalfields. A party of forty guests had been invited to meet them, staying in the 365-room Palladian mansion with its five miles of passages, eating thirteen-course dinners cooked by French chefs. This Edwardian royal entertainment meant that 'one could not get away early', wrote the Queen, and the packed royal schedule of visits to the industrial areas from 10 a.m. until 7 p.m. was 'awfully tiring'.[45]

On the morning of 9 July news reached the King at breakfast at Wentworth of a pit explosion which had killed more than seventy miners eight miles away at Cadeby. The royal party stuck to their programme; cancelling was unthinkable. Defying advice that he should reconsider, George insisted on descending a mine at Elsecar nearby as planned. 'Whatever happens,' he declared, 'I have got to show I want to do all I can at this time to see for myself, as far as I can, the risks to which my miners are exposed.'[46]

That evening at 6.30 the King and Queen made an impromptu visit to Cadeby 'to express our sympathy personally'.[47] The parallel timelines of the tragic pit disaster and the stately royal progress – narrated by Catherine Bailey in her book *Black Diamonds* – for a brief moment intersected. The royal Daimler, driven at walking pace, edged towards the pit office through crowds which lined the road four deep. When George and May emerged from the office they were visibly affected. The stony-eyed Queen was in tears. 'It was awfully upsetting seeing the poor people who had lost relatives,' she later wrote.[48] As they left, the women sobbed, and people were uncertain whether to cheer or clap.

Doubtless, wrote the Yorkshire grandee Lord Halifax, father of the Conservative politician, the visit to Cadeby 'did no end of good'.[49] But this was a spontaneous gesture, not a cynical PR exercise, and there is no denying the genuineness of George's and May's emotions. For them, this sort of connection was so much more authentic than showing themselves to the crowds on the balcony at Buckingham Palace, dismissed by May as 'all very touching & "émouvant", but we seem to live in an atmosphere of that kind of thing which is rather a trial'.[50]

John Lavery, the Irish artist, was commissioned by the publisher Hugh Spottiswoode to paint the royal family in 1912. The commission was for a family picture in the manner of Winterhalter's painting *The Royal Family in 1846*. Both George and May took an unusual interest in this vast canvas; they gave Lavery several sittings early in 1913, and they twice visited the artist's studio. They were so pleased with the canvas, Lavery recorded, that the King said 'he would like to have a hand in it', and both King and Queen dabbed some royal-blue paint on their Garter ribbons.[51]

Winterhalter's painting included all the royal children, but the only children in Lavery's picture are David and Mary. Bertie was away at sea, and the King and Queen decided not to include the three younger boys. This prevented Lavery from depicting the intimacy and spontaneity of children at play. 'His figures are stiff, isolated and formal. Lavery's portrait falls between the public and private image, the symbolic and the documentary.'[52] George stands to one side, wearing the uniform of an admiral of the fleet with epaulettes, his hand on his sword: the father of the nation perhaps, but a distant father of his family. There is no eye contact between the figures, and they are dwarfed by Lavery's luminous, impressionistic painting of the vast dirty-white and gold spaces of the White Drawing Room at Buckingham Palace.

Unwittingly perhaps, Lavery captured the family dynamic. Queen Mary sits bolt upright wearing her jewels, with her daughter Mary leaning awkwardly on her knee. Mary was George's favourite child – they would ride together before breakfast – but she was often made miserable by hay fever, and she was the shyest of the children. When George was at York Cottage on his own with the children, May had to write to Mary, 'begging her to be nice' and sit with him, which she did, though she refused to speak.[53]

In the painting, David stands apart from his father and looks out beyond him. Their relationship, never easy, was becoming fractious. George nagged his son for smoking too much and taking too much violent exercise. May remained curiously detached, confiding her hopes and anxieties for the prince in long talks with Lord Esher. When he was nineteen, David started to lose weight. 'We have great trouble in getting our boy to <u>eat</u>, therefore he is dreadfully thin,' wrote May.[54] Lord Esher noted: 'The Prince of Wales is very thin, I cannot make out what is wrong with him. Arrested puberty I <u>think</u>.'[55] The Duchess of Devonshire, mistress of the robes, noted that the prince's weight had fallen to seven stone four pounds and wrote: 'The poor boy is evidently suffering from hysteria and I am sure they don't manage him well. He was given a big scolding yesterday and threatened with a rest cure and forcible feeding ... I thought he looked even more miserable than usual.'[56]*

David's eating problems brought him closer to May. Mother and son had long friendly talks together; as May said: 'It is useless your bottling

---

*George recorded family weights in a weighing book, and he told David in 1913 that 'on December 22, 1910, you weighed 7st. 13 lbs., and when I weighed you at Balmoral you were 7 st. 8 lbs., so instead of increasing you have lost 5 lbs. in nearly three years, that is certainly not as it should be' (Edward, Duke of Windsor, *A Family Album* (Cassell, 1960), p. 63).

up your feelings & never giving vent to what you really feel & I am so glad you spoke out so freely as I am sure you feel all the better for doing so.'[57] David, who had gone up to Magdalen College, Oxford in October 1912, was prescribed a fattening regime.

> I am indeed glad to hear that you really intend to stick to the food diet & to do your best to get strong & well for I feel sure that the depression you unluckily suffer from is due principally to your brain not being properly nourished & this must be put an end to or you will get worse.[58]

The possibility that David's symptoms of depression, 'arrested puberty' and refusal to eat were linked seems not to have occurred to anyone at the time, though today doctors would surely have become involved.

Then there was Johnnie, now aged seven. Lala reported from Sandringham that he had 'two or three severe attacks each day & that they sometimes last fully 10 minutes, she says they are very painful to see, as he struggles so much, poor child'.[59] May found Johnnie's state 'very agitating . . . poor little boy how distressing & worrying'.[60] But there was little she could do, beyond moving him from overcrowded York Cottage when visitors stayed. She took him to the doctors, who changed his medicine and then gave him a stronger dose but, as George pointed out, they had little effect. 'I am quite sure the doctors can do no earthly good with him, he takes his medicines & nothing can be done, they said so before. But if it will make you happier for them to see him, I don't mind.'[61]

That winter Johnnie's cousin the Tsarevich, aged eight, suffered a bad fall and nearly died. A medical bulletin was issued, announcing the little boy's illness, which had been kept a state secret until then. This confirmed May's suspicions that 'the unfortunate child has the cruel illness' – haemophilia. 'What a tragedy,' she wrote.[62] 'Like Leopold, I suppose,' George replied.[63]* He sympathised with Nicky – 'another anxiety & worry added to his many' – but made no connection between the plight of the two little boys.[64] Johnnie was fifth in line to the throne; his illness was a family tragedy, not a dynastic catastrophe.

On 13 February 1913 George had an interview with his private secretary Francis Knollys. He wrote in his diary:

---

*Leopold, Duke of Albany, Queen Victoria's youngest son, suffered from haemophilia, which he inherited from his mother. He died from a fall aged thirty. The Tsarina was a carrier for haemophilia, as was her mother, Princess Alice, Queen Victoria's second daughter. The Tsarevich inherited the illness from his mother.

Saw Francis and told him that I feared my having two private secretaries was not satisfactory and that perhaps he might consider whether it was not best for him to resign. He took it very kindly and said he thought I was perfectly right. Very disagreeable for me to have to say this to such an old friend as Francis, but I am sure it is for the best.[65]

Knollys, now seventy-five, was 'a real typical mid Victorian', and it was generally agreed, even by him, that his retirement was overdue.[66] For over a year George had meant to sack him and postponed the interview time after time – though it is to the King's credit that he was determined to speak to Knollys himself rather than doing it 'in a cowardly way' through a third person.[67] But Knollys did not go quietly. He telephoned George's sister Princess Victoria, and complained that he had been dismissed in 'the most unpleasant manner, exactly as an unsatisfactory butler might be dismissed', and that he felt 'exceedingly badly used'.[68] When Knollys returned later the same day to do the King's letters, he gave him a 'very unpleasant time'. George confided in Davidson, and confessed that he was 'dreadfully unhappy' about the matter.[69]

The bad feeling went back to the King's conditional pledges to create peers in November 1910. Knollys, as we have seen, had concealed from the King the information that the opposition leader, Balfour, was willing to form a government; this was vital because it meant that George felt he had no alternative to agreeing to Asquith's request for guarantees. When George discovered that Knollys had duped him he was enraged, and he never forgave him. In September 1913, several months after Knollys's resignation, George told Esher:

> It was like treating me like a child, I suppose he thought I had not the intellect to deal with a matter of such importance. He was my private secretary, bound to me by every tie, and he never so much as told me a word of what had been happening ... But what ought Francis to have done? Why didn't he insist that I should get in writing the views of the Ministers and say that they should have an answer next day at 12? He was in a conspiracy with them. I know it now ... Do you suppose that if I had been a little longer on the throne that they would have coerced me as they did? Let them try it again. I shall never forget it, and never forgive any of them.[70]

In the summer of 1911, after the Tories had discovered Knollys's role in advising the King over the guarantees, Balfour, usually the coolest of men, embarked on an angry correspondence with the private secretary. When Lady Desborough asked him whom he would like as a fellow guest at a house party, Balfour replied: 'My dear Ettie, I should enjoy meeting any man in England, except Lord Knollys; him I will not meet.'[71] Having a private secretary who was not on speaking terms with the opposition was 'most embarrassing', complained the King.[72]

Lord Stamfordham, who was a Tory, had made plain his disagreement with Knollys over the guarantees in November 1910, and by the summer of 1911 relations between the two men had grown so bad that Stamfordham considered resigning. George found the 'jealousy' between them 'intolerable'.[73] Knollys told Asquith that his position had become impossible because of 'the strong divergence of opinions which existed between the King and his surroundings (not the Queen) on one side and myself on the other'.[74]

The appointment of the 63-year-old Stamfordham as private secretary was not universally welcomed. Lord Carrington (now promoted to Marquess of Lincolnshire) dismissed him as 'a narrow-minded soldier who was the son of a Parson, and who married a Parson's daughter; and who held strong Tory opinions; and not much command of temper; and who besides is not in the best of health'.[75] One historian has argued that the appointment was a 'dangerous move' at a time when Stamfordham's Unionism was becoming more strident.[76] Certainly the government felt this. At Cabinet, everyone 'lamented the loss of Knollys, and the influence of Stamfordham whose wings the P.M. earnestly desired should be clipped'.[77] The Tories were threatened by him too. When Stamfordham appeared in the leader's office around this time and cross-questioned the chief whip about the party's attitude towards Irish Home Rule, Balcarres was so taken aback that he was at a loss as to what to say.[78]

Today, coming across one of Stamfordham's memos in the Royal Archives, written in a clear hand in bold black ink, is like striking gold. His notes on interviews with politicians, or his chronological narratives of crises, such as the thirty-two pages he penned on the Parliament Bill, give a rich, clear-headed analysis of the tangled politics of George's reign. 'The great figure in the whole story was Stamfordham,' John Gore told Harold Nicolson.[79] This was the golden age of the private secretary, and Stamfordham was the greatest of them all.

Home Rule or self-government for Ireland, with its own parliament in Dublin, had been a live political issue for forty years. Two Home Rule bills had been defeated in Parliament: the first one, in 1886, was voted down in the Commons when the Liberal Party split; and the second fell in the Lords in 1893. The Asquith government was determined to get a third bill through both houses. The bill was accordingly introduced in the Commons in 1912 and aroused furious hostility from the Unionists, above all in Ulster, where Protestants saw government from Dublin as 'Rome Rule'.

In May 1912 Andrew Bonar Law, the mild-mannered, pipe-smoking Glasgow businessman who had succeeded Balfour as leader of the now formally unified Conservative and Unionist Party, gave the King 'the worst five minutes he has had for a long time' after a dinner at Buckingham Palace. He warned the King that he must either accept the Home Rule Bill or use his prerogative to veto it and dismiss his ministers, ' "and in either case half your subjects will think you have acted against them". The King turned red; and Law asked "Have you ever considered that, Sir?" "No," said the King, "it is the first time it has been suggested to me." '[80]

The Parliament Act had been the prelude to the Irish Home Rule Bill, which was introduced in April 1912, passed its third reading in the Commons on 16 January 1913 and was rejected by the House of Lords on 30 January. Under the terms of the Parliament Act, which reduced the House of Lords to a suspensory two-year veto, Home Rule was due to pass in the summer of 1914. In Ulster the Volunteers rallied and drilled, and as the deadline loomed it became evident that the Ulstermen preferred to meet their forcible expulsion from the Union with civil war rather than elect representatives to an Irish parliament in Dublin.

Archbishop Davidson saw George in February 1913 and found him in a state of deep anxiety about the government's plan to carry Home Rule. The bill had been introduced after the second election in 1910, and therefore had no electoral mandate. George showed the archbishop a 'crudely written' and 'injudicious' letter he had written, threatening to refuse his assent to Home Rule unless the bill was put to the electorate. He assured Davidson that the letter had been seen by no one, but the archbishop observed that 'considering the warmth of his feeling on the subject, and the stentorian tones in which he described it all to me', the secret would get out if any listener were within a hundred yards. George told Davidson 'in dramatic tones, and at the top of his voice' of the conversations he had had with Asquith and others. Davidson considered that the King was exaggerating his own contribution in these meetings. 'I greatly doubt whether he had really said it all.'[81]

Hensley Henson, the Dean of Durham, was another churchman in whom George confided. Staying at Windsor for the first time, he found the King 'in much confusion and distress of mind' about whether he should veto Home Rule, and complaining bitterly that he had been badly treated by ministers over the guarantees. Henson worried that the

King should 'pour himself out thus freely'; he found him 'a well-intentioned but weak man, who was conscious of an obligation to take some decisive action, but unable to determine what precise action that should be'. Lacking in 'personal magnetism', he gave 'an impression of feeble perplexity, which must needs alarm a considering patriot. I find it difficult not to think that he is at the mercy of the latest speaker.'[82]

It was Stamfordham who calmed George's nerves. In the summer of 1913 he held a series of interviews about the King's position with politicians on both sides, taking careful notes. The Liberals told him that the King should follow the government's advice. The Conservatives, on the other hand, argued that the Parliament Act had created a gap in the constitution by stripping the House of Lords of its power to refer Home Rule to the electorate. The responsibility for referring fundamental legislation to the voters now lay with the King.[83] To an extent, the Conservatives were playing party politics and trying to use the King to force an election which they believed they could win. But many people considered that in destroying the veto of the House of Lords the Parliament Act had changed the balance of the constitution, and in the columns of *The Times* constitutional authorities such as Sir William Anson, the warden of All Souls, opined that the King had a right to call for a dissolution of Parliament.[84]

That was certainly George's understanding. In 1914 he wrote that

> the Parliament Act places me in a false position, & one never contemplated by the framers of our Constitution. As I regard it, the King alone can now compel a Government to refer to the Country any measure which hitherto would have been so referred by the action of the Lords.[85]

How the King was to cause an election was far from clear. George by now had grown to like Asquith; as he wrote, 'I don't want him to resign particularly & I don't think he will agree to a dissolution'.[86] Worried that he was placed in an impossible position, George summoned Stamfordham to Cowes in August 1913, and together they composed a memo for the prime minister. Asquith, who had been avoiding the King, was summoned to an audience on the 11th of that month and presented with a paper written in George's schoolboy handwriting, which he asked to take away. Asquith told the King that his position was 'absolutely unassailable so long as he does nothing unconstitutional'.[87] George did not agree. The danger of civil war in Ulster was real, in his view, and it was his duty to prevent it.

'Whatever I do I shall offend half the population,' George told

Asquith in his handwritten memo. 'No sovereign has ever been placed in such a position, & this pressure is sure to increase during the next few months. In this period I have a right to expect the greatest confidence & support from . . . my Prime Minister. I cannot help feeling that the Government is drifting & taking me with it.'[88]

The solution George proposed was to hold a conference of representatives of all the parties, following the example of the Constitutional Conference on the Parliament Bill in 1910. He favoured an arrangement allowing Ulster to contract out of Home Rule. George's Tory instincts had inclined him to use his veto to throw out Home Rule; but his proposal for a conference pointed to a non-partisan monarchy acting as mediator. 'Would it not be better,' asked the King, 'to try to settle measures involving great changes in the Constitution . . . not on Party lines, but by agreement?'[89] After months of turmoil and discussions, George had reached a new understanding of his role as monarch.

Asquith responded by sending George two papers: a lawyerish lecture on his constitutional position, and a second paper dismissing the resistance in Ulster as organised disorder rather than civil war. In response a lengthy essay emanated from Balmoral, outlining the sovereign's duty in the event of civil war. So cogent was the argument that Harold Nicolson printed the entire document, three-and-a-half pages of small print.[90] It was a prime example of the new style which Stamfordham had brought to the monarchy, reasoned and pragmatic. Little wonder that the Asquiths dubbed the private secretary an old cuttlefish, 'flooding [the King's] mind with ink'.[91]

At Balmoral that autumn the King discussed the Irish question with each politician who stayed. To his mother he confessed that politics was causing him 'great worry & anxiety . . . I must say I have had a most difficult & hard time during the last three years.'[92] Asquith visited and made no attempt to soothe the King's anxiety. George wrote in his diary: 'Had a conversation with him on the political situation. He owned it was serious but was optimistic as usual.'[93] Churchill, by contrast, was helpful, reporting that 'the King has been extremely cordial & intimate in his conversations with me, and I am glad to think that I reassured him a good deal about the general position.'[94]

In Cabinet a few days later Asquith boasted that the 'rudimentary truths' about the constitutional position of the monarch to which he had drawn the King's attention at Balmoral had 'had a marked effect, and at the end of his visit the King used a very different language'.[95] In private, Asquith liked to dismiss the King as a dunce. He told his daughter Violet that the King was 'in an awful state' about Home Rule: 'he is just in a blue funk. Poor little man he isn't up to his position.'[96]

The truth was that George's understanding of the situation was sharper than that of the supercilious Asquith. As Vernon Bogdanor has written, on these matters 'the king's judgement was superior to that of his prime minister'.[97] Contrary to what Asquith liked to think, the Ulstermen were not bluffing when they threatened civil war. Ulster's resistance to its forced ejection from Westminster meant that Home Rule could not be treated as an ordinary piece of legislation as Asquith pretended. George understood this. And he deserves credit for pushing the government to agree to a conference, and for encouraging Asquith to hold secret conversations with Bonar Law.

CHAPTER 15

Buckingham Palace

1914

King George was a man of simple habits. His daily routine at Buckingham Palace was ordered and domestic. He rose at 8.00, rode in the park with Princess Mary if the weather was fine; if the day was wet he went through his letters before breakfast at 9.15 with the Queen. This was a frugal meal of tea, toast and marmalade, and fish or eggs, and by 9.30 he was back in his study, where he received Stamfordham and other members of his household. 'The King's writing-table is kept in perfect order,' wrote one journalist, 'so that His Majesty can always lay his hand upon any letter or document which he requires.' The London papers were brought in at 11.00. 'Certain articles and paragraphs are marked with a blue pencil, but the papers are all laid before the King unmutilated; for His Majesty always insists upon seeing everything himself.'[1] Before lunch the King gave audiences to ambassadors, colonial governors and military officers. He returned to his study after eating lunch at 1.30, and by quarter to three the work left over from the morning was finished, and he gave brief audiences to ministers.

In the afternoon there was a visit to Queen Alexandra. Most afternoons he walked three times round the gardens at Buckingham Palace, a distance of three-and-a-half miles. Tea with the Queen was served at 5.00, and from half-past five until after eight 'the King is hard at work in his study'.[2] After dinner with the family, he liked to spend his evenings reading a book. Augustus Birrell, who discussed novels with the King, considered that he had 'excellent literary taste ... He <u>hates</u> R. Kipling, finding him coarse' (later he changed his mind about Kipling); he enjoyed Captain Marryat's navy yarns, but his favourite was the historical novelist Harrison Ainsworth.[3]

The King preferred simple food. According to Gabriel Tschumi, a royal chef who later wrote a memoir, His Majesty consumed soup in large quantities. Consommé was served at eleven, and he sometimes called for two or three bowls of soup while he worked. For lunch when no guests were present he ate curry, for which he had acquired a taste in India. He preferred it made from beefsteak and served with Bombay duck, a sun-dried fish from the Indian Ocean which was split and grilled. He enjoyed nursery dishes such as Irish stew and cottage pie followed by apple

Charlotte or pancakes. He and the Queen ate food eight times a day – early-morning tea, breakfast, something at eleven o'clock, luncheon, milk (for the King) at four o'clock, tea, dinner, and biscuits at bedtime.[4]

Queen Mary preferred the *cuisine classique*. Having 'a great feeling for royal traditions', she continued the elaborate French menus of Edward VII. Members of her household later claimed that she was indifferent to food and seldom saw the chef at Buckingham Palace, but Tschumi regarded her as a connoisseur of *haute cuisine*.[5] George's mashed potatoes were served alongside the Queen's dishes such as *Côtelettes de saumon à la Montpellier* or *Asperge d'Argenteuil, sauce mousseline*.[6]

George was a considerate employer. His equerries were poorly paid but they lived in substantial grace-and-favour houses. Stamfordham and Fritz Ponsonby had houses in St James's Palace. Bryan Godfrey-Faussett lived at the Mill House, Dersingham, which the King had built specifically for him at a cost of £2,000 when he married. Godfrey was not a rich man, and his equerry's salary of £600 (£70,000 in today's values) was not enough to pay the ten servants he needed to run the house – a valet, footman, lady's maid, cook, kitchen maid, housemaid, under-housemaid, nurse, gardener and boy.* His wife Eugenie (whom he always called Babs) Dudley Ward disliked living there and found Norfolk very dreary. Dersingham was a mile away from Sandringham, and the King and Queen had a disconcerting habit of dropping in unannounced and inspecting the house all over. Once the royal motors approached while Godfrey was eating luncheon in his slippers. Another time the servants were just about to start their Christmas meal.

In 1913 Godfrey decided to leave Norfolk and move to London. He ducked telling the King and instead informed Sir William Carington, comptroller of the household. This was a mistake. When George found out he was furious. With trepidation Godfrey asked for an interview. The King told him that he 'ought to have come to me in the first place', but to Godfrey's relief he was 'in a very good temper and was perfectly charming to me throughout my interview'.[7] A few days later, 'a wonderful thing happened'. Godfrey received a message to telephone the King, who told him that Rangers Lodge in Hyde Park had come vacant and he could have it for free. Rangers Lodge is a delightful small Georgian house in the middle of the park, and the news made Babs 'wild with delight'. The King wanted Godfrey to keep Mill House, and when he protested that he couldn't afford it, George offered to pay the annual

---

*His equerry's salary had been £400 in 1902 (George Godfrey-Faussett, *Royal Servant, Family Friend: The Life and Times of Naval Equerry Captain Sir Bryan Godfrey-Faussett RN* (Bernard Durnford, 2004), p. 117).

rent of £110 on condition that Godfrey told no one. 'Neither of us slept much last night, thinking of the King's offer,' wrote Godfrey.[8]

For the opening of Parliament in March 1913 George wore his crown. No sovereign had done this since Queen Victoria before Albert died, and George was so worried about it that he asked the Cabinet's advice. 'As we none of us cared what he wears,' wrote the Liberal minister Charles Hobhouse, 'we agreed to the crown.'[9] In The Mall on the way there, five suffragettes rushed out and tried to present petitions to the King calling for votes for women. 'Of course the police caught them,' wrote May, 'but it caused a scene & looked undignified.'[10] The suffragettes were more than a nuisance; they targeted the monarchy for good reason. Not only did this tactic guarantee publicity, but they claimed an ancient right to petition the sovereign.

At the Epsom Derby on 4 June the suffragette Emily Davison dashed out of the stands as the horses thundered round Tattenham Corner and tried to catch the bridle of Anmer, the King's horse. She was knocked unconscious with a fractured skull, and both horse and jockey were sent flying. Davison never regained consciousness, dying four days later. The suffragettes constructed her as a martyr who had deliberately laid down her life in an attempt to petition the King. But she had a return train ticket in her pocket, and it was doubtless a lucky accident that the horse which caused her death was the King's. To single out and throw herself at a particular horse galloping downhill at thirty-five miles per hour would have been an almost impossible athletic feat.[11]

The royal party left before the last race ended, 'their Majesties and everyone else feeling very depressed'.[12] In his diary George showed no sympathy for Miss Davison. He thought her jump 'a most regrettable & scandalous proceeding', and he sympathised with the jockey (who recovered) and the horse (which was unhurt).[13] May called her 'a horrid woman', but, to be fair, when she wrote that she was under the impression that Davison was 'injured but not seriously'.[14]

The lack of sympathy shown by the royals to Emily Davison seems callous today. But the anger of the King and Queen was in line with opinion at the time. Tommy Lascelles recalled that the incident made a profound impression: 'it seemed the most outrageous interruption of sacred proceedings since Jenny Geddes threw her famous stool in St Giles's Cathedral'.[15]*

---

*Jenny Geddes threw her stool at the minister's head in St Giles's Cathedral, Edinburgh, in protest against Charles I's new prayer book in 1637, sparking a Scottish rebellion.

Princess Sophia Duleep Singh, daughter of the deposed Maharajah Duleep Singh, lived in a grace-and-favour house at Hampton Court. She was a suffragette, and to demonstrate her sympathy for Emily Davison she stood outside the gates of Hampton Court selling the *Suffragette* newspaper. This enraged the King, who wanted her evicted, and he asked Lord Crewe who, as secretary of state for India, was responsible for Sophia's security, to expel her. Crewe refused, claiming that the India Office was not answerable to the King; but the King dared not evict Sophia himself for fear of the adverse publicity. So George fumed, and Princess Sophia continued her campaign. When the *Daily Mail* printed an account of her appearance in court, Crewe sighed: 'Buck Pal will probably write again full of rage and grief. They read the *Mail* assiduously there.'[16]

By the spring of 1914 George and May were almost under siege from the suffragettes. On 21 May Emmeline Pankhurst led a march of 200 suffragettes on Buckingham Palace to present a petition to the King. It ended in violence and fifty-seven arrests. Lawyers dismissed the suffragettes' claim of a right to petition the monarch as fiction, but the attacks continued nonetheless.[17]

On 4 June during an evening court a young woman named Mary Blomfield, daughter of the architect Sir Reginald Blomfield, fell on her knees before the King. In a loud, shrill voice which could be heard all over the Throne Room, she cried: 'For God's sake, Your Majesty, won't you stop torturing the women?' Before she could finish her sentence, this protestor against the forcible feeding of jailed suffragettes was 'gently escorted out' by Sir Douglas Dawson, the comptroller of the Lord Chamberlain's Department. According to *The Times*, Their Majesties carried on with the presentations with 'dignity and composure'.[18] 'I don't know what we are coming to,' was George's comment in his diary on Miss Blomfield's outburst.[19]

May described the suffragettes as 'horrid' and 'tiresome', though it would be wrong to infer that she was opposed to women's rights.[20] She dreaded being the target of suffragette attacks. When George and May toured Scotland in July they were mobbed. At Dundee a suffragette ran up to the royal carriage, brandishing an umbrella at the Queen, and at Perth another rushed on to the running board of the car, and 'it took several police to get her off'.[21] As May told her aunt, the women were 'a constant & additional anxiety to our Tour & tho' outwardly I mercifully look calm, inwardly my heart goes pit a pat when a female dashes out to throw papers into the carriage'.[22] Perhaps the surprising thing today is that the King and Queen appear to have had no security to protect them from the radicalised women.

* * *

Because of the Balkan Wars, often seen as a prelude to the First World War, George and May were advised by the government to make no official state visits in 1913, but they accepted an invitation to Berlin in May for a 'family gathering': the wedding of the Kaiser's daughter Victoria Louise to Ernest of Hanover. The King did not bring a minister in attendance, as he would have done on a state visit, and the King and Queen were not the central figures, with every hour programmed; as guests they were left to themselves for much of the time. The marriage ended the feud between the houses of Hohenzollern and Hanover which dated back to Prussia's annexation of Hanover in 1866. It was the last gathering of the royal mob. May thought Ernest 'extremely attractive', and the previous year she had considered him as a possible husband for her fifteen-year-old daughter Mary. 'He will have a great fortune,' she told Count Mensdorff, George's cousin the Austrian ambassador, 'and could be in England a lot'.[23] This dynastic marriage to the inevitable German prince would have united the 'old' royal family to which May belonged with George's dynasty of Saxe-Coburg-Gotha. Fortunately, given that Britain and Germany were soon at war, Ernest had other ideas. 'I can quite understand Victoria Louise falling in love with him at first sight,' wrote May. 'He looks so like the Gainsborough portraits of the old royal family.'[24]

As usual on her German trips, May was preoccupied by dynastic genealogy. A visit to Aunt Augusta made her 'quite agitated ... My mind goes back to our Mecklenburg descent & our being the first English King and Queen to visit the home of our mutual Gt Grandmother & Gt Gt Grandmother [Queen Charlotte, wife of George III].'[25]

George insisted on meeting 'dear Nicky' at the station, where the Tsar arrived with over 100 policemen in attendance. George had a 'long & satisfactory talk' with his cousin: 'he was just the same as always'.[26] The two men were photographed together, George dressed in the uniform of the Prussian regiment, the 8th Cuirassiers, of which William had made him colonel-in-chief, with the long patent-leather boots that he wore for the wedding. This involved standing from 3.45 until 10.30 p.m., which made him very tired.

'Whether the visit was a success, I really don't know,' wrote Fritz Ponsonby, who came as equerry.[27] George was polite to William, but he avoided talking politics with him. William let himself go in a hair-raising rant to an astonished Stamfordham, attacking Britain for deserting the Teutonic races in favour of the Latins, and forecasting an escalation of the ongoing Balkan war into a war of all the European great powers.[28] When George inspected his regiment he rode a horse that was so well schooled he couldn't make it canter, so he arrived at a trot which, said

Fritz, 'did not look well'.[29] George talked a lot to the Kaiser's master of the horse, and the foreign diplomats found him unimpressive.[30]

In November 1913 the Archduke Franz Ferdinand and his morganatic wife the Duchess of Hohenberg made an informal visit to Windsor. Cultivating good relations with the heir to the Austrian empire was a way of undermining the Dual Alliance of Austria-Hungary and Germany; but the chief purpose of the visit was sport. Franz Ferdinand rivalled George as the best royal marksman in Europe. George's diary entry is characteristically non-committal: 'The Archduke shot quite well, but he uses 16 bores & light charges.'[31] (A sixteen-bore is a slightly smaller-calibre shotgun than the normal twelve-bore.) What George omitted to say was that he shot better than the Archduke.

Because of the duchess's morganatic status no princesses were asked, as they would have taken precedence over her. May found the duchess 'very nice, agreeable & quite easy to get on with, very tactful which makes the position easier'.[32] The visit was a success. Franz Ferdinand was amiable and appreciative. Formerly, wrote May, he was 'very anti-English, but that is quite changed now, & her influence has been & is good they say in every way'.[33]

The shooting at Windsor was not so good as Sandringham's – there were only two weeks of pheasant shooting, one in November and one in January – and in the winter George spent little time there. But he stayed at Windsor more than Edward VII, who often managed only two weeks in the whole year – a state visit in November and Ascot in the summer. Some found evenings at Windsor rather stiff. After dinner, the King and the men withdrew to the further White Drawing Room, where they smoked standing up. The Queen and the ladies retired to the nearer Green Drawing Room and sat down. 'About 10.15 the King comes into the nearer drawing room and the Queen and everybody else stand up and remain standing for the rest of the evening that is until about 11.30 while the King moves about talking to people; at 11.30 or a little earlier the Queen and the ladies retire; the King goes back to smoke again for a short time and then to bed.'[34]

Windsor was May's idea of paradise. 'I like living here enormously,' she wrote in 1910. 'I always knew I should. I love every inch of the old castle with its glorious & historical associations so fully appreciated by me.'[35] The castle was a living museum, stuffed with treasures, and the Queen liked nothing better than 'looking through old things & apportioning the various articles to the Library, the room where family papers are kept & so on ... I have always wished to get these things into order some day.'[36] She spent hours searching through old inventories and books to find the history of innumerable small things at Windsor, it has been a great pleasure doing this, tho' rather a trouble as it has taken so much time. However if the things continue to be properly catalogued & taken care of as they are now I shall be rewarded for any trouble I have taken to ascertain their origin.[37]

Queen Mary's name is hallowed in the Royal Collection today; her curating and cataloguing were the foundation of the collection. Inspired by the Carnavalet Museum at Paris and the Hohenzollern Museum at Berlin, at Kensington Palace she created the London Museum, to which she sent items such as her wedding dress and the dress she had worn for King Edward's coronation or the chair from Kew Palace upon which Queen Charlotte had died.[38]

At Windsor the scholar-queen spent her mornings 'arranging or doing things in the Castle', ignoring her guests while she sorted out a room for private family souvenirs belonging to Queen Victoria with the help of the librarian, John Fortescue, 'a perfect treasure to us and so keen and interested and knowledgeable about our collections'.[39] In 1914, as the crisis over Home Rule worsened, with increasing bitterness on both sides, 'to take my thoughts off graver subjects' the Queen studied the Carlton House catalogues of George IV's furniture and china, 'trying to ascertain where they are now placed. This interests me & I make frequent excursions to the State rooms & drawing rooms.'[40]

Buckingham Palace was refaced in 1913 with a façade in Portland stone designed by Aston Webb. The gleaming white Victoria Memorial, also in Portland stone, made the dull east front of Buckingham Palace, designed by Edward Blore in 1847, look 'so black and ugly' that it was generally felt 'something must be done to improve the appearance of the front of the Palace'.[41]

'I think you will be pleased with the new façade which looks very handsome,' May told George, who was away shooting.[42] The new front completed the processional route which still forms London's grandest axis. Writing in 1966, the architectural historian Ian Nairn described it better than anyone else:

Here is an axis of exactly the right length, with a circumstantial entry from the bustle of Trafalgar Square and with the royal palace at the other end – still an inaccessible home and not a museum, its bulk and gravity just enough to control the lavish stone expression of fountains and gate piers in front, yet not enough to overshadow it ... The particular Recessional flavour, an Indian summer of Empire fanned up briefly to be hotter than mid-July, is very poignant just now: not a museum piece but a living expression of 1910, calling to the Edwardian hidden in every person's character.[43]

King George, the sovereign at the apex of this Imperial splendour, working dutifully at his desk, was a troubled man. At a shooting party at Chatsworth, Lord Curzon found him excited in manner and intemperate in language. 'Forgetting . . . that Lady Crewe was the wife of an eminent Cabinet Minister he poured into her astonished ear terrific denunciations of Lloyd George on the subject of pheasants and mangold worzels.'[44]* The winter of 1913/14 was perhaps the best pheasant-shooting season ever. George himself counted 80,000 pheasants which he saw shot and fired 40,000 cartridges (since becoming king he had ceased to note in his diary the annual tally of birds he had shot himself).[45] Accompanied by David, George attended Lord Burnham's High Barn when 3,937 pheasants were killed, a record which still holds. The King was 'deadly' that day; shooting with three guns, he killed 1,000 birds himself. In the car on the way home he remarked: 'Perhaps we went a little too far today, David.'[46]

In 1935 a young British writer living in New York named George Dangerfield published a book entitled *The Strange Death of Liberal England*. It attracted little attention at the time, but it has since become recognised as a classic analysis of the ills of Edwardian Britain. Influenced by Jung and also by Lytton Strachey, Dangerfield linked the three rebellions of 1910–14 – the women, the unions and the Tories – and characterised them as symptomatic of a democracy in crisis. The only figure who emerges with credit from this narrative of political implosion is King George V. According to Dangerfield, George 'had one of the most active consciences in England; he was conscientiously determined to do his duty; his whole disposition was towards peace'. Writing in the last year of George's life, he observed: 'England has had more brilliant and more spectacular monarchs than King George, but surely no monarch more suited to assist its democracy through a period of what was beginning to look very like nervous breakdown.' Over Home Rule, 'that unique capacity for doing his duty, which has since been recognised by the world, was never more bitterly tested than in 1914, when nobody recognised it at all'.[47]

---

*Lloyd George had launched his campaign attacking landowners by claiming that whole fields of mangold worzels were devoured by pheasants.

By January 1914 the talks between Asquith and Bonar Law over Home Rule had broken down and, unless an agreement could be reached, civil war in Ulster loomed. Archbishop Davidson spent over two hours with the King at Windsor on the 21st. Davidson had come to play the role of secular confessor to the monarch, and his diary gives a revealing account of George's state of mind. He found the King 'more upset and vehement than I had ever seen him'. If anyone was close to nervous breakdown, it was George.[48]

The King held an audience with Asquith at Windsor on 5 February. They spoke for an hour and a half and, according to Asquith, they parted 'on very friendly terms'.[49] George gave a different account: 'We were very frank with one another about Ireland, it was not particularly pleasant.'[50] When Asquith insisted that responsibility for settling the Irish question lay with the government, not the King, George replied that he could not allow bloodshed among his loyal subjects without doing all in his power to stop it. According to Stamfordham's note, the King then said that 'although at the present stage of the proceedings he could not rightly intervene, *the time __would__ come when the Bill was presented for Assent, and then* he should feel it his duty to do what in his own judgement was best for his people generally'.[51] The words in italics suggest that the King was threatening to refuse his assent to the Home Rule Bill, and in Nicolson's biography they were cut from the quotation. The omission is a significant one, perhaps the only instance of fudging in the book.

While he was working on his life of King George, Nicolson had lunch one day with Owen Morshead, the royal librarian, and he asked what he should do if he came across something really damaging, such as George threatening to abdicate over Home Rule.* Morshead pursed his lips and replied: 'Your first duty will always be to the Monarchy.'[52] At this uncharacteristically stuffy response, Nicolson felt all the contrariness in him surge up in a wave of sudden republicanism.

What Nicolson didn't know was that four years earlier, in the course of preparing his entry on King George for the *Dictionary of National Biography*, Morshead had come across Stamfordham's note of the 5 February 1914 audience. The King's threat to refuse the assent worried him so much that the Cabinet secretary was consulted as to whether the

---

*Rumours persisted that the King had threatened to abdicate over Home Rule. In 1930 the writer Ford Madox Ford claimed that the King had forced the Liberals into co-operating with the Constitutional Conference by threatening abdication, provoking furious headlines and a denial from the palace (Alan Judd, *Ford Madox Ford* (Collins, 1990), p. 403).

document should be suppressed. After an exchange of learned letters, the Cabinet secretary ruled that no grounds existed for suppressing the document, as the sovereign still retained the power of veto though it had not been used since the reign of Queen Anne.[53]

Whatever the constitutional theory, the reality was that George had no intention of deploying the archaic power of refusing the assent. He set out his views in a letter drafted in July 1914, in which he claimed that the assent should not be withheld 'unless there is convincing evidence that it would avert a national disaster, or at least have a tranquillizing effect on the distracting conditions of the time. There is no such evidence.'[54]

Refusing the assent and forcing an election would have pleased the Tories, but George was determined to suppress his Tory sympathies, at any rate in his official role. Davidson was impressed by his political neutrality: 'The King himself is honestly striving to keep perfectly free from party complications, and not to let his anti-Home Rule sentiment lead or drag him into unwise action.'[55] George's position was a simple one, as he explained to Asquith: 'Whether Ireland had Home Rule or not was a matter of indifference to him: the politicians must settle that question. But as King he held that it was his duty by every means in his power to prevent civil war or bloodshed in any part of this kingdom.'[56]

George's aim was to broker a settlement, and in pursuing this he actually helped Asquith to resolve the political deadlock over Ulster. Asquith had begun secret negotiations with John Redmond, leader of the Irish nationalist MPs, and when Redmond agreed to a three-year exclusion of Ulster, the King declared that this was not enough. This enabled Asquith to go back to Redmond and ask for more. With Asquith's knowledge George wrote to Bonar Law asking him to tone down his violent speeches on Home Rule, such restraint being needed 'if we are to hope for a peaceful settlement'.[57] Stamfordham called on the Irish Unionist leader Edward Carson to express the King's hope that he would refrain from delivering a bitter speech which would 'make it still more difficult for the Prime Minister to propose a settlement acceptable to the Opposition'.[58]

At the opening of Parliament on 10 February 1914 the lord chancellor blundered and failed to hand the King the specially printed large-type version of his speech. George was annoyed. He claimed that he needed large type because nervousness made his hand shake, but the print grew steadily bigger as he got older, and 'at the end of his reign the type was enormous'.[59] He had no wish to use pince-nez while wearing uniform, and court protocol forbade the monarch from wearing spectacles. In spite of the small type, George managed to lay great stress on the paragraph in the speech about Home Rule, 'in which I appeal for a peaceful settlement', and he wrote to Asquith to say how pleased he was with the passage, which 'seems to have created a very good impression on all sides'.[60]

On the morning of 19 March Asquith had an audience at Buckingham Palace which lasted almost an hour. In this 'long and intimate talk' (as Harold Nicolson described it), the prime minister remarked how 'deeply grateful' he was to the King for helping to promote a settlement. 'Throughout, the King had, he considered, behaved in exactly the manner a Constitutional Sovereign should act.'[61] Asquith, ever the optimist, thought the King was in 'a gloomy mood' and exaggerated the danger of civil war in Ulster.[62] Gloomy George certainly was. He considered the audience 'not at all satisfactory, the position looks bleaker than ever; if neither side gives in there must be civil war'.[63]

The same morning Asquith attended a conference of ministers to brief General Sir Arthur Paget, the officer commanding the army in Ireland. The 63-year-old Paget was a hot-tempered old warhorse 'who should have been put out to grass years ago'; both he and his American wife Minnie Stevens had been members of the court of Edward VII.[64] Paget returned to Ireland that night in a highly excitable state, and the next morning gave orders to the officers stationed at the Curragh army base, many of them sympathetic to the Unionist cause, that they must either agree to take part in 'active operations' in Ulster or be dismissed from the service. Fifty-eight cavalry officers resigned.

'Had a most harassing day,' wrote George on 21 March, the day the news broke of an apparent mutiny in the Curragh, and a succession of generals were summoned to Buckingham Palace.[65] It was soon established that there had been no mutiny, that Paget had misunderstood his ministerial briefing; and the officers' resignations were set aside. 'I am glad to say,' wrote George, that 'the officers who had resigned have been told to return to their commands in Ireland, so all is as before, so the danger for the moment is over.'[66]

George himself soon came under attack. As Stamfordham wrote, 'the chief complaint of the Army is against the King. They say he ought to have asserted himself and prevented all this trouble. On the other hand the Radicals [Liberals] are denouncing "Buckingham Palace" and its evil influences.'[67] Neither of these charges had any substance. The King had nothing to do with the Curragh incident – the first he heard of it was reading the newspapers the next day. As for the attack on 'Buckingham

Palace', this annoyed George intensely because it impugned his political neutrality, and implied that the King was plotting with the Tories.[68]

Stamfordham was 'full of indignation at the way in which the King had been misinterpreted and censored for the very things he had not done'.[69] But though Asquith agreed that the attacks on the King were unfair, he was not sympathetic. After an audience with the King on 26 March, he reported to his mistress Venetia Stanley: 'I found the main preoccupation of the Other Party . . . was with his own position and the "terrible cross-fire" to which he conceives himself to be exposed.'[70]

The anxiety levels at Buckingham Palace can be gauged from an exchange between the Queen and the Prince of Wales, then at Oxford. May wrote giving what David described as an 'admirable' account of the 'present appalling crisis' and the 'dreadful time' she and George were having.[71] Worried that she had been indiscreet, she asked David to burn her letter, which he did, alas. 'It occurred to me that in the days to come a letter like mine might do harm & not be understood when one is supposed to hold aloof from politics which is not easy when one feels so strongly on the subject,' she told her son.[72]

To Queen Mary the Home Rule Bill seemed 'like the sword of Damocles hanging over one's head & one can think of nothing else & feels quite weighed down by it all'.[73] In fact, by demonstrating that the Ulster crisis wasn't bluff but seemed to pose a real threat of civil war, the Curragh incident brought a settlement nearer.

George and May made their first state visit, to Paris, in May 1914. The Queen would have preferred to give the honour of the first state visit to Vienna, but the foreign secretary, Sir Edward Grey, 'will not hear of it': paying this compliment to France was a way of nurturing the Anglo-French entente.[74] The royals were reluctant to travel after the Curragh incident, but Grey insisted that the visit went ahead. 'How I hate having to go when things are so unsettled here,' wrote May (she was referring to Home Rule), 'especially as one feels so acutely how England has fallen in prestige abroad. I really feel so ashamed I would prefer to hide – certainly not to smile & make oneself agreeable.'[75]

Fritz Ponsonby, who accompanied the royals as equerry, was full of foreboding and acid remarks. He worried that the Queen was too dowdy. She laughingly declared that she had bought a gown of the latest fashion, but when she turned to show him it was evident to his 'untutored' (and ungallant) eye that the dress was the style of years before. The French, grumbled Fritz, 'do not understand how to marshal a procession', and carriages lost their places and disappeared in the crowd.[76] But none of this mattered because, as May reported, 'to our great surprise ... the French people met us à bras ouverts & this continued until we left. Nothing could have exceeded the warmth of our reception everywhere & it really was very touching.'[77] Driving in an open carriage through the sunlit boulevards, the King-Emperor was cheered enthusiastically. Indeed, as George remarked, the cheering was 'just the same as England'.[78]

The last state ball of the Season took place on 16 July. The King and Queen had even less inclination for socialising than usual 'with all the anxiety of the dreadful political situation here which is such a constant source of distress to us – God knows how it will end'.[79] The next day Asquith informed the King that the time for a conference over Home Rule had arrived. 'I found the royal person in a tent in the garden,' he wrote, 'and had nearly ½ an hour with him. He was full of interest and excitement about the Conference.'[80]

At Buckingham Palace the English and Irish party leaders met four times in the Forty-Four Room between 21 and 24 July.* Their discussions broke down over the geographical limits of Ulster. The radical and socialist press attacked the King for interfering, but George's role in peacemaking strengthened him in the country at large – though as Geoffrey Robinson of *The Times* wrote in a letter to Stamfordham, 'this feeling is less vocal than the other'.[81]† Queen Mary poured out her feelings in a letter to her aunt:

> We certainly have had the most dreadfully bad luck since George succeeded, such momentous questions, such difficulties on all sides, & such impossible people to deal with, never being able to make them see the patriotic view of the question instead of the <u>party</u> one. It is such a pity when George really works like a slave for the good of the country, makes himself quite ill over it all, & then being abused for his pains. I confess it all makes me furious.[82]

When the Home Rule Bill eventually passed in September 1914 (but suspended for the duration of the First World War), Stamfordham composed a memorandum in which he described how for over a year the King had devoted 'quiet, patient, unremitting work' to help find a peaceful settlement.[83] He had corresponded with and talked to politicians on

---

*The Forty-Four Room, a vision of blue and gold and the grandest of the palace's reception rooms, was named for the visit of Tsar Nicholas I in 1844.

†Geoffrey Robinson, editor of *The Times* between 1912 and 1919 and again between 1923 and 1941, changed his name to Dawson in 1917, the name by which he is better known.

all sides. Indeed, wrote Stamfordham, 'I doubt whether anybody has a more comprehensive view of the whole question than that of the King, but this if I may say so, is as it should be.'[84]

The boxes of papers, of letters and chronologies on Home Rule neatly filed by Stamfordham testify to the emergence of a new type of monarchy: politically neutral but intervening to promote the public good and broker agreement. The political and constitutional crises of 1910–14 have been described by David Cannadine as 'the most testing domestic challenge' faced by any twentieth-century British sovereign.[85] King George was forced to learn on the job, and by 1914, with Stamfordham's help, he had reinvented the public role of the sovereign.

During the Buckingham Palace Conference George was worried by Lady Warwick, his father's ex-mistress, who threatened to publish Bertie's love letters unless she received a large sum of money. 'The most horrible fiend of a woman,' wrote George, she 'must be mad.'[86] Determined not to give in to blackmail, he instructed Charles Russell, the King's solicitor, who served an injunction on Daisy Warwick, forbidding her from publishing the letters. This ruthless use of the law to silence his enemies was another new feature of George's reign.

Soon Lady Warwick was banished from George's mind by a greater worry. On 25 July he noted: 'Had a long talk with Sir Edward Grey about Foreign Affairs, it looks as if we were on the verge of general European war, caused by the sending of ultimatum to Servia by Austria, very serious state of affairs.'[87] This is the first reference in his diary to what became known as the July crisis. Preoccupied by the Irish question, George had shut his eyes to the diplomatic storm. Both he and May had noted the assassination of Franz Ferdinand at Sarajevo on 28 June, which outraged Vienna and provoked the ultimatum, but they saw it as a private tragedy – 'a terrible shock to the dear old Emperor' – rather than the potential cause of war.[88] Both George and the Kaiser had accepted a pheasant-shooting invitation with Franz Ferdinand that autumn, and the archduke was busy extending his dining room in the weeks before the assassination.[89] As Harold Nicolson observed, 'it is curious how they never seemed to have realised until the Austrian ultimatum that war might result. The King's remarks on the affair are childish in the extreme.'[90]

At 9.30 a.m. on 26 July Prince Henry of Prussia came to see George at Buckingham Palace. Prince Henry was the Kaiser's younger brother, a naval officer like George, and May thought him 'extremely nice'.[91] Prince Henry stayed in George's study for only eight minutes. He reported back to the Kaiser that George said: 'We shall try all we can to keep out of this and shall remain neutral.'[92]

The effect of these off-the-cuff remarks was 'catastrophic'. William chose to interpret George's words as 'a clear official declaration of neutrality', and this emboldened him in pushing for war during the July crisis.[93] George, however, denied that he had used the words Prince Henry attributed to him. In a note written later, he claimed to have told his cousin: 'I hope we shall remain neutral. But if Germany declared war on Russia, & France joins Russia, then I am afraid we shall be dragged into it.'[94] George had a remarkably good memory, and his account of the conversation was probably accurate. It seems very unlikely indeed that he gave Prince Henry an official assurance of neutrality. Apart from anything else it was not within his power to do so.[95]

Over foreign policy George's views counted for little. His personal relations with the Kaiser were friendly, far more so than his father's had been. But his influence was less. He took little interest in foreign relations, and made no attempt to appoint his own nominees as King Edward had done. He fretted about the danger of war with Germany and claimed to prefer an anachronistic policy of splendid isolation.[96]

George's role in the July crisis was marginal. Foreign Office telegrams flooded into Buckingham Palace, and George diligently read them; but his diary gives no sense of agency. He didn't strive to prevent war as he had done with Home Rule. May confessed that she was 'torn in two'.[97] She had close ties to Germany through her aunt Augusta, and she had a soft spot for the Kaiser. She told her aunt: 'God grant we may not have a European war thrust upon us & for such a stupid reason too, no I don't mean stupid but to have to go to war on behalf of tiresome Servia beggars belief!'[98]

On 1 August George noted that opinion was dead against Britain joining the war. However, Edward Grey's speech on 3 August, declaring that 'we should not allow Germany to pass through English Channel or into North Sea to attack France & that we should not allow her troops to pass through Belgium, has entirely changed public opinion & now everyone is for war & our helping our friends'.[99] Large crowds flocked to the Palace, and the King and Queen were forced to appear several times on the new balcony to tremendous cheering. Doubts and rational politics were swept away by the roaring crowds. On 4 August George noted:

> I held a Council at 10 45 to declare war with Germany, it is a terrible catastrophe but it is not our fault. An enormous crowd collected outside the Palace, we went on the balcony both before & after dinner.

When they heard that war had been declared the excitement increased & it was a never to be forgotten sight when May & I with David went on the balcony, the cheering was terrific. Please God it may soon be over, & that he will protect dear Bertie's life.[100]

George had written to 'Dear Bertie', now a midshipman on the battleship HMS *Collingwood*, a week before when he learnt that all leave had been stopped on account of the European crisis. Asked by the captain whether the prince should come home, the King said no. He explained his decision to Bertie: 'Of course you could not have leave until the situation became normal again. I am sure you would be the last to wish to be treated differently to anybody else.'[101]

PART FIVE

WAR

1914–1918

CHAPTER 16

George at War

1914–1915

'Come at once. You may not be able to travel tomorrow,' the Queen telegraphed her woman of the bedchamber Lady Bertha Dawkins the day before war was declared.[1] Lady Bertha arrived to find the Queen speaking in a firm, strong voice, determined to avoid the chaos of overlapping voluntary organisations that had occurred during the Boer War. As president of Queen Mary's Needlework Guild, the charity which she had inherited from her mother, the Queen co-ordinated needlework guilds all over the country. The gorgeous state apartments at Friary Court in St James's Palace were lent by the King as a warehouse for garments, and the room where Charles I spent his last night was piled high with pyjamas and flannel shirts. Spearheaded by the Queen, sewing for the troops 'took on a quasi-religious character'.[2]

But this 'perfect epidemic of needlework' by 'the well-intended and well-to-do' had unintended consequences.[3] The Labour Party's Workers' War Emergency Committee objected that the glut of voluntary sewing by middle-class women was swamping the market, causing employers to make women textile workers redundant. Mary Macarthur, Labour firebrand and organiser of women's trade unions, begged: 'Stop these women knitting!'[4]

Queen Mary quickly grasped that voluntary work need not cause unemployment, and that for working women 'employment is better than charity'.[5] She wrote to the prime minister and, aided by the capable Lady Crewe, she invited the Workers' Committee to send women representatives to advise the Queen's Fund for unemployed women which she proposed to establish. This combination became the Central Committee on Women's Employment, a body which combined Edwardian battleaxes such as Mrs H. J. Tennant and Violet Markham with Labour women. Queen Mary was the president, and it was financed by the Queen's Work for Women Fund, as the Queen's Fund had now become.

Queen Mary summoned Mary Macarthur to Buckingham Palace. The two women formed an instant understanding. 'Here is someone who can and who means to help!' Macarthur shouted for joy after their first meeting.[6] She gave the Queen books to read, and dared to lecture her on the inequality of the classes. 'The Queen simply does understand

and grasp the whole situation from the Trades Union point of view,' said Mary M. of Mary R.[7]

The war gave May an exhilarating opportunity to *do* something. With the Central Committee and her friendship with Macarthur she broke out of the box of conventional royal charity and initiated a new version of welfare monarchy. When Kathleen Woodward wrote a celebratory life of Queen Mary at the suggestion of Lady Crewe in 1929, she listed the Central Committee as the Queen's greatest achievement.

'Here I am in this bloody gt [*sic*] palace,' wrote David the day after war was declared, 'doing absolutely nothing but attend[ing] meals.'[8] For the King and Queen, however, war brought ceaseless activity. 'Both of us are trying to do our level best for our beloved country,' May told a friend.[9] They stayed at Buckingham Palace for the first weeks, cancelling holidays and shutting up Balmoral for the duration of the war. 'You must be very sorry at not being able to go up to Scotland this year as usual,' wrote Bertie to his father. 'You must be very tired after all this very trying time with so much work to do and so many people to see and never getting a rest.'[10]

Throughout August the German armies swept relentlessly into France, until the invaders' advance on Paris was halted by the French, supported by the British Expeditionary Force (BEF), at the miracle Battle of the Marne (6–12 September). This was a decisive battle of the war. It smashed the Schlieffen Plan, which envisaged a knock-out blow on the Western Front, and so ultimately secured Germany's defeat, but at the cost of a four-year war of attrition. Little wonder that George was 'ceaselessly worried, constantly at work, sometimes unwell'.[11] No longer at the centre of politics, as he had been since 1910, it was far from clear what his role should be. Urged by his assistant private secretary Clive Wigram, from early on he wore uniform, which he did throughout the war.[12] When he visited troops at Aldershot, General Sir Douglas Haig observed: 'The King seemed anxious but he did not give me the impression that he fully realised the grave issues both for our Country as well as for his own house.'[13]

The First World War is a problem for George's biographers. As Frank Prochaska pointed out, 'royal biographers with their high political interests have difficulty with the role of constitutional monarchs in modern wars'.[14] Harold Nicolson's solution was to consider 'how the King's influence was brought to bear' during the war. Rather than catalogue the King's 'wearisome' routine duties in wartime, he wrote a high-politics narrative, focussing on his relations with politicians and generals.[15] One of the effects of the war, however, was to bring more ordinary people into direct contact with the sovereign than ever before, making the monarchy seem more accessible than ever before.[16]

George's diary, never an easy document to read, becomes particularly impenetrable during the war years. Day after day the entries fill with troop inspections, hospital visits, factory visits and medal pinning. The statistics are: 400 troop inspections, 300 hospital visits, 50,800 decorations conferred. The diary, as John Gore observed, is 'a curious blending of the trivial and the important'.[17] Constructing a narrative or tracing the outlines of a life from these bald, clotted entries isn't easy, but it's clear that the war years witnessed a transformation of the monarchy. To the arbitrator-monarch of 1910–14 was added a service monarchy, making direct contact with ordinary people, similar to the institution as it is today.

At the first Battle of Ypres (19 October to 22 November 1914) the British under Sir John French held the line, resisting the German advance at a catastrophic cost of over 55,000 casualties. 'Not Mons nor the Marne but Ypres was the real monument to British valour as it was also the grave of four-fifths of the original BEF.'[18] Three members of George's household were killed within a week: Lord Charles Mercer-Nairne, Lord Crichton and Lord John Hamilton.* Ypres convinced the King that it was his duty to visit his troops. The trip was meticulously planned by Stamfordham. Plain-clothes policemen provided security, and the details of the itinerary were concealed from the press. Unlike his bombastic cousin William II, George arrived neither with pomp nor with any intention of influencing the direction of the war.[19] 'I felt that it was my duty to go, & that it will do good,' he wrote.[20]

May had accompanied George on almost all his journeys since their marriage, but there was no question of her coming with him this time. George did not approve of women at the front. When he heard of Margot Asquith or the Duchess of Sutherland visiting France, he wrote begging the government to 'put a stop to these female excursions to the theatre of war: they must cause inconvenience & especially to the doctors as His

---

*On a letter from Mercer-Nairne dated 25 October 1914, the King wrote: 'Poor Charlie was killed on Oct. 30th by a shell' (RA PS/PSO/GV/C/Q832/263, 264, Lord Charles Mercer-Nairne, 'Report on our Brigade', 25 October 1914). Lord Crichton's death in October 1914 was not confirmed until 1916. 'Dolly has seen his poor widow who had hoped against hope that Ld C would be found somewhere at the end of the War! He was such a delightful person,' wrote Queen Mary (RA QM/PRIV/CC26/113, M to Augusta, 14 July 1916).

Majesty understands these lady visitors go to the hospitals but merely as sightseers!'[21]

The King arrived in France on 29 November feeling depressed by this 'awful wicked war', not helped by a rough crossing, during which 'I was sick all the time, besides getting some heavy seas over me on deck'.[22] George stayed in Saint-Omer, the headquarters of the British army, in the same street as the commander-in-chief, Sir John French, in a comfortable house with nice rooms 'including a big bath'. He found the army 'cheerful & optimistic, much more so than we are at home'.[23] After a packed four days driving in his motor, he managed to see all the troops except for those in the trenches. 'I must say the men look fit & well in spite of the cold & wet & all they have to go through in the trenches, some really like it they tell me.'[24] He told May that the men 'all seemed pleased to see me by the way they cheered & their smiling faces' – due, he thought, 'to the excellent food that they are getting, never has an army been half so well fed'.[25] The visit left him feeling confident that 'the Germans will not break through our lines now, however many fresh troops they may bring up, as we are so strongly entrenched'.[26]

The visit brought the King into informal contact with his soldiers, far more so than he ever had been before the war.[27] Perhaps he was too easily taken in by cheering troops and men telling him what they thought he wanted to hear. Haig dined with him at Saint-Omer, and found him 'very cheery but inclined to think that all our troops are by nature brave and [he] is ignorant of all the efforts which Commanders must make to keep up the "morale" of their men in war' and the training needed to enable a company to go forward in the face of almost certain death. Haig told the King of the deserters from Ypres coming down the Menin road with 'a look of absolute terror in their faces'.[28] This was not a side of the war that George understood.

'The King's Christmas: No Material Change of Plan,' announced *The Times*.[29] This was propaganda: the reality (wrote May) was that 'we can have no real festival this year, only do what we can to make others as comfortable as possible under the sad circumstances'.[30] At Sandringham, six bullocks were slaughtered, and George watched as the traditional joints of beef – two pounds for an adult and one pound for a child – were distributed to the 1,557 people on the estate on Christmas Eve.[31] Plum pudding was served at Christmas dinner and the shooting went on as before. There were no guests, but the bag was 2,000 pheasants most days.[32]

The royal family stayed only two weeks at Sandringham. When they returned to York Cottage at the end of January 1915 they found a guard of 120 Grenadiers and two naval guns, deployed for their protection after a Zeppelin raid the previous week. 'It is tiresome,' wrote May, 'that even there one cannot get away from the feeling of uncertainty which constantly haunts one. Really the behaviour of the Germans is beyond everything.'[33] The officers dined with the King and Queen, 'a pleasant change for us,' wrote May, 'as we don't see many people'.[34]

Godfrey Thomas, equerry to the Prince of Wales, stayed at York Cottage in December 1914 and described the King after dinner wearing big tortoiseshell spectacles and reading out bits from the newspapers, 'generally adding explosive comments about the Germans'.[35] George had at first resisted the anti-German clamour. When he was pushed to take down the heraldic banners in St George's Chapel, Windsor which belonged to the eight Garter knights who were enemies of Britain in the war, he refused. In October 1914 he had been forced to yield to the demand for the sacking of Prince Louis of Battenberg, the first sea lord. That a German should head the Royal Navy was unacceptable in wartime even though (as George wrote) 'there is no more loyal man in the Country'. He noted: 'I saw poor Louis, very painful interview, he quite broke down.'[36] George received 'heaps' of abusive letters about his first cousins who were fighting against Britain. Charles Edward, Duke of Coburg had chosen the German side, and so had the son of Princess Christian, Albert of Schleswig-Holstein, an officer in the Prussian army. George explained to Asquith that cousin Albert wasn't really fighting on the side of the Germans, as he had been put in charge of English prisoners in a camp near Berlin. 'A nice distinction,' observed the prime minister.[37]

The war tore apart the dynastic realm of Queen Victoria's extended family. What caused George's feelings to harden was the Germans' conduct of the war. German cruisers shelled Scarborough and Hartlepool on 16 December, killing 110 civilians. 'This is German *"kultur"*,' was George's grim comment.[38] The sinking of the Cunard liner *Lusitania* on 7 May 1915, killing over 1,100 civilians, many of them Americans, was 'a most dastardly crime'.[39] George was outraged by the way the Germans treated their prisoners of war: 'It is a perfect scandal & the Germans call themselves civilised.'[40]

Such war crimes, violating the code of honour, made the enemy's Garter banners untenable. Queen Alexandra, whose hatred of the Germans stretched back over half a century to the Prussian invasion of Denmark in 1863, wrote to her son that 'the time has come when I must speak out' about 'those hateful German banners'.[41] On 14 May 1915 behind locked doors at St George's Chapel, Sir Alfred Scott-Gatty, Garter king of arms, ordered a gang of workmen to dismantle the eight enemy banners – large flags hoisted high up in the choir. The King was not present. The event was private because 'a public ceremony of degradation' was thought to be 'repugnant' to the public.[42]*

At Buckingham Palace austerity reigned. The King and Queen gave the lead to the country in this respect. On a visit to a hospital George was shown the central heating. 'How lucky you are,' he exclaimed. 'You know we have to live in the corner of one room to keep warm?' He joked: 'And you can have hot baths every day! I only get a hot bath once a week now – and – well, you just cannot lather soap in cold water, can you?'[43]

Strict rationing was ordered at the Palace. Menus were slashed from twelve to three courses, and the use of wine or sherry was forbidden in cooking. Queen Mary ordered that meat was to be served to the royal family and the household staff no more than three times a week. This edict caused a fluster in the kitchens as the French-trained Edwardian chefs knew no vegetarian recipes. They improvised with fish dishes, such as toast Ivanhoe: a purée of smoked haddock cooked in béchamel, sieved and served on toast.[44]

For George the passing of the *cuisine classique* was no hardship. He far preferred simple food. Occasionally he sent messages to the kitchen. '*Saturday*. Minced chicken for lunch. *Sunday*. Boiled chicken for lunch. A small piece off the breast. Don't send up a whole bird.'[45]

Only recently fitted with false teeth, the King was perhaps more than ever averse to grand dinners. Virginia Woolf recounted a story of the King at the Royal Academy asking Princess Victoria where she got her false teeth. 'Mine,' George exclaimed, 'are always dropping into my plate: they'll be down my throat next. My man is a rascal. I am going to leave him.'[46]†

Queen Mary sent down orders every day to the chefs, and soon after the war broke out she launched an offensive against the Edwardian breakfast. Banished were the silver chafing dishes filled with kippers,

---

*The Garter banners removed were those of the Emperor of Austria, the German Emperor, the King of Württemberg, the German Crown Prince, the Grand Duke of Hesse, Prince Henry of Prussia, the Duke of Saxe-Coburg and the Duke of Cumberland, father of Ernest of Hanover, Duke of Brunswick, who had married the Kaiser's daughter in 1913. Apart from the Emperor of Austria, these were all relations of the King or Queen.

†George saw his dentist, Harry Baldwin, frequently in 1914–15. In 1915 Baldwin pulled out three teeth, but George did not wear a full plate of false teeth. Woolf's authority was Walter Lamb, secretary to the Royal Academy.

kidneys and scrambled eggs. To reduce waste the Queen introduced a system of portion control. Each person's breakfast was decided arbitrarily by the Queen and ordered in advance. She made sure that she was the first down to breakfast. 'If anyone was tempted to help themselves to fish when they also had sausage and bacon one look from her was sufficient to make them change their minds.'[47] Only Prince Henry was allowed the privilege of two eggs for breakfast, which he claimed he needed for health reasons. Punctuality was crucial. The household soon discovered that in order to be sure of getting something to eat one had to be there before time. Godfrey-Faussett once came in late for breakfast, and seeing all the food had gone he rang the bell and ordered a boiled egg. The King was enraged. He 'accused him of being a slave to his inside, of unpatriotic behaviour, and went so far as to hint that we should lose the war on account of his gluttony'.[48]

Lloyd George saw the King on 29 March 1915, and (George noted) 'we had an interesting conversation about the drink question', which was the chancellor's current obsession.[49] Lloyd George insisted that excess alcohol consumption was damaging the war effort by reducing the productivity of workers in armament factories. The next day the King wrote to Lloyd George offering to 'set an example' by giving up alcohol himself and banning it in the royal household.[50] Lloyd George promptly sent the letter to *The Times*, and the King was trapped. There was no going back. 'This morning we have all become teetotallers until end of the war,' wrote George on 6 April. 'I hate doing it, but hope it will do good.'[51] It didn't. Few in public life followed his example, the public did not respond, and the King came to feel that 'he had been made a fool of'.[52]

'Awful balls the whole thing,' was David's verdict.[53] Lloyd George, who was no admirer of the monarch – 'I wonder what my little German friend has got to say to me!' he remarked when summoned to the palace – had duped the King into rushing into a pledge which the household regretted even if the King did not.[54] Forced to give up the small bottle of sparkling Moselle which she drank for dinner each evening and sip Perrier water instead, the Queen declared: 'We have been carted.'[55] The servants arranged a wreath of empty bottles outside the locked cellar door with a crepe bow and a placard with the word 'Dead' written on it.[56] For George, however, giving up wine was no hardship: 'he doesn't miss it at all,' wrote May, '& feels less sleepy'.[57] According to a mischievous tale told by David, the King after dinner would leave his guests for five minutes and retire to his study 'to attend to a small matter of business', which was generally supposed to be 'the consumption of a small glass of port'.[58]

*   *   *

The court spent Easter 1915 at Windsor. Clive Wigram, assistant private secretary – tall, athletic, ex-Indian army, an improbable Wykehamist, known to the Queen as Wiggy – was in attendance, and he brought his young wife Nora, who wrote daily to her parents.* It was a quiet family party. The only guests were Balfour and Rosebery. They drank home-made orangeade at dinner and afterwards sang songs such as 'Tipperary' for hours standing round the piano, the Queen 'enjoying herself immensely' while others longed to go to bed. Nora couldn't get over 'how stupid all the courtiers are'. The only one with brains was Fritz Ponsonby; 'the others are all wonderfully ill-informed & never seem to know anything'. Lady Fritz, a beauty, was hated by the other court ladies, who thought her a snob: 'She wears a perpetually bored look but she is good looking.'[59]

One afternoon Nora drove with the Queen and the children to play in the woods. 'It was so nice seeing the Queen under these conditions with all the children in fits of laughter.' Prince George slithered down tree trunks and made his trousers green. 'The Queen [shook] her umbrella at his head saying, Come off that at once. Papa hates you spoiling your clothes!'[60]

Once Nora went driving alone with the Queen for two hours. 'Never ceased talking for half a minute!' She talked about the Delhi Durbar, 'and it seemed so curious hearing the Queen of England describing her feelings when she sat on the parapet where the old Mogul Emperors had wandered'. On the subject of building New Delhi, she said 'she thought Lutyens was going to make a hash of it as being too visionary'.[61]

The next day the Queen ('As usual she was charming to me') showed Nora her rooms. Her sitting room, hung with a soft reseda-green bro-cade, led into her drawing room, 'rather an ugly Empire paper and ugly Royal portraits'. Opening out of that was her bedroom, 'not a very big room, hung with pale pink silk'. In it was 'a wonderful ormolu dressing table on which was the whole toilet set which used to belong to Queen Anne – massive gold' and, to Nora's eyes, hideous. 'I couldn't admire it.' Next was the Wedgwood room, a little gem, Adam walls and recesses filled with blue Wedgwood. 'The poor Queen she heaved a heavy sigh and said I do trust some other Queen won't arise and undo all this room. For it is my all my own idea and I do love it so'. Nora's verdict:

---

*'Who is this wonderful Wigram?' asked George when Wigram was appointed his assis-tant chief of staff in India in 1905–6 (John Gore, *King George V: A Personal Memoir* (John Murray, 1941), p. 198). In 1910 Wigram joined the royal household as assistant to Stamfordham.

'The Queen is a dear if one can venture to describe her so and such a grande dame.'[62]

The great excitement was when the Asquiths came to stay. The court ladies disliked Margot intensely and 'banded together to be rude to her'. Margot didn't disappoint. 'What a woman – the cheek of her,' wrote Nora. She appeared in a little dinner dress: 'black, long sleeves, high collar at the back ... open at the front, a tousled head, no jewels – and a marvellous pair of red heeled shoes about 4 inches high. Such a contrast to the Queen, who had her best brocade on and diamonds galore!'[63]

'We were a dull lot!' wrote Margot of the dry court.[64] There were no other guests. No one talked except Margot, who 'took copious swigs from a medicine bottle'. After the Queen said goodnight and the party broke up, Margot 'lit a particularly strong cigarette and walked airily down the long picture gallery, the holy of holies'. Lady Minto in her most bland lady-in-waiting tones pursued her, saying, 'You know dear Mrs Asquith it isn't usual to smoke here but of course it doesn't matter in your case!' Subdued giggles from the maids of honour in the distance.[65]

Nora particularly liked sitting next to the King at dinner. 'He is so charming and easy.' These were not words usually used of George, but sophisticated women were captivated. 'My passion for him grows to an obsession,' wrote Ettie Desborough. Nora noticed that the King 'appeared to be highly entertained' by Margot at dinner, and the appreciation was mutual. 'He is a dear little fellow,' wrote Margot, 'and fundamentally humble in spite of his manner (noisy and crude).'[66]

'David's gone to the Front and Bertie's gone back to sea, and I sit here and knit, knit, knit,' wailed Prince John. 'I call this a bloody war.'[67] As a serving naval officer on HMS *Collingwood* Bertie seemed in pole position when the war broke out, but his health gave way. An operation to remove his appendix failed to cure his stomach problems. This was not surprising as he suffered from a gastric ulcer which had not been diagnosed, and his return to the *Collingwood* in February 1915 was short-lived. Nora Wigram found him 'extraordinarily attractive – such a charming smile and so much easier to talk to than the Prince of Wales'. The latter was 'the only member of the Royal Family I have found difficile'. Sitting next to him at dinner, 'I couldn't make any headway'.[68]

Twenty-year-old David was consumed with one ambition, and that was to get to the front. He persuaded his father to find him a commission in the Grenadier Guards, in spite of being at five feet seven inches 'a pygmy among giants', well below the regulation height of six feet.[69] At first he was blocked by his father from accompanying the brigade to

France, but in November he was given a post on the staff of Sir John French. He complained that he was kept occupied with made work which concealed his non-combatant role under a show of activity. In letter after letter to his father – lengthy epistles which often took two or three hours to compose – he harped on a single theme: to be allowed to fight. He appealed to Lord Stamfordham. 'I have no real job except that of being Prince of Wales,' he grumbled, as if being Prince of Wales wasn't enough.[70]

It's easy to judge the prince as spoilt and petulant. The reasons why the heir to the throne was not allowed to fight in the trenches were obvious enough. In his memoir he recalled that 'the concept of duty was part of my inheritance': was it surprising, he asked, that he should rebel against being held back when his peers bore the shock of the battle?[71] What was surprising, perhaps, was not his sense of duty or honour but his obsessiveness. The trenches were a forbidden world, 'ghastly beyond conception', to which he yearned to belong. His minders deplored his uncourtly habit of swearing. But peppering his speech with intensifiers such as 'fuck' was a badge of belonging to that band of brothers.[72] Foul-mouthed and baby-faced, the prince was stranded in a psychological no man's land between the court and the trenches. As the prince at the front, however, he achieved film-star popularity.

David had always been closer to his mother, and during the war he became her confidant. May complained that George discussed David's arrangements without her being present:

Papa never likes me to be with him when he discusses things with people about all of you children, such a pity as first of all I ought to know, & secondly it makes it more difficult to me just to hear in a cursory way from Papa a few facts in a few short minutes.[73]

When George refused to show David's letters to May, she asked him to write his confidential news on a separate sheet.[74] 'I miss our little talks,' she told him, 'for it is nice for me to feel I can talk so openly with you & that you understand certain little difficulties one has which make times like the present ones, rather more difficult.'[75]

Letters such as these have caused biographers to accuse May of mischief making between David and his father. Members of the household could never understand why she failed to confront her husband over the children.[76] But this deeply royal woman was no ordinary wife. She was also a consort, and as such it was her duty to avoid confrontations with the sovereign; instead she used courtly diplomacy to get her way. The war made her relations with George fraught. Her letters hint at his low moods, refusal to talk and grumpiness. 'I am afraid from what you tell me Papa writes rather despondingly to you,' she told David, 'but certainly he has been in better spirits lately & rather more talkative.'[77] For the Queen, lonely and isolated at Buckingham Palace, it was indeed a blessing, as she told David, that 'I can write & talk to you openly knowing you will see my point of view'.[78]

George's diary filled with troop inspections as Australian and Canadian soldiers poured into England, and Kitchener's army trained two-and-a-half million recruits destined for France. It was the King's duty to maintain morale, visiting the men in their camps and inspecting them before their departure to France. 'First you're trained; then you're polished up; then the King comes; and then you're off,' was the saying.[79]

Leaving London after breakfast and steaming at speed on a special train to Winchester or Salisbury Plain, George could review thousands of troops and return to Buckingham Palace in time for lunch. On these trips he was usually accompanied by Lord Kitchener, and in his diary he often noted: 'Had a long talk with Kitchener in the train.'[80]

A vast figure, six feet two inches tall, red-faced, heavy and fat, Lord Kitchener of Khartoum was George's rock. As secretary of state for war, Kitchener was uncomfortable in the Cabinet, and ministers found him ponderous and slow-witted. Many agreed with Margot Asquith, who quipped that he was 'more of a great poster than a great man'.[81]* Kitchener's only fault in George's eyes, however, was that he talked so much that even George couldn't get a word in. Travelling back from Winchester once, the voluble king was reduced to silence.[82]

The war work that the King and Queen did together was visiting hospitals. As the wounded from France and later from the Dardanelles filled Britain's hospitals, many of them hastily improvised for the war, the King and Queen struggled to keep pace. On more than forty days in 1915 George's diary records visits to hospitals, sometimes seeing two or three in an afternoon. There was no press coverage and little preparation for these visits, but the informality and lack of publicity was congenial to George. A telephone message received at noon would announce that the King and Queen had an hour to spare when they would like to see the hospital. A flustered matron might protest that fresh cases from the front were about to arrive at Victoria, and please could the King come an hour later. 'That is exactly how the King wants

---

*The 'great poster' showed a picture of Kitchener above the words 'WANTS YOU'.

to see you, when you are busy,' came the reply on the telephone. 'He does not want you to make especially ready for him.' The King and Queen would walk from room to room, talking freely to everyone, and the young wounded men 'forgot to be awed'.[83]

Society ladies converted their houses into hospitals or nursing homes, and royal social life became a matter of visiting wounded officers in houses in Belgrave Square, where Lady Bathurst, Mrs Eyres Monsell and Lady Aberconway had hospitals, or Lady Ridley's house in Carlton House Terrace. At Polesden Lacey in Surrey, Mrs Ronnie Greville entertained royalty in wartime fashion. 'She has got 10 wounded officers there who she has made most comfortable,' wrote George. 'May & I had a long talk with her, she gave us tea & showed us her lovely garden.'[84]

The visits to hospitals filled with hundreds of wounded and mutilated men, some without limbs or eyes, some shell-shocked, were traumatic. 'You can't conceive what I suffered going round those hospitals in the War,' George later remarked.[85] For the Queen hospital visits were even more of an ordeal. Naturally squeamish, and lacking Queen Alexandra's empathy with the sick, she forced herself to talk calmly to horribly disfigured men. 'Sometimes when we left the ward,' wrote Lady Airlie, 'I would see tears glistening in her eyes but she never allowed them to fall.'[86] Never before had hospital visits exposed the King and Queen to such broken, shattered men, and they both found the experience hard to bear.

'Life is very monotonous,' wrote May. 'I hardly see anyone, go nowhere except to hospitals, or to my work rooms or centres, so that one thinks and talks of nothing but of this dreadful war.'[87] She found distraction in reading old family letters – such as those to George IV from his mother, Queen Charlotte, 'so affectionate and nice', and from his daughter, Princess Charlotte.[88] Every day at Buckingham Palace George wrote in his diary: 'Read all the evening. Bed at 11.30.' After a silent, spartan dinner, he retired to his study and worked. No guests came. 'Papa won't have anyone to dinner. More's the pity,' wrote May to David.[89] In March 1915 George joined a men's dinner at the Marlborough Club. 'Quite a pleasant dinner,' he wrote, 'first time I have dined out since the War began.'[90]

The King had become almost invisible. The newspapers reported his visits to troops or hospitals, but, as the novelist Rider Haggard observed, 'in all the private discussion on the war at which I have been present, I have never heard his name mentioned. No one asks what does the King think.'[91] It wasn't that anyone doubted that he was doing his duty, but he failed to provide the leadership that some felt the nation needed.

Cigarettes helped ease the tension, and it was probably during the war that George, once a moderate smoker, became a heavy one.[92] He himself later declared that his stamps 'saved his life' during the war.[93] They offered an escape: as May observed, George was 'more than ever interested in his stamps which is a good thing'.[94]

John Tilleard, George's stamp keeper, had died in 1913, and he was succeeded by E. D. Bacon, a professional philatelist with an illustrious career as an organiser of famous collections. Bacon was a member of the household with the title of curator of the King's philatelic collection, and he had a room on the ground floor at Buckingham Palace next to the Billiards Room. On two or three days a week during the war the King walked downstairs from his office to the Stamp Room, a high space lit by a large window facing on to an internal courtyard. 'Arranged stamps with Bacon before & after luncheon' is a frequent diary entry; he worked on stamps on eighty-five days in 1915.

'Papa is doing his beloved stamps, so good for him,' wrote May. 'He is looking thro' a wonderful collection of British Empire stamps.'[95] Choosing 'some very good stamps' to buy from the twenty-five volumes of William Mann's famous collection of British Colonial issues was utterly absorbing.[96] When Britain took Germany's African colonies Kamerun and Togoland or annexed Egypt, the King was quick to add the relevant new stamps to his collection as well as old stamps overprinted with 'GR'. Sitting in the Stamp Room, peering through his magnifying glass with Bacon at his side, King George calmly mapped the rise of his new empire beyond the seas in Africa and the Near East, a welcome distraction from the bloodletting in France.

'I must say', George told May on 17 May, 'I have been terribly depressed in the last few days & have so many extra worries besides all the anxieties.'[97] George was writing from the train after visiting Glasgow, where he walked several miles inspecting the shipbuilding yards on the Clyde. Back in London the shortage of shells combined with the disastrous failure of the Dardanelles campaign in north-west Turkey to produce a crisis about the direction of the war. Esher gave a trenchant summary in a letter to the King:

> If I live to write the history of this War!! I shall point to . . . 10th May, a day when we were fighting for our existence in Flanders. When . . . the Board of the Admiralty was crumbling to pieces. When the biggest soldier of the Emperor [Kitchener] was hesitating whether he could carry on. And the King's Prime Minister was out of town playing golf.[98]

Admiral Fisher, the first sea lord, was a man whom George had always disliked and distrusted. He had objected strenuously to Fisher's appointment in October 1914. After resigning over the mismanagement of the Dardanelles, withdrawing his resignation several times, pretending to go to Scotland and hiding in the Charing Cross Hotel, Fisher left the government on 16 May 1915, to George's mixed fury and relief.* Fisher's resignation prompted Asquith to form a coalition government with the Conservatives a few days later. This was welcomed by George chiefly because it allowed Asquith to get rid of Churchill, first lord of the Admiralty, 'who has become impossible'.[99] The one-time friend of the King had disgraced himself again. Not only was Churchill to blame for the fiasco of the Dardanelles, but 'he is intriguing with French against Kitchener, he is the real danger'.[100]

The shell scandal of May 1915 was orchestrated by Sir John French, the commander-in-chief, who inspired a press campaign in *The Times* against Kitchener. In the quarrel between Kitchener and French, the Palace was firmly on the side of the secretary of state. 'Really the behaviour of Sir J F passes all comprehension,' wrote the Queen, 'and how can he be so petty fathoms belief – it is a great pity for a clever man to act like this. The "Times" outburst against Ld K of K has had just the opposite effect to what was desired I am so delighted for anything more outrageous than such an uncalled for attack has never been done.'[101] Walking round the garden at Buckingham Palace with Esher, the King 'declared over and over again that he would support Ld K'.[102] He lent Kitchener York House in St James's Palace and, as a special mark of favour, created him a knight of the Garter.

George's loyalty to Kitchener was problematic, however. Supporting Kitchener meant opposing French. The King was arguably too willing to listen to complaints about French, rather than attempting to repair relations between the two field marshals. By the summer of 1915 the King had lost confidence in French. 'I don't think he is particularly clever & he has an awful temper,' wrote George.[103] General Sir William Robertson, one of French's enemies, had a long talk with George, who noted afterwards: 'I am convinced it would be better for all concerned if the C-in-C were changed.'[104]

French's nemesis was the Battle of Loos (25 September to 8 October

*Fisher's bad behaviour rankled with the King for many years. In the 1920s he got so angry while talking about Fisher that he became red in the face and declared that the admiral should have been hanged from the yardarm for desertion (Robert Rhodes James, ed., *Memoirs of a Conservative: J.C.C. Davidson's Memoirs and Papers* (Weidenfeld & Nicolson, 1969), p. 108).

1915). Under pressure from the French leaders, he led a doomed attempt to break the German defences. He took part against his better judgement, knowing that shortages of ammunition made the German line impossible to break. The attack failed, and the British suffered 60,000 casualties, twice as many losses as the Germans. The defeat at Loos sealed French's fate.

A fortnight later, on 21 October, the King, dressed in khaki, slipped out of Buckingham Palace at 9.20 a.m. in a motor car, accompanied only by Fritz Ponsonby and Charles Cust. At Victoria he boarded a discreet special train to Dover. Elaborate precautions had been taken to conceal the King's visit to France, and his luggage was sent in hired vans.

At Boulogne the King's party was reunited with Henri Cédard, the head chef at Buckingham Palace, and his deputy Tschumi, who had travelled ahead with two lorries loaded with eggs, butter and game. They brought with them King Edward VII's purpose-built hot box designed to supply piping-hot refreshments out shooting. George plunged into a packed schedule of visits to military hospitals filled with terribly mutilated men or gassed soldiers blue in the face and gasping for breath. Behind his car trundled a lorry dispensing hot food, more than ever welcome after the rations of the trenches.

The King stayed at a small chateau in the town of Aire. David arrived to accompany him on his inspections, and Ponsonby noticed that he was very nervous before his father: 'He remained singularly silent, only opening his mouth when he was addressed and then weighing carefully each word he uttered.'[105] His private war with his father to be allowed to serve in the trenches had encountered a setback during the Battle of Loos a few weeks before. When he left his car in order to inspect the front line with General Cavan, who had been put in charge of him, he returned to find that his driver had been killed. The King was also annoyed with David for refusing to wear the orders given him by Uncle Nicky and the French. David's insistence that he hadn't earned the decorations as he hadn't fought in the trenches made little impression on his father.

The generals who came to dine with the King told him what he had come out to France to hear – namely, that everyone had lost confidence in Sir John French and he must go. Douglas Haig dined at the chateau and, though never very communicative, he went much further than the others and told the King that French was 'a great source of weakness'.[106] General Robertson stuck the knife in too and told the King that Haig would be 'excellent' as C-in-C.[107]

On the morning of 28 October the King set out in drenching rain to inspect the Guards Division. People had complained on his previous visit to France that no one could see him, as he was always on foot or in a motor car, and to avoid disappointment he agreed to inspect troops riding a horse. Haig insisted on lending him a handsome charger but, like all generals' horses, it was very fresh.

Back at the chateau, the cooks had succeeded in sourcing six local chickens for dinner that evening. They were supervising the plucking when an equerry rode up, breathless and incoherent. There had been an accident to the King. The staff at the chateau thought he had been shot by the Germans.

The King's horse had reared, frightened by cheering troops, and fallen backwards, crushing the King. For two or three minutes, George lay motionless. David thought he was dead.[108] He might have been killed if the ground had been dry and hard, but he was saved by the soft mud.[109] He stood up and was carried to his car, and then was driven to the chateau in excruciating pain.

CHAPTER 17

The King and the Generals

1915–1916

Back at the chateau, they carried the King awkwardly upstairs to his bedroom and laid him on a sofa. He refused to see the army doctors sent by Haig, and waited for the royal physicians Sir Bertrand Dawson and Sir Anthony Bowlby, who were working in army hospitals nearby. A bulletin was issued signed by five doctors confirming that the King was suffering from severe bruising. 'Few bruises have had so much attention,' was Haig's dismissive comment.[1]

George dictated his diary entry for 28 October several days after his fall, and the handwriting seems to be David's. The diary records that he suffered great pain and hardly slept for three nights. Two days after the accident, 'I was X-rayed & the pelvis was found to be intact'.[2] The doctors were deliberately withholding the gravity of the King's condition from the public. As Dawson later wrote, 'the injuries were more serious than could then be disclosed'.[3] The King had fractured his pelvis in two places. When informed that Sir John French was imploring him to move in case the chateau was bombed by Germans, the King replied: 'You can tell French to go to hell and stay there. I don't intend to move for any bombs.'[4]

Lying on his back in the hospital train in France, the injured King insisted on decorating Sergeant Brooks of the Coldstream Guards, who had won the Victoria Cross, but he was too weak to push the pin through the khaki uniform.[5] The drawing by Samuel Begg of Sergeant Brooks kneeling at the King's bedside imagined George as a saintlike figure. Not all the comments were kind, however. One officer wrote: 'The din caused by the men's enthusiasm . . . rather upset the king's horse, and old Georgie came off.'[6] By making himself accessible, the King exposed himself to ridicule and scorn, leading (it has been suggested) to 'desacralization' of the monarchy.[7]

The Channel crossing was very rough, and 'naturally I was seasick which did not make my pains less.'[8] In spite of the injury, protocol was observed. 'I will wait in my room until you send for me,' wrote the Queen in advance of his homecoming, 'for I presume you would rather be settled in your bed before you see me.'[9]

It was two weeks before the King could put his feet to the ground and three weeks before he was able to dress. After six weeks the nurses left, and Sir Frederick Treves paid his last doctor's visit.[10] The doctors issued a bulletin saying that on medical grounds the King should 'take a little stimulant daily during his convalescence', temporarily interrupting his dry war.[11] At York Cottage for Christmas he was able to shoot, and on his first day he killed 333 birds himself, including 161 pheasants in one stand, 'not bad after my accident'.[12] But the pain persisted. In April, May reported him 'rather lame still & the weather affects the nerves of the right leg'.[13] When Churchill saw him some months after the accident he was shocked by his 'shattered condition and evident physical weakness', which had been hidden from the public.[14]

George's biographers agree that 'he was never the same man again' after his accident.[15] His keepers and loaders testified that he never shot as well. He was often in pain which, coupled with his workload, made him irritable. Queen Mary begged David not to bother his father with complaints about his role. 'Papa has so much to worry him that I think we ought to keep our own little troubles and vexations to ourselves, instead of troubling him with them.'[16]

John Gore believed that the King's diary changed. 'It reveals much more of the character of the writer', and after the accident the picture grows of 'a great gentleman and a true Christian'.[17] This is not a reading of the diary that everyone will recognise.

George's visit to France had convinced him, as we have seen, that Sir John French must go, 'otherwise we shall never win this war'. He told Stamfordham: 'This has been my opinion for some time.'[18] From his sickbed at Buckingham Palace the King played a 'pivotal' role in pressing Asquith and Kitchener to dismiss French.[19] He saw both men within days of his return, while he was still lying on his back and racked with pain. Asquith needed no persuading, but the King kept up the pressure, urging him to act.[20] On 6 December French resigned, and soon afterwards Haig was appointed commander-in-chief. At the same time another of the King's favourites, General Sir William Robertson, was appointed chief of the Imperial General Staff and sole military adviser to the War Council, thus restoring the control of the military experts over strategy and eliminating the strategic amateurs such as Churchill, whom the King, as an ex-naval officer, deeply distrusted.

The appointments of Haig and Robertson marked what has been described as the 'apogee' of the King's real influence over military affairs.[21] Their rise owed much to the King's support, a fact which (as one historian wrote) 'has not received adequate attention'.[22] When he saw Maurice Hankey, secretary to the War Council, the King 'told me all about the forthcoming changes ... and rather hinted that he had done the whole thing'.[23]

As he had done over Home Rule, George conducted a voluminous correspondence, this time with generals and royal relatives serving in France. He became exceptionally well informed. 'The King's knowledge of all the details of what goes on is remarkable,' wrote Esher, 'and he never seems to forget anything that he is told.'[24] But the King was also used by the generals, who exploited the influence that his confidence gave them and whispered criticisms of their rivals into the royal ear.

Haig was quick to court the King's favour. In the very first week of the war he had told George ('I felt it my duty to do so') that he had grave doubts whether Sir John French was fit to command the army in France.[25] Haig sent diary letters home to his wife Doris, who typed them up. When Wigram suggested that the diaries might be sent first to the King and then forwarded to Lady Haig, Doris objected, as she considered that the diaries were written 'for me alone'.[26] So she was entrusted with the duty of selecting passages for the King, which she sent on to Wigram. 'Had I known that Your Majesty would care to read these notes, I would of course have written them with greater care!' said Haig.[27] Allowing Doris to control the diaries seems a bizarre arrangement in the male-dominated military world of the Great War, but the arrangement continued, and Doris was instructed by Haig to use her own judgement and not to forward details of future military operations.

In 1915 Haig's criticisms of French became more frequent, undermining the King's confidence in the latter, and George encouraged Haig to write directly to Wigram with his complaints. After his appointment as C-in-C, Haig was invited by the King to write to him 'quite freely and tell me how matters are progressing. Naturally I shall consider your letters in the strictest confidence.'[28] Haig, who was fluent on paper but a poor speaker, wrote 'often and without reserve'.[29]

Whether George's intervention over French's removal and Haig's appointment was constitutional or wise is debatable. George took seriously his titular position as head of the armed services. Asquith recognised that 'all our sovereigns (I have now dealt with three) believe that in Army & Navy appointments they have a special responsibility & a sort of "divine right of Kings" prerogative ... they have to be humoured & brought in'.[30] In the First World War, as the politicians battled the generals for control over the strategic direction of the war, this prerogative took on a greater significance. When the King and prime minister were in agreement, as George and Asquith were over French and Haig, there was no problem. But when the politicians quarrelled with the generals, as Lloyd George did with Haig, and the King supported the generals, the King's intervention risked involving him in a damaging conflict with the government.[31]

Backing Haig meant endorsing the conventional strategy of concentrating Britain's forces on the war in France. The King had no time for 'sideshows', especially after the disaster of the Dardanelles, as he explained in December 1915:

> The British Empire must make haste and concentrate all our strength and all our energy to produce as strong an army as possible to take the offensive in France in the spring and the Allies must deliver their attacks simultaneously and by then the Central Powers [Germany, Austria-Hungary, the Ottoman Empire and Bulgaria] I am sure will not be able to stand the strain.[32]

Generals such as Haig were worshipped as demi-gods during the war and afterwards. Criticism was unthinkable. Not until the 1930s did people come to see the First World War as a wicked, needless waste of life. In his 1936 novel *The General* C. S. Forester pilloried Haig and his generals for their iron will and blinkered vision. 'Men without imagination were necessary to execute a military policy devoid of imagination, devised by a man without imagination.'[33] If this was true of Haig, it applied to King George as well. What he did, he did very well; but he was a Westerner, committed to defeating the Germans on the Western Front, and he could see no alternative to the catastrophic slaughter taking place in France.

In one week in March 1916 the King and Queen gave three huge tea parties for the wounded. Over 2,000 men came from London hospitals to Buckingham Palace, where they were waited on by duchesses (Devonshire, Sutherland, Buccleuch) who poured the tea instead of flunkeys. The King and Queen walked quietly from one table to the next, talking to the men. There followed an entertainment in the Riding School featuring Harry Lauder, the singer and comedian, and the actress Gladys Cooper, and at the end the King and Queen were cheered to the roof. 'Those who watched the King, who still used a stick in getting about, could see his face lighten with joy and pride, for he was among his own men again,' wrote a patriotic journal.[34]

The Queen was much involved with women's wartime employment, inspecting new enterprises where women did the work in order to release the men. 'One really feels very proud of the women who have come forward most valiantly to help,' she wrote.[35] 'It appears to encourage them, my visiting them, so I gladly do this.'[36] After inspecting a factory in Notting Hill which trained women in welding for the manufacture of aircraft, the Queen paid an impromptu call on another workshop. Ray Strachey, the women's leader, recounted:

> There had been no preparation at all there, & the atmosphere was much more agreeable, & suddenly she thawed, & laughed, & joked & listened to stories & poked into everything. Then she agreed to have tea, & sat down on our only chair (which had no seat) & drank out of our broken cups & eat [sic] cakes off a tin lid, & evidently thought she was seeing life. She seemed really to be enjoying it – & stayed ¾ hour.[37]

Informal visits such as these continued the accessible style pioneered by the monarchy in the years before the war.

At York Cottage at Christmas there were songs after dinner. 'I had to play accompaniments for comic songs sung by the Queen, Princess Mary & 3 Princes till we went to bed,' wrote Lady Bertha Dawkins. 'They did make a noise!'[38] On the Sunday walk, Nora Wigram described 'the little Prince of Wales, such a baby still – he and P. Albert walking about arm in arm singing comic songs'.[39]

Life at Buckingham Palace by contrast was dreary. Princess Mary described 'those rather silent dinners' when 'Papa will read the paper'.[40] George's uncle and aunt the Duke and Duchess of Connaught came to dinner in October, and (said May) they were 'the first guests we have had to dine with us here since the war began'.[41] The only form of social life was tea parties, which the Queen encouraged for her children as 'they give a little enjoyment to this otherwise dull & serious life of which I confess I am heartily sick!!! Our meals are very blighty [presumably referring to 'blight', the family name for depression]!!!'[42] There were no tiaras in wartime.

In the autumn the King and Queen resumed hospital visits, and May confessed in an unguarded moment to David: 'They are "assommant" [tiresome] & I dislike them more than words can describe!' She found relief on 'off days' in shopping, often at Goode's, the china shop, 'which thoroughly amuses me as well as Mary & is a distraction for us both'.[43] From an amusement and a distraction, shopping was to grow into an obsession.

On Friday 2 June 1916 George wrote in his diary: 'Heard from [Admiral] Jellicoe that a large naval action took place in North Sea on evening of

May 31st, apparently the whole Grand Fleet took part in it.'[44] He added a list of the fourteen ships sunk in the Battle of Jutland. George had been warned that a naval battle was imminent, and the first news of Jutland was indeed discouraging, especially for a naval officer. It 'cast a terrible gloom' over his fifty-first birthday the following day.[45]

Jutland was made more unbearable for the King and Queen because of worry over Bertie. He had returned to his ship *Collingwood* after several months' illness but he was still not recovered. His pain and sickness came back just before the battle. On the morning of Thursday 1 June the King and Queen heard that *Collingwood* was in action, but not until the Friday morning did they learn there were no casualties on board. 'It was indeed a relief, for Papa & I had never admitted to each other how anxious we were!!!' May told David.[46] Bertie was able to take his place in 'A' turret, watching the action and at one point being fired at by a German ship. When George went to inspect the Grand Fleet at Scapa Flow in the Orkney Islands a fortnight later, he told May: 'I have been with Bertie all day, he is a splendid fellow . . . they all love him in the fleet.'[47]

On the morning of 6 June, only four days after Jutland, Stamfordham came to tell the Queen (George was away inspecting submarines in Felixstowe) that Lord Kitchener had drowned when the ship in which he was travelling on a mission to Russia was sunk by a German mine. This came as a hammer blow. 'I feel quite stunned by the news & so sorry for poor G. who will feel his death terribly,' wrote May in an uncharacteristically long and emotional diary entry. Later: 'Went to G. who was dreadfully upset. Stayed some time with him . . . Spent a very sad evening.'[48] Not only had George lost 'a great personal friend' – as May wrote, 'a real friend, like a rock & always straight & full of confidence'.[49] But the ducks which George had lined up so carefully in a row – Haig, Robertson, Kitchener – had been blown apart, and the direction of the war was no longer controlled by a triumvirate of generals. 'It is indeed a heavy blow to me & a great loss to the Nation,' wrote George.[50]

Lloyd George, who as minister of munitions claimed the credit for solving the shell shortage, was the obvious successor to Kitchener as secretary of state for war. But the generals didn't want him and nor did the King. General Robertson campaigned to keep Lloyd George out of the War Office. He told Stamfordham that he worried that the Welshman would interfere with military appointments with 'fatal results', especially as he was known to dislike Haig, 'though his judgement can only be the result of tittle tattle gossip'.[51] Hankey recorded that when he saw the King he 'went into a most violent diatribe against Ll George'.[52] But it was no use. Lloyd George got the job. On 23 June, the King noted: 'The

Prime Minister came to see me & I had a long talk with him about choosing S of S for War & other important subjects.'[53] To make Lloyd George's appointment more acceptable to the generals, Asquith gave the job of under-secretary for war to the Earl of Derby, a good friend of the King. This was not enough to mollify George. 'The King was in despair when [Henry] told him of his intention,' wrote Margot.[54] She considered Lloyd George's appointment to the War Office the greatest blunder of her husband's career. 'We are out,' she wrote: 'it can only be a question of time now when we shall have to leave Downing Street.'[55]

In France on 1 July, the first day of the Battle of the Somme, British troops advanced into the jaws of the German guns and suffered a tragic 57,000 casualties including 19,000 dead – the greatest loss of life ever recorded in a single day in British military history. 'Kitchener's Army found its grave on the Somme just as the old Regular Army had done at Ypres.'[56] George knew of the heavy losses, though the figures he received were not accurate, but he remained tight-lipped.* Only seventeen years before, George's grandmother Queen Victoria had wept over the lists of casualties in the Boer War.[57] King George, working through a heatwave in a tent in the garden at Buckingham Palace, gave expression to no grief. Only Queen Mary paused to reflect: 'How one regrets the terrible losses the offensive has again caused us – it is tragic.'[58]

On 7 August 1916 George wrote in his diary: 'Finished arranging my War stamps with Bacon, they are a fine lot & worth over £8000' (£710,000 in today's values).[59] The following day he departed on his third visit to France, leaving the Queen at Buckingham Palace, where she preferred to stay, 'as I like being as close as possible to news & in touch with everything'.[60]

In France, some way behind the line, in a clearing in a small wood, the officers of the Guards regiments were summoned to meet the King on the morning of an attack. As the thud and muted thunder of the guns charged the air with doom, the King shook hands with every officer. The prime minister's son Raymond Asquith, no admirer of the monarch and given to sardonic remarks, thought he looked 'as glum and dyspeptic as ever', but Oliver Lyttelton, who had been dreading a battle speech, was agreeably surprised by the King's tactful, down-to-earth manner.

---

*He wrote on 3 July: 'The fighting in France is progressing, but our casualties are heavy 1300 officers & 41,000 men' (RA GV/PRIV/GVD/3 July 1916). Casualty figures varied according to the criteria for including wounded men, and they were also fiddled for political reasons.

What sort of food do the men carry into an attack? asked the King. 'Cold chicken, I expect.'[61]

The King had tea with Haig and found him 'in capital spirits & pleased & satisfied with what our troops are doing'.[62] Haig noted that the King 'spoke a great deal' (code for very angrily) about a paper which Churchill had written for the Cabinet, in which he criticised the Battle of the Somme as a disaster.[63] Churchill was the first to call attention in Cabinet to the appalling human cost of the Somme campaign, and at the time he was dismissed as a self-seeking meddler. Haig, with his gleaming boots, his perfectly trimmed moustache and his fine grey eyes, seemed to float calmly above the human tragedy and military catastrophe of the Somme, guided (as he told his wife) by a higher Power and an inner voice.[64] The King had no such inner voice, but for him criticism of the losses was unthinkable and dishonourable.

Before he left France, the King gave Haig the GCVO as a mark of support.* 'How proud I am that the King has said He has confidence in me,' wrote Haig, and 'what a real pleasure it has been to every one of us to see Your Majesty moving about amongst the troops.'[65] One young officer, watching the King pass slowly through the lines of a regiment in a closed car, described him as looking like a big, rather worn penny.[66]

Back in England, the court adjourned to Windsor. Guests complained that the wine-free dinners were heavy going, and veterans of the Edwardian court such as Lord Lincolnshire rubbed their eyes with amazement when the King and Queen went to bed promptly at 10 p.m. 'They sensibly retire to read quietly,' wrote the diplomat Lord Carnock.[67] Nora Wigram found herself seated next to the King most nights, 'for you see there are no other ladies'. She had enjoyed sitting next to George the previous year, but now, she wrote, 'dear as he is, it is always rather a tax'.[68] The King claimed that he had given away most of his wardrobe, and had ordered no new clothes since the war began. Unfortunately, as Carnock observed, 'all this most excellent example is I fear but little known – and, if known, is in some circles regarded with a smile'.[69]

They watched the official film of the Battle of the Somme. The King approved, and 'he enlarged with much energy on the achievements & sufferings of the troops, and of the importance of bringing these home

---

*The Royal Victorian Order, founded in 1896 by Queen Victoria, is an order of knighthood in the gift of the sovereign. The GCVO (Grand Cross of the Victorian Order) confers the rank of knight, but Haig, whose chest was stiff with medals, had already received four knighthoods, so this last one made little difference.

to the people'.[70] The troops in the film, which can be seen in surviving footage, seem suspiciously clean and cheerful as they march to an almost certain death. Like the troops who paraded before the King on his visits to the front, they had perhaps been cherry-picked.[71]

Hensley Henson, Dean of Durham, one of the clerics invited to preach, found the King 'so loquacious that it is difficult to get a word in'; but he spoke 'with a candour and naturalness which is very taking'. The Queen's occasional remarks were 'always sensible'.[72] Henson noticed a 'weedy looking youth': this was Bertie, home on sick leave once more. The royal doctors had diagnosed a burst internal abscess, which was discharging from the navel.[73] Bertie pleaded with his father to agree to an operation to get it over and done with, but the royal doctors hesitated for two months. In the meantime, Bertie was confined to bed, and on several days his father came and sat with him in his room.

The King attended to more congenial topics. As head of the army, he was asked by the adjutant general, Sir Nevil Macready, to approve a change in the rule which decreed that officers and men should wear moustaches. This had become unenforceable as many of the recruits in Kitchener's army were too young to grow convincing moustaches. Most conspicuous was the smooth-faced Prince of Wales, who didn't even shave in the morning, let alone sport a moustache. George, who held conservative views on matters of facial hair, reluctantly agreed to General Macready's order (8 October 1916), which allowed soldiers to clean-shave if they so desired. 'But remember, Macready,' was his parting shot as the adjutant-general left the room, 'no Charlie Chaplins!'[74]

'Of course Greece exercises the mind of His Majesty,' wrote Lord Carnock, who was acting adviser to the King on foreign affairs.[75] The crisis which blew up in Greece that autumn presented George with an acute dilemma – a conflict between his family loyalties and the national interest. King Constantine of Greece was George's first cousin, and Queen Sophia was the Kaiser's sister and therefore also a first cousin of George's. The difficulty was that Constantine refused to join the Allies. He acted 'in a very devious and unsatisfactory way'.[76] He sacked his prime minister, who wanted to enter the war, and split his country. When the Allies intervened and sent troops into Greece, George wrote to Asquith, complaining that these harsh measures threatened to destroy the Greek monarchy, and 'this I am sure is <u>not</u> the policy of my Government'.[77]

The 'shameful' treatment of Greece provoked howls of protest from Queen Alexandra and her sister Minny (their brother had ruled as King George of Greece until he was assassinated in 1913).[78] 'Grannie is terribly agitated about Greece,' May told David, '& is making herself miserable about it all, why we can't think – the stupid little country is not worth the trouble.'[79] Perhaps she was right, but George's loyalty to Constantine did him no good. Queen Sophia was alleged to be a German agent with an underwater petrol station for submarines on the beach at Athens. This was untrue, but it was a fact that Sophia passed on information to the Kaiser about Greek negotiations with the Triple Entente.[80] George himself was damaged by the perception that he supported the pro-German Constantine and kept him on his throne.[81] Greece was a warning, the first sign of the danger that dynastic loyalties posed to the British crown.*

'Saw Bigge, there is another political crisis on,' George wrote wearily on Sunday 3 December 1916. 'Read all evening.'[82] On Tuesday the 5th: 'At 7 p.m. the Prime Minister came to see me & placed his resignation in my hands, which I accepted with great regret.'[83]

'G. much worried,' wrote the Queen; and well he might be.[84] This was the first time a prime minister had resigned since George became king. The circumstances were exceptional. None of the usual rules applied. In normal times the resignation of a prime minister would prompt a general election. The last election had been held in December 1910, and another was overdue, as the Parliament Act had reduced parliamentary terms from seven years to five; but in wartime a general election was not practicable.

Since May 1915 the Conservatives under the leadership of Bonar Law had been in coalition with the Liberals, as was the Labour Party under Arthur Henderson, who had become the first Labour Cabinet minister. Asquith fell because his conduct of the war lost him the confidence of his Cabinet colleagues, and MPs no longer believed in him as war leader. Lloyd George had demanded that he be made head of the War Council, which would give him control of the war. When Asquith insisted that he as prime minister should chair the War Council, Lloyd George resigned. It then emerged that Bonar Law and also Edward Carson, the Irish Unionist leader, supported Lloyd George over that issue. A further three Conservative Cabinet ministers deserted the prime

---

*George benefited from the Allies' intervention in Greece in one respect. When the British seized the Greek post office, the Army printing office in Salonica overprinted a certain number of current British stamps with the word 'LEVANT'. These stamps were rare and valuable, and George was given a set. It turned out that the stamps were not officially authorised and could not be treated as genuine, but George nevertheless included them in his collection (Nicholas Courtney, *The Queen's Stamps: The Authorised History of the Royal Philatelic Collection* (Methuen, 2004), pp. 177–83).

minister, and Asquith suddenly found himself with no alternative but to offer his resignation.

On Monday 4 December, the day before Asquith resigned, Stamfordham had dinner with Archbishop Davidson, who kept a record which reveals the thinking of the Palace. The King, said Stamfordham, was 'strongly averse' to Asquith's resigning. Even if Asquith did resign, Stamfordham was confident that he would survive. The private secretary believed that, lacking sufficient support in the Commons, neither Bonar Law nor Lloyd George would be able to put a new government together, 'and in that case Asquith wd come back . . . The risk of course is that one or other of these might succeed in getting a Cabinet [that is, forming a government] & A wd then be wholly "out of it".' However, noted Davidson, Stamfordham 'is on the whole in favour of A's resignation feeling pretty sure that he wd come back'.[85] Earlier in the day Stamfordham outlined this secret agenda to Maurice Hankey. The aim was to block Lloyd George. 'Apparently [Stamfordham] and the King are intensely indignant with Ld. G., whom they regard [as] a blackmailer, whom it is better to tackle and have done with,' wrote Hankey.[86]

Stamfordham wrote a diary of events in which he detailed the King's actions. Understandably, this formal document makes no mention of Project Asquith. At first, things seemed to go according to plan. Immediately after Asquith resigned on 5 December, the King, acting in accordance with constitutional convention, summoned Bonar Law, who appeared after dinner at 9.30. The King asked him to form a government. Stamfordham noted: 'The King mooted the question of a dissolution, to which, however, he added he would not give his consent, if asked.'[87] Constitutional experts have questioned whether the King really meant to make a commitment in advance that he would not grant a dissolution once Bonar Law was in office.[88] But the fact was that an election in wartime would be divisive and disruptive.

The meeting ended tetchily. Bonar Law declared that the war had been mismanaged. In a display of what Davidson ponderously described as his 'dangerous overcommunicativeness with Ministers unaccustomed to this sort of familiarity', the King disagreed, and said that the politicians should leave the conduct of the war to the experts.[89] Bonar Law said that 'the soldiers were all wrong, with the result that we have lost Serbia, Romania and very likely Greece. The King expressed his entire disagreement with these views.'[90] Law then departed, having undertaken to attempt to form a government.

After leaving the King, Bonar Law, who believed his only hope of putting a government together was to make a deal with Asquith, went round to Number 10 and asked Asquith if he would join him. Asquith declined. Next morning (6 December) Bonar Law and Lloyd George called on Arthur Balfour at 4 Carlton Gardens, where they found the 68-year-old hypochondriac statesman ill in bed. Balfour suggested that the King should be asked to hold a conference; as we have seen, George believed in conferences as a way of resolving political deadlocks.

At 1.00 p.m. Bonar Law arrived at Buckingham Palace and (wrote the King) 'asked me to have a Conference here this afternoon which I agreed to'.[91] The conference took place immediately, at three o'clock that afternoon, and the King 'commanded' Balfour to come half an hour before.[92] Dragging himself from his sickbed, Balfour explained to the King 'his views of the situation and what seemed a possible solution' and agreed to start the discussions.[93]

In the Forty-Four Room at Buckingham Palace, Asquith, Bonar Law, Lloyd George and Arthur Henderson held a general conversation, very moderate in tone, according to Balfour, but so far as Lloyd George and Asquith were concerned, with a 'sub-acid flavour'.[94] Balfour, Bonar Law, Henderson and even Lloyd George appealed to Asquith to serve under Bonar Law, but Asquith declined. As he listened Balfour drew on his blotting paper a sketch of a bridge among hills. The King later pasted it into his diary. But Balfour's mind was not wandering. Asked by the King at the end for his opinion, he suggested that Bonar Law should attempt to form a government and, failing this, he proposed that Lloyd George should do so. The King dismissed the conference at 4.30, and at 7.00 Bonar Law returned and reported that he was unable to form a government. Asquith had consulted his Liberal colleagues, and they had resolved not to join a government but to go into opposition. As agreed, the King then sent for Lloyd George, who accepted the commission. Though he had little support in the Liberal Party, Lloyd George could count on the votes of Conservative MPs. Next day at 7.30 p.m. Lloyd George came and informed the King that he was able to form an administration. There is no record that he kissed hands: it seems he was the first incoming prime minister not to attempt this ritual.

Stamfordham's plan had failed, and Asquith was indeed 'out of it'. Stamfordham had underestimated the dissatisfaction of the Conservative leaders with Asquith's leadership. Ministers such as Curzon were exasperated by Asquith's chaotic and disorganised chairing of Cabinet meetings and his chronic indecisiveness.[95] This failure of judgement by Stamfordham was due in part to the wartime isolation of the monarchy. George's regime of early bed, no court and no dinner parties left him dangerously out of touch with domestic politics. Nor did Stamfordham allow for Asquith's exhaustion. As Asquith told Davidson: 'I have not had one single day . . . without the burden pressing ceaselessly upon me and I have found, especially since Raymond's death, a lack of resilience (that was his exact phrase) which makes everything terribly trying'.[96] (His son Raymond had been killed three months earlier in the Battle of the Somme.)

Asquith felt he had been 'stabbed'.[97] It was a political assassination; it split the Liberal Party and left lasting bitterness. Balfour played the part of kingmaker, enabling Lloyd George to become prime minister and, incidentally perhaps, avenging himself on Asquith for the dirty deed of the 1910 November pledges. In Churchill's phrase, Balfour resembled 'a powerful graceful cat walking delicately and unsoiled across a rather muddy street'.[98] When Bonar Law, acting on behalf of Lloyd George, went to Balfour's house to offer him the job of foreign secretary in the new government, he found him in his bedroom sitting in an armchair wearing a dressing gown. Jumping up at once, Balfour declared: 'Well, you hold a pistol to my head – I must accept.'[99]

The role of the King was important too. He had acted as 'a valuable facilitator' in the formation of the new government,[100] presiding over an orderly (if undemocratic) process which legitimised the result he most dreaded: the accession of Lloyd George.

'It has been a trying day for me,' wrote George that night. 'We got the sad news that dear Augusta died yesterday at the age of 94.'[101] It was a severe blow for May. For almost twenty years Aunt Augusta, the last surviving granddaughter of George III, had filled the place left by the death of her mother. 'We had corresponded ... each week for 19 years & I shall miss her letters dreadfully,' wrote May. 'Poor old lady, she made a gallant fight to live on to the end of the war.'[102]* But it was perhaps fortunate that she didn't survive to see the suicide of her beloved grandson Fred, Grand Duke Adolphus Frederick VI, in 1918, nor the abolition of the German monarchies and the establishment of the Free State of Mecklenburg-Strelitz. She died with these words on her lips: 'Tell the King it is a stout old English heart that is ceasing to beat.'[103] Yet another link in the dynastic chain was broken.

Asquith's fall was also the end of an era. By contrast with the King, the prime minister had barely changed his Edwardian way of life during the war. At Number 10 Margot gave lunch parties and dinner parties,

---

*Lady Mary Cambridge, Queen Mary's niece, later Duchess of Beaufort, was less reverential: 'In the war Aunt Augusta turned very pro-German and wrote the Queen such dreadful letters that the Queen gave up answering them in the end' (James Pope-Hennessy, *The Quest for Queen Mary*, ed. Hugo Vickers (Zuleika, 2018), p. 302).

and most weekends she entertained house parties at Walmer Castle in Kent; the champagne flowed, and Asquith played bridge after dinner every night. 'Mr Asquith,' asked Lady Tree after a weekend at Walmer, 'do you take an interest in the War?'[104]

George was nonetheless reluctant to part with Asquith. He told him on 4 December that 'he had the fullest confidence in him'.[105] According to the former prime minister's daughter-in-law Cynthia Asquith, the King was 'terribly distressed' at Asquith's leaving and said: 'I shall resign if Asquith does.'[106] At the Buckingham Palace Conference, Asquith 'referred in touching terms to the unquestioning confidence the King had invariably placed in him'.[107] But Asquith had not always treated the King well. He often sneered behind his back, he had shafted him over the November pledges and he considered him out of his depth, fussy and indiscreet. Asquith's succinct, lawyerly letters to the King formed the official minutes of the Cabinet, and they revealed little – though, as George remarked, they were 'his only means of knowledge . . . of what is really going on'.[108] The two men were not close friends – Queen Mary remarked in November 1916 that she hadn't seen Asquith for over a year.[109] But they settled into a working relationship, the more so when George turned out not to be the Tory monarch that Asquith had expected.

For the King almost anyone was better than Lloyd George. Britain's first working-class prime minister had no time for inherited privilege and ceremonial. '"I must say I did treat [the King] abominably at first,"' said Lloyd George. His secretary recalled: 'Many a letter from G.R. he never even answered, and once he even forgot an appointment with him!'[110]

There was friction over government appointments. The Office of Works dealt with royal palaces, and it was traditionally headed by someone who was acceptable to the sovereign. When Lloyd George suggested Sir Alfred Mond, the Jewish scion of a chemical dynasty who went on to found ICI, Stamfordham was horrified: 'He is of German extraction' (like the King, it could be said) 'and speaks English with a German accent. I declared that I really felt almost unable to submit his name to the King.'[111] The King had twice refused to make him a privy counsellor, before relenting at the third request. Only when Lloyd George explained that Mond's work in wartime would consist not of maintaining palaces but of building accommodation for temporary officers did the King reluctantly give his approval while strongly protesting.*

---

*The King was not pleased either by the appointment of Sir Edwin Cornwall, a self-made tea merchant, as comptroller of the household, but consented as this was a war government,

Even more infuriating was Lloyd George giving a peerage to Sir Max Aitken without consulting the King. Aitken, the Canadian millionaire who was Bonar Law's intimate friend, had already been made a knight, and the only reason for promoting him to the peerage (he became Lord Beaverbrook) was that he had given up his seat in Parliament to a friend. Stamfordham declared the King to be 'surprised and hurt': 'He trusts that in future no honours whatever will be offered by any Minister until his approval has been informally obtained.'[112] Faint hope.

'during which time no Court functions will be held' (RA PS/PSO/GV/C/K/1048/A/1, 'Fall of Mr Asquith's Administration').

CHAPTER 18

Unrest in the Country and within the House of Windsor

1917

The only member of the royal family whose life was largely unaffected by the war was Prince John. He lived with Lala at Frogmore, the Georgian *petit trianon* where generations of royals had found seclusion since the daughters of George III had done so. He was affectionate and 'awfully pleased to see us', but (as May wrote) while 'he looks well [he] does not grow up at all, I mean his brain. It is such a pity.'[1] When Johnnie was ten a tutor was engaged. Mr Lyon, a 28-year-old officer with a strained heart recommended by Henry Hansell, 'seems to us to be just the right man', wrote May.[2] But Mr Lyon was not the right man. His arrival in the spring of 1916 'rather upset Johnnie and made him more excited than ever'.[3] Within a few days it was plain that Mr Lyon had failed. Johnnie needed a male keeper, not a tutor.

'It is a sad conclusion to have arrived at,' wrote the Queen, 'but I fear we must make up our minds to the fact that poor Johnnie will never get really normal, & that the only thing we can do is to make the boy's life as happy as possible.'[4] This was realistic and sensible, but her detachment was chilling. June 1916 was a crisis for Johnnie. 'There is no doubt that Johnnie has got worse of late which is very sad,' May told Bertie. 'Don't say anything to Papa about it, I thought you would like to know.'[5] The last sentence is revealing. George didn't want to know about Johnnie, and nor did David. Bertie was the son in whom May could confide. Johnnie's deterioration created a silence between husband and wife.

The royal family spent Christmas 1916 in London. For the first time, the war was allowed to interrupt their iron routine; as May explained, 'Papa feels it wiser to be on the spot when so much is going on'.[6] On Christmas Day they visited King George's Hospital in Waterloo Road, where there were 1,600 wounded soldiers. This was the new style of monarchy at work. The family divided up the wards, each of them taking a floor and handing out copies of *The*

Queen's Gift Book.* 'We think this a nice idea for spending Xmas,' wrote May.[7]

At Sandringham, where they escaped for the month of January 1917, the Queen arranged a new home for Johnnie at Wood Farm near Wolferton. 'We can make it quite nice & comfortable, & we can take in a good piece of ground for him to play in & plant vegetables,' she wrote.[8] Watching Johnnie with the gramophone when 'he seemed awfully pleased but walked round the table the whole time & each time a tune finished wanted to change the records himself, much to David's dismay', May was saddened 'to see this great strong boy with the mind of a child of six'.[9] Installed at Wood Farm with Lala, however, 'he seemed very happy'.[10]

At York Cottage, the King and Queen lived in startling simplicity. When Nora Wigram arrived for lunch, she rang the front door bell, 'and who should come up and open the door to me but the King! I little thought I should live to have the door opened to me by the King of England!' At lunch, a simple meal of pheasant and chocolate mousse, the King grumbled about napkin rings. 'I quite refuse to use one <u>and</u> I like a clean napkin every day.' This royal homeliness could be disconcerting. Once Nora returned to her house to find the Queen was there. 'My dear' – how Nora enjoyed being on 'My dear' terms with the Queen – 'we have been inspecting your room and I <u>do</u> apologise that you have no cushions on your sofa,' said Her Majesty. The Queen bounced into Nora's maid's room, 'had a chat to her, sat in her chair & asked if she was comfortable', leaving the maid pink with excitement.[11]

On a snowy Sunday afternoon the King asked Nora to join them for the ritual Sandringham walk. 'I don't mean it in a blasé way,' she wrote, 'but really I got rather bored.' They dawdled through the gardens, it was bitterly cold and the children got lost. 'The King said they were always trying to avoid him! (quite true!) Then the dog got lost! Then [Godfrey-Faussett] got lost looking for the dog!! By that time the King was awfully cross!' As soon as the King and Queen had gone home, Princess Mary, the Prince of Wales and Prince Albert became 'quite cheerful & entirely flippant, writing their names in the snow'.[12]

One day a mysterious Dane named Mr Anderson appeared. He was

The Queen's Gift Book: In Aid of Queen Mary's Convalescent Auxiliary Hospitals for Soldiers and Sailors Who Have Lost Their Limbs in the War (Hodder & Stoughton, 1915). This was an illustrated anthology of poems and stories by Somerville and Ross, Jerome K. Jerome, Arthur Conan Doyle, Joseph Conrad, John Buchan, J. M. Barrie and others to raise money for the Queen's charity.

the confidential adviser of the King of Denmark, and he had long conversations with King George. Nora was asked to entertain him for tea
and, thinking she was a grand friend of the royals, he told her a lot
about Russia where 'the Empress is mad' and 'anything' may happen.
'One is inclined to wonder if he is quite "all right",' wrote Nora.[13]

The King was a worried man. Since the assassination of the Siberian
monk Rasputin on 30 December 1916, the tsarist autocracy had tee-
tered on the edge of the abyss. Rasputin had seemingly possessed the
power to stop the bleeding of the haemophiliac Tsarevich, and this gave
him control over the Empress Alexandra. In a doomed attempt to save
the Russian war effort, Emperor Nicholas II had put himself at the head
of the army in 1915, leaving the Empress to govern as regent in St
Petersburg (known as Petrograd since the outbreak of war). Under the
influence of Rasputin, the 'man of God', she created chaos, appointing
four prime ministers in sixteen months. Queen Mary was forthright in
her criticism of Alicky: 'What mischief the Emp. A. is making in Russia,
she must be insane to act as she is doing, why do stupid women have
such a bad influence on men!'[14]

Heedless of the universal discontent and economic collapse, Nicky
thought of nothing but avenging the murder of Rasputin. The Foreign
Office telegrams which the King received made alarming reading. In the
first week of 1917 George wrote out a deciphered telegram from Sir
George Buchanan, the British ambassador in Petrograd: 'If the Emperor
continues in his present course . . . danger of anti-dynastic movement . . .
assassination of Empress is a common topic of conversation.'[15]

As Nicky sleepwalked towards disaster, Buchanan begged the government to allow him to warn the Tsar in the name of the King. 'All that
I ask is that I may be charged with some message from the King,' he
wrote, 'that would show that His Majesty both as the Emperor's kins-
man, and as Russia's Ally, is seriously preoccupied by the turn events
are taking.'[16] Foreign Secretary Balfour wired a cagey reply: 'I am
unwilling to press the King to send a private telegram to the Emperor,
especially as he is at Sandringham and I cannot personally consult him.'
However, he agreed to Buchanan asking for an audience with the Tsar.
'You may add that the whole subject is causing the King very great
anxiety.'[17]

Buchanan was granted an interview on 12 January, but the Tsar was
stiff and repellently formal. Matters were made worse by the sudden
death of Count Benckendorff, the Russian ambassador in London. 'I
was terribly shocked,' wrote George, 'he will be a great loss to me, as he
was the only one I could talk to quite openly about Russia . . . I own
that I am very anxious.'[18]

Hence Mr Anderson's visit to Sandringham. Desperate to get a message to Nicky, George proposed to send the Dane on a mission to Petrograd, bearing a letter from him in a last attempt to avert catastrophe. But Anderson never reached Russia.

George hesitated to open Parliament with the Queen in wartime. The Queen, however, was ready to go, 'and to wear any kind of dress he wishes suitable in time of war'. She wrote privately to Stamfordham: 'I just tell you this as it may be a guide to you to know what line I take, & no doubt you may be inclined to think that this is a moment for us to be seen by the public once more!'[19] The King and Queen drove in an open carriage drawn by six bay horses to the opening of Parliament on 7 February. The King wore an admiral's uniform, the peers wore uniform or plain clothes, and the sick and wounded filled the royal gallery.

George's relations with his new prime minister were tetchy. Harold Nicolson thought Lloyd George 'really behaved very badly'.[20] When Stamfordham rebuked Number 10 for attempting to take over the royal prerogative of granting honours, Lloyd George didn't bother to answer his letter.[21] Lloyd George's secretaries, William Sutherland and J. T. Davies, treated the royal private secretaries with calculated insolence, refusing to get up from their chairs when Stamfordham came into the room on the King's business. Lloyd George, in the view of the Conservative politician J.C.C. Davidson, was 'a republican, and not a monarchist, at heart ... he disliked any show of pomp and dignity on the part of the Crown and its servants'.[22] Of all twentieth-century prime ministers, Lloyd George was perhaps the rudest to the sovereign; and he did his best to cut out the King from the running of the war.

Lloyd George was determined to break the generals' control over the war and remove Haig as commander-in-chief. On 26 February 1917 at a conference with the French at Calais, he sprang his plan to put Haig's army under the command of the French general Robert Nivelle. For Lloyd George, this was a way of preventing yet another massacre of British troops in a new Haig offensive, but the coup was seriously flawed. For a British prime minister to give away control of his country's army, then at peak fitness, to the struggling, demoralised French was a half-baked idea.

The King was not informed of Lloyd George's plan until two days after the Calais conference, when Haig fired off a furious letter to the King threatening to resign.[23] 'I am very worried about it all,' wrote George after a meeting with Lord Derby, the war minister.[24] George saw

Haig on 11 March and begged him not to resign because (according to Haig's account) Lloyd George would then call an election and probably win a great majority. 'The King's position would then be very difficult. He would be blamed for causing a General Election.' It's hard to see how the King could be blamed if Haig resigned; but George was evidently anxious. The King, noted Haig, 'was furious with Lloyd George'.[25]

J.C.C. Davidson sometimes wondered why the King tolerated the 'humiliating treatment handed out to him by Lloyd George' without speaking his mind.[26] On this occasion he did. On 12 March he saw Lloyd George, who by now had been forced to abandon his plan by his colleagues in the War Cabinet. (The War Cabinet was a committee of four ministers under Lloyd George responsible for the direction of the war – a body very similar to the War Council proposed in 1916.) The King tore strips off him. As head of the army he 'objected to being kept in ignorance' of such matters. The whole army would strongly resent being placed 'under the command of a foreign general', and the country would agree.[27]

The King's fury with Lloyd George masked a visceral fear. The mentality at Buckingham Palace can be seen from a remark made by Wigram the same day. He told one of the generals that Lloyd George's reason for wishing to place the British army under Nivelle

> is based on his ultimate intention of breaking up the Monarchy and introducing a republic with himself at the head and . . . he foresees the loyal adherence of the Army to the Monarch as his chief obstacle – For this reason he desires to weaken it by breaking it up and distributing it among the French Armies.[28]

This sounds hysterical. But the very next day George wrote in his diary: 'Bad news from Russia, practically a revolution has broken out in Petrograd.'[29] To understand George's reaction to these events in Russia we need to realise how threatened he felt by Lloyd George and his blundering attempt to hand over the command of the British army to the French.

The February Revolution in Russia plunged the British monarchy into an existential crisis, but this was not apparent at first. George reacted initially in the way that British rulers had done in the past to deposed monarchs such as Louis Philippe and Napoleon III, offering sympathy and support. On 15 March he heard that the Tsar had abdicated. 'I fear Alicky is the cause of it all & Nicky has been weak,' he wrote. 'I am in despair.'[30] After a delay of four days, Stamfordham sent a telegram on behalf of the King: 'Events of last week have deeply distressed me. My thoughts are constantly with you and I shall always remain your true and devoted friend, as you know I have been in the past.'[31] George had seemingly contrived at last to make contact with his cousin Nicky.

Sir George Buchanan, the British ambassador in Petrograd, was an old-school diplomat, pictured by Somerset Maugham (then working in Russia as an intelligence officer) wearing a perfectly cut tail coat, while on the other side of the embassy wall was 'a restless, turbulent population that might at any moment break into bloody revolution'.[32] On 20 March Buchanan reported that Pavel Miliukov, the foreign minister of the liberal Provisional Government, expected the British government to offer the Tsar residence in England.[33] This was the first mention of the request, and Balfour sent a wary reply: 'No invitation has been sent to His Majesty to come to England, and it seems very doubtful whether such a course would be desirable. Has the Emperor thought of either Denmark or Switzerland?'[34] Buchanan's next telegram came as a bombshell. Miliukov was 'most anxious' that the Emperor should leave Russia immediately: 'he would be grateful if the King and His Majesty's Government would at once offer Emperor asylum in England'.[35]

Stamfordham hurried round to Downing Street the next morning, insisting that 'the King would wish to be consulted before his Government gave a definite reply to this suggestion'. After discussion with Lloyd George, it was agreed that 'the proposal that we should receive the Emperor in this country (having come from the Russian Government which we are endeavouring with all our powers to support) could not be refused'.[36] Lloyd George was prepared to rescue the Romanovs if that was the price of keeping Russia in the war. Later that day a telegram was sent to Buchanan: 'In order to meet the request made by the Russian Government, the King and H.M. Government readily offer asylum to the Emperor and Empress in England.'[37]

The offer of asylum was stillborn, merely a statement of intent, floating above events. On the day it was sent, the Tsar returned from Pskov, where he had abdicated, to Tsarkoe Selo, thirty miles from Petrograd, where he was reunited with his family. Here they lived in the splendour of Catherine the Great's Alexander Palace under house arrest, guarded by 300 soldiers and close to a barracks of 40,000 troops. Escape would have been impossible, even if they had wished it. The Petrograd Soviet of workers was determined that the Romanovs should be prevented from leaving Russia. When the revolutionary Marxist Bolsheviks penetrated the soviet, the Provisional Government became powerless to resist. The idea of exiling the Tsar was quietly dropped. Even Miliukov recognised that the offer had come too late.[38]

Back in London, the King and his government were slow to realise the ascendancy of the Petrograd Soviet, and the escape of the Romanovs seemed a matter of when rather than if. At Buckingham Palace views were hardening against asylum. The first sign was a spat over George's telegram of 19 March ('Events ... have deeply distressed me'). After some confusion, this was delivered to Buchanan, who showed it to Miliukov, who refused to give it to the Tsar on the grounds that the King's words might be misinterpreted. George's private message to his cousin had been blown up into an official communication, and George himself was furious. Stamfordham sent a stinging rebuke to Buchanan and ordered the telegram to be cancelled.[39]

The next day Stamfordham wrote a letter to Balfour which began: 'The King has been thinking much about the Government's proposal that the Emperor and his Family should come to England ... His Majesty cannot help doubting,' said Stamfordham, 'on general grounds of expediency, whether it is advisable that the Imperial Family should take up their residence in this country.'[40] On the draft of this letter which is preserved in the Royal Archives, Stamfordham wrote a pencil note: 'submitted to the King 30.3.17.'[41] These few words are hugely significant. They establish that George agreed with Stamfordham that the offer of asylum should be withdrawn.

The refusal of asylum to the Tsar was sensationally revealed by Kenneth Rose in his 1983 biography, and since then it has become the dark stain on George's reputation.[42]* Even before the documents were released, King George and Queen Mary were blamed for failing to help their Russian cousins, which, said 'Chips' Channon, the diarist and socialite, was 'the one blot on their lives'. Queen Mary was alleged to feel 'sorely conscience stricken' about it.[43] Although the offer came too late, the decision to withdraw it tells us much about the King's moral compass.

One recent, comprehensive study has blamed Stamfordham for the U-turn, accusing him of frightening the King and forcing him to change his mind, 'vigorously stoking the fires of George's anxiety' by feeding him hostile press cuttings.[44] But George showed no enthusiasm for rescuing the Romanovs. On the contrary, he seems to have been against it from the start. 'As you know,' Stamfordham told Balfour on 6 April,

---

*The episode is covered in Harold Nicolson's biography too (pp. 300–2), but in such a matter-of-fact way that the reader easily slides over it.

'from the first the King has thought the presence of the Imperial Family (especially the Empress) in this country would raise all sorts of difficulties.'[45]*

The Duke of Windsor told a story to Gore Vidal many years later. One day he was having breakfast alone with his parents when an equerry came in. 'Not done, you know, ever. The king was furious, but the man went up to him with this note, which the king read and gave my mother, and she read it and gave it back and said, "No". The king gave it to the equerry and said, "No".' Later that day David asked his mother what it was all about, and she replied that the government was willing to send a ship to rescue the Tsar, but she did not think it would be 'good for us' to have them in the country.[46] Gore Vidal is not a reliable witness, but perhaps on this occasion he was accurate.

Stamfordham's agenda can be traced from the papers he preserved in the file which he labelled 'Russia 1917'. If the Lloyd George government wanted the Romanovs to come to Britain in order to please the Provisional Government and keep Russia in the war, the King as constitutional monarch could not stop them. It was in Britain's interest for Russia to stay in the war. Not until March 1918 did it pull out. The most that Stamfordham could do as private secretary was to distance the King from the decision to offer asylum, and point out the King's objections. Lord Carnock, the royal foreign policy adviser, wrote to Stamfordham: 'So far as I understand the question, the Emperor will not be allowed to leave Russia, so the question of his residence here will not arise – but from what I can ascertain there would be a good deal of disagreeable criticism were he to come here.'[47] Stamfordham pencilled a note on the letter: 'ansd [answered] quite agree but Govt are determined that TIM [Their Imperial Majesties] shall come here if the Russ Govt wish S 2/4/17'.[48]

Balfour in his reply to Stamfordham's letter of 30 March expressing doubts ('The King has been thinking much') reiterated the government's policy of offering asylum. The nub of Balfour's letter was this:

> His Majesty's Ministers quite realize the difficulties to which you refer in your letter, but they do not think, unless the position changes, that it is now possible to withdraw the invitation which has been sent,

*Wigram wrote on 9 April 1917 to General Sir William Lambton: 'You have probably heard rumours of the Emperor and Empress of Russia . . . coming to . . . find asylum here. As a matter of fact His Majesty has been opposed to this proposal from the start, and has begged his ministers to knock it on the head' (Helen Rappaport, *The Race to Save the Romanovs: The Truth behind the Secret Plans to Rescue Russia's Imperial Family* (Hutchinson, 2018), p. 81).

and they therefore trust that the King will consent to adhere to the original invitation, which was sent on the advice of His Majesty's Ministers.[49]

On the surface, this appears to be a rebuff, and that is how some have read it. In fact there seems to have been an understanding between the two men. Balfour's letter contains the crucial phrase distancing the King from the asylum offer that Stamfordham wanted him to write. Stamfordham noted in pencil: 'I think this letter says all that is required viz: that the invitation was <u>sent on the advice of H.M.'s Ministers</u>.'[50]

But then Stamfordham changed his mind. On 6 April he wrote again to Balfour: 'Every day the King is becoming more concerned about the question of the Emperor and Empress coming to this country.'[51] Later the same day he fired off a second, much stronger letter, demanding that the invitation be withdrawn.[52] What had happened? It seems Stamfordham had seen an article in *Justice* by H. M. Hyndman, leader of the Independent Labour Party. This article, titled 'The Need for a British Republic', claimed that 'if the King and Queen have invited their discrowned Russian cousins here' they had entirely misunderstood the feelings of the people.[53] These words Stamfordham underlined in red. He could feel the ground shifting beneath his feet. The virus of republicanism was spreading to Britain, and the very survival of the British monarchy was at stake.

Balfour forwarded Stamfordham's two letters to the prime minister with a covering note, of which Stamfordham received a copy. 'I think the King <u>is</u> placed in an awkward position,' he wrote. 'If the Czar is to come here we are bound to state that we (the Government) have invited him – and to add (for our own protection) that we did so on the invitation of the Russian Government (who will not like it).'[54]

With the prime minister forewarned by Balfour, Stamfordham swept into Downing Street on 10 April. Brandishing Hyndman's article, he 'tried to impress upon [Lloyd George] the King's strong opinion that the Emperor and Empress of Russia should not come to this country', and demanded that the government withdraw their invitation. 'I pointed out to Mr Lloyd George that it would be most unfair upon the King (who is closely related to both the Emperor and the Empress) if Their Imperial Majesties came here when popular feeling against their doing so is so pronounced.' Stamfordham's tirade succeeded. Lloyd George 'admitted that evidently the matter was more serious than he was aware'.[55] There was talk of sending the Tsar to France, but the reality was that the invitation to England was cancelled.

A Foreign Office telegram whizzed along the wires to Sir George Buchanan, who still clung to the hope of rescuing the Tsar: 'There are indications that a considerable anti-monarchical movement is developing here . . . if the Emperor comes here, it may dangerously increase that movement.'[56] Buchanan cabled back the only answer that was possible: 'I entirely share your view that, if there is any danger of anti-monarchist movement, it would be far better that the ex-Emperor should not come to England.'[57]

George was ruthless in his concern to protect the Crown and secure Britain's political stability. He didn't scruple to drop 'dear Nicky', to whom he claimed to be devoted – 'the best, straightest, most clear and decided man I know'.[58] The two cousins were very similar characters – uxorious, domestic, chain-smoking. When Princess Margaret read Robert Massie's *Nicholas and Alexandra*, published in 1967, she said with a shudder: 'They're so perfectly ordinary. I mean, it could be *us*.'[59] But for George the lesson of the Russian Revolution was that the monarchs' trade union no longer counted. When Queen Wilhelmina of the Netherlands asked him to visit her country, which itself was on the verge of revolution, he refused: 'I am not going to be used to bolster up monarchies which are shaky, that is not my metier.'[60]

How real were the fears of an anti-monarchical movement in Britain? This was the question that Stamfordham now set out to investigate, and his research is documented in the Royal Archives.[61] Hyndman's article prompted him to begin a new file, gathering intelligence, which he labelled 'Unrest in the Country'. He pasted into it republican newspaper cuttings, underlining the key passages in red. 'I do not believe,' he wrote, 'that there is any Sovereign in the world to whom the truth is more fearlessly told by those in his immediate service, and who receives it with such good will – and even gratitude – as King George. There is no Socialistic newspaper, no libellous rag that is not read and marked and shown to the King if they contain any criticisms.'[62] Stamfordham also collected intelligence from correspondents, notably John Watts-Ditchfield, the Bishop of Chelmsford, who had worked in Bethnal Green and was 'thoroughly in touch with the working classes'.[63] Colonel Unsworth of the Salvation Army reported a change in attitudes towards the King and Queen since the Russian Revolution: 'One hears talk . . . which is very painful . . . to listen to.'[64]

Similar findings reached the War Cabinet, which discussed the matter of the invitation to the Tsar on 13 April. Lloyd George reported that there was a strong feeling hostile to the Czar in certain working-class circles in the country, and that articles tending to associate the King with the Czar had appeared in the Press; it was felt that if the Czar should take up residence, there was a danger that these tendencies might be stimulated and accentuated.

The War Cabinet therefore agreed that the best solution was for the Tsar to live in France.[65]

A letter from H. G. Wells to *The Times* on 21 April calling for the formation of a Republican Society seriously alarmed the Palace. As Lord Derby pointed out, 'the revolution in Russia has given all monarchies a knock. Wells's letter to *The Times* would not have been printed a year ago, but now it undoubtedly represents the view held by a very considerable class'.[66] A second broadside from Wells in the *Penny Pictorial* declared that 'the European dynastic system, based upon intermarriage by a group of minority German Royal Families, is dead today'. The security of the British monarchy, said Wells, depended upon its severing itself 'definitively from the German dynastic system with which it is so fatally entangled by marriage and descent'.[67]

The court moved to Windsor for Easter 1917. Queen Mary welcomed the chance to entertain as a break from 'the monotony of our present dull routine'.[68] One of the guests on the day Wells published his *Times* letter calling for a Republican Society was Lady Maud Warrender, a six-foot-one aristocrat, singer and patron, and a lesbian who had left her husband to live with an American opera singer.* According to her account, someone mentioned that the King must be pro-German because he had a German name, and George 'started and grew pale'.[69] When Wells wrote the year before in *Mr Britling Sees It Through* of 'an uninspiring and alien Court', George had quipped: 'I may be uninspiring, but I'll be d—d if I'm alien.'[70] Now he was not so sure.

Watts-Ditchfield had observed that 'Labour has not been sufficiently recognised', adding: 'If His Majesty could <u>see</u> the Labour Leaders more the benefit would be enormous' (Stamfordham's underlining).[71] Accordingly invitations were sent to Labour ministers in the coalition government, among them the pensions minister, George Barnes. For Lady Bertha Dawkins, the Queen's woman of the bedchamber, entertaining Mr Barnes made the evenings 'ever so much more pleasant, and I do not have to sit

---

*She was the rather improbable sister of Lord Shaftesbury, a member of the household.

by the King at dinner!'[72] (The King was no doubt just as relieved not to have Lady Bertha as his neighbour – see above, page 188.) Mr and Mrs Barnes were both 'so nice: she is a dear old thing, and was much pleased with her long talk with the Queen; she does not pretend to be a lady, so it must have been difficult for her'.[73]

As food shortages tightened, the Queen rationed bread and ordered one meat-free day a week even when there were guests.[74] (It seems her earlier attempt to cut meat to three days a week had been too ambitious.) The royal household conformed to the same rations as everyone else – four pounds of bread and two-and-a-half pounds of meat per head per week. Gone were the stately footmen in powdered wigs, most of whom had joined up.[75] 'Only at Grannie's table alas I see no difference!!!' the Queen reported to David, '& her silly little dog is still fed on meat & milk. I am afraid I am naughty,' telling tales on her mother-in-law.[76] Alexandra refused to listen when May explained the importance of saving petrol, 'constantly repeating, it is very hard on people, I can't walk so must use my car for getting about!!!'[77]

Some of the aristocracy were just as blinkered as the Queen Mother. When the son of Lord Derby the King's friend married Sybil (Portia) Cadogan, a maid of honour and the daughter of Lady Meux, a terrific row blew up between the two families about which side of the Guards' Chapel the King and Queen should sit on. Godfrey-Faussett spent twenty minutes attempting to pacify Lady Meux, seated with her in her car on the forecourt at Buckingham Palace.[78] No one would have guessed that a quarter of a million British soldiers were set to lose their lives at the Battle of Passchendaele in the next four months.

For their war work at Windsor, the royal family planted potatoes. On 25 April the King and Queen, Princess Mary and Princes Henry and George dug hard in the blazing sun for two hours. (Was it a coincidence that this happened when the Labour MPs were staying?) 'It was a funny sight,' wrote Lady Bertha, '& they all got so red & hot; the King's valet had to come, & the Head Gardener nearly died of it!!'[79]

Back in London, Stamfordham opened another new file which he called 'Change of Name', and he began discussions with two former Liberal prime ministers, Rosebery and Asquith, about dropping the German name of Saxe-Coburg-Gotha and renaming the dynasty. The funny thing, wrote Harold Nicolson, was that the King and Queen 'did not know what their real name was'. Henry Farnham Burke of the College of Heralds was consulted, and he advised that the family name of Prince Albert was not Wettin, as they thought, but Wipper, which was 'not a good name for any Royal Family to possess'.[80]* The German names were discarded, and the search for a new one began.

The Hanoverian family name was Guelph, but that was 'too foreign' and 'not at all liked' by the King and Queen.[81] Stamfordham then suggested Tudor-Stewart (*sic*).[82] 'The King is for Stewart,' wrote Stamfordham, and 'the Queen strongly supports Stewart and cannot see the objections raised to it' – namely that the Hanoverians had been called in (in 1714) to keep the Stuarts out.[83] Rosebery and Asquith both argued strongly against Stewart and Tudor-Stewart, but they failed to come up with an alternative.[84] This, said Stamfordham, was 'disastrous': 'the King is all for a prompt settlement', and 'the matter must be pushed on'.[85]

The impasse was broken by Stamfordham, who hit upon a new name: the House of Windsor. Rosebery and Asquith both agreed it, and on 15 June the King wrote from his train: 'I am quite sure that Windsor is the best for my family name.'[86] Rosebery sent Stamfordham a letter of congratulation: 'Do you realise that you have christened a dynasty? . . . It is really something to be historically proud of.'[87]†

The House of Windsor was inaugurated at a council held in the Forty-Four Room at Buckingham Palace on 17 July. 'I declared that my House should have the name of Windsor & that I relinquished all my German titles for myself & family,' wrote George.[88] Not everyone liked the new name. Some of the courtiers grumbled, and Rosebery now said that he preferred the name of Lancaster.[89] 'It was quite an historical occasion,' wrote George; but it hardly seemed so at the time.[90] Labour's George Barnes arrived without a frock coat and Godfrey-Faussett had to lend him one. Balfour and Asquith, who were both invited to attend, failed to appear. Balfour's secretary mislaid the piece of paper, and Asquith 'thought it of no particular importance'.[91]

One Bavarian nobleman remarked: 'The true royal tradition died on that day in 1917 when, for a mere war, King George V changed his name.'[92] But George was not an ideologist of monarchy. He was a pragmatist, and on 17 July he did everything that H. G. Wells had called for. This was dynastic public relations. Out went Saxe-Coburg-Gotha. British names and titles were found for the German relations. Prince Louis of Battenberg became Marquess of Milford Haven with the anglicised

---

*These were matters which fell within the province of the Garter King of Arms, the seventy-year-old Sir Alfred Scott-Gatty, but he seemed unable to give any help, though 'happily he abandons his positions as hastily as he formulates them' (Sir Almeric Fitz-Roy, *Memoirs*, vol. 2, p. 655).

†Not consulted were the family of the Earls of Plymouth, whose surname was Windsor-Clive. 'The King said that theirs was a double name,' wrote Nicolson, 'and that they ought to feel honoured in any case' (Sissinghurst, Nicolson to Vita, 10 August 1950).

family name of Mountbatten.* May's two brothers dropped Teck and adopted Cambridge as their family name. Alge was transformed from Prince of Teck to Earl of Athlone, and Dolly the elder brother, the Duke of Teck, became Marquess of Cambridge. He considered this a poor exchange, and (according to May) he was 'tiresome' about his new name and even threatened to 'revert to Teck as a surname in a few years'.[93]

The King also informed the council that 'May & I had decided some time ago that our children should be allowed to marry into British families'.[94] To prevent the proliferation of princes in continental fashion, it was later announced that the rank of prince and of royal highness was now limited to the children of the sovereign, the children of their sons and the eldest living son of the eldest son of the Prince of Wales – a ruling that is still relevant more than a century on.[95]

Some have suggested that the de-Germanification of the royal family was prompted by the horrific German air raid of 13 June, when the new Gotha bombers killed 140 in the East End of London, including forty schoolchildren in Poplar. The King drove at once to the hospitals to visit the injured – something which Lord Rosebery was very pleased to see: 'I have long waited in hope for such an occasion,' he told Stamford-ham.[96] But no one made the connection between the Gotha bombers and the King's name. Talks about the change of name had begun months before. The paper trail contained in Stamfordham's files reveals that the House of Windsor was born, not in the devastation of London's East End by Gotha bombers, but in the panic of kings that followed the fall of the Romanovs.

Watts-Ditchfield told Stamfordham in July that 'the position of the throne has been strengthened during the last month and ... the worst of the present crisis has passed'.[97] The recalibration of the monarchy certainly helped, but other factors were at work as well. On his bedroom wall George hung 'a splendid new map which shows everything most clearly', wrote May, 'and the progress of the blue line is most refreshing'.[98] The map showed Haig's victory at Arras, and the Canadians' capture of Vimy Ridge – 'this news bucks one up,' wrote George.[99]

On 7 April the United States entered the war, just as the Russians left it. A service was held at St Paul's Cathedral where (in Derby's words) 'we thanked the Almighty for having at last made the Americans realise their duty'. The King was cheered; 'although not very popular, he always has a good reception'.[100] Watching the service, Rider Haggard observed that

---

*The new titles necessitated a new precedence for the family which, wrote George, 'is not very easy to settle'; he spent two days discussing it with Louis Mountbatten (RA GV/PRIV/GVD/23–24 July 1917).

he had never before realised how small the King was. Beside the Queen, with a tall feather in her hat, he looked 'tiny and unimpressive . . . To be frank he did not look half an inch a King, notwithstanding his Field Marshal's uniform.'[101]*

Relations improved with Lloyd George, humbled perhaps by the failure of the Nivelle offensive. Visiting the royal family at Windsor, he found it 'all so homely', and was amused by the Queen and her account of Prince John, who refused to eat his suet pudding. 'What's the matter with the pudding, John?' asked the Queen. 'It's lumpy,' said the prince. The idea of the King's son complaining of lumpy pudding tickled Lloyd George immensely.[102]

---

*Hence the joke, 'King George the Fifth and Queen Mary the Four-Fifths'.

CHAPTER 19

The Nonentity King

1917–1919

Lady-in-waiting Ettie Desborough stayed at Windsor in August 1917. 'It is sad to see what a very heavy burden is carried there,' she wrote. 'There is such an intense desire to do right – it is like the piteous spectacle of watching a very good child under an almost unsurmountable handicap.'[1]

The good children undertook punishing visits to the industrial north. Sleeping and dining in the comfort of the royal train, which had been fitted out on the orders of King Edward VII to resemble the royal yacht, allowed them to dispense with stays in great houses.* In May they spent a week inspecting munitions factories in Lancashire. While the King spoke to the men and presented medals, the Queen visited hospitals and women workers. In June the royal train took them to the shipyards of the north-east. 'I feel I could almost make a ship,' wrote May, after long, tiring days spent inspecting shipbuilding yards and ironworks.[2] 'So much walking on such rough uneven ground,' wrote Lady Bertha Dawkins, '& the Queen got quite worn out.'[3]

Queen Mary insisted on accompanying George on his fourth visit to France in July 1917. At Calais they parted, George leaving to inspect troops, while the Queen accompanied by Mabell Airlie visited hospitals at a safe distance from the front. May told George: 'You cannot think how glad I am that I came out here, it is all too interesting for words.'[4] On one occasion May 'had the luck to see 1500 of our men coming back from the line'.[5] She told the officer accompanying her: 'I want to speak to those men,' and crossed over amid tremendous cheers.[6] This was her only chance to stray from the 'terrible sameness' of young faces and broken bodies into the man's sphere of combat. The closest the two women came to the front was when they visited one of the battlefields on the Somme, twelve miles from the German line. Climbing over a mound composed of German dead buried by their comrades horrified them. Mabell Airlie described the scene: 'The Queen's face was ashen and her lips were tightly compressed. I felt that like me she was afraid of breaking down.'[7]

---

*Bathrooms for the King and Queen were added to the train for these tours, which lasted several days (Edward, Duke of Windsor, *A Family Album* (Cassell, 1960), p. 68).

With David, the Queen motored to the site of the English victory over the French at the Battle of Crécy (1346) and saw the cross put up to King John of Bohemia. In a moment of military patriotism, she noted in her diary: 'It was probably the first time that a Prince of Wales had visited the scene since Edward the Black Prince was there at the time of the battle.'[8] George meanwhile suffered a bout of violent diarrhoea, sent for Bertrand Dawson and spent the day in bed.

'Both George & I are feeling dreadfully tired after all our hard work the past 3 months,' wrote May.[9] George looked ten years older and, at fifty, May's hair was streaked with grey and she suffered from neuritis in her right arm, which was treated with electricity.[10] The doctors ordered rest, but in wartime this seemed impossible.

Even at Sandringham there was war work. Every morning and afternoon the Queen and her ladies picked horse chestnuts for making into acetone, a chemical used by munitions factories. Bertha Dawkins found it backbreaking work, and so did the Queen. They collected over three tons of conkers in a fortnight, and the Queen declared it 'great fun'.[11]

George's work seemed to increase every day. 'You have no idea of the masses of papers I am expected to read,' he reported to his mother. 'I am so tired in the evening that I go to bed at 11.0.'[12] When Alix told him that he was doing too much, he replied: 'I am not too tired. In these days I must go about & see as many people as possible . . . I am quite ready to sacrifice myself if necessary as long as we win this war.'[13]

'Very often I feel in despair,' George told May, '& if it wasn't for you I should break down.' When they were apart he felt 'tired, worried & depressed'.[14] In her letters to George, May created a domestic life. The chief inhabitants of this world were two characters named Charlotte and Jack, a parrot and a dog, the King's pets, whom the Queen mentioned frequently in her letters. But though George needed May to be there, he confided in her less and less.

May complained how hard it had become to discuss arrangements with the King. 'I cannot help laughing to myself,' she told David, 'at the mystery which surrounds any new plan which any of us have to put before Papa, it all requires such a lot of thought, writing, choosing the right moment etc, really comical in a way but so tiresome.'[15] Bertie too grumbled that his father never told him things, 'which is really rather a bore at 21'.[16] Making plans with the King was rather like negotiating with a foreign potentate. When May complained to Stamfordham about her husband's 'tiresome secrecy', he agreed, but neither of them could think how to stop it.[17] The loneliness of life with George led the Queen to despair. 'I have no one to help me, no one intimate enough & discreet enough to understand,' she wrote. 'How I miss my dear Duchess' – that is, Evelyn, Duchess of Devonshire, who had given up being mistress of the robes the previous year to accompany her husband as governor-general of Canada. 'I do not feel I can confide in my new Duchess [of Sutherland] in the same way.'[18] One person she felt that she could confide in was David. They had long talks which 'cleared up clouds which were gathering on the horizon'.[19]

May is usually seen as slavishly devoting herself to her royal husband, mesmerised by the mystique of the Crown. In reality the relationship was both more complex and more human. The war imposed a terrible strain on the marriage. George retreated into depression and overwork, excluding May from his confidence. Buckingham Palace in wartime became for her a lonely prison.

In March 1918 Germany launched the first wave of hammer blows known as the Ludendorff offensive. 'I have never in my life suffered so much <u>mentally</u> as I am suffering now,' May told George.[20] 'These are very anxious days,' wrote George, as the news came in of the Germans breaking through the British lines and the troops falling back.[21] In the spring of that year they lived under the shadow of defeat. This was the summer of the Spanish flu, which infected one in four of the population of Britain, causing 228,000 deaths; but the King and his advisers were fixated on the war, never mentioning the killer virus.

The King made a three-day visit to France to restore morale (28–30 March). He brought with him Wigram, Stamfordham, Derek Keppel, a police inspector, a press man and a photographer. 'This is what he calls "travelling light",' commented Philip Sassoon, Haig's sharp-tongued private secretary.[22] Lord Esher, who had spent the war directing British intelligence in Paris, wrote caustically about the King, picturing him 'laid up in bed with a pain in his tummy, having his head held by Derek Keppel'. Though he was only fifty-two

> they think of him as though he were Queen Victoria <u>after</u> her Diamond Jubilee . . . Poor little King! I think he is right from the point of view of saving what skin he has left, to go out . . . It is wonderful that the whole affair has not crumbled under an avalanche of ridicule.[23]

No one could doubt the King's conscientiousness, but in Esher's view his work was a waste of time. The troops, said Esher, dubbed the royal couple 'Fertile and Futile'.[24] At Buckingham Palace Esher found a 'Rip Van Winkle' scene. 'The same routine. A life made up of nothings – yet a busy scene: constant telephone messages about trivialities.'[25]

In February 1918 Esher visited Archbishop Davidson, whom he found in bed in a room full of flowers at Lambeth Palace. Esher complained that the King was 'making himself a nonentity' at a time when it was vitally important for him to be before his people, showing himself at public functions. 'He seems virtually a recluse, steadily devoting himself to good purposes and little works of a good kind, but with no conspicuousness, no assertiveness of the King's position.' As for the Prince of Wales, 'he might be doing all kinds of good in France, if he were there as Prince of Wales and treated ... as heir to the throne'. But the King made no attempt to promote his son.[26]

Esher's jaundiced view of the King was perhaps influenced by his failure to gain the monarch's ear. He had been one of the few friends of Edward VII who remained welcome at George's court before 1914, and he was on particularly friendly terms with Queen Mary. After the war he failed to keep the King's confidence. To manly men like King George V and Stamfordham, the homosexual Esher resembled a 'medicated tom cat', and they 'felt their skin prickle when he entered the palace, as some people react to the unseen presence of a cat in the room'.[27] Esher was perhaps aware that his days of royal service were numbered.* But he was not the only member of the old guard to criticise the King and the new style of informal, face-to-face royal visits. The longer the war dragged on, the more vulnerable the King became to criticism of this sort.

In May 1918 Lord Rosebery wrote a memorandum addressed to Stamfordham, claiming, as Esher did, that the King was becoming a 'nonentity in the National life'. Stamfordham decided not to show this 'vicious' document to the King, 'for it would be more likely to irritate without helping'.[28] Instead he passed it on to Archbishop Davidson, who was staying at Windsor, and also to the Queen. She pencilled a message to the Archbishop, telling him to ask to see the King and Queen together, and to advise the King to have small dinners, 'and explain the feelings of the upper classes, also that the King should do more things in public'.[29] Sitting next to Davidson at dinner that night, the Queen spoke freely on the matter.

At the interview the next morning in the King's room, Davidson found the Queen present. The King was a little nervous, and asked 'what it was all about'. Davidson explained that public men outside the government 'now never saw the King at all', and while this was tolerable in wartime,

---

*In 1919 Esher was replaced as keeper of the archives by John Fortescue, who combined this post with the office of royal librarian. Esher was appointed to the honorary post of constable and governor of Windsor Castle.

'it could not rightly go on for years'. He urged the King to hold dinner parties, and 'rather scouted his lame excuses that he had too many papers and documents to read'. The Queen backed the Archbishop, and 'after a good deal of bickering about it, the King said "Very well we will do it. I think I understand but it will be much more difficult than you think."' Davidson pressed for more publicity to be given to investitures – 'why not before a few thousand people, instead of before twenty in the Throne Room?' The King reluctantly consented to drive through London in an open carriage; the Queen complained that 'open carriages disturb one's hair', but she agreed. Davidson noted: 'All this was the outcome of pro-longed conversation, the King talking most of the time, and I succeeded only by great determination in getting in my remarks, and declining to be interrupted.' Afterwards, Davidson walked down the corridor with the Queen, and 'she said it had been a triumph, and that I had succeeded better than she dared to hope'.[30]

Like his grandmother Queen Victoria, George was in danger of becoming invisible, and the Queen played a crucial role in digging him out of his wartime bunker mentality and forcing him to accept the need to be seen to behave as sovereign. The dinner parties of twenty or so duly took place. 'Quite a success,' May told David, 'Mary & I enjoy them but Papa pretends he is bored & that it is a waste of time!'[31] George took refuge in Eeyorish self-pity. 'I don't think any Sovereign of these realms has had a more difficult or more troublous 8 years than I have,' he wrote on the anniversary of his accession.[32] His troubles were far from over.

Rumours reached London in July of the death of the Tsar, and on 24 July the Foreign Office confirmed that he had been shot. But it was not until 28 July that George learnt that Nicky had been murdered on the 16th.[33] 'It is too horrible & heartless,' wrote May. 'Mama & Toria came to tea, terribly upset.'[34]

Stamfordham fussed about whether the King should attend the memorial service for his first cousin, fearful that the public would accuse the King of being anti-democratic and sympathising with the counter-revolutionaries in Russia.[35] Balfour reassured him that the tragic circumstances of the Tsar's death made the King's attendance all the more necessary.[36] The service in the Russian chapel at Welbeck Street was 'crammed', and afterwards court mourning was ordered for a month, a 'dreadful bore' in the hot summer weather, wrote the Queen.[37]

'I was devoted to Nicky, who was the kindest of men,' wrote George in his diary (yet again).[38] People have often suggested that, because he refused to offer asylum to Nicholas and Alexandra, George was responsible for their deaths. This is unfair. The Romanovs were surrounded by guards and kept under tight house arrest. Escape was impossible.[39] An offer of asylum from George would have made no difference. We know this now, but at the time in March 1917, when Russia was imploding, things were much murkier. George probably did believe that his cousins could have been smuggled out of Russia. In March 1917 the decision to save the British monarchy rather than risk unrest or even revolution by inviting the Tsar to live in Britain made sense. George was sorry for Nicky's death, but there's no reason to believe that he felt remorse.

Stamfordham was 'one of the wisest and most decent people of that restless, disturbed period'.[40] He too made no connection between the refusal of asylum and the murder of the Tsar. He blamed the Bolsheviks and the British public. 'Was there ever a crueller murder,' he asked Esher, 'and has this country ever before displayed such callous indifference to a tragedy of this magnitude?'[41]

Communication with the Tsar had broken down after the refusal of asylum in April 1917. Reviewing the file in 1932, assistant private secretary Alec Hardinge was surprised to find that correspondence 'comes to a dead end towards the end of April [1917] and is not resumed until the end of July'.[42] As Nicky and his family travelled into the void, journeying into the depths of Siberia, George found it easy to ignore them. His silence stands in stark contrast with Alix's desperate attempts to keep open communications with her sister Minny the Dowager Empress, ignoring warnings to cease sending telegrams and badgering Balfour at the Foreign Office.[43]

The fate of Alicky and their five children was still unknown, and the Bolsheviks spread false information that they were alive. On 31 August a Foreign Office telegram confirmed that a heap of charred bones had been found in a mineshaft twenty miles from Ekaterinburg. Among the ashes were shoe buckles, corset ribs and diamonds. These were identified by a courtier as belonging to the Empress and her children. A summary of this telegram, 'omitting gruesome details', was wired to Stamfordham at Windsor.[44] George wrote in his diary: 'For poor Alicky, perhaps it was best so. But those poor innocent children!'[45]

The next day was a Sunday, and George's cousin Princess Marie Louise and her mother Princess Helena, a daughter of Queen Victoria, came to lunch as they often did when the King was at Windsor. The King walked slowly down to where they stood waiting in the corridor, and he looked so 'grave and distressed' that they imagined a terrible defeat in France. 'Oh, George, is the news very bad?' asked Princess Helena. 'Yes,' said George, 'but it is not what you think,' and he told them about the Romanov murders.[46]

Marie Louise's story suggests that George was genuinely upset. David later wrote that the murder of the Tsar had 'shaken my father's confidence in the innate decency of mankind'.[47] In the spring of 1919 a British battleship was sent to rescue the Dowager Empress and her daughter Xenia from the Crimea. George behaved with generosity and warmth, sending affectionate messages to his aunt. Perhaps this was some sort of atonement for his abandonment of Nicky.

Fifteen years later, George bought a Fabergé Easter egg from Cameo Corner in London, and gave it to May for her birthday. One of Fabergé's most sophisticated creations, the Mosaic Egg of gold and platinum mesh set with tiny diamonds, pearls and many other stones was given by Nicky to Alicky for Easter in 1914. It contains a 'surprise': an ivory medallion, painted with portraits of the five children. Seeing the egg at an exhibition much later the diarist James Lees-Milne wondered: 'Did George V feel guilty when he purchased it?'[48]

George was in France inspecting troops when the Allies broke through the German lines, advancing six miles in places. 'Very good news & it has bucked us up,' he wrote.[49] This was the start of Haig's Hundred Days (8 August to 11 November 1918), when the German army was beaten back by an Allied offensive combining infantry, tanks, planes and artillery. Within four weeks of the start of Haig's offensive, the Germans recognised that they were incapable of fighting back. Aided by fresh troops from the US, sent in at the rate of 10,000 a day, the Allied advance was remorseless, and the German army moved towards surrender.

The Armistice was signed at 5 a.m. on 11 November, and at 11 a.m. the fighting ceased. At Buckingham Palace the King and Queen went out on the balcony to greet the crowds, and the people surged all day as the Guards' bands played patriotic songs and the royals showed themselves on the balcony twice more. On five successive days the King and Queen drove in an open motor car or carriage through packed cheering crowds in the poorer districts of London. 'The demonstrations of the people are indeed most touching,' wrote George.[50] As Harold Nicolson wrote, the King had become the Hierophant or high priest of his people – a new and potentially fruitful role for the monarch.[51]

Not everyone rejoiced. Esher scorned the undignified spectacle of the poor Queen in an open car 'waving a silly little flag like the baby in [Madame] Butterfly'.[52] Behind the scenes, Buckingham Palace vied with Lloyd George to announce the peace and claim credit for victory. On 11

November, as the household were about to hang placards declaring the armistice on the Palace railings, the press bureau told them to stand fast as Lloyd George thought the news should be kept for him to announce in the House of Commons that afternoon. 'Did you ever hear anything so monstrous?' wrote Wigram.[53] But he was well aware that 'we must not lose our heads in this tremendous wave of loyalty and enthusiasm. Bad times are ahead.'[54]

The Kaiser abdicated on 9 November and fled to the Netherlands. 'How the mighty are fallen,' wrote George. He thought his cousin had 'utterly ruined his country & himself & I look upon him as the greatest criminal known for having plunged the world into this ghastly war which has lasted 4 years & 3 months with all its misery'.[55] George 'felt very deeply' that the end of the war had come about with William escaping justice, and regretted that 'we should not be able to bring to book the Kaiser'.[56] But his anger against his cousin soon cooled. When Lloyd George campaigned to extradite the Kaiser and put him on trial for war crimes, the King was furious. To his relief, the Dutch refused all attempts at extradition, and the Kaiser lived on as a country gentleman at Doorn.

The Kaiser's abdication together with the resignation of Emperor Charles of Austria and the murder of the Tsar destroyed the dynastic system, leaving George the only sovereign of a great power still on his throne. But in spite of winning the war his position was not secure. The most immediate threat was democracy. The 1918 Representation of the People Act tripled the electorate, and eighty per cent of the population over twenty-one now had the vote, including women over thirty. Many of the new voters were demobilised, traumatised soldiers. As Esher perceived, 'the Monarchy and its cost will have to be justified in the future in the eyes of a war worn and hungry proletariat, endowed with a huge preponderance of voting power'. Democracy brought the threat of republicanism, popularised by President Woodrow Wilson of the United States. But as Esher saw, 'the strength of Republicanism lies in the personality of Wilson! . . . He has made the "fashion" of a Republic. We can go one better if we try.'[57] Put another way, the monarchy must be 'sold' to the democracy.

On 5 November Lloyd George saw the King and asked him to dissolve Parliament. George was reluctant. 'We discussed the question from all sides & at last I agreed to the proposal being against it before.'[58] The King objected to the risk from 'unknown factors' such as the women's and soldiers' votes. Lloyd George countered that the existing parliament was dead and did not represent the new electorate. Perhaps his real aim was to cash in on victory in order to secure a mandate for his coalition, but the King was on weak ground. As we have seen, under the Parliament Act an election should have been held within five years of the last one in December 1910. An emergency statute had allowed an extension of three years on account of the war, but now that the war was all but over a dissolution was hard to resist.

'The general election is dreadfully upsetting & has come at a very bad time,' wrote May.[59] The spectacle of Labour trade unionists at the Royal Albert Hall calling for a bloody revolution and making speeches about flying the red flag over Buckingham Palace was not encouraging.[60] At the polls Lloyd George's Liberal–Conservative coalition won a landslide victory of 522 seats, due in large measure to the 'coupon', a letter of endorsement issued to candidates who supported the government. These candidates were almost all returned. The Liberals were split, with Asquith's Independent Liberals gaining only thirty-six seats. Labour, which had refused to support the coalition, won fifty-seven seats – a breakthrough which positioned it to replace the Liberals as the party on the left.

The lessons were not lost on the Palace. Modernisers such as Wigram thought the monarchy must reform if it was to survive a future Labour government. 'I am very keen that all the old Court and State functions should be revived and opened up to more classes of the community,' he wrote. 'People of all classes should have an opportunity of coming into Buckingham Palace and its garden ... school teachers, civil servants should have the entrée. I go as far as saying that trains and feathers at Court should be abolished.'[61] Wigram wanted to remove the dead wood from the household – the so-called Troglodytes of the old court party who blocked change.[62]

Stamfordham watched carefully. He consulted Esher, who proposed a radical reform of the household on the lines of the General Staff, headed by the private secretary.[63] Taking advice from Watts-Ditchfield, Stamfordham urged a policy of neutralising dangerous Bolshevik elements in south Wales and on the Clyde by persuading the 'thinking' working classes to see the Crown 'not as a mere figurehead ... but as a living power for good'.[64]

From Scotland Yard, Sir Basil Thomson, the bristling, bustling director of intelligence, composed a memorandum intended for the King's desk. Pointing out that the monarchy was the only important national institution lacking an intelligence system, Thomson urged that its need was the greatest. As the only major monarchy surviving the war, 'it will appear as an isolated and conspicuous relic'. The collapse of dynastic channels left the King dependent for information on the prime minister. Even if the prime minister was loyal, it was 'to the personal advantage of any ambitious Prime Minister to keep the King in the background to prevent his being thoroughly kept informed . . . the less the King appears, the greater in the eyes of the world is Lloyd George'.

The crown's only other information channel (said Thomson) was even worse: the courtiers of the household, 'honourable and pleasant' but Victorian and incompetent. 'If the monarchy is to survive, its representative must be known, namely must be constantly in the public eye, and must know, namely have an intelligence organisation.' The King, argued Thomson, needed a security officer 'directly in touch with the ordinary life of the country', and the chief obstacle to this was the Victorian courtiers, who could only liaise with a limited public through the court.[65]

Clearly the dynasty's change of name in 1917 had not proofed it against revolution. Nor was it enough to hold investitures and pin on medals. In May 1919 George calculated that he had given over 40,000 medals since the war began. By December the tally was 50,668.[66] Of these 25,000 were medals of the Order of the British Empire, which was first awarded in September 1917. It was open to men and women, with civil and military divisions, and with five ranks from knight or dame to officer and member. 'By turns, national and imperial, hierarchical yet also popular, the Order of the British Empire connected the King with his People in new and novel ways.'[67]

The modernisers called for further reform. But how far the reforms should go and what form they should take was ultimately up to the King.

May was sympathetic. Wigram noted 'a most interesting talk' with the Queen, 'who understands thoroughly the problems we have to face' and was 'full of ideas'.[68] But he grew impatient at the lack of progress. 'It is very hard to get a move on here,' he grumbled. 'Stam [sic] produces the most excellent suggestions which he picks up dining out – these must wait till the King says yes. I stand by like a Bookie's clerk.'[69]

The Wykehamist Wigram was his own worst enemy. His manner, wrote May, was 'a little brusque . . . he gets impatient with stupid people who do not see his point of view, & the necessity of gradually changing things, this annoys people & then the rows begin'.[70] Godfrey-Faussett was one who incurred the wrath of Wigram, who thought him 'the fussiest, stupidest little fellow I have ever met but with the very best intentions'.[71] One can't help sympathising with Godfrey-Faussett. But the real obstacle was the King. As May told David, 'I sadly fear Papa does not yet realise how many changes this war will have brought about'.[72]

George resisted modernising the household because he didn't believe it was needed. 'I fear at this moment Monarchies are pretty cheap,' he told his mother.

> But please God this dear old country will remain calm & collected, I have great faith in the British race who are full of common sense & I believe a monarchy suits them best . . . I shall do my best to keep in close touch with the people, & help them all I can & do what I consider to be my duty.[73]

This was George at his best, the father of his people, benevolent and trusting. When the diarist Lord Crawford saw the King, however, he found him excited, shrill-voiced and 'syncopated' or jerky in his gestures, but confident of the monarchy's future. '"Why should our people have a revolution? We are the victors, we are the Top Dog" (this on a top note).'[74]

In December George crossed to France for a victory tour of the battlefields. As he walked through scenes of muddy desolation, he was cheered by rain-sodden troops. David, who accompanied him, thought his father in wonderful form:

> This trip has done him worlds of good & he is quite human; it's getting away from Buckhouse [sic] & the real court life that does it! Oh!! that court life . . . that's what's going to hasten the end of it if it isn't vastly modified; people can't & won't stand it nowadays.[75]

Back in London, the Queen found George 'awfully tired & with such a bad cold, looking really ill'.[76] But George's hopes of escaping to Sandringham for Christmas were dashed by Lloyd George, who had invited President Wilson for a state visit without consulting Buckingham Palace. When Stamfordham telephoned Sir Maurice Hankey, the Cabinet secretary, to protest, the King could be heard in the room grumbling loudly about losing his holiday.[77] George was overruled by the Imperial War Cabinet – 'too tiresome', he wrote in his diary.[78]

The president, with his tall black silk hat and his wide, acid smile, was enthusiastically received by the London crowds. Queen Mary found the presidential couple 'very nice & easy to get on with', and so did George, who had a talk with the president after dinner.[79] At the state dinner Mrs Wilson wore a plain black velvet dress, making no attempt to compete with the Queen, who was resplendent in pale blue brocade and diamonds. The president, however, seemed to Lady Airlie 'determined to undermine the prestige of the British monarchy'.[80] In his reply to the King's toast, he failed even to mention the sacrifice made by the British Empire in the war. In retrospect George thought him an odious man: 'I could not bear him, an entirely cold academical professor.'[81]

The King and Queen retreated to Sandringham and its pheasants, and 'very nice & quiet it is too, a great rest & Papa is better already,' wrote May.[82] By order of their father, Bertie and David, who had accompanied him on his victory tour in France, remained there for Christmas, which they spent among the troops. 'It will never do', wrote George, for the princes to return home before the other troops: 'our boys ought to set the example ... in these democratic days, it will be all in their favour later on.'[83]

At 5.30 p.m. on Saturday 18 January 1919 Queen Mary was writing a letter to Bertie when Lala telephoned from Wood Farm to say that Johnnie had just died in his sleep. The thirteen-year-old prince had suffered a severe epileptic attack the night before, and he had another bad fit that afternoon. The King and Queen motored at once to Wood Farm, where they found Johnnie lying peacefully and Lala calm but heartbroken. Back at her desk by 7.00 after a very brief visit, and showing iron self-control, May continued her letter to Bertie. It was a 'merciful release to the poor little soul of unrest', but 'simply heartrending', and she felt 'rather stunned'. Mary and Georgie were 'awfully upset, their first real sorrow'.[84] As for the King, he showed no emotion. 'It is of course very sad but no one could have wished him to have gone on living, but he was quite happy poor boy.'[85] Within days George had started shooting again. 'I am thankful,' wrote May, 'it is so good for him & gets him out.'[86]

The letter that David wrote from France in response to the news upset May so much that she destroyed it. His feelings can be gauged from a letter that he wrote to Freda Dudley Ward, who had recently become his mistress, in which he described Johnnie's death as 'the greatest relief imaginable & what we've always secretly prayed for'. Johnnie had become 'more of an animal than anything else'.[87] His mother didn't answer his letter, and when David realised how upset she was, he apologised: 'I feel such a cold-hearted and unsympathetic swine for writing all that I did.'[88] David's callousness contrasts sharply with Bertie's intuitive sympathy over Johnnie's death. 'I can see from your letter that it has upset you very much and I don't wonder either,' he told his mother. 'When I received the telegram from Papa it upset me too, especially as I had not seen him since this time last year.'[89]

Together in Belgium, the two brothers had packed to travel home for the funeral when a telegram arrived from the King telling them not to come. David, desperate to see his mistress, was furious. Bertie was miserable. 'I felt that it would have been so nice to have come home for a few days and then to have been with you,' he told May. 'Here it is so far away.'[90] The funeral at Sandringham was arranged for 21 January so that Queen Alexandra and Queen Maud could be present, but leaving no time for the brothers to travel. 'I hope you and David understand,' wrote May to Bertie, but this putting duty above brotherly grief seems a sad error of judgement.[91]

'It was an awfully trying moment when the coffin was lowered & we were terribly upset,' wrote May to Bertie after the funeral.[92] 'Upset' means 'tearful' in Queen Mary's code. Her grief contradicts Pope-Hennessy's opinion that 'the general lack of maternal feeling becomes a complete void where Prince John is concerned'.[93] Yet she could hardly bear to see him when he was alive. No one had visited him except the family, and then only once or twice a year. On afternoon walks the royal party would head off towards Wood Farm, but only get near enough to see Prince John jumping about in 'a loony way'.[94] When Queen Alexandra visited him eighteen months before he died he was playing football with Lala and three women of his household. 'He was so hot but came rushing over to me & showed me his garden & all over the house . . . & he seemed quite happy but all the same I think he is longing for a companion.'[95] Poor lonely Prince John.

PART SIX

POST-WAR

1919–1927

CHAPTER 20

The Divine Right of Kings

1919–1921

The King had nothing to do with the peace negotiations, but when the treaty was signed at Versailles at 4 p.m. on 28 June 1919, a crowd of 100,000 people surged round the palace, and the King and Queen appeared on the balcony for forty minutes. The next day, defying protocol, the King drove to Victoria Station to meet Lloyd George on his triumphant return from signing the peace treaty. George wrote in his diary: 'Please God this dear old country will now settle down & work in unity.'[1] This was wishful thinking in the new post-war world of demobilised, angry soldiers, strikes and Bolshevism.

Outwardly, things seemed to revert to normal. After an absence of six years, the royal family returned to Balmoral, 'this dear place' as George called it, in August 1919.[2] Asquith's daughter Violet Bonham Carter found the scene 'pure Victoria & Albert . . . Tartan curtains, glass door handles, Landseer watercolours' and seven pipers screeching after dinner. Wearing sky-blue tweed the Queen walked through the woods, tapping fir cones with a stick. The King, whom Violet sat next to at dinner, was 'rather pathetic' about the possibility of a Labour government. 'They may want to get rid of <u>me</u>,' he said.[3]

When a railway strike paralysed the country, the King found himself cut off from all London letters and papers. There was no minister in attendance at Balmoral, and the only source of news was an Aberdeen paper that arrived by bicycle. J.C.C. Davidson, Bonar Law's private secretary, telephoned Stamfordham and asked if he had news of the strike. 'Not a word,' replied Stamfordham. 'I have sent telegram after telegram from the King, and I have not had a single reply for days.'[4] This was shabby treatment of the King by Lloyd George, though why Stamfordham didn't telephone Downing Street himself is not explained. 'It is all most sad,' wrote the Queen, '& God knows how it will end.'[5]

The King and Queen, who were 'most anxious to get to London, and be in the midst of things', made a panicky decision to travel south by car.[6] They took with them only the private secretaries, a valet and a lady's maid, leaving the rest of the household behind at Balmoral. The journey took three days. George recorded times and burst tyres, calculating the average speed at thirty-five miles per hour, while the Queen organised country-house tourism, stopping for meals at Welbeck Abbey in Nottinghamshire and Hatfield House in Hertfordshire, even though the owners were away.[7]

The strike was settled the day after they reached London, but Bolshevism remained a threat. At least the succession seemed secure. After the war ended, the Queen wanted David to stay in England, 'to learn how to govern'.[8] She told him:

> Do please remember there is an awful lot for you to do in England in every kind of way when you do come home & now is the moment for you to get hold of our people here, who are in a restless mood & need much care & attention & you will be able to help Papa and me in this. I feel sure you will see this yourself & that the 'cause' is the great thing in these days.[9]

For David, staying in England meant taking on roles such as the presidency of King Edward's Hospital Fund or of the Royal College of Music, or becoming a trustee of the British Museum – public duties listed in a letter from Stamfordham which could hardly fail to make the 24-year-old prince's heart sink.[10] After the excitement of the war years, when the charismatic prince had enjoyed celebrity status on the front line, settling down to the Victorian job description of the Prince of Wales did not appeal.

One morning in March 1919 the prince dropped in on Lady Airlie in her London flat. He sat for an hour on a stool in front of the fire, chain-smoking cigarettes and talking about himself. 'I shall have to work to keep my job,' he told her. 'I don't mind that, but the trouble is they won't let me have a free hand.' Lloyd George had proposed a new plan: a series of empire tours, using the young prince's popularity to bond the loyalty of the dominions. The prince preferred this idea to staying at home. The King liked it too. Meanwhile, David had persuaded his father to allow him to have his own establishment at York House in St James's Palace. 'I don't want to marry for a long time,' he told Lady Airlie, 'but at twenty-five I can't live under the same roof as my parents.'[11]

This was about the time when David's affair with Freda Dudley Ward began in earnest. Unhappily married to a Liberal MP sixteen years older than her, Freda possessed the indefinable gift of charm. Every day for sixteen years when he was in London, the prince met Freda at five o'clock and spent the evening with her. They were the same age and both tiny – he weighed nine stone four pounds, and she was two stone lighter.[12] When they were apart he scrawled long letters to her. Often written in baby language, they reveal him as anxious, oversensitive to criticism, petulant and needy, but besotted. Mrs Dudley Ward, the daughter of a Nottingham glove maker, became one of the great royal mistresses. 'Be like Mrs Keppel,' Lord Esher advised her. 'Be discreet.'[13]* She played her role to perfection, acting as the mother figure that the prince so badly needed. 'She has absolutely been a mother to him,' wrote Louis Mountbatten, 'and he has brought all his troubles to her and she has comforted and advised him.'[14] In doing so, however, she prevented him from performing the fundamental dynastic function of the Prince of Wales: to marry and beget an heir.

David's first tour to Canada and the United States (August to December 1919) was a triumph. 'What wonderful things of all sorts & kinds you have done & are doing!' wrote his mother. 'They quite take my breath away.'[15] There were warning signs, however. 'One's head almost reels at the amount you are doing & I feel angry at the amount of hand-shaking & autograph writing you seem compelled to face!'[16] Too much hand shaking was disapproved of. In one place David had to use his left hand as his right was swollen. 'This does not sound dignified,' wrote the Queen.[17]

George did remarkably little to prepare his son for becoming king. He did, however, warn him that, though the war had made it possible for him to mix with many people, 'don't think that this means you can now act like other people. You must always remember your position and who you are.'[18] For George this was easy; there was no gap between his public persona and his private self (though in private he was more Tory than he was in public). For David, on the other hand, the public role of Prince of Wales was unendurable. As he later wrote, 'I was in unconscious rebellion against my position.'[19]

The year 1919/20 was a record one for woodcock shooting in Norfolk, and over Christmas at Sandringham the King counted 404 killed, 'of which I got 174'.[20] David meanwhile dashed off a running commentary to Freda from 'York Cottage (F—ck it!!!!) [sic]'. His mother was 'divine', but his father was 'the most extraordinary man ... he isn't a man at all he is so queer in many ways' (this was an original take on George V). His parents interrogated him about Freda, but David assured her that 'they know nothing, darling one', although they only needed to glance at the post to see that something was up.[21]

David embarked on his second tour, to New Zealand and Australia, in March, half hoping that Freda was pregnant and swearing that he

---

*Freda Dudley Ward's husband William was well connected at court. His uncle was Lord Esher; and his sister Eugenie was married to Bryan Godfrey-Faussett.

'would never marry any other woman but YOU!!!!'[22] 'The day for Kings and Princes is past,' he declared: 'monarchies are out-of-date though I know it's a rotten thing for me to say & sounds Bolshevik!!'[23] Certainly these sentiments would have infuriated his father.

The young Louis Mountbatten accompanied David on the tour. He was loathed by the prince's staff for sucking up to David, whose confidant he became. David told Louis that 'he <u>hates</u> his father & mother'.[24] This of course went straight back to Louis's mother. 'His father's letters might be the letters of a Director of some business to his Assistant Manager,' wrote Louis, 'and even his mother seems so stiff and unnatural.'[25] Queen Mary adored her eldest son, but she remained 'tragically inhibited' with him, a prisoner of protocol.[26]

George opened Parliament in state in February 1920, bedizened in robes and crown, but the troops wore khaki. Not until 1921 was the opening of Parliament the same as before the war. 'May & I went in the Coronation coach with 8 black stallions (the creams have been done away with) & the Household Cavalry & Guards were in their full dress again, red coats & bearskins & they looked splendid.'[27]

The first court for six years was held in June 1920. It lasted one hour twenty minutes, George noted, and 'went much quicker as there were no trains or veils'.[28] The Queen reached once more for her book of 'Gowns and Jewels', which had remained closed during the war; her lady-in-waiting recorded that she wore an opalescent sequin gown, and a train of green and gold brocade. For the next court she wore a new white and gold gown and a diamond crown with the Koh-i-noor.[29] The King held his first levee since the war; how 'refreshing' it was, he wrote, to see the old full-dress uniforms again.[30] So many debutantes had accumulated during the war years that the only way to get through the backlog of presentations was to hold a series of garden parties which functioned as extra courts.[31]

Ceremonial at court was restored against a background of economic collapse. The slump of 1920–21 was the deepest since the Industrial Revolution (until the recession of 2020), caused by severe cuts in government spending coupled with a spike in unemployment as demobilised troops returned home. Royal anxiety about Bolshevism and revolution was stoked by the reports of Basil Thomson, director of intelligence at the Home Office. One report, which claimed that the Russian Trading Delegation posed a greater revolutionary threat than anything since the Armistice, sent a chill down the King's spine.[32] After reading another of Thomson's reports, George became convinced that communists were 'behind all the troubles such as have recently occurred in Dundee, Liverpool and . . . Aberdeen, and what is still more odious is that, probably, their activities are made possible by Russian money'.[33] But Thomson's reports were opinionated and exaggerated, and he was sacked as head of intelligence later in 1921.

The miners came out on strike in April 1921, in protest against wage reductions prompted by the slump. The royals cut short the Windsor court and returned to London in a fright. George considered that 'we are passing through as grave a crisis as this country has ever had' and worried about the extremists, who 'hoped to bring on a revolution'.[34] Rather than call for troops, however, the conciliator King urged the government to provide a scheme of 'emergency works' for the unemployed who wanted to work.[35]

George had found a new way of connecting with the working class. He had first attended the Football Association Cup Final in 1914 and, when the competition was resumed after the war, Cup Finals became fixtures in the royal diary. The King was transformed into 'an enthusiastic schoolboy, gripping his hat with excitement'.[36] In April 1921 when the royal cars arrived unexpectedly at Stamford Bridge for the Cup Final between Tottenham Hotspur and Wolverhampton Wanderers, the King was cheered by a crowd of 72,000 men waving cloth caps in the air as they sang the National Anthem. He found it 'very moving'.[37] After the match, spectators rushed on to the pitch to see the King present the cup. He told his mother: 'There were no bolshevists there, at least I never saw any. The country is all right, just a few extremists are doing all the harm.'[38]

The King made one important political intervention: over Ireland. The Home Rule legislation had passed in September 1914, but had been postponed for the duration of the war. This was regarded as a betrayal by Irish nationalists. When the 1916 Easter Rebellion broke out in Dublin, it was mishandled by the British, and support surged for Sinn Féin (the Irish republican movement). As a result, Sinn Féin won 73 of 105 Irish seats in the 1918 election, and the following January, having set up Ireland's own parliament (the Dáil), declared independence, while embarking on a campaign of murder and terrorism against the British.

A fourth Home Rule Bill, which created Southern Ireland and Northern Ireland, each with its own parliament, was passed in November 1920. Meanwhile the armed struggle, which came to be known as the Irish War of Independence, had continued unabated. The government sent paramilitaries – nicknamed the 'Black and Tans' because they wore a mix of police and military clothing – who fought a bloody and indiscriminate guerrilla war against the nationalists. George was outraged, considering the protection of his Irish subjects to be his duty. 'Are you going to shoot all the people in Ireland?' he asked Lloyd George. 'I cannot have my people killed in this manner.'[39] When the King was asked to open the new Ulster parliament in Belfast in June 1921, he saw a chance to intervene with a message of peace for the Irish people. The King's initiative was not welcomed by ministers, who had intended the royal visit to be purely formal. Nagged by Stamfordham, however, Lloyd George agreed that the King should deliver an important speech. A suitable text was drafted by the prime minister's private secretary and approved by Lloyd George and the Cabinet.

Queen Mary unexpectedly decided to accompany George to Belfast only ten days before the visit took place, puzzling her household, as her usual practice was to plan her engagements down to the last detail as far ahead as possible. As the King and Queen drove through the Belfast crowds in heavy open barouches at walking pace, the home secretary worried about a terrorist attack. Afterwards, Mabell Airlie heard the Queen murmur: 'They could have got any of us.' Mabell observed: 'And then I thought I knew the reason which had made her suddenly decide to go with the King to Belfast.'[40]

The King's speech, a moving appeal for peace and unity, delivered from the throne with intense feeling, was perfectly pitched, and the royal party drove the two miles back to the quay to the accompaniment of a continuous wave of cheering. But George's satisfaction was short-lived. On the journey home in the royal yacht, he read *The Times'* report of a speech by the lord chancellor, Lord Birkenhead, in the House of Lords declaring that peace in Ireland was impossible and Britain was at war with Ireland. In a fury he hurled the newspaper away, shouting: 'The government have broken faith with me.'[41]*

All was not lost. At Euston the King was met by Lloyd George and greeted with thunderous cheers from the crowds who thronged the

---

*Such was the King's anger with the government for sabotaging his Belfast speech that Stamfordham leaked the story to Wickham Steed, the editor of *The Times*. When the story was published in the *New York Times* in July, Lloyd George summoned Stamfordham, who admitted that he had told Steed that the King and the prime minister 'had been at variance'. Lloyd George was 'simply furious', and said to Stamfordham: ' "This means that the King's secretary is seeing the Editor of the chief Opposition newspaper, & gives him the impression that there is a difference of opinion between the King & his Prime Minister. I cannot allow this to happen again." [Lloyd George] said S. was very frightened' (Frances Stevenson, *Lloyd George: A Diary*, ed. A.J.P. Taylor (Hutchinson, 1971), pp. 232–3).

station. Stamfordham dashed off a memo to Lloyd George urging him to grasp the 'psychological moment and it is a fleeting moment' to make use of the King's success and negotiate with the Irish government.[42] Enabled by the King, a conference took place in October at Downing Street between Lloyd George and delegates of the Irish government. An Anglo-Irish Treaty, giving dominion status to the newly founded Irish Free State and excluding six Ulster counties, was agreed and passed by both the British parliament and the Irish Dáil.

George was jubilant. 'The happiest & greatest event that has happened for many years is the signing of the agreement,' he declared. 'It means peace in Ireland. For 700 years the Statesmen have all failed to find a solution.'[43] He spoke too soon. Dominion status was unacceptable to many nationalists, and the treaty was fatally divisive, plunging Ireland into a bloody civil war, with republicans on one side and supporters of the Anglo-Irish Treaty on the other. Nevertheless, the King had played his part impeccably; as Harold Nicolson wrote, it was 'a classic example of correct constitutional behaviour and of the proper functioning of Monarchy in a parliamentary State'.[44] Once again, the King had acted as arbitrator.

The King's attempt to broker peace echoed his efforts to prevent civil war over Ulster by convening the Buckingham Palace Conference in 1914. But in 1921 nothing could stop the drift towards civil war in Ireland. British rule was in retreat, and this was not something that the King could prevent. He was sent the proofs of the stamps of the Irish Free State for approval, but even here the King's powers were small. 'I am afraid,' wrote Winston Churchill's private secretary Eddy Marsh, 'that it will not be possible to persuade the Irish Government to include the King's head among their designs.'[45] Increasingly George's efforts were directed towards the consolidation and strengthening of the monarchy at home.

In August 1921 the King stayed at Bolton Abbey to shoot grouse with the Duke of Devonshire. He hadn't been there since 1912, and he enjoyed his stay 'immensely', himself shooting 766 birds over seven days.[46] As was traditional, no women except the duchess and the duke's sisters were asked. There was no electricity, and smoking oil lamps blackened the walls of Pugin's drawing room. The King filled the house with his own staff and his own post office, and he brought a hill pony to carry him to the butts. At 2 a.m. on 19 August ministers arrived from London and he held an emergency council to cancel the prorogation of Parliament, allowing MPs to sit for one more day for an emergency debate on the Irish question. 'Bed at 2.15 very sleepy & rather grumpy,' he wrote.[47]

In 1920 for the first time in seven years, the King attended Cowes week, announcing his decision to race again with the royal yacht *Britannia*. Built in 1892 for the then Prince of Wales, the *Britannia* had beaten all her rivals in her first five years, winning 122 out of 289 races. She had ceased to race in 1897, when she was beaten at Cowes by the Kaiser in his more powerful yacht *Meteor*, an embarrassing humiliation that mirrored the Anglo-German naval rivalry. 'The Regatta used to be a pleasant relaxation for me,' said the prince. 'Since the Kaiser took command, it is a vexation.'[48] He sold *Britannia*, then bought her back in 1902 and used her as a pleasure boat. Now the Kaiser was gone and the German fleet was scuttled, and *Britannia* could once more rule the waves. Working with Major Philip Hunloke, whom he had appointed to the post of the King's sailing master in 1913, George rerigged *Britannia* as a racing cruiser.

Britannia's 1920 season was a success. Cowes, which had stagnated during the war, revived thanks to the King's involvement. *Britannia* sailed in nine races and won five firsts and three seconds. Fritz Ponsonby told Hunloke: 'The King appeared in London delighted with his yachting and said to me as he struck me a violent blow "You'll be pleased with me I have been winning you money £800 (then another blow) what do you think of that." '[49] George's habit of hitting people as he spoke to them in a friendly but painful way seems to have developed since the war.

The year 1921, as George's biographer John Gore observed, was 'perhaps the happiest, as it was one of the most successful in King George's yachting history'.[50] In his diary, normally a bare record of facts, George let his pen run on when describing his yacht racing. Here he is in July 1921: 'We got a capital start, the others were all behind & we went right away from them at the beginning & gained time on them each time & won easily. I never saw the old boat sail better ... Enjoyed my sail immensely.'[51] *Britannia*'s statistics were excellent: 'She has started a race 290 times, has won 15 first prizes & 36 other prizes ... I am sure no other yacht has got a record like that in 28 years, 16 of which she didn't race.'[52]

Britannia was always steered by Hunloke when she raced, but George was no dilettante sailor. According to the coxswain on *Victoria and Albert*, the King was 'a terrific martinet in naval matters' and 'his knowledge was terrifying ... he could handle a boat better than most naval officers'.[53] Yacht racing was a man's sport which the Queen did not enjoy, especially (as she once wrote) because 'I managed to be sick and spent most of the time in Major Hunloke's cabin'.[54] At Cowes she took motor drives round the Isle of Wight inspecting Osborne or visiting antique shops. 'The *Britannia* has just passed us,' she wrote on one occasion in 1925, 'and I saw the King looking very wet and uncomfortable in oilskins – what a way to enjoy oneself.'[55]

George refused to buy a new yacht. Instead *Britannia* was refitted in successive years, and the improvements were supervised by the King in correspondence with Hunloke. 'I don't care what anyone says,' George told Hunloke, 'she is probably the best racing yacht ever built.'[56] Modernising *Britannia* cost money. Fritz Ponsonby as keeper of the Privy Purse complained in 1925 that 'money has been spent pretty freely on the "Britannia" of late years and either there have been mistakes or it is not humanly possible to make a yacht built 40 years ago as fast as these modern yachts'.[57] He was proved right in 1926, when the alterations were a failure and 'ruined her in a strong wind, which makes me sad', as the King lamented.[58] 'Such a disappointment for you after all that expense, what can be done now I wonder,' wrote the Queen to the King.[59]

The new normal at Cowes in the early 1920s cost considerably more than normalcy had done before the war. King George was a simple soul but, as his eldest son explained, this did not mean that he lived in discomfort. On the contrary, 'everything about him was always of the best – his clothes, his fine hammer guns by Purdey, his food, his stationery, his cigarette cases by Fabergé'.[60] Perhaps the sole exception was his bed at Sandringham. One day when the King was out, bedchamber woman Lady Cynthia Colville slipped into his room and jumped up and down on his bed to test how hard it was: 'it was like jumping on the floor'.[61]

Court ceremonial was expensive, and the King complained that he couldn't afford it. George had made economies during the war. His outgoings were significantly reduced – no entertaining or wine, no carriage horses or liveries, no Balmoral, no state visits. Mindful perhaps of how unpopular hoarding taxpayers' money had made Queen Victoria, George gave a voluntary payment to the Exchequer of £100,000 (£8.7 million today) in 1916. He also contributed £77,000 to charities during the war. These generous gifts were overlooked at the time. But he nevertheless made a net saving of £78,000 which was not returned to the Treasury.[62]

Peacetime brought more bills. The livery of each uniformed servant cost an annual £100 (£8,763 today). For the opening of Parliament fifty-two horses were required, 'and I could do it much easier in two motor cars', said the King.[63] Entertaining the King of the Belgians on a state visit and taking *Britannia* to Cowes cost 'immense sums'.[64] Stamford-ham reckoned that the King needed an increase of £100,000 on the Civil List 'to keep things up as they are at present'.[65] The alternative was that the King should cease to exercise hospitality on a large scale, rid himself of his horses and carriages and dismiss over 100 servants.

Fritz Ponsonby wrote to Lloyd George claiming that rising costs had created a deficit on the Civil List for 1919/20 of £60,000. Unless 'vast cuts' were made, the deficit would be unaffordable in future years. In order to avoid the spectre of the 'the King going to open Parliament in a taxi-cab', Ponsonby asked for an increase of £100,000 on the Civil List.[66]

As one historian has pointed out, Ponsonby made no mention of the savings which the King had made on the Civil List, amounting to £220,000 over the years 1910–18. Exactly what happened to this money is unclear, but the suggestion is that most of it 'seems to have gone into George V's private pocket'.[67] To be fair, however, the King's income from the Duchy of Lancaster had fallen from £64,000 in 1911 to £44,000 in 1921. Lord Crawford, chancellor of the Duchy of Lancaster, reported that net receipts from the duchy had dropped 40 per cent since 1914 on account of new taxation.[68]

There was no crisis on the Civil List. The monarchy was not going bankrupt in 1920/1, but George worried that increased expenditure would eat into his private savings.

Lloyd George resisted the King's demand for an increase on the Civil List. This infuriated Stamfordham and Ponsonby, who demanded the matter be put before Parliament. But Lloyd George was right. Economic recession made 1921 the worst time to discuss the riches of the Crown. Instead, a one-off transfer of £100,000 was made from the Duchy of Lancaster to pay off the debt on the Civil List. In Parliament the chancellor of the Exchequer, Austen Chamberlain, praised the King's public-spiritedness in declining to ask Parliament for money.

The Treasury set up a committee to inquire into spending in the royal household. The committee recommended cuts in servants' wages, which had been increased by the scheme known as the 'war bonus'. Twenty-two staff at the Royal Mews or stables were made redundant. The greatest savings were made in food, where the committee uncovered a racket. Inflated prices were being paid for excessive quantities (the daily allowance was an astonishing three pounds of meat or fish per person). Either the food was not delivered, or once delivered it was smuggled out. This scandal happened on the watch of the master of the house-hold, Derek Keppel, who was criticised for his laxness, though the committee acknowledged that as a courtier he could hardly be expected to read accounts. The committee recommended economies which saved £40,000 a year.

The King's pleas of poverty need to be put in perspective. True, wages in the royal household were notoriously low. Wigram complained in 1918 that the £300 he received as assistant private secretary (he earned a further £500 as equerry) was not sufficient for him to 'live up to the position'. His wages had not increased since his appointment in 1910, 'when the income tax had been 1/- in the pound, and my contract was to serve for 6 months and 6 months off whereas during the last 4¼ years I had been in full time & sacrificed all for my sovereign'.[69]* But the Crown was growing richer. No mention was made of the King's exemption from taxation; if he had paid tax on the Civil List it would have cost him £478,000 for the war years.[70] This compares starkly with the catastrophic decline in landed incomes during and after the First World War. Hammered by death duties of 40 per cent from 1919 coupled with income tax at 30 per cent and supertax, the aristocracy sold off much of its land. As the aristocracy was cut to the bone, the tax-exempt monarchy 'quietly fattened'.[71]

On 11 November 1920 at 11 a.m. King George unveiled the permanent Cenotaph, designed by Lutyens (the 1919 original was a temporary structure), and there followed two minutes' silence throughout the empire. 'The whole ceremony was most moving & impressive,' wrote George.[72] Wearing a field marshal's uniform at the burial of the Unknown Warrior he walked down Whitehall behind the gun carriage to Westminster Abbey, where the burial took place.

Laying a wreath on Armistice Day either at the Cenotaph or on the grave of the Unknown Warrior became an annual royal event, marked by two minutes' silence. Initially secular, Armistice Day soon developed into a religious ceremony and an increasingly formal one. In 1924 a short service took place, and (wrote George) 'all the members of the Government, Guards of Honour of the three services & an enormous crowd were there: it was most impressive'.[73] Leading the commemoration for the war dead gave the King the role of chief mourner for the nation and, as the ceremony assumed a religious form, George took his place as leader of the nation's public religious life.[74]

---

*In 1923 the Wigrams went to live at Windsor in the Norman Tower, and their staff consisted of a butler/valet, footman, hall boy, cook, kitchenmaid, housemaid, under-housemaid, nanny, nursemaid and lady's maid. In 1927 they bought a car (G.N.C. Wigram, 'Some Memoirs of My Early Life'). Presumably Wigram was given a rise.

The King's role as chief mourner was strengthened by his visit to the war graves in France. This was urged on George by Rudyard Kipling, who was a member of the Imperial War Graves Commission. Kipling made a rule of refusing honours, and in December 1921 when he was offered the Order of Merit he turned it down. Stamfordham leaked the story to the press, and when Kipling discovered what had happened he angrily demanded an interview with Stamfordham. Kipling took the opportunity to point out how important it was that the King should visit the war graves in France and Flanders. Stamfordham minuted: 'Mr Kipling is in touch with republican propaganda and knows what capital is made out of this omission in unfortunately criticising the King, especially in Australia and South Africa ... I mentioned this to the King.'[75]

The King took note. After a state visit to Belgium in May 1922, he made a three-day 'pilgrimage' to the war graves. The speech he delivered was written in a different register from the usual empty platitudes. He expressed eloquent sentiments: 'In the course of my pilgrimage, I have many times asked myself whether there can be more potent advocates of peace upon earth through the years to come than this massed multitude of silent witnesses to the desolation of war.'[76] The monarchy had become more vocal than ever before. Convention dictated that the King's speeches were 'written by him personally'.[77] But the pilgrimage speech is widely considered to be Kipling's work; with his clever pen he defused the republican threat by making an inspirational appeal for peace.

The lord chamberlain's power to censor plays was a historic survival dating back to the time of Robert Walpole in the eighteenth century. Usually exercised to protect theatregoers from obscenity and profanity, after the First World War the lord chamberlain's power was also wielded to veto plays featuring the monarchy.

Brigadier-General Sir Douglas Dawson had been appointed comptroller of the Lord Chamberlain's Office in 1907. He was a reactionary, banning plays about the empire, the monarchy or the army; according to Wigram, he 'grows more "gugga" daily', and Nora Wigram thought him 'the most consequential [sic] old donkey I have ever met'.[78]

The Earl of Cromer, who became lord chamberlain in 1922, brought new vigour to the censor's role. He had worked as assistant private secretary to the King, and in 1918 he wrote that 'the position of the Monarchy is not so stable now ... as it was at the beginning of the War', urging that 'no stone should be left unturned in the endeavour to consolidate the position of the Crown'.[79] As lord chamberlain, Cromer sidelined the blimpish Dawson and exercised his power over the theatre with shrewdness and authoritativeness. Over any drama connected with the monarchy, he consulted the King; and the Palace urged a policy of rejecting all portrayals of the royal family, sympathetic or not.[80] In 1921 the royal advisers intervened to ban a play about George III and his relationship with the Quaker Hannah Lightfoot: 'In these days when some Thrones have disappeared, others are shaking and the wave of democracy appears to be rising, it seems to His Majesty undesirable that the story should be given on the stage.'[81] Cromer ruled in 1923 against a play about Queen Victoria, arguing that it was too soon for her to be portrayed on stage, and Stamfordham confirmed that 'the King will not hear of this play being produced'.[82] Cromer refused to license any play about Queen Victoria during George's reign.

But the King couldn't censor books. When Lytton Strachey published his brilliantly irreverent and ironic life of Queen Victoria in 1921, the King, said the Prince of Wales, was 'very angry and got quite vehement over it'.[83] The prince, by contrast, was discovered roaring with laughter over the description of the queen and John Brown. Nor was George's disapproval confined to books about the royal family. When Margot Asquith published an indiscreet autobiography, he commented: 'People who write books ought to be shut up.'[84]

Rather than modernise the court, the King made it a beacon of moral rectitude. The aristocracy was expected to provide an example of good behaviour. The rules excluding divorced people from appearing at court were strictly enforced, as indeed they had been before the war. Ethel Beatty, the rich American divorcee who had married Admiral Beatty, flew into a tantrum and threatened to force her husband to leave the navy when she was barred by the Lord Chamberlain's Office in 1911, and only after considerable lobbying was she invited to a court ball.[85] The divorce rate spiked after 1919, and more people were excluded. The actor Arthur Bourchier was refused a knighthood; the lord chamberlain opined that 'having been divorced by his wife, he certainly could not be received at Court: and this was considered sufficient reason why he should not be made a knight'.[86]

Bendor, the fabulously rich 2nd Duke of Westminster, was closely connected to the royal family, and as lord lieutenant of Cheshire he was expected to play a part at court. The Grosvenors were related by marriage to the royal family – Bendor's aunt Meg was the wife of Queen Mary's brother Dolly, Marquis of Cambridge. Bendor's sister Constance (Cuckoo), Lady Shaftesbury was a lady of the bedchamber to Queen Mary for forty-seven years; her husband Lord Shaftesbury was lord steward. And, as we have seen, many of Bendor's relations held positions in the household.

Bendor, however, was not an ideal duke. In 1913 he separated from his first wife Shelagh. He wrote to tell the King, and the King saw Meg, who 'told me all about Bendor & his wife who are now separated'.[87] Bendor was allowed to remain in his post, but George wrote a threatening letter: 'I do implore you to remember your great position; not only that of your family but as my representative in the County of Cheshire & that in these days the example from those like yourself may do infinite good or harm in the country.'[88]

But Bendor, who was nothing if not wilful, ignored the warning. In 1919 he divorced his wife in a sensational court case. He wrote to Stamfordham offering to resign his position as lord lieutenant of Cheshire. Lord lieutenants were appointed on the recommendation of the prime minister, and, following correct procedure, Stamfordham wrote to Lloyd George recommending that Bendor should be asked to resign. This was ignored by the prime minister, who not only didn't reply to Stamfordham but told Bendor to sit tight and wait for the rumpus to blow over. When several months later Stamfordham discovered that Lloyd George had failed to sack the duke, he was horrified and so was the King. George considered that the prime minister had 'let him down badly' and he overruled Lloyd George, insisting that the duke 'cannot come to Court' and forcing him to resign.[89] Bendor was unceremoniously expelled. Small wonder that Bendor's third wife considered that 'ever since his first divorce had made him *mal vu* at Buckingham Palace, Benny had had a complex about the Royal family and everyone connected with them'.[90]

Sometimes the aristocracy pushed back. Perhaps the most ostentatious rebel was Lord Birkenhead. The King had objected to the appointment of the witty, fast-living, hard-drinking F. E. Smith as lord chancellor aged only forty-seven.[91] In October 1921, when the King spotted a newspaper photograph of Birkenhead wearing a soft hat instead of morning dress for the Downing Street Conference on Ireland, he instructed Stamfordham to write a letter complaining that the lord chancellor was incorrectly dressed and should have been wearing a silk hat. Instead of grovelling, Birkenhead responded by ridiculing the King's small-mindedness, and pointing out that 'it was never the custom to appraise the adequacy or dignity of Lord Chancellors in terms of head-gear'. George noted: 'I consider this a very rude letter.' The row was patched up by Stamfordham. George wrote: 'I only wanted him to keep up the dignity of his position. For a Conference of this kind he ought to be properly dressed.'[92] The King had assumed a new role of protecting standards in public life. But perhaps his moral leadership had gone slightly to his head; some of his household thought that he really 'believed in the divine right of kings'.[93]

CHAPTER 21

Grasping the Nasty Nettle

1920–1923

In January 1951 Harold Nicolson wrote to Tommy Lascelles explaining that he had reached the point in his biography where he needed to grasp the 'nasty nettle' of George's relations with his sons. 'I approach this subject with distaste,' he wrote, 'partly because I find it sad and dull myself, and partly because, upon the picture of a genial and high-minded monarch which I have so carefully constructed is suddenly superimposed the picture of a marine bully.'[1] Nicolson claimed that he would prefer 'not to mention the subject at all, but as everybody knows about it and will be on the lookout for it, it may diminish my credit if I do not make some allusion'.[2]

The section in Nicolson's biography which deals with George's relations with his sons consists of a single long paragraph of speculation and rhetorical questions. George 'may have felt' that, 'bred . . . in the artificial atmosphere of a Court', the princes needed a discipline which he alone could give. Alternatively, 'he may have exaggerated the contrast between the remembered ordeals of his own youthful training and what seemed to him the softer slackness of a degenerate age'. Again, 'he may have sought – sometimes by irritated disapproval, more often by vociferous chaff – to check in them what he vaguely recognised as the revolt of post-war youth against the standards and conventions in which he himself had been nurtured'. Finally, there is the marine bully: 'He may even have regarded his immediate family as a ship's company of whom he was the master and the martinet, and have adopted towards them a boisterous manner which, however suited to the quarter-deck, appeared intimidating when resounding amid the chandeliers and tapestries of palatial saloons.'[3]

Nicolson's excuse for writing so briefly and so allusively about the King's relations with his sons was that the matter had been discussed by John Gore in his 1941 personal memoir. But Gore's account had been heavily censored. To the dismay of his publisher, John Murray, Gore was ordered by King George VI to cut out the chapter on 'the late King's relations with his sons'.[4] In its place, Gore wrote an anodyne passage attributing George V's difficulties as a father to the happiness of his own childhood, which made him unable to accept the deviations of the

post-war generation from the standards of his youth. This was sentimental tosh, but it won the approval of Queen Mary and the King.[5]

Nicolson knew that King George VI, who was very loyal to his
father's memory, 'will not want me to say much about his ill-treatment
of his children.'[6] When he sent his draft to Lascelles, the latter approved
it at once. 'You have handled the subject with perfect delicacy and
regard for truth,' he wrote.[7] 'How well H.N. has grasped the nettle of
K. George's relations with his sons,' wrote the courtier Sir Godfrey
Thomas. 'I can't believe that anything in it is likely to cause pain or
irritation to Q. Mary or the present King.'[8]

In his diary, however, Nicolson recorded a very different version. One
after another, the members of George V's household whom Nicolson
interviewed testified to the King's shortcomings as a parent. Indeed for
the household George's quarrel with his eldest son represented his
greatest failure as king, far worse than his refusal of asylum to the
Romanovs, which was never mentioned. Alec Hardinge, son of the viceroy, who entered George's household as assistant private secretary in
1920, told Nicolson: 'It remains a problem ... why the King, who was
one of the most kind-hearted people in the world, should have been
such a brute to his children.'[9] Owen Morshead observed memorably
and acutely: 'The House of Hanover produce bad parents. They are like
ducks, they trample on their young.'[10]*

Lord Cromer considered that George believed that 'princes ought to
be brought up in fear of their father. "I was always frightened of my
father; they must be frightened of me." '[11] This is a version of the well-
known story of Lord Derby's exchange with his friend the King, which
was told to Harold Nicolson by Duff Cooper as follows:

'I think you make a mistake, Sir, not making greater friends of your
children. Now that my own sons and daughters are grown up I find
them delightful companions who add to the pleasures of life.' 'Not at
all,' said King George, 'my father was terrified of his mother, I was
terrified of my father, and I am determined that my own children shall
be terrified of me.'[12]†

---

*When Nigel Nicolson edited his father's diaries for publication in 1967, he wrote to
Morshead asking for permission to include this quote. Morshead begged him to cut the
sixteen words about Hanoverian ducks. 'I don't think the Queen today would care to
read it,' he wrote, 'though to be sure it would not be new to her either' (Nicolson Diary,
Owen Morshead to Nigel Nicolson, 1 March 1967). Nicolson obliged.
†Clementine Churchill commented on Lord Derby: 'People think he is bluff & independent & honest & John Bullish but he is really a fat sneak (Mary Soames, ed., *Speaking for*

The story may well be apocryphal but, as Philip Ziegler observed, 'like most apocryphal stories it contains an essential truth' – namely, that George was a bad-tempered father who believed he was entitled to bully his sons.[13] He seems to have believed that this was the right thing for a royal father to do. In 1923 George told Clive Wigram that the tradition of royal families, especially the English and the German, was 'that parents and children were estranged ... HM then said that he thought every father had the privilege of criticising the actions of his children.'[14] To which Wigram replied that fathers should remember that times change, an idea that the King strenuously dismissed.

In 1920 George launched a crackdown on his two eldest sons. To Bertie, who was dating a married woman, Sheila, Lady Loughborough, the King said that if he broke up with the glamorous Australian he would make him Duke of York. Bertie obeyed, and duly became Duke of York that June. 'I know that you have behaved very well, in a difficult situation for a young man,' wrote his father, '& that you have done what I asked you to do.'[15]

As for David, when he visited New Zealand and Australia in 1920 the King peppered him with criticisms. 'You might as well be photographed <u>naked</u>,' wrote George of a picture of David in a swimming pool.[16] On David's return, the King insisted that he should embark on a tour of India almost immediately. Unable to break up his son's relationship with Freda Dudley Ward, the King endeavoured to punish him by keeping him out of the country. David must be prevented from enjoying London nightclubs, which the King imagined to be dens of vice – 'dimly lit, smoky, disreputable dives'.[17] Unlike Bertie, however, David did not obey. He retaliated by declaring war on his father. 'I am not going to be wet-nursed or interfered with any more,' he told Philip Sassoon. 'I've got to win and come out on top or it'll be the end of me.'[18] He annoyed his father by going behind his back to Lloyd George and asking him to plead on his behalf for a rest after his return from Australia. George's demand was unreasonable; David was genuinely exhausted by his packed Australian programme, and the King was forced to relent and allow his son a year's break before he travelled to India in October 1921.

By now even Stamfordham was in despair. 'There <u>must</u> be a happier condition of affairs between the King and his eldest son,' he wrote.[19]

Themselves: The Personal Letters of Winston and Clementine Churchill (Black Swan, 1999), p. 252, 3 February 1922).

Some thought the King envied his son's success and popularity. 'His great complaint against you is due to jealousy,' Bertie told David. 'He knows too well what a success you have been ... I must tell you that at times his jealousy is quite apparent.'[20] Archbishop Davidson worried about the King's envy of his son, who upstaged him: while the prince was 'evoking enthusiasm everywhere', the King was 'retaining the people's respect but not doing anything to correspond with the élan and charm of the Prince of Wales'.[21]

The prince was volatile, indiscreet, loose-tongued and immature. He said or wrote the first thing that came into his head, and he overreacted to his father's criticisms. His idea of modern monarchy was very different from his father's manly, preachy style of kingship. As George acknowledged, 'you seem to have evolved a technique of your own ... and while I do not altogether approve your informal approach, I must concede that you have done very well'.[22] Though the two men quarrelled, the prince had no desire to take his father's place. This was not a power struggle between father and son such as the early Hanoverians had fought. On the contrary, David dreaded his accession.

At Sandringham in the autumn of 1920 Nora Wigram joined the royal shooting party. The Queen appeared wearing 'a very long dress with a very unsuitable crimson feather toque and ... an absurd little tweed cloak wrap'. She trudged gamely along over the ploughed fields, being pushed through the hedges by two of the gamekeepers. The Queen and Nora sat on their shooting sticks beside the King. 'Howlet the King's big fat valet loads for H.M., a little boy slips in the cartridges. A man with 2 beautiful Labradors and fat Spencer the detective completes the party.' Driven partridges flew like bullets. 'The King gets a brilliant right and left. "Well done George", from the Queen.'[23]

At the hunt ball that winter where 'the whole of Norfolk prostrated itself, while the Queen and Royal Family processed through the rooms', Nora watched the Prince of Wales dance foxtrots 'really quite beautifully' with his aunt Queen Maud of Norway, and he was 'awfully good talking to all the people and dancing with all the localites [sic]'.* The Queen looked lovely in pale pink and silver, and 'was in great form,' wrote Nora. 'I stood beside her some of the time and she put her arm on mine and just rocked with laughter.'[24]

---

*The prince gossiped about his aunt Louise, the Princess Royal: 'She is quite "dippy". You know, quite quite mad. She ought to be shut up, she really ought. I can manage her all right but she is raving!'

The prince stayed at Sandringham shortly before he sailed for India in October 1921. Nora watched him playing billiards with the King after dinner. 'They both looked delightful types of English gentlemen each wearing white carnation buttonholes and were on such good terms with one another.' The King played some excellent shots. 'What a topping shot, Papa,' said the prince.[25] But father and son were walking on very thin ice. A day or two later the prince exploded. 'I've turned Bolshie tonight,' he told Freda, 'as H M [*sic*] has been the absolute limit, snubbing me and finding fault sarcastically on every possible occasion. It really isn't fair, darling, particularly as I've been playing up to him all I can since I arrived.'[26]

Princess Mary was the least visible of the royal children. So low was her profile that she escaped the acid keys of Pope-Hennessy's typewriter and the waspish reminiscences of Queen Mary's household. Painfully shy, she liked horses, dogs and living in the country. The favourite child of George V, she was also the constant companion of Queen Mary and the only one of her children with whom the Queen was intimate. David adored her; 'she is such a darling really, & such a marvellous friend & confidante to me, although she may not appear to be!!'[27] It was she who had forwarded David's almost daily letters to Freda from France, slipping out to post them when the French governess turned her back.[28] Everyone loved Princess Mary; she was the centre who held this emotionally dysfunctional family together.

Now twenty-four, the matter of her marriage prospects had become fraught.* Queen Mary had once earmarked Ernest of Hanover, heir to the Duke of Brunswick, as a potential spouse, but the King's renunciation of the family's German identity had ended the days of arranged marriages to German princelings. George declared in 1917 that his children should be allowed to marry into British families. But David worried that his sister would be prevented from marrying at all by his father 'imprisoning her at court'.[29]

'If only she was allowed to dress decently,' wrote David, lamenting his sister's frumpish wardrobe.[30] At Sandringham she insisted on knitting 'a peculiarly hideous grey sweater' which the Queen 'kept going on at: "My dear child, why <u>can't</u> you knit yourself a pretty jumper. Clothes are so expensive – and a pretty jumper would be most becoming."'[31] Spotting her with the Queen at a charity matinée, Cynthia Asquith wrote: 'I was

---

*Dorothy Parker wrote a poem in 1923 which described the 'maiden blush' in the cheek of Princess Mary ('Shall we say a royal flush?') (*The Times*, 7 February 2020).

surprised by the prettiness of [Princess Mary] – she has a lovely complexion. <u>She</u> laughed very little, but her mother <u>rocked</u>.'[32]

Marrying a commoner was uncharted territory for the royal family, and there were no exact precedents for Mary's engagement to Harry Lascelles.* Fifteen years older than Mary, Lascelles was heir to the Earl of Harewood and fabulously rich, having unexpectedly inherited a fortune of £2.5 million (£200 million today) from his great-uncle, the miserly Marquis of Clanricarde. Some joked that Lascelles proposed to the princess in order to win a bet at his club. 'Of course he is too old for her and not attractive,' wrote David.[33]

When the future Conservative MP Duff Cooper met Lascelles in the trenches as an officer in the Grenadier Guards he found him 'extraordinarily elegant, beautifully clean and rich', a connoisseur, surrounded by copies of *Country Life* and the *Burlington Magazine*.[34] He affected specially high stiff collars, rounded not pointed and with a narrow opening which left little space for the knot of the tie.[35] 'I study "Harry Lascelles",' wrote Nora. First impression: 'No beauty but well-groomed looking with nice hair and a pleasant friendly manner'. Later she wrote: 'I think he is quite nice – but he is rather ladylike. There is nothing of "L'homme Brutale" about him . . .'[36]

Osbert Sitwell, who got to know Lascelles well in the trenches, liked him 'for he knew a great deal about pictures and art . . . and he was broadminded and kind as well as intelligent', but 'he was not generally liked', and Sitwell could never make out why this was.[37] A one-time suitor of Vita Sackville-West, Lascelles appears in Virginia Woolf's *Orlando* as the Romanian Archduke Harry, who had transformed himself into a woman in order to make love to Orlando, who was at that point a man (was Lascelles bisexual?): 'Falling on his knees the Archduke Harry made the most passionate declaration of his suit. He told her that he had something like twenty million ducats in a strong box at his castle. He had more acres than any nobleman in England. The shooting was excellent . . .'[38]

'I only hope it isn't too much arranged,' wrote David.[39] Queen Mary's account doesn't suggest that it was. She related that Mary had returned from a visit to Chatsworth 'very pleased with herself', and 'I thought something was up but of course said nothing'. Lascelles then came to stay at York Cottage.

---

*Harry Lascelles was a cousin of Tommy Lascelles. When Tommy married in 1920 Harry gave him a wedding present of £30,000 (£1.3 million today).

I felt that now possibly things might move a bit fast, but when she came & told me on the Sunday evening when I was resting that he had proposed I nearly fell off my sofa with astonishment! Down we went to Papa, me in a kimono, and announced the fact to him, he was delighted.[40]

The Queen was overjoyed. 'My head is in a whirl,' she wrote.[41] 'They are constantly together & she is not at all shy with him and most natural: very talkative, even with Papa, full of jokes, fun, in fact completely changed.'[42] 'I am snowed under with things to see,' she said in another letter, 'but nothing matters for Mary is radiant & I am getting so fond of him & we get on very well.'[43] George was not so pleased. 'It has come as a shock, & I shall be miserable to lose her,' he wrote.[44] As for David, he rejoiced for that very reason – at last the 'poor girl is going to be free and let out of Buckhouse prison'.[45]

The wedding on 28 February 1922 took place in Westminster Abbey, following the example of Princess Patricia of Connaught, who in 1919 was the first royal to marry in the abbey for over 500 years. Princess Mary's wedding was the first major royal carnival since the coronation in 1911, and news footage shows the streets bursting with cheering crowds. Never before had the marriage of one of the monarch's children outside the direct line of succession been a day of national celebration, and Princess Mary's wedding created a new tradition. As Bertie wrote, 'it is no longer Mary's wedding but (this from the papers) it is the "Abbey Wedding" or the "Royal Wedding" or the "National Wedding" (I have heard it called) "of our beloved Princess"'.[46]

The transformation from court ceremony to people's celebration was reflected in confusion over the dress code. Guests were initially commanded to wear full court evening dress with feathers and veil. However, the Dean of Westminster objected to women not covering their heads in the abbey, arguing that this would encourage the deplorable feminist practice of women attending church bare-headed. The result was that 'morning dress and hats' was substituted at the last minute for 'low necks', to the fury of the many guests who had already ordered expensive evening dresses for the event.[47] Rather than a closed court service, the wedding became a public demonstration of royal domesticity, managed by Queen Mary, who showed a 'shrewd awareness of the importance of modern PR in promoting the House of Windsor as ... a model of Christian family life'.[48]

The reality of royal family life contrasted sadly with the fairy tale of the wedding. For both George and May the marriage of their only daughter came as a wrench. After the wedding luncheon at Buckingham Palace, George related, he 'went up to Mary's room & took leave of her & quite broke down'.[49] The Queen, controlling her feelings as ever, 'managed to keep up as I so much feared Mary wld break down', but Mary's departure 'left a terrible blank'.[50] George wrote in his diary: 'I miss darling Mary too awfully.'[51]

'You wouldn't think it possible but Mama actually talked about marriage to me the other day!!!!!!!' Bertie told David in May 1920.[52] The marriage of the Duke of York to Lady Elizabeth Bowes-Lyon was a love match, but it was also arranged, and Queen Mary played a significant part in making it happen.

Weeks after breaking up with Sheila Loughborough, Bertie met the nineteen-year-old Elizabeth Bowes-Lyon at a ball given by the courtier and fraudster Sir Horace Farquhar.* He later claimed he had fallen in love with her that evening, 'although he did not realise it until later'.[53] After an uproarious house party at Glamis Castle of late-night games, dancing, sing-songs and apple-pie beds, Bertie determined to marry her. Early in 1921 he warned Queen Mary that he intended to propose.

Lloyd George had recently advised the King that the public would not tolerate a foreign alliance for the Prince of Wales, and the Duke of York should marry a British aristocrat. No doubt David's relationship with Freda Dudley Ward meant that Queen Mary was all the more determined that Bertie should make a suitable marriage as soon as possible. She consulted her lady-in-waiting Mabell Airlie, whose Scottish home was close to Elizabeth's family, the Strathmores, at Glamis.

Lady Airlie reassured the Queen that Elizabeth was a young woman destined for marriage and motherhood and not one of the 'cocktail-drinking, chain-smoking' girls of the Roaring Twenties.[54] But Elizabeth was a flirt, pursued by fleets of suitors, at least one of whom was serious – the handsome war hero James Stuart, an equerry to the Duke of York. Irresistibly attractive to men, Elizabeth had received more proposals than she could remember, and her dizzy life of dances and house parties left her with little inclination to settle for the stuttering duke.

---

*Sir Horace Farquhar was one of the few friends of Edward VII who remained in favour with George V. In his will, he bequeathed large legacies to minor members of the royal family, but when he died he turned out to be penniless and heavily in debt (Hugo Vickers, *Elizabeth the Queen Mother* (Hutchinson, 2005), pp. 69–70). He embezzled funds from the Conservative Party. That George should have been a close friend of such a rogue while expelling divorced people from his court seems perverse.

In February 1921 Bertie proposed and Elizabeth refused him. But the letter she wrote to him afterwards hardly suggests that the refusal was final. By repeatedly saying how sorry she was, and asking to remain friends, she kept her options open. Lady Strathmore wrote to Lady Airlie: 'I do hope the Queen is not very much annoyed with E. [sic] & me, altho' it wd be quite natural that she shd be,' adding: 'I hope "he" will find a very nice wife . . . I feel he will be "made or marred" by his wife.'[55]

The Queen was not annoyed. On the contrary she did what she could to promote the match. She invited herself to stay with Lady Airlie in September 1921 in order to visit the Strathmores at Glamis. Mabell Airlie was very grand and (according to Chips Channon) beautiful in a *dix-huitième* fashion, 'with her snowy white hair piled like an edifice'.[56] She had known Queen Mary since they were children; she was the Queen's favourite lady-in-waiting and constant companion, but she was not overjoyed by the royal invasion.

The Queen announced that she was bringing Derek Keppel, two maids, a footman, a police inspector and two motor men. 'I am sure I shall be most comfortable, & shall not find your house too small,' wrote the Queen. Mabell scrawled crossly over the letter in pencil: 'The servants could sleep anywhere I suppose.'[57] Detailed instructions followed from the Queen: 'One line to say that I drink a particular kind of sparkling wine for dinner only, I will bring some with me to save trouble.'[58]

'I always felt,' wrote Lady Airlie, 'that the visit to Glamis was inspired by her desire to help [her son]'.[59] The Queen returned from her lunch at Glamis satisfied that Elizabeth was the right wife for Bertie. She told Lady Airlie: 'I shall say nothing to either of them. Mothers should never meddle in their children's love affairs.'[60] But meddle she did. James Stuart, the rival for Elizabeth's affections, resigned as Bertie's equerry, and took a job in America in the oil business. He later claimed that Queen Mary had intervened to get him out of the country. 'That bitch Queen Mary,' said he, 'that cow, she ruined my life! I was in love with the Queen Mother and she with me, but Queen Mary wanted her for the Duke of York.'[61] Meanwhile, Elizabeth was a bridesmaid at Princess Mary's wedding, a sign of royal favour, and the Queen authorised Lady Airlie to act as matchmaker and go-between for Elizabeth and Bertie.

Bertie proposed for the second time on 7 March 1922. Again Elizabeth refused him. At first Bertie kept it secret from his mother, and when she discovered she was not pleased. She told Lady Strathmore that she was 'much disappointed . . . I hope you and E. will not reproach yourselves in any way,' she wrote, meaning perhaps that they should do just that.[62] Bertie confided his unhappiness in her, and she told him: 'You have made me very happy telling me what you have, and I greatly appreciate it.'[63]

As far as the Queen was concerned, the romance was over. Protocol forbade further contact between the couple. Bertie explained his predicament in a chance meeting with the Conservative MP J.C.C. Davidson, who seemed to make a habit of popping up when the royals were in trouble. 'The King's son cannot propose to the girl he loves,' wrote Davidson, 'since custom requires that he must not place himself in the position of being refused, and to that ancient custom the King, his father, firmly adhered.'[64]

Blithely unaware of the royal disapproval, Elizabeth continued to write to Bertie and to meet him at dances. Always one to shirk unpleasant conversations, the Queen withdrew her confidence from Bertie and communicated with him through Lady Airlie. Elizabeth was warned by Lady Airlie, acting on the Queen's instructions, to stay away from a hunt ball where Bertie would be present. A note of panic crept into Elizabeth's letters to the prince: 'I do hope you don't think I've behaved badly . . . Please tell me, have I done right?'[65]

The person who thought Elizabeth really had behaved badly in 'this tiresome matter' was the Queen. She told Mabell on 9 January 1923: 'The King & I quite understand . . . what is going on. I confess now we hope nothing will come of it as we both feel ruffled at E's behaviour!'[66] Perhaps a hint of royal displeasure helped bring Elizabeth into line. Bertie wrote to his mother asking for permission to propose once more, and this time Elizabeth said yes. Elizabeth told her brother: 'I could hear the door clanging behind me – never to open again.'[67]

'Bertie is a very lucky fellow,' wrote the King in his diary after his meeting with his future daughter-in-law.[68] Queen Mary's role has been overlooked, but her discreet matchmaking had been critical in ensnaring the reluctant and much-admired Elizabeth for her son.

The wedding took place on 26 April 1923 at Westminster Abbey, following the precedent of Mary's wedding the year before. As parents of the bride, the Earl and Countess of Strathmore expected to pay, and they were no doubt relieved to learn that the Crown would foot the bill for a royal wedding, which was really a national celebration. Bertie's wedding was a smaller affair than Mary's. To keep costs down, the King ruled out the construction of special stands in the abbey, and the congregation numbered 1,780, significantly fewer than the 2,680 who attended Mary's wedding.[69]

On the day of the wedding King George wrote to Bertie: 'You have always been so sensible & easy to work with & you have always been ready to listen to any advice & to agree with my opinions about people & things that I feel we have always got on very well together. Very different to dear David.'[70] The last sentence is revealing. King George VI once remarked that his father was only really impossible when his sons were bachelors: 'he was terrified of their getting into trouble with women; but ... once they married respectably his whole manner changed'.[71] The wedding-day letter makes clear that George V had always found his second son easier to deal with than his first. That letter should be set beside Queen Mary's wishful observation to Harold Nicolson in 1951: 'Bear in mind that it was only to David that he was really unkind.'[72]

David had returned from his tour of India in June 1922 after eight months away. Through no fault of his own, the visit was a mixed success. His attempt to break through the wall of imperial protocol and connect with the Indian people was frustrated by Gandhi. The Congress Party intimidated the people, stopping crowds from appearing to welcome the prince. David disliked India. He had no sympathy with the independence movement, and he refused to go tiger shooting with the Indian princes.

Back in England, David was exposed to the full blast of his father's disapproval. The unspoken cause was once again the affair with Freda Dudley Ward. At her insistence, the relationship was now platonic, but she remained his closest friend and loyal confidante. When Queen Mary reported that she had dined with David and they had talked a lot but 'nothing very intimate', George snorted: 'Curious that David does not confide in you any more, I suppose he only does to her.'[73] A year before, the King had written: 'If only he could settle his affair I am sure his health would be improved & weight taken off his mind.'[74]

Such brief, cryptic remarks are all we have to assess George's view of his son's infatuation with the woman he dismissed as 'the lacemaker's daughter'.[75]* We can only guess at the rows that took place. George had never learnt to control his temper. As John Gore diplomatically remarked:

---

*Freda Dudley Ward was the daughter of Lieutenant Colonel Charles Birkin, a wealthy Nottingham lace manufacturer. Winston Churchill commented: 'How odd the Birkins should have produced this delightful little Sèvres porcelain shepherdess' (Soames, ed., *Speaking for Themselves*, p. 313). Her husband William Dudley Ward was treasurer of the royal household 1909–12 and vice chamberlain 1917–22.

His trust in the discretion of all his Household ... was so complete that he did not stop to mince his words even in the presence of the servants, and his loud and trenchant chaff or criticism would ring out, not sparing the object of his wrath, in a publicity which obviously increased the embarrassment of his youthful victim.[76]

The Duchess of York once compiled a list of hints 'in case of anything happening to me' for her husband Bertie. 'Remember how your father, by shouting at you, & making you feel uncomfortable lost all your real affection,' she wrote. 'None of his sons are his friends, because he is not understanding & helpful to them.'[77]

David's biographer Philip Ziegler considered that Queen Mary was the one person who could have healed the quarrel between the King and his heir, but with the ascendancy of Freda Dudley Ward she had forfeited her influence.[78] 'My mother is sweet to me and so sensible,' David told Freda, 'there's really no rot about her though she is a martinette. But that is her upbringing and no fault of hers, and she really is a wonderful woman.'[79] But Freda's coolness drove the prince to chase other women, and to spend too much time in nightclubs, with the result that a rift opened between the Queen and her son.

George's anger against his son was visceral. 'So David is in London,' he wrote to the Queen in mid-August 1922, 'how long is he going to remain & what on earth is he doing there ... I have only had one line from him since July 24th ... since that not a word, he is certainly not a good letter writer, I think it is very <u>rude</u> as he entirely ignores me. I shall take no notice of him.'[80] To which the Queen mildly replied: 'I scolded David for not writing to you, & he promised to do so.'[81]*

The departure of Princess Mary had left a hole in her parents' lives at Buckingham Palace, and with Bertie's marriage the upper-floor rooms overlooking The Mall designated for the 'children' were empty. 'I feel that [Papa and Mama] can't possibly stay in and dine together every night of their lives,' wrote Bertie after Mary's marriage.[82] But stay in they did, and in London almost every night they dined alone. Family meals were formal, nevertheless. When David came to dinner, both he and his father wore a white tie and tails and the Garter star, and the Queen put on a tiara.[83] When the King was alone with the Queen, he relaxed and

---

*At Christmas 1922 at York Cottage George noted: 'David & Harry came by motor & only arrived at 8.25 which we thought very rude' (RA GV/PRIV/GVD/23 December 1922). Being called 'very rude' by George V must have been truly terrifying.

wore a dinner jacket. After dinner, they sat by the fire and read. At Balmoral, the King dined in a kilt and wore the Order of the Thistle.[84] At family dinners, the Marchioness of Cambridge recalled, the King would say: 'We won't talk, will we?'[85]

George in his fifties grew 'less and less inclined for social life'.[86] The royal couple seldom accepted invitations to dinner parties, and then only to a few great houses. Their contact with London society was confined to the four or five evening courts which they held each summer, when the King's chief concern was to race through the presentations as quickly as possible. The great houses of London reopened, their windows blazing with light as hostesses entertained the dance-crazed youth of the twenties, but Buckingham Palace remained silent and dark.

A replacement was found for Mary as young companion to the King: Queen Mary's niece, the 26-year-old Lady Mary Cambridge. George wrote from Aldershot: 'I miss dear Mary dreadfully here, as she has always been here with us. But I am glad to have Mary Cambridge who is a nice girl & rides with me each day.'[87] The King was 'especially fond' of Mary Cambridge, 'and loved to bring out her gifts of banter'. As for Mary Cambridge, she had a 'heavenly time . . . she particularly loved the King and didn't mind the shouting'.[88]

Fighting a one-man war against the twentieth century, the King deplored the 'New Woman' and disapproved of Soviet Russia, painted fingernails and women who smoked in public. One day as an experiment the Queen, who secretly longed to wear fashionable clothes, asked Lady Airlie to raise the hem of her skirt by an inch or two, but the King declared it was too short. Lady Airlie hastily lowered the hem again, and the Queen never dared to show her perfect legs.[89] The Queen liked to sing at the top of her voice (some said with a German accent) 'Yes, We Have No Bananas', the hit song of 1923.[90] But once when she asked Fritz Ponsonby to teach her the new dance steps, the King entered the room and exploded with rage, and the lesson was not repeated.[91]

George never liked to leave his wife. Writing from York Cottage in 1923 he told her: 'It is quite ridiculous how much I miss you here, the House seems altogether different, & I was very lonely last night.'[92] On a state visit to the King of the Belgians in 1922 he wrote in his diary: 'May lives at one end of the Palace & I at the other, it is not very convenient.'[93] In the middle of the night May heard her bedroom door opening. She switched on the light and there, peering round the screen, was his 'dear, sad little face', having found his way to her rooms on his own in the dark from the other end of the palace.[94]

Pope-Hennessy claimed that in the 1920s Queen Mary achieved what he described as the 'supreme feminine happiness of knowing that she was indispensable'.[95] According to him, she was 'perfectly contented' with George's social seclusion, and enjoyed her 'peaceful, dignified' life as consort.[96] It is true that she was indispensable, but the idea that for her this was supreme happiness is a patronising piece of unconscious gender bias. May was a perfect consort. She even pretended to be fond of George's pets, always sending him news of Charlotte the parrot and Jack the terrier when he was away. But perhaps the Queen did not find fulfilment in this Darby and Joan regime of compulsory domesticity. Prevented by the killjoy King from creating a social background for her children or introducing them to anyone outside the court, she sought new forms of escape. If the King would not entertain the aristocracy at Buckingham Palace, the Queen would invite herself to visit her subjects.

CHAPTER 22

The Influence of the Crown

1922–1924

'I have got to go to London tomorrow I regret to say on account of the political situation & shall lose my day's shooting at Six Mile Bottom,' wrote the King on 18 October 1922.[1] The Lloyd George coalition fell over the Chanak crisis, when Mustafa Kemal Atatürk threatened to drive the Allied army of occupation out of Turkey and restore Turkish rule over Constantinople. Lloyd George called for war against Turkey, but neither the Conservative Party nor the dominions supported him. The Queen was so depressed by the prospect of war that she stayed in bed, and 'worried all day over the troublous times'.[2]

The King returned to London from Sandringham on 19 October. He arrived at Buckingham Palace just in time to hear that at the Carlton Club meeting that morning Conservative MPs had voted by 187 to 87 to smash the coalition. At 4.15 Lloyd George appeared at the Palace and offered his resignation. A few days earlier the King had told Lloyd George: 'I trust you will remain my Prime Minister', but he was not sorry to see him go.[3] Nor did Lloyd George show much affection for his monarch.

Research in the Lloyd George Papers reveals files filled with querulous complaints from Stamfordham about matters such as honours and protocol. As Kenneth Rose observed, 'it must have been profoundly irritating for the PM, charged with the supreme direction of the Great War, to receive such a stream of irritating pinpricks from the Palace'.[4] Nevertheless, in 1921 when Bonar Law, the Conservative leader, resigned from the government on health grounds, and the survival of the coalition seemed at risk, the King sent warm assurances to Lloyd George via Stamfordham: 'I firmly believe he is now more necessary to this country than he ever was.' He added: 'I have complete confidence in him and will do everything in my power to help him.'[5]

The King's confidence was severely tested. Lloyd George's preferred method of party fund raising was the sale of honours. The rascal Maundy Gregory acted as a tout on his behalf, setting up an office in Parliament Street and charging £10,000 for a knighthood and £40,000 for a peerage. Stamfordham's letters to Number 10 show mounting royal concern over the inflation of honours. In 1919 he noted that 100 new peerages had been conferred since 1910, some of them 'contrary to what would have been the King's personal wish'.[6]

The King's birthday honours of June 1922 were flagrantly corrupt. Five new peers were listed, four of whom were crooks or tax evaders. The King wrote a stern letter to Lloyd George, describing the ennoblement of the notorious South African swindler Joseph Robinson as 'an insult to the Crown'.[7] Robinson was forced to decline the honour. Lloyd George had become a liability to the King, contaminating the court as the fount of honour, and his corruption was the more damaging because it compromised the moral standing of the post-war monarchy.

Back at York Cottage on 19 October, Nora Wigram and lady-in-waiting Mary Trefusis waited 'on tenterhooks' for news of the change of government, 'and then the Queen came in and disclosed all that the King had just told her on the telephone – and nothing but politics was discussed at dinner'.[8]*

In truth the King had little choice in the matter of the new prime minister. Austen Chamberlain, the leader of the Conservatives, had lost his party's confidence when he was defeated at the Carlton Club over his support for continuation of the coalition. The obvious choice was Bonar Law, Chamberlain's predecessor as party leader. 'I sent for Bonar Law who came at 6 & asked him to form a Government,' noted the King. 'He can't give me an answer until he has had a meeting with his party.'[9] By dinner time on 19 October it was clear that, once the party meeting had been held and he had been confirmed as the new Tory leader, Bonar Law would become prime minister.

This was a simple change of government, more straightforward than the formation of the Lloyd George coalition in December 1916, when the King had called a conference at Buckingham Palace. But in 1922 the King was choosing a prime minister only for the interim period up to the general election which now had to be held because Bonar Law did not have a parliamentary majority. Bonar Law duly called an election, which the Conservatives won with 344 seats. The Liberals were split into sixty-two supporters of Asquith and fifty-three Lloyd George Liberals, and Labour emerged as the second largest party with 142 MPs.

If George believed that normalcy had been restored, he was badly

---

*Nora, who was not a member of the royal household, worried whether she should remain at Sandringham without Clive, who had gone to London. '"Don't be a goose my dear," said the Queen, "I love having you with me," and she embraced me warmly' (Wigram Papers, Nora to parents, 22 October 1922).

mistaken. After Lloyd George's fall there ensued three prime ministers in fifteen months, and in the process the party system was reconfigured and the crown's power of appointing a prime minister severely tested.

The King was making his annual visit to the Royal Pavilion at Aldershot – a fixture that he particularly enjoyed – on Whit Sunday, 20 May 1923, when he received a visit from Bonar Law's son-in-law and his secretary Colonel Waterhouse. They brought a letter of resignation from Bonar Law. After only seven months in office, the pipe-smoking prime minister had been diagnosed with terminal throat cancer. He was too ill to travel to Aldershot and unable to resign in person. George wrote in his diary: 'It places me in a difficult position, as it is not easy to make up my mind whether to send for Curzon or Baldwin to succeed him.'[10] Today, a successor would be chosen by the party. But in the unusual circumstances of 1923, when the retiring prime minister was too sick to name his successor, and no obvious single candidate had emerged, responsibility for choosing the new prime minister rested with the Crown. This was an exceptional situation. George must decide between two candidates: Lord Curzon, the foreign secretary, and the chancellor of the Exchequer, Stanley Baldwin.

There followed two days of intense political drama choreographed by Stamfordham, who reported his activities in a black-ink memorandum that reads like a thriller. As this document makes abundantly evident, he took soundings and held interviews in London while the King remained at Aldershot, communicating with his private secretary at Buckingham Palace by telephone. He returned to London only when the choice of prime minister had been made.[11]

The views of the dying Bonar Law as to his successor were unclear. He seems to have thought that Curzon was the inevitable choice as the vastly experienced senior statesman, though he may have preferred the little-known Baldwin. With the prime minister 'not in a position to be consulted about his successor', Stamfordham sought advice from Lord Balfour, 'the outstanding person to whom HM could in confidence turn'.[12] On Sunday he wired the 74-year-old ex-prime minister at the Grand Hotel, Sheringham, where he had gone for a Whitsun golfing holiday. Stamfordham asked Balfour to come to London the following day. 'The matter is most urgent.'[13] Balfour had succumbed to an attack of phlebitis and was unable to walk or stand but, defying his doctor's advice, he agreed to motor from Norfolk to London.

At 3 p.m. on Monday 21 May Stamfordham saw Balfour, who was lying on his back at his house, 4 Carlton Gardens. Balfour claimed to speak 'regardless of the individuals in question'. While his opinion of George Curzon was 'based upon an intimate, life-long friendship, and the recognition of his exceptional qualifications', he knew little of Baldwin, whose public career had been 'uneventful and without any signs of special gifts or exceptional ability'.[14] But he considered that Curzon was ruled out, not on personal grounds, but because he was a member of the House of Lords. Insisting that the new prime minister should be a member of the House of Commons, not least because five or six secretaries of state already sat in the Lords, he advised the King to send for Baldwin.

Kenneth Rose observed that 'no man played a more decisive part than Balfour in clarifying the King's mind'.[15] This was because Balfour told the King what he wanted to hear. As he wrote in a memorandum, Balfour understood from Stamfordham that the views he expressed were 'probably in very close conformity to those already held by His Majesty'.[16]

Curzon had seemed the inevitable successor to Bonar Law on Sunday, but by Monday the odds were turning against him. Twice that day Stamfordham saw Geoffrey Dawson, editor of *The Times*, a man upon whose judgement he was becoming reliant. The first time Dawson was pro-Curzon, but by 8 p.m. opinions in *The Times* office were equally divided and the younger men were rooting for Baldwin. The case for a prime minister in the House of Commons was greatly strengthened by the consideration that the Labour Party, which as the second largest party was now the official opposition, had no representatives in the Lords.

Dawson told Stamfordham that he proposed writing a non-committal article, but (said the private secretary) 'if I could intimate the King's probable line of action he might be able to help'. To which Stamfordham replied that 'the King so far was convinced that his responsibility to the country made it almost imperative that he should appoint a Prime Minister from the House of Commons'. If he didn't and 'the experiment failed the country would blame the King for an act which was entirely his own, and which proved that H.M. was ignorant and out of touch with public opinion'.[17] Insisting on a prime minister from the Commons was a convenient cover. The King's dealings with Curzon had not always been harmonious. In 1911 when Curzon criticised George for supporting the reversal of his partition of Bengal, the King 'abused Lord C violently and said that he hoped <u>never</u> to see him in any important position again'.[18]

That afternoon, Stamfordham dictated a telegram to Curzon, who was at Montacute, his house in Somerset: 'Would it be possible for me to see you in London tomorrow Stamfordham'. The wording was carefully chosen in order to avoid giving the impression of a summons by the King.

On Tuesday 22 May Stamfordham saw Baldwin at 10.30 a.m., and asked whether he would be prepared to retain Curzon as foreign secretary if the King invited him to form a government. Baldwin replied that he would welcome such an arrangement, though he doubted whether Curzon would be willing to serve under him.

Lord Stamfordham was having a busy morning. At 11.00 he saw Balfour, who was leaving for Sheringham. Balfour reiterated his support for Baldwin. According to the story which appeared in Winston Churchill's *Great Contemporaries*, when Balfour returned to Sheringham his friend Ettie Desborough asked him: ' "And will dear George be chosen?" "No," he replied placidly, "dear George will not." '[19]

This famous anecdote implies that Balfour the elegant, manipulative, feline elder statesman had intervened to block his old friend and rival from the premiership. But the King, as we have seen, would probably have appointed Baldwin in any case. In making this 'delicate and difficult' choice he clung to the safety of a newly emerging constitutional convention that the prime minister must be a member of the House of Commons.[20] This was a development which the King and Balfour had instinctively understood; it was not a formal convention until the Earl of Home gave up his peerage in 1963.

On Tuesday morning Lord Curzon travelled to Paddington by train, making plans on the journey for the government which he confidently expected the King would ask him to form. Only now did the King appear on the scene, motoring up from Aldershot. He reached Buckingham Palace at 12.20, when he saw Stamfordham, who 'took His Majesty's orders to summon Mr Baldwin to be at Buckingham Palace at 3.15 p.m. and for me to see Lord Curzon as soon as I could and before the King received Mr Baldwin'.[21]

Stamfordham's narrative depicts the constitutional machinery moving with stately precision, as statesmen in frock coats and silk hats rode in their Daimlers up and down The Mall and spoke calmly in grammatical sentences. This was a polite fiction. The meeting that ensued with Curzon was anything but smooth.

Stamfordham arrived at Curzon's house, 1 Carlton House Terrace, at 2.30. He 'endeavoured gradually to break to Lord Curzon' that, in spite of the latter's high position, His Majesty 'felt compelled, though with great regret, to ignore the personal element, and to base his choice upon what he conceived to be the requirements of the present times: viz. the continuance of the Prime Minister in the House of Commons'.[22] According to Curzon's account, he spoke 'with obvious embarrassment and in halting language'.[23]

Stamfordham in his record of the interview noted that Curzon listened quietly and then replied 'with considerable feeling but with restraint and without bitterness'.[24] He declared that Stamfordham's message was the greatest conceivable blow and slur on him and his career, and he threatened to leave public life at once.

Stamfordham later told Curzon's first biographer, Lord Ronaldshay, that, had he known Curzon's extraordinary character, he would not have had the courage to face a personal interview. 'I shall never forget the two different men, the Curzon who received me and the Curzon that I left.'[25] The reality was that Curzon the All-High was 'perfectly furious'. It had never occurred to him that any alternative to himself as prime minister existed. The news that the King was sending for Baldwin 'produced explosions of wrath'.[26] As Ronaldshay observed, this incident was 'the most distressing in Ld Curzon's life'.[27]

Curzon had too many enemies. When he had heard the rumour of Bonar Law's retirement, he 'reacted in the worst possible manner', writing a pompous letter reminding the prime minister of his claims to succeed him, which he followed with a barrage of complaints and criticism.[28] As chairman of Cabinet in Bonar Law's absence he was 'unbearable', and in the Foreign Office his 'brutality', his scoldings and violence, were 'beyond belief'.[29] He had little support in the Conservative Party. Colonel Jackson, the party chairman, told Stamfordham that 'from all parts of the country his agents were telegraphing in hopes that Mr Baldwin would be the prime minister'. He estimated that at a meeting of Tory MPs Curzon would gain no more than fifty votes.[30]

At 3.15 the King saw Baldwin, who agreed to form a government. George noted drily in his diary that Curzon 'says he will retire into private life & his career is at an end; we shall see. I much regret having hurt his feelings.'[31] The King was right to discount Curzon's rage. The next day he changed his mind and agreed to remain at the Foreign Office, which Baldwin had asked him to do on the King's prompting. Five days later Curzon made an admirable speech at a meeting of Conservative MPs proposing Baldwin as party leader. On 29 May the King sent for Curzon and thanked him for the generous way in which he had accepted Baldwin as prime minister. But Curzon's snub still rankled, and in his interview with the King he 'argued against every point which had been urged against his appointment', and protested vigorously against what he described as 'the bar which had now been placed against any peer being made Prime Minister'.[32]

However, as the King made clear in an interview with Neville Chamberlain, he did not say that a peer could never be prime minister. 'What I said,' observed George, 'was that there were circumstances in which it was very undesirable that a peer should be Prime Minister and in my view this was such a case.'[33]

In opting for Baldwin, George probably made the right choice. Curzon the bombastic, arrogant grandee was a survivor from a vanishing Edwardian age and almost a comic figure. In 1927 Harold Nicolson brilliantly lampooned him in *Some People*, a book which made the King shout with laughter.[34] The process by which the Crown appointed a new prime minister, however, was revealed by the crisis to be flawed and outmoded. In a democracy it was not appropriate that the prime minister should be chosen by the sovereign's private secretary in a series of secret conclaves.

Stanley Baldwin, George's fourth prime minister, was inexperienced and unimpressive. 'He is no orator, scarcely even a debater,' wrote the Conservative politician and diarist Lord Crawford: 'he has no presence, a rather thick and husky voice ... and what is called a stocky stubby figure – altogether a very uninspiring person.' But Crawford recognised that Baldwin possessed what he called character, 'firm, staunch, honourable', and in the long run character counted more than brilliance.[35]

The King was at York Cottage for a men's shooting party on 12 November 1923 when Baldwin arrived to ask for a dissolution. The King wrote afterwards that he 'strongly deprecated' an election only a year after the last one; it risked plunging the country into turmoil and might result in Baldwin's defeat. So opposed was the King that he had told the prime minister that he 'was prepared to take the responsibility of advising him to change his mind'.[36]* But Baldwin insisted that he needed an election in order to gain a mandate for his policy of protectionist tariffs. On 16 November the King came home from shooting at 1.00 '& held a Council at which I dissolved Parlt', after which he joined the shooters in time for lunch.[37] According to Crawford, who was present at the council, the King did not conceal his opposition to the election: 'The King is really afraid of a Labour government, probably more so than circumstances justify.'[38]

Back at Sandringham again in December for another shooting party, the King watched the election campaign closely, deploring the behaviour of the Countess of Warwick, who stood as a Labour candidate.[39]

---

*Crawford heard that the King had told Baldwin that he would refuse a dissolution and allow Baldwin to say so (Earl of Crawford, *The Crawford Papers: The Journals of David Lindsay, 27th Earl of Crawford and 10th Earl of Balcarres (1871–1940), during the Years 1892 to 1940*, ed. John Vincent (Manchester University Press, 1984), p. 488).

The shooting had been improved by dint of cutting clearings or 'rises' in the woods, and the birds, which had flown unsportingly low before the war, were now 'screamers', flying 'as high as the most ambitious gun could hope for', with the King standing in the best place.[40] At dinner the King entertained his guests with royal table talk, telling stories about Queen Victoria's marvellous powers of hearing, which allowed her to follow three conversations at once.[41] On polling day, 6 December, the shooting stopped early to allow time to vote. 'I shall be thankful,' wrote George, 'when I hear what the Govt's majority is over the other two parties, as I firmly believe they will get a majority.'[42]

Along with Baldwin as well as 'the experts both on the Conservative and Liberal sides', George predicted the election wrongly.[43] The result on 8 December came as a shock: the Conservative Party lost its overall majority and a hung parliament was elected, in which no party had an absolute majority, comprising 258 Conservatives, 191 Labour MPs, 158 Liberals and 8 others. 'It is a very serious state of affairs,' wrote George, 'and will give me great difficulties to get out of the impasse, as another election is now out of the question.'[44]

How, in such circumstances,' asked Harold Nicolson, 'was the King to exercise his prerogative?'[45] Choosing a new prime minister from two men belonging to the same party had been hard enough, but now the King was expected to decide the composition of the new government. Lords Stamfordham and Esher were both 'much concerned' about the King's position, and 'eager that the private secretary should not have to go scouting from one person to another in secret trying to find out who should be sent to succeed Baldwin', as had happened when Bonar Law resigned.[46] Far from clinging to the royal prerogative of appointing a prime minister, they considered that, as a constitutional monarch, the King should be guided by a party meeting or by Parliament. The journal memo which Stamfordham began when Baldwin resigned enables us to watch the process of decision making that took place at Buckingham Palace.

Baldwin had failed to obtain the mandate that he needed for his policy of tariffs, and at first he wanted to resign at once. This would have left the King dangerously exposed. Stamfordham consulted Balfour, his constitutional guru, who advised him that

> I have come to the very definite opinion that it is Baldwin's duty to King and country, to say nothing of his own party, to carry on till he is defeated in the House of Commons ... at this moment Baldwin still commands the strongest party, and it seems to me that the King has a right to press him to carry on ... and when he is beaten, as he will and ought to be beaten, the choice of his successor becomes almost automatic.[47]

Balfour's advice was percipient. The King saw Baldwin on 10 December and 'asked him not to resign but to meet Parliament & see what happens'.[48] As Parliament was not due to meet until January, this left a month in which to appoint a new government. More importantly, it protected the King. Esher observed: 'A nice mess we should have been in, had Baldwin resigned. All responsibility would have been thrown, most unfairly, on the King. Who would have been without guidance by the only body qualified to offer it, that is to say the H. of C.'[49] Fortunately, Baldwin changed his mind, and when his leadership was challenged by a party plot decided not to resign as prime minister.

Two alternative scenarios emerged. One was a Liberal–Conservative coalition led by Asquith. This was scuppered by Asquith, who refused to accept the premiership either to keep the Conservatives in or to keep Labour out. That left the second alternative: a minority Labour government under Ramsay MacDonald. The palace had dreaded a Labour government ever since the war, and the King worried that Labour would introduce a Budget imposing a levy on capital and taxing the rich, which would be thrown out by Parliament, allowing them to go to the country and win a landslide election.[50]

Over the next few days the King changed his mind. On 14 December Stamfordham wrote a letter which gives an indication of the King's thinking. 'At the present moment,' he said, 'I feel that His Majesty should do his utmost not to hamper in any way Ramsay MacDonald in, what we must all admit will be, a task of almost incalculable magnitude.' In sending for MacDonald, he was confident that 'the King would be interpreting the general feeling of the people of the country that, true to British ideas, the Government, whoever they may be, should have a fair chance'.[51]

George meanwhile was struck down by sciatica. 'Had an awful night,' he wrote on 14 December, 'great pain & practically never slept at all, kept May awake all night'.[52] (Evidently the royal couple shared a bed.) For six weeks the King complained of pain, especially at night, and he slept badly though his symptoms were relieved by 'electrical treatment'.[53] George had never before suffered from sciatica, which can be triggered by stress, and perhaps he was haunted by the spectre of Bolsheviks at Number 10.

Over Christmas, Ramsay MacDonald endeavoured to put the King's mind at rest. He sent messages via Stamfordham assuring the King that 'there was no necessity for any anxiety on His Majesty's part', and if 'the King asks Mr Ramsay MacDonald to form a government he will undertake to do so'. There would be no extreme legislation, '"no playing up to the Clyde division!" [the radicalised Red Clydesiders of Glasgow, several of whom won seats in the 1922 election] but an endeavour to carry on the Government on sound lines'.[54] The trade unionist and MP J. H. Thomas asked Stamfordham point blank whether the King was alarmed at the prospect of a Labour government. Stamfordham replied, as he told the King: 'My answer was positive that Your Majesty was not in the least alarmed: that you had profound faith in your people.'[55]

George scrawled in blue pencil on a ponderous memorandum by the lord chancellor, Lord Cave: 'There are really no precedents for present situation. I must use my own judgement as each case arises.'[56] Stamford-ham agreed, advising that 'the one and safest course is to keep silent and await events'.[57] The reality was that as a constitutional monarch the King had no choice but to ask MacDonald to form a government.

The King opened Parliament on 15 January 1924. Baldwin was duly defeated and resigned on the 22nd at 11.15 a.m. With clockwork precision, the King held a council at 12.15 at which Ramsay MacDonald was sworn a member. The King then asked him to form a government, which he undertook to do. In his audience with MacDonald, the King mentioned the question of giving diplomatic recognition to Russia and (recorded MacDonald) said he 'hoped I would do nothing to compel him to shake hands with the murderers of his relatives'.[58] He complained that MacDonald had presided over a meeting at the Albert Hall where 'The Red Flag' was sung. 'King plays it straight,' wrote MacDonald, 'though I feel he is apprehensive. It would be a miracle were he not.'[59]

George wrote in his diary: 'He impressed me very much, he wishes to do the right thing. Today 23 years ago dear Grandmama died, I wonder what she would have thought of a Labour government.'[60] Still more startled might the old queen have been to see the role her grandson played in enabling that government. As for Aunt Augusta, she would have spun in her grave.

What did King George think of a Labour government? J.C.C. Davidson, the Conservative chancellor of the Duchy of Lancaster, considered the King a 'marvellous' man: 'it was remarkable how he hid from the world that he was an absolutely dyed-in-the-wool conservative'. Especially admirable was the way the King managed to persuade the Labour Party that he was 'entirely neutral ... He managed to keep his relations with Ramsay MacDonald and the rest of them so well that they became – and particularly some, like Jimmy Thomas – more royalist than the King. I always felt this was an extraordinary *tour de force*.'[61] Davidson's insight was shrewd. The King's ability to suppress his inner Tory was critical to the success of the first Labour government.

George dreaded republicans and loathed Bolsheviks, but he firmly believed in the good sense of the ordinary British people – the troops who had greeted him with hurrahs at the front, and the men who cheered him at football matches. When Davidson handed in his seals of office in January 1924 the King told him 'that a Socialist Government would have an opportunity of learning their administrative duties and responsibilities under favourable conditions, and that it was essential that their rights under the Constitution should in no way be impaired'.[62] Neville Chamberlain, another outgoing minister, found that the King's language about the Labour Party was no longer 'violent': 'he had evidently been favourably impressed by R. Macdonald [*sic*] and at the same time relieved by his assurances'.[63]

George saw all the Labour ministers in turn, and considered them 'very intelligent'. He told his mother: 'They have different ideas to ours as they are all socialists but they ought to be given a chance.'[64] This was not political calculation; the truth was that George found MacDonald and the Labour government 'easier to get on with and far readier to listen to the King's advice' than Baldwin was.[65]

The King was insistent on one point. Labour should not give Soviet Russia diplomatic recognition. Stamfordham explained the King's feelings to Lord Haldane, lord chancellor in the Labour government. The King was concerned that

> in the event of our recognising the Russian Government, an Ambassador would be sent here, as it would be indescribably abhorrent to H.M. to have to shake hands with anyone who was, directly or indirectly, concerned with the brutal murder of his cousins, the Emperor and Empress of Russia and their children. If a Minister came there would be no difficulty: but with an Ambassador H.M. would have to shake hands.[66]

Labour challenged the monarchy at one of its most sensitive points: the protocol of dress. The martinet King had rebuked the Conservative lord chancellor Lord Birkenhead for failing to wear a silk hat, and he exploded with indignation when he saw George Colville, husband of Cynthia, walking down The Mall wearing a top hat and short black coat, 'a sartorial innovation he thought abominable'.[67] But he bit his lip when the new Labour ministers arrived at Buckingham Palace to be sworn in, having been drilled by Maurice Hankey, clerk of the Privy Council, wearing suits because they didn't possess frock coats. John Wheatley, a bowler-hatted revolutionary and minister of health, was so overcome that he went down on both knees, 'actually kissing the King's hand'.[68] George wrote in his diary: 'He is an extreme Socialist & comes from Glasgow. I had a very interesting conversation with him.'[69]

'I really am ashamed to trouble you with such trivialities as dress when you are deciding weighty matters of State,' wrote Stamfordham to MacDonald, but dress had become a political issue.[70] Labour ministers refused to wear court dress of white breeches and white stockings at a levee. Newspaper headlines hailed the 'King's Democratic Revolution: Evening Dress and Knee Breeches'.[71] The King showed unwonted tolerance, declaring that 'whatever decision the Cabinet ministers come to, I will agree to, but they must all do the same. It would look very odd if some were in uniforms & some in evening clothes at a Levee.'[72] The matter was discussed in Cabinet, which agreed that ministers attending levees should be permitted to wear black evening dress and knee breeches.[73] The King ruled that 'full dress is not necessary on account of the expense'; it cost £73 2s 6d (roughly £4,500 in today's money).[74] Ever practical, Stamfordham discovered that Messrs Moss Bros stocked full levee dress, complete with sword and cocked hat, for £30 (£1,850 today).[75] Cheerfully ignoring the King's request that they should wear the same, at the first levee 'the PM, Mr Henderson & Mr Thomas came in uniform (levee dress) [and] the other ministers came in evening dress with tights'.[76]

The advent of Labour forced an overdue reform in the royal household. Ramsay MacDonald had no wish to appoint his own nominees to court offices. No Labour peers existed to fill the household posts in the House of Lords, so he asked the King to allow existing household officers to remain in post.[77] This seemed a sensible arrangement of a minor issue. However, as Fritz Ponsonby pointed out, the risk was that the matter might be politicised. 'The very existence of the Monarchy may depend on what is done now and a mistake or even a misunderstanding might put the King in a most awkward position later.' For the King to surround himself with Conservative peers, now in opposition, 'smacks of the reactionary policy in Russia'.[78]

The solution, as Stamfordham saw, was to introduce a reform he and the King had urged for some time, namely to 'do away with the "political" element altogether'.[79] The three great officers – the lord chamberlain, the lord steward and the master of the horse – should be appointed by the King, not by the prime minister, along with such Ruritanian officials as the captain of the bodyguard, the captain of the gentlemen at arms and three lords-in-waiting. The Cabinet agreed that if the existing holders of the three great offices gave 'an undertaking not to speak, vote or act against the Government in the House of Lords' they would be retained in their offices.[80] Lord Cromer became permanent lord chamberlain, Lord

Shaftesbury became lord steward and Lord Granard (a Liberal unlike the other two) master of the horse. The household was uncoupled from party politics, and future Conservative governments lost a useful source of patronage.*

How to treat the wives of the Labour ministers was another worry. Mrs Beatrice Webb, upper-middle class, wealthy and socially confident, acted as 'doyenne' among ministers' wives, organising their social intercourse with the court. She accepted that ministers should attend levees and audiences to pay their respects to the King. But she considered 'there is not the remotest reason why the <u>wives</u> and <u>daughters</u> should be dragged into Smart Society, with the inevitable "dressing up" and extravagant expenditure'.[81] The King and Queen gave afternoon parties at Buckingham Palace at four o'clock. 'The ladies can come to these if the evening parties alarm them,' wrote the Queen. 'A pity Mrs W is so obstinate!'[82] Mrs Webb spurned this well-intentioned if patronising initiative, ostentatiously refusing an invitation to a Buckingham Palace afternoon party. But ministers' wives such as Ethel Snowden, despised by Webb as 'a "climber" of the worst description', had no such scruples.[83]

Ramsay MacDonald, as Nicolson wrote, was a combination of 'silk and tweed': small, immaculately dressed, combining cosmopolitan distinction with Scots good sense, he was 'a fundamentally simple man'.[84] So was the King, and perhaps this is why they understood each other. Royalty, wrote MacDonald, 'has been considerate, cordially correct, human and friendly. The King has never seen me as a Minister without making me feel that he was also seeing me as a friend.'[85] He stayed at Windsor in April and was received, he wrote, with the 'kindly homeliness of a cottage'. MacDonald's respect for royalty was driven by political calculation. He needed royal approval if his party was to break through from its working-class base. The King for his part needed MacDonald in order to contain the deferential, respectable working class within a moderate Labour Party and split them off from the Bolsheviks and Red Clydesiders.

---

*Not all household officers agreed with the new policy. The Earl of Bradford resigned as lord-in-waiting in protest at being powerless to assist his party, and the Earl of Mount Edgcumbe refused to accept a position which would prevent him from voting against a Labour government (RA PS/PSO/GV/C/K/1918/198, Bradford to Stamfordham, 28 January 1924. RA PS/PSO/GV/C/K/1918/297, Lord Mount Edgcumbe to Stamfordham, 15 February 1924).

CHAPTER 23

The Dolls' House

1923–1925

'I am dying to see it,' wrote George to May of the Queen's Dolls' House, the miniature palace designed by Edwin Lutyens as a tribute to the Queen.[1] The idea originated with Princess Marie Louise, who proposed it to Lutyens in 1921 and then enlisted the Queen, and the house was completed in time to be exhibited at the 1924 British Empire Exhibition at Wembley. The Queen, who collected miniature objects and shared the royal cult for Fabergé, embraced with enthusiasm Lutyens's project for a palace in the scale of one inch to one foot.

A Georgian façade inspired by Wren opened to reveal palatial interiors: not reproductions of existing royal residences, but a palace designed and decorated in the style of the 1920s. The painted ceilings by artists such as William Nicholson and Glyn Philpot were supervised by the Queen, for once abandoning her usual conservatism and promoting the avant garde.

Harold Nicolson, who was invited to contribute one of the 200 miniature books in the royal library handwritten by their authors, observed in his volume on 'The Detail of Biography': 'I am stirred with envy for the biographer of 2023.' The works of art in the Dolls' House could be found in other collections. 'But with what illumination will he [sic!], the future biographer, gaze upon the detailed domestic appliances of 1923!'[2]

The American electric lifts are fully functioning, hoisted by fishing lines. The bathrooms have running water. The six motor cars in the garage include the King's favourite Daimler limousine and a Daimler station wagon, and they are customised with the royal livery colours of black and maroon and fitted with real petrol engines. The King's shotguns are here – three-inch miniature Purdeys able to shoot a fly. Here too is the King's red box. 'How did you get hold of my despatch boxes?' the King asked Marie Louise. 'I borrowed them,' she replied. 'Who gave you permission?' 'No one did,' she said. 'And you [yourself] got them?' said the King. 'Yes!'[3]

Where else would the biographer of today find such an intimate item as the King's WC, a miniature wooden throne or 'valve closet' with a handle at the side to pull up for the flush, made by John Bolding & Sons, and supplied with tiny sheets of bromo loo paper? Queen Mary's WC was disguised as an eighteenth-century wooden armchair.

A hint for the biographer of today was given by the tiny pillowcases on the Queen's bed embroidered M.G. and G.M. When the Queen asked what the letters stood for, Lutyens replied: 'For "May George?" Ma'am, and "George May!"'[4] Lutyens was an inveterate punner, and when he showed the pillowcases to Queen Mary, he said: 'I am afraid this is Lazy Majesty, Ma'am.' She replied: 'Lèse Majesté.' 'No,' said Lutyens, 'Lazy Majesty – the King's in bed.'[*]

The biographer of 2023 might be struck by an absence: there are no dolls in the Dolls' House. The aesthetically beautiful house is empty of family figures – something that, as one writer has observed, was 'extremely revealing' of the Queen. The strong room, containing a miniature of the Imperial State Crown, adorned with the Koh-i-Noor, took up almost as much space as the nursery.[5]

The Dolls' House acted as a vehicle for royal patronage. More than 700 watercolours were commissioned by living artists. Not everyone agreed to play. Sir Edward Elgar, who was invited to send a score, declined, and Siegfried Sassoon in his diaries described him spitting with rage: 'We all know that the King and Queen are incapable of anything artistic,' fulminated Elgar. 'But as the crown of my career I'm asked to contribute to – a Dolls' House for the Queen! . . . I wrote and said I hoped they wouldn't have the impertinence to press the matter any further.'[6] Elgar was no doubt absurdly pompous, but the wider point he made about the failure of the King and Queen to act as patrons of the arts could not be gainsaid.

In *Mrs Dalloway* (1925) Virginia Woolf describes a great motor car gliding slowly down Bond Street one June morning in 1922 with its blinds drawn, stared at by the people in the street. 'Was it the Queen in there – the Queen going shopping?' they wondered. 'But there could be no doubt that greatness was seated within; greatness was passing, hidden, down Bond Street, removed only by a hand's-breadth from ordinary people.'[7][†]

The Queen's massive Daimler, with its high roof to allow her to alight while wearing her toque hat, was a familiar sight drawn up to the kerb

---

[*]Lutyens claimed that he said this in order to verify a story that Queen Mary always corrected French pronunciation. Visiting a hospital during the war, she asked a wounded soldier: 'And where were you wounded, my poor man?' 'Wipers,' said the Tommy, and the Queen corrected him by saying 'Ypres'. 'We were just advancing on Wipers—' 'Ypres,' said the Queen. After she left the hospital the Tommy said to the matron: 'It's a pity the poor dear had the hiccups' (Ursula Ridley Papers).

[†]Woolf was invited to contribute a book to the Dolls' House but refused (Lucinda Lambton, *The Queen's Dolls' House* (Royal Collection Trust, 2010), p. 98).

of a Mayfair street. Unlike the King, whose tailors and tradesmen came to him, the Queen loved to shop. Leaving Buckingham Palace punctually each afternoon at 2.45 and always returning in time for tea with the King, the Queen sallied forth with her lady.[8] On days when she had no official engagement, she visited exhibitions and prowled antique shops or picture dealers. She was a regular customer at Mayfair dealers such as Thomas Goode, John Sparks, Albert Amor, Wartski, Partridge, Mallett, Dreyfus and Spink, who bowed to her expertise.[9]*

Nothing gave her a greater thrill than finding an object for her collection – usually porcelain or a painting and 'often something with a tenuous royal connection'. The Queen's reconnoitre would be followed by a summons to a lady-in-waiting or relative, whom she would charge with beating down the price. 'He's asking £350 but if you can get it for £250 . . .' was the royal command.[10]

The Queen seems to have believed that royal items belonged almost by right to the monarch. She wrote in 1917 to Lord Lee, the owner of Chequers, to say that she 'greatly admired a little portrait of her ancestor Charles II and would we consider selling it to her for the Royal Collection at Windsor?' Lee's account continued:

> There was of course only one possible answer to this request, and I wrote back to say that we would be honoured if she would accept the picture as a gift 'with our humble duty'. This she did without demur, and later sent us her own autographed photograph framed, as she explained, 'in Indian brocade, which I brought myself at Benares'.[11]

The Queen's excitement in the chase can be seen from a breathless letter which she penned to George after a visit to Crichton Brothers, the Bond Street silver dealers:

> I am so much thrilled at the wonderful English Cumberland plate I saw at Crichton's today I must tell you about it – Crichton is not selling the plate in sets but piece meal, & he will let us buy anything we like at a reduced price. There are several things we positively must buy, as they are the best examples & were made for George I for use in Hanover, ditto for George II when Prince of Wales, everything beautifully engraved & just the shapes we two admire the most.[12]

---

*Albert Amor was appointed antiquary to the Queen in 1921, the first holder of the post. Sparks was awarded the Royal Warrant of Antiquary of Chinese Art to Queen Mary in 1926.

Sotheby's was a favourite hunting ground. The Queen's contact with Sotheby's was her son-in-law Harry Lascelles. Since inheriting a vast fortune from Lord Clanricarde, Lascelles had collected Old Masters, and his adviser was the Finnish art historian Tancred Borenius, 'an old-fashioned savant' and excellent company.[13] It was widely believed that Borenius had 'made a very good thing out of it', and that 'he combined great knowledge with a strong "£ove" of art'.[14] In 1923 Borenius was appointed expert on Old Master prints at Sotheby's, and he acted as a consultant and cataloguer. After Lascelles introduced her to Borenius, 'the Queen constantly sought his advice in her voracious collecting activities'.[15]

The richest pickings came from the Romanovs. From around 1921 Queen Mary can be seen in photographs wearing a spectacular tiara of interlaced diamond ovals hung sometimes with pearl droplets, sometimes with emeralds.* This was the Vladimiri tiara, which was made for the Grand Duchess Vladimir, a duchess of Mecklenburg-Schwerin who married the Grand Duke Vladimir, uncle of Nicholas II. She was a fanatical collector of jewels, and her palace functioned as an alternative court and the centre of fashionable society in St Petersburg before 1914. When the grand duchess fled Petrograd in 1917 she left her jewels behind. How Queen Mary must have enjoyed the story of Bertie Stopford, the grand duchess's English agent, smuggling the jewels out of a secret safe in the Vladimiri Palace and travelling back to London with 244 priceless items wrapped in newspaper and stuffed into two shabby Gladstone bags.† Reunited with her bling, the grand duchess died in 1920, and her jewels were divided between her children. Queen Mary 'bagged all the best' and bought the tiara, which had been the grand duchess's most prized possession, from her only daughter Helen, the wife of Prince Nicholas of Greece.[16] When Prince George married Princess Marina, Helen's daughter, in 1934, her family was reunited with the tiara, but the Vladimiri was far too precious to be gifted to the wife of a younger son, and today it remains the most prized of all the Queen's tiaras.

Richard Molyneux, who was a groom-in-waiting to the King (1919–36), told Harold Nicolson that 'Queen Mary had no taste at all; what

---

*Was this the 'new pearl & diamond tiara, pearl & diamond ornaments' which she wore with new pale blue and gold moiré gown and the Garter for an evening party in 1922? (RA QM/PRIV/CC58/163, Queen Mary's Dress Book, vol. 2, 23 February 1922).
†There are several versions of the story of Stopford's escape with the Vladimiri jewels. According to Lady Airlie, he disguised himself as an old woman, hid the tiara in his black bonnet and stuffed fifteen pearl droplets into cherries which were sewn on as a trimming (Leslie Field, *The Queen's Jewels: The Personal Collection of Elizabeth II* (Harry N. Abrams, 1987), p. 117).

she did possess was an amazing faculty for accumulating and remembering facts. Thus she learned about furniture from the dealers. She acquired extensive knowledge: nothing could give her taste.'[17] Waspish comments of this sort are characteristic of a certain type of embittered old courtier. Lord Claud Hamilton, another member of the household, remarked that the Queen's collections when valued for probate were not worth much, and 'she never bought a good picture nor was she interested in them'.[18] It's true that she was perhaps more concerned with the sitter than the artist, but her ability to identify the subjects of royal miniatures was unequalled.[19] Viewing the magnificent collection at Petworth House in Sussex, famed for its Turners, the painting that she most admired was one representing the Apotheosis of Princess Charlotte by a little-known artist.[20]

Queen Mary's life's work – her 'one great hobby', as she described it – was the cataloguing and curating of the Royal Collection, and in particular objects connected with the Guelph or Hanoverian family.[21] 'There is hardly a piece of furniture, picture or print in the remotest bedroom or back passage of the royal palaces and houses on which a label is not to be found in Queen Mary's handwriting describing its subject and origin,' wrote one woman of the bedchamber.[22]

Here are the contents of just one corner of the Queen's boudoir, taken from a 1912 catalogue of Buckingham Palace:

> The first [Vitrine table] contained two gold salvers which had belonged to Queen Charlotte, pieces of a silver-gilt toilet service made for Lady Charlotte Finch, who was governess to the children of George III, an inkstand created from a box for an Order of the Garter, and an inkstand which had belonged to Adolphus, Duke of Cambridge. On the desk was a screen mounted with 13 miniatures of family members. A second group of miniatures on the desk included images of George V, Queen Victoria, Queen Charlotte and Queen Louise of Prussia, together with a bust of George V on a pedestal of lapis lazuli. In a kidney-shaped table was a pencil holder, a paperknife with a topaz handle and ring containing a miniature, all relating to Princess Charlotte.[23]

Collecting was a proper vocation for a monarch, but for Queen Mary it had become 'the major preoccupation', one might say the obsession, of her life. Perhaps, as Pope-Hennessy suggested, preserving the artefacts of royal history made her feel secure in the post-war world of change and disintegration.[24] No doubt she was making up for time lost during the war years, when collecting had not been possible. But perhaps the emotional urge to accumulate went deeper. This child of spendthrift parents, damaged by her father's indebtedness and disgrace, but inheriting his insatiable appetite for precious things, had learnt to measure her own self-worth in terms of the treasures she collected. Beautiful objects perhaps filled the place of human relationships, and priceless jewels such as the Vladimiri tiara were perhaps emotional substitutes for departing children.[25]

'As a matter of fact the Queen is never bored,' wrote May, annotating a tiresomely inaccurate biography of herself.[26] When in the country, the Queen and her lady would set off each afternoon in the motor to visit country houses and castles that were within range. 'I saw more of Great Britain,' reflected one exhausted bedchamber woman, 'than could normally have been my good fortune in several lifetimes.'[27] Staying at Goldsborough Hall in Yorkshire with her daughter Mary and Harry Lascelles, the Queen spent little time with her two small grandsons, but packed in a full itinerary of visits to the neighbouring great houses and antique shops. On one such visit, Molyneux wrote: 'To Harrogate shops in morning; Queen bought "Slingsby" cabinets.' The Queen particularly enjoyed Castle Howard ('The Queen in good spirits,' wrote Molyneux).[28] 'You can't think how nice Mr Geoffrey Howard was, I was quite surprised, he adores the place,' wrote the Queen.[29] She stayed at country houses such as Westonbirt in Gloucestershire ('too Italian for my taste') where Sir George Holford laid on country-house tourism, or Alnwick Castle with the Duchess of Northumberland.[30] 'Helen [Northumberland] is one of the most charming women I know & I am sure she did everything to amuse you & for your comfort,' wrote George.[31] The Queen was 'petrified' by the cold of Alnwick, but appreciative – 'I had forgotten what a lot of nice pictures & things there are here.'[32]

Queen Mary made her royal progresses in August when George was away shooting grouse. She stayed in great houses without the King, in rather the same way as her father-in-law had stayed without Queen Alexandra, and though some aristocrats complained that her admiration for their treasures verged on the predatory, she certainly didn't bankrupt them nor make them install bathrooms and telephones nor cause scandals as Edward VII had done.

In 1923 Lady Cynthia Colville became a woman of the bedchamber to Queen Mary. She was a daughter of the King's friend Lord Crewe, but she owed her appointment to her role as a social worker in the East End of London. Lady Cynthia came to the attention of the Queen when she invited Her Majesty to open a nursing home in Shoreditch. Cynthia's professional expertise on the subject of 'the child at risk' impressed the Queen. On the same day that the letter arrived from the mistress of the robes, the Duchess of Devonshire, inviting her to serve as a woman of the bedchamber, Cynthia was asked to stand in the 1922 election as Liberal candidate for Shoreditch. She didn't hesitate to accept the Queen's offer and turn down the chance of becoming an MP. She never regretted her decision; on the contrary, her post in the Queen's household raised her profile as a spokesperson for maternal and child welfare.[33]

When she joined the royal household Lady Cynthia was struck by the hierarchy which still governed court appointments as it had done before the war. The four ladies of the bedchamber were all peeresses, and they were of a higher social rank than the women of the bedchamber, who were the daughters of marquesses or earls but not married to peers. There were at the time four women of the bedchamber – Lady Bertha Dawkins, Lady Elizabeth (Bessie) Dawson, Lady Joan Verney and Lady Mary Trefusis, who, exceptionally, job-shared with Lady Cynthia.*

The women of the bedchamber were equivalent to the equerries in the King's household. Their role was to reply in handwriting to letters which the Queen would have answered herself had she not been Queen. Lady Cynthia recalled:

> At 9.30 the Queen's bell went in the sitting room of the current Woman, who then went in with all her letters in her hand.† She would find the Queen seated at her desk, having opened, as she always did, every letter addressed to herself, no matter who from. Very few lunatics, many begging letters (these she would initial for the alternative charities to deal with); marvellous memory 'I thought I knew that handwriting' and it would be some woman who [had] written from Australia eleven years before. The Queen would deal efficiently and quickly with these and with those brought by her Lady – 'Say yes,' 'say no' etc. The Lady would take everything away after the business was finished (seldom more than ½ hour), and then settle down to the work of answering . . .‡[34]

The Queen drove her women hard. After accompanying the Queen on her afternoon expeditions and sometimes to evening functions, Cynthia

---

*Lady Joan Verney was the wife of Sir Harry Lloyd Verney, who was groom-in-waiting to George V (1911–31) and private secretary to Queen Mary (1919–35).
†These were letters intended for the Queen but addressed to her ladies.
‡The quote uses 'Lady' and 'Woman' interchangeably, perhaps because addressing the Queen's women of the bedchamber as 'Women' was not considered polite.

often sat up writing letters until 1 a.m., occasionally working right through the night.

The Queen organised her charity work through the bedchamber women, and this meant a heavy workload. The London Needlework Guild, renamed Queen Mary's Needlework Guild, had flourished during the war, supplying clothing to the troops as well as the poor, and in 1918 the guild launched a successful fund-raising campaign to commemorate the Queen's silver wedding. The Queen used this money in 1919 to found Queen Mary's Maternity Home for the wives and children of servicemen, housed in a handsome building in Heath Street, Hampstead, built on a site given by Lord Leverhulme. This was intended to set a trend: 'The Queen's view is that Maternity homes and hospitals should be provided in all parts of the country, and her hope is that the establishment of the Hampstead institution will encourage the extension of its objects.'[35]

The Queen tasked Lady Bertha Dawkins with managing this project. 'Thank you for all the trouble you are taking,' she wrote. 'I approve of all proposals ... Glad the Matron impressed you favourably.'[36] Lady Bertha was commanded to request a meeting with the government's chief medical officer, Sir George Newman:

> As I do not wish him to think I took up this scheme for the Q.M.N.G. money on a whim may I ask you to see him yourself & explain how the whole matter arose & how it has been carefully thought out & being under the Ministry of Pensions & approved by them I thought it a good scheme to help.[37]

This was a Queen who clearly understood how the charity sector worked.

The Queen was always formidably well prepared for her visits to hospitals and homes, sometimes embarrassing her hosts with acute questions they were unable to answer. She had a disconcerting habit of departing from schedule. At the opening of the British Medical Association building in Tavistock Square in July 1925, Neville Chamberlain, the minister of health, rode with the King and Queen in an open carriage; he noticed that they kept up a constant flow of conversation all the time they were bowing to the cheering crowds. The opening was a shambles, even by the standards of the 1920s, when royal functions were more relaxed than today's strictly choreographed and policed ceremonies. Lutyens, the architect, forgot where he had put the key and was unable to produce it when summoned to present it to the King. It was discovered in the pocket of the Archbishop of Canterbury, who had taken it because Lutyens couldn't be trusted, but then forgot about it.[38]

The Queen disappeared, having gone on alone ahead of the official procession to see the exhibits in the hall by herself.[39] There was a last-minute
change of plan when the King agreed to visit the disabled children in the
Mary Ward Settlement adjoining the new building. When the Queen
discovered that the gate in the railings between the school and the BMA
was locked, she asked for the key, and she and the King went inside and
spoke to the children. 'The incident touched all who witnessed it very
much,' observed the *British Medical Journal*. 'Thoughtful actions of this
kind have done more to establish the royal family in the hearts of our
people than all the ceremonies in which they take part.'[40]

The King and Queen were at Balmoral on 2 October 1924 when Stamfordham received a letter from Ramsay MacDonald warning that the
government was likely to be defeated on a motion of no confidence, in
which case the prime minister would need to ask the King to dissolve
Parliament.[41]

On the 6th Stamfordham departed on a fact-finding mission to London. That morning, Lady Bessie Dawson fell on her walk and fractured
her hip.[42] She crawled back to the castle with much difficulty and in
great pain, and a surgeon and a nurse were summoned. Downstairs a
bizarre scene ensued, recounted by Helen Hardinge, the wife of Alec
Hardinge, the King's assistant private secretary: 'The King then read
about a woman who had suffered a similar accident and had needed
both legs amputated. This led to a long conversation about people who
had come to untimely and unlikely ends, the Queen ending with the
complaint: "It all comes from this mania for exercise".' Sir Derek Keppel, master of the household, arrived at the castle and asked to go to bed
as he was suffering from lumbago. 'The King thundered: "Why should
they all want to come here to be ill!" He launched into a tirade about
how unsuitably dressed Lady Bessie had been when she fell. "Of course
the shoes ladies wear nowadays I don't wonder they fall down."'[43]

It would have been funny if it hadn't ended in tragedy. On 8 October
the King and Queen cut short their holiday and hastened to London to
deal with the political crisis. Lady Bessie was taken into an Aberdeen
nursing home, and she died there on 13 October aged fifty-five from
heart failure.* 'It is too sad,' wrote the King.[44] Contrary to Helen
Hardinge's account, the Queen *did* care. She wrote to Bertha Dawkins:

---

*Lady Bessie had been appointed a woman of the bedchamber in 1920. *The Times* published a eulogy: 'More wise than clever, more humorous than witty, she added to remarkable
distinction in appearance an unconscious nobility of mind' (21 October 1924).

'Poor Bessie's death is indeed a shock & blow to us, I can't get over it, for she was in such good spirits & we really had great fun at Balmoral & she seemed so happy & well.'[45] The lesson was not lost on the Queen. 'I think H.M. does not want another lady to die,' wrote Lady Bertha in 1927, 'so she is very careful of me!!!'[46]

'I am thankful beyond words that Your Majesty will be at the seat of government,' wrote Stamfordham when he received the telegram announcing the King's return to London.[47] As in previous crises, Stamfordham interviewed the other party leaders, Baldwin and Asquith, and asked whether they were prepared to form a government. Stamfordham wired Hardinge, who was at Balmoral: 'Baldwin is entirely in favour of a General Election and could not undertake to form Government. Shall report Asquith's condition later on.'[48]*

Travelling overnight, the King reached Buckingham Palace at 8.15 on 9 October, changed into a frock coat, breakfasted with the Queen at 9.00 and saw Ramsay MacDonald at 10.00. The Labour government had been defeated the previous night, and the King gave his consent to a dissolution 'with regret as it means an immediate general election, & the last one took place only 9 months ago, & the country are tired of these constant elections'.[49]

MacDonald's private secretary, Sir Ronald Waterhouse, had warned Stamfordham on 7 October of the dangers of rejecting the prime minister's request: 'Refusal of Dissolution would be regarded as a slap in the face to the Labour party who in office form the best buffer to Communism. This anti-Communism undoubtedly represents the present Labour mentality – to affront it might result in a rapprochement to Communism in the future.'[50] As a constitutional monarch, the King had little choice but to agree. According to MacDonald, the King was cordial and the interview 'almost touching as we assured each other that we had done the best we could for each other'. The King remarked at the end: 'You have found me an ordinary man, haven't you?'[51]

The election was dominated by the Bolshevik threat. The Zinoviev Letter, purportedly written by the head of the Communist International, and claiming that Labour's resumption of diplomatic relations with Russia would accelerate Communist penetration of the British working class, torpedoed the Labour campaign. The letter was a forgery, as the King himself suspected, but MacDonald botched his response and the

---

*Stamfordham sent this message in code in a second telegram to Hardinge: 'Livy entirely drunk and frivolous shall report Virgil's condition later on' (RA PS/PSO/GV/C/K/1958/11, Stamfordham to Hardinge, 7 October 1924). This was presumably to baffle the Bolsheviks.

Tories won a thumping majority, returning 412 MPs, against 151 Labour and 40 Liberals.[52]

Ramsay MacDonald resigned at 5.30 p.m. on 4 November. 'I like him,' wrote George, '& have always found him quite straight.'[53] Mac-Donald complained to the King that Churchill had attacked the Labour ministers for slavishly rushing to wear court dress, when they had done so only reluctantly and 'out of anxiety to fall in with the King's wishes'.[54] John Wheatley defiantly ignored Stamfordham's advice to wear a morning tail coat when he took leave of the King and turned up in a short jacket.[55] The sartorial bickering masked the game-changing political shift that had taken place. The first Labour government had established Labour as the progressive party, replacing the Liberals, and capable of holding office, and the King had facilitated this realignment.

At 7 p.m. on 4 November the King saw Baldwin and asked him to form a government. He then gave the new prime minister a lecture about avoiding class war with the Labour extremists, leading to 'unruly disorder' in the House of Commons.[56] 'I hope at last we have got a stable government who will remain in for some years,' wrote the King.[57] Baldwin was an indolent but instinctive politician who would 'sniff and snuff at problems like an elderly spaniel', and he was far less amenable to royal control than MacDonald had been.[58] 'I've got the people's mandate & that makes me very independent,' he declared.[59] Lord Esher remarked: 'I am sure that the King is sorry to part with MacDonald. Radicals and Socialists are much nicer to Sovereigns than Tories.'[60] Esher was right about the socialists but not about the radicals; Asquith and Lloyd George had treated the King with far more contempt than Baldwin did.

Chips Channon reported in his diary a feeling among peers and others of disappointment with the King's lack of initiative. 'He is so uninspiring and does nothing to stem the socialist tide every day swelling.'[61] This could hardly be further from the truth. George had managed the political crisis with a sure touch. His dealings with his eldest son were less assured. David returned from a holiday in America and Canada the day after the election. Summoned to his father's office, he found the King sitting at his desk with a heap of American press cuttings with headlines such as 'Here He Is Girls – The Most Eligible Bachelor Yet Uncaught, Oh! Who'll Ask H.R.H. What He Wears Asleep?'[62] In vain did the prince attempt to explain that the extravagant front pages of American papers were forgotten the next day. For the King, who knew only the British press, which respectfully abstained from comment on the private life of the royal family, this publicity was shocking and humiliating.

On Long Island David spent two weeks playing polo, dancing, partying and staying up until 5 a.m. He had an attention-grabbing affair with a 'comet' named Pinna Cruger, a divorced Hollywood actress. His roistering earned him a reprimand from his mother:

> What a hectic time you have had . . . almost too much going on, & the newspaper reports were too silly each day giving details of what you did practically every hour – it all sounded terribly frivolous for these anxious times in the world & sitting up dancing till 5 each night must have been most tiring for you.[63]

It might have been much worse. No one had anticipated the boatload of seventy-five pressmen who greeted the prince on his arrival. Tommy Lascelles, the prince's assistant private secretary, had the resourcefulness to ask the newspaper owners to tea, and the prince enlisted their sympathy. Lascelles considered that the prince had promoted Anglo-American relations and 'done as much good to the British Empire as the Baldwin debt settlement'.[64]* The King reached the opposite conclusion. 'If this vulgarity represents the American attitude towards people in our position,' he told his son, 'little purpose would be served in your exposing yourself again to this kind of treatment.'[65] There were to be no more trips to America in the King's lifetime.

King George was fifty-nine but he dressed like a Victorian. He still wore a frock coat, the formal dress of the nineteenth-century statesman, cut with a squared-off skirt above the knee. He insisted on the frock coat being worn at court (except in the case of Labour ministers) though it had fallen out of fashion since the war. He never wore a soft collar. His shirts were seldom striped and never coloured. His trousers were ironed with a sideways crease. He rarely wore shoes, preferring old-fashioned buttoned boots. He passed his tie through a ring instead of tying it in a knot.[66]

Clothes were one of the King's favourite topics of conversation, and his talk usually took the form of a diatribe against men who dressed differently from himself, whom he dismissed as 'cads'. Foremost among the cads was his son. David understood the semiotics of dress better than

---

*Baldwin visited America in 1923 in an attempt to settle Britain's war debt with the US.

anyone – indeed he wrote a book about it. His memoir *A Family Album* is concerned 'almost exclusively with elaborately detailed recollections of the clothes he wore on various occasions and his father's uncomplimentary views on them'.[67] David's rebellion against his father was expressed entirely in sartorial terms. One of his first acts on becoming king was to abolish the frock coat at court – truly an act of patricide.[68]

For George the informality of David's clothes was symptomatic of his unwillingness – perhaps his inability – to prepare himself to be king. Rather than confront the inadequacy of his flibbertigibbet son, the King blamed the prince's friends, especially Captain Edward 'Fruity' Metcalfe. An Irish outsider ('Who is this "Juicy" Metcalfe?' asked the deaf Queen Alexandra), Metcalfe was a genial rogue – an impecunious cavalry officer David brought home from India and a man to whom George took an instant dislike.[69] Metcalfe was a superlative horseman, and as the prince's equerry he acted as unofficial master of the horse, running his stables.

King George had encouraged his son to learn to ride when he was at Oxford, 'as the English people like riding and it would make you very unpopular if you could not do so'.[70] Surprisingly, the princes were not taught to ride as children. But George was dismayed when, encouraged by Metcalfe, David developed a craze for riding in point-to-point races. David was not a natural horseman; his courage and enthusiasm outran his skill, and he often fell. After David had a fall and suffered concussion in March 1924 at a point-to-point near Aldershot, George wrote to Queen Alexandra: 'It is too bad that he should continue to ride in these steeple chases. I have asked him not to, on many occasions, everyone thinks it is a great mistake, as he runs unnecessary risks.'[71] George had stopped his son from exposing himself to unnecessary risks by serving in the front line during the First World War, but David was now thirty, and George still treated him like a schoolboy. 'Dearest David,' he wrote, 'the time has come when I must ask you to give up riding in the future in steeplechases & point to point races.'[72]

When David returned from America the King pressed him to get rid of Metcalfe. 'Had a talk with David . . . about Metcalfe,' wrote the King, 'I found him very obstinate.'[73] George succeeded in blocking David's strenuous attempts to appoint Metcalfe to his staff when he visited South Africa in 1925. Fruity was sent back to India, but his ambitious marriage to Lord Curzon's daughter Alexandra (Baba) meant that he could afford to leave the army and return to the prince's side.[74]

Fruity was David's only real male friend. The two men 'thought, dressed, ate, talked alike – one was never seen without the other'.[75] Fruity had a room in York House, and on the evenings when the prince was free 'Fruity and I would go out and have a good time', escaping the

King's spies at Society balls and dancing to jazz bands at the Embassy Club.[76] No one except Fruity treated the prince as an ordinary human being. He called him 'The Little Man'. Out hunting once and in need of a cigarette, Fruity lit a match on the sole of the prince's riding boot, a familiarity which no one else would have presumed, and which, said the prince, 'amused and delighted me'.[77]

Fruity played Falstaff to David's Prince Hal. The question was whether David had the character to become Henry V. Neither of his parents discussed the matter of marriage with him, though he was well aware that his father was troubled by his continuing bachelorhood.[78] The King's unspoken fear, which he hardly dared contemplate, was that David didn't want to become king. Certainly others doubted the prince's desire to succeed. As early as 1925 Chips Channon wrote: 'The P of W would not raise his finger to save his future sceptre, many of his intimate friends think he would be only too happy to renounce it.'[79]

The King was ill with influenza followed by bronchitis in early 1925. 'Cough rather bad,' he wrote. 'Nights rather restless & disturbed. See hardly anyone just do the boxes. May sat with me whenever she could every day.'[80] For thirteen days he was too ill to write his diary and the entries are in May's hand.

The doctors ordered the King to take a Mediterranean cruise. Queen Mary's diary records her carefully plotted itineraries, landing each day to inspect the treasures of Naples and Sicily, but the trip was not a success. George spent his time reading Sidney Lee's biography of Edward VII: 'very interesting and well written but not always quite accurate', was his verdict.[81]

'The King is bored, as one would expect,' wrote Harry Lascelles. 'The Queen angry because nobody else cares to sight-see.' The King's sister Princess Victoria, who accompanied them, was 'very restless & no sooner begins one thing than she wants to do another'.[82] The Queen claimed that the trip was ruined for her by the King and Princess Victoria ('a bitch of the first order', according to David): 'Whenever *she* organised trips to Pompeii, etc., *they* spoiled it all by silly jokes and laughter.'[83]

The royal doctor Sir Stanley Hewett prescribed that the King must 'go abroad every year in future', as Edward VII and Queen Victoria had done, but his advice was ignored.*[84] 'My father did not care for travelling,' wrote David, and the older the King became the more reluctant he was to leave

---

*Hewett had succeeded Sir Francis Laking as surgeon-apothecary to the King in 1914.

home.[85] Like Nancy Mitford's Uncle Matthew in *The Pursuit of Love*, another 'violent, uncontrolled man' who also roared at his children and insisted on the strictest punctuality, King George believed that abroad was bloody. No one but the doctors suspected that the King's health was already compromised, and that he was suffering from an incurable lung disease.

'I dread Sandringham,' wrote Lady Bertha Dawkins before departing there for Christmas in 1924. Now in the advanced stages of dementia, the old Queen Alexandra didn't realise it was Christmas, and thought it was her birthday.[86] 'Her graciousness of manner long survived her brain,' noted Channon. Queen Olga of Greece stayed with her, and whenever she went to London for the day, Alexandra would weep and bid her farewell and load her with jewels and photographs – and the next day they would dine together as though nothing had happened.[87] Lady Bertha was shocked to find her bowed and bent and looking vacant. 'The Queen is so sad over her,' she wrote, '& minds dreadfully seeing her in this childish state; as she says, it is so hard that that beautiful woman should have come to this.'[88]

Age was cruel to the beautiful queen. Since the war, Queen Alexandra had complained of feeling depressed and unwell. Frail, stone deaf with noises in her head, and losing her sight and her memory, she retreated to Sandringham, where she lived in sad, silent seclusion with her daughter Victoria. Tea in the hall at Sandringham was 'a nightmare with ghosts', wrote Fritz Ponsonby, with Alexandra, old and shrivelled, pouring out the tea and her faithful retainers Charlotte Knollys and Dighton Probyn sitting in their same places, all terribly old.[89]

George considered that the death of Alexandra's favourite son Eddy in 1892 had 'completely knocked her out, and she has never been the same since'.[90] She addressed her letters to him as 'King George', though she knew very well that the correct form was to write 'The King'.[91] George described this foible as 'characteristically feminine', but the truth was he could never replace Eddy in his mother's affection. He was a dutiful son. He continued to visit her, even though, as May wrote, 'it will be so distressing I know for you to see her in this sad state'.[92] He could be spotted in church sitting next to his mother, finding the place in the psalms as though she were a child.[93]

Alexandra wrote to George on the Mediterranean cruise: 'I feel completely collapsed, I shall soon go.'[94] Princess Victoria found life with her demented mother distressing: 'She dreads going back [to Sandringham] yet knows she must, how sad it all is,' wrote the Queen.[95]

At Sandringham on 19 November 1925 Queen Alexandra suffered a heart attack. The King and Queen were at York Cottage, and George left the shooting to see his mother. She rallied a little, and (wrote May) 'G. therefore returned to his shooting.'[96] No one seemed to think this odd. George and May went back to the big house later. May wrote: 'Saw darling Mama who knew us & I kissed her hand & her forehead.'[97] Alexandra died the following evening. She was nearly eighty-one. 'It is really a happy release for the poor darling,' wrote George, 'as she was getting worse & worse.'[98]

Alexandra's death was devastating for her woman of the bedchamber, ninety-year-old Charlotte Knollys, who had served her for sixty-three years. Nora Wigram found her pathetically clutching a long string of pearls. They were the pearls that Alexandra had worn every day of her life, and after her death a letter was found in her dressing-table drawer saying that when she died she wished them to be given at once to Charlotte.[99]

For George the death of his mother broke the last link with the older generation. The funeral service at Westminster Abbey was 'most trying for me standing alone at the head of the coffin'.[100] The committal service was held the next day at Windsor, and now, wrote May, 'darling Mama lies near dear Eddy'.[101]

At last the house which Edward VII had left to his widow for her lifetime was George's. On 2 January 1926 George noted: 'May & I went up the house & we spent two hours sorting out dear Mama's jewels.'[102] A week later May wrote: 'At 11 to [Sandringham] where Toria and Maud with G. & me divided dear Mama's jewels – it was interesting but sad.'[103]

CHAPTER 24

Safe Haven

1925–1927

By 1925 the court was restored to its full magnificence. Four or five courts were held each Season when the King, wearing the full-dress uniform of an admiral of the fleet or a field marshal, and the Queen, blazing with jewels, her train carried by two pages in scarlet, processed through the State Rooms at Buckingham Palace, with the lord steward and lord chamberlain walking backwards before them, holding white staves. At 9.30 precisely they entered the ballroom, the band played the National Anthem, and they advanced to their crimson and gold thrones, while the princes and princesses and members of the household took up their places on the dais behind them.

The ladies waiting in a long line to be presented all wore three white ostrich feathers in their hair. Trains were compulsory but for reasons of economy they were allowed to trail no more than eighteen inches on the ground. Loelia Ponsonby, the daughter of Fritz Ponsonby, who was presented in 1925, remembered the ceremony being over in a flash. 'One reached the head of the queue, handed one's invitation to a splendid official, he shouted aloud one's name and tossed the card into a rather common-looking little wastepaper-basket, one advanced along the red carpet, stopped and made two curtsies to the King and Queen . . . and then walked on.'[1]

Presentation at court was traditionally the entrée into Society, but Society and the court had diverged since the Great War. The monarchy had severed its dynastic links, and its social and intellectual range had narrowed. Queen Victoria and her daughter the German Empress had access to the mental world of the European upper-middle class, and perhaps so did Queen Mary. But this was closed to George, who was poorly educated and spoke little French and less German. Since the First World War the dynastic cosmopolitanism of Edward VII's court had been replaced by a Tory landowner culture. George V shared the tastes of any British hereditary landowner – though his world-class stamp collection suggests that given a better education the results might have been very different.[2] In politics, as we have seen, George owed his success to his ability to bite back his Tory instincts and act as peacemaker and arbitrator.

Rather than marry German royals, two of his children had chosen spouses from the Tory landowner class that dominated the Court. At Balmoral and Sandringham, the King lived the life of a Tory squire – though not all the local grandees appreciated the royal invasion. Queen Mary once rang old Lady Leicester suggesting that she and the King should come over to Holkham, only for the earl 'to be heard bellowing, "Come over? Good God, no! We don't want to encourage them!"'[3]

Society had changed too. It was less political and more 'open'. Only two of the most successful hostesses (Mrs Ronnie Greville and Sybil Colefax) were British; the rest were Americans, such as Lady Astor and Lady Cunard. Society still embraced the court and territorial aristocracy, it still revolved around the events of the Season such as Ascot and Cowes. But it was smart, metropolitan and American, its glamour fuelled by the oxygen of the gossip columns. This was not a world where the King and Queen felt comfortable and, as we have seen, they rarely attended Society events. Particularly alien were the younger generation of Bright Young People, the social rebels whose frantic activities were blown up in the press and satirised by Evelyn Waugh in *Vile Bodies* (1930).

Loelia Ponsonby was on the fringes of the Bright Young People. She confessed to being petrified by the Queen, and the shy Queen was probably frightened of her too. At Balmoral she was once told to kiss the Queen's hand; when her turn came, she 'seized Queen Mary's hand and pressed it ardently to my lips – to perceive immediately that I had left a perfect print of a scarlet mouth on the back of her white kid glove. She gave me one withering look that said all and I slunk away in disgrace'.[4] The generation gap could hardly be better dramatised than by Loelia and the lipstick kiss.

At a charity matinée performance of *No, No, Nanette* the Queen ostentatiously turned her head away from the bathing-suit chorus.[5] No wonder Waugh wrote about the Presence of Royalty as being 'as heavy as thunder in the drawing-room'.[6] At the Royal Academy the Queen innocently persuaded Lord Lee to escort her into a room of erotic fleshy nudes by Norman Lindsay. After a few glances through her lorgnette, she flushed pink and whispered to Lee: 'Dear! Dear! You must take me away,' and Lee forced a passage through the gaping-eyed crowd to get her out of the room. The Queen was not amused, on the contrary: 'She seemed quite cross with me,' wrote Lee, 'and bade me a frigid goodbye when I bowed her into her car.'[7]

But if the court seemed dull, tweedy, Tory and slightly ridiculous, this was only in the small world of Society. After 1918, the monarchy gained a 'cultural centrality to British life' which was equalled by hardly any political institution. 'It became more public, ceremonial and glamorous, but also more obviously domestic'.[8] The film-star celebrity of the Prince of Wales was one reason for this. Another was the new media of news-reels and mass-circulation newspapers. How the grumpy, home-loving, Tory monarch and his reserved consort effected this transformation is the conundrum of the second half of the reign of George V.

The King applied himself to the work of maintaining standards in public life. Baldwin, who was not Kipling's cousin for nothing, let his pen run away with him in a letter to the King describing a late-night sitting in July 1925. 'The House bore many resemblances to St James's Park at midday,' he wrote. 'Members were lying about the benches in recumbent positions, some being overcome by sleep and completely oblivious to their surroundings.'[9] The monarch was not amused. A ponderous rebuke whizzed from Stamfordham's pen: 'It must be remembered that Members of Parliament now include ladies and such a state of things as you describe seems to His Majesty hardly <u>decorous</u> or worthy of the dignity and tradition of the Mother of Parliaments.'[10] But Stamfordham overstepped the mark when he added that 'His Majesty's first intention was for me to write direct to the Speaker'.[11] For the King to complain to the Speaker was an infringement of parliamentary privilege, warned Baldwin, and 'one of the earliest historical objects of the House of Commons was to exclude the Crown from interfering in its proceedings'.[12] After an agitated meeting with the prime minister's private secretary, Stamfordham agreed to withdraw the letter to Baldwin. This sharp pushback irritated the King, who disliked being reminded by Baldwin of King Charles I, something that Ramsay MacDonald would surely never have done.

Any mention of royalty in print was pounced on. Sir Almeric Fitz-Roy, retired clerk of the Privy Council, published two volumes of flatulent diaries in 1925. Stamfordham ticked him off for including a story about Edward VII receiving an address from the House of Commons while having his corns cut. FitzRoy was reprimanded for being 'impertinent' in presuming to express his approval of Queen Mary's intelligence. When he presented a copy of his *Memoirs* to Queen Mary, it was politely returned.[13]*

The King deplored divorce and he was outraged by the case of

---

*FitzRoy had been convicted of 'wilfully interfering' with a woman in Hyde Park, but the conviction was dismissed on appeal, and the King was supportive; Lord Salisbury, however, urged Stamfordham that FitzRoy should be removed, and he resigned as clerk of the Privy Council in 1923.

Russell v. *Russell* in 1922. John Russell sued for divorce on grounds of adultery as evidenced by the birth of a child. He claimed that his marriage to Christabel Hart, a Bright Young Person, was not consummated, and he was not the father of her child. Christabel denied adultery and insisted that the child was conceived through 'incomplete intercourse'. The intimate details of the Russells' so-called Hunnish practices were revealed in court and reported at length in the newspapers, enthralling the public and enraging the King. The case was particularly distasteful because it was uncomfortably close to the court: John Russell was the son of Lady Ampthill, Queen Mary's lady-in-waiting.

Stamfordham set to work. A letter was fired off to the lord chancellor, Lord Birkenhead: 'You will not be surprised to hear that the King is disgusted at the publication of the gross, scandalous details of the Russell divorce case.' Never before had there been so 'repulsive an exposure of [the] intimate relations between man and woman'.[14] Since Lord Campbell's Act of 1857 divorce cases had been reported in the press, and Stamfordham suggested a change in the law: 'His Majesty asks whether it would be possible in future to try such cases in Camera.'[15] Birkenhead enjoyed a fractious relationship with the King, whose interference he usually resisted, and the royal request received a dusty answer from the Lord Chancellor's Office.

In 1925 the King returned to the attack over the case of *Dennistoun* v. *Dennistoun*. This was not actually a divorce, but a dispute between a divorced couple, and in court it was revealed that the wife had had an affair with a military officer in order to advance her husband's career. This revelation moved the King to fury, and Stamfordham wrote to the new lord chancellor, Lord Cave: 'The King deplores the disastrous and far reaching effects throughout all classes and on all ranks of the Army of the wholesale press advertisements of this disgraceful story.'[16] This time the lord chancellor responded more sympathetically to the King's request for a change in the law, and in 1926 the Judicial Proceedings Act allowed publication of no more than an outline of the proceedings in divorce cases.

As for Lady Ampthill, she survived as lady-in-waiting in spite of *Russell* v. *Russell*. She had refused to attend her son's wedding, and in her evidence in court she made no attempt to conceal her dislike and disapproval of his wife. She was rewarded with royal favour, remaining a lady-in-waiting until Queen Mary's death. According to her obituary, her life's work centred on her sixty years' friendship with the Queen, and the two women resembled one another, being tall, dignified and stiffly agreeable. It was qualities such as these, wrote Lord Templemore, a lord-in-waiting, 'that made King George's court a model of all courts'.[17] The Russell divorce case was thus neatly swept under the carpet.

'They're changing guard at Buckingham Palace – / Christopher Robin went down with Alice,' wrote A. A. Milne in 1924. 'A face looked out but it wasn't the King's. / "He's much too busy a-signing things." '[18] Some hailed the return of normalcy at court in 1925, but the fact was the new normal involved more ceremonial than before the war – more carriage horses, more brightly coloured full-dress uniforms. Perhaps, as Cynthia Colville suggested, 'because King George V made fewer public appearances than his son or grand-daughter (and certainly saw far less of his Empire and indeed of the remoter parts of the British Isles), he was more often inclined to do things "in State" '.[19]

The King travelled less and attended fewer functions than before 1918. Not only did the empire tours of the Prince of Wales relieve him of the need to visit his Dominions beyond the Seas in person, but the Duke of York played a vital part in reducing the King's workload at home. Since taking on the presidency of the Boys' Welfare Association in 1919, Prince Albert had expanded his role to become the prince who dealt with what he called industrial relations – the working conditions of industrial labourers. Hating ceremonial and prevented by his stutter from speech making, he agreed to do the job 'provided that there's no damned red carpet about it'. Known as 'the Foreman' by his brothers, he went down coal mines, drove locomotives, inspected new machinery.[20] The Duke of York's annual camps where working-class boys mixed with public schoolboys all wearing shorts were a PR masterstroke.

Beneath the stateliness of the King's annual routines, however, the rumbling of discontent could still be heard. The King was at Goodwood on 29 July 1925 when an impending coal strike threatened to force him to return to London to hold a council to allow troops to be called out. The King suggested holding the council in the drawing room at Goodwood House, but the home secretary, William Joynson-Hicks, a priggish killjoy, objected that the public would be shocked by the supposed frivolity. 'I never seem to get any peace in this world. Feel very low & depressed,' groaned the King. 'Just like my luck.'[21]

'I know all this will spoil your Goodwood,' wrote the Queen from London, 'as you will be full of anxiety & worry.'[22] Cut off from Stamfordham at Buckingham Palace by a bad telephone line, George wrote to May outlining the scenario of a coal strike. 'Matters . . . would be so bad that I should have to remain in London.' Cowes would be cancelled, all the guests put off, the servants would need to be stopped from travelling to Portsmouth. In short, 'If the strike should take place now, I look upon it as one of the greatest catastrophes that could happen to the country.'[23] The Queen was more realistic: 'It would hardly do for us to be so to speak enjoying ourselves [at Cowes] when the country would be going through a very serious crisis.'[24]

The strike was called off, and the King resumed his programme. From Balmoral he sent the Queen a cutting from the *Daily Express*, congratulating him on his well-earned holiday after months of hard work: 'Let us suppose ourselves ... governed by a King ... slack in his duties ... only then would the people realise what they had lost.'[25]

The King stayed most years at Newmarket for the spring meeting, when the One Thousand Guineas was run. He took little interest in racing until Major Fetherstonhaugh succeeded Lord Marcus Beresford as manager of the royal stables in 1922. Fetherstonhaugh understood – as did the King's sailing master, Major Hunloke – that the King needed to be kept thoroughly informed, and he managed to spark George's interest. 'Fether [*sic*] came to see me' becomes a frequent entry in his diary.[26] Staying in the elegant Jockey Club Rooms, going for early-morning rides on the heath, watching his horses and playing poker after dinner: Newmarket for the King was a convivial sporting Tory world.*

The King was at Newmarket in April 1926 when the government's negotiations with the miners broke down, threatening a general strike. On Newmarket Heath the King encountered the coal-rich racehorse owner Lord Durham, who blasted the miners as a 'damned lot of revolutionaries'. The King exploded: 'Try living on their wages before you judge them.'[27] He expressed his frustration with the miners in a letter to the Queen: 'What hopeless people they are, it will throw everything back just when they were beginning to improve, will cost the country many millions & cause a lot of bad blood & give great pleasure to our communists & the Russian Soviet.'[28] These were not the words of a man who feared revolution.

On 30 April after watching his horse Alosia run a disappointing race in the One Thousand Guineas, the King motored up to London to hold a council at Buckingham Palace at 5.30.[29] The miners rejected the wage

---

*The King bet but in moderation. Mrs Fetherstonhaugh placed his bets and kept the account, the King compiled his own account, and the London office made another. Winnings were paid by cheques drawn to cash to hide the source, but the King couldn't understand the procedure, so they were made out in his name. He spent his profits on stamps. His father had given his racing winnings to his mistresses.

cuts demanded by the government, and on 4 May the Trades Union Congress called a general strike and 1.7 million workers came out. At Buckingham Palace the sentinels exchanged red coats for khaki. The King gave audiences to ministers daily, and the boxes 'coming in at all times with reports from all over the country' kept him busy.[30] 'I have passed through some anxious times during the last 16 years,' he wrote, and, as Harold Nicolson observed, he displayed a 'buoyant optimism' throughout the strike.[31]

When someone suggested that the Crown should intervene, as it had done over the Irish question with the Buckingham Palace Conference, Stamfordham replied that the King 'absolutely declines' unless invited by the government.[32] What his attitude actually was towards the General Strike – whether he saw the strikers as a communist revolutionary threat or as desperate, starving men – has been disputed.[33] The King was inconsistent, and his views changed as the strike went on. At first, he was hawkish, calling on day two (5 May) for emergency legislation to prevent peaceful picketing in order to allow food ships to be unloaded (this was out of the question, as it would have meant amending the 1906 Trade Disputes Act). In a further blast on 7 May Stamfordham wrote to Number 10 anticipating martial law and demanding protection for strike breakers from intimidation. These views were hardly compassionate. Lord Crawford, a leading coal owner, noted on 8 May: 'I was glad to gather from Stamfordham that the Court is not bringing pressure on the Government to weaken. Stamfordham who is apt to be timorous is quite bellicose.'[34]

The King's views soon shifted. On 10 May he objected to a bulletin in the *British Gazette*, the strike newspaper edited by Churchill, chancellor of the Exchequer in Baldwin's government, which declared that all ranks of the armed forces would receive full support from the government in any action they took to aid the civil power. 'His Majesty cannot help thinking that this is an unfortunate announcement.'[35] On 9 May an emergency council was held at Buckingham Palace to consider issuing an order preventing banks paying out Russian money to trade unions. The King protested vigorously at any attempt to 'touch the pockets' of the strikers, which in his view was likely to cause panic and provoke reprisals.[36] The order was dropped – a royal intervention which, in the view of one historian, justified the institution of monarchy.[37] In spite of his sympathy for the hungry strikers, George kept up pressure on the government to suppress revolutionary groups. 'Could these not be arrested?' he wrote in red ink beside a list of communist organisations.[38]

When the General Strike collapsed on 12 May George wrote in his diary: 'Our old country can well be proud of itself, as during the last 9 days there has been a strike in which 4 million men have been affected, not a shot has been fired & no one has been killed, it shows what wonderful people we are.'[39] His view was perhaps over-optimistic, and he overlooked several thousand prosecutions for incitement and violence. But the failure of the General Strike seemed to suggest that the revolutionary danger which had preoccupied the King ever since 1917 was finally receding. At last the monarchy was entering a safe haven.

In the early hours of 21 April 1926 Joynson-Hicks, the home secretary, was summoned to witness a royal birth. The Duchess of York was delivered of a girl at 2.40 a.m. in her parents' house, 17 Bruton Street. Tradition dictated that the home secretary should be present even at the birth of the child of a second son. For Joynson-Hicks, who was working night and day to reach a settlement with the miners, the summons to Bruton Street was an unwelcome distraction.

The King and Queen were at Windsor. Reggie Seymour the equerry had much difficulty in getting to their room; it was 'pitch dark and no one about'.[40] The King and Queen were woken at 4.00 a.m. 'Such a relief & joy,' wrote the Queen.[41] Three days before, Bertrand Dawson (now Lord Dawson of Penn) the King's physician had explained to them that the baby would be induced. Queen Mary decided not to go to Bruton Street for the birth on account of the press interest that her presence would attract. 'I hope you will both understand & not think me a heartless wretch,' she wrote, in a letter which must have come as a relief to her daughter-in-law.[42] After a difficult labour, 'a certain line of treatment was successfully adopted' in the words of *The Times* – that is, a Caesarian section.[43]

The King and Queen motored up from Windsor and arrived at Bruton Street at 2.30 p.m. to see their new granddaughter.[44] When Bertie suggested that the baby's names should be Elizabeth Alexandra Mary the King approved at once, even though Victoria was not one of the names. No princess had been called Elizabeth since one of the daughters of George III.[45]

The King already had two Lascelles grandsons, George, born in 1923, and Gerald, who was born the following year. He had been in the house when George was born, 'pacing up and down and regaling them with tales of the wives of his friends who had died in childbirth'.[46] Thereafter he saw his grandsons occasionally, but he rarely visited Goldsborough, and he was given to ranting about 'how he hated Harewood House', the Lascelles family seat in Yorkshire. During one of these tirades at York

Cottage someone asked Queen Mary: '"But what sort of house <u>does</u> he like, then?" To which [she] replied, "This damned house!"'[47]

The King said his grandson George Lascelles was 'a delightful boy', but no more than that.[48] With baby Elizabeth it was different. She was third in line to the throne, and most people still expected the Prince of Wales to marry and produce children, but her arrival guaranteed the continuity of the dynasty. For the ageing King the princess offered a way out of the succession deadlock caused by David's refusal to marry. Even as a newborn baby, Elizabeth was a celebrity. When Lady Airlie went round to Bruton Street a few days after the General Strike to deliver some Jordan water for the christening, the crowd in front of the house was so big that the baby had to be smuggled out of the back door when she went out in her pram.[49]

It's tempting to dismiss stories of George V's closeness to his grand-daughter as a royal myth, but his special affection for the child was evident from the start. When she was only nine months old he wrote: 'Our sweet little grandchild Elizabeth arrived ... yesterday, & came to see us after tea.'[50] On 21 April 1927: 'Dear little Elizabeth is one year old today ... The baby came to breakfast as usual, & we gave her some toys.'[51] George's affection for his granddaughter was touching to behold. Even as a baby Elizabeth seemed remarkable.

In August 1926, with the King safely out of the way on the Yorkshire moors, the Queen descended on Sandringham. Queen Alexandra had grown old surrounded by sixty years of clutter. Her private sitting room was too crowded to turn round in, and 200 objects filled her writing table.[52] (As Queen Mary had ninety-three objects on her desk, she was not really one to talk.)[53] During a 'tremendous fortnight' Queen Mary cleared out the clutter and hung countless pictures, 'so that one now has the feeling of space & air that was sadly lacking before. We have practically redone our own rooms, Victoria's & old Charlotte's, otherwise the rooms remain more or less the same with regard to carpets & curtains which we had not time to do.'[54]

King George regretted the move from York Cottage. 'I am miserable at the idea of leaving that dear little house,' he wrote, 'where we have been together for ... 33 very happy years.'[55] The Queen dutifully echoed her husband's sentiments about leaving 'our dear little old home', but the truth was she couldn't wait to move out of York Cottage, 'this damned house'.[56]

Lady Bertha noticed at Balmoral how much pleasure the King took in the garden improvements: 'You would almost think that he had planned it all, whereas it was the Queen . . . All the same it is nice to see how His Majesty adopts all the Queen's ideas & makes them his own.'[57] Similarly, at Sandringham Queen Mary assured her change-averse husband that she had done nothing to alter the 'essential character' of the house.[58] The bathroom with three basins marked 'head and face', 'hands' and 'teeth' remained to puzzle guests. So did the bathroom lined with seven mirrors which old Dighton Probyn had given Charlotte Knollys for her seventieth birthday. 'I am never lonely in my bath as there are seven other Charlottes looking on,' said she.[59] Lady Bertha reported that 'mercifully' the steam from the bath clouded the mirrors, 'so I could not see my elderly form reflected too often'.[60]

'You would be surprised to see how comfortable the Queen has made this beastly house,' Ettie Desborough told Arthur Balfour, 'my great-uncle's, as you will remember, and sold at a ramp price by Lord Palmerston.'[61]* Everyone agreed that the Queen had worked wonders. 'One would not recognise some of the rooms which used to be so over-crowded and overloaded with trifles,' wrote Lady Bertha, though 'nothing can change the ugliness of some of the rooms'.[62] The Duchess of York concurred. 'It is a million times better here than at York Cottage,' she wrote. 'Plenty of room and a much better atmosphere.'[63]†

John Fortescue, the royal librarian, retired in 1926 after more than twenty years in the position. He had published a thirteen-volume *History of the British Army* (1899–1929) as well as *The Correspondence of King George the Third* in six volumes (1927–8), and the feeling was that 'he has given to the writing of his books what he ought to have spent on his job'.[64] This was perhaps a blessing as Fortescue attempted to raise funds for the library by selling off what he mistakenly considered to be unimportant prints and documents, including the seventeenth-century collections of Cassiano dal Pozzo, which had been acquired in 1762.[65] Fortescue's much younger wife Winifred was an actress, which was awkward as it meant she could not be received at court. She set up a clothes shop, advertising herself as 'the Hon. Mrs

*Ettie's great-uncle Spencer Cowper, who was Palmerston's stepson, had owned the house, but he lived abroad. The King corroborated Ettie's story that Palmerston sold the house and 6,000 acres at an exorbitant price. The Prince of Wales had paid £240,000 when the actual value was £80,000 (Wigram Papers, Clive to Nora, 3 December 1923).
†Pope-Hennessy, who saw the house in 1956, couldn't resist being poisonous: 'This is a hideous house with a horrible atmosphere in parts . . . It was like a vast morgue, and everywhere were their faces, painted, drawn or photographed' (James Pope-Hennessy, *The Quest for Queen Mary*, ed. Hugo Vickers (Zuleika, 2018), p. 96).

Fortescue, the impoverished wife of the King's Librarian, who is so underpaid that she has to keep a hat shop in Mayfair'.[66]

Owen Morshead, Fortescue's successor, was a young Cambridge librarian who had had a good war. His DSO and MC 'completely captured' the King, who insisted on his appointment, but, as Stamfordham explained, the job 'affected the Queen more than the King'. He told Morshead over lunch: 'She has, I understand, a certain amount of taste, in art matters, particularly perhaps in miniatures; but she needs someone just to ... you know ... keep her right.'[67]

One of Morshead's first decisions was to invite the 25-year-old Kenneth Clark to catalogue the Leonardo drawings in the Royal Collection bought by Charles II. This was one of the most important assignments that could be given to a scholar, and Morshead took a frightening risk in appointing an unknown amateur but, as Clark wrote, 'I think it came off'.[68] Morshead acted as artistic adviser to the Queen, planning her country-house itineraries and going through the sales catalogues for her.[69]

'Chatty and long-winded', Morshead was 'a strange man – a Victorian in many ways – the sort of person who enjoyed Calvary', but he was a sharp observer of the royal marriage.[70] He considered that the Queen was more intelligent than the King, but she didn't have mastery over him. 'He was master in his own house, and She [sic] was quickly shewn where she got off if she overstepped her province – which, being a sensitive and tactful woman, she never did.' Being a 'stupid' man ('let me so express it for brevity,' wrote Morshead), the King could be obstinate. 'Even if he didn't always understand all the business that was laid before him, it was nevertheless his business, and if he wanted Her [sic] advice he'd ask for it.' Far from being terrified of the King, she controlled him in the way that an effective consort does.

> Like a wise and experienced wife, she evolved means of 'managing' him. She'd get X or Y (or even me! ... whatever weapon lay to her hand for the purpose) to suggest things to Him [sic] – reserving her own fire for the really important things. She was a very, very good wife – but always the submissive spouse.[71]

Others read the marriage differently. Lord Cromer, the long-serving lord chamberlain, considered that Queen Mary was terrified of the King. 'All suggestions that it was she who managed him are false. She would get Cromer and others to put to him the things she wanted. She would not ever put them to him herself.'[72] In fact Cromer was making

Morshead's point about the Queen managing the King, but he was see-ing it from another angle. Daisy Bigge, Stamfordham's clever daughter, who worked in her father's office, disliked Queen Mary. She told James Pope-Hennessy that the Queen was 'frightened to death' of the King. Stamfordham used to say: 'The Queen is the biggest moral coward I've ever met in the whole of my life.'[73] Princess Alice of Athlone was damn-ing about this household gossip. It was 'nonsense' to say the Queen was frightened of him. 'She wasn't. They must be awfully stupid, the whole lot of them.'[74]

The dynamic of the royal marriage fascinated royal watchers such as Chips Channon. He considered that it was wrong to suppose that 'the King is entirely led by the Queen'. Though she had the stronger charac-ter 'and does to a great extent influence and soften him', in reality 'she is terrified of him'. He noted: 'Apparently she is never quite at her ease with him and always gives in.' Whether this was in fact her way of man-aging the King, Chips did not discuss. He added: 'They still and always sleep in the same bed', the result of habit or lust perhaps, or merely 'as an example to the bourgeoisie of Britain'.[75]

Queen Mary failed to restrain the King in one vital respect: his relations with his sons. Allegedly she never once stood up to the King when he shouted at the children. Daisy Bigge remarked: 'If she had done it once, he would have given it up. He just didn't know it upset them, but she did.'[76]

These were not easy years for Queen Mary. The King had other con-fidantes. Each morning at 9.30 he telephoned his sister Princess Victoria and gave her all the news. He joked that one morning she answered the telephone at the usual time and said: '"Hullo, you old fool." And the voice of the operator broke in, "Beg pardon, Your Royal Highness, His Majesty is not yet on the line."'[77] But May felt excluded from these con-spiratorial conversations, during which Princess Victoria, who was resentful, manipulative and contemptuous of May's morganatic breed-ing, 'poured mischief into the King's ear'.[78]

Another person who enjoyed the confidence of the King was the seventy-year-old Sister Agnes Keyser, a wealthy spinster who ran a nurs-ing home for officers in Grosvenor Gardens. She had been a favourite of Edward VII; as the Duke of Windsor recalled, she owned 'a little house in Mayfair to which she used to invite King Edward and at which he could be with Mrs Keppel in peace'. George gave Sister Agnes a key to the gar-den at Buckingham Palace. 'Round and round that garden they would walk together while she told him tales about his sons.'[79] She was 'noisy & vulgar', and courtiers agreed she was the 'most evil' of the King's friends.[80]

According to the Marquis of Carisbrooke, George's first cousin, Sister Agnes was a pernicious influence, injecting the King with 'poison and suspicion against the Prince of Wales'.[81] Princess Victoria also encouraged him to be harsh with his sons.[82] But the Queen did not agree.

May's role as queen and wife depended on having access to the King, but it seems that George was drifting, and no longer kept her in the know. Daisy Bigge considered that 'she was not told much'.[83] According to Cromer, 'the King kept his own confidence and never told the Queen anything . . . His valet was his main confidant.'[84] Without the King's ear, the Queen's position was fatally weakened. She dared not confront her husband as she might have done before.

Some of the most damning verdicts on Queen Mary's character date from these years. 'I don't believe she was ever fond of any human being in the whole of her life,' said Daisy Bigge. 'She wasn't capable of it. The King was very warm-hearted.'[85] Lord Claud Hamilton, a lifelong member of the household, concurred: 'She was fundamentally cold, had no use for people when they became infirm . . . Quite unlike King George who stood by his friends to the end.'[86] Testimony such as this from members of the household in interviews with Pope-Hennessy in the 1950s is at odds with the evidence of her warm-heartedness during and before the 1914–18 war. Lonely and isolated, she had retreated into majestic frigidity.

George considered the four princes to be his responsibility because, as head of the family, it was his duty to ensure the succession to the throne. David and Bertie were especially exposed to his stifling, disciplinarian regime. Less is known about the two younger princes, but neither of them escaped their father's wrath.

Prince Henry (born 31 March 1900) was a knock-kneed, nervous child who was small for his age and, like Bertie, suffered from a speech impediment. He was sent to a prep school in Broadstairs and then to Eton, making him the first son of a reigning monarch to attend a major public school. His house master found him lacking in self-confidence, but he was good at sport, and after a wasted year at Magdalene College, Cambridge he was allowed to do what he wanted: join the army. But his career in the 10th Royal Hussars was interrupted by royal duties, and as the son of the King he was prevented from joining his regiment overseas. 'My father was the most terrible father, most terrible father you can imagine,' he would later say.[87]

The first of the younger princes to break ranks was Prince George (born 20 December 1902). He was forced into the navy by his father, who wanted a sailor son: Dartmouth was followed by seven years as a naval officer. Prince George loathed the sea. Tall and athletic, with piercing blue eyes, he was dazzlingly good-looking. When he was twenty-one the Queen wrote to Bertie from Cowes: 'Georgie is having high jinks, tennis all day & dancing all night, he is very popular with the ladies & Papa & I are rather nervous.'[88] He was the only son to share his mother's interests in furniture and collecting. On a sightseeing trip, she wrote: 'He asks most intelligent questions & appears to be much interested.'[89] As David perceived, George was 'sharply different in outlook and temperament from the rest of us. Possessed of unusual charm of manner and a quick sense of humour and talented in many directions, he had an undoubted flair for the arts.'[90]

In December 1926 George returned home from the China station, having been away for one-and-a-half years. Six weeks later he announced to his horrified parents that he wished to propose to a Bright Young Person named Poppy Baring. 'It is a regular bombshell & will require careful consideration,' wrote the King. 'He is much too young.'[91]

'It is all a great worry,' said the King.[92] George's diary and the letters exchanged between him and the Queen reveal the panic that the Poppy Baring affair inspired. It preoccupied the royal parents for months. A member of the powerful Baring family, Poppy couldn't be rejected out of hand. If Elizabeth Bowes-Lyon was allowed to marry a prince, why not Poppy? The Barings were richer than the Strathmores and closer to the throne – not only was Lord Cromer the lord chamberlain, but Lord Revelstoke was one of the King's best friends and looked after his private finances. But Poppy was 'fast': she had had several affairs, including one with the Duke of York, who proposed to her in 1921. She accepted, but Queen Mary swiftly intervened and forbade the engagement.[93] Another of her lovers was Duff Cooper, who thought she was what 'Josephine must have been when young', and found her discreet and reserved.[94]* The King's concern was that if the older sons were wiped out, 'the public would not accept her as queen'.[95] After a long talk with Cynthia Colville, who was a cousin of Poppy's, the King and Queen told George that 'we could not consent to his proposing to "Poppy" Baring'.[96]

But Poppy was 'sleeping peacefully in the arms of Prince George', and he refused to leave her.[97] There was still talk of marriage, though Poppy didn't help her prospects by saying 'she couldn't bear the Royal Family'. Duff Cooper thought Prince George was 'really very nice and rocks with laughter at the jokes about his family which Poppy never stops making'.[98]

---

*'She thinks she is a virgin,' wrote Duff after spending the night with her. 'I don't know why she thinks so' (Duff Cooper, *The Duff Cooper Diaries*, ed. John Julius Norwich (Weidenfeld & Nicolson, 2005), p. 188).

The King consulted Lord and Lady Crewe, who advised him that 'the marriage was quite impossible', and he had a long talk with his friend Lord Derby, who said the same.[99] Poppy's worst enemy was 'that vile old Revelstoke – who apparently has an old grudge against her father. So the girl's sunk.'[100] When the King wrote what he called a 'difficult letter' to his son, however, he received no answer. 'I can't understand his behaving in this way,' wrote the King, 'he must know that I shall never allow it.'[101] The Queen blamed Poppy for her son's behaviour: 'It only shows the bad influence those kind of decadent girls have on the young men of the present day.' What their next move should be was a problem: 'we cannot sit down calmly & let G go on seeing & writing to her – it is indeed worrying for us both & one feels so helpless'.[102] When Queen Mary consulted the Yorks, seemingly forgetting Bertie's fling with Poppy, they spoke with horror of the idea of a marriage and said they had received several letters 'saying how foolish George was to go on in the way he did with such an impossible young person!'[103]

The King reached for the panic button and asked Prime Minister Baldwin to write to Prince George. 'I only hope it may have the desired effect & stop this infernal thing going on.'[104]* George was bundled off to Canada with the Prince of Wales, who made an official visit there in July 1927. According to Chips, Poppy's 'heart is still Prince George's and [he] would have married her but for the violent objections of the King and Queen'.[105]

David was charged with looking after Prince George, although the King worried, rightly, that he 'may be helping his brother'.[106] David's relations with his father were as bad as ever. The King forced him to abandon his plan to visit the USA. 'I don't see that he could have done otherwise, I should have had nothing more to do with him, if he had done otherwise, after what I told him,' raged the King.[107]

Unexpectedly Baldwin chose to accompany the two princes on the Canada tour. Tommy Lascelles, David's assistant private secretary, was so angered by his master's louche behaviour that he told the prime minister that the Prince of Wales was 'rapidly going to the devil' and 'would soon become no fit wearer of the British crown'.[108] Baldwin listened but did nothing. In spite of this rocky start the trip was a success.

---

*Ramsay MacDonald had written to David, presumably at the King's behest, when David disobeyed his father's orders to give up riding in point-to-points (Edward, Duke of Windsor, *A King's Story: The Memoirs of HRH the Duke of Windsor* (Cassell, 1951), pp. 195–6).

PART SEVEN

HOME STRAIGHT

1928–1936

CHAPTER 25

'Sir, the King of England is Dying'

1928–1929

On their thirty-fifth wedding anniversary George wrote to May:

> I suppose no two people really suit each other better than we do, although I fear sometimes you must think me rather dull, but I have learnt to look to you to help me in my busy life & you never fail me, indeed I thank God for all the happiness that you have brought me during these 35 years.[1]

Though he rarely spoke about his feelings, he could write a letter which was disarmingly self-aware. By suggesting that 'you must think me rather dull', the King perhaps acknowledged that he had drifted.

He wasn't dull, even if his court was. More than anything he was ordinary, and his ordinariness was one reason why he had succeeded in making the monarchy so central to the nation's life. After sixteen turbulent years, the period between the General Strike and the formation of the National Government in 1931 was the least politically eventful of the reign. The King proceeded uninterrupted on his stately royal routine.

At breakfast, punctually at nine o'clock, Charlotte the King's parrot would walk around the table and dig her beak at random into the boiled egg of a guest or member of the household. When she made a mess on the table the King guiltily covered it up with a silver mustard pot. After breakfast the King invariably walked out of the front door to inspect the weather with a cigarette in a holder in his mouth, and Charlotte perched on his left wrist, followed by Snip, the cairn terrier who had succeeded the faithful Jack.[2]

He was a man of disconnected feelings. A brilliant shot, he thought nothing of killing thousands of pheasants, but his eyes filled with tears when he found a dead bird on the slopes at Windsor.[3] A man who seemed 'lovable, sincere and straightforward' to those around him, he inspired fear and loathing in his sons.[4]

The only son who didn't quarrel with his father was the Duke of York. He turned away the King's anger by becoming as much like his father as possible.[5] Bertie and Elizabeth lived an uxorious domestic life, as George and May had done. The Duke of York shared his father's territorial aristocratic lifestyle. Like the King he was a first-class shot, and in politics he was as Tory as the King. Born left-handed and forced to write with his right hand, the prince developed handwriting which was almost identical to his father's schoolboy script.

'Now, Bertie, no more babies for a while – you have got to go to Australia,' said the King to the Duke of York.[6] Unlike the other brothers, however, the Yorks were able to manage the King. On their state visit to Australia in 1927, the King fired off his usual furious telegrams, complaining of the press coverage. The Earl of Cavan, the Yorks' chief of staff, wrote privately to Stamfordham, imploring him to ask His Majesty to send an encouraging word, as the duke and duchess were both sensitive and 'frightfully anxious to do well'.[7] The King listened. The reproofs ceased.

In a Commons debate on the cost of the tour, a Labour MP objected that the Duke of York was making a 'pleasure trip' paid for by the taxpayer at a time of industrial depression. The palace leapt to the duke's defence. A letter whizzed from Stamfordham on behalf of the King reprimanding Baldwin for allowing these 'flippant, discourteous, if not insulting allusions to his Family'.[8] In future, warned Stamfordham, no member of the royal family would undertake a state visit unless 'the expenses were borne by the Dominions visited or under an arrangement by which Parliament was not called upon to vote the money'. The royal family should not be 'exposed to attacks which they are unable to answer'.[9] One wonders whether the King would have defended the Prince of Wales with such vigour.

On his return the King ordered the duke to wear 'frock coat & epaulettes with star'. He added: 'We will not embrace you at the station before so many people. When you kiss Mama take your hat off.'[10] The formalities belied the King's warmth towards his second son and his appreciation of the success of the tour. In August the King wrote from Balmoral: 'Delighted to have Bertie with me ... have had several talks with him & find him most sensible, very different to D.'[11]

Contemporary biographers portrayed the Yorks, now living at 145 Piccadilly, as the ideal young modern family. They gained a reputation for being dull, but the duchess was an extrovert and socialite by nature, and the home-loving image of the Yorks was deliberately cultivated, distancing them from the playboy bachelor princes.

King George enjoyed the company of young women, and the duchess, who always preferred the company of men, was a compulsive flirt. The pair hit it off. 'The better I know & the more I see of your dear little wife, the more charming I think she is & everyone fell in love with her here,' George wrote to Bertie soon after the marriage.[12] She was even allowed to commit the cardinal royal sin of being unpunctual. Once when she was late for dinner the King said: 'You are not late, my dear, I think we must have sat down two minutes too early.'[13] None of his sons could have got away with that. As she once confided in a letter written shortly after the King's death: 'Unlike his own children I was never afraid of him ... he never spoke one unkind or abrupt word to me.'[14] When the King told her that he disliked her fringe, 'much to everyone's surprise all she said was "Oh I *am* so sorry", and didn't take the hint'.[15] The duchess used her ascendancy over the King to shield her vulnerable, stuttering husband. Whether she intended it or not, her strategy of pleasing the King advanced her husband in the race that was opening up for the succession.

In August 1928 Prince George was in trouble once more for his 'stupid behaviour' over an 'unfortunate affair'.[16] It's clear from their agitated letters that he had lied to his parents about a girlfriend. Possibly this was the occasion when George told his father he was going to stay with his friend Louis Mountbatten when in fact he was seeing a girl. The King found out and was very angry with George for deceiving him and with Mountbatten for being a party to the deception. 'When Mountbatten reproached George for having dragged him unfairly into a family row, George replied: "I am sorry. But my father is so bloody to me that I might as well lie to him on the chance of getting away with it as tell him the truth." '[17] George was banished to the North America and West Indies station on board HMS *Durban*, pursued by a letter which the King found 'not easy to write', and no wonder. 'I only said I was absolutely ashamed of his behaviour & hoped he was ashamed too, he must turn over a new leaf & become straight, else no one would trust him & have anything to do with him.'[18] From Bermuda, George wrote 'anything but happy letters' to the Queen – 'he hates the place, climate & people, he is difficult to please which distresses Papa & me very much indeed'.[19]

David was summoned by his father and reprimanded for covering up his brother's affair. The King wrote to the Queen: 'I told him it was a pity he didn't tell us about it before, as we were bound to hear of it sooner or later & might have stopped it.'[20] David for once was not in the firing line, and his relations with his father improved. 'I have had several talks with David,' wrote the King, '& I have got on capitally with him, better than for a long time.'[21]

What the royal parents did not know, however, was how wild Prince

George had become. Known as 'PG' or 'Babe', the prince was immature and easily led. 'George is such a baby for his age,' said the Yorks.[22] George knew no boundaries in his pursuit of pleasure. The rumours that spread about his drug taking and his homosexual affairs were true. At York House in St James's Palace, where he lived with David when on leave, George came under his brother's influence. 'We became more than brothers,' wrote David. 'We became close friends.'[23]

David and his brother Harry, on the other hand, never got on. They had 'one hell of a row' in 1927 when Harry told someone: 'I didn't think he'd ever be King, and it was repeated. [David] said to me, "Did you say it or didn't you?" So I said, ". . . I'm going to tell you the truth. I did say it and I still think it." Then we had the row.'[24] In September 1928 David and Harry, by now Duke of Gloucester, embarked on a visit to Kenya. Harry went on a separate safari while David made an unofficial visit to Happy Valley, shooting elephants with Denys Finch Hatton and partying until 3 a.m. in the Muthaiga Club with Lady Delamere, who once rolled him around on the floor.

Tommy Lascelles, who accompanied the Prince of Wales as assistant private secretary, grumbled about the prince's frivolity and futility. 'His personal charm has vanished irretrievably so far as I am concerned, and I always feel as if I were working, not for the next King of England, but for the son of the latest American millionaire.'[25] But Lascelles's plan to have it out with the prince and resign from his job was pre-empted by events. On 27 November alarming telegrams from Baldwin reached the prince imploring him to return home at once on account of the illness of the King. 'We hope that all may go well,' cabled Baldwin, 'but if not, and you have made no attempt to return, it will profoundly shock public opinion.'[26] The prince was sceptical. 'I don't believe a word of it,' said he. 'It's just some election dodge of old Baldwin's.' 'Sir,' replied Lascelles, or so he recalled, 'the King of England is dying; and if that means nothing to you, it means a great deal to us.'[27] The prince left the room without a word and spent the evening seducing the wife of the local commissioner.

At Buckingham Palace on the evening of Wednesday 21 November the King had complained of a chill. Too feeble to finish writing his diary for the day, he dictated to the Queen: 'I was taken ill this evening. Feverish cold they called it & retired to bed.'[28]

Since the King's illness of 1925 Sir Stanley Hewett had monitored George's health, forbidding him from leaving the house in bad weather for fear of catching a cold. 'Horribly cold East wind so Hewett wouldn't let me go out,' grumbled George one day in March 1928.[29] At a dinner at Admiralty House a few days later, Neville Chamberlain found the King 'in great spirits roaring with laughter & jabbing the First Sea Lord in the ribs with immense gusto'.[30] In September, staying at Balmoral, Winston Churchill noted: 'The King is well – but ageing. He no longer stalks but goes out on the hill where the deer are "moved about for him", & it may be that some loyal stag will do his duty.'[31]

When Hewett and Lord Dawson of Penn were summoned to Buckingham Palace on 21 November, they realised as soon as they saw the King lying in his plain brass bed that 'there was something seriously wrong'.[32] Dawson privately confided that 'there is something he cannot quite understand about the King's condition': he looked like a doomed man.[33] A bulletin was issued saying that the King was suffering from 'cold with some fever'. But the doctors feared septicaemia, and a 'bacteriological' specialist named Lionel Whitby arrived at midnight on an emergency mission to take the King's blood. Not until 24 November was this mentioned in *The Times*, and then the investigation was passed off as 'habitual', a routine procedure.[34] By that time Whitby's cultures – together with small clots of blood which the King coughed up in his sputum – had confirmed the doctors' suspicions that the King was indeed suffering from septicaemia, but this was not mentioned in *The Times* until 10 December.[35]

Dawson, physician-in-ordinary to the King, the senior doctor of the royal household, was media-savvy, far more so than the Palace. *The Times* claimed that the King's physicians were 'taking the public into their confidence' but this was only partly true.[36] Not only did Dawson endeavour to manage public expectations and dampen panic and damaging speculation. But for the ambitious doctor the King's illness offered a fantastic PR opportunity – so long as the outcome was good.

For ten days the press bulletins charted the King's oscillating symptoms, his zigzagging fever, his restless nights and disturbed days. Congestion of the right lung was diagnosed, and then plastic pleurisy, causing pain and a spike in temperature. Outside the Palace a 'hushed and utterly silent crowd' waited for the bulletins, which were posted at three- or four-hourly intervals in a glass-fronted mahogany frame hung on the railings.[37] They watched as a heavy lorry carrying an X-ray machine parked under the King's bedroom window, and great coils of tubing were passed into the room, the first time the new technology had been used outside a hospital.[38]

For several hours each day the Queen sat in George's room. According to Sister Catherine Black, who was one of the team of four top nurses and a devoted royalist, the Queen 'showed no hint of the anxiety she was undergoing', but radiated strength and serenity to the King. 'Even when he was too ill to talk his face would brighten when she entered the room and his eyes would never leave her.'[39] Queen Mary is a *'real tough guy'*, murmured Hewett.[40] Her children marvelled that 'she has never once revealed her feelings to any of us'.[41]

On Sunday 2 December Queen Mary's calm turned to panic. 'G was very ill in the evening as the heart began to give out. Terribly anxious,' she wrote.[42] The bulletins announced that 'anxiety concerning the heart still exists'.[43] Dawson wrote privately that 'the crux is the <u>heart</u>, and while the lung trouble is practically over there remains a fight between whatever poison remains and the heart'.[44] The Duke of York told the Prince of Wales that 'the whole cause of the anxiety has been the heart': the King had somehow damaged the valves of his heart over the past few months, possibly 'overdoing the shooting'. It was touch and go on Sunday night and all day Monday whether he would live.[45] On Monday Hewett told Bryan Godfrey-Faussett that he didn't think the King's heart would hold for many days longer, and 'the poor Queen is prepared for the worst to happen . . . It is all very terrible.'[46]

As the King slipped in and out of consciousness, the Prince of Wales, recognising at last the seriousness of his father's illness, rushed home from Kenya, travelling 6,700 miles in nine days, first by train to Dar es Salaam and then boarding a cruiser. The journey home of the estranged heir echoed Queen Victoria's dash to the bedside of her son Bertie, stricken by typhoid in 1871. But the drama that transfixed the nation was not the reconciliation of the King and his heir, but the King's struggle to live.

As the doctors battled against time to find the source of the infection on the lung which was causing the fever and exhausting the heart, the nation held its breath. The doctors' bulletins were transmitted by telegraph to every post office in the land, and broadcast by the BBC. At one o'clock and nine o'clock people all over England sat listening to the chimes of Big Ben and waiting for the announcer's voice.[47] Watching the continuous stream of people moving in front of Buckingham Palace to read the bulletins, Joan Lascelles, Tommy's wife, wrote: 'It is really rather wonderful to think of the King, living quietly and unobtrusively all these years, doing his job, and then to realise at moments like these what he means to the whole nation, and it is all utterly spontaneous.'[48]

On Tuesday 4 December a Privy Council was held to nominate six counsellors of state, including the Queen and the Prince of Wales, to act on the King's behalf.* The Council took place in the Audience Room,

---

*The others were the Duke of York, the Archbishop of Canterbury, the prime minister and the lord chancellor.

which adjoined the King's bedroom, and the home secretary, William Joynson-Hicks, read the order paper standing in the open door a few feet away from where the King lay ill in bed.

That day Princess Victoria somehow managed to slip in through the Audience Room before anyone could stop her and sit down on George's bed. Seeing the change in her brother she could not hide her distress, 'and her lamentations made him conclude that he was dying'. He was so tired by this display that the Queen decided not to visit him in the evening. The next morning he greeted her:

'You didn't come to see me last night.'
'Did you miss me?' she asked.
'Of course I did. What do you think?'[49]

Lady Airlie, who noticed that the King's dependence on the Queen made her 'in a way happy', thought that his reply gave her immense pleasure.

Throughout the week the King deteriorated. 'The strain is very wearing,' wrote the Queen.[50] Neither needles nor X-rays could locate the 'mischief' in the lung, which meant that the abscess could not be drained, and the King grew more and more exhausted by his fever.[51] On Monday 10 December, the King was 'rather worse' and the evening bulletin announced a return of the 'general infection', or septicaemia, 'with its necessary effect on the heart'.[52] 'All feel very anxious,' wrote the Queen.[53] At 10.30 the following evening David arrived, 'to our great relief', and the Queen took him to George's room. 'He recognised him & spoke to him quite clearly.'[54] Baldwin told a story that when the prince entered the room, 'the old King, who had for nearly a week been practically unconscious, just opened half an eye, looked up at him and said: "Damn you, what the devil are you doing here?"'[55]*

On the afternoon of 12 December as Sister Black sat beside his bed the King seemed only hours from death. Lord Dawson entered the room. 'Will you give me a syringe?' she remembered him asking. 'I think I will make one more try to find that fluid.'[56] In a moment of high drama, the doctor took the syringe, and in a few seconds he located the infection. Sixteen ounces of pus were drained from the abscess immediately. That evening an operation was performed for the emptying of the remaining fluid and removal of one rib. The family sat together waiting

---

*Another version is that the King said to David: 'How about the lions, tell me all about them' (George Godfrey-Faussett, *Royal Servant, Family Friend: The Life and Times of Naval Equerry Captain Sir Bryan Godfrey-Faussett RN* (Bernard Durnford, 2004), p. 302).

in the Queen's room until Dawson appeared and announced that 'all had gone off successfully'.[57]

George's recovery was slow, and the illness dragged on for weeks. He was sometimes delirious, his speech was thick and slurred, he slept badly and he refused to eat. Christmas at Buckingham Palace was a subdued affair. Then on 6 January 1929, he sent for the Queen, who wrote: 'He was perfectly clear & we had a talk for 20 minutes which cheered me much after not having spoken to me for practically 6 weeks. George signed his name just to show me he could do so.'[58] Dawson declared that 'never in all his experience had he known any patient, old or young, to be so ill and yet survive'.[59]

The next day George saw Stamfordham for the first time since his illness. Sister Black, who was sentimental, described how 'the old secretary entered the room of the King whom he had never thought to see again, and . . . tears splashed onto His Majesty's hand as he kissed it fervently. King George's eyes too were wet . . .'[60] According to Godfrey-Faussett, however, Stamfordham broke down because he was shocked by the terrible change in the King, 'and this made the King do the same'.[61] So distressed was Stamfordham that he went to bed for four days.

A month later, on 9 February, the King moved to the south coast on Dawson's orders to convalesce in the sea air. Sir Arthur Du Cros offered the King Craigweil, his house near Bognor to rent.* Dawson oversaw the medical modifications of the house and had the King's bedroom fitted with newly invented Vitaglass, which admitted therapeutic ultraviolet light.

When Bertha Dawkins glimpsed the King, she was shocked by the change in his appearance – 'such a long, thin face, all eyes'.[62] He soon gained eight pounds in weight, and began to listen to the gramophone once more. After four days at Bognor he smoked his first cigarette since November.[63] Neither the King nor his doctors realised that smoking was the chief cause of the 'mischief' in his lungs, which today would probably be diagnosed as chronic obstructive pulmonary disease.

The Queen spent the time scouring the antique shops within range of Bognor, and she adopted the habit of entering unexpectedly into the houses of complete strangers, 'frequently causing alarm, but always with the best of intentions'. Once she looked in on a house where a fete was being held, taking over the selling at a stall of toys, 'and within half an hour the stall was cleared'.[64]

---

*Du Cros, who made a fortune out of Dunlop tyres, was created a baronet for paying off Lady Warwick's debts in 1916.

Randall Davidson, who had recently retired as Archbishop of Canterbury aged eighty-one, visited Craigweil and found the King dressed and up and smoking cigarettes 'rather vigorously' through an elaborate holder. The King spoke of the welcome he had received from the people on a drive to Bognor, and Davidson felt he was 'affected through and through' by his illness. 'I cannot help believing that his illness is going to intensify a closer relation with his people,' he wrote. For the King, his illness was almost a religious experience; as he told Davidson, 'it was the sympathy & prayers of my people which enabled me to pull through & I am indeed grateful to God that he spared me that I might still work for the benefit of my Empire & people'.[65]

The King, thought Davidson, was 'moved deeply' by the Prince of Wales's new-found loyalty and enthusiasm for public work.[66] But his faith in David was only skin-deep. Many years later, the Queen Mother recalled that when she and Bertie visited the King at Bognor, he said 'he thought David would never take over from him. We were astonished,' she said, 'and hardly understood what he meant.'[67]

On 15 May the King returned to Windsor after three months at Bognor. Before his departure a deputation of the citizens of Bognor came to ask that their town should be known as Bognor Regis. The King, who was in another room, replied: 'Bugger Bognor,' while Stamfordham politely informed the deputation that their request was granted.[68]* The royal connection was double-edged, as soon afterwards 'the cornfields gave way to villadom'.[69]

By the King's orders the royal motor car drove at walking pace through the villages on the route to Windsor, where he was received by cheering crowds.[70] But his recovery was not complete, and on 27 May he suffered a relapse: 'Felt seedy in evening & have temp 100.'[71] The doctors sent him to bed, and he recorded bad nights, shivering and rising temperature. Then on 31 May 'an abscess burst through the old wound, which was great relief & temp went down at once, probably caused by small pieces of bone from the rib'.[72]

'It is dreadfully disappointing H.M. being ill again,' wrote the King's groom-in-waiting Dick Molyneux after spending an hour with the Queen.[73] Even worse, the King's relapse coincided with a political crisis. Baldwin had called an election which he confidently expected to win.

---

*The story that the King's last words, on being told by one of his doctors that he would soon be well enough to recuperate at Bognor, were 'Bugger Bognor' is much better but sadly not correct.

The result, declared on the day the King's abscess burst, came as a shock: a hung parliament, comprising 287 Labour MPs, 260 Conservative and 59 Liberal, plus nine others. As after the 1923 election the King was faced with appointing a government when no party had an overall majority.

Stamfordham followed his usual practice and opened a file on the change of government. Unlike previous files, this one has been vetted. The royal librarian, Robin Mackworth-Young, read the file in preparation for the visit to the archives of Keith Middlemas, Baldwin's biographer, in 1966. Mackworth-Young inserted typewritten notes recommending the withholding of documents which appeared to reveal the King and Stamfordham to be biased against Labour. The file was then read by two other people, one using biro, the other writing in pencil. Against one of Mackworth-Young's notes the reader with the pencil has written: 'Geo V papers as a corpus hereunto do not show anti-Labour bias on Stamfordham's part.'[74] Letters by Stamfordham agreeing with Baldwin's decision to resign before meeting Parliament are annotated by Mackworth-Young: 'Should be withheld as they seem to show that Ld Stamfordham wants Baldwin returned to power.'[75] The person with the biro has commented, in a small neat hand: 'I'm not sure that they do show this!' The pencil annotator adds that the correspondence indicates that 'HM and Stamfordham rather liked "Ramsay Mac".'[76] Indeed it does. Mackworth-Young's comments tell us more about the paranoia of the palace during the Wilson government than about the political views of George V in 1929. In spite of his salty Tory talk, the King was resolved to act on the verdict of the election and appoint a Labour government.

For King George the pressing anxiety was whether he would be strong enough to endure the ordeal of appointing a new government with an open wound discharging in his back. Baldwin came to Windsor on 4 June and resigned. 'Very sorry to part with him,' wrote the King, but Baldwin's determination to do the sportsmanlike thing and resign at once, rather than meet Parliament and attempt to make a deal with the Liberals, simplified the King's task.[77] Next day Ramsay MacDonald arrived for an audience to find the King in his bedroom, wearing a brightly coloured Chinese dressing gown. On Stamfordham's advice MacDonald kissed hands while the King remained seated on a sofa. This was fortunate because the King forgot to ask MacDonald to form a government, but it was implied by kissing hands. MacDonald thought the King's face seemed longer, his eyes staring and his speech too loud.[78] '"Nothing", H.M. said, "could have been nicer than [MacDonald's] manner and all that he said about my illness and the attitude of his party towards me during the long and anxious time." '[79] These were not the words of a monarch who was desperate to keep Labour out of office.

The King was dressed and up on 7 June when the Baldwin Cabinet arrived to deliver their seals. He spoke to each minister separately but found it 'rather tiring' and went to bed afterwards.[80] When the incoming Labour government arrived the next day to be sworn in, Wigram found them in the Red Drawing Room on their knees, solemnly rehearsing for kissing hands. 'Clive said he nearly died of laughing!' wrote Nora. They were admitted one by one into the King's smoking room, and the King 'looked so smart in his frock coat & wearing the Guards tie'. J. H. Thomas remarked to Wigram on the brave show the King made. 'It is his bloody guts that have done it!'[81] The King charmed them one and all, and he was even nice to Margaret Bondfield, minister of labour, who was sworn in as the first woman privy counsellor. She telephoned Stamford-ham the night before, asking what she should wear, and he replied that he really couldn't advise. She chose sober black and white, and when she was sworn in the King broke his customary silence and said: 'I am pleased to be the one to receive the first woman minister.'[82]

The thanksgiving service at Westminster Abbey on 7 July was simple and brief but an ordeal for the King. 'Fancy a Thanksgiving Service with an open wound in your back,' he remarked to Dawson and Hewett on returning to Buckingham Palace. After appearing on the balcony before the cheering crowds, the King was examined by his doctors. They advised him to postpone his departure for Sandringham, which had been planned for the following day. 'I am more than disappointed,' wrote George.[83]

A second operation was needed to drain the cavity. This operation was bigger than the one in December. 'They removed another rib, part of the old one & an abscess which was below them & cleaned it all out.'[84] Dawson was anxious about the anaesthetic: the King's illness had been so dangerous, he said, '(at least 60 per cent of patients die) that it had of necessity left his heart poisoned and very weak'.[85] The procedure had been thought a success the first time, but on this occa-sion it really succeeded. On 25 July the King wrote: 'Smoked my first cigarette which I enjoyed.'[86] The next day Neville Chamberlain dined at the Palace and found the King in tremendous spirits. 'After dinner he beckoned me up and then we went & sat down together and had quite a long conversation. He was exceedingly indiscreet about his present ministers but evidently delighted that Jimmy Thomas has got back into the Dominions office again.'[87] On 9 August George wrote: 'Had my first bath today for 25 days, very pleasant it was too.'[88] By 24 August he was sufficiently recovered to be allowed to leave for Sandringham.

*　*　*

After the King had recovered, Sister Black was asked to stay on indefinitely as his nurse. Dawson watched the King's health more carefully than before, often dropping in to examine him. The local doctors at each of the King's residences reported back to Dawson on a regular basis. In his diary, George recorded every symptom of cough or cold. He was a worried patient. The medical surveillance suggests that the King was effectively an invalid after 1929. But this was hotly denied by Dawson.

In 1940 when John Gore had finished writing his biography of the King, galleys of the sections on the King's illness of 1928–9 were sent to Dawson for approval. Dawson rewrote the account, adding technical medical detail. These changes infuriated Gore, who complained bitterly about Dawson's interference. Dawson for his part threatened to 'wash his hands of the whole affair and publicly repudiate the medical portion of the book'.[89] As head of the King's medical household and a personal friend of George VI, Dawson was a man Gore could not afford to antagonise, and he accepted most of the changes.

For Dawson the sticking point was that Gore gave a misleading impression of the King's last years. John Murray, Gore's publisher, explained:

> Dawson will not have it that he was an invalid obviously breaking up . . . He was of course a delicate man then, but able to fulfil all the duties which an elderly king can be expected to fulfil and not lead an invalid life . . . if you have a limited amount of petrol in your car and can't get more, you can go ahead normally as before without unduly stepping on the accelerator and give no outward sign of the shortage you know of. Your journey will be shorter and come to a more sudden end. Or you can husband every drop, go very slowly and last rather longer, making quite obvious what you are doing.
>
> The former was the deliberate policy of the King's doctors and they think it very important that the normalcy of the King's last years should be stressed, while you, I think, stress too much the invalid side.[90]

Dawson's professional reputation was at stake. By his skilful treatment he had saved the King's life, and this made him a national celebrity. He was a leader of his profession, and the King rewarded him by making him a privy counsellor, the only doctor to receive that honour, for which the King had to make a special case.[91] Dawson's decision to opt for 'normalcy' in managing the King's health after the 1928–9 illness meant that there was always a danger that he would come to a sudden end, in the same way as Edward VII, who suffered from a similar condition, had done.

If George had died in 1928 Dawson considered that the King would not have 'earned his peculiar place in our history' as the founder of the modern monarchy that he achieved in the last years of the reign.[92] Some people thought his near-death experience changed him. Ivan Maisky, the Soviet ambassador, heard a story that before the illness the King was very depressed and 'felt that he was coping poorly with his duties and steadily losing authority and respect among his subjects'. During the illness, the sympathy displayed by the public impressed him deeply. 'He became calmer, having decided that the Empire needed him; his will to live came sharply into focus. This psychological state greatly facilitated the king's almost miraculous recovery.'[93]

If George had died in 1928 would the Abdication have taken place? Without Mrs Simpson in the picture, David might have behaved differently, but he had already forfeited much of his reputation and lost the respect of his advisers. The letter that Bertie sent to David welcoming the news of his return from Kenya was written in jest, but with hindsight it seems prophetic: 'There is a lovely story going about which emanated from the East End that the reason of your rushing home is that in the event of anything happening to Papa I am going to bag the Throne in your absence!!!! Just like the Middle Ages.'[94]

CHAPTER 26

Queen Mary Takes Control

1929–1931

The King returned to Windsor in May 1929 to find unfinished business awaiting him. The month before he became ill, his aunt Minny, the Dowager Empress of Russia, had died aged eighty in Copenhagen. Her death opened up the snake pit of the Romanov jewels.

Ever since he refused asylum to his cousin Nicky, George had behaved impeccably towards his Romanov cousins. When Ramsay MacDonald formed the first Labour government in 1924, Stamfordham warned against restoring diplomatic relations with Russia, because it would be indescribably abhorrent to the King to shake the hands of anyone concerned with his cousins' murders.[1] When MacDonald formed his second government in 1929 Stamfordham again begged him to spare the King 'feelings of repulsion' at shaking hands with a Russian envoy, but the government insisted on recognising the Soviet ambassador.[2] At the levee in March 1930 the King was therefore compelled to receive the Soviet envoy, but he demanded that they shake hands beforehand in private, refusing to do it in public, thus making plain his disapproval of the regime.[3]

Back in 1919 George had sent the dreadnought HMS *Marlborough* to rescue the Dowager Empress and her daughter Grand Duchess Xenia from the Crimea. When 'dear Aunt Minny' arrived in England, he paid her the compliment of meeting her at Victoria station.[4] Embarrassingly, one of the Romanov servants mistook the King for the Emperor and threw himself at George's knee.[5] Minny moved in with Alexandra at Marlborough House, but the two sisters didn't get on, and Alexandra complained that she couldn't afford to keep the Empress's Russian servants.[6] Minny went to live in Denmark. King George gave her a substantial allowance of £10,000 a year (£640,000 in today's money). She brought with her the last remaining casket of Romanov jewels which she had smuggled out of Russia. The King kept a careful watch on the jewels: he ordered Fritz Ponsonby to attend to the safekeeping of the box, and in order to prevent the Empress from giving the gems away, Ponsonby made elaborate arrangements to ensure that when she was in Denmark the key of the safe was not in her possession.[7]

From time to time packing cases arrived at Buckingham Palace which purported to contain the valuables of the Dowager Empress or things belonging to Tsar Nicholas. The boxes sent to the Dowager Empress in November 1919 turned out to be nothing but worthless trash.[8] Twenty-nine packing cases which supposedly contained the possessions of Nicholas and Alexandra appeared in October 1919, but the boxes had been looted on the journey from Yekaterinburg to Vladivostok, and there were no items of value, only rubbish such as old cooking pots.[9]*

Xenia remained in London. The cousin who had flirted with George in the long-ago days of Fredensborg, Xenia had wide-apart, protuberant eyes and a doll-like figure which belied her mental toughness. Growing up as a Romanov princess of fabulous wealth meant that she never learnt the value of money, and her generosity to her family and the hangers-on from the Russian court left her penniless. In 1922 a fraudster swindled her out of pearl necklaces worth £10,000.[10]

'Poor Xenia's financial affairs . . . are in a very bad state & I am going to help her,' wrote George in 1925.[11] Peter Bark, the last tsarist foreign minister, was commissioned to sort out Xenia's debts. George gave her £2,400 a year and a grace-and-favour cottage at Frogmore (it had twenty-three rooms). Xenia was pathetically grateful and wrote George an ecstatic letter of thanks. 'I longed to write at once & have written & torn up many sheets of paper but felt shy! & didn't quite know what was going on.'[12]

At Frogmore, George insisted on paying himself for much-needed improvements, overriding the rule that repairs to grace-and-favour houses should be the responsibility of the occupants. 'The King has expressed a wish that the Grand Duchess be made as comfortable as possible,' noted the Office of Works.[13]

How much Xenia knew about George's role in her brother Nicky's fate is unclear. As Frances Welch has pointed out, if Xenia had known the truth about Georgie's refusal to offer asylum to her brother, 'she would hardly have felt so well disposed to him'.[14] She must have been aware of the rumours, however. Prince George of Greece wrote to her in 1920:

---

*Not all the contents were trash. The Tsarina's lady-in-waiting Baroness Buxhoeveden later wrote to Grand Duchess Xenia telling her that the Tsarina's jewels were concealed in a roll of cloth in one of the boxes, and these were retrieved. In April 1919, the baroness had come to tea with George and Mary '& told us some most interesting things' (RA GV/PRIV/GVD/19 April 1919).

There is one, who might have stuck to principal [*sic*] and to nobel [*sic*] acts, and this is English Georgie, but he, hiding behind the words 'constitutional King' allows the evil to conquer over everything that is good and right, so as to stick to his d—d throne, which nowadays is no better than a WC.[15]

But if the price of silence was grace-and-favour accommodation for her lifetime and friendly relations with George and May, this was perhaps something that the pragmatic Xenia was willing to pay – the more so if she realised that Nicky could never have been rescued.

The funeral of the Dowager Empress in Copenhagen in 1928 was the last gathering of the old Russian court in exile. King Christian of Denmark sniffed treasure and so did the Romanovs' Russian relations. Crooks circled, plotting to grab the fabled jewels, which the Empress had left to her daughters Xenia and Olga. On the advice of Fritz Ponsonby, who enjoyed masterminding cloak-and-dagger operations of this sort, King George sent the wily Peter Bark to Copenhagen. Bark outwitted the enemy by persuading Xenia to hand over the jewels and entrust them to his safekeeping before the Empress's funeral took place. On 28 October 1928 a messenger arrived at Buckingham Palace carrying the sealed casket of jewels. Ponsonby breathed a sigh of relief and locked them into his safe at the palace.[16]

Before the jewel box could be unsealed the King became ill, and it was not until over six months later, on 22 May 1929, that he was back at Windsor and well enough to oversee the opening of the box. He wrote: 'Xenia came from Frogmore & we looked at all Aunt Minny's jewels, some lovely things & she had luncheon with us.'[17] The Queen and Xenia watched as seventy-six pieces of jewellery cascaded out of the casket, including two graduated natural pearl necklaces with some pearls as big as cherries, each valued at £50,000 (£3.2 million today). Mr Hardy of the Bond Street jewellers Hennell was asked to make a provisional valuation, and he priced the jewels at £156,674 (£10 million today).[18]

This was a private sale and few knew what went on, but whispers later began to circulate that Queen Mary had taken advantage of Xenia and helped herself to the jewels. The rumours intensified after the death of Xenia's sister Olga in 1960. Grand Duchess Olga ended her days in a flat above Ray's Barbershop in East Toronto. Unsurprisingly perhaps, she felt that she had not received her fair share of Romanov wealth, and she complained that she had been cheated of her full inheritance. Her grievance was published by her biographer, who claimed that the Dowager Empress's jewels had been sold for a total of £350,000 but the two grand duchesses had received only £100,000 between them.[19] Olga's two sons tried to find out what had happened to the missing £250,000. It was rumoured that in 1968 Elizabeth II had paid compensation to one of Olga's sons, thus implying that the Queen accepted that the family had been cheated. This was firmly denied by Buckingham Palace.[20]

Once again the finger pointed at Queen Mary, adding to her reputation as the kleptomaniac queen. One historian of the royal jewels writing in 1985 described Queen Mary's behaviour over the Romanov gems as follows: '*She had picked out the choicest items for herself and had offered half the Hennells' valuation price or had simply never paid up at all.*'[21]

Recent research has shown this story to be untrue. What really happened to the Romanov jewels was discovered by William Clarke, the historian of the lost fortune of the tsars. Researching in the Hennell archive, he found a comprehensive and professional inventory of the Xenia/Olga jewels. This lists the valuations of the seventy-six jewels, the names of the purchasers and – crucially important – the prices that were paid. From this document, it is evident that Queen Mary bought only four pieces of jewellery, and for each piece she paid the valuation price or slightly more.[22] As for the allegedly missing £250,000, it turns out that the full price realised by the jewels was £136,621, and the sisters presumably each received half of this. The figure of £350,000, which Fritz Ponsonby quoted in his memoirs, was just plain wrong.[23]

The discovery that Queen Mary bought the Romanov jewels at valuation prices or above has far-reaching significance. This is perhaps the only occasion where documentary evidence has been found which exonerates her from malicious gossip. But if the rumours about her are not substantiated on this occasion, there is reason to question the hearsay in other cases where no hard evidence exists. The perception of the Queen as a rapacious predator appropriating jewellery and precious things needs to be radically revised.

According to Queen Mary's biographer, the winter of 1929 and the whole of 1930 were overshadowed by her perpetual concern for the King's health.[24] In her diary she diligently reported his symptoms, and she remained outwardly calm as she had done throughout his illness. When Xenia praised her for showing no anxiety, the Queen replied: 'George wouldn't like it.'[25] Bertie worried that she 'never once revealed her feelings to any of us. She is really far too reserved; she keeps too much locked up inside herself. I fear a breakdown if anything happens.'[26]

Faced with the prospect of widowhood and demotion to queen dowager, Queen Mary showed no sign of cracking.

Kenneth Rose described the Queen's position as one of 'dignified slavery'.[27] This was the public perception, but it was only part of the story. After his return from Africa, the Prince of Wales deputised for the sick King. Behind the scenes, however, Queen Mary, who was one of the counsellors of state, managed David just as she did the King. It was she who persuaded the prince to give up riding in steeplechases. She told him: 'With Papa so ill and unable to get around and your having to do so much more, it would seem better if you did not take these chances.'[28] This helped to repair David's relations with the King, who believed that his son had sold his horses on his own initiative, in order to leave more time for public affairs.[29]

The Queen held four courts on her own that Season. 'I dread the . . . Courts without you as you can imagine,' she told George, 'but for the sake of the "trade" I feel it is right to hold them.'[30] Magnificent in a gown of silver grey diamanté with the Koh-i-Noor, or a gold lamé gown with the Star of Africa in a diamond coronet, the Queen swept into the Throne Room at 9.30 precisely on the hand of the Prince of Wales, who escorted her to her solitary gilt chair on the dais.[31]* General Charles Dawes, the incoming American ambassador, threatened not to wear the black velvet knee breeches which were customary when the Queen was present. David, whose rebellion against his father was largely a matter of rejecting formal dress, refused to intervene. When Dawes appeared at court wearing long trousers, the Queen gave him a glacial look. Afterwards she murmured to David, 'Papa will not be pleased.'[32]

The Queen also had to deal with Prince Harry, who returned from his African safari in December 1928. Back in London he was reunited with his pregnant mistress Beryl Markham, daredevil and aviatrix from Kenya's Happy Valley. The baby was not Harry's – it was conceived months before they met. Regardless of appearances, Harry installed Beryl as his mistress in the Grosvenor Hotel, a few minutes' walk from his apartments at Buckingham Palace. David noted that 'for once Queen Mary's blue-eyed boy was in trouble instead of himself' – this was particularly gratifying because, unknown to Harry, David was also conducting an affair with Beryl.[33]

The King tried to put an end to the affair by sending Harry abroad on a mission to Japan, to give the Emperor the Garter, but Harry attempted

---

*While deputising for his father, it was David's duty to hold levees on behalf of the King and to act as escort to the Queen when she had to hold courts (Edward, Duke of Windsor, *A King's Story: The Memoirs of HRH the Duke of Windsor* (Cassell, 1951), p. 234).

to wriggle out of it. He appealed to David, who approached the Foreign Office and asked for the visit to be postponed on account of the Duke of Gloucester's increased public duties at home. When Queen Mary discovered what was going on, she asked Lord Stamfordham to intervene. He told the Foreign Office that the matter was not for the Prince of Wales but for the Queen, 'who alone I regard as the mouthpiece of the King'. He continued:

> Her Majesty told me that the previous evening she had explained to the Prince of Wales that what had been arranged by the King could not be changed, and that H.R.H. understood that it must now be settled that the Duke of Gloucester goes as previously arranged with the Garter Mission.[34]

David was firmly put in his place. Harry sailed to Japan.

That was not the end of the matter. When Harry returned from Japan, he resumed his affair with Beryl, who was spotted running barefoot along the corridors of Buckingham Palace. Armed with love letters from Harry which he had found in Beryl's desk drawers, her husband Mansfield Markham threatened to divorce her, citing the prince. His elder brother Sir Charles Markham was summoned to Buckingham Palace and warned off by the Queen: 'One simply could not cite a Prince of the Blood in a divorce petition.'[35] Mansfield Markham was also summoned and lectured by an angry Queen, who didn't even ask him to sit down. Blackmailed by the Markham brothers, the Palace paid up. A capital sum of £15,000 was placed in a trust fund, providing Beryl with an annuity of £500 (around £32,000 today). The money was said to be paid not by the Queen but by the Duke of Gloucester.[36]

At least Prince Harry was not the heir. King George's illness gave the 35-year-old David the opportunity to prove his fitness to be king. It would be wrong to say that he failed altogether. He took up the cause of unemployment, he toured the mining districts of Durham and Northumberland, raised funds and made radio broadcasts.[37] His relations with the King improved. He was reported to have said that 'I now feel for the first time that I have a father', and the King acknowledged his son's help and comfort during his illness.[38] But the prince's advisers were mutinous. Tommy Lascelles resigned, unable to stand any more. Early in 1929 Godfrey Thomas, the prince's private secretary, analysed the reasons for his unpopularity:

> If the monarchy is to continue a certain amount of aloofness and mystery – call it what you like – must hedge a king. The Duke of York,

with half HRH's charm, is daily gaining popularity at his expense. The King and Queen lead what some people are pleased to consider a humdrum, old-fashioned life. And that's why they're so popular. It's what people want of their sovereign. [There is an] almost universal feeling of dismay at the prospect of the Prince of Wales coming to the throne at the present moment.[39]

Queen Mary must surely have realised that David was not up to the job, She, on the other hand, most certainly was, and George acknowledged how much he owed his wife. He wrote to her: 'I can never sufficiently express my deep gratitude to you, darling May, for the way you have helped & stood by me in these difficult times. This is not sentimental rubbish but is what I really feel.'[40]

'You know I have never got on with my father,' David remarked, 'but when, on getting back, I found him a little, shrunken old man with a white beard, the shock was so great that I cried.'[41] At sixty-four the King had indeed become an old man. He had lost all his teeth except for two – seven were extracted during his illness – and he complained of the discomfort of his false teeth.[42] He suffered from neuritis in his arm, for which he received electrical treatment. He was afflicted by back pain, the legacy of his fall in 1915, which his doctor diagnosed as arthritis.[43] He was deaf, the result no doubt of firing countless thousands of cartridges.[44] He had always been a hypochondriac, and every cold was now potentially life-threatening. On wintry days, as already noted, the doctors forbade him from going out of doors.[45] Unable to take exercise, he put on weight, and his uniforms became 'too tight alas'.[46]

At Sandringham, where he stayed for six months, he struggled to recover his strength for shooting.[47] He started to ride the white shooting pony again, and was 'none the worse' after one-and-a-half hours.[48] Purdey, the royal gunsmiths, built him an exact wooden replica of his shotguns which was fitted with batteries and lenses, so that he could see where he was firing and practise shooting in his rooms.[49] He experimented with a light twenty-bore gun, but 'shot very badly'.[50] By December he was strong enough to use his normal twelve-bores. 'I got on better,' he wrote after shooting 232 head one day.[51]

The King's convalescence was shadowed by anxiety about Prince George, whose name appears often in the diary. George had become addicted to cocaine and morphine, and David took it upon himself to cure his brother of his craving. He banished Kiki Preston, the pusher from Happy Valley with the silver syringe who had corrupted George,

State portrait of George V in coronation robes by Luke Fildes. In this conventional image, the King's knock knees are ignored.

Left: The Downey Head. George the philatelist king was disappointed with this stamp design, based on a three-quarters face photographed by Downey, which he thought made him look like a monkey.

Right: Coronation photo, 22 June 1911. For Queen Mary in particular the coronation was 'a very real solemn thing.'

George at the helm of *Britannia*. He was an accomplished sailor but when *Britannia* raced, Philip Hunloke, the King's sailing master, always took the helm.

George and May in Delhi, wearing their hot, heavy robes, about to show themselves to the people at the Red Fort. It was George's idea to make a state visit to India and to crown himself in Delhi.

Lavery's 1913 painting of the royal family in the grandeur of the White Drawing Room at Buckingham Palace shows only two of the children, David and Mary. The King and Queen took a special interest in the painting, dabbing on the blue of the Garter ribbon in the artist's studio.

Left: Queen Mary wearing the Vladimiri tiara, which she bought after the death of the Romanov Grand Duchess Vladimir in 1920. The tiara was smuggled out of Russia after the Revolution, and it remains the most prized of Queen Elizabeth's headpieces today. It can be hung with pearls or, as in the photograph, emerald droplets.

Right: Prince John, the youngest of the royal children, who died from epilepsy aged thirteen in 1919.

Wentworth Woodhouse, South Yorkshire, 1912: Queen Mary visits Silverwood Colliery on a trolley to inspect the surface workings.

Above, left: George, wearing a steel helmet, on a visit to the Western Front in 1917, surveying the ruin of the battlefield after the British victory at Wytschaete Ridge.

Above, right: Flouting protocol, George met Lloyd George at Victoria Station on his return from signing the Treaty of Versailles in June 1919 and drove him in his carriage to Buckingham Palace. 'History will not overlook the significance of this act,' wrote Churchill.

Right: Ramsay MacDonald, perhaps George's favourite prime minister and certainly the one he found easiest to deal with.

On Kipling's urging, George made a 'pilgrimage' to the war graves in 1922. Here he inspects the temporary graves of soldiers killed at Passchendaele.

A happy family snap. Prince George and Princess Marina staying at Balmoral after their engagement in 1934. The King wears tweed from top to toe – even his socks.

The King's last visit to the East End. His appearances there were 'like the arrival of Father Christmas,' with a cheerful atmosphere and almost no security.

George made his first Christmas broadcast from Sandringham in 1932. The table was covered in a thick cloth to muffle the sound of rustling papers in the King's shaky hands. His three-minute speech was a triumph.

The King with his shooting pony Jock. He rode Jock when he could no longer walk, right up to his last illness.

King and Queen at the Jubilee, June 1935. 'I'd no idea they felt like that about me,' said the King after driving past the cheering crowds. 'I am beginning to think they must really like me for myself.'

The princes. Left to right: George, Duke of Kent; David, Prince of Wales (in kilt, posing for the camera); Bertie, Duke of York; and Harry, Duke of Gloucester.

On the balcony at the Jubilee. Margaret stands beside George, who jokes with his son-in-law Lord Harewood. Elizabeth is the only one in the group to wave.

and he incarcerated his brother in the country, acting as 'doctor, gaoler and detective combined'.[52] David claimed credit for saving George, but the addiction can hardly have been serious if it was so easily ended. David arrived at Sandringham by plane to report progress to his father, and King George wrote to him: 'I think it was wonderful all you did for him.'[53] Sir Maurice Craig, the pioneering psychiatrist who treated Virginia Woolf, was consulted, and he told the King that George 'was not at all an easy case'.[54] Meanwhile, rumours circulated of a passionate homosexual affair with Noël Coward as well as encounters with an Argentinian diplomat and an Italian aristocrat.[55] The only member of the royal family who 'made any pretensions to be cultivated and well-read – and the only one who wrote an educated hand', Prince George had considerable social charm. But in Lascelles's censorious view, 'the air of a "spoilt child" never quite deserted him'.[56]

Beside the shenanigans of the delinquent dukes of Gloucester and Kent, and the growing realisation of the inadequacy of the Prince of Wales, the Yorks stood out as a shining beacon of domestic rectitude. Their second child was born at Glamis in August 1930. The birth was late, and the waiting was made intolerable by the presence of the obstetricians and the gynaecologist, who stayed at the castle for over a fortnight beforehand. J. R. Clynes, the Labour home secretary, was also stranded, staying nearby with Lady Airlie, determined not to miss his constitutional duty of witnessing the birth of a child in direct line of succession to the throne.

The news of the birth of a second girl, soon to be christened Margaret Rose, was telephoned through to Wigram at Sandringham at 10.15 p.m. on 21 August. When Wigram brought the message to the King and Queen, he said: 'I wish the baby had been a boy and the Queen agreed but the King said, "I am glad it is a girl. One can play with them longer than with boys. The parents are both young and have lots of time to have a son!"'[57]

A boy would have taken precedence over the adored and precocious Princess Elizabeth. Even Churchill thought the little princess had 'an air of authority and reflectiveness astonishing in an infant'.[58] Each morning after breakfast at Buckingham Palace the King fitted his cigarette in its holder and trained his binoculars on Number 145 Piccadilly, where the little Princess Elizabeth waved to him from the window.[59]

The King's sister Louise the Princess Royal died on 4 January 1931. 'A bad beginning for a new year & I feel very depressed,' he wrote.[60] Two weeks later George was 'terribly shocked & grieved' on getting home from shooting to hear of the sudden death of Charles Cust.[61] The King's oldest friend – 'I had known him for 54 years' – Cust was an eccentric figure. 'He walks about with his cloak on & paints flowers in his book,' wrote the King.[62] Cust was the only man who dared complain about the parrot Charlotte at breakfast, and the only man who could answer the King back. 'They used to have tremendous quarrels. They loved each other,' recalled David.[63] Then the King's terrier Snip died – 'I miss him terribly'. [64] Snip was succeeded by another cairn terrier, named Bob.

The worst blow was the death on 31 March 1931 of Lord Stamford-ham, still in service at eighty-one. The Victorian private secretary had steered the monarchy through the two tumultuous decades of George's reign. How much was initiated by Stamfordham, how many decisions were made by the King himself, was never clear: the seamlessness of the relationship is testimony to Stamfordham's success at the job. As Gore wrote, 'in saving his master he forgot himself. Every good idea which emanated from his experience was the King's, every successful outcome or decision he took was at the King's instigation.'[65]

The King was 'quite knocked out' by the blow. His cough was made worse by 'depression & grief' and he took to his bed with a sharp attack of bronchitis.[66] As the Queen remarked, Stamfordham's death left the King in a state of loneliness 'such as comes to a child parting with a devoted Nanny'.[67] On the day of Stamfordham's death, George pro-moted his deputy, 58-year-old Clive Wigram, as private secretary. Almost the first matter that Wigram and the weakened King were called upon to deal with was a homosexual scandal.

Earl Beauchamp was an amiable Liberal peer and politician with close ties to the court. He had served as lord steward of the household (1907–10), he had carried the Sword of State at the coronation of George V, he was made lord lieutenant of Gloucestershire in 1911, and he was appointed lord warden of the Cinque Ports in 1913 and a knight of the Garter in 1914. His homosexuality and in particular his predilection for footmen became a scandal when his brother-in-law Bendor, Duke of Westminster determined to destroy him in 1931.

People turned a blind eye to homosexual affairs so long as they were conducted with discretion, but Beauchamp had become careless.* From Australia, where he travelled in 1930, gossip reached home that the earl

---

*At dinner with Beauchamp Harold Nicolson was asked by an astonished guest: '"Did I hear Beauchamp whisper to the Butler, 'Je t'adore'?" "Nonsense," said Nicolson, "he said 'Shut the door'"' (Paula Byrne, *Mad World: Evelyn Waugh and the Secrets of Brideshead*

was living openly with his nineteen-year-old valet. No doubt the Duke of Westminster was envious of his brother-in-law's public offices as well as his domestic happiness – Beauchamp was a devoted father and, unlike the duke, whose only son had died aged four, he had produced an heir. But, as we have seen, Bendor resented the way in which George V had forced him to resign as lord lieutenant of Cheshire in 1920. He thought he had been treated unfairly by the King, and he regretted his resignation when the Duke of Marlborough refused to surrender his office of lord lieutenant of Oxfordshire after he divorced Consuelo, the first duchess in 1921. Beauchamp's position was still more galling: he continued to attend court, remaining a lord lieutenant and a Garter knight, in spite of flaunting his homosexuality, which, unlike divorce, was illegal.

According to Loelia Ponsonby, who was his wife at the time, Bendor was 'utterly ruthless' in his breaking of his brother-in-law.[68] He hired private detectives to collect evidence of Beauchamp's affairs. He attempted to make Beauchamp's children testify against him (they refused). He forced his sister Lettice, Lady Beauchamp to leave her husband, and he confronted her with brutal evidence of Beauchamp's homosexuality which drove her to a mental breakdown.

The petition of divorce, recently discovered by Paula Byrne, lists the acts of gross indecency committed by Beauchamp with his manservants.[69] The descriptions are 'simply revolting', suggesting to one writer that Bendor paid these men enormous bribes to induce them to swear testimony for legal purposes.[70]

There can be no doubt that Westminster was deeply involved in the destruction of Beauchamp. The conundrum at the heart of the affair is this: was he acting on his own initiative, driven by malice against Beauchamp, or was Beauchamp's downfall instigated by someone else – that is, the King? We may never know the answer. The box marked 'Beauchamp Papers' in the Grosvenor archive was destroyed in 1960.[71] The story has developed a life of its own, morphing into fiction, providing Evelyn Waugh with the material for *Brideshead Revisited*. The feud between the Grosvenor and Lygon families means that there exist two versions of the story.

The version which emanates from the Grosvenor family claims that Bendor acted on behalf of the King. Of course Beauchamp's open homosexuality disqualified him from the court, but (according to the Grosvenor family) the King had another motive: to protect his son Prince George.

(HarperPress, 2009), p. 131). The schoolboy joke was a ruse: Nicolson knew very well that the guest had heard correctly.

Since the summer of 1930 George had been walking out with Beauchamp's daughter Lady Mary (Maimie) Lygon, and there was allegedly talk of an engagement. In hounding the gay earl out of the country, Bendor was helping to avert a scandal which would have been damaging to the royal family.[72]

This story shifts some of the blame away from Bendor, and it was furiously denied by the Lygon family. According to Lady Sibell Lygon, her sister Maimie and Prince George 'did have a fling but no engagement'.[73] The story is not easy to untangle even today, but of the two versions the Lygon one, which blames the vengeful Bendor, seems the more plausible. The Lygons were right to play down the affair between Prince George and Maimie. Certainly Maimie Lygon did not hit the radar of the royal family as Poppy Baring had done. No mention is made in the King's diary of a possible proposal to her. If a proposal had been imminent it would surely have caused alarm. According to Chips Channon, 'she has slept with every man one knows in London . . . she cannot say "no"'.[74] Prince George, as we have seen, was kept under close surveillance in 1929–30. Concern focussed on his drug addiction: Queen Mary reported in February 1930 that Sir Maurice Craig was pleased with his progress, 'but of course he can't go out alone yet, that would be unwise'.[75]

At some point in 1931 Bendor informed the King of Beauchamp's homosexuality. Allegedly George responded: 'I always thought people like that shot themselves.'[76] If George remembered the Cleveland Street gay scandal in which his brother Eddy was implicated, he would have recalled that Lord Arthur Somerset didn't shoot himself; he was forced to leave the country and live in exile to avoid standing trial. The same happened to Beauchamp.

The King wanted to prevent a scandal. The feud involved two aristocratic families with close ties to the court. Bendor's aunt Meg was sister-in-law to Queen Mary and, as we have seen, members of the Grosvenor family clustered thickly round the throne. On the Beauchamp side, the earl's sister Lady Mary Lygon, later Trefusis, had served Queen Mary as lady-in-waiting until her death in 1927 aged fifty-eight. The Queen wrote to Beauchamp saying how much she had valued Lady Mary 'as her best friend as well as her faithful, devoted, clever and wonderful servant, and she is very, very sad'.[77] If Lady Mary had still been alive, she might have prevailed on her sister-in-law not to leave her husband.

The King asked his legal adviser Lord Buckmaster, former lord chancellor, to investigate. On 14 May 1931 Lady Beauchamp, pressured by her brother Bendor, filed the petition for divorce. If the scandal was to be hushed up, Lord Beauchamp would have to leave the country instantly to avoid appearing in court. On 28 May the King noted in his diary: 'Had a long conversation with Crewe on a very unpleasant subject connected with B [*sic*].'[78] 'B' was presumably Beauchamp, and Lord Crewe was the King's friend. This brief and cryptic note is the only reference to the affair in the King's diary. However, on 2 June at the annual Jockey Club dinner at Buckingham Palace – an event which was not a court function, and which the twice-divorced Duke of Westminster was therefore allowed to attend, thanks to his father-in-law Fritz Ponsonby – the King wrote: 'Richmond & Bendor sat on each side of me', a sign that Bendor had been restored to favour.[79]

One warm evening early in June, Lord Beauchamp sat dozing over his embroidery in the garden at Madresfield, his idyllic country house. A motor car drew up, and out stepped three peers, each of them friends of Beauchamp – Lord Crewe, Lord Chesterfield and Lord Stanmore.[80]* They announced that they had been sent by 'the highest authority in the land', that is to say the King. No written account survives of the meeting, but the Lygon children understood that a Home Office warrant for Beauchamp's arrest on the charge of committing acts of gross sexual indecency had been issued, and that he was obliged to leave the country in order to escape prosecution and disgrace.[81]

Beauchamp was forced to sign an undertaking not to return, and on 9 June he fled. The King 'brokered a deal' whereby in exchange for Beauchamp going into exile, Bendor would not press for prosecution. Bendor wrote Beauchamp a note: 'Dear Bugger-in-Law, You got what you deserved.' (This may be apocryphal.)[82] It was the King who had engineered Beauchamp's escape in order to prevent a lurid divorce case. The scandal was effectively buried. Instead of disgracing himself and tarnishing the court, Beauchamp was banished. His nemesis was his brother-in-law, but the King intervened to protect the honour of the court. Arthur Ponsonby (brother of Fritz) summed it up in a conversation with Hugh Dalton (son of the canon) about 'the sad case of Lord Beauchamp, who has had a persistent weakness for footmen ... The King didn't want a scandal because he was a Knight of the Garter!'[83] Fortunately the scandal escaped the newspapers, thanks to Lady Sibell Lygon, who was the mistress of the press magnate Lord Beaverbrook.

---

*Most versions of this story state that three knights of the Garter arrived, but only Crewe and Chesterfield were Garter knights; Lord Stanmore, Liberal chief whip in the Lords, was not a KG.

CHAPTER 27

King George's Last Stand

1931–1932

On 20 August 1931 the King travelled overnight in his special train from Sandringham to Balmoral in a state of uncertainty. As the global economic blizzard of the Great Depression took hold, the fall of the minority Labour government seemed imminent. The number of unemployed increased from one million to three million, exports halved and government revenue fell: Britain was on the verge of bankruptcy. Ramsay MacDonald's Labour government needed to slash spending and balance the budget in order to obtain vital loans from New York, but the Cabinet split over proposals for cuts to the dole. However, when the royal secretaries telephoned Number 10 to confirm whether the King should travel north as planned, they were advised that cancelling the journey 'would only give rise to alarming rumours and cause consternation'.[1]

The King had been concerned for some time about the impending financial crash. The industrialist Arthur Balfour (not to be confused with the Tory politician) had warned of the dangers ahead and suggested a coalition government back in October 1930 in a letter which 'profoundly impressed' the King.[2] Wigram warned the King in July 1931 that 'we are sitting on the top of a volcano': 'If a crash comes in Germany we shall have a financial situation something like that at the outbreak of war … A Minority Government will hardly be able to deal with the situation, and it is quite possible that Your Majesty might be asked to approve of a National Government [that is, a coalition].'[3] That autumn George ordered five new Daimlers, more than any king had ordered before, in an attempt to keep the works in business over the winter months.[4]

The King's private investments were in good shape. Sir Edward Peacock, the self-made Canadian banker who succeeded Lord Revelstoke as head of Barings, managed the King's private portfolio in his Number 4 account. In July he told the King 'how well No. 4 account was getting on in spite of these bad times'.[5]

On 22 August, the day after George reached Balmoral, the Prime Minister's office telephoned to say that it might be necessary to ask the King to return to London. George declared that 'shilly-shallying' on an occasion like this was no use, and he travelled south that night.[6] His special train had already returned, but a railway official managed to locate the King's carriage, which was hitched on to the scheduled over-night train at 11.15, and he slept well in his own very comfortable bed.[7]

The Queen remained at Balmoral. She told George how 'dreadfully sad' she felt at seeing him go without her, 'as we have always been together so far in all the many crises you have had to go through since 1910'. The truth was she was 'furious' that the politicians had made the King go to Balmoral: 'It was too bad your having come all the way here, only to have to return South at once, of course we ought never to have left Sandring-ham with the Government in such a plight, but the Gov. always think of itself first & its own position.'[8] She was even crosser at being left behind, raging (in Lady Bertha Dawkins's account) that she '"will not be left sit-ting on a mountain" which she hates'.[9]

The King reached London at 8.10 a.m. on Sunday 23 August, and received the prime minister at 10.30. Ramsay MacDonald 'looked very rattled' and was 'very gloomy about the situation'.[10] According to Wigram's account, MacDonald told the King that if his colleagues resigned it would be impossible to carry on the government.[11] In his diary MacDonald gave a fuller and very different version of the conversation. He told the King that he intended to resign and

> I [MacDonald] advised him in the meantime to send for the leaders of the other two parties and have them report [the] position from their points of view. He said he would & would advise them strongly to support me. I explained my hopeless Parlty. position . . . He said that he believed I was the only person who could carry the country through. I said that did I share his belief I should not contemplate what I do, but that I did not share it.[12]

MacDonald's diary shows that the first suggestion of a coalition gov-ernment of three parties came from the King, who refused to accept the prime minister's resignation.[13] According to Wigram, however, the first person to mention a national government under MacDonald was not the monarch but the deputy Liberal leader, Sir Herbert Samuel, whom the King saw next at 12.30. (Lloyd George, the official Liberal leader, was ill.) Wigram's narrative of the crisis continues: 'His Majesty thought that Sir Herbert Samuel had given a very clear exposition of the situ-ation, and explained the necessity for a National Government.'[14] At 3 p.m. the King saw Stanley Baldwin, who as a loyal Tory had no choice but to obey his sovereign's command to serve under MacDonald, even though as leader of the second largest party in the House of Commons he might reasonably have expected the King to ask him to form a government. 'The King was greatly pleased with Mr Baldwin's readiness to meet the crisis which had arisen; and to sink Party interests for the sake of the Country,' wrote Wigram.[15]

That evening Peacock dined with the King, and briefed him on the financial crisis. 'We had an interesting talk,' wrote George.[16] After dinner Peacock telephoned the Bank of England to discover whether the American bankers were prepared to bail out the government.[17] Meanwhile, at Number 10 Ramsay MacDonald failed once more to persuade the Cabinet to agree to cuts, and eight ministers resigned. At 10 p.m. MacDonald telephoned Buckingham Palace to say that he wished to see the King. 'I'm off to the Palace to throw in my hand,' he said.[18] Looking 'scared and unbalanced' (according to Wigram), the prime minister told the King that 'all was up', and he had no alternative but to resign. For the second time – if we believe MacDonald's version of events on 23 August, that it was the King and not Herbert Samuel who first suggested a national government – the King told him that 'he was the only man to lead the country through this crisis' and hoped he would reconsider.[19] At MacDonald's request, the King agreed to hold a meeting the next day with the three party leaders 'to see what can be done'.[20]

MacDonald was conflicted. He minded deeply breaking with the Labour Party, but he was a snob and sensitive to royalty. According to his secretary, when on 23 August 1931 'the King put his arm on his shoulder it was too much for him … he had an almost mystic feeling about his own position, regarding it as the decree of destiny that he should remain Prime Minister and leave his party'.[21]

At the conference with Baldwin, Samuel and MacDonald at ten the following morning (24 August) at Buckingham Palace, the King asked MacDonald for the third time to stay on as prime minister. 'The King assured the Prime Minister that, remaining at his post, his position and reputation would be much more enhanced than if he surrendered the government of the country at such a crisis.'[22] The King virtually instructed the three leaders to form a national government. He left the room at 10.35 a.m., and when he was asked to return at 11.45 by the party leaders they had obediently drawn up terms.

After the meeting, the King told Godfrey-Faussett: 'MacDonald has burnt his boats and can never be Labour Prime Minister again but he has acted in the only right and strong way by [sic] the good of the Country.'[23] George's role in this was clear. As one authority wrote: 'Had the King simply accepted MacDonald's resignation, either there would have been no National Government, or, if there had been, it would not have been led by MacDonald.' As MacDonald's diary reveals, the King was 'not merely the facilitator of the National Government, but the instigator of it'.[24]

At Balmoral the Queen watched events anxiously, keeping Lady Bertha tightly in attendance. She worried about Buckingham Palace, where the rooms were being repapered, and there were no taps on the King's bath.[25] Lady Bertha was with the Queen nearly the whole day on 24 August, 'and she was very kind in telling me what she knew by letter & telephone'. It is all very exciting, wrote Lady Bertha, 'as it has been such a race against time', with only a few hours between England and bankruptcy.[26] Setting aside Lady Gwendolen Cecil's life of Lord Salisbury, which she had been reading to the Queen for four hours each day, Lady Bertha now read aloud from the Scottish papers and *The Times*, pausing only when the King telephoned, which he did 'at length every day'.[27]

When the outgoing Labour minister J. R. Clynes surrendered his seals of office to the King at Buckingham Palace on 26 August, he thought 'his face looked grey and lined'.[28] The King held a council to swear in his new Cabinet, and then returned to Balmoral. 'Felt rather tired,' he wrote.[29] However, Lady Bertha found him 'very well & vigorous ... I really think he is all the better for having been able to play the Sovereign for once, & give a lead to his rattled Minister[s]!'[30] Ethel Snowden, wife of chancellor of the Exchequer Philip Snowden, the Queen's friend in the Labour Party, wrote to 'Your Majesty, Dearest Ma'am' to say: 'The K will have told Your Majesty everything which is pertinent to the present political situation. What he will not have told you, for he cannot know, is how enormously his already great prestige has been enhanced by his coming to London to help.'[31]

Clive Wigram, who was a talented games player, likened the making of the National Government to a Test match. 'Our Captain (the King) played one of his best innings with a very straight bat. He stopped the rot and saved his side.' For Wigram this was his first test as private secretary. 'I went in pale but determined,' he wrote.[32] A sense of his nervousness can be glimpsed from the file. Beside Lord Stamfordham's magisterial confidence and bold black ink, Wigram seems uncertain, perhaps out of his depth. As one observer wrote, he 'is always very genial, but it seems to take a good deal to make him understand things'.[33]

In summing up his impressions of the crisis, Wigram opined that when the history came to be written, everyone would acclaim 'the calm, impartial, constitutional part the King had played in saving the country from ruin'.[34] The King himself certainly considered that he had acted constitutionally. 'I have only done my duty,' he told Archbishop Cosmo Lang. 'Nothing could have been nicer than the leaders of the three parties were, when I [sic] suggested the formation immediately of a National Govt.'[35]

Constitutional questions continued to nag, however. Had the King acted constitutionally in virtually ordering Ramsay MacDonald to stay on as prime minister after he lost the support of his own party? Acting as the instigator of the National Government was hardly consistent with Bagehot's three rights of a constitutional sovereign – the right to be consulted, the right to encourage, the right to warn.

From the Marxist wing of the Labour Party, Harold Laski argued in 1932 that the National Government was born of a Palace revolution 'brilliantly concealed' from the public. MacDonald was appointed not because of his party support, which had disintegrated, but because he was the King's favourite. Just as George III had appointed his favourite Lord Bute prime minister, MacDonald was in office merely as a person, not as a representative leader.[36]

Harold Nicolson considered the appointment of the National Government 'the most controversial incident in the whole Reign'.[37] The crisis had taken place only eighteen years before he began his book, and he was concerned about confidentiality. Many of the protagonists were still alive, and Nicolson managed to interview several of them. He wrote a draft chapter on 1931 at the start of his research which he submitted to the Cabinet secretary, Sir Norman Brook, asking for permission to quote from Cabinet minutes.[38] Nicolson found the file in the Windsor archives 'far more informative than I expected. It is quite clear that MacDonald lost his head, that Arthur Henderson headed a revolt against him, that Samuel persuaded the King to press for a National Government and that the latter (although acting quite constitutionally) really did decide the matter.'[39] Nicolson, however, did not have access to Ramsay MacDonald's diary, which showed that the idea of the National Government originated with the King, and not with Herbert Samuel.

The royal advisers remained nervous. In 1965 when Keith Middlemas asked to see the papers for his biography of Baldwin, he was blocked from accessing the 1931 file. 'I think better not,' wrote one adviser. 'This is very confidential inter private secretary stuff.'[40]

The rights and wrongs of George V's intervention in 1931 continue to be debated. One view is that the King's action was questionable because it ignored the crucial role played by political parties in forming a modern democratic government. Ramsay MacDonald was appointed prime minister as a person, and not as the representative of a party.[41] However, the debate is largely academic. The appointment of MacDonald did not set a precedent. It was not the prelude to a resurgence of royal power. The part played by the Crown in the formation of governments has become a passive one. For the monarch to initiate a coalition in the way that George V did is unimaginable today. Nor do we consider the formation of the National Government the most controversial event of the reign. Most people view the refusal of asylum to the Romanovs as George's dirtiest deed.

The appointment of the National Government was the right thing to do in the circumstances of the 1931 economic catastrophe. The alternative was to ask Baldwin to form a coalition government, which would have caused uncertainty and delay leading to a drain of gold. The crisis of 1931 was an episode of panic bordering on hysteria, and the King's leadership helped to restore calm and confidence.

From Balmoral, the King watched the political situation with dismay. He found it 'very worrying & quite spoils my holiday'.[42] Sister Agnes arrived and kept the King amused, 'striding over the heather wearing bright mauve and an orange wig'.[43] Lady Bertha, who couldn't abide Sister Agnes, noted that 'behind her back, we all laugh at her'.[44] The Yorks came to stay, bringing with them the two little princesses, and George found Lilibet 'delightful and full of conversation'.[45] Lady Bertha waspishly remarked that 'Lilibet is no longer pretty, her face is long & lanky', while Margaret 'is not really pretty, but has good eyes'.[46]

At Balmoral, talk about politics was not allowed, and 'one got away from the usual melancholy conversation of "how can one economise"'.[47] In private, however, people spoke about little else but the new taxes introduced by the National Government. The Duchess of York told Queen Mary: 'I really feel rather worried about everything, Mama. The world is in such a bad way.'[48]

The King volunteered to take a cut in the Civil List of £50,000 (£3.4 million in today's values). This gave a 'splendid' lead to the nation and, according to Peacock, 'struck the imagination of everyone, and has already done a great deal of good'.[49] George could afford to make this generous gesture because, under Peacock's management, his private investments had flourished. But he introduced economies nonetheless. He gave up the shooting in Windsor Great Park, 'as I can't afford it, I am sorry as the birds fly so well there'.[50] Ethel Snowden told the Queen: 'With what pride we read the announcement of the lead given by the King and other members of the Royal family in the Economy campaign. It has put to shame those false leaders of the people who are capable of shame.'[51]

The National Government was supported by only a handful of Labour MPs. Led by Arthur Henderson, the Labour Party broke away, and MacDonald, Snowden and Thomas were expelled from the party. The King anticipated 'hectic' times in the House of Commons. He sent a message to the Serjeant-at-Arms that 'he should always have at least six stalwart constables at hand to do any chucking out required instead of using the proper attendants – all of whom were old and . . . stout'.[52] Wigram took fright at this attempt to interfere, remembering the rebuke Stamfordham had received in 1925 from Baldwin, who had made it very clear 'that the House of Commons could do and act as they liked, and to all intents and purposes it was no business of the Sovereign's to comment on what happened in the House of Commons'.[53] Fortunately Colin Keppel, the Serjeant-at-Arms, was 'particularly discreet and experienced and would never mention HM's name'.[54] The matter was quietly buried, but it shows how high the King's anxiety levels were running.

As the situation worsened, Wigram began using cricket metaphors once more, a sure sign of alarm. 'I foresee that the King will still have some sticky wickets to bat on,' he wrote, 'but I am sure that he will play as fine a game as he did at the end of last month.'[55] He was soon proved right. On 15–16 September the Atlantic fleet at Invergordon staged a strike against pay cuts which the newspapers described as a mutiny. George was 'much put out' by the disturbances but not unduly worried: 'I suppose the rotten press have telegraphed all over the world, "mutiny in British Navy", this sort of thing does harm to the old country abroad, & merely because the matter has been badly handled.'[56]

Invergordon caused a stock-market panic, and a further run on the banks. The King held a council on 20 September (not announced in the press) to enable a bank holiday to be declared 'any day next week' if the run on the Bank of England by foreign countries continued. 'The situation is an anxious one,' he wrote.[57] On 21 September Britain was forced to abandon the gold standard – this had been widely dreaded, but rather than a disaster it turned out to have a positive effect on the economy, as the depreciation of sterling helped exports.

Wigram worried whether the King should return to London immediately in view of the crisis. He asked Peacock – on whose advice the King was increasingly reliant – and Peacock counselled against:

His Majesty's sudden return on his own initiative some time ago was just the right thing and made all the difference. On this occasion it seems to me the circumstances call for the other course, as a sudden return might cause alarm at a moment when we wish to adhere as nearly as may be to the normal course of events.[58]

The King complied.

The King returned to London on 29 September, and saw Ramsay Mac-Donald at 2.25 p.m. for thirty-five minutes. 'We talked about a general election,' he wrote, 'the National Government making the appeal to the electors.'[59] This was a departure from what had been publicly agreed when the National Government was set up – namely, that once emergency meas-ures had been passed to restore confidence in the economy, an election would take place which each party would fight 'on its own lines'.[60] As the so-called guardian of the National Government, the King might have been expected to follow the agreement and urge an election on party lines, but he did nothing of the sort.[61] He told MacDonald that 'party differences should be sunk. If a Socialist Government came into power and carried out their extravagant promises to the electorate, this country would be finished.' Once more he flattered MacDonald: 'The King was sure that his present Prime Minister was the only man who could save the country, and His Majesty himself was prepared to support him.'[62]

When the King saw Baldwin and discussed a national appeal to restore the stability of the country, 'no one could have been nicer'.[63] The Tories stood to gain from such an election. The Liberals did not. When the King saw Sir Herbert Samuel, he was 'quite impossible, most obstin-ate', refusing to accept the National Government's policy of tariffs. 'God knows what can be done!' wrote George. 'Am much worried by political situation & I can't see a way out.'[64] Once again, his solution was to put pressure on MacDonald. On 3 October MacDonald told him that the Conservatives and Liberals were deadlocked, and 'he had better clear out'. The King replied that 'he must at all costs find the solu-tion himself, and His Majesty would refuse to accept his resignation'. This was the fourth time that the King had refused to allow MacDonald to resign. The prime minister 'must brace himself up to realise he was the only person who could tackle the present chaotic state of affairs'.[65]

At 8.30 a.m. on 6 October Ramsay MacDonald rang Buckingham Palace and asked to see the King as soon as possible. At 9.15 he told the King that the Cabinet had agreed late the night before to fight the elec-tion on a so-called doctor's mandate, allowing MacDonald to use any measures he thought fit to stabilise the country.[66] 'I am very pleased & congratulated him,' wrote the King.[67]

At the election on 27 October the National Government won a landslide of 554 seats. Of these 470 were Tories. For Labour it was a disaster. The Labour opposition was reduced to fifty-two MPs. The Liberals did even worse, winning only thirty-two seats. The election realigned the party system, establishing the Tories as the party of government.

The King's insistence on MacDonald staying in office was partly for personal reasons. He found MacDonald easier to deal with than Baldwin. He 'understood and liked Ramsay far more than he liked Baldwin'.[68] In George's eyes, MacDonald resembled a Highland servant or ghillie – a relationship they both understood. There were echoes here of Queen Victoria's friendship with her servant John Brown. But in urging MacDonald to go to the country at the head of the National Government, the King made an astute electoral calculation. A Tory government would have been perceived by Labour voters as a bankers' government. MacDonald was reviled as Judas for deserting his followers by the Labour parliamentary party, but his charismatic leadership still counted among working-class voters.

In the 1931 election, Labour lost all but two of the eleven Durham mining constituencies. Probably the most important factor in the collapse of the Labour vote was the Labour government's failure to redeem its promise to cure unemployment. But MacDonald himself was returned with a majority of 6,000 in his Durham constituency of Seaham, a personal vote of confidence (his constituency association had fired him) and a vote for the National Labour Party which he had founded. Some likened him to Lenin, the leader of the mute working class.[69] But MacDonald the people's hero was also the King's favourite; he was Lenin rolled into John Brown.

On polling day the King and Queen dined alone: 'We listened to the returns of the elections on the wireless, which made us happy, as the National Government have won seats everywhere.'[70] The next day George wrote: 'I am indeed happy at the results of this election, and please God I shall have a little peace & less worries.'[71]

By strange coincidence, the King and Queen attended Noël Coward's *Cavalcade* at Drury Lane the day after the election. Coward's patriotic pageant of the years 1900 to 1930 ends with the Union Jack and 'God Save the King'. George thought it 'very interesting & well done; we got a wonderful reception from a crowded house, which sang the National Anthem at the end'.[72]

No sooner had the King dealt with the political crisis than he was forced to accept unsettling changes in the constitution of the empire. At the time of his accession he had declared that his mission as monarch would be to promote tighter bonds between the mother country and the empire. The war and its aftermath had diverted him, and he was forced to focus on domestic issues. Disliking travel, he declined to visit the dominions after 1918, and the Prince of Wales made spectacular tours in his stead. Nevertheless, the King corresponded regularly and at length with the viceroys and the governors-general, and he played an active part in making new appointments. No British monarch was so well informed about the empire and its people.

The Statute of Westminster of 1931 gave the dominions – Australia, Canada, the Irish Free State, New Zealand, Newfoundland and South Africa – legislative autonomy and established the principle of the Commonwealth nations' direct allegiance to the Crown.* The King disliked the new constitution because it clipped his power to appoint governors-general. Leo Amery, the colonial secretary, lunched with the King to discuss the constitutional changes. He found 'a George III atmosphere' at Buckingham Palace. The King was 'more talkative not to say noisy than usual' and 'quite incapable of understanding that the Governor General is no longer the British Government's representative'.[73]

When the Australian prime minister James Scullin nominated an Australian, Isaac Isaacs, for the post of governor-general, and claimed to be acting in accordance with the new principles, the King was furious. He was accustomed to choosing governors-general from a list submitted by the British prime minister of royals, aristocrats and public servants, and he resented Scullin's challenge to his patronage. Scullin had an audience with the King. 'He argued with me for some time, he is vain, obstinate & narrow-minded,' wrote George, '& with great reluctance I had to approve of the appointment, I should think it will be very unpopular in Australia.'[74] It was. The next governor-general was a British aristocrat, Lord Gowrie.

There was a positive side to the Statute of Westminster, though the King was slow to see it. The direct link of the Crown to the Commonwealth nations gave the monarch a new role as head of the Commonwealth. As Leo Amery remarked, 'King George was not an imaginative man; it took him some time before he grasped the fact that the Statute of Westminster would increase the importance of the Crown'.[75]

Still more upsetting to the King was the rise of Indian nationalism

---

*The Statute of Westminster gave effect to the so-called Balfour formula, which was agreed at the Imperial Conference of 1926, and which declared the dominions to be autonomous communities within the British Empire, equal in status and united by common allegiance to the Crown.

and the success of Mahatma Gandhi's civil disobedience campaign. British attempts to grant dominion status to India were undermined by Gandhi's refusal to co-operate. George was not a diehard, and he welcomed the 1930 Simon Report, which proposed a federation of self-governing states. When Viceroy Lord Irwin held negotiations with Gandhi, the King congratulated him for bringing about a temporary truce which 'no one but you could have achieved'.[76]

In November 1931 Gandhi came to London for the Indian Round Table Conference, and Samuel Hoare, the Indian secretary, asked the King whether he would receive him. 'What!' roared George. 'Have this rebel fakir in the Palace after he has been behind all these attacks on my loyal officers?'[77] Nevertheless, the King at once assumed that Gandhi would be invited. At the party, the King spoke to Gandhi, who stood out wearing dhoti and sandals among the black morning coats. Hoare became nervous when he saw the monarch glaring resentfully at Gandhi's bare knees, and when Gandhi took his leave the King couldn't resist warning him: 'Remember, Mr Gandhi, I won't have any attacks on my Empire!' To which Gandhi diplomatically replied: 'I must not be drawn into a political argument in Your Majesty's Palace after receiving Your Majesty's hospitality.'[78]

The King was instrumental in securing the appointment of Lord Willingdon as viceroy of India in 1931. He telephoned personally to Willingdon in Canada, where he was governor-general, insisting on his becoming viceroy. The call was put through at midnight, and Willingdon said he must first consult his wife. 'Tell her from me,' said George, 'that she will have a good smacking if she refuses.'[79] Perhaps George was joking, but the context was hardly jocular, and the threat of violence towards a wife certainly hints at a disturbing view of marriage, even if he behaved with perfect decorum towards Queen Mary. When civil disobedience broke out once more, Willingdon ordered Gandhi's arrest, thus ending the attempt to co-operate.

On fine mornings, the King rode before breakfast in Hyde Park. To avoid the crowds, his horse was brought for him to mount in the gardens of Rangers Lodge, the grace-and-favour house of Bryan Godfrey-Faussett in the park. For the Godfrey-Faussett family the arrival at an early hour of several horses with grooms, a royal Daimler containing the King, the riders accompanying him and a bevy of policemen was not a welcome sight, especially as the King's temper was famously bad before breakfast. If Godfrey-Faussett was at home, his family stayed in their beds, but if he was away the family either drew lots to choose which of them was to greet the King or pretended to be asleep. Peeping out on one occasion when they had decided all to stay hidden, they spied the irate monarch prowling round the house, looking into the downstairs windows and evidently longing to bang on the front door.[80]

He was terrified of catching cold, and he was said to 'fly into a rage if anyone coughs or sneezes in his presence'.[81] George Lascelles, his eight-year-old grandson, suffered from hay fever and when he went to say goodbye to his grandfather one day in April 1931, he started to sneeze. 'Get that damn child away from me,' shouted the King which, as Lascelles later wrote, 'made rather a strong impression on an awakening imagination'.[82]

Christmas 1931 was made miserable by a cold. 'I never went out of my rooms, feel very depressed,' wrote George.[83] When after two weeks he eventually ventured out shooting, riding his white shooting pony, Jock, he wrote: 'I was so cold that I went home after luncheon, alas I can't walk now & therefore get warm.'[84] His only consolation, as usual, was playing with the 'sweet little grandchildren' Lilibet and Margaret (who didn't sneeze). 'I shall miss them dreadfully,' he wrote when they left.[85]

On the Thursday before Easter 1932 the King and Queen attended the Royal Maundy service at Westminster Abbey. For the first and only time in his reign, the King distributed the money in little red and white bags to the sixty-six old men and sixty-six old women, one for each year of the King's age, lined up in the abbey. 'James II was the last King who performed the rite in 1685,' wrote George, who attended at the suggestion of his cousin Marie Louise.[86] The ceremony originated in the medieval ritual of the monarch washing the feet of twelve old men as the servant of his people. George's presence, said *The Times*, was 'the fitting symbolic expression of his attitude to his people'.[87] No doubt the King drew comfort from it, but this ancient ritual symbolising the divine right of kings was hardly calculated to relieve the mass unemployment of almost three million workers.

There was a growing sense that George's monarchy was out of touch and outdated. He had nothing to say to the legions of unemployed, the dejected men gathering at street corners in boarded-up northern manufacturing towns and pit villages. Even Queen Mary, the *grande dame* of charity, was discombobulated by the marches of hungry men who invaded London. 'We did not go out on account of the "Hunger Marchers" – Procession to the Hse of Commons,' she wrote on 21 October 1932, the day the biggest hunger march reached London to be met by massed police and scenes of violence. 'Apparently it was a failure.'[88]

To his credit, the Prince of Wales attempted to reach out. A speech at the Royal Albert Hall (27 January 1932) appealing for voluntary efforts to relieve unemployment made a remarkable impact. Within a year 2,300 clubs, canteens and playing fields had appeared. The prince followed up with tours of slums and mining villages.[89] Sometimes in working-men's clubs he met with a 'reproachful, almost sullen silence', a new experience for a prince accustomed to cheers. 'But I had the feeling that empty as was my mission, my appearance among them was in large measure appreciated and taken as a sign that the Monarchy had not forgotten them in their misfortunes.'[90]

The King attempted to make contact with his people too. On Christmas Day 1932 George wrote in his diary: 'At 3.35 I broadcasted a short message of 251 words to the whole Empire from Francis' room.'[91] He sat at a table in Lord Knollys's ugly little office underneath the stairs at 3.35 Sandringham time, which was 3.05 GMT.[92] At Sandringham the clocks ran thirty minutes fast to allow more daylight for shooting, as they had in King Edward's day. A thick cloth was spread over the table to muffle the noise of rustling paper as the King's hands shook with nerves.

The broadcast was the brainchild of Sir John Reith, the first director-general of the BBC, who had been pressing the King to address his people for some years. George disliked the idea. When Wigram tried to persuade him to broadcast in 1932, he replied that Wigram was 'too modern', and he agreed to speak only when the prime minister endorsed the proposal.[93]

The three-minute speech was a triumph. 'The King spoke more personally and effectively than I had ever heard him,' wrote Reith.[94] Never before had the King's voice been heard by so many. One critic thought it 'such an odd, hoarse voice as if roughened by weather'.[95] Harold Nicolson considered it 'very virile, rather bronchial, very emphatic'. The royal voice was not aristocratic. Nicolson noted the 'closed "o" as in "those"', which he thought was 'what the BBC call "off white" meaning thereby slightly Cockney'.[96]

Kipling, the King's trumpeter, wrote the words. The speech began with an appeal for the unity of the empire, but it came alive when the King said: 'My life's aim has been to serve ... I speak now from my home and from my heart to you all; to men and women so cut off by the snows, the desert or the seas, that only voices out of the air can reach them.'[97]

Kipling wept when he heard the King intone his words, listening to the wireless at his home.[98] The speech conjured a picture of the grandfather king, sitting beside his fire, speaking to his people – an image of a family man that was both domestic and intimate.[99] At Sandringham, however, things were far from homely. The Prince of Wales, who had heard several rehearsals of the speech, disappeared into the garden when the King made his broadcast. 'I confess I was rather hurt that you should have gone out to play golf just when I made my short broadcast,' complained the King.[100]

CHAPTER 28

That Woman!

1933–1935

The entries in George's diary become briefer and more perfunctory during the 1930s, chronicling his failing health. Far more business-like than most people realised, he continued to work conscientiously on his boxes, measuring his days by the clocks which chimed in unison on the mantelpieces of all his palaces (except Sandringham, where they ran fast). 'Don't feel too grand,' he wrote one day in 1933, 'did my work as usual.'[1] He rarely went out when the weather was bad. At Sandringham in January 1933 the lake froze and he tried to skate, but 'my ankles hurt so much I soon gave it up.'[2] Two days later: 'I never went out, so I read "Uncle Tom's Cabin" all day.'[3] In the summer of 1933 George was too unwell to attend four of the five courts of the Season.[4]

Little wonder that some writers have concluded that the King's last years were a time of unremitting gloom, when he was depressed, 'discouraged and perplexed'.[5] But there was another side to the King – bluff, jovial, even funny. As he told his stories, the Queen Mother recalled, 'he would bang you on the arm. By the end of the visit it would be black and blue.'[6] He liked his family to join him in his dressing room ten minutes before dinner to watch his ritual dressing. Like a baroque sovereign, 'he would put a little scent on his handkerchief, and wind up all his watches'.[7] His drives through the East End resembled the arrival of Father Christmas, with a cheerful atmosphere, people holding up little children and almost no security.[8] At Balmoral in 1932, Neville Chamberlain found him 'in great form, shouting and guffawing away'.[9] Sometimes he went too far. At Windsor he would look down on the public visiting the terraces below and make rude comments in a loud voice about women wearing trousers or bobbed hair, until the Queen, 'embarrassed beyond endurance, called upon him peremptorily to be silent. He obeyed with a guilty smile'.[10]

Lord Crawford recorded a surreal tea party given by Philip Sassoon in 1932. The King was offered a boiled egg, tactfully prepared in anticipation, and he refused it. Sassoon 'got more and more fussy, we all laughed':

Some wonderful grouse sandwiches arrived, the King refused them because he could not stop eating haddock sandwiches: more laughter, and then I suddenly realised I was in the noisiest party I could recall. The whole house might have shaken with the shindy which reached its height when the King denounced the new tariffs which caused him to pay an extra ten per cent on any foreign stamps ... I confess I was immensely amused though nothing witty was said from beginning to end. I am quite sure the King was thoroughly amused (with himself).[11]

One Sunday in March 1934 the King and Queen descended on the National Gallery. This was the first ever visit by a reigning monarch, but the trustees were not invited. The ostensible reason was to see the pictures, but the King thought little of them, waving his stick at a Cézanne and declaring that 'Turner was *mad*, my grandmother always said so'. The King's real purpose was to recruit the gallery's thirty-year-old superstar director, Kenneth Clark, to become surveyor of the King's pictures. Clark had been hotly tipped by the royal librarian, Owen Morshead, but he declined the post, so the King went to Trafalgar Square and offered it to him in person.

'Why won't you come and work for me?'
'Because I wouldn't have time to do the job properly.'
The King snorted with benevolent rage: 'What is there to do?'
'Well, sir, the pictures need looking after.'
'There's nothing wrong with them.'
'And people write letters asking for information about them.'
'Don't answer them. *I want you to take the job*.'[12]

And so of course he did. Clark found the Queen stiff and the King 'much jollier'; he recalled that 'staying at Windsor was the best thing in the world'.[13]

The King's views on art were robust. At the opening of the Tate Gallery in 1926 he called out to the Queen, 'May, here's something to make you laugh.' It was a Cézanne.[14] Of the Royal Academy Summer Exhibition in 1931 he remarked: 'I never saw a worse lot of pictures, modern art is becoming awful I think.'[15] When Augustus John was elected an academician and the King had to sign the diploma, he exclaimed: 'What, *that* fellow; I've a damn good mind not to sign it!'[16]

Perhaps the most surprising thing about the King's last years is that he became a dedicated reader. George V was an even more unlikely royal bookworm than Elizabeth II, as portrayed in Alan Bennett's novella *The*

Uncommon Reader (2006). Wits joked about his philistinism. When H. H. Asquith's private secretary telephoned the palace to say that it was Thomas Hardy's seventieth birthday and he might appreciate a telegram, the royal congratulations were sent to a bemused Hardy of Alnwick, the maker of the King's fishing rods.[17]*

The role of supplying the monarch's unwonted and worrying appetite for books was played by the royal librarian, Owen Morshead. At Buckingham Palace the King would sit in his north-facing study, reading in a low armchair with his back to the window. The man who once wrote 'People who write books ought to be shut up' was now a voracious reader.[18]

The King read 159 books in 1933–5, an average of one book a week, and each title was listed in the notebook recording 'Books I Have Read' which he had kept since 1890.[19] One surprising item on the list is *Lady Chatterley's Lover*, which was smuggled in by Lady Cynthia Colville, who gave it to the Queen to read. In a towering rage, the King snatched the 'disgusting thing' from the Queen, and was soon discovered reading it himself. When Prince George laughed at him, he flung it into the fire.[20]

The King had mellowed. Books on royal subjects no longer provoked explosions of kingly wrath. Of Philip Guedalla's edition of Queen Victoria's outrageous letters to Gladstone, he merely remarked: 'Rather a pity raking out all my Grandmother's letters to old Gladstone I think, but perhaps I'm getting old-fashioned.' Of E. F. Benson's slim volume on Edward VII he observed: 'Amusing writer, but I didn't find that a very nice book I'm sorry to say.'[21]

Books about the Great War were another matter. The King deplored the publication of material relating to contentious episodes. When he learnt of Lloyd George's decision to publish his war memoirs, he asked Maurice Hankey, the Cabinet secretary, to dissuade him. 'He can go to hell,' Lloyd George retorted. 'I owe him nothing. He owes his throne to me.'[22]

In 1934 Lloyd George submitted his memoirs to the Cabinet secretary for approval. Hankey objected to the chapter on the failure to offer asylum to the Tsar. He worried about Lloyd George's account of the change of mind, and he had reservations about revealing the strength of feeling against the monarchy in 1917. This he thought would 'carry little conviction to the public who will not readily believe that there was any real danger to the throne here' – a comment which shows how much stronger the monarchy had grown since the war.[23] Objections were made on behalf of the court by Wigram, described by Lloyd George as 'very jumpy

---

*To be fair, George had read *Tess of the d'Urbervilles* back in 1892.

and nervy'.[24] The Cabinet Office recommended that Lloyd George's entire chapter on asylum for the Romanovs should be suppressed for fear of upsetting the King. Two months later Lloyd George wrote a new chapter omitting all reference to the King, and stating that the invitation was not withdrawn, but the Russian government decided the matter by preventing the Tsar's departure.[25] Lloyd George's rewriting of history to protect the King went down well. The King read all six volumes of the memoirs and found them very interesting. 'You see, he's written in them (look there's his handwriting) and very kindly too, I must say.'[26]

The King protected the reputation of the officers he had supported. Over the Battle of Jutland, he took the side of Admiral Beatty, and declared himself 'disgusted' by Sir Reginald Bacon's *Jutland Scandal* (1925), a pro-Jellicoe account which 'criticises and runs down Beatty the whole way through, & can only do harm, a great pity he ever wrote it'.[27] The King ordered Godfrey-Faussett to read the book and report back. Godfrey-Faussett dutifully obeyed, in spite of the fact that his wife Eugenie, always known as 'Babs', who was one of the racier members of George's court, had been Beatty's mistress for the past seven years.

A still more controversial subject was Earl Haig, who died suddenly in 1928 at a moment when his reputation was coming under attack. The King had been a staunch supporter of Haig, playing a key part in his appointment as commander-in-chief, and the choice of Haig's biographer was a political question in which Buckingham Palace had an interest. It was complicated by Haig's widow Doris, who was in possession of the C-in-C's war diaries which were known to be dynamite, and who was trying to do what her husband would have wished, which was to publish the diaries in full.

Wigram intervened on behalf of the King, and told the trustees of Haig's estate that if Lady Haig tried to publish the diaries, 'I hope you will take out an injunction against her'.[28] (Not until 1952 did a volume of lengthy extracts from the diaries appear, under the title *The Private Papers of Douglas Haig*.) Duff Cooper was appointed official biographer, and he found Lady Haig 'half sane and impossible to deal with'.[29] Lady Haig at first agreed to Cooper's appointment, then changed her mind and decided to bring out her own memoir. 'I need hardly say how sorry His Majesty is to hear that . . . Lady Haig wishes to publish,' wrote Wigram.[30] Undaunted by the royal disapproval, Lady Haig worked obsessively, 'typing and correcting – never even changing her dress for dinner' (this last made her family think she really *was* mad).[31] In spite of a legal battle with Cooper, she published *The Man I Knew* in 1936. It is hard not to feel sorry for Doris Haig, persecuted by lawyers and demoralised by royal bullying. The King does not emerge with glory from this episode – the less so as Lady Haig had once been a maid of honour and a favourite of Queen Alexandra.

King George never much liked Windsor until the end of his life. When he caught cold and stayed indoors, he would spend hours in the Library, looking at the treasures of the Royal Collection.[32] Morshead marvelled that 'one with his limitations should have taken such an interest in the Library'. The King was not an educated man, but like King George III he had 'a great sense of kingship' and felt that the Crown's possessions should be cherished and increased.[33]

The Library occupied the rooms which had once been the bachelor quarters where King George III had been confined during his madness. Each morning the mad monarch would toddle to the window and salute, and the ensign would call 'eyes right'. A week after George III's death there he was. The ensign hesitated and then called 'eyes right'. The ghost saluted. Morshead once asked the King if the story was true. He replied: 'Perfectly. I was told of it by the ensign in question.'[34] Nor was this impossible: suppose the ensign was born in 1800, the episode took place in 1820 and he told King George in 1884.

Windsor gave the King a sense of connectedness with his ancestors which none of his other residences could match. George's sitting room at Windsor was the blue room where George IV, William IV and Prince Albert had all died. After Albert's death, Queen Victoria preserved it as a death chamber for forty years, with everything in the place it had been when the prince died. George V insisted on keeping the room exactly as it was when his father died. Once a housemaid put things back in the wrong place and the King erupted in a Hanoverian rage and summoned the housekeeper, Mrs Rawlings. Like everyone else in his service, Mrs Rawlings was devoted to him 'even (or perhaps especially) in his tantrums', and she sensibly suggested that the room should be photographed.[35]

Richard Molyneux, who acted as the Queen's adviser on matters of taste, recorded in his diary days at Windsor spent moving carpets or furniture with the Queen, sparring with her over the discarding of gilded statuettes from the Guard Room or reorganising the furniture in the Van Dyck Room ('got rid of awful sofa and ghastly coal box').[36] He persuaded the King and Queen to agree to his suggestions for hanging paintings, arranging china or repositioning bronzes. 'We had trouble with the Queen moving bronzes', but next day she was friendly again.[37]

This ritual moving of precious things happened year after year. The stakes were high. Once Molyneux rearranged all the objects in the Green Drawing Room. The King, upset by his possessions being disturbed, was 'furious, and ordered them all to be put back as they had been'.[38] Night after night of the Easter Windsor court, Molyneux recorded wearisome dinners, followed by 'fun' and 'wild rags' in the corridor with the Yorks and the Harewoods after the King and Queen had gone to bed at 10.30.[39] The court was enlivened by the mischievous 'little Duchess' of York, the patron of the Windsor Wets, a secret society dedicated to drinking wine. Molyneux was treasurer, and their motto was *Aqua vitae, non aqua pura*.[40]

Six miles from Windsor castle, on the other side of Windsor Great Park, stands Fort Belvedere, a castellated folly built by Jeffry Wyatville for George IV. In 1929 the Prince of Wales asked his father if he could live there. 'What could you possibly want that queer old place for? Those damn week-ends I suppose,' said the King. 'Well if you want it, you can have it.'[41]

For the bachelor prince the Fort provided the home he didn't have. He redesigned and modernised the interior, installed central heating and ensuite bathrooms, built a swimming pool and became a manic gardener, hacking out the undergrowth surrounding the house and cutting paths through the trees. This 'child's idea of a fort' was the scene of his alternative court, the antithesis of his father's: a Camelot where everything was a few hours later than other places and dinner was at ten, and the prince wore azure socks with plus-four knickerbockers so exaggerated that they were known as plus-twenties, changing for dinner into a dress kilt with an immense white leather purse and playing the bagpipes.[42]

By 1930 the prince's decade-long affair with Freda Dudley Ward was cooling, though she remained the most important woman in his life. A new mistress appeared at weekends at the Fort. She was Thelma Furness, the rich and beautiful American wife of Viscount Furness, a shipping magnate. Thelma 'modernised' and Americanised the prince, rendering him (according to Chips Channon) 'over-democratic, casual and a little common'.[43] Unwittingly, Thelma made the prince even more incapable of marrying the British aristocrat that his parents wished for.

George watched his son's affair with dismay. He wrote to the Queen in September 1931: 'I see by the papers that David is in Paris and has postponed his return home until today by air. I suppose Lady F wished him to spend another night with her in Paris!'[44] Ulick Alexander, a member of the prince's household, was one of George's informants. 'I have had a long talk with Ulick,' wrote the King, '& he told me many things I didn't know, which I will tell you when we meet.'[45]

In March 1932 King George had an unusually long and intimate conversation with his son. He warned David that his popularity would not survive the revelation of his private life, especially his affair with Lady Furness. He told the prince how important it was to have a wife to share the burden of the throne. David confessed that the only woman he had ever wanted to marry was Freda Dudley Ward. George asked David whether he was happy, and David replied that he was not. The King then asked David whether he had considered marrying 'a suitable well-born English girl', and the prince answered that he had never supposed it would be possible.[46] It was an extraordinary admission, given Bertie's marriage to Elizabeth Bowes-Lyon, and it shows how far apart David had drifted from his parents. This was the last time that George discussed the topic of marriage with his son. David took no notice. Thelma remained the mistress of the Prince of Wales for another two years.

Chips Channon thought the dullness of the court was partly to blame for the Prince of Wales's failure to marry. The King and Queen 'practically saw no one except their old courtiers, and they made no social background whatever for any of their children'.[47] Even the ultra-loyal Duchess of York conceded that 'Balmoral was not very lively for the younger ones', as the guests were the King's oldest friends such as Canon Dalton and the Archbishop of Canterbury.[48]

At Cowes in July 1933 the King mentioned to the Duchess of York that 'a certain person' had been staying at the Fort in January when the Yorks were skating nearby, and he intended to speak to David about it. The 'certain person' was Wallis Simpson, already a figure of dread on account of being an American divorcee, though Thelma remained the mistress. The duchess was appalled by the King's suggestion that he should reprimand David for allowing Mrs Simpson to come near her. 'David would *never* forgive me,' she told Queen Mary: 'relations are already a little difficult when naughty ladies are brought in, and up to now we have not met "the lady" at all, & I would like to remain quite outside the whole affair.'[49] The Queen agreed that 'it would never do to start a quarrel, but I confess I hope it will not occur again for you ought not to meet D's lady in his own house, that is too much of a *bad* thing!!!'[50]

It was unthinkable that Wallis Simpson should formally 'meet' the Duchess of York. She was instantly perceived as a 'naughty lady' and social pariah, in spite of belonging to an aristocratic Baltimore family. A socially ambitious poor relation, she married the dull and wealthy Ernest Simpson as her second husband, came to London and attempted to launder her reputation by getting herself presented at court.* Introduced to the prince by her friend Thelma Furness in January 1931, Wallis entertained him at her flat in Bryanston Court, a smart new block in Marylebone. The prince was enchanted by the pale green drawing room and the glass-topped dining-room table – the last word in 1930s chic.[51] In 1933 the Simpsons became regular weekend guests at the Fort, and the prince dined often at Bryanston Court on Wallis's American cooking. Unlike British hostesses, who never ventured behind the green-baize door, Wallis, who was a superb cook, spent the afternoon in the kitchen before a dinner party.[52] So often did Wallis see the prince that she was obliged to reassure her aunt Bessie that 'Thelma is still the Princess of Wales'.[53]

Wallis was everything the King disliked about the modern world: a divorced American with painted nails and plucked eyebrows living in a flat. We can gauge his state of mind from a note made by Neville Chamberlain, who travelled down from Scotland in September 1933 with J. H. Thomas. Thomas had been staying at Balmoral, and he related that on long walks the King had poured out his family troubles, 'no doubt about his sons'. 'By God he is a great yewman [sic] creature,' said Thomas. When he went to say goodbye to the Queen, she burst out: 'I can't tell you what a lot of good you've done the King and how you've cheered him up.'[54]

At Sandringham that Christmas the King gave a second broadcast. The stuffier members of his household warned that the broadcasts were becoming 'too familiar', but the King was persuaded to address his people by Wigram, who told him that he was sixty-eight and 'had not got many years to look forward to'.[55]

At the Fort, meanwhile, Wallis staged a putsch. Thelma Furness had departed on a trip to the United States, and when she returned in March 1934 she found that Wallis had dethroned her and established herself as the prince's favourite. 'I'm not in the habit of taking my girlfriends' beaux,' wrote Wallis; but she was a predator, and that was precisely what she did.[56]

How long the news took to reach Sandringham is not clear. We can judge the atmosphere prevailing there from an anecdote relating to this time. Penelope Maffey, later Aitken, a young protégée of the King, was the daughter of John Maffey, a distinguished colonial administrator. He lived at Anmer Hall on the Sandringham estate, a grace-and-favour house which the King had given him, allegedly because of the accuracy

---

*Divorced women could be presented at court provided they could prove that they were not the guilty party.

of his shooting. Ever since she was a teenager and the King had happened upon her as her spaniel chased a royal pheasant, Penelope had been a special friend of the King. They discussed spaniel breeding together. One night around this time, she was invited to dinner at Sandringham, in itself frightening enough, but on this occasion a terrifying experience, as she witnessed at first hand the monarch becoming incandescent with rage when he discovered that the Prince of Wales had gone AWOL with Wallis Simpson.[57]

In August 1934 Prince George became engaged to Princess Marina of Greece. Queen Mary was 'delighted & excited' but worried about her son's playboy life. 'I hope all will be for the best & that he will settle down.'[58] She approved of Marina, who was a great-niece of Queen Alexandra. 'The women of that Danish family make good wives,' she told Lady Airlie. 'No bread-and-butter miss would be of any help to my son, but this girl is sophisticated as well as charming, and she will be.'[59] If the glamorous Marina was welcomed at Buckingham Palace, the arrival of her family, a horde of displaced royals who spent their lives in the lounges of continental hotels, was awaited with dismay.[60]

These displaced and impecunious royals included Marina's thirteen-year-old first cousin Philip, who travelled to the wedding from Gordonstoun where he was a pupil. He was the son of Prince Andrew of Greece, one of George's first cousins. When revolution broke out in Greece in 1922 a British man-of-war was sent to rescue the King and Queen of Greece and Prince Andrew, the king's brother, as 'their lives might have been in danger'.[61] Andrew, however, stayed behind in order to join his wife and children, and he was soon arrested. At this point George V intervened, and it was allegedly as a result of his 'personal action' that Andrew's life was saved. Exactly what George did to help his first cousin is not known, but a mysterious British naval officer named Gerald Talbot was sent to rescue Andrew, who escaped on a British cruiser with his wife and children, including his eighteen-month-old son Philip.[62] At Prince George's wedding Philip first set eyes on the eight-year-old Princess Elizabeth, who was a bridesmaid.

Playing down Marina's status as a penniless exiled royal, her press campaign presented the engagement as a true modern romance. She and George were the first royal couple to kiss (on the cheek) on camera, and Marina broke convention by smoking in public.[63] Marina's troubles as a member of the Greek royal family, despised by their British cousins as an 'inferior tribe', were eased by King George, who 'fully realised the difficulty of her position' and treated her with kindness and imagination.

'She could not understand how a man who could be so considerate and sensitive to her, could be such a devil to his sons.'[64]

On 27 November, two days before the royal wedding at Westminster Abbey, an evening party was held at Buckingham Palace. The Prince of Wales included Wallis's name on his list and the King scratched her out, but somehow or other she was reinstated. At the party, the prince introduced her to his mother, and Wallis recalled the thrill of him bringing the Queen up to her, 'in front of all the cold jealous English eyes'.[65] David was heading towards the King to present Wallis when he was cut off by an aide. This incident was a decisive moment in George's relations with his son. Later he complained furiously that Wallis had been smuggled into Buckingham Palace. 'That woman in my own house!' he shouted.[66]

Scarcely less welcome than Wallis was Ivan Maisky, the ambassador of the Soviet Union, who was also a guest. He watched the King speaking to Baldwin:

> The king – short, balding, frail, his arms almost straight down by his sides – moved his lips slowly and, bending slightly forward, gazed ingratiatingly at the Conservative leader. Baldwin – solidly built with a paunch, red hair and a confident, grinning face – was leaning back arrogantly and listening to the King in a calm and somewhat majestic manner.[67]

Observing the two, he asked, which was the master? It certainly didn't seem to be the King.

By now Baldwin was effectively leader of the government. Ramsay MacDonald was still prime minister, but he had faded into irrelevance, a shadow of a leader, reviled by the Labour Party as a traitor and failing in health. The King, moved by the vast cheering crowds at the wedding, wrote to Archbishop Lang: 'If only the politicians would give up their party quarrels and would rally round and support the National Government, what could one not do in this country. We [sic] have done our bit, it is now for the country to do the same.'[68] Maisky noticed how the wedding was turned into a 'real national event' – though he was pleased to observe that most of the people in the crowd were women.[69]

The National Government was a bulwark against fascism in Britain, but in Germany the rise of Hitler already worried the King. George's attitude towards Nazi Germany was not wholly consistent, as Kenneth Rose pointed out.[70] The First World War had left him with a horror of Germany. The Kaiser was anathema to him. He shunned his German cousins. Ernest Cassel, the financier who had done so much to rescue his father's finances as well as being one of Edward VII's closest friends, was ostracised at court on account of his German origins. Not until 1927 did George restore to favour his cousin and friend Albert Mensdorff, the former Austrian ambassador – described by Chips as 'deaf, snobbish, social and soft, with perfect manners and a horror of the untitled' – inviting him to Sandringham and allowing him to wear once more his Royal Victorian Order.[71] Only in 1935 did George write to his first cousin Ernie, or Ernst Ludwig, Grand Duke of Hesse (Darmstadt): 'That horrible and unnecessary war has made no difference to my feelings for you.'[72]

But George's reconciliation with cousins such as Mensdorff does not mean that he favoured appeasing Hitler. He refused to allow the Prince of Wales to attend the wedding in 1932 of the daughter of his cousin the Duke of Saxe-Coburg to the Crown Prince of Sweden because the duke was Hitler's henchman.[73] He warned the German ambassador in 1934 that rearming Germany could only end in war.[74] When the foreign secretary, the appeaser Sir John Simon, urged a reconciliation with Germany in January 1935, the King demurred. 'His Majesty feels that we must not be blinded by the apparent sweet reasonableness of the Germans, but be wary and not taken unawares.'[75] In the last months of his life his attitude changed. He became violently anti-war. But this is because he was ill and tired, not because he wanted to appease Hitler.[76]

The idea of celebrating the Silver Jubilee to mark the twenty-fifth anniversary of George's accession in 1935 originated not with the King but with his ministers, anxious to put on a show of national unity ahead of the election.* To restore the King's health, the King and Queen spent a month at Eastbourne, borrowing the Duke of Devonshire's Compton Place, after Lord Dawson had pronounced that the air would suit the King.[77] It was not a house of happy memories. George had stayed there after Eddy died, perhaps the most wretched time of his life. For May it brought memories of Eddy too. She had spent the day chosen for their wedding here. Marking out her life in jewels (just as George measured his life in numbers) she recalled that her parents-in-law had given her a row of diamonds intended as a wedding gift. 'I write these details as I think them so interesting,' she noted.[78] They watched Greta Garbo and

---

*Winston Churchill was commissioned by Alexander Korda to write the script for a film on the life of George V to appear in time for the Jubilee, but the project was dropped because it ran out of time. Judging from the surviving script, which is in the Churchill Archive, the film was more about Churchill than the King.

Hitchcock films in the cinema installed in the house, and the Queen took walks on the esplanade and went for drives. 'Unfortunately the King does not care for driving,' she told Evie, Duchess of Devonshire, and 'the weather is far from grand, rain and wind'.[79]

The court moved to Windsor in April, the King's cough became worse, and he took to dining alone in his rooms.[80] His advisers urged him to confront his son over Mrs Simpson but he refused, saying that he had tried and failed over Lady Furness.[81] Back in January the King had been informed by a member of his household that the prince had given jewels worth £10,000 (over £700,000 today) to an unnamed woman. Fearing blackmail, the King allegedly asked Stanley Baldwin to authorise Special Branch to conduct a surveillance operation on the prince and the woman, who was of course Wallis Simpson. For the monarch to ask the security services to spy on his own son was an unprecedented step, and, if this is true, an indication of how far relations between the King and the prince had deteriorated.[82]

The King gave orders that Mrs Simpson was not to be invited to the Silver Jubilee functions nor to Royal Ascot.[83] David demanded that the Simpsons should be asked to the Court Ball. When the King replied that that he refused to invite his son's mistress, David swore that Wallis was not his mistress. An invitation was sent to Wallis but the household were convinced the prince had lied. Certainly the King believed that this was the case.[84]

David was then forty, and the spectacle of the ageing King challenging his middle-aged bachelor son as to whether he had slept with his mistress seems bizarre. It was as if the prince was infantilised by being a bachelor without a domestic life. Queen Mary played no part in these exchanges. Her failure even to attempt to grasp the nettle was badly judged. As her biographer observed, 'this, we may think, was one case in which silence was not golden. The unmentioned, which was at the same time the all-important, was left floating like a submerged mine beneath the surface of the life of the Royal Family during the last months of the reign of King George V.'[85]

At five minutes to eleven on the morning of Monday 6 May 1935 the King and Queen left Buckingham Palace in the big open carriage drawn by six Windsor Grey horses in procession to St Paul's. This jubilee was not as grand as Queen Victoria's jubilees had been. For one thing, most of the royal cousins had lost their thrones. Gone too were the splendid Hanoverian Cream horses which had drawn the state carriages since the reign of George I, destroyed by the King in 1921 in a drive to economise and purge the royal mews of German blood.[86] But the route was lined with cheering crowds, and the royal carriages were greeted with thunderous applause, especially the Yorks'. 'The Kents and Wales nowhere,' wrote Nancy Mitford, who considered that Princess Marina, wearing an enormous, unsuitable hat, was wrongly dressed and looked like a mannequin.[87] The roars reached a crescendo when the King and Queen came into sight. All eyes were on the Queen in her shimmering, silvery dress and white fur stole. 'Never has she looked so serene,' wrote Chips Channon, who got up at 7.15 to witness the spectacle, 'so royally majestic, more, so attractive. From being a dowdy joke (*qua* clothes I mean) she has become the best-dressed woman in the world. I fear she eclipsed the King.'[88]

'The greatest number of people in the streets that I have ever seen in my life,' wrote the King, for once at a loss for a numeral.[89] Footage shows him saluting repeatedly to the crowds, while the Queen smiled (just) and bowed her head in thanks – neither of them did anything so vulgar as to wave.* The temperature was seventy-five degrees in the shade, and 7,000 people fainted and had to be rescued by ambulances.[90] The crowds were orderly and good-natured. In the emergency room which had been set up at Scotland Yard, linked by telephone to all the police stations, no calls came through.[91]

George seemed 'almost overcome' by the warmth of his reception.[92] Broadcasting that night from Buckingham Palace, he struck a note of unprecedented emotion. 'I can only say to you, my very dear people, that the Queen and I thank you from the depths of our hearts for all the loyalty and – may I say? – the love with which this day and always you have surrounded us.'[93]

Some thought the most moving event was the reception for the diplomatic corps and dominions' representatives at St James's Palace on Wednesday 8 May. When George mentioned his 'happy partnership' with the Queen his voice cracked, and the Queen wept. At last the King said: 'Well, Mary [*sic*], when you have stopped crying we'll go home.'[94]

At Westminster Hall on the Thursday the King and Queen were received by the members of both houses. They sang the National Anthem and gave three cheers for the King and Queen, which 'moved me much', wrote George.[95] For his speech of thanks he had told his secretary to put the paragraph mentioning the Queen at the very end. 'I can't trust myself to speak of the Queen when I think of all I owe her.'[96] Sure enough when he came to that passage his voice broke, as could be clearly heard by those

---

*However, footage also shows the little princesses being encouraged by their grandparents to wave from the balcony at Buckingham Palace.

present.[97] MP Robert Bernays thought the Queen looked superb: 'There is no woman in England who at that age would have dared to dress in pink. She carried it off superbly.' The only flaw was the Prince of Wales, who rustled his programme and talked throughout the King's speech. 'I gather it has been a bad Jubilee for him,' wrote Bernays. 'He likes being at the centre of the picture and was very annoyed, rightly I think, that he was not given a carriage to himself during the procession.'[98]

On three days the Queen and the King, wearing field marshal's uniform, drove through the streets of the East End and the poorer districts of London, which the people had decorated spontaneously with flowers and messages and flags. For once Sister Black was not sentimentalising when she recalled him saying on his return from one of these drives: 'I'd no idea they felt like that about me ... I am beginning to think they must really like me for myself.'[99] It was as if he had died and gone to heaven. But new worries about dangers both to the monarchy and to the country clouded his Jubilee celebrations.

Wallis Simpson was becoming impossible to ignore. At the Court Ball (14 May) she danced with the Prince of Wales, and as they whirled past the King she felt his eyes rest 'searchingly' on her. She recalled in her memoirs: 'Through the panoply of pomp I discerned that here was a frail old man ... A premonitory shiver ran through me.'[100] The King for his part made his feelings very clear. When he left after supper, the prince followed him as far as the private door, but the King said nothing, not even good night.[101]

By now 'war to the knife' had broken out between the prince's past mistress Freda Dudley Ward and Wallis Simpson. The prince's friends took sides. Chips was officially on the side of Freda, but secretly delighted that Mrs Simpson was winning. Having first referred to her as 'a nice, quiet, well-bred mouse of a woman' (this was very badly out) with a 'a huge, huge mole', he now thought her jolly, unprepossessing, witty and 'madly Americanly anxious to storm society' – and he should know.[102] He also noted the prince's growing Nazi leanings, encouraged by Emerald Cunard, who was in thrall to Ribbentrop.[103] The outlook for the next reign did not look promising.

Still more concerning was the threat of European war. In his speech at Westminster Hall the King spoke of 'these days, when fear and preparation for war are again astir in the world'. When Hitler telegraphed his congratulations on the Jubilee, the King replied thanking him for 'the friendly reference to my efforts and the efforts of my Government in the interest of peace. The cause of peace is very dear to me,' he wrote.[104] But fine words didn't stop Hitler, and the threat to peace posed by the dictators loomed ever larger in the King's mind.

CHAPTER 29

Lord Dawson's Syringe

1935–1936

The King was seventy on 3 June 1935. Chips Channon watched him Trooping the Colour on his birthday. 'Alone, aged, sad and incredibly dignified,' he rode a tired horse. Much of the time he was unattended. 'Anyone could have murdered him.'[1]

Ramsay MacDonald recommended Clive Wigram for a peerage in the birthday honours, but the King blocked it on the grounds that he couldn't make Wigram a peer without ennobling the long-serving Fritz Ponsonby, keeper of the Privy Purse. As he explained to Nora Wigram, 'Clive has been gold, Fritz has been lead.' Speaking in a crowded room at the Royal Academy ('I only pray it wasn't overheard for his voice carries for miles'), the King told Nora: 'I do not want to make Fritz a peer. He hasn't served me well.' As for his wife, 'she is a horrid vulgar climbing woman (!!)'. Naturally the Wigrams were miffed. 'I can't help thinking he has displayed a little weakness,' wrote Nora.[2] Refusing a peerage to Wigram in order to spite Ponsonby was not good management. MacDonald persuaded the King to change his mind, and both men were made peers. Fritz died a few months later. The King then caused a scandal by refusing to grant Fritz's widow a pension, and turning her out of St James's Palace, where she had lived all her married life. 'The Court is dead and out of date,' wrote Channon, shocked by the King's vindictiveness towards his old retainer.[3]

Ramsay MacDonald, ridiculed in the House of Commons as a nincompoop, resigned on 7 June, and was succeeded as prime minister by the inevitable Baldwin, though MacDonald remained in the Cabinet as lord president. Mussolini's threatened invasion of Abyssinia and the danger of a European war obsessed the King. In an 'extraordinary' outburst, he told Lloyd George: 'I *will* not have another war. I *will* not. The last war was none of my doing, and if there is another one . . . I will go to Trafalgar Square and wave a red flag myself sooner than allow this country to be brought in.'[4] Samuel Hoare, foreign secretary in the Baldwin government, was frequently summoned by the anxious monarch to discuss the Abyssinia crisis. 'I am an old man,' said the King. 'I have been through one world war. How can I get through another? If I am to go on, you must keep me out of one.'[5]

Lord Dawson was concerned that the King had 'surrendered himself to invalid habits'.[6] He would sit hunched up in an armchair, taking little interest in those around him. Dawson recommended showing films to rouse the King out of his lethargy. At a drawing room at Buckingham Palace Robert Bernays noticed that 'the King showed signs of having taken to the rouge pot'.[7] The artist Duncan Grant observed at the Jubilee that the King was *tremendously* made up. Every eyelash stuck together just like any debutante.'[8] After the Jubilee George couldn't throw off a cold, and he remained at Sandringham on doctor's orders, while Queen Mary carried out Ascot alone ('a great bore') as well as holding a court without the King ('to my great regret').[9] The King suffered from sleepiness, often dropping off, the result, said Dawson, of 'the narrowing of the cerebral vessels and failing myocardium'.[10] By now Sister Black was in attendance, often giving the King oxygen when he woke at 3 a.m.

At Cowes that year the King didn't race. The *Britannia* was too old to compete against modern yachts. But he was happy sailing, spending days in the 'wonderful peace' of the *Britannia* – 'no noise but the creaking of the sails & the cooing voice of Sir Philip [Hunloke], softly inviting the crew to Lee-o!'[11]

Balmoral was enlivened by the surprise engagement of Prince Harry to Lady Alice Scott, 34-year-old daughter of the Duke of Buccleuch, 'a plump, dull as ditchwater girl', according to Chips.[12] The King grumbled that 'Harry really ought to have written to me before', but he was pleased, as the Duke of Buccleuch was one of his oldest friends.[13] The Queen thought Alice 'charming & intelligent' and 'quite nice looking tho' she is rather short', adding: 'I think she will suit perfectly in our family.'[14] Alice was placed next to the King at dinner because her stories kept him awake and made him laugh.[15]

Nothing could assuage the King's anxiety about Wallis Simpson. J. H. Thomas stayed at Balmoral and boasted afterwards (to the irritation of the snobbish Lord Lee of Fareham) that Queen Mary had begged him to intervene with the prince, saying: 'You *must*'elp us, Jim; this'*ere* bloody thing'as got to *stop*!'[16] The King spent an hour with Archbishop Lang, 'outpouring all his troubles'.[17] That those troubles concerned David's affair with Wallis Simpson is confirmed by Lady Airlie, who saw the archbishop shortly afterwards.[18] Perhaps it was on this occasion that Lang congratulated the King on having raised the monarchy to a position higher than ever before, and George replied: 'What is the use, when I know my son is going to let it down.'[19]

The Queen later endorsed the envelope of a letter from the King dated 26 August 1935 'The last letter George wrote me'.[20] After Balmoral they were never apart again. The wedding of the Duke of Gloucester and Alice Scott took place in the private chapel at Buckingham Palace owing to the death of the Duke of Buccleuch. Afterwards the King wrote in his diary: 'Now all the children are married but David.'[21]

It was around this time that the King predicted that David would abdicate. He said this to several people. To Baldwin he remarked: 'After I am dead the boy will ruin himself within twelve months.'[22] To Ulick Alexander he said: 'My eldest son will never succeed me. He will abdicate.'[23] Blanche Lennox, a socialite and friend of the King's, told Lady Airlie that George had said: 'I pray to God that my eldest son will never marry and have children, and that nothing will come between Bertie and Lilibet and the throne.'[24]

The King deplored the pact which Samuel Hoare negotiated with the French prime minister, Pierre Laval, in Paris, surrendering territory in Abyssinia to appease Mussolini. Hoare was forced to resign, and when he took leave of the King he was shocked by his appearance. 'He looked very ill and spoke as if he was weighed down by anxiety.'[25] This didn't stop the King chaffing Hoare. He joked: 'You know what they're all saying, no more coals to Newcastle, no more Hoares to Paris.' Later, he remarked: 'The fellow didn't even laugh.'[26]*

On a bitter day before Christmas Anthony Eden went to Sandringham to be sworn in as foreign secretary. He found the King coughing painfully but in good spirits. No longer worried about war with Italy, he was robustly opposed to appeasing Mussolini.

Christmas at Sandringham was quiet. For once there was no shooting for the King – his last day was 14 November, when over 1,000 pheasants were killed. The King mourned his sister, Princess Victoria, who died on 3 December. 'How I shall miss her & our daily talks on the telephone,' he wrote.[27] 'G. terribly upset,' noted the Queen.[28] He cancelled the opening of Parliament on his sister's account. At Sandringham, the King watched while the Queen arranged Princess Victoria's collection of Fabergé in vitrines.[29]

George gave his Christmas broadcast. His voice was guttural and

---

*Another George V joke concerned Lord Kemsley. When given a peerage he was asked what title he would take. He replied: 'Lord Farnham-Royal', the name of his estate. 'The Crown Office informed him that he could not have the title of "Lord Farnham-Royal" but might take that of "Lord Farnham-Common"' (Kenneth Rose, *Who's In, Who's Out: The Journals of Kenneth Rose, Vol. 1*, ed. D. R. Thorpe (Weidenfeld & Nicolson, 2018), p. 12).

strong as ever, and he got through the script without coughing. He spoke of 'the personal link between me and my people which I value more than I can say'. At a time of European anxiety, 'it is good to think that our own family of peoples is at peace in itself and united in one desire to be at peace with other nations'.[30]

His own family, however, was far from united. David arrived on Christmas Eve, joining a family party depleted by flu. He wrote to Wallis on Boxing Day: 'It really is terrible here and so much the worst Xmas I have ever had to spend with the family, far worse than last year and that was bad enough.'[31] Consumed by self-pity and envious of his brothers' domestic happiness, David made no attempt to speak to his father. 'This was hardly the time or the place,' he wrote.[32] His father was bent, thin and frail, and the news that David wanted to tell him was explosive. Since his return from holiday in October he had determined to marry Wallis Simpson.[33] Moreover, he was prepared to abdicate if necessary. As he later wrote: 'I could not discount the possibility of my having to withdraw from the line of succession.'[34] Little did he know that his father had already reached the same conclusion.

For the first two weeks of January 1936, the Queen's diary records a normal Sandringham routine. Most days she walked beside George, who rode his white shooting pony, Jock. Looking back, however, she felt that George's 'weakness & wretchedness' had begun at the New Year.[35] Sister Black reported to Dawson on 7 January that the King 'was going through one of his phases of sleepiness and breathlessness and generally feels "cheap"'.[36] Dawson looked in a week later and found the King unwell, but he was not sufficiently alarmed to stay or summon more doctors.

On Wednesday 15 January the Queen recorded that 'poor George who had not been feeling well for some days, felt worse & had to go to bed before dinner'.[37] That night the King's legs became swollen, and though the swelling went down the next day, he stayed in his room. 'Most worrying,' wrote the Queen.[38]

Still carrying on as normal, the Queen summoned Bertie to help her with the house party. Travelling on the same train to Sandringham on Thursday the 16th Bertie found Tommy Lascelles, the newly appointed assistant private secretary to the King (he had returned to royal service two years after leaving the Prince of Wales's household). 'What's all this about the King not being well?' asked the duke, but Lascelles knew nothing. On arrival, he learnt that 'the King was in a lower and more depressed state than they had ever seen him'.[39]

That day the Queen wrote to David, who was shooting at Windsor when he received her understated message: 'I think you ought to know that Papa is not very well.'[40] The Queen suggested that David should 'propose himself' for the weekend; but David returned at once to Fort Belvedere and, after showing his mother's letter to Wallis, telephoned his pilot and arranged to fly to Sandringham the next day.[41]

Friday 17 January was cold and snowy, and the Queen wrote: 'George very ill ... G. very drowsy all day.'[42] The King sat in his favourite chair in front of a crackling fire wearing an old Tibetan dressing gown, the same dressing gown perhaps that he had worn when he appointed Ramsay MacDonald prime minister in 1929. He was comatose, almost semi-conscious, and his kidneys were not functioning properly.[43] When David arrived he seemed to be asleep, and barely noticed that his son was in the room. Dawson, who had also been sent for, 'gave a bad account which distressed us very much', wrote the Queen.[44] Dawson noted in his diary: 'I realised at once that the Queen did not think the King could live.'[45]

The King wrote the last entry in his diary: 'Dawson arrived this evening, I saw him & feel rotten ...'[46] The entry then trailed off. A later annotation by the grieving Queen reads: 'My dearest husband was much distressed at the bad handwriting above & begged me to write his diary for him next day.'[47]

Just before midnight on Friday the BBC broadcast the first worrying bulletin, signed by three doctors: 'The bronchial catarrh from which His Majesty the King is suffering is not severe, but there have appeared signs of cardiac weakness which must be regarded with some disquiet.'[48]

Saturday 18 June was 'a very sad day' according to the Queen.[49] The grandchildren departed, and all the guests were turned out of the house. Tommy Lascelles wrote to his wife asking her to send his black mourning trousers. In the afternoon the Queen went for a walk with David and Bertie and she broached the subject that none of them dared mention – the changes that would follow from the King's death. For once the Queen confronted reality. It was probably on this occasion that David 'horrified' his mother by saying that Sandringham was only a 'hobby' or holiday house which he might not continue with.[50]

Sir Maurice Cassidy, the heart specialist summoned by Dawson, confirmed that 'the heart was not functioning properly' and he added his name to the 3.30 bulletin.[51] Outside Buckingham Palace, the anxious crowd thickened round the gloomy notice: 'The cardiac weakness and the embarrassment of the circulation have slightly increased and give cause for anxiety.'[52]

While the nation prepared to mourn, the heir apparent wrote love letters to Mrs Simpson. 'I do long long [*sic*] to see you even for a few minutes my Wallis it would help so much . . . You are all and everything I have in life and WE must hold each other so tight. It will all work out right for us.'[53]

Wigram arrived, having been sent for by the Queen. Realising that the King was expected to die, he brought the file of the secret committee which had made arrangements in case of the monarch's demise.

On Sunday 19 January, the King was 'about the same', and the Queen sat with him 'from time to time'. It was another 'very sad day'. None of the royal family went to church, as it was surrounded by photographers and reporters – 'too heartless', said the Queen.[54] David and Bertie motored up to London and, after visiting Wallis at her flat, David saw Baldwin at 10 Downing Street. The meeting left the prime minister 'very much disturbed' about the prince's relations with Mrs Simpson. As he told Duff Cooper, 'the country won't stand it'. If she were 'a respectable whore', explained Baldwin, 'he wouldn't mind'.[55]

Archbishop Lang invited himself to Sandringham and arrived there at about seven. As the end approached, the household melted into the background, and two shadowy figures slipped in and out of the King's room – Dawson and the archbishop, 'a noiseless spectre in black gaiters'.[56] On his arrival Lang saw Dawson, who told him he had little hope, but 'the chances were 75 p.c. in favour of the King lasting for days or even weeks, 25 p.c. in favour of hours'. At dinner with the household, the Queen was 'wonderfully calm and talked freely on all sorts of subjects'.[57]

On Monday morning, 20 January, the King was 'clearer after a fair night but weak'.[58] On the insistence of the Cabinet, who seemed to Dawson 'unduly nervous', a pathetic farce was played out in the dying sovereign's bedroom.[59] In order to appoint a council of state, consisting of the Queen and her four sons, empowered to act in the King's name, three black-coated privy counsellors arrived from London at 11.30. Ramsay MacDonald, the lord president, Lord Hailsham, the lord chancellor, and Sir John Simon, the home secretary, assembled in the room adjoining the King's bedroom, and solemnly witnessed the undignified spectacle of the King attempting to sign his approval, though he could no longer use his right hand. With Dawson kneeling beside him and guiding his hand, he was 'able to sign 2 little crosses as he was unable to sign his name which distressed him'.[60]

'G became weaker during the evening,' wrote the Queen, '& we realised the end was approaching.' The family dined alone and then 'went to G's room at intervals'.[61] Dawson, dining alone in his suite, was visited by Wigram, who worried that the last bulletin issued at 5.30 that afternoon – 'The condition of His Majesty the King shows diminishing strength' – had not prepared the nation for his impending death.[62] Dawson picked up a menu card and wrote the famous one-liner: 'The King's life is moving peacefully towards its close.' He looked in on the royal dinner party, and they approved the words.[63] The bulletin was issued at Sandringham at 9.25 and broadcast on the BBC at 9.30. At once the BBC's programmes were silenced. Every fifteen minutes the bulletin was read. The wireless brought the nation to a vigil at the King's deathbed.

What happened next was not revealed until 1986, when Dawson's biographer, Francis Watson, wrote an explosive article for *History Today*. In his secret notes, Dawson recorded that 'at about 11 o'clock it was evident that the last stage might endure for many hours'. In order to ensure a brief final scene, 'I therefore decided to determine the end, and injected (myself) morphia gr. ¾ & shortly afterwards cocaine gr. 1 into the distended jugular vein'. He performed the injections himself because Sister Black was 'disturbed' by the procedure.[64]

Dawson's motive was to ensure that the King's death was reported in *The Times* the following morning rather than in the evening papers later in the day. He telephoned his wife in London and told her to ask *The Times* to hold the presses until midnight, as the death was imminent. His timing was precise. The scene as recorded by Dawson was more like an Agatha Christie murder story than the solemn demise of the monarch. At 11.15 Archbishop Lang was called to the King's bed by one of the doctors to say final prayers. Gliding silently into the room, he found the Queen and Princess Mary already there – they must have entered the room only minutes after Dawson had administered his lethal jabs.[65] Within fifteen minutes of the injections Dawson noted: 'Breathing quieter – appearance more placid – physical strength gone.'[66]

Punctual as ever, the King died on schedule at 11.55 on 20 January. 'My darling husband passed peacefully away,' wrote the Queen.[67] The bulletin announcing the death was broadcast by the BBC at 12.10, only minutes after the King had died. By the time the news reached *The Times*, the presses had started to roll, and 30,000 copies had already been printed, but the change was quickly made, and a leader, memoir and pictures appeared in 300,000 copies.[68]

Dawson claimed that the Prince of Wales had told him that neither he nor the Queen wished the King's life to be prolonged if he was mortally ill.[69] But it is debatable whether that rather general remark gave

Dawson the authority to inject the King with a lethal overdose of morphia and cocaine. As a medical reviewer observed, the killing of an unconscious patient without the patient's prior knowledge or consent cannot be described as a mercy killing. Rather it was a convenience killing, timed to suit the purposes of the arrogant Lord Dawson, who consulted no one, and considered that only he had the right to decide when the King should die.[70] One lawyer with whom Kenneth Rose discussed the case declared emphatically that Dawson was guilty of murder, as the King was in no pain and Dawson knowingly hastened his death.[71]*

'When a King starts to die,' wrote the Duke of Windsor, 'the whole world crowds in for the death-watch.'[72]

Driving past Buckingham Palace on the night the King died, Virginia Woolf noticed 'a cluster, like a swarm of bees, around the railings'.[73] The MP Robert Bernays walked home past the Palace, and saw vast crowds, 'standing sad and silent'.[74] Maisky woke his chauffeur and drove to the Palace to observe the long black queue slowly filing past the gates. 'There was a restrained, intent silence, but there were no tears or hysterics.'[75] Fleet Street was full of boys carrying newspapers with stories and editorials about the King only an hour after his death. So much for *The Times* being the first.

Richard Norton (later Lord Grantley), a film maker, was about to release a comedy entitled *Where's George?* He was telephoned early on the morning after the King's death by an agitated official from United Agents. 'Do you realise that overnight we put up a thousand posters on advertising hoardings in London, all saying *Where's George?*' A horrified Norton ordered the posters to be immediately ripped down, and the film was hastily retitled.[76]

The King's last words were eagerly awaited. Wigram, who was in the King's bedroom on the morning before he died, claimed that he heard His Majesty saying the word 'empire' with a query in his voice that seemed to mean 'How goes the empire?' 'All is well, Sir, with the empire,' said Wigram.[77] This anecdote suggests a monarch conscious of his duty even on his deathbed, which was how the establishment wanted to remember him. Baldwin repeated it in his BBC tribute to the King. Bernays thought it savoured too much of the *Daily Mail*, and Virginia

---

*The clerihew 'Lord Dawson of Penn / Killed many men / That's why we sing / "God Save the King"', which circulated during Dawson's lifetime, suggests that people already suspected Dawson of hastening the King's death.

Woolf mocked it in her diary: '[The King] had said to his Secretary "How is the Empire?" – an odd expression. "The Empire, Sir, is well"; whereupon he fell asleep. And then of course, he ended with God Save the King.'[78]

Nor was the anecdote typical of the salty-mouthed King, who once remarked of a politician attacking Buckingham Palace influence: 'What does he mean by saying that Buckingham Palace is not me? Who else is there I should like to know? Does he mean the footmen?'[79] When towards the end Stanley Hewett injected the King with painkilling morphia the King exclaimed: 'God damn you.' The Queen laughed and said how humorous to be able to say that 'when you are dying'.[80] These were the last words of a monarch who once roared at a footman who dropped a loaded tea tray: 'That's right, break up the bloody palace.'[81]

The moment the King died Queen Mary took David's hand in hers and kissed it. Prince George did the same. The new King Edward VIII 'became hysterical, cried loudly, and kept on embracing the Queen', wrote Wigram.[82] His first act as king was to order the Sandringham clocks, still running thirty minutes fast, to be put back to GMT. Contrary to Virginia Woolf's suggestion that the new King was taking revenge on his dead father, the order was probably prompted by irritation at the confusion caused by Sandringham time when King George lay dying.[83] But the thoughtlessness was typical of the new King. All through the night the lights burnt in the house as the clockmen went from room to room changing the clocks.

'Am broken hearted,' wrote the Queen.[84] She begged David not to repeat the protracted grieving for Edward VII, and to bury his father within a week.[85] At 5 p.m. on Tuesday 21 January George's coffin, made of oak grown on the Sandringham estate, was closed (he had been embalmed earlier in the day to Dawson's satisfaction). The coffin was placed on a bier and wheeled across the park to Sandringham church. Headed by the King's piper, a tiny procession of no more than a dozen people – the Queen, her family and household – walked to the church along the narrow path which the late King had always used. The men of the King's Company, 1st Battalion Grenadier Guards slung the coffin on their shoulders and laid it before the altar. There they left it, after a very brief service, to be watched over by gamekeepers and gardeners of the Sandringham estate for thirty-six hours. That small, simple ceremony on a dark, wet and windy evening remained in the minds of some of those who were there as the most impressive of all.[86] 'It is curious,' reflected the Queen, 'my having been present in this house at the death beds of 2 brothers Eddy & George'.[87]

On the morning of Thursday 23 January the coffin was taken in a gun carriage drawn by six horses of the Royal Horse Artillery to Wolferton station. The princes followed on foot, and the Queen and Princess Mary followed in carriages. Behind them walked Jock, the King's pony, and hundreds of people from the Sandringham estate. A single cock pheasant rocketed ahead, very high, immediately above the gun carriage.[88]

The royal train arrived at King's Cross at 2.34. Here the royal standard was draped over the coffin, and the Imperial State Crown secured to the coffin lid. The simple family procession followed the gun carriage on foot through the streets lined by silent, black-coated crowds – more impressive, thought David, than the state cortège on the day of the funeral. Arriving at Westminster Hall, the great door opened, and the coffin was carried in. There followed the new King, 'boyish, sad and tired', observers thought, and the Queen, 'erect, more magnificent than ever'.[89] In dead silence the coffin was placed on a catafalque. Then the choir unaccompanied sang the hymn 'Praise, my soul, the King of Heaven'. The coffin lay in state for four days, and over 800,000 people filed past.* At David's suggestion the four sons wearing full-dress uniform stood guard round the catafalque at midnight on the Monday, bent over their reversed swords, motionless for twenty minutes – a gesture of brotherly solidarity that was soon to dissolve.

The King's funeral at Windsor on Tuesday 28 January was 'a terrible day of sadness' for the Queen.[90] Vast silent crowds surged along the route from Westminster to Paddington, jostling and battling the police. The procession of thousands of troops seemed unending. At last came the massed bands and swirling pipers, and then the gun carriage bearing the King's coffin. It was drawn by sailors, marching with such precision that they seemed not to strain the rope at all.[91] People noticed how tiny the coffin was: 'the monarch of the world in that small coffin'.[92] Men fainted, men wept. The new King walked behind the gun carriage, heading the procession of princes and kings. Then came the coaches, the Queen's glass coach with its striking red trappings at the rear. She could be seen, all in black, 'incredibly magnificent and composed', holding a handkerchief.[93] At the service in St George's Chapel, she stood alone by the open vault, wearing the peaked coif and thick

---

*Some 400,000 were estimated to have attended Edward VII's lying-in-state.

417

crepe veils of German royal mourning.[94] 'We left him sadly,' she wrote, 'lying for the present with his ancestors in the vault.'[95]

People marvelled at her courage and calm composure. But the Queen was an expert at masking her feelings in public. The lying-in-state at Westminster Hall she found 'so lovely & peaceful just what G. would have liked'.[96] Far more upsetting than the public ceremonies was going into George's rooms. The business room was exactly the same as it had been before Christmas, but the fire was not lit, the parrot Charlotte was not there and nor was the cairn terrier Bob. 'Very painful,' wrote the Queen, seeing the rooms empty, '& all his little things about.'[97]

Conclusion

As King George's coffin processed at foot pace through wintry streets on 23 January 1936 to the lying-in-state at Westminster Hall with the Imperial State Crown fixed to the lid, the Maltese cross at the top of the crown fell off into the gutter. The new King Edward VIII, walking behind the gun carriage, spotted the cross with its flashing square sapphire and hundreds of diamonds, and walked on. The gems sparkling on the street caught the eye of a sergeant major who swiftly scooped up the cross. 'Christ! What will happen next?' the King was heard to say.[1]

The Imperial State Crown had been made for Queen Victoria in 1837. It weighed three-and-a-half pounds, and the Queen soon abandoned wearing it. Edward VII never used it. In 1913 George donned the crown for the opening of Parliament, and he wore it almost every year except in wartime. The Imperial State Crown became part of the mystique of his monarchy. By 1936 the century-old crown was in poor condition, its frame gradually collapsing, patched by various repairs.[2] It seemed emblematic of the condition of the monarchy and a bad omen that the Imperial State Crown, so closely identified with George V, should fall to pieces at his funeral.

The sense of an end of an era was captured by John Betjeman in his poem 'Death of King George V':

> Spirits of well-shot woodcock, partridge, snipe
>   Flutter and bear him up the Norfolk sky:
> In that red house in a red mahogany book-case
>   The stamp collection waits with mounts long dry.
>
> The big blue eyes are shut which saw wrong clothing
>   And favourite fields and coverts from a horse;
> Old men in country houses hear clocks ticking
>   Over thick carpets with a deadened force;
>
> Old men who never cheated, never doubted,
>   Communicated monthly, sit and stare
> At a red suburb ruled by Mrs Simpson
>   Where a young man lands hatless from the air.[3]

Old men in country houses weren't the only people who mourned George's death. Writing in 1937 Kingsley Martin considered that the high point of royal popularity had been reached by George V. The Jubilee was a national carnival equalled only by the Armistice in 1918. The King's death revealed the strength of popular affection for him. 'No one who talked to his neighbour on a bus, to the charwoman washing the steps, or to a sightseer standing at the street corner could doubt the almost universal feeling of loss.'[4]

On the day of the Abdication, 10 December 1936, Virginia Woolf encountered the Society hostess Lady Ottoline Morrell in Whitehall, and the two women walked past the Banqueting House together. Morrell pointed to the window through which Charles I had stepped to have his head cut off. 'I felt I was walking in the 17th Century with one of the courtiers,' wrote Woolf, '& she was lamenting not the abdication of Edward . . . but the execution of Charles. It's dreadful, dreadful, she kept saying.'[5]

King George was not expected to die as soon – nor as suddenly – as he did. If he had lived longer the Abdication crisis might not have happened. Chips Channon for one believed that Edward never wished to be king, and if his father had been ill for a long time he would have renounced the succession.[6] Lascelles thought that King Edward had been 'caught napping' by his father's sudden death. He had, 'in all probability, already made up his mind to renounce his claim to the throne, and to marry Mrs S'.[7]

Edward claimed in his autobiography that he had intended to discuss his marriage to Wallis Simpson with his father in the months before his death.[8] When it came to the point, however, he would most likely have lacked the courage to confront the old King. As Frances Donaldson wrote, 'what is more curious is that King George did not speak to him'.[9] As we have seen, in spite of pressure from his advisers, and in spite of praying that his son would renounce the succession, George could not bring himself to intervene, and he lived his last months with the 'unexploded mine' of Mrs Simpson floating uncomfortably beneath the surface.

The rift with his son David must count as George's greatest failure. Not only did his bullying and hectoring push David into rebellion, but by giving up on him in the last months of his life George left unresolved the issue that was to detonate the Abdication. However, dreadful though the Abdication seemed, it was nothing remotely like the execution of Charles I.

On the contrary, the change of monarch was accomplished remarkably smoothly. The removal of Edward VIII now seems increasingly fortunate in view of mounting evidence of his Nazi sympathies. The success of George VI, as Bertie elected to be styled, in restoring continuity with his father's reign is testimony to the robustness of the institution. The monarchy was not breaking up in the manner of the Imperial State Crown. The Abdication can be seen as 'triumphant proof' of the success of the life's work of George V.[10] As Queen Mary wrote a few days afterwards, 'it was all managed in such a dignified way that things are beginning to settle down after that terrible upheaval, in any other country there would have been riots, thank God people did not lose their heads'.[11] This was George's achievement.

He was an ordinary man. He was neither glamorous nor charismatic and he was woefully badly educated. The 'dear little man' with his light-blue eyes, his nicotine-stained beard and his guttural laugh was not distinguished.[12] He shared the cultural and educational attitudes of the Tory landed aristocracy with military connections delineated in Betjeman's poem.[13] Among these men he was famed on account of his brilliant accuracy as a shot.

In a speech at his Silver Jubilee, the King recalled that Queen Victoria at her jubilees had given thanks for a long period of unbroken prosperity. In looking back over his own reign, he recorded thankfulness for escapes from existential perils and 'danger greater than ever before [that] threatened our land'.[14] George had steered the monarchy through the turmoil of the First World War, emerging stronger from a crisis which caused the fall of the three great empires of Russia, Germany and Austria-Hungary. He played the role of mediator over Irish Home Rule, concerned above all to prevent civil war. He intervened to enable the appointment of prime ministers at times when, either through war or through political realignment, the party system was not functioning as it should to produce agreed candidates for the office. The King and his private secretary, Lord Stamfordham, would descend in their frock coats and set to work to fix the problem and find a new prime minister.

Born a Victorian (he was thirty-five when his grandmother died) George managed to adapt to the new world of democracy brought about by the 1918 Representation of the People Act. In his tribute in the House of Commons, the Labour leader, Clement Attlee, a perceptive monarchist, described King George as a democrat. The King had succeeded in a reign of twenty-five years of rapid transition because he was prepared to accept change. Most significant of all was his decision to enable the first Labour governments, whose members were drawn from manual workers, 'an event almost unthinkable only a few decades ago'.

According to Attlee, the King offered 'a point of stability in a distracted world'. One of the reasons why Britain avoided the 'mass hysteria' of other nations, he said, was because of 'the presence of a King who commanded the respect and affection of his people, who was beyond the spirit of faction'. Thus 'there has been no need to elevate some individual party leader to a national hero because the King was there to express the views of his people'.[15] In other words, it was at least in part because of the heroic stature of the King that the British people didn't turn to a fascist leader.

George presided over profound changes in the monarchy too. He reinvented it as the House of Windsor, cutting its links with the dynastic realm of European monarchies. Edward VIII, an acute critic of the institution, observed that the internal contradiction of monarchy in the twentieth century was the need 'to be remote from, yet at the same time to personify the aspirations of, the people'. The monarch must appear 'aloof and distant' to sustain the illusion of a sovereign who stands above politics, and at the same time 'share intimately' the ideals of the public.[16] George resolved this tension by transforming the Crown into a beacon of traditional family values. Part of the problem of Edward VIII was that neither his lifestyle nor his relationship with an American divorcee fitted his father's domestic monarchy.

George V was an ordinary man who achieved extraordinary things – so much so that it seems he was not really ordinary at all. Certainly, Lascelles was right when he wrote – as quoted in the Preface to this book – 'his reign (politically and internationally) never had a dull moment'.[17]

'I do wonder how she is, and if that matchless strength has stood the strain,' wrote Ettie Desborough of Queen Mary after the King's funeral.[18] But Queen Mary's troubles did not end with George's death. Nineteen thirty-six must surely have been the worst year of her life. Her diary records long, sad days at Buckingham Palace sorting things – and few people possessed more things than she did (according to one source her rooms contained over a thousand objects) – in preparation for her move to Marlborough House.[19] 'I think I shall be quite contented here,' she wrote of her new home, 'though there must always be the fearful blank.'[20] Almost as sore as the wrench of leaving Buckingham Palace was the pain of handing over to Garrard the Crown Jewels, 'which have been in my care since 1910. Felt very sad at the parting.'[21]

The Queen saw King Edward often during the months after George's funeral and before the Abdication, and though their relations were friendly, she never mentioned the name of Mrs Simpson. The story of Wallis's divorce broke in early December 1936, and Edward told his mother that he was determined to marry Mrs Simpson and abdicate. The Queen, according to Channon, was 'shy, nervous and ineffectual'.[22] On the contrary, the Queen was furious. The next day she received Baldwin. She came into the room with her hands stretched out, saying: 'Well, Mr Baldwin, this is a pretty kettle of fish.'[23]

Her rage persisted. 'This really might be ROUMANIA!!' she stormed on another occasion.[24] She was 'very angry' with Edward, and (said Lady Bertha Dawkins) 'I really think that helps her to bear what she calls "the Humiliation" of it all'.[25] She told Edward: 'All my life I have put my Country before everything else, and I simply cannot change now.'[26] When Lord Salisbury saw her after Edward had signed the Instrument of Abdication, he expected to find her weeping. But she was incensed and outraged. 'The person who needs most sympathy is my second son,' she reminded him indignantly. 'He is the one who is making the sacrifice.'[27] As Lady Airlie perceived, Queen Mary, who was so gentle in her private life, 'had a side which was as steel'.[28]

One day at the height of the crisis, the Queen's Daimler drew up in Warwick Street, Soho outside the Roman Catholic church. A plain brick Georgian box, in the eighteenth century it had been the church of the Portuguese and then the Bavarian legations. Accompanied by a lady-in-waiting the Queen entered the church and sat or knelt in front of the Virgin. Five minutes later, she departed. From that date until her death in 1953 flowers were delivered to the church every week from the Queen.[29]

That Queen Mary should seek comfort in a Catholic church was extraordinary. Brought up a strict Protestant, she had become more High Church later in life. But she was sternly Anglican – her position as queen consort depended on it. 'If I wasn't I wouldn't be here,' she once remarked.[30] The episode at the church in Warwick Street is perhaps a measure of how desperate she had become. She confided in her sister-in-law Princess Alice that the Abdication made her 'more unhappy than she had ever been in her life. "Even worse than when George died."'[31]

Queen Mary threw her influence behind the new King George VI. Defying the convention that the queen dowager should not attend the coronation of her husband's successor, she made a sensational appearance. Erect and regal in a silver gown and Garter ribbon she advanced slowly to the royal box, 'the very symbol of the solidity of the British monarchy'.[32] To the family she gave advice and leadership. 'Thank God we have all got you as a central point, because without that point [the family] might easily disintegrate,' said one of them.[33]

Adjusting to her new role as queen mother was hard for Queen Mary, as it had been for Queen Alexandra before her.* Her magnificent self-control meant that few knew what she really felt. Some thought that she was 'never able to establish her own personality until she became a widow', and she was happier then 'than at any other time in her life'.[34] But people close to her realised how much she regretted not being at the centre of things. She 'suffered agonies of unhappiness from a sense of powerlessness. Nothing she asked was done.'[35]

As Osbert Sitwell observed, a 'film-star glamour' overtook her appearance in advanced age. Her Transylvanian eyebrows, set at an angle, her love of jewels and the way she wore them and the stylisation of her clothes 'made her an attractive as well as an imposing figure'.[36] Sitwell admired the way she smoked her cigarettes – she who had once written of a German princess, 'Fancy dying of over smoking. Such a pity people can't do things in moderation', was now often seen smoking her particular brand of Egyptian cigarettes.[37] And the beautifully waved silver hair which elicited so many compliments was a wig – silver by day and gold at night.[38]

At Marlborough House she established her own court. Seemingly incapable of downsizing after Buckingham Palace, she insisted on keeping a staff of sixty servants. Knee breeches were compulsory at her dinners, unlike at Buckingham Palace where men were allowed to wear trousers.[39] Worried about money, the Queen considered doing without her ladies-in-waiting, managing only with her women of the bedchamber. The Duchess of Devonshire volunteered to stay on as mistress of the robes without taking a salary, and this allowed the Queen to keep on Lady Ampthill and Lady Airlie as her ladies at £300 a year.[40]

In May 1939 Queen Mary's Daimler was involved in a collision with a lorry. The Queen had just pointed out a caterpillar on the leg of equerry Lord Claud Hamilton, and they were watching him pick it off

---

*According to Lady Airlie, Queen Mary chose the title of Queen Mother rather than Queen Dowager because the former 'has certain rights whereas a Queen Dowager has no particular privileges except those voluntarily accorded to her by the existing sovereign' (Mabell, Countess of Airlie, *Thatched with Gold: The Memoirs of Mabell, Countess of Airlie*, ed. Jennifer Ellis (Hutchinson, 1962), p. 207).

when the lorry rammed the car and it turned over. Bedchamber woman Lady Constance Milnes Gaskell found herself

> doubled up in a corner against a window which was against the road, and the seat which the Queen had been sitting on, on top of me. I could see nothing at first then screwing my head round I saw the Queen's head at my feet, imagine my agony of mind I thought the Queen was dead!

The Queen was saved by falling partly on Lord Claud; her head would otherwise have hit the door or the glass. She was extricated with a ladder, and when Lady Constance herself emerged from the wreckage she found the Queen standing on the pavement with 'not one hair out of place, looking as if she had just left her room'.[41] At seventy-two, the Queen was still (in the words of Sir Stanley Hewett) 'a *real tough guy*'.[42]

The Queen spent the Second World War at Badminton in Gloucestershire, bringing with her fifty servants, as the guest of her niece Mary Cambridge, now Duchess of Beaufort. This was the first time she had lived in the country, and here she stayed for six years, spending her afternoons destroying ivy or 'wooding' – cutting down elder and planting trees with her suite. Some of her projects such as sorting out the Somerset family papers dismayed her hosts, as did her 'ivy mania'. The life suited her. She would appear in a sequinned dress with an ostrich-feather cape for a sparse dinner which was over by 9.00, when she would listen to the news on the wireless while knitting.[43] She made a habit of stopping her car to give a lift to airmen or soldiers on the road: 'she discovered democracy and loved it'.[44] During air raids she was to be seen in the shelter in the middle of the night 'perfectly dressed with her pearls, doing a crossword puzzle'.[45] She was tearful when she left. 'Oh I *have* been happy here,' she said. 'Here I'm anybody to everybody and back in London I shall have to be Queen Mary all over again.'[46]

In London Queen Mary sallied forth once more to the Victoria and Albert Museum and the Wallace Collection, she went to films, she was cheered in the street.[47] But Marlborough House was cold and increasingly lonely. Few visitors came. Often the only person she saw was the lady-in-waiting with whom she ate dinner.[48] She defied old age by pretending it wasn't happening. Her household were not allowed to grow old or become ill, and she avoided visiting retired loyal retainers.[49] The faithful Lady Airlie, her closest friend, narrowly escaped being sacked after forty-three years as a lady-in-waiting because the Queen couldn't abide her becoming deaf and acquiring false teeth.[50]*

Queen Mary's reputation has suffered from stories about her alleged 'kleptomania'. Typical of these is a visit she paid to Lady Islington during the Second World War. First she admired a large vase bearing the Teck arms. Lady Islington was silent. The Queen then praised a little table. Silence. As she got into her car, the Queen said: 'I really must go back and say goodbye to that charming little table.' She did. But Lady Islington still said nothing, and the Queen departed.[51] In the wake of such unsuccessful attempts, she might write and offer to buy the object, and this was a coded royal command to make it a gift.[52]

It's hard to know whether these stories are apocryphal. The fact that they follow the same pattern may be taken as corroboration or, per contra, may suggest that their authenticity is doubtful. Very few end in victory for Queen Mary. The object usually remained in the house of its owner. People learnt to put away the Fabergé before she arrived and hide the carriage clocks. Old Monsignor Gilbey, the famous Roman Catholic priest, once asked James Lees-Milne whether he had ever come across an authentic case of Queen Mary demanding to be given an antique from someone she was visiting. 'I hadn't,' replied Lees-Milne.[53] Perhaps the truth is that she behaved like this once or twice and gossip then took over.

Her disconcerting habit of descending on people in their houses with very little notice did her reputation no good. Often these expeditions were successful, however. Just after the outbreak of the Second World War she made a visit with only one day's notice to Mark Gambier-Parry at Highnam Court in Gloucestershire. The rush and panic to get the house ready was stressful. But 'from the moment H.M. entered the house all was serene and no one could have imagined the awful scrimmage . . . She saw everything . . . Although a Queen she is entirely homely in manner and speech despite a regal carriage and a very reserved manner.' Afterwards Gambier-Parry was deeply touched to receive a signed photograph from his unexpected guest with the message 'In Memory of a very charming afternoon'.[54]

Queen Mary's eccentricities in later life should not obscure the very

---

*It was fortunate for Queen Mary that Lady Airlie was reprieved. Her posthumously published memoir, *Thatched with Gold*, is by far the most perceptive and sympathetic account of Queen Mary's career as queen consort.

real historical significance of her years as consort. It is impossible to understand the monarchy of George V without realising the importance of the Queen Consort. George V created the first modern family monarchy. Edward VII had sidelined Queen Alexandra, and Prince Albert had tried to appropriate Queen Victoria's power rather than walk two steps behind her. Queen Mary achieved a working partnership as consort with George V. As she reflected, 'all through the years the King always told me everything *first*. I do miss that.'[55]

When she died aged eighty-five in March 1953, in the reign of her granddaughter, Queen Mary had survived her husband by seventeen years, a symbol of rectitude and resilience, evoking a past that had been overtaken by another world war and the end of empire. But King George, and his Queen Consort, deserve to be remembered for the dramatic changes his reign helped to bring about. He was an unexpected king, but the way he handled the crises that came at him one after another showed him to be one of the most thoughtful and one of the most successful monarchs in British history. He may have ducked the issue of his immediate successor, but the Crown's stability in the twenty-first century – and that of Britain's system of government – surely owes much to him.

Acknowledgements

My greatest debt is to Her Majesty Queen Elizabeth II for permission to make use of the papers of King George V and Queen Mary in the Royal Archives at Windsor. Working in the impressive new research room at the top of the Round Tower has been a privilege and a pleasure. Invariably friendly and helpful, the staff have made the many days I have spent working in the archives especially enjoyable. I am grateful to Bill Stockting, the Archives Manager, for his wise guidance and advice. Special thanks to Senior Archivist Julie Crocker for all her help with my research, for her efficiency in supplying me with documents, and for her accuracy and speed in checking footnotes.

I would like to thank Her Majesty Queen Elizabeth II for permission to quote from documents of which she holds the copyright outside the Royal Archives. These include James Pope-Hennessy's transcripts from the Royal Archives now in the Getty Research Library in Los Angeles.

I am grateful to the Getty Research Library for granting me permission to make use of the James Pope-Hennessy papers. Julia Armstrong-Totten identified the papers for me and her enthusiasm encouraged me to visit the Getty. My thanks to the Getty for making my two research trips to their calm and serene research room so enjoyable and productive. The Getty awarded me a Getty Library Research Grant, for which I would like to record my thanks.

My thanks to the Harold Nicolson Literary Estate for permission to quote from Harold Nicolson's Diary at Balliol College, Oxford, from his letters to Vita Sackville-West at Sissinghurst, and from the Harold Nicolson papers at the Beinecke Library at Yale. Thank you to Timothy Young of the Beinecke for help with the Nicolson letters there. I am especially indebted to Juliet Nicolson. I spent a memorable summer's day at Sissinghurst, reading Harold's letters while sitting at his desk in his room looking out on his garden.

I should like to thank Lady Webb-Carter for generously giving me access to the Wigram papers and for permission to quote. Thank you to the Devonshire Collections at Chatsworth for permission to quote from the papers of Evelyn, Duchess of Devonshire. Extracts from the papers of Lord Esher are reproduced by kind permission of the Churchill Archives Centre on behalf of the 5th Viscount Esher. Thanks also to the Churchill Archives for permission to quote from the papers of Sir Bryan Godfrey-Faussett. I am grateful to Charles Gore for permission to quote from his private papers, and also from the John Gore Papers in the John Murray Archive in the National Library of Scotland in Edinburgh.

Richard Davenport-Hines provided me with invaluable suggestions and information. I am especially grateful to Lord Luce. Jane Roberts was generous with her time and expertise; after spending an afternoon with her at Windsor, I began to realise the importance of Queen Mary's role in enlarging and curating the Royal Collection. Michael Sefi, Keeper of the Royal Philatelic Collection, showed me King George's mind-boggling collection of stamps. With Sally Bedell Smith I visited White Lodge and Frogmore, and had many entertaining conversations over sandwiches in the Round Tower. Ian Shapiro gave me access to his collection, and he and Sue Woolmans supplied invaluable information about Queen Mary.

My MA students at Buckingham have probably heard more than they would like about royal biography, but they have greatly helped me to clarify my ideas. I am especially grateful to Christina Dykes whose research has informed my understanding of certain episodes in the book.

The following have provided information, stories and contacts, and helped in all sorts of ways with the book: Jonathan Aitken, Catherine Armitage, Caroline Behr, Vernon Bogdanor, John Brown, Lady Myra Butter, Clarissa Campbell Orr, David Cannadine, Anne de Courcy, the Marquess of Donegall, Alistair Ferguson, Frank Field, Nicholas Gibbs, Lord Grantley, Marion (Patsy) Grigg, Lady Raina Haig, Rear-Admiral Michael Harris, Jeremy Howard, Simon Jenkins, Aidan Jones, Kathryn Jones, Alan Judd, Bev Kelly, Andrew Lownie, Andrew Lycett, Sarah Mahaffy, Philip Mansel, Clarissa Mitchell, Frank Mort, Jason Pemberton-Piggott, Dominic Pierce, Sir Charles Ponsonby, Iain Scott, D. R. Thorpe, Hugo Vickers, Lady Doune Wake, Philip Williamson, Joan Winterkorn. Special thanks to Piers Russell-Cobb.

I have greatly enjoyed working with Becky Hardie, my editor at Chatto, and I am grateful for her patience with my repeated requests for more time and for her amazing skill in managing the final stages of the book. Thanks to Peter James, for his superb editing, and to Jonathan Wadman for his swift and rigorous copy-editing. At the publishers, my thanks to Etta Voorsanger-Brill for the wonderful jacket, to Fiona Brown for her meticulous proof reading and to Tom Atkins. Jo Evans did a great job with the picture research. Most of all I want to thank my marvellous agent Caroline Dawnay, who has come to the rescue on so many occasions. I am indeed fortunate to have Caroline as my agent.

Huge thanks to my sons Toby and Humphrey for putting up both with me and with the book. No sooner had they survived my immersion in Edward VII than George V appeared on the scene. Thanks again to Toby, who was the first person to read the typescript. This book is dedicated to Toby and Humphrey.

List of Illustrations

First section

Alexandra with Albert and George © Look and Learn/Bridgeman Images

George as a young boy, courtesy of the Library of Congress, Prints and Photographs Diction, LC-B2-1114-2

The Wales children © Universal History Archive/UIG/Bridgeman Images

The Waleses © Universal History Archive/UIG/Bridgeman Images

George in naval uniform © Look and Learn/Valerie Jackson Harris Collection/Bridgeman Images

Eddy in collars and cuffs © Look and Learn/Bridgeman Images

Eddy and May of Teck's engagement © Granger/Bridgeman Images

The Duchess of Teck and her children © Universal History Archive/ UIG/Bridgeman Images

Wedding of George and May © Royal Collection/Royal Collection Trust © Her Majesty Queen Elizabeth II, 2021/Bridgeman Images

George and May's wedding-day photo © Look and Learn/Valerie Jackson Harris Collection/Bridgeman Images

George at Sandringham with his children © Look and Learn/Valerie Jackson Harris Collection/Bridgeman Images

Arthur Bigge, later Lord Stamfordham © Look and Learn/Peter Jackson Collection/Bridgeman Images

York Cottage, Sandringham © Look and Learn/Elgar Collection/ Bridgeman Images

George shooting grouse © PA Images/Alamy Stock Photo

Nicky and Georgie © Granger/Bridgeman Images

433

The cousins' last meeting © CSU Archives/Everett Collection/Bridgeman Images

Four generations © Historic Royal Palaces/Bridgeman Images

Bertie and George © Look and Learn/Valerie Jackson Harris Collection/Bridgeman Images

Shooting party at Sandringham © Historic Royal Palaces/Bridgeman Images

Second section

Coronation portrait of George V by Luke Fildes © Galerie Bilderwelt/Bridgeman Images

The Downey Head. Stamp design © Royal Mail Group Limited

Coronation of George V and Mary. Digital image courtesy of Getty's Open Content Program

George sailing *Britannia* © Spaarnestad Photo/Bridgeman Images

Coronation of George and Mary in Delhi © akg-images

John Lavery's painting of the royal family © Stefano Baldini/Bridgeman Images

Queen Mary wearing the Vladimiri tiara © Bridgeman Images

Prince John © Universal History Archive/UIG/Bridgeman Images

Queen Mary visits Silverwood Colliery © Bridgeman Images

George at the Western Front © The Stapleton Collection/Bridgeman Images

George and Lloyd George at Victoria Station © Universal History Archive/UIG/Bridgeman Images

Ramsay MacDonald © SZ Photo/Bridgeman Images

George visits the Passchendaele war graves © National Army Museum/Bridgeman Images

Prince George and Princess Marina at Balmoral © Peter Newark Pictures/Bridgeman Images

King George's last visit to the East End © The Stapleton Collection/Bridgeman Images

George making his first Christmas broadcast © The Stapleton Collection/
Bridgeman Images

The King with his shooting pony Jock © The Stapleton Collection/
Bridgeman Images

King and Queen at the Jubilee © Universal History Archive/UIG/
Bridgeman Images

The princes © Bridgeman Images

On the balcony at the Jubilee © Spaarnestad Photo/Bridgeman Images

Notes

Archives and Abbreviations

Mabell, Countess of Airlie	British Library (BL)
Albert Victor, Duke of Clarence (Eddy)	Royal Archives, Windsor (RA)
Queen Alexandra (Alix)	Royal Archives, Windsor and Danish National Archives, Copenhagen
Herbert Asquith	Bodleian Library, Oxford
Margot Asquith	Bodleian Library, Oxford
Augusta, Grand Duchess of Mecklenburg-Strelitz	Royal Archives, Windsor
A. J. Balfour	British Library, London
Maurice Baring	Harry Ransom Centre, Austin, Texas
Prince Louis of Battenberg	Southampton University, Southampton
Norman Brook	The National Archives, Kew (TNA)
Lord Carnock	The National Archives, Kew
Archbishop Davidson	Lambeth Palace, London
Lady Bertha Dawkins	Getty Research Library, Los Angeles
King Edward VII	Royal Archives, Windsor
King Edward VIII (D, David, Duke of Windsor, EDW)	Royal Archives, Windsor
Lord Esher (ESHR)	Churchill Archives Centre, Cambridge
Evelyn, Duchess of Devonshire	The Devonshire Collections, Chatsworth
Foreign Office Files, 1917–18	The National Archives, Kew
King George V (G, GV)	Royal Archives, Windsor
GVD	Diary of George V
Bryan Godfrey-Faussett (BGGF)	Churchill Archive Centre, Cambridge
John Gore	John Murray Archive, National Library of Scotland and by kind permission of Charles Gore
Bishop Hensley Henson	Durham Cathedral Library
Viscount Knollys	Royal Archives, Windsor
Archbishop Cosmo Lang	Lambeth Palace, London
Marquess of Lincolnshire (Lord Carrington until 1895)	Bodleian Library, Oxford
David Lloyd George	Parliamentary Archives, House of Lords, London

Philip Magnus	By kind permission of Charles Sebag-Montefiore
Princess Mary Adelaide, Duchess of Teck	Getty Research Library, Los Angeles
Queen Mary (May of Teck)	Royal Archives, Windsor and Getty Research Library, Los Angeles
Schomberg McDonnell (Pom)	Public Record Office of Northern Ireland, Belfast
Hon. Richard (Dick) Molyneux	Liverpool Library, Liverpool
Harold Nicolson	Balliol College Archive, Oxford (Diary); Beinecke Library, Yale (Papers); Sissinghurst, Cranbrook (Sissinghurst Papers)
James Pope-Hennessy (Pope)	Getty Research Library, Los Angeles
Sir Edward Sieveking	Royal College of Physicians, London
Lady Geraldine Somerset	Getty Research Library, Los Angeles
Queen Victoria (QV, V)	Royal Archives, Windsor and http://www.queenvictoriasjournals.org/home.do
Vicky (Dowager Empress Frederick of Germany)	Royal Archives, Windsor
Clive Wigram, Nora Wigram	Wigram Papers by kind permission of Lady Webb-Carter

Preface

1 Sir Alan Lascelles, *King's Counsellor: Abdication and War – The Diaries of Sir Alan Lascelles*, ed. Duff Hart-Davis (Phoenix, 2007), p. 433.
2 Balliol College Archive, Harold Nicolson Diary, Nicolson to Vita Sackville-West, 8 June 1948.
3 Nicolson Diary, 26 July 1951.
4 Nicolson Diary, 16 August 1949.
5 Nicolson Diary, Nicolson to Vita Sackville-West, 17 August 1949.
6 Sissinghurst Papers, Nicolson to Vita Sackville-West, 9 September 1948.
7 Nicolson Diary, 4 November 1948 (Kenneth Clarke).
8 National Library of Scotland, John Murray Archive, John Gore Papers, Acc. 13328/171 EE6, Gore to Murray, n.d. [1939].
9 John Gore, *King George V: A Personal Memoir* (John Murray, 1941), p. xv.
10 Kenneth Rose, *King George V* (Phoenix Press, 2000), p. 96.
11 Gore, *King George V*, p. 232; Jane Ridley, *Bertie: A Life of Edward VII* (Chatto & Windus, 2012), p. 364.
12 Diary of George V, RA GV/PRIV/GVD/6 May 1910.
13 Nicolson Diary,18 December 1948.
14 Nicolson Diary, 27 July 1949 (Lord Carisbrooke); Ridley, *Bertie*, pp. 240, 305–6.
15 Kenneth Rose, *Who's In, Who's Out: The Journals of Kenneth Rose, Vol. 1*, ed. D. R. Thorpe (Weidenfeld & Nicolson, 2018), p. 516.
16 Kenneth Rose, *Who Loses, Who Wins: The Journals of Kenneth Rose, Vol. 2*, ed. D. R. Thorpe (Weidenfeld & Nicolson, 2019), p. 103.
17 Rose, *Who Loses, Who Wins*, p. 264.
18 Rose, *King George V*, p. 300.
19 James Pope-Hennessy, *Queen Mary* (Phoenix Press, 2000), p. 23.
20 John Gore Papers, Acc. 13328/141 DV10, Stanley Went of G. P. Putnam's to Murray.

CHAPTER I

My Darling Little Georgie

1 *The Times*, 3, 5 June 1865; Jane Ridley, *Bertie: A Life of Edward VII* (Chatto & Windus, 2012), p. 93.
2 Royal College of Physicians, Shelfmark 718, Diaries of Sir W. Sieveking, 3 June 1865.
3 Sieveking Diary, 5 February, 4 June 1865.
4 RA VIC/MAIN/QVJ (W) QVJ online, 3 June 1865.
5 Getty Research Library, Pope 194/3, V to Vicky, 22 February 1865.
6 Pope 194/3, V to Vicky, 5 June 1865.
7 Pope 194/3, V to Vicky, 17 June 1865.
8 *Queen Victoria's Letters*, Second Series, Vol. 1, V to Bertie, 13 June 1865, p. 268.
9 RA VIC/MAIN/Z/448/110, Bertie to V, 16 June 1865; Z488/111, Phipps to V, 17 June 1865.
10 Pope 194/3, V to Vicky, 8 July 1865.
11 Pope 194/3, V to Vicky, 23 September 1865.
12 RA VIC/MAIN/Y/111/24, V to King Leopold, 11 March 1864.
13 RA VIC/MAIN/Z/449/27, Bertie to V, 5 November 1868.
14 RA VIC/ADDC18/93, Lady Macclesfield Diary, 11 November 1864.
15 Copenhagen Letters, Box 102, Alix to Minny, 4 September 1866.
16 Georgina Battiscombe, *Queen Alexandra* (Constable, 1969), p. 144.
17 Pope 194/3, V to Vicky, 23 February 1867.
18 Roger Fulford, ed., *Your Dear Letter: Private Correspondence of Queen Victoria and the Crown Princess of Prussia 1865–1871* (Evans Brothers, 1971), p. 186, V to Vicky, 2 May 1868.
19 RA VIC/MAIN/T/5/13, V to Bertie, 4 May 1868.

20 RA VIC/ADDA3/108, Bertie to V, 1 May 1868.

21 RA VIC/MAIN/Z/449/20, V to Bertie, October 1868.

22 RA VIC/MAIN/Z/449/26, Bertie to V, 1 November 1868.

23 Fulford, ed., *Your Dear Letter*, p. 221, V to Vicky, 27 January 1869. *The Times*, 23 January, 11 May 1869.

24 RA VIC/MAIN/A/3/128, Bertie to V, 26 February 1869.

25 Roger Fulford, ed., *Darling Child: Private Correspondence of Queen Victoria and the Crown Princess of Prussia 1871–1878* (Evans Brothers, 1976), p. 93, V to Vicky, 2 June 1873.

26 Battiscombe, *Queen Alexandra*, pp. 122–3 (17 March 1872).

27 Fulford, ed., *Your Dear Letter*, p. 277, V to Vicky, 30 April 1870.

28 RA VIC/MAIN/QVJ (W) QVJ online, 5 February 1871.

29 Ben Pimlott, *Hugh Dalton* (Jonathan Cape, 1985), pp. 7, 77–9, 644.

30 Pimlott, *Hugh Dalton*, p. 71.

31 RA VIC/MAIN/QVJ (W) QVJ online, 1 June 1874.

32 Fulford, ed., *Darling Child*, pp. 140–1, V to Vicky, 2 June 1874.

33 Pope 194/8, V to Vicky, 8 April 1874.

34 RA VIC/ADDA 36/776, Ponsonby to V, 9 August 1874.

35 Balliol College Archive, Nicolson Diary, 21 March 1949.

36 John Gore, *King George V: A Personal Memoir* (John Murray, 1941), p. 42n.

37 Gore, *King George V*, p. 19, Nicolson, *King George the Fifth*, p. 7.

38 Harold Nicolson, *King George the Fifth: His Life and Reign* (Constable, 1952), p. 8.

39 Sissinghurst Papers, Nicolson to Vita, 11 March 1949. Gore, *King George V*, p. 19.

40 Ian Shapiro collection, G to Dalton, 19 August 1877.

41 Sissinghurst Papers, *King George the Fifth* royal proofs, Vol.1, p. 7. Nicolson Diary, 5 January 1950.

42 Hugh Dalton, *Political Diary of Hugh Dalton*, ed. Ben Pimlott (Jonathan Cape, 1981), p. 11, 17 August 1931.

43 Gore, *King George V*, pp. 9, 11, 54, 116, 367.

44 Marie, Queen of Roumania, *The Story of My Life* (Cassell, 1934), vol. 1, p. 43.

45 RA GV/PRIV/AA28/8, Alix to G, 11 August 1877.

46 Nicolson Diary, 12 August 1949 (John Gore).

47 Marie, *The Story of My Life*, vol. 1, pp. 6–7.

48 Wigram Papers, Clive to Nora, December 1923

49 Lady Geraldine Somerset in Battiscombe, *Queen Alexandra*, p.139.

50 Fulford, ed., *Your Dear Letter*, p. 223, V to Vicky, 10 February 1869.

51 James Pope-Hennessy, *The Quest for Queen Mary*, ed. Hugo Vickers (Zuleika, 2018), p. 164.

52 John Van der Kiste, *Edward VII's Children* (Alan Sutton, 1989), pp. 33–40.

53 RA VIC/MAIN/QVJ (W) QVJ online, 7 February 1877.

54 Fulford, ed., *Darling Child*, p. 141, Vicky to V, 6 June 1874.

55 RA VIC/MAIN/Z/459/90, 11 February 1877, Dalton's Memorandum on Education of 'Bertie's Boys', 11 February 1877.

56 Dalton's Memo, 11 February 1877, in Nicolson, *King George the Fifth*, p. 13.

57 RA VIC/MAIN/QVJ (W) QVJ online, 16 February 1877.

58 QV's Memorandum, 15 February 1877 in Nicolson, *King George the Fifth*, p. 14.

59 RA GV/PRIV/AA28/5, Alix to G, 2 May 1877.

60 *The Times*, 19 May 1877. Nicolson, *King George the Fifth*, p. 12. Andrew Cook, *Prince Eddy: The King Britain Never Had* (History Press, 2008), p. 62.

61 *The Times*, 5, 28 July 1877. Anna Keay, *Landmark: A History of Britain in 50 Buildings* (Frances Lincoln, 2015), pp. 243–7.

62 RA GV/PRIV/AA28/8, Alix to G, 11 August 1877.

63 Van der Kiste, *Edward VII's Children*, p. 49.

64 RA VIC/MAIN/Z/452/108, Alix to V, 15 October 1877.

65 *The Times*, 19 October 1877. Kenneth Rose, *King George V* (Phoenix Press, 2000), p. 7. Andrew Gordon, *The Rules of the Game: Jutland and British Naval Command* (Penguin, 2015), p. 218.

66 RA GV/PRIV/AA39/6, Eddy to G, 4 November 1883.

67 Commander E. P. Statham, *The Story of the 'Britannia': The Training Ship for Naval Cadets* (Cassell, 1904), Appendix IV, loc. 3992–4030 [Gutenberg]. Gordon, *The Rules of the Game*, p. 172.

68 Battiscombe, *Queen Alexandra*, p. 140.

69 Queen Victoria, *The Letters of Queen Victoria, Second Series: A Selection from Her Majesty's Correspondence and Journal Between the Years 1862 and 1878*, ed. George Earle Buckle (John Murray, 1926), vol. 2, p. 575, Dalton to V, 14 November 1877.

70 RA VIC/MAIN/Z/452/167, Bertie to V, 23 April 1878.

71 Statham, *The Story of the 'Britannia'*, loc. 1766.

72 Captain S.W.C. Pack, *Britannia at Dartmouth* (Alvin Redman, 1966), p. 51.

73 Statham, *The Story of the 'Britannia'*, loc. 1597.

74 George recorded by Owen Morshead, January 1932 in Gore, *King George V*, p. 31.

75 Pack, *Britannia at Dartmouth*, p. 51.

76 Gore, *King George V*, p. 31. Gordon, *The Rules of the Game*, p. 216.

77 RA VIC/MAIN/Z/473/1, Ramsay to Bertie, 3 December 1878.

78 Battiscombe, *Queen Alexandra*, p. 153.

79 Dalton to Bertie, 9 April 1879 in Philip Magnus, *King Edward the Seventh* (John Murray, 1964) p. 158.

80 RA VIC/MAIN/Z/453/30, Bertie to V, 14 July 1879.

81 Dalton to Bertie, 9 April 1879 in Magnus, *King Edward the Seventh*, p. 158.

82 Sissinghurst, HN to Vita, 11 March 1949.

CHAPTER 2:

A Disgraceful Education

1 John Gore, *King George V: A Personal Memoir* (John Murray, 1941), pp. 56–7. RA GV/PRIV/AA 37/3, G to Alix, 14 September 1901.

2 Queen Victoria, *Advice to a Grand-Daughter: Letters from Queen Victoria to Princess Victoria of Hesse*, ed. Richard Hough (Readers Union, 1976), p. 29.

3 RA VIC/MAIN/Z/453/104, V to Bertie, 26 May 1880.

4 RA VIC/MAIN/Z/453/118, V to Bertie, 6 July 1880.

5 RA VIC/MAIN/Z/453/96, Bertie to V, 22 May 1880.

6 *The Times*, 17 September 1879. Gore, *King George V*, p. 40.

7 Captain S.W.C. Pack, *Britannia at Dartmouth* (Alvin Redman, 1966), pp. 55–6. Andrew Gordon, *The Rules of the Game: Jutland and British Naval Command* (Penguin, 2015), p. 218.

8 Harold Nicolson, *King George the Fifth: His Life and Reign* (Constable, 1952), p. 22. Balliol College Archive, Nicolson Diary, 21 March 1949.

9 Nicolson, *King George the Fifth*, p. 28.

10 Ben Pimlott, *Hugh Dalton* (Jonathan Cape, 1985), p. 11. Gore, *King George V*, p. 40.

11 RA GV/PRIV/AA28/39, Alix to G, 15 January 1880.

12 Dalton, 1 May 1880 in Philip Magnus, *King Edward the Seventh* (John Murray, 1964) p. 169.

13 RA GV/PRIV/AA28/32, 2 June 1879. Nicolson, *King George the Fifth*, p. 23.

14 Sissinghurst Papers, Nicolson to Vita, 3 March 1949.

15 Nicolson Diary, Nicolson to Vita, 31 August 1948. Gore, *King George V*, p. 9.

16 Georgina Battiscombe, *Queen Alexandra* (Constable, 1969), p. 142.

17 RA GV/PRIV/AA28/25, Alix to G, 26 January 1879.

18 RA GV/PRIV/AA28/43, Alix to G, 15 September 1880.

19 RA GV/PRIV/AA36/2, G to Alix, 19 September 1880. Gore, *King George V*, p. 41.

20 *The Times*, 14 September 1880.

21 G to Alix, 15 September 1880 in Nicolson, *King George the Fifth*, pp. 24–5.

22 Prince Albert Victor, Duke of Clarence and Avondale and Prince George of Wales, *The Cruise of Her Majesty's Ship 'Bacchante'* (Macmillan, 1886), vol. 1, p. viii.

23 Nicolson Diary, 21 March 1949.

24 Dalton to Bertie, 16 May 1882 in Nicolson, *King George the Fifth*, p. 20.

25 Nicolson, *King George the Fifth*, p. 20.

26 Edward, Duke of Windsor, *A King's Story: The Memoirs of HRH the Duke of Windsor* (Cassell, 1951), p. 35.

27 *The Times*, 31 May 1886.

28 RA GV/PRIV/AA36/3, G to Alix, 19 December 1880.

29 RA GV/PRIV/AA36/3, G to Alix, 19 December 1880.

30 Albert Victor and George, *The Cruise of HMS 'Bacchante'*, vol. 1, pp. 257–8. *The Times*, 5 August 1882.

31 Nicolson, *King George the Fifth*, pp. 32–3.

32 Gordon, *The Rules of the Game*, pp. 172, 175–6, 222.

33 Nicolson Diary, 21 March 1949.

34 Nicolson, *King George the Fifth*, p. 29.

35 RA GV/PRIV/AA36/11, G to Alix, 5 April 1882.

36 RA VIC/MAIN/Z/475/16, V to Bertie, 4 August 1891.

37 RA GV/PRIV/AA28/54, Alix to G, 10 March 1881.

38 RA GV/PRIV/AA29/1, Alix to G, 22 April 1881.

39 RA GV/PRIV/AA28/54, Alix to G, 10 March 1881.

40 RA GV/PRIV/AA29/16, Alix to G, 3 March 1882.

41 Windsor, *A King's Story*, p. 37.

42 Nicolson, *King George the Fifth*, p. 34. John Wheeler-Bennett, *King George VI: His Life and Reign* (Macmillan, 1958), p. 26n.

43 Nicolson, *King George the Fifth*, p. 34.

44 Alix to Dalton, 11 March 1883 in Battiscombe, *Queen Alexandra*, p. 162.

45 RA GV/PRIV/AA29/32, Alix to G, 23 March 1883.

46 RA GV/PRIV/AA29/36, Alix to G, 15 June 1883.

47 RA GV/PRIV/AA39/1, Eddy to G, 15 June 1883.

48 RA GV/PRIV/AA39/2, Eddy to G, 20 June 1883.

49 George to Dalton, 22 April 1884 in Gore, *King George V*, p. 60. RA GV/PRIV/AA39/12, Eddy to G, 1 March 1884. RA GV/PRIV/AA 39/13, Eddy to G, 30 March 1884. Nicolson, *King George the Fifth*, p. 6.

50 Dalton to G, 11 July 1883 in Gore, *King George V*, p. 57.

51 Sissinghurst, bound proof annotation by George VI, vol. 1, p. 8.

52 Nicolson Diary, 4 January 1950.

53 Gore, *King George V*, pp. 9, 74.

54 Nicolson, *King George the Fifth*, p. 38.

55 Dennis Friedman, *Darling Georgie: The Enigma of King George V* (Peter Owen, 1998), p. 72.

56 Friedman, *Darling Georgie*, pp. 50, 67–8.

57 RA GV/PRIV/AA29/35, Alix to G, 12 June 1883.

58 Friedman, pp. 68–9.

59 Nicolson Diary, Nicolson to Vita, 31 August 1948. Gore, *George V*, p. 9.

60 Theo Aronson, *Prince Eddy and the Homosexual Underworld* (John Murray, 1994), p. 64.

61 RA GV/PRIV/AA39/4, Eddy to G, 29 July 1883.

62 Andrew Cook, *Prince Eddy: The King Britain Never Had* (History Press, 2008), p. 102.

63 RA GV/PRIV/AA39/5, Eddy to G, 27 September 1883.

64 RA VIC/MAIN/QVJ (W) QVJ online, 15 September 1883.

65 RA GV/PRIV/AA39/6, Eddy to G, 4 November 1883.

66 *Punch*, 24 November 1883. Aronson, *Prince Eddy and the Homosexual Underworld*, pp. 66–73. Henry Wilson had been one of the young men picked to coach Eddy at Sandringham, and he was expected to become Eddy's private secretary. Instead, he joined the colonial service and served as private secretary to Joseph Chamberlain.

67 Deborah Cadbury, *Queen Victoria's Matchmaking: The Royal Marriages That Shaped Europe* (Bloomsbury, 2017), p. 112.

68 RA GV/PRIV/AA39/6, Eddy to G, 4 November 1883.

69 RA GV/PRIV/AA39/12, Eddy to G, 1 March 1884.

70 RA GV/PRIV/AA39/6, Eddy to G, 4 November 1883.

71 RA GV/PRIV/AA39/7, Eddy to G, 28 November 1883.

72 Cook, *Prince Eddy*.

73 'X' (Herbert Vivian), *Myself Not Least: Being the Personal Reminiscences of 'X'* (Thornton Butterworth, 1925), p. 36.

74 'X', *Myself Not Least*, p. 37.

75 RA GV/PRIV/AA39/2, Eddy to G, 20 June 1883.

76 RA GV/PRIV/AA29/34, Alix to G, 19 April 1883.

77 Nicolson Diary, 1 March 1949.

78 Nicolson Diary, 3 November 1948. James Pope-Hennessy, *The Quest for Queen Mary*, ed. Hugo Vickers (Zuleika, 2018), p. 129.

79 RA GV/PRIV/AA30/15, Alix to G, 26 February 1886.

80 RA GV/PRIV/AA30/17, Alix to G, 10 May 1886.

81 RA GV/PRIV/AA30/17, Alix to G, 10 May 1886.

82 RA GV/PRIV/AA30/27, Alix to G, 16 February 1887.

83 RA GV/PRIV/AA39/36, Eddy to G, 9 August 1887.

84 Gore, *King George V*, p. 67.

85 RA GV/PRIV/AA36/16, G to Alix, 4 January 1888.

86 Gore, *King George V*, pp. 75–6.

87 Battiscombe, *Queen Alexandra*, p. 143.

88 RA GV/PRIV/AA30/19, Alix to G, 3 June 1886.

89 Vin Vincent, *Olga; or, Wrong on Both Sides* (Griffith Farran Browne, [1885]).

90 Nicolson, *King George the Fifth*, p. 39. He read it aloud to his wife shortly after his marriage (RA GV/PRIV/GVD/21, 24 August 1894).

91 Nicolson Diary, 7 September 1949. Sissinghurst, HN to VSW, 8 September 1949. Nicolson, *King George the Fifth*, p. 39.

CHAPTER 3

Naval Lieutenant

1 RA GV/PRIV/AA15/38, Bertie to G, 14 October 1885.

2 RA GV/PRIV/AA30/16, Alix to G, 17 April 1886.

3 G to Stephenson, 4 January 1886 in John Stephenson, ed., *A Royal Correspondence: Letters of King Edward VII and King George V to Admiral Sir Henry F. Stephenson* (Macmillan, 1938), pp. 62–3.

4 Bertie to Stephenson, 4 January 1886 in *Stephenson*, p. 64.

5 RA GV/PRIV/AA15/41, Bertie to G, 5 March 1886.

6   G to Bertie, 7 March 1886 in
    Harold Nicolson, *King George the
    Fifth: His Life and Reign*
    (Constable, 1952), p. 38.

7   RA GV/PRIV/AA36/14, G to Alix,
    18 December 1887.

8   Balliol College Archive, Nicolson
    Diary, 12 August 1949.

9   Andrew Gordon, *The Rules of the
    Game: Jutland and British Naval
    Command* (Penguin, 2015), p. 192.

10 Bertie to Stephenson, 27 July 1887
    in Stephenson, ed., *A Royal
    Correspondence*, p. 100.

11 Knollys to Stephenson, 19 May
    1886 in Stephenson, ed., *A Royal
    Correspondence*, p. 75.

12 Marie, Queen of Roumania, *The
    Story of My Life* (Cassell, 1934),
    vol. 1, p. 105.

13 RA GV/PRIV/AA36/16, G to Alix,
    4 January 1888.

14 Churchill Archives Centre, Bryan
    Godfrey-Faussett Papers, CHAR/
    BGGF 1/19, Diary 6,7 January, 2
    February, 25 April 1887.

15 Gordon, *The Rules of the Game*,
    p. 177.

16 Friedman, Dennis, *Darling Georgie:
    The Enigma of King George V*
    (Peter Owen, 1998), pp. 70–1.

17 Nicolson, *King George the Fifth*,
    p. 34.

18 Churchill Archive Centre, Godfrey-
    Faussett Diary, 1 May 1887.

19 Lytton Strachey, *Queen Victoria*
    (Collins, 1958), p. 226.

20 RA GV/PRIV/AA30/25, Alix to G,
    21 November 1886.

21 Pope 194/3, Pss Victoria to Empress
    Frederick, 8 June 1892.

22 RA GV/PRIV/AA39/34, Eddy to
    G, 27 December 1886.

23 RA GV/PRIV/AA30/25, Alix to G,
    21 November 1886.

24 RA GV/PRIV/AA13/43, Bertie to
    G, 13 August 1887.

25 G to Stephenson, 24 December
    1887 in Stephenson, ed., *A Royal
    Correspondence*, pp. 106–7.

26 RA GV/PRIV/AA39/41, Eddy to
    G, 31 December 1887.

27 RA GV/PRIV/AA36/14, G to Alix,
    18 December 1887.

28 RA GV/PRIV/AA31, Alix to G, 31
    January 1887.

29 Nicolson, *King George the Fifth*,
    pp. 30, 39. RA GV/PRIV/AA30/35,
    Alix to G, 4 April 1888

30 Nicolson Diary, 21 March 1949.

31 RA GV/PRIV/AA36/17, G to Alix,
    23 January 1888.

32 RA GV/PRIV/AA36/18, G to Alix,
    2 February 1888.

33 John Gore, *King George V: A
    Personal Memoir* (John Murray,
    1941), p. 88.

34 RA GV/PRIV/AA36/21, G to Alix,
    2 October 1888. This letter is
    addressed from Naplia (Nafplion),
    which is fifteen miles from
    Mycenae: he talks of a twelve-mile
    walk inland to the site.

35 G to Stephenson, 23 June 1888 in
    Stephenson, ed., *A Royal
    Correspondence*, pp. 134–5.

36 Nicolson Diary, 20 July 1949.

37 RA GV/PRIV/AA31/9, Alix to G,
    2 September 1889.

38 G to Stephenson, 6 September 1888
    in Stephenson, ed., *A Royal
    Correspondence*, p. 135.

39 Gordon, *The Rules of the Game*,
    p. 321.

40 RA GV/PRIV/AA13/43, Bertie to
    G, 13 August 1887.

41 RA GV/PRIV/AA13/28, Bertie to
    G, 2 February 1887.

42 Gordon, *The Rules of the Game*,
    p. 237.

43 RA GV/PRIV/AA31/12, Alix to G,
    22 May 1890.

44 RA GV/PRIV/AA36/27, G to Alix,
    15 June 1890.

45 RA GV/PRIV/GVD, 27 February
    1891.

46 RA GV/PRIV/GVD, 1 January;
    24, 25, 26, 28 February
    1891.

47 G to Missy, 7 January 1891 in
    Hannah Pakula, *The Last
    Romantic: A Biography of Queen
    Marie of Roumania* (Weidenfeld &
    Nicolson, 1985), p. 57.

48 Marie, *The Story of My Life*, vol. 1, p. 140.

49 G to Missy, 2 January 1888 in Pakula, *The Last Romantic*, p. 47.

50 RA GV/PRIV/AA31/1, Alix to G, 17 October 1888; RA GV/PRIV/AA31/11, Alix to G, 11 April 1890.

51 Pakula, *The Last Romantic*, p. 57, letter wrongly dated 3 January 1890.

52 Queen Victoria, *Advice to a Grand-Daughter: Letters from Queen Victoria to Princess Victoria of Hesse*, ed. Richard Hough (Readers Union, 1976), p. 120.

53 RA GV/PRIV/AA36/24, G to Alix, 24 May 1890.

54 RA GV/PRIV/AA36/31, G to Alix, 23 December 1890.

55 RA GV/PRIV/AA31/16, Alix to G, 10 January 1891.

56 RA GV/PRIV/AA31/16, Alix to G, 10 January 1891.

57 RA GV/PRIV/AA31/16, Alix to G, 18 April 1891.

58 RA GV/PRIV/AA31/5, Alix to G, 28 February 1889.

59 Getty Research Library, Pope 194/3, V to Vicky, 2 June 1891.

60 E.g. James Pope-Hennessy, *Queen Mary* (Phoenix Press, 2000), p. 249.

61 *The Times*, 27 August 1891. Nicolson, *King George the Fifth*, p. 44. Gordon, *The Rules of the Game*, p. 230.

62 *The Times*, 20 October 1891.

63 RA GV/PRIV/AA30/32, Alix to G, 3 October 1887.

64 Simon Sebag Montefiore, *The Romanovs 1613–1918* (Weidenfeld & Nicolson, 2016), pp. 474–5.

CHAPTER 4

Eddy

1 Getty Research Library, Pope 193/4, V to Vicky, 16, 19 November 1891. RA GV/PRIV/GVD, 31 December 1891.

2 Pope 193/4, V to Vicky, 19 November 1891.

3 Pope 203/6, Dr Broadbent's Report for QV, n.d. [?January 1892].

4 RA GV/PRIV/GVD/8 January 1892.

5 Pope 203/6, Broadbent to Miss Butterworth, 14 January 1892. Broadbent was afterwards appointed physician-in-ordinary to the Prince of Wales for his service to the two princes during their illnesses. He later persuaded George to become president of St Mary's Hospital and, with Bertie's agreement, he named a new wing after the Duke of Clarence (*ODNB*).

6 Pope 203/6, Broadbent's Report for QV.

7 Pope 203/6, Broadbent's Report for QV.

8 Pope 203/6, Broadbent's Report for QV. *British Medical Journal* quoted in *Bury and Norwich Post*, 19 January 1892.

9 RA VIC/Z/95/5, Bertie to V, 14 January 1892.

10 RA GV/PRIV/GVD, 13 June 1892.

11 Pope 203/6, Broadbent's Report for QV.

12 RA GV/PRIV/GVD, 13 January 1892.

13 Pope 203/6, Broadbent to James Reid, 14 January 1892.

14 RA GV/PRIV/GVD, 14 January 1892.

15 Princess Maud to Princess Hélène, 21 January 1892 in Prince Michael of Greece, *Eddy and Hélène: . . . An Impossible Match* (Rosvall Royal Books, 2013), p. 79.

16 Pope 203/6, Duchess of Teck to QV, 14 January 1892.

17 RA GV/PRIV/GVD, 17 January 1892.

18 Pope 203/6, Aunt Augusta to Duke of Cambridge, 24 January 1892.

19 *The Times*, Duke of Clarence obituary, 15 January 1892.

20 'The Duke of Clarence at Cambridge', *Pall Mall Gazette*, 15 January 1892.

21 James Edward Vincent, *His Royal Highness Duke of Clarence and Avondale: A Memoir* (John Murray, 1893), pp. 9–11, 25–28.

22 *Pall Mall Gazette*, 14 January 1892.

23 *Reynolds's Newspaper*, 24 January 1892.

24 Sissinghurst, Nicolson to Vita, 17 February 1949.

25 Balliol College Archive, Nicolson Diary, 16 February 1949.

26 Theo Aronson, *Prince Eddy and the Homosexual Underworld* (John Murray, 1994), pp. 82–115. Stowell's story was decidedly fishy. When someone pointed out that Eddy's schedule, published in the Court Circular, showed that he was not in London on the days of the Ripper murders, Stowell retracted in a letter to *The Times*. This was published the day after his death, and shortly after his son claimed to have destroyed the Ripper file unread (*The Times*, 4, 9, 14 November 1970).

27 Sissinghurst Papers, Nicolson to Vita, 3 March 1949.

28 Eddy to Dr Roche, 21 November 1885, 18 December [1886], International Autograph Auctions, 5 March 2016, https://web.archive. org/web/20160304071305/http:// www.autographauctions.co.uk/ bidcat/detail.asp?SaleRef=0061& LotRef=4 (accessed 4 June 2016). See Deborah Cadbury, *Queen Victoria's Matchmaking: The Royal Marriages That Shaped Europe* (Bloomsbury, 2017), pp. 34–5.

29 RA GV/PRIV/AA39/50, Eddy to G, 29 November 1888. RA GV/ PRIV/AA36/20, G to Alix, 13 September 1888. RA GV/PRIV/AA 30/39, Alix to G, 12 August 1888.

30 Southampton University, Mountbatten Papers, T77, Eddy to Louis Battenberg, 6 September, 7 October 1889. Cadbury, *Queen Victoria's Matchmaking*, pp. 95–110.

31 James Pope-Hennessy, *Queen Mary* (Phoenix Press, 2000), p. 190.

32 RA GV/PRIV/AA31/15, Alix to G, 23 October 1890.

33 RA GV/PRIV/AA33/11, Alix to G, 10 November 1905.

34 Aronson, *Prince Eddy and the Homosexual Underworld*, p. 198.

35 Eddy to Hélène, 2 September 1890 in Michael, *Eddy and Hélène*, p. 19.

36 Eddy to Hélène, 19 October 1890 in Michael, *Eddy and Hélène*, p. 34. See Michael Holroyd, *A Book of Secrets: Illegitimate Daughters, Absent Fathers* (Chatto & Windus, 2010), p. 72.

37 Pope 204/1, Eddy to Sybil, 19 April, 28 June 1891.

38 Michael, *Eddy and Hélène*, p. 62.

39 Pope-Hennessy, *Queen Mary*, p. 199.

40 Pope 204/1, Eddy to Lady Sybil, 21 June 1891.

41 Pope 204/1, Eddy to Lady Sybil, 28 June 1891.

42 Pope 205/5, Knollys to Ponsonby, 2 September 1891, annotated by Pope-Hennessy: 'These M.S. letter[s], Knollys–Ponsonby, were given J P-H to keep by John Gore, who had been given them by Arthur Ponsonby.'

43 *Reynolds's Newspaper*, 11 October 1891. *Lloyd's Weekly Newspaper*, 11 October 1891. *West Australian*, 27 November 1891, available at https://trove.nla.gov.au/newspaper/ article/3027954 (accessed 22 June 2021). Cadbury, *Queen Victoria's Matchmaking*, p. 157.

44 These two letters, dated November 1890 and December 1891, were auctioned at Bonhams in 2002 and quoted by Patricia Cornwell in *Portrait of a Killer: Jack the Ripper – Case Closed* (Sphere, 2003), pp. 135–6. Their authenticity has been disputed, and there is confusion about the dates (Andrew Cook, *Prince Eddy: The King Britain Never Had* (History Press, 2008), pp. 297–8). Assuming the December 1891 date is right, this fits with Maud Richardson's claim in 1900 that she threatened to cancel Prince Eddy's engagement to Princess May ('Adventures of a Chorus Girl', *Auckland Star*, 7 April 1900, available at http://paperspast.

natlib.govt.nz/cgi-bin/paperspast?a=
d&d=AS19000407.2.49.29
(accessed 22 June 2021)).

45 Pope 204/1, Eddy to Sybil, 28 June
1891.

46 Pope-Hennessy, *Queen Mary*, p. 194.

47 Pope 204/1, Eddy to Sybil, 29
November 1891.

48 Nicolson Diary, 29 July 1949
(Carisbrooke).

49 Princess Louise to Hélène, 22
January 1892 in Michael, *Eddy and
Hélène*, p. 83. See Cadbury, *Queen
Victoria's Matchmaking*, p. 193.

50 Pope 203/5, typed note by
Pope-Hennessy, n.d.

51 Pope 196/16, in James Pope-
Hennessy, *The Quest for Queen
Mary*, ed. Hugo Vickers (Zuleika,
2018), p. 191.

52 Pope 178/10, Pope-Hennessy, to
Mrs Waterfield, 24 April 1958.

53 *Pall Mall Gazette*, 15 January 1892.
Hampshire Advertiser, 23 January
1892.

54 *Reynolds's Newspaper*, 24 January
1892.

55 *Pall Mall Gazette*, 16 January 1892.

56 John Wheeler-Bennett, *King George
VI: His Life and Reign* (Macmillan,
1958), p. 294.

57 Pope 203/6, G to Duke of
Connaught, 16 January 1892.

58 John Gore, *King George V: A
Personal Memoir* (John Murray,
1941), p. 348n.

59 Pope 194/3, Vicky to V, 24 March
1892.

60 Gore, *King George V*, p. 99n.

61 RA GV/PRIV/GVD, 21 February,
24 March 1892.

62 RA GV/PRIV/GVD 24 May 1892.

63 Harold Nicolson, *King George the
Fifth: His Life and Reign*
(Constable, 1952), p. 47. Victoria
preferred the title Duke of London
(Gore, *King George V*, p. 104n).

64 Kenneth Rose, *King George V*
(Phoenix Press, 2000), p. 24.

65 Churchill Archives Centre, Godfrey-
Faussett Diary, 6 May 1892.

66 Godfrey-Faussett Diary, 12 July 1892.

67 RA GV/PRIV/GVD/5 February
1892.

68 Hannah Pakula, *The Last
Romantic: A Biography of Queen
Marie of Roumania* (Weidenfeld &
Nicolson, 1985), p. 57.

69 Pope 194/3, V to Vicky, 5, 7, 13
June 1892.

70 RA GV/PRIV/AA10 /37, V to G, 6
March 1892

71 Pope 194/3, V to Vicky, 5 June
1892. Cadbury, *Queen Victoria's
Matchmaking*, pp. 201–7.

72 Pope 194/3, V to Vicky, 5 June
1892.

73 RA GV/PRIV/AA10 /38, V to G, 6
April 1892.

74 Pakula, *The Last Romantic*,
pp. 55–9.

75 Pope 195/3, Diary of Lady
Geraldine Somerset, 3 June 1892.

76 Pope-Hennessy, *Queen Mary*,
p. 253.

77 Pope 194/3, V to Vicky, 13 June
1892.

78 RA GV/PRIV/AA31/21, Alix to G,
28 June 1892.

79 RA GV/PRIV/GVD/26, 28, 29
August; 1, 3, 6, 7, 8 September
1891.

80 Pope-Hennessy, *The Quest for
Queen Mary*, pp. 161–2.

81 Pope 194/3, note 'Prince George's
Diary': two extracts in another
hand, presumably Xenia's.

82 RA GV/PRIV/AA31/22, Alix to G,
July 1892. Pope 194/3, pencil note
on this letter: 'Pss Xenia, no doubt'.

83 G to Dalton, 9 June 1892 in
Andrew Gordon, *The Rules of the
Game: Jutland and British Naval
Command* (Penguin, 2015), p. 234.

84 Gordon, *The Rules of the Game*,
p. 234.

85 Gordon, *The Rules of the Game*,
235.

86 RA GV/PRIV/GVD/27 July 1892.

87 *The Times*, 17 August 1892.

88 RA GV/PRIV/GVD/6, 10 August
1892.

89 Godfrey-Faussett Diary, 18 August
1892.

90 RA GV/PRIV/AA19/35, 36, Bertie to G, 24, 27 August 1892.
91 G to O. Montagu, 28 September 1892 in Gore, *King George V*, 106.
92 RA GV/PRIV/AA31/23, Alix to G, 3 October 1892. Yale, Beinecke, Gen. MSS 614, Box 17, Nicolson to Lascelles, 6 March 1951.
93 Austin, Texas, Harry Ransom Center, Maurice Baring Papers, G to M. Baring, 20 October 1892.
94 Gore, *King George V*, p. 106.
95 RA GV/PRIV/GVD, 9 November 1892.
96 RA GV/PRIV/GVD, 30 November 1892.
97 Pope 203/6, V to Ponsonby, 14 January 1892; Vicky to Sophie, 14, 15 January 1892.
98 RA GV/PRIV/AA10/37, V to G, 6 March 1892.
99 Pope 194/3, V to Vicky, 14 June 1892.
100 RA GV/PRIV/AA10/38, V to G, 6 April 1892.
101 Wigram Papers, Clive to Nora, 7 February 1931.
102 See Chapter 3, p. 40.
103 RA GV/PRIV/AA31/21, Alix to G, 28 June 1892.
104 RA GV/PRIV/GVD, 19 August 1892.
105 RA GV/PRIV/AA19/35, Bertie to G, 24 August 1892.
106 RA GV/PRIV/GVD/13 December 1892.

CHAPTER 5

May of Teck

1 Getty Research Library, Pope 196/16, Lady Juliet Duff, in James Pope-Hennessy, *The Quest for Queen Mary*, ed. Hugo Vickers (Zuleika, 2018), p. 132.
2 Pope 196/16, Hon. Daisy Bigge, in Pope-Hennessy, *The Quest for Queen Mary*, p. 236.
3 James Pope-Hennessy, *Queen Mary* (Phoenix Press, 2000), p. 135.
4 Pope 196/16, Lady Estella Hope, in Pope-Hennessy, *The Quest for Queen Mary*, p. 99.

5 Pope 200/11, V to Vicky, 26 May 1894.
6 Pope-Hennessy, *Queen Mary*, pp. 28, 144.
7 *Standard*, 25 July 1883. Pope 200/8, Teck to Ponsonby, 4 June 1883, Teck to Ponsonby 16 June 1883, Teck to Ponsonby 25 July 1883, Ponsonby to QV, 27 July 1883.
8 Pope-Hennessy, *Queen Mary*, p. 136.
9 Pope-Hennessy, *Queen Mary*, p. 137.
10 Pope-Hennessy, *Queen Mary*, p. 163.
11 Pope-Hennessy, *Queen Mary*, p. 183.
12 Pope-Hennessy, *Queen Mary*, p. 232. Pope 201/10, QMD, 27 February 1892; and 1947 note.
13 Pope-Hennessy, *The Quest for Queen Mary*, p. 99.
14 Pope 196/16, Cynthia Colville, Lady Estella Hope, in Pope-Hennessy, *The Quest for Queen Mary*, pp. 53, 99–100.
15 Pope-Hennessy, *Queen Mary*, p. 160.
16 Pope 196/16, Lady Estella Hope, in Pope-Hennessy, *The Quest for Queen Mary*, p. 101.
17 Pope 196/16, Duchess of Devonshire, in Pope-Hennessy, *The Quest for Queen Mary*, p. 104.
18 Pope 196/16, Lady Reid, in Pope-Hennessy, *The Quest for Queen Mary*, p. 153.
19 Arthur Hamilton Lee, 'A Good Innings': The Private Papers of Viscount Lee of Fareham, ed. Alan Clark (John Murray, 1974), p. 286 (Sir George Arthur, 3 March 1928).
20 Pope-Hennessy, *The Quest for Queen Mary*, p. 156.
21 Pope-Hennessy, *The Quest for Queen Mary*, p. 230. Lady Cynthia Colville, *Crowded Life* (Evans Brothers, 1963), pp. 116–17.
22 Pope-Hennessy, *The Quest for Queen Mary*, p. 138.
23 Pope 194/8, M to Augusta, 26 February 1886.

24 Frank Prochaska, 'Mary Adelaide, Princess [Princess Mary Adelaide of Cambridge], Duchess of Teck (1833–1897)', *Oxford Dictionary of National Biography* (2004).

25 Pope 200/9, extract from Mrs Hunt, 'Record of a Friendship'.

26 Pope-Hennessy, *Queen Mary*, p. 186.

27 Pope 200/9, extract from Mrs Hunt, 'Record of a Friendship'.

28 Pope 200/11, QV to Vicky, 6 December 1891.

29 Pope 203/5, M to Aunt Augusta, 9 December 1891.

30 Pope 200/12, M to Bricka, 24 March 1892.

31 Pope-Hennessy, *The Quest for Queen Mary*, pp. 101, 122–4. Pope 196/3, Lady Estella Hope, 15 July 1956. Hopetoun married in 1886.

32 Pope-Hennessy, *The Quest for Queen Mary*, p. 101.

33 RA QM/PRIV/CC24/101, M to Augusta, 1 March 1908.

34 Pope 196/16, Lady Cynthia Colville interview, 16 August 1955.

35 Pope 200/12, M to Augusta, 24 February, 6 August 1891.

36 Pope 194/10, extract from Mrs Hunt, 'Record of a Friendship'. Pope 178/10, Pope to Mrs Waterhouse, 23 April 1958.

37 *Birmingham Daily Post*, 8 December 1891 quoting 'One who Knows the Princess Well'.

38 Pope-Hennessy, *Queen Mary*, pp. 173, 203.

39 Balfour to Salisbury, 30 August 1890 in Robin Harcourt Williams, ed., *The Salisbury–Balfour Correspondence: Letters Exchanged between the Third Marquess of Salisbury and His Nephew Arthur James Balfour 1869–1892* (Hertfordshire Record Society, 1988), p. 321.

40 Pope 200/11, QV to Vicky, 12 November 1891.

41 Pope 203/5, M to Augusta, 9 December 1891.

42 Pope 200/11, Princess Victoria of Schaumburg-Lippe to Vicky, n.d.

43 Pope-Hennessy, *Queen Mary*, pp. 208–9. Pope 195/3, Lady Geraldine Somerset Diary, 15 November 1891.

44 Pope 200/11, V to Vicky, 19 November 1891.

45 See Chapter 4, pp. 48–9.

46 Pope 203/5, M to Augusta, 9 December 1891.

47 Pope 203/5, QMD, 3 December 1891.

48 Pope 203/5, M to Augusta, 9 December 1891.

49 Pope 196/3, Interview with Lady Cecilia Goff, March 1956.

50 Pope 195/3, Lady Geraldine Somerset Diary, 7 December 1891.

51 Pope 195/3, Lady Geraldine, 7 December 1891. *Hampshire Advertiser*, 9 December 1891. *Freeman's Journal*, 8 December 1891.

52 Pope 203/5, M to Augusta, 9 December 1891.

53 'One who Knows the Princess Well' in *Birmingham Daily Post*, 8 December 1891.

54 Pope 203/5, M to Augusta, 9 December 1891.

55 Pope 196/3, Maggie Wyndham, in Pope-Hennessy, *The Quest for Queen Mary*, pp. 113–14.

56 Pope 204/10, Duchess of Teck to Mrs Hunt, 31 December 1891.

57 Pope 203/6, QMD, 8 January 1892.

58 Pope 203/6, QMD, 10 January 1892.

59 Pope 195/3, Lady Geraldine, 17 January 1892.

60 Pope 203/6, QMD, 14 January 1892.

61 Pope 203/6, Dss of Teck to QV, 14 January 1892.

62 Pope 203/6, Alix to M, 29 January 1892.

63 Pope 203/6, M to Emily Alcock, 13 February 1892.

64 Pope 203/6, M to Emily Alcock, 13 February 1892.

65 Pope 195/3, Lady Geraldine, 4 February 1892.

66 Pope 195/3, Lady Geraldine, 2
March 1892. See also Princess
Victoria to Hélène, 22 January
1892 in Prince Michael of Greece,
*Eddy and Hélène: . . . An Impossible
Match* (Rosvall Royal Books,
2013), p. 82.

67 'Albert Victor', *The Times*, 15
January 1892.

68 Pope 203/6, Augusta to Duke of
Cambridge, 20 January 1892.

69 Pope 203/6, QMD, 20 January
1892.

70 Pope 203/6, Augusta to Duke of
Cambridge, 20 January 1892.

71 Pope 195/3, Lady Geraldine, 9
February 1892.

72 Pope 195/3, Lady Geraldine, 6
March 892.

73 Pope 203/6, M to V, 16 January
1892.

74 RA GV/PRIV/AA10/36, V to G,
14 February 1892.

75 Pope 203/6, Duchess of Teck to V,
14 January 1892.

76 Pope 203/6, M to Emily Alcock, 13
February 1892.

77 Pope 201/10, QMD, 27 February
1892.

78 Pope 201/10, Duchess of Teck to V,
201/10

79 Pope 200/12, M to Bricka, 24
March 1892.

80 E.g. *Liverpool Mercury*, 6 April
1892. *North-Eastern Daily Gazette*,
25 April 1892. *Dundee Courier and
Argus*, 16 April 1892.

81 Pope 195/3, Lady Geraldine, 11
April 1892.

82 RA GV/PRIV/AA10/38, V to G, 6
April 1892.

83 Pope 201/10, QMD, 23 April 1892.

84 Pope 201/10, M to Bricka, 12 May
1892.

85 Pope 201/10, M to Bricka, 23 May
1892.

86 Pope 201/10, Interview with
Princess Alice of Athlone, 29 April
1957.

87 Pope 201/10, Interview with
Princess Alice of Athlone, 29 April
1957.

88 Pope 201/10, M to Bricka, 23 May
1892.

89 Pope 201/10, M to G, 31 May 1892.

90 Pope 200/12, M to Bricka, 21 June
1892.

91 Pope 201/10, QMD, 23 June 1892.

92 Pope 203/6, M to Emily Alcock, 21
February 1893.

93 Pope 201/10, QMD, 3 June 1892.

94 Pope 201/10, Duchess of Teck to
Princess Amelie, 10 November 1892.

95 RA VIC/MAIN/QVJ (W), 7
December 1892.

96 Pope 178/10, Pope to Mrs
Waterhouse, 3 April 1958.

97 *Freeman's Journal*, 8 December
1891.

98 Pope 195/3, Lady Geraldine,
11 July 1892.

99 Pope 196/16, Lady Shaftesbury, in
Pope-Hennessy, *The Quest for
Queen Mary*, p. 128.

CHAPTER 6

George and May

1 Peter Quennell, ed., *Lonely
Business: A Self-Portrait of James
Pope-Hennessy* (Weidenfeld &
Nicolson, 1981), p. 231.

2 Getty Research Library, Pope
201/10, G to M, 15 January 1893.
RA GV/PRIV/GVD/14 January
1893.

3 Pope 204/10, G to M, 4 March
1893.

4 RA GV/PRIV/AA31/27, Alix to G,
1 February 1893.

5 Pope 204/10, Vicky to Pss F.C. of
Hesse, 23 February 1893. James
Pope-Hennessy, *Queen Mary*
(Phoenix Press, 2000), p. 257.

6 Pope 204/10, extract from Empress
Frederick, *The Empress Frederick
Writes to Sophie: Letters 1889–
1901*, ed. Arthur Gould Lee (Faber
& Faber, 1955), p. 140, February
1893.

7 Pope 204/10, Vicky to Pss F.C. of
Hesse, 23 February 1893.

8 RA GV/PRIV/GVD/15 March
1893.

9 M to Bricka, 20 February 1910, in Pope-Hennessy, *Queen Mary*, p. 113.

10 Pope 204/10, Queen Olga to G, 6/18 April 1893.

11 Pope 204/10, Sophie to Vicky, 29 March/10 April 1893.

12 Pope 204/10, G to M, 17 March 1893.

13 Pope 204/10, G to M, 31 March 1893.

14 RA GV/PRIV/AA31/30, Alix to G, 29 April 1893.

15 RA GV/PRIV/GVD/3 May 1893.

16 Pope 204/10, QMD, 3 May 1893.

17 Pope 204/10, G to M, 3 May 1893.

18 Pope 204/10, M to G, 3 May 1893.

19 RA GV/PRIV/AA31/31, Alix to G, 6 May 1893.

20 Pope 204/10, *The Empress Frederick Writes to Sophie*, p. 147 (April 1893).

21 Pope 204/10, Princess Adolf of Schaumburg Lippe to Vicky, 24 February 1893.

22 *Reynolds's Newspaper*, 21 May 1893.

23 *The Times*, 14, 15 June 1893.

24 Sir William Harcourt in the House of Commons, 27 June 1893, *The Times*, 28 June 1893.

25 Lambeth Palace, Davidson Papers, Vol. 12, M to Davidson, 19 June 1893.

26 *The Times*, 7 July 1893. Pope-Hennessy, *Queen Mary*, pp. 264–5.

27 Pope 202/6, M to Duchess of Teck, 20 August 1893.

28 Pope 204/10, G to M, 24 May 1893. The Angeli was a present from Queen Victoria to the Duchess of Teck. Fildes's painting was a wedding present from the proprietors of the *Graphic* (*The Times*, 21 June, 5 July 1893).

29 Kenneth Rose, *King George V* (Phoenix Press, 2000), p. 82.

30 Deborah Cadbury, *Queen Victoria's Matchmaking: The Royal Marriages That Shaped Europe* (Bloomsbury, 2017), pp. 225–8, 235.

31 See Jane Ridley, *Bertie: A Life of Edward VII* (Chatto & Windus, 2012), p. 306n.

32 Harold Nicolson, *King George the Fifth: His Life and Reign* (Constable, 1952), p. 144.

33 Pope 204/10, M to G, 20 June 1893; G to M, 19 June 1893

34 Pope 204/10, G to M, 13 June 1893.

35 Pope 204/10, G to M, 13 June 1893.

36 Pope 204/10, M to G, 20 June 1893.

37 Pope 204/10, M to G, 28 May 1893.

38 Pope 195/3, Lady Geraldine, 14 May 1893.

39 RA GV/PRIV/GVD/23 June 1893.

40 RA GV/PRIV/GVD/24, 25 June 1893.

41 Pope 196/16, Cynthia Colville, in James Pope-Hennessy, *The Quest for Queen Mary*, ed. Hugo Vickers (Zuleika, 2018), p. 53.

42 Pope 196/16, Maggie Wyndham, in Pope-Hennessy, *The Quest for Queen Mary*, p. 114.

43 *Reynolds's Newspaper*, 7 May 1893.

44 Pope 204/10, G to M, 3 July 1893.

45 Pope 202/6, G to M, 12 August 1894.

46 Pope 196/16, Maggie Wyndham, in Pope-Hennessy, *The Quest for Queen Mary*, p. 114.

47 Pope 204/10, G to M, 24 May 1893.

48 Bodleian, Lincolnshire Diary, Microfilm 1101, 18, 20 May 1893.

49 *Liverpool Mercury*, 7 July 1893.

50 RA GV/PRIV/GVD/30 June 1893.

51 Andrei Maylunas and Sergei Mironenko, *A Lifelong Passion: Nicholas and Alexandra – Their Own Story* (Weidenfeld & Nicolson, 1996), p. 27.

52 RA GV/PRIV/GVD/3 July 1893.

53 Edward, Duke of Windsor, *A King's Story: The Memoirs of HRH the Duke of Windsor* (Cassell, 1951), p. 129.

54 Pope 196/3, Maggie Wyndham, in Pope-Hennessy, *The Quest for Queen Mary*, p. 117.

55 Pope-Hennessy, *Queen Mary*, p. 268.

56 Lady Geraldine, quoted in Pope-Hennessy, *Queen Mary*, p. 269. RA VIC MAIN QVJ (W), 6 July 1893.

57 Pope 195/3, Lady Geraldine, 6 July 1893.

58 Pope-Hennessy, *Queen Mary*, p. 290, Duchess of Teck to M, 20 October 1893.

59 Pope 202/6, M to QV, 13 July 1893. RA GV/PRIV/GVD/6 July 1894.

60 Pope 195/9, Kitty Waterhouse to Pope, n.d. [?1958].

61 John Gore, *King George V: A Personal Memoir* (John Murray, 1941), pp. 111–12. RA GV/PRIV/GVD/6 July 1893.

62 Pope-Hennessy, *The Quest for Queen Mary*, p. 84.

63 Nicolson Diary, 4 October 1949.

64 Frances Donaldson, *Edward VIII* (Weidenfeld & Nicolson, 1974), p. 5.

65 Nicolson Diary, 4 October 1949. Sissinghurst Papers, Nicolson to Vita, 5 October 1949.

66 RA GV/PRIV/GVD/22 November, 3 December 1892, 27 June 1893, 31 July 1894.

67 Nicolson Diary, 4 October 1949. Pope 196/16, Lady Juliet Duff, in Pope-Hennessy, *The Quest for Queen Mary*, p. 133.

68 Pope 196/16, Duke of Gloucester, in Pope-Hennessy, *The Quest for Queen Mary*, p. 187.

69 Pope 195/6, G to M, 11 October 1893.

70 Pope-Hennessy, *Queen Mary*, p. 277.

71 George and Weedon Grossmith, *The Diary of a Nobody* (Penguin, 1965), p. 19.

72 Sir Sidney Lee, *King Edward VII: A Biography, Vol. 1: From Birth to Accession, 9th November 1841–22nd January 1901* (Macmillan, 1925), pp. 602–3. Benjamin Sacks, 'The Prince of Wales's Children Act 1889', *Albion*, vol. 5, no. 4 (1973).

73 Pope 202/6, G to Duchess of Teck, 10 July 1893.

74 Pope 202/6, M to Bricka, 9 July 1893. M to Emily Alcock, 12 July 1893.

75 Pope 202/6, G to M, 10 October 1893.

76 Pope 202/6, M to G, 15 August 1894.

77 Pope 202/6, Princess Alice interview, 29 April 1957.

78 Pope-Hennessy, *Queen Mary*, pp. 105, 279.

79 Pope-Hennessy, *Queen Mary*, p. 279.

80 Pope 194/8, M to Bricka, 9 July 1893.

81 Pope 202/6, M to G, 25 October 1894.

82 Pope 202/6, M to Duchess of Teck, 12 August 1893.

83 Pope 202/6, M to Duchess of Teck, 3 August 1893.

84 Pope 202/6, G to M, 10 October 1893.

85 Pope 202/6, G to M, 12 October 1893. M to G, 12 October 1893.

86 Pope 202/6, M to G, 7 November 1893.

87 Pope 202/6, M to G, 1 November 1893.

88 Nicolson Diary, 30 June 1948 (George Gage's remark to HN).

89 Windsor, *A King's Story*, p.137.

90 Pope 195/3, Lady Geraldine Diary, 30 April 1893.

91 Pope 202/6, G to M, 19 August 1894.

92 Pope 202/6, G to M, 19 August 1894.

93 Pope 195/6, G to M, 24 August 1894.

94 Pope 196/16, Duke of Gloucester, in Pope-Hennessy, *The Quest for Queen Mary*, p. 184.

95 Maylunas and Mironenko, eds, *A Lifelong Passion*, p. 61, Alicky to Nicky, 24 April 1894.

96 RA GV/(PRIV)/AA20/43, Bertie to G, 5 November 1894.

97 RA GV/PRIV/GVD/1, 12 November 1894. Pope 202/6, G to M, 17 November 1894.

98 Pope 202/6, G to M, 12 November 1894.

99 Lincolnshire Diary, 12 November 1894.

100 Pope 202/6, G to M, 15 November 1894. Lincolnshire Diary, 16 November 1894.

101 Pope 202/6, G to M, 17 November 1894. Lincolnshire diary, 17 November 1894.

102 Pope 202/6, G to M, 17 November 1894.

103 Pope 202/6, G to M, 26 November 1894.

104 Pope 202/6, M to G, 26 August 1894.

105 Pope 202/6, G to M, 30 November 1894. M to G, 25 August 1896.

106 Pope 202/6, M to G, 8 January 1895.

107 Pope 202/6, M to G, 13 November 1894.

108 Pope 202/6, M to G, 15 August 1894.

109 Pope-Hennessy, *Queen Mary*, p. 307.

110 Pope 194/5, V to Vicky, 19 June 1894.

111 Windsor, *A King's Story*, p. 1.

112 RA GV/PRIV/GVD/23 June 1894.

113 Philip Ziegler, *King Edward VIII: The Official Biography* (Collins, 1990), p. 4.

114 Pope 194/5, G telegram to V, 24 June 1894. RA GV/PRIV/GVD/23 June 1894.

115 Pope 194/5, Mrs Hunt's 'Record of a Friendship': note on Lady Eva Greville.

116 Pope 196/16, Duke of Gloucester.

CHAPTER 7

The Wasted Years

1 John Gore, *King George V: A Personal Memoir* (John Murray, 1941), p. 128.

2 Sissinghurst Papers, Nicolson to Vita, 17 August 1949. Harold Nicolson, *Diaries and Letters of Harold Nicolson 1945–62* (Collins, 1968), p. 174.

3 Lambeth Palace, Nicolson Diary, 16 August 1949.

4 Sissinghurst, Nicolson to Vita, 17 August 1949.

5 Lord Riddell, *More Pages from My Diary* (Country Life, 1934), p. 218.

6 Vernon Bogdanor, *The Monarchy and the Constitution* (Clarendon Press, 1995), pp. 40–1.

7 Walter Bagehot, *The English Constitution* (Chapman & Hall, 1867), pp. 57, 62, 86.

8 RA GV/PRIV/GVD/15 March 1894. Bogdanor, *The Monarchy and the Constitution*, pp. 40–1.

9 RA GV/PRIV/GVD/7, 16 March, 12 April 1894.

10 Sir Edward Walter Hamilton, *The Diary of Sir Edward Walter Hamilton 1885–1906*, ed. Dudley W. R. Bahlman (University of Hull, 1993), 14 March 1894, p. 251.

11 Getty Research Library, Pope 204/9, G to M, 20 March 1896. RA GV/PRIV/GVD/1–30 March 1898.

12 RA GV/PRIV/GVD/17 April 1898.

13 RA GV/PRIV/AA13/43, Bertie to G, 13 August 1887.

14 RA GV/PRIV/GVD/February 1897. 'Game Killed by Me During Season 1896–97'.

15 J. Wentworth Day, *King George V as a Sportsman* (Cassell, 1935), p. 16.

16 Day, *King George V as a Sportsman*, p. 27.

17 Sir Alan Lascelles, *King's Counsellor: Abdication and War – The Diaries of Sir Alan Lascelles*, ed. Duff Hart-Davis (Phoenix, 2007), pp. 433–4.

18 Lincolnshire Diary, 8 January 1895. Gore, *King George V*, p. 231.

19 Jonathan Garnier Ruffer, *The Big Shots: Edwardian Shooting Parties* (Debrett's Peerage, 1977), pp. 23, 50. Gore, *King George V*, p. 233.

20 RA GV/PRIV/GVD/February 1897. Ruffer, *The Big Shots*, p. 50.

21 See Jane Ridley, '"The Sport of Kings": Shooting and the Court of Edward VII', *Court Historian*, vol. 18, no. 2 (2013).

22 RA GV/PRIV/GVD/19 November 1896.

23 RA GV/PRIV/GVD/8 December 1896.

24 Gore, *King George V*, p. 131.

25 RA GV/PRIV/GVD/12 August 1896.

26 Pope 202/6, G to M, 16 August 1896.

27 Pope 202/6, M to G, 16 August 1896.

28 Pope 202/6, M to G, 18 August 1896.

29 James Pope-Hennessy, *Queen Mary* (Phoenix Press, 2000), p. 330.

30 Pope 202/6, G to M, 6 September 1896.

31 Pope 202/6, M to G, 18 August 1896.

32 Marion Crawford, *The Little Princesses* (Orion, 2003), pp. 47–8.

33 Pope 202/6, G to M, 8 September 1896.

34 RA GV/PRIV/AA 21/8, Bertie to G, 10 September 1896. RA GV/PRIV/GVD/22 September 1896.

35 Ronald W. Clark, *Balmoral: Queen Victoria's Highland Home* (Thames & Hudson, 1981), p. 112. RA GV/PRIV/GVD/25 September 1896. See Frances Welch, *The Imperial Tea Party: Family, Politics and Betrayal – the Ill-Fated British and Russian Royal Alliance* (Short, 2018), pp. 22–86.

36 RA GV/PRIV/GVD/22 September 1899.

37 Clark, *Balmoral*, p. 110.

38 Pope 194/5, Lady Eva Greville's comment in Mrs Hunt, 'Record of a Friendship'. Empress Frederick, *The Empress Frederick Writes to Sophie: Letters 1889–1901*, ed. Arthur Gould Lee (Faber & Faber, 1955), p. 210.

39 Pope 205/9, M to G, 13 November 1895.

40 Pope 200/4, Vicky to Pss Frederick Charles of Hesse, 2 February 1897.

41 Pope 200/4, Vicky to Pss Frederick Charles of Hesse, 5 October 1898.

42 Pope 196/16, Lady Juliet Duff, in James Pope-Hennessy, *The Quest for Queen Mary*, ed. Hugo Vickers (Zuleika, 2018), p. 132.

43 Frances Donaldson, *Edward VIII*, p. 92.

44 Pope 202/6, M to G, 3 August 1894.

45 Pope 200/4, Vicky to Pss F. C. of Hesse, 2 February 1897. Pope 205/9, Mrs Peters to Mrs Masters, 28 August 1895.

46 John Wheeler-Bennett, *King George VI: His Life and Reign* (Macmillan, 1958), p. 17.

47 Edward, Duke of Windsor, *A King's Story: The Memoirs of HRH the Duke of Windsor* (Cassell, 1951), p. 7.

48 Pope-Hennessy, *Queen Mary*, p. 392, M to G, 29 November 1895.

49 Pope 194/5, Bricka to Prince Alge, 8 May 1896: 'La Princesse de Galles trouve que David lui rappelle tant Prince Eddy; elle adore cet enfant, qui est si sage avec elle.'

50 RA GV/PRIV/AA 32/3, Alix to G, 2 May 1896.

51 Pope 194/5, M to G, 29 October 1896.

52 Pope 194/5, G to M, 30 October 1896.

53 Pope, p. 392, M to G, 28 October 1896.

54 Pope 194/5, Duke of Teck to Prince Alge, 18 March 1897.

55 RA GV/PRIV/AA 32/7, Alix to G, 12 April 1897.

56 RA GV/PRIV/AA 36/37, G to Alix, 18 March 1897.

57 RA GV/PRIV/AA 36/37, G to Alix, 18 March 1897. RA GV/PRIV/GVD/17 March 1897.

58 Pope 194/5, M to G, 13 August 1897.

59 Pope 194/5, Duke of Teck to Prince Alge, 17 May 1897.

60 Pope-Hennessy, *The Quest for Queen Mary*, pp. 88–9.

61 *The Times*, 28 October 1897.

62 C. Kinloch Cooke, *A Memoir of HRH Duchess of Teck* (John Murray, 1900), vol. 2, p. 298.

63 Mrs Hunt, 'Record of a Friendship', Bricka to Mrs Hunt, December 1896.

64 Pope 196/5, Duchess of Teck to M, 8 May 1897.

65 Pope 196/5, M to Dss of Teck, 7 May 1897.
66 Pope 196/5, G to M, 16 May 1897.
67 Pope 196/5, Lady Eva Dugdale to M, 30 October 1897.
68 Pope 196/5, M to G, 9 August 1897.
69 Pope 196/5, M to G, 10 August 1897.
70 RA GV/PRIV/GVD, 4 October 1897.
71 Pope 194/3, G to M, 5 October 1897.
72 Pope 194/3, G to M, 5 October 1897.
73 Lincolnshire Diary, 29 October 1897.
74 RA GV/PRIV/GVD/27 October 1897.
75 Lincolnshire Diary, 27 October 1897.
76 Pope 196/5, M to G, 25 October 1897. QMD, 25 October 1897.
77 Pope 196/5, M to G, 26 October 1897.
78 Pope 196/5, Princess Helena to QV, 27 October 1897.
79 Pope 196/5, Eva Dugdale to M, 27 October 1897.
80 Pope 196/5, Princess Helena to QV, 27 October 1897; Prince Arthur to QV, 27 October 1897.
81 Pope 196/5, Duchess of Albany to QV, 27 October 1897.
82 Pope 196/5, G to M, 26 November 1897.
83 RA GV/PRIV/GVD/4 November 1897.
84 RA GV/PRIV/GVD/23 November 1897.
85 Pope 202/6, G to M, 19 November 1897.
86 Pope 196/5, Augusta to Duke of Cambridge, 28 October 1897.
87 Pope 196/5, M to QV, 27 November 1897.
88 Pope 196/5, G to M, 19 January 1898.
89 Pope 196/5, King of Württemberg to Prince Dolly, 21 July 1898.
90 Pope 196/5, M to Prince Alge, 4 August 1898.
91 Pope 196/5, M to G, 11 October 1898.

CHAPTER 8

'I Find Life in General Very Dull'

1 Getty Research Library, Pope 205/2, Vicky to Princess Frederick Charles of Hesse, 28 October 1898. Augusta to M, 6 April 1898.
2 Pope 205/2, QV to Vicky, 16 October 1897.
3 Pope 205/2, QV to Vicky, 9 January 1898.
4 Pope 205/2, QV to Vicky, 21 December 1898.
5 Pope 205/2, QV to Vicky, 15 December 1897.
6 Marie Mallet, *Life with Queen Victoria: Marie Mallet's Letters from Court*, ed. Victor Mallet (John Murray, 1968), p. 168.
7 Pope 205/2, M to G, 4 March 1898.
8 Pope 205/2, M to Alge, 5 March, 10 March 1898.
9 Pope 205/2, M to G, 16 March 1898; V to Vicky, 21 March 1898.
10 *The Times*, 30 March 1898.
11 RA QM/PRIV/CC23/14, M to Augusta, 12 January 1902. RA QM/PRIV/CC23/39, M to Augusta, 5 April 1903. RA QM/PRIV/CC23/53, M to Augusta, 14 February 1904.
12 Pope 205/2, von Sellheim to Pope-Hennessy, 9 and 20 June 1960.
13 RA QM/PRIV/CC22/23, M to Augusta, 3 April 1898.
14 Pope 205/2, Augusta to Alge, 14 April 1898.
15 Pope 200/4, Augusta to Lady Eva Dugdale, 28 May 1910.
16 Pope 204/9, M to G, 11 February 1898.
17 Pope 204/9, G to M, 10 February 1898. M to G, 11 February 1898.
18 Pope 204/9, G to M, 28 March 1898.
19 Pope 204/9, M to G, 24 March 1898.
20 Pope 204/9, M to G, 13 March 1898.
21 Pope 204/9, G to M, 16 March 1898.

22 Pope 204/9, M to G, 19 March 1898.

23 Pope 204/9, G to M, 19 March 1898.

24 Pope 204/9, M to G, 22 March 1898.

25 Pope 204/9, M to G, 31 March 1898.

26 RA GV/PRIV/GVD/12, 13, 15 April 1898.

27 Pope 204/9, G to M, 28 March 1898.

28 Pope 204/9, M to G, 31 March 1898.

29 Pope 204/9, M to G, 24 March 1898.

30 Pope 199/4, M to G, 22 March 1899.

31 Pope 204/9, M to G, 12 March 1898; G to M, 15 March 1898.

32 Pope 204/9, M to G, 18 March 1898.

33 *The Times*, 6 June 1898.

34 Pope 204/9, G to M, 14 July 1898.

35 Pope 204/9, G to M, 17 July 1898.

36 RA GV/PRIV/GVD/21 June 1898.

37 *The Times*, 22, 25 June 1898.

38 RA GV/PRIV/AA32/16, Alix to G, 9 February 1899.

39 Mallet, p. 158.

40 Mallet, pp. 156, 159.

41 Nicolson Diary, 18 August 1949.

42 RA GV/PRIV/GVD/15 December 1899.

43 RA GV/PRIV/GVD/16 December 1899.

44 RA GV/PRIV/AA22/31, Bertie to G, 8 January 1900.

45 Pope 204/9, G to M, 18 October 1898.

46 Pope 194/8, undated note by Pope-Hennessy.

47 Pope 205/9, M to Dolly, 11 February 1900.

48 RA QM/PRIV/CC22/36, M to Augusta, 11 April 1900.

49 Pope 194/8, Vicky to Princess Frederick Charles of Hesse, 8 November 1898.

50 RA GV/PRIV/GVD/2 August 1900.

51 Pope 194/8, G to M, 3 August 1900.

52 RA GV/PRIV/GVD/2 August 1900.

53 RA GV/PRIV/GVD/2 August 1900.

54 RA GV/PRIV/GVD/19 January 1901.

55 Pope 199/4, G to M, 18 January 1901.

56 RA GV/PRIV/GVD/19 January 1901.

57 RA QM/PRIV/CC22/54, M to Augusta, 20 January 1901.

58 Pope 199/4, G to M, 21 January 1901.

59 RA GV/PRIV/GVD/22 January 1901.

60 RA QM/PRIV/CC22/55, M to Augusta, 27 January 1901.

61 RA QM/PRIV/CC22/57, M to Augusta, 3 February 1901.

62 Nicolson Diary, 24 August 1949.

63 RA QM/PRIV/CC22/57, M to Augusta, 3 February 1901.

CHAPTER 9

The Heir Apparent

1 RA QM/PRIV/CC22/59, M to Augusta, 8 February 1901.

2 Getty Research Library, Pope 194/6, M to Alix, 16 September 1900.

3 Pope 194/6, Augusta to Duke of Cambridge, 18 March 1901.

4 RA GV/PRIV/GVD/16 March 1901.

5 RA GV/PRIV/AA36/48, G to Alix, 21 March 1901.

6 Pope 194/6, Augusta to Duke of Cambridge, 18 March 1901.

7 Pope 194/6, M to Bricka, 30 March 1901.

8 RA QM/PRIV/CC22/61, M to Augusta, 21 March 1901.

9 Pope 194/6, G to M, 27 November 1900.

10 Pope 194/6, M to Bricka, 16 April 1901.

11 RA QM/PRIV/CC22/61, M to Augusta, 30 March 1901. RA QM/PRIV/CC22/65, M to Augusta, 30 April 1901.

12 RA QM/PRIV/CC22/63, M to Augusta, 8 April 1901.

13 Pope 196/16, Duke of Gloucester, in James Pope-Hennessy, *The Quest for Queen Mary*, ed. Hugo Vickers (Zuleika, 2018), p. 184.

14 RA GV/PRIV/AA36/50, G to Alix, 11 April 1901.

15 RA GV/PRIV/GVD/17, 23 April 1901. Nicholas Courtney, *The Queen's Stamps: The Authorised History of the Royal Philatelic Collection* (Methuen, 2004), pp. 62–3.

16 John Gore, *King George V: A Personal Memoir* (John Murray, 1941), p. 66.

17 Harold Nicolson, *King George the Fifth: His Life and Reign* (Constable, 1952), p. 64.

18 Pope 200/11, Fritz Ponsonby to mother, 26 August 1898.

19 Pope 200/11, Ponsonby to mother, 26 August 1898.

20 RA GV/PRIV/GVD/20 April 1901.

21 RA GV/PRIV/AA36/49, G to Alix, 30 March 1901.

22 See Steve Harris, *The Prince and the Assassin: Australia's First Royal Tour and Portent of World Terror* (Melbourne Books, 2017).

23 RA QM/PRIV/CC22/66, M to Augusta, 8 May 1901.

24 Godfrey-Faussett Diary, 1/49, 7 May 1901. RA GV/PRIV/GVD/7 May 1901.

25 Pope 194/6, M to Bricka, 20 July 1901. RA QM/PRIV/CC22/67, M to Augusta, 12 May 1901.

26 Pope 194/6, M to Bricka, 17 May 1901.

27 RA GV/PRIV/AA36/55, G to Alix, 8 July 1901.

28 Godfrey-Faussett, 1/49, Diary, 10 July 1901. RA GV/PRIV/GVD/10 July 1901.

29 Pope 194/6, Lady Mary Lygon to Lady Ampthill, 20 July 1901.

30 RA QM/PRIV/CC23/5, M to Augusta, 22 September 1901.

31 RA QM/PRIV/CC23/6, M to Augusta, 28 September 1901.

32 Godfrey-Faussett, 1/50, Diary, September 1901.

33 *The Times*, 6 December 1901.

34 RA QM/PRIV/CC23/10, M to Augusta, 10 November 1901. Nicolson, *King George the Fifth*, p. 65.

35 Pope 204/9, G to M, 12 November 1901.

36 Pope 204/9, M to G, 13 November 1901.

37 Sir Edward Walter Hamilton, *The Diary of Sir Edward Walter Hamilton 1885–1906*, ed. Dudley W. R. Bahlman (University of Hull, 1993), pp. 400–1.

38 Gore, *King George V*, p. 157.

39 Pope 195/15, Augusta to M, 22 November 1901.

40 RA GV/PRIV/AA32/30, Alix to G, 28 June 1901.

41 RA GV/PRIV/AA37/1, G to Alix, 11 August 1901.

42 RA GV/PRIV/AA23/16, Bertie to G, 9 December 1901.

43 RA GV/PRIV/AA23/16, Bertie to G, 9 December 1901.

44 RA GV/PRIV/AA22/61, Bertie to G, 11 April 1901.

45 RA GV/PRIV/GVD/January 1897, January 1903, January 1904.

46 Bigge to Esher, 2 August 1901 in Reginald, Viscount Esher, *Journals and Letters of Reginald, Viscount Esher, Vol. 1: 1870–1903*, ed. Maurice V. Brett (Ivor Nicholson & Watson, 1934), p. 303.

47 G to Bigge, 1 January 1902 in Gore, *King George V*, p. 175.

48 RA GV/PRIV/GVD/9 November 1902. Sir Frederick Ponsonby, *Recollections of Three Reigns* (Odhams Press, n.d.) p. 102.

49 Hamilton, *The Diary of Sir Edward Walter Hamilton*, p. 427, 7 November 1902.

50 RA GV/PRIV/AA16/28, Bertie to G, 26 February 1887. RA GV/PRIV/AA20/10, Bertie to G, 10 July 1893. RA GV/PRIV/AA22/47, Bertie to G, 20 August 1900.

51 RA GV/PRIV/AA23/15, Bertie to G, 9 November 1901.

52 Lambeth Palace, Nicolson Diary, 21 April 1949.

53 Pope 204/9, G to M, 12 November 1901.

54 Lincolnshire Diary, 27 March 1902.

55 Esher, *Journals and Letters of Reginald, Viscount Esher, Vol. 1*, pp. 324, 345, 14 February, 27 July 1902.

56 Hamilton, *The Diary of Sir Edward Walter Hamilton*, p. 427.

57 Esher, *Journals and Letters of Reginald, Viscount Esher, Vol. 1*, 324.

58 RA VIC/ADDU/28, Treves, 'Illness of Edward VII', p. 64.

59 RA VIC/ADDU/28, Treves, 'Illness of Edward VII', p. 74.

60 RA GV/PRIV/GVD/24 June 1902.

61 RA GV/PRIV/AA26/9, G to Bertie, 3 August 1902.

62 RA VIC/ADDU/28, Treves, 'Illness of Edward VII', p. 89.

63 Pope 205/6, G to M, 16 July 1902.

64 Pope 204/9, M to G, 17 July 1902.

65 Lincolnshire Diary, 15 July 1902.

66 RA QM/PRIV/CC23/11, M to Augusta, 30 November 1901.

67 M to Mabell Airlie, 24 November 1901 in Mabell, Countess of Airlie, *Thatched with Gold: The Memoirs of Mabell, Countess of Airlie*, ed. Jennifer Ellis (Hutchinson, 1962), pp. 100–1.

68 Airlie, *Thatched with Gold*, p. 102.

69 RA QM/PRIV/CC22/62, M to Augusta, 30 March 1901.

70 RA QM/PRIV/CC22/71, M to Augusta, 17 June 1901.

71 Pope-Hennessy, *Queen Mary*, pp. 394–5, Alix to M, 19 July 1901.

72 RA QM/PRIV/CC22/36, M to Augusta, 4 January 1903

73 RA QM/PRIV/CC23/35, M to Augusta, 23 November 1902.

74 Pope 205/9, M to Bricka, 22 September 1902.

75 Pope 195/7, M to G, 18 August 1902.

76 RA GV/PRIV/AA32/41, Alix to G, 20 December 1902.

77 RA QM/PRIV/CC23/19, M to Augusta, 1 March 1902.

78 Pope 199/5, QMD, 28 February 1902.

79 RA QM/PRIV/CC23/23, M to Augusta, 6 April 1902. RA QM/PRIV/CC23/24, M to Augusta, 13 April 1902.

80 RA GV/PRIV/AA32/23, Alix to G, 27 September 1900.

81 Pope 195/6, Lady Mary Lygon to Lady Ampthill, 23 October 1902.

82 Esher, *Journals and Letters of Reginald, Viscount Esher, Vol. 1*, pp. 324, 341.

CHAPTER 10

Family Life

1 Getty Research Library, Pope 195/14, QMD, 20 April 1902.

2 Pope 195/14, M to G, 12 November 1901.

3 Pope 195/14, Augusta to M, 12 November 1902.

4 Pope 195/14, G to M, 20 July 1902.

5 Pope 195/15, M to G, 23 July 1902.

6 RA QM/PRIV/CC23/39, M to Augusta, 5 April 1903.

7 RA GV/PRIV/AA26/23, G to Bertie, 5 April 1903.

8 Pope 195/14, Augusta to M, 14 May 1903.

9 Mabell, Countess of Airlie, *Thatched with Gold: The Memoirs of Mabell, Countess of Airlie*, ed. Jennifer Ellis (Hutchinson, 1962), p. 106.

10 RA QM/PRIV/CC23/41, M to Augusta, 31 May 1903.

11 RA QM/PRIV/CC23/43, M to Augusta, 21 June 1903.

12 RA QM/PRIV/CC23/109, M to Augusta, 10 November 1901.

13 James Pope-Hennessy, *Queen Mary* (Phoenix Press, 2000), p. 303.

14 Pope-Hennessy, *Queen Mary*, p. 303.

15 Pope-Hennessy, *Queen Mary*, p. 303.

16 George Godfrey-Faussett, *Royal Servant, Family Friend: The Life*

and Times of Naval Equerry Sir Bryan Godfrey-Faussett RN (Bernard Durnford, 2004), p. 117.

17 RA QM/PRIV/CC23/50, M to Augusta, 8 November 1903.

18 RA QM/PRIV/CC23/50, M to Augusta, 8 November 1903.

19 RA QM/PRIV/CC23/53, M to Augusta, 14 February 1904.

20 Pope 196/16, Pss Alice of Athlone, in James Pope-Hennessy, *The Quest for Queen Mary*, ed. Hugo Vickers (Zuleika, 2018), p. 181.

21 M to Duchess of Teck, 30 April 1896, in Pope-Hennessy, *Queen Mary*, p. 319. Kenneth Rose, *King George V* (Phoenix Press, 2000), pp. 37–8.

22 Pope-Hennessy, *Queen Mary*, p. 427.

23 RA QM/PRIV/CC23/31, M to Augusta, 8 June 1902.

24 Pope 205/2, Augusta to M, 29 January 1902.

25 RA QM/PRIV/CC23/33, M to Augusta, 5 October 1902.

26 RA QM/PRIV/CC23/37, M to Augusta, 1 March 1903.

27 RA QM/PRIV/CC23/56, M to Augusta, 27 March 1904.

28 RA QM/PRIV/CC24/7, M to Augusta, 3 July 1904.

29 Michael L. Nash, *Royal Wills in Britain from 1509 to 2008* (Palgrave, 2017), p. 158.

30 RA QM/PRIV/CC24/61, M to Augusta, 6 July 1906.

31 Pope 205/2, M to G, 1 August 1904.

32 Pope 205/2, Augusta to M, 16 September 1903.

33 Pope 205/2, M to G, 11 August 1904.

34 RA QM/PRIV/CC24/1, M to Augusta, 26 April 1904.

35 Pope 199/5, Lady Mary Lygon, 26 April 1904.

36 RA GV/PRIV/GVD/20 April 1904.

37 RA GV/PRIV/GVD/21, 22 April 1904.

38 RA GV/PRIV/GVD/14 January 1904.

39 Harold Nicolson, *King George the Fifth: His Life and Reign* (Constable, 1952), p. 61.

40 RA QM/PRIV/CC23/3, M to Augusta, 11 August 1901.

41 Godfrey-Faussett Papers, G to GF, 17 January 1904. *The Times*, 14 January 1904.

42 Sir Frederick Ponsonby, *Recollections of Three Reigns* (Odhams Press, n.d.), p. 281. See Nicholas Courtney, *The Queen's Stamps: The Authorised History of the Royal Philatelic Collection* (Methuen, 2004), pp. 80–96; Helen Morgan, *Blue Mauritius: The Hunt for the World's Most Valuable Stamps* (Atlantic, 2006).

43 Courtney, *The Queen's Stamps*, p. 98.

44 Earl of Crawford, *The Crawford Papers: The Journals of David Lindsay, 27th Earl of Crawford and 10th Earl of Balcarres (1871–1940), during the Years 1892 to 1940*, ed. John Vincent (Manchester University Press, 1984), p. 312.

45 Pope 204/9, G to M, 13 August 1903.

46 Pope 200/5, QV to Vicky, 31 May 1898.

47 Pope 200/5, QV to Vicky, 4 June 1898.

48 Pope 200/5, G to M, 10 February 1898.

49 Pope 200/5, QV to Vicky, 31 May 1898.

50 Tor Bomann-Larsen published these claims in 2004: *The Times*, 15 October 2004. Pope 200/5, M to G, 4 January 1900.

51 Pope 200/5, G to M, 29 January 1905.

52 RA GV/PRIV/AA33/3, Alix to G, 2 February 1905.

53 RA GV/PRIV/GVD/1 May 1909.

54 Pope 200/6, G to M, 20 August 1908.

55 Pope 196/16, Lady Juliet Duff, in Pope-Hennessy, *The Quest for Queen Mary*, p. 133.

56 Pope 196/16, Pss Alice of Athlone interview.
57 Pope 200/6, M to G, 7 April 1901.
58 G to Bigge, 22 September 1904, in John Gore, *King George V: A Personal Memoir* (John Murray, 1941), p. 191.
59 RA GV/PRIV/GVD/6 April 1905. See RA GV/PRIV/GVD/2–15 April 1905.
60 Lincolnshire Diary, 3 April 1905.
61 See Ronald Hyam, *Empire and Sexuality: The British Experience* (Manchester University Press, 1990), pp. 75–8.
62 RA GV/PRIV/AA32/30, Alix to G, 28 June 1901.
63 RA GV/PRIV/AA37/1, G to Alix, 11 August 1901.
64 Gore, *King George V*, p. 184.
65 Edward, Duke of Windsor, *A Family Album* (Cassell, 1960), p. 24. Frances Donaldson, *Edward VIII* (Weidenfeld & Nicolson, 1974), p. 16. Edward, Duke of Windsor, *A King's Story: The Memoirs of HRH the Duke of Windsor* (Cassell, 1951), p. 29.
66 Pope 205/9, G to M, 10 August 1896.
67 Gore, *King George V*, p. 184.
68 Sarah Bradford, *King George VI* (Weidenfeld & Nicolson, 1989), p. 29.
69 Airlie, *Thatched with Gold*, p. 113.
70 Windsor, *A Family Album*, p. 24.
71 RA GV/PRIV/GVD/15 April 1905.
72 Windsor, *A King's Story*, pp. 20–1. Donaldson, *Edward VIII*, p. 17. Windsor, *A Family Album*, p. 9.
73 Windsor, *A King's Story*, p. 18.
74 Philip Ziegler, *King Edward VIII: The Official Biography* (Collins, 1990), p. 14.
75 RA QM/PRIV/CC24/33, M to Augusta, 3 September 1905.
76 Windsor, *A King's Story*, p. 57.
77 J. Bryan III and Charles J. V. Murphy, *The Windsor Story* (Granada, 1979), p. 44.
78 Windsor, *A King's Story*, p. 27.
79 Donaldson, *Edward VIII*, p. 12.
80 Windsor, *A King's Story*, p. 24.
81 Airlie, *Thatched with Gold*, p. 112.
82 Airlie, *Thatched with Gold*, p. 113.
83 RA QM/PRIV/205/9, Augusta to M, 12 January 1905.
84 RA QM/PRIV/CC24/20, M to Augusta, 28 July 1905.
85 RA GV/PRIV/GVD/12 July 1905.
86 RA GV/PRIV/AA24/15, Bertie to G, 18 July 1905.

CHAPTER 11

George's Progress

1 RA GV/PRIV/AA33/7, Alix to G, 24 September 1905.
2 Getty Research Library, Pope 206/3, M to G, 29 September 1905.
3 Pope 206/3, M to G, 24 August 1905. G to M, 25 August 1905.
4 Pope 206/3, G to M, 30 September 1905.
5 *The Times*, 26 September 1905.
6 Sir Walter Lawrence's memo, n.d., in John Gore, *King George V: A Personal Memoir* (John Murray, 1941), p. 199.
7 Kenneth Rose, *King George V* (Phoenix Press, 2000), p. 62.
8 Bertie to G, 26 January 1906 in Rose, *King George V*, p. 62. David Gilmour, *Curzon* (John Murray, 1994), pp. 341–4.
9 Godfrey-Faussett Diary, January 1906.
10 G to Bertie, 8 January 1906 in Rose, *King George V*, p. 63.
11 Lawrence in Gore, *King George V*, pp. 204, 206.
12 Harold Nicolson, *King George the Fifth: His Life and Reign* (Constable, 1952), p. 86. See Rose, *King George V*, p. 61.
13 Lawrence in Gore, *King George V*, p. 205.
14 RA QM/PRIV/CC24/65, M to Augusta, 8 September 1906.
15 Martin Gilbert, ed., *Servant of India: A Study of Imperial Rule from 1905 to 1910 as Told through the Correspondence and Diaries of Sir James Dunlop Smith* (Longmans, 1966), p. 32, Dunlop Smith Diary, 10 January 1906.

16 Lawrence in Gore, *King George V*, p. 208.

17 RA GV/PRIV/AA33/16, Alix to G, 22 December 1905.

18 G to Bertie, 8 January 1906 in Shrabani Basu, *Victoria and Abdul: The True Story of the Queen's Closest Confidant* (History Press, 2010), p. 248.

19 Gore, *King George V*, pp. 207–8.

20 Nicolson, *King George the Fifth*, pp. 88–9.

21 RA GV/PRIV/AA33/21, Alix to G, 26 January 1906.

22 RA QM/PRIV/CC24/40, M to Augusta, 30 January 1906.

23 RA QM/PRIV/CC24/41, M to Augusta, 3 February 1906.

24 Pope 196/16, Lord Carnock, in James Pope-Hennessy, *The Quest for Queen Mary*, ed. Hugo Vickers (Zuleika, 2018), p. 78.

25 Gilbert, ed., *Servant of India*, pp. 31–2, 10 January 1906.

26 RA QM/PRIV/CC24/44, M to Augusta, 28 February 1906.

27 RA QM/PRIV/CC24/45, M to Augusta, 6 March 1906.

28 Pope 196/16, Lady Shaftesbury, in Pope-Hennessy, *The Quest for Queen Mary*, p. 128.

29 RA EDW/PRIV/MAIN/A/1825, M to David [D], 29 March 1916.

30 Churchill Archives Centre, Godfrey-Faussett Diary, May 1906.

31 Pope-Hennessy, *The Quest for Queen Mary*, p. 116.

32 RA QM/PRIV/CC1136, Prince John Baby Book.

33 RA QM/PRIV/CC24/66, M to Augusta, 23 September 1906.

34 RA QM/PRIV/CC24/114, M to Augusta, 12 July 1908.

35 RA GV/PRIV/AA37/11, G to Alix, 22 January 1909.

36 RA GV/PRIV/GVD/18 February 1907 in Gore, *King George V*, p. 218.

37 Philip Ziegler, *King Edward VIII: The Official Biography* (Collins, 1990), p. 21.

38 Edward, Duke of Windsor, *A King's Story: The Memoirs of HRH the Duke of Windsor* (Cassell, 1951), p. 58.

39 Windsor, *A King's Story*, p. 59.

40 Windsor, *A King's Story*, p. 63.

41 RA QM/PRIV/CC24/70, M to Augusta, 3 February 1907.

42 RA QM/PRIV/CC24/71, M to Augusta, 10 February 1907.

43 RA QM/PRIV/CC25/14, M to Augusta, 29 November 1908.

44 RA GV/PRIV/AA33/17, Alix to G, 29 December 1905. Sir Frederick Ponsonby, *Recollections of Three Reigns* (Odhams Press, n.d.), p. 153.

45 RA GV/PRIV/GVD/24 December 2008. Pope 199/8 Lady Bertha Dawkins, 25 December 1924.

46 Ponsonby, *Recollections of Three Reigns*, p. 153.

47 RA GV/PRIV/GVD/24, 25 December 1908.

48 G to Bigge, 25 December 1908 in Gore, *King George V*, pp. 220–1.

49 RA QM/PRIV/CC25/18, M to Augusta, 27 December 1908. RA GV/PRIV/GVD/25 December 1908.

50 Lawrence in Gore, *King George V*, p. 205.

51 *Monthly Weather Report of the Meteorological Office*, December 1908, https://digital.nmla.metoffice.gov.uk/IO_9229466c-0f5d-43b6–8783–19fbff1e8188/ (accessed 23 June 2021).

52 RA QM/PRIV/CC24/18, M to Augusta, 29 January 1905.

53 Pope 199/5, M to G, 26 February 1906. Pope 206/3, G to M, 4 March 1906.

54 Pope 199/5, M to Bricka, 15 April 1906.

55 Pope 199/5, G to M, 25 February 1906; M to G, 26 February 1906.

56 RA QM/PRIV/CC24/57, M to Augusta, 10 June 1906.

57 RA QM/PRIV/CC24/31 May 1906 in Gore, *King George V*, p. 212.

58 *The Times*, 5 February 1908.

59 RA QM/PRIV/CC24/14, M to Augusta, 20 November 1904.

60 RA QM/PRIV/CC24/98, M to Augusta, 2 February 1908.

61 RA QM/PRIV/CC24/99, M to Augusta, 9 February 1908.

62 RA GV/PRIV/GVD/2 February 1908 in Gore, *King George V*, p. 222. See John Villiers, 'Sir Francis Villiers and the Fall of the Portuguese Monarchy', http://www.mod-langs.ox.ac.uk/files/windsor/7_villiers.pdf (accessed 23 June 2021).

63 RA QM/PRIV/CC24/101, M to Augusta, 1 March 1908.

64 Pope 203/7, Augusta to M, 10 August 1905.

65 Pope 203/7, Augusta to M, 28 November 1905.

66 RA QM/PRIV/CC24/59, M to Augusta, 24 June 1906.

67 RA GV/PRIV/GVD/22 June 1906. James Pope-Hennessy, *Queen Mary* (Phoenix Press, 2000), pp. 407–9.

68 Pope-Hennessy, *The Quest for Queen Mary*, p. 68.

69 RA QM/PRIV/CC25/18, M to Augusta, 27 December 1908.

70 RA QM/PRIV/CC25/22, M to Augusta, 14 March 1909. RA QM/PRIV/CC25/49, M to Augusta, 9 January 1910.

71 RA QM/PRIV/CC24/106, M to Augusta, 19 April 1908.

72 RA QM/PRIV/CC24/94, M to Augusta, 24 November 1907.

73 RA QM/PRIV/CC25/24, M to Augusta, 25 March 1909.

74 RA QM/PRIV/CC25/14, M to Augusta, 29 November 1908.

75 RA QM/PRIV/CC25/3, M to Augusta, 1 August 1908. This visit was to Sir Edgar Sebright.

76 RA QM/PRIV/CC24/105, M to Augusta, 11 April 1908.

77 RA QM/PRIV/CC24/105, M to Augusta, 11 April 1908.

78 James Lees-Milne, *The Enigmatic Edwardian: The Life of Reginald, 2nd Viscount Esher* (Sidgwick & Jackson, 1986), p. 188.

79 RA GV/PRIV/AA37/8, G to Alix, 10 April 1908.

80 Reginald, Viscount Esher, *Journals and Letters of Reginald, Viscount Esher, Vol. 2: 1903–1910*, ed.

Maurice V. Brett (Ivor Nicholson & Watson, 1934), p. 207. *The Times*, 1 May 1908.

81 RA GV/PRIV/GVD/30 April 1909.

82 RA QM/PRIV/CC24/39, M to Augusta, 19 January 1906.

83 RA QM/PRIV/CC24/43, M to Augusta, 22 February 1906.

84 RA QM/PRIV/CC25/26, M to Augusta, 4 April 1909.

85 Frank Mort, 'Safe for Democracy: Constitutional Politics, Popular Spectacle, and the British Monarchy 1910–1914', *Journal of British Studies*, vol. 58, no. 1 (2019), p. 118.

86 Lees-Milne, *The Enigmatic Edwardian*, p. 191. Rose, *King George V*, pp. 71–3.

87 Lees-Milne, *The Enigmatic Edwardian*, p. 188.

88 Jane Ridley, *Bertie: A Life of Edward VII* (Chatto & Windus, 2012), p. 417.

89 RA GV/PRIV/AA23/44, Bertie to G, 14 March 1906.

90 RA GV/PRIV/GVD/24 April 1908. Andrew Roberts, *Churchill* (Penguin, 2019), pp. 120–1.

91 RA QM/PRIV/CC25/31, M to Augusta, 6 June 1909.

92 Pope 204/9, M to G, 31 July 1906.

93 Pope 204/9, G to M, 31 July 1906.

94 Pope 204/9, G to M, 2 September 1907.

95 Gore, *King George V*, p. 218.

96 Esher, *Journals and Letters of Reginald, Viscount Esher, Vol. 2*, p. 387, 9 May 1909. Lees-Milne, *The Enigmatic Edwardian*, p. 187.

97 Bodleian, Margot Asquith Papers, MS Eng d.3206, Diary, 15 November 1909.

98 RA GV/PRIV/GVD/2 August 1909.

99 Pope 199/6, QMD, 2 August 1909.

100 Pope 199/6, QMD, 3 August 1909.

101 RA GV/PRIV/GVD/4 August 1909. RA QM/PRIV/CC25/39, M to Augusta, 6 August 1909. See Frances Welch, *The Imperial Tea*

Party: Family, Politics and Betrayal –
the Ill-Fated British and Russian
Royal Alliance (Short, 2018), pp.
175–231.

102 RA QM/PRIV/CC25/30, M to
Augusta, 30 May 1909.
103 Pope 199/6, Augusta to M, 2 June
1909.
104 The Times, 6 January 1906.
105 Ridley, Bertie, pp. 450–1.
106 See Ridley, Bertie, pp. 441–4.
107 RA GV/PRIV/AA33/44, Alix to G,
26 March 1910.
108 RA GV/PRIV/AA25/72, Bertie to
G, 29 March 1910.
109 RA GV/PRIV/GVD/27 April 1910.
110 RA GV/PRIV/GVD/3 May 1910.
111 RA GV/PRIV/GVD/4 May 1910.
112 RA GV/PRIV/AA37/16, G to Alix,
4 May 1910.
113 RA GV/PRIV/GVD/4 May 1910.
114 RA GV/PRIV/GVD/5 May 1910.
115 RA GV/PRIV/GVD/6 May 1910.
116 Richard Holmes, Edward VII: His
Life and Times (Amalgamated
Press, 1911), vol. 2, p. 599.
117 RA GV/PRIV/GVD/6 May 1910.

CHAPTER 12

King

1 RA GV/PRIV/GVD/7 May 1910.
2 Lambeth Palace, Davidson Papers,
581, Dictated Memoranda about
the Deathbed and Funeral of King
Edward VII, 25 August 1910, pp.
11–12.
3 Harold Nicolson, King George the
Fifth: His Life and Reign
(Constable, 1952), p. 123. In his
diary George had written: 'I have
lost my best friend & the best of
fathers, I never had a word with
him in his life' (RA GV/PRIV/
GVD/6 May 1910).
4 Sir Almeric FitzRoy, Memoirs
(Hutchinson, 1925), vol. 2,
pp. 404–5.
5 Edward, Duke of Windsor, A King's
Story: The Memoirs of HRH the
Duke of Windsor (Cassell, 1951),
p. 70.

6 Churchill Archive Centre, Godfrey-
Faussett Diary, 5–26 May 1910.
John Gore, King George V: A
Personal Memoir (John Murray,
1941), p. 241.
7 Lambeth Palace, Davidson Papers,
581, Dictated Memoranda about
the Deathbed and Funeral of
King Edward VII, 25 August
1910, pp. 3–4.
8 Bodleian, Lincolnshire Diary, 6 May
1910.
9 Nicolson, King George the Fifth,
p. 105.
10 RA QM/PRIV/CC25/58, M to
Augusta, 15 May 1910.
11 RA QM/PRIV/CC25/58, M to
Augusta, 15 May 1910.
12 The Times, 9 May 1910.
13 Earl of Crawford, The Crawford
Papers: The Journals of David
Lindsay, 27th Earl of Crawford and
10th Earl of Balcarres (1871–
1940), during the Years 1892 to
1940, ed. John Vincent (Manchester
University Press, 1984), p. 153, 9
May 1910.
14 Edward David, ed., Inside Asquith's
Cabinet: From the Diaries of
Charles Hobhouse (John Murray,
1977), p. 91, 15 May 1910.
15 Nicolson, King George the Fifth,
p. 123.
16 RA QM/PRIV/CC25/58, M to
Augusta, 15 May 1910.
17 Crawford, The Crawford Papers,
p. 153.
18 RA QM/PRIV/CC25/58, M to
Augusta, 15 May 1910.
19 David, ed., Inside Asquith's Cabinet,
p. 91.
20 Getty Research Library, Pope 204/9,
G to M, 30 October 1910.
21 Nicolson, King George the Fifth,
p. 130.
22 RA GV/PRIV/GVD/18 May 1910.
23 Roy Jenkins, Asquith (Collins,
1964), p. 213.
24 Sam Knight, '"London Bridge is
down": the secret plan for the days
after the Queen's death', Guardian,
17 March 2017.

25 RA QM/PRIV/CC25/62, M to Augusta, 12 June 1910.

26 RA QM/PRIV/CC25/58, M to Augusta, 15 May 1910.

27 James Lees-Milne, *The Enigmatic Edwardian: The Life of Reginald, 2nd Viscount Esher* (Sidgwick & Jackson, 1986), p. 210.

28 Public Record Office of Northern Ireland, Schomberg McDonnell Papers, D/4091/A/6/6/1–8, McDonnell, 'Death and Funeral of King Edward VII', May 1910, p. 1. Lincolnshire Diary, 7 May 1910.

29 Davidson Papers, 581, Dictated Memoranda about the Deathbed and Funeral of King Edward VII, 25 August 1910, pp. 29–30.

30 Schomberg McDonnell Papers, D/4091/A/6/6/1–8, McDonnell, 'Death and Funeral of King Edward VII', May 1910, p. 30.

31 RA QM/PRIV/CC25/59, M to Augusta, 22 May 1910.

32 RA GV/PRIV/GVD/20 May 1910.

33 RA GV/PRIV/GVD/20 May 1910.

34 John C. G. Röhl, *Wilhelm II: Into the Abyss of War and Exile 1900–1941* (Cambridge University Press, 2014), p. 785.

35 Pope 194/2, Augusta to M, 24 May 1910. Augusta to Eva Dugdale, 28 May 1910.

36 Pope, Augusta to M, 24 May 1910.

37 RA QM/PRIV/CC25/60, M to Augusta, 29 May 1910.

38 RA QM/PRIV/CC25/60, M to Augusta, 29 May 1910.

39 RA QM/PRIV/CC25/61, M to Augusta, 5 June 1910.

40 RA QM/PRIV/CC25/63, M to Augusta, 18 June 1910.

41 Churchill Archives Centre, Esher Journal 2/12, 25 August 1910.

42 RA GV/PRIV/AA37/17, G to Alix, 29 August 1910.

43 *The Times*, 9 August 1910. Kenneth Rose, *King George V* (Phoenix Press, 2000), p. 296.

44 Esher Journal, 21 August 1910.

45 Esher Journal, 21 August 1910.

46 RA QM/PRIV/CC25/77, M to Augusta, 16 October 1910.

47 RA QM/PRIV/CC25/77, M to Augusta, 16 October 1910. *The Times*, 24 October 1910.

48 Godfrey-Faussett Diary, 22 October 1910.

49 RA GV/PRIV/GVD/22 October 1910.

50 James Pope-Hennessy, *The Quest for Queen Mary*, ed. Hugo Vickers (Zuleika, 2018), p. 181.

51 Pope 204/9, G to M, 30 October 1910.

52 James Pope-Hennessy, *Queen Mary* (Phoenix Press, 2000), pp. 427–8.

53 Michael L. Nash, *Royal Wills in Britain from 1509 to 2008* (Palgrave Macmillan, 2017), pp. 152–79. Suzy Menkes, *The Royal Jewels* (Grafton, 1985), pp. 67–9. 'I am thankful to say Frank's affairs are now finished & settled, such a mercy after a whole year,' May told George on 2 November 1911 (RA GV/PRIV/CC8/136).

54 Derby's Memo, 20 August 1911 in Randolph S. Churchill, *Winston S. Churchill, Vol. 2: Young Statesman 1901–1914* (Heinemann, 1967), p. 342.

55 RA PS/PSO/GV/C/K/2552(1) Bigge memo, 11 November 1910.

56 Jenkins, *Asquith*, p. 218.

57 RA GV/PRIV/GVD/11 November 1910. RA PS/PSO/GV/C/K/2552(1)/41, Bigge's note, 11 November 1910.

58 RA VIC/ADDC07/2/H, Bertie to Knollys, 9 April 1910.

59 Knollys to Esher, 17 April 1910 in Philip Magnus, *King Edward the Seventh* (John Murray, 1964), 453.

60 RA PS/PSO/GV/C/K/2552(1)/49, Knollys to G, 14 November 1910.

61 Bigge's memo for G, 15 November 1910 in Nicolson, *King George the Fifth*, pp. 137–8.

62 RA PS/PSO/GV/C/K/2552(2)/72, Stamfordham Memo, 10 August

1911, quoting Elibank to Knollys, 14 November 1910.

63 Bigge Memo, 18 November 1910 in Nicolson, *King George the Fifth*, 138.

64 Knollys to G, 15 November 1910 in Nicolson, *King George the Fifth*, 137.

65 RA GV/PRIV/GVD/15 November 1910.

66 RA GV/PRIV/GVD/16 November 1910.

67 Nicolson, *King George the Fifth*, p. 138.

68 RA PS/PSO/GV/C/K/2552(2)/99, Memo by Wigram, 9 November 1931.

69 Balliol College Archive, Nicolson Diary, 19 October 1949: interview with Cromer.

70 RA VIC/ADDC07/2/11, Bertie to Knollys, 23 April 1910.

71 Derby in Churchill, *Winston S. Churchill*, p. 343.

72 RA GV/PRIV/GVD/16 November 1911.

73 Bigge memo, 18 November 1910 in Nicolson, *King George the Fifth*, p. 139.

74 Nicolson Diary, 2 November 1949.

75 Rose, *King George V*, p. 141.

76 RA VIC/ADDC7/2/H, Nash to Knollys, 16 November 1910. Carrington, 10 May 1910.

77 Rose, *King George V*, p. 124.

78 Esher Journal, 19 November 1910. Significantly, the second sentence praising Knollys was deleted from the printed version of the journal.

79 Vernon Bogdanor, *The Monarchy and the Constitution* (Clarendon Press, 1995), pp. 117–19.

80 Nicolson Diary, 2 November 1949.

81 RA PS/PSO/GV/C/K/2552(2)/99, Memo by Wigram, 9 November 1931.

82 Godfrey-Faussett Diary, 18 November 1910.

83 RA PS/PSO/GV/C/K/2552(2)/89, Note by G, 7 January 1914.

84 Davidson Papers, Davidson's Memo 'Irish Question', 21 January 1914.

85 RA PS/PSO/GV/C/K/2552(2)/99, Memo by Wigram, 9 November 1931.

86 Yale Beinecke, Gen MSS 614, Box 17, Nicolson to Lascelles, 23/27 January 1953.

87 Frank Mort, 'Safe for Democracy: Constitutional Politics, Popular Spectacle, and the British Monarchy 1910–1914', *Journal of British Studies*, vol. 58, no. 1 (2019), pp. 118–21.

88 Esher Journal, 2/12, 14 October 1911.

89 Esher Journal, 2/12, 21 August 1910.

90 RA QM/PRIV/CC25/82, M to Augusta, 18 December 1910.

91 RA QM/PRIV/CC25/82, M to Augusta, 18 December 1910.

92 RA QM/PRIV/CC25/84, M to Augusta, 1 January 1911.

93 RA QM/PRIV/CC25/70, M to Augusta, 7 August 1910.

94 Philip Hall, *Royal Fortune: Tax, Money and the Monarchy* (Bloomsbury, 1992), pp. 33–6.

95 Schomberg McDonnell Papers, D/4091/A/6/6/1–8, McDonnell, 'Death and Funeral of King Edward VII', May 1910, pp. 5–6.

96 Hall, *Royal Fortune*, p. 40.

97 Rose, *King George V*, p. 92.

98 H. H. Asquith, *Letters to Venetia Stanley*, ed. Michael and Eleanor Brock (Oxford University Press, 1982), p. 43, Asquith to Margot, September 1912.

99 Godfrey-Faussett Diary, 21 October 1910.

100 Godfrey-Faussett Diary, 3 November 1910.

101 See Rose, *King George V*, pp. 82–7.

102 RA GV/PRIV/AA37/22, G to Alix, 6 February 1911.

103 Churchill, *Winston S. Churchill*, vol. 2, p. 420.

104 Rose, *King George V*, p. 84.

105 Robin Callender Smith, 'The Missing Witness? George V, Competence, Compellability and the Criminal Trial of Edward Frederick Mylius', *Journal of Legal History*, vol. 33, no. 2 (2012), pp. 209–39.

106 George Dangerfield, *The Strange Death of Liberal England* (Constable, 1936), pp. 31–2.

107 RA GV/PRIV/AA37/22, G to A, 6 February 1911.

CHAPTER 13

Constitutional Monarch

1 RA GV/PRIV/GVD/22 June 1911.
2 *The Times*, 23 June 1911.
3 George had nagged the government, getting his private secretary to write to Number 10: 'The King is very anxious that the new road [in The Mall] should be used at the Coronation.' (Bodleian, Asquith Papers, 2, Knollys to Nash, 2 November 1910. See Steven Brindle, 'Buckingham Palace and the Victoria Memorial, 1901–14', *Court Historian*, vol. 11, no. 1 (2006).)
4 Sir Almeric FitzRoy, *Memoirs* (Hutchinson, 1925), vol. 2, p. 450.
5 Lambeth Palace, Davidson Papers, Vol. 280, Davidson to Duke of Norfolk, 13 June 1911.
6 Davidson Papers, Vol. 280, Bigge to Davidson, 3 March 1911.
7 *The Times*, 23 June 1911.
8 RA GV/PRIV/GVD/22 June 1911 in Harold Nicolson, *King George the Fifth: His Life and Reign* (Constable, 1952), p. 147.
9 Nicolson, *King George the Fifth*, p. 147.
10 RA QM/PRIV/CC25/107, M to Augusta, 25 June 1911.
11 *The Times*, 23 June 1911.
12 V. Sackville-West, *The Edwardians* (Hogarth Press, 1930), p. 344.
13 Earl of Crawford, *The Crawford Papers: The Journals of David Lindsay, 27th Earl of Crawford and 10th Earl of Balcarres (1871–1940), during the Years 1892 to 1940*, ed. John Vincent (Manchester University Press, 1984), p. 188.
14 *The Times*, 23 June 1911.
15 RA GV/PRIV/GVD/22 June 1911.
16 Suzy Menkes, *The Royal Jewels* (Grafton, 1985), p. 65.
17 RA QM/PRIV/CC25/100, M to Augusta, 7 May 1911.
18 Getty Research Library, Pope 201/9, QM's List of Dresses for Coronation Festivities. Vickers, p138.
19 'Queen Mary's Coronation Dress, 1911', Royal Collection Trust website, www.royalcollection.org. uk/collection/75030 (accessed 23 June 2021).
20 Pope 195/8, M to G, 6 December 1910; G to M, 7 December 1910.
21 James Pope-Hennessy, *The Quest for Queen Mary*, ed. Hugo Vickers (Zuleika, 2018), p. 143.
22 'Queen Mary's Coronation Dress, 1911'.
23 RA QM/PRIV/CC25/61, M to Augusta, 5 June 1910.
24 RA QM/PRIV/CC25/89, M to Augusta, 11 February 1911.
25 Pope 201/9, QMD, 28 June 1910. Menkes, *The Royal Jewels*, pp. 66–7.
26 RA QM/PRIV/CC58/162, Gowns and Jewels Worn by Her Majesty at Important Functions during 1911–14.
27 Pope 201/9, QM's List of Dresses for Coronation Festivities.
28 RA QM/PRIV/CC58/162, Gowns and Jewels Worn by Her Majesty.
29 RA PS/PSO/GV/PS/ STAMP/2090/1, Ponsonby to Matthew Nathan, 28 June 1911.
30 RA GV/PRIV/GVD/5 August 1910.
31 RA GV/PRIV/4130/59, Bigge to Tilleard, 30 November 1910.
32 Nicholas Courtney, *The Queen's Stamps: The Authorised History of the Royal Philatelic Collection* (Methuen, 2004), pp. 112ff.

33 *The Times*, 23 June 1911.

34 RA PS/PSO/GV/PS/ STAMP/2090/1, Ponsonby to Matthew Nathan, 28 June 1911.

35 Courtney, *The Queen's Stamps*, p. 116.

36 Edward, Duke of Windsor, *A King's Story: The Memoirs of HRH the Duke of Windsor* (Cassell, 1951), p. 79.

37 RA QM/PRIV/CC25/109, M to Augusta, 15 July 1911.

38 Churchill Archives Centre, Esher Papers, 2/12, Journal, 25 August, 26 November 1910.

39 Windsor, *A King's Story*, p. 76.

40 RA QM/PRIV/CC25/96, M to Augusta, 9 April 1911.

41 RA GV/PRIV/GVD/22 June 1911.

42 Esher Journal, 2/12, 26 November 1910.

43 Windsor, *A King's Story*, p. 74.

44 Sarah Bradford, *King George VI* (Weidenfeld & Nicolson, 1989), p. 45, quoting Nicolson Diary, 20 September 1943.

45 RA QM/PRIV/CC45/380, Maud to M, 30 November 1911.

46 RA PS/PSO/GV/C2548/21, M to Alix, 26 February 1911.

47 RA GV/PRIV/CC8/130, M to G, 25 August 1911,

48 RA QM/PRIV/CC04/76, G to M, 27 August 1911.

49 RA QM/PRIV/CC45/380, Queen Maud to M, 30 November 1911.

50 RA GV/PRIV/AA37/31, G to Alix, 24 April 1911.

51 Esher Journal, 2/12, 14 October 1911.

52 Esher Journal, 2/12, 14 October 1911.

53 Davidson Papers, Vol. 12, Memorandum 22 July–1 August 1911, p. 5.

54 Roy Jenkins, *Asquith* (Collins, 1964), p. 229.

55 Davidson Papers, Vol. 12, Memo 'Obviously "Unfit for publication"', Easter 1913.

56 Davidson Papers, Vol. 12, 22 July–1 August 1911, pp. 2–3.

57 Davidson Papers, Vol. 12, 22 July–1 August 1911, p. 5.

58 David Gilmour, *Curzon* (John Murray, 1994), p. 389.

59 Gilmour, *Curzon*, p. 392.

60 RA GV/PRIV/GVD/25 July 1911.

61 Esher Journal, 2/12, 14 October 1911.

62 Earl of Midleton, *Records & Reactions 1856–1939* (John Murray, 1939), p. 275.

63 Davidson Papers, Vol. 12, Memo, 13 August 1911, p. 23.

64 *The Times*, 11 August 1911.

65 Davidson Papers, Vol. 12, 13 August 1911, p. 22.

66 Esher Journal, 2/12, 14 October 1911. Gilmour, *Curzon*, p. 392. RA GV/PRIV/GVD/10 August 1911.

67 Gilmour, *Curzon*, p. 393.

68 George Godfrey-Faussett, *Royal Servant, Family Friend: The Life and Times of Naval Equerry Sir Bryan Godfrey-Faussett RN* (Bernard Durnford, 2004), p. 170 (10 August 1911).

69 RA GV/PRIV/GVD/10 August 1911.

70 RA GV/PRIV/GVD/18, 20 August 1911.

71 RA QM/PRIV/CC04/70, G to M, 13 August 1911.

72 RA GV/PRIV/CC8/126, M to G, 14 August 1911.

73 RA QM/PRIV/CC04/71, G to M, 15 August 1911.

74 RA GV/PRIV/CC8/129, M to G, 22 August 1911.

75 Esher Journal, 2/12, 4 October 1911.

76 James Pope-Hennessy, *Queen Mary* (Phoenix Press, 2000), p. 425.

77 Mabell, Countess of Airlie, *Thatched with Gold: The Memoirs of Mabell, Countess of Airlie*, ed. Jennifer Ellis (Hutchinson, 1962), p. 128.

78 RA QM/PRIV/CC04/73, G to M, 20 August 1911. Frank Mort, 'Safe for Democracy: Constitutional Politics, Popular Spectacle, and the British Monarchy 1910–1914', *Journal of British Studies*, vol. 58, no. 1 (2019), p. 120.

79 Kenneth Rose, *King George V* (Phoenix Press, 2000), p. 92.

80 Mary Soames, ed., *Speaking for Themselves: The Personal Letters of Winston and Clementine Churchill* (Black Swan, 1999), pp. 55–6.

81 RA QM/PRIV/CC04/76, G to M, 27 August 1911.

82 RA QM/PRIV/CC25/117, M to Augusta, 6 October 1911.

83 Churchill, Godfrey-Faussett Diary, 12 November 1911.

84 RA GV/PRIV/AA37/31, G to Alix, 19 November 1911.

85 Esher Journal, 2/12, 25 August 1910.

86 Esher Journal, 2/12, 17 February 1912. Asquith also understood that the King was responsible for the move: see Edward David, ed., *Inside Asquith's Cabinet: From the Diaries of Charles Hobhouse* (John Murray, 1977), p. 107.

87 David, ed., *Inside Asquith's Cabinet*, p. 107.

88 Esher Journal, 2/12, 17 February 1912.

89 The Devonshire Collections, Chatsworth, Evelyn Duchess of Devonshire Evelyn Papers, J10, Duchess Evelyn to Duke Victor, 22 November 1911, typed transcript of letters from India, November 1910/ January 1911.

90 Chatsworth, J10, Duchess Evelyn to Duke Victor, 20 November 1911, typed transcript.

91 Chatsworth, J10, Duchess Evelyn to Duke Victor, 16 December 1911, typed transcript.

92 Sir John Fortescue, *Narrative of the Visit to India of Their Majesties King George V and Queen Mary* (Macmillan, 1912), p. 121. Jessica Douglas-Home, *A Glimpse of Empire* (Michael Russell, 2011), pp. 47–52.

93 RA QM/PRIV/CC25/126, M to Augusta, 6,7 December 1911.

94 RA QM/PRIV/CC58/162, Gowns and Jewels, 12 December 1911.

95 Pope-Hennessy, *Queen Mary*, p. 460. Menkes, *The Royal Jewels*, pp. 71–2.

96 Nicolson, *King George the Fifth*, p. 172.

97 Chatsworth, J10, Duchess Evelyn to Duke Victor, 18 January 1912, typed transcript.

98 RA GV/PRIV/GVD/12 December 1911.

99 RA QM/PRIV/CC25/127, M to Augusta, 13 December 1911.

100 Esher Journal, 2/12, 17 February 1912.

101 RA QM/PRIV/CC04/85, G to M, 19 December 1911.

102 RA GV/PRIV/CC8/141, M to G, 24 December 1911.

103 RA QM/PRIV/CC26/1, M to Augusta, 1 January 1912.

104 RA GV/PRIV/AA37/40, G to Alix, 15 January 1912.

105 RA QM/PRIV/CC04/86, G to M, 22 December 1911.

106 Chatsworth, J10, Duchess Evelyn to Duke Victor, 16 December 1911, typed transcript.

107 RA GV/PRIV/GVD/11 January 1912.

108 David Cannadine, *Ornamentalism: How the British Saw Their Empire* (Penguin, 2001), pp. 51–4.

109 RA QM/PRIV/CC04/86, G to M, 22 December 1911.

CHAPTER 14

'The King is Duller than the Queen'

1 Violet Bonham Carter, *Lantern Slides: The Diaries and Letters of Violet Bonham Carter 1904–1914*, ed. Mark Bonham Carter and Mark Pottle (Weidenfeld & Nicolson, 1996), p. 305, 5 February 1912.

2 Richard Davenport-Hines, *Ettie: The Intimate Life and Dauntless Spirit of Lady Desborough* (Weidenfeld & Nicolson, 2008), p. 155.

3 James Pope-Hennessy, *Queen Mary* (Phoenix Press, 2000), p. 432.

4 RA PS/PSO/GV/C2548/21, M to Alix, 26 February 2011. RA QM/PRIV/CC25/70, M to Augusta, 7 August 1910.

5   Princess Marie Louise, *My Memories of Six Reigns* (Evans Brothers, 1956), p. 45. Adrian Tinniswood, *Behind the Throne: A Domestic History of the Royal Household* (Jonathan Cape, 2018), pp. 240–44.

6   RA GV/PRIV/GVD/14, 15 March 1912.

7   RA GV/PRIV/GVD/19 July 1912.

8   Bonham-Carter, *Lantern Slides*, p. 272, 10 May 1911.

9   RA QM/PRIV/CC58/162, Queen Mary's Gowns, 1st Court 1912.

10 RA QM/PRIV/CC26/7, M to Augusta, 17 March 1912.

11 Tinniswood, *Behind the Throne*, p. 127.

12 The Devonshire Collections, Chatsworth, CC59/AA12/12045, M to Dss of Devonshire, n.d. [December 1910]. CC59/AA12/12044, M to Dss of Devonshire, 17 December 1910.

13 Chatsworth, CC59/AA12/12051 12051, Miss Rossiter to Dss of Devonshire, 17 December 1910.

14 Chatsworth, CC59/AA12/12055, Ly Katherine Coke to Dss of Devonshire, 3 January 1911.

15 Chatsworth, CC 12057, Dss of Buccleuch to Dss of Devonshire, 9 January 1911. CC 12059, Duchess of Buccleuch to Duchess of Devonshire, 21 January 1911.

16 James Pope-Hennessy, *The Quest for Queen Mary*, ed. Hugo Vickers (Zuleika, 2018), p. 126.

17 RA QM/PRIV/CC25/87, M to Augusta, 29 January 1911.

18 Davenport-Hines, *Ettie*, p. 153.

19 Chatsworth, CC59/AA12/12047, Lady Bertha Dawkins to Dss of Devonshire, 17 December 1910.

20 Lady Shaftesbury in Pope-Hennessy, *The Quest for Queen Mary*, p. 130.

21 RA QM/PRIV/CC24/103, M to Augusta, 22 March 1908. Lady Bertha Dawkins (née Bootle-Wilbraham) was the daughter of the Earl of Lathom, lord chamberlain 1885–92 and 1892–5.

22 Pope-Hennessy, *The Quest for Queen Mary*, p. 286. See below Chapter 18, p. 261.

23 Pope 195/15, Note of Conversation with Cynthia Colville, 31 January 1958.

24 Chatsworth, CC59/ AA12/ 12047, Lady Bertha Dawkins to Dss of Devonshire, 17 December 1910. Getty Research Library, Pope 195/15, Lady Mary Trefusis to Lady Bertha Dawkins [1907].

25 Pope-Hennessy, *The Quest for Queen Mary*, p. 129.

26 RA QM/PRIV/CC26/11, M to Augusta, 20 April 1912. Pope-Hennessy, *The Quest for Queen Mary*, p. 129.

27 Mary Soames, ed., *Speaking for Themselves: The Personal Letters of Winston and Clementine Churchill* (Black Swan, 1999), p. 57.

28 Kenneth Rose, *King George V* (Phoenix Press, 2000), p. 96.

29 Rose, *King George V*, p. 87.

30 Rose, *King George V*, p. 96.

31 RA QM/PRIV/CC26/6, M to Augusta, 18 February 1912.

32 RA QM/PRIV/CC26/7, M to Augusta, 17 March 1912.

33 RA QM/PRIV/CC26/8, M to Augusta, 24 March 1912.

34 Knollys to Asquith, 6 September 1911, in Catherine Bailey, *Black Diamonds: The Rise and Fall of an English Dynasty* (Penguin, 2008), p. 116. Roy Jenkins, *Asquith* (Collins, 1964), pp. 233–4.

35 Frank Prochaska, *Royal Bounty: The Making of a Welfare Monarchy* (Yale University Press, 1995), p. 170.

36 RA GV/PRIV/CC8/129, M to G, 22 August 1911. See RA QM/PRIV/CC04/74, G to M, 23 August 1911.

37 Bailey, *Black Diamonds*, p. 121. See Prochaska, *Royal Bounty*, p. 174.

38 Stamfordham to Halifax, 29 June 1912 in Bailey, *Black Diamonds*, p. 143. *The Times*, 28 June 1912.

39 *The Times*, 26 June 1912.

40 Frank Mort, 'Safe for Democracy: Constitutional Politics, Popular

Spectacle, and the British Monarchy 1910–1914', *Journal of British Studies*, vol. 58, no. 1 (2019), pp. 123–9.

41 RA QM/PRIV/CC26/20, M to Augusta, 29 June 1912.

42 RA QM/PRIV/CC04/74, G to M, 23 August 1911. *The Times*, 15 June 1912. Prochaska, *Royal Bounty*, p. 174.

43 *The Times*, 29 June 1894.

44 Bailey, *Black Diamonds*, p. 151.

45 RA QM/PRIV/CC26/22, M to Augusta, 14 July 1912.

46 Bailey, *Black Diamonds*, p 145.

47 RA QM/PRIV/CC26/22, M to Augusta, 14 July 1912.

48 RA QM/PRIV/CC26/22, M to Augusta, 14 July 1912.

49 Bailey, *Black Diamonds*, p. 147.

50 RA QM/PRIV/CC26/5, M to Augusta, 11 February 1912.

51 Sir John Lavery, *The Life of a Painter* (Cassell, 1940), p. 162.

52 'Sir John Lavery (1856–1941), *The Family of King George V*, Signed and Dated 1913', Royal Collections Trust website, https://www.rct.uk/collection/407134/the-family-of-king-george-v (accessed 24 June 2021).

53 RA GV/PRIV/CC8/159, M to G, 2 November 1912. RA QM/PRIV/CC4/108, G to M, 3 November 1912.

54 RA QM/PRIV/CC26/57, M to Augusta, 4 July 1913.

55 Churchill Archive Centre, Esher Papers, Journal, 10 September 1913. George Godfrey-Faussett, *Royal Servant, Family Friend: The Life and Times of Naval Equerry Captain Sir Bryan Godfrey-Faussett* (Bernard Durnford, 2004), p. 194.

56 The Devonshire Collections, Chatsworth, L13, Duchess Evelyn to Duke Victor, 20 May 1913.

57 RA EDW/PRIV/MAIN/A/1205, M to David, 26 January 1914.

58 RA EDW/PRIV/MAIN/A/1205, M to David, 26 January 1914.

59 RA QM/PRIV/CC4/108, G to M, 3 November 1912.

60 RA GV/PRIV/CC8/160, M to G, 4 November 1912.

61 RA QM/PRIV/CC4/109, G to M, 4 November 1912.

62 RA GV/PRIV/CC8/157, M to G, 23 October 1912.

63 RA QM/PRIV/CC4/104, G to M, 23 October 1912.

64 RA GV/PRIV/AA37/54, G to Alix, 23 October 1912.

65 Rose, *King George V*, p. 140.

66 H. H. Asquith, *Letters to Venetia Stanley*, ed. Michael and Eleanor Brock (Oxford University Press, 1982), p. 51.

67 Lambeth Palace, Davidson Papers, Vol. 12, Memo, 16 February 1913, p. 3.

68 Davidson Papers, Vol. 12, 16 February 1913, p. 2, note of conversation with King, 14 February 1913.

69 Davidson Papers, Vol. 12, 16 February 1913, pp. 3–4.

70 James Lees-Milne, *The Enigmatic Edwardian: The Life of Reginald, 2nd Viscount Esher* (Sidgwick & Jackson, 1986), pp. 242–4.

71 Rose, *King George V*, p. 143.

72 Esher Journal, 24 December 1912.

73 Esher Journal, 24 December 1912. Davidson Papers, Memo, 22 July–1 August 1911.

74 Rose, *King George V*, pp. 140–1.

75 Bodleian, Lincolnshire Diary, 11 May 1912.

76 H.C.G. Matthew, 'King George V (1865–1936)', *Oxford Dictionary of National Biography* (2004).

77 Edward David, ed., *Inside Asquith's Cabinet: From the Diaries of Charles Hobhouse* (John Murray, 1977), p. 145, 8 August 1913.

78 Earl of Crawford, *The Crawford Papers: The Journals of David Lindsay, 27th Earl of Crawford and 10th Earl of Balcarres (1871–1940), during the Years 1892 to 1940*, ed. John Vincent (Manchester University Press, 1984), p. 282, 31 October 1912.

79 Nicolson Diary, 12 August 1949.

80 Harold Nicolson, *King George the Fifth: His Life and Reign* (Constable, 1952), pp. 200–1.

81 Davidson Papers, 16 February 1913, pp. 7–8.

82 Henson diary, vol. 18 [Durham Cathedral Library], 2 February 1913.

83 RA PS/PSO/GV/C/K/25553(1)/36, Stamfordham's note of interview with Lansdowne, 1 July 1913.

84 Vernon Bogdanor, *The Monarchy and the Constitution* (Clarendon Press, 1995), p. 125. *The Times*, letters from Sir William Anson (10 September 1913), A. V. Dicey (15 September 1913).

85 RA PS/PSO/GV/C/K/25553 (5)/98a, Memo by G [1914].

86 RA PS/PSO/GV/C/K/25553(1)/57, G to Stamfordham, 3 August 1913.

87 RA PS/PSO/GV/C/K/25553(1)/68, Stamfordham's note of Asquith audience, 11 August 1913.

88 G to Asquith, 11 August 1913 in Nicolson, *King George the Fifth*, p. 223.

89 Nicolson, *King George the Fifth*, pp. 223–4. See Mort, 'Safe for Democracy', p. 121.

90 Nicolson, *King George the Fifth*, pp. 225–9.

91 Bonham-Carter, *Lantern Slides*, p. 393, 8 October 1913.

92 RA GV/PRIV/AA37/20, G to Alix, 20 September 1913.

93 Nicolson, *King George the Fifth*, p. 231, 6 October 1913.

94 Soames, ed., *Speaking for Themselves*, p. 76.

95 David, ed., *Inside Asquith's Cabinet*, pp. 146–7, 17 October 1913.

96 Bonham-Carter, *Lantern Slides*, p. 391, 13 September 1913.

97 Bogdanor, *The Monarchy and the Constitution*, p. 128.

CHAPTER 15

Buckingham Palace

1 Bruce Graeme, *A Century of Buckingham Palace 1837–1937* (Hutchinson, 1937), pp. 129–31.

2 Graeme, *A Century of Buckingham Palace*, p. 129.

3 Birrell to Violet Asquith, 7 September 1911 in Violet Bonham Carter, *Lantern Slides: The Diaries and Letters of Violet Bonham Carter 1904–1914*, ed. Mark Bonham Carter and Mark Pottle (Weidenfeld & Nicolson, 1996), p. 283.

4 The Devonshire Collections, Chatsworth Archive, Duchess Evelyn Papers, J10, Duchess Evelyn to Duke Victor, 23 January 1912, typed transcript.

5 Lord Claud Hamilton in James Pope-Hennessy, *The Quest for Queen Mary*, ed. Hugo Vickers (Zuleika, 2018), p. 131.

6 Gabriel Tschumi, *Royal Chef: Recollections of Life in Royal Households from Queen Victoria to Queen Mary* (William Kimber, 1954), pp. 129–32.

7 George Godfrey-Faussett, *Royal Servant, Family Friend: The Life and Times of Sir Bryan Godfrey-Faussett* (Bernard Durnford, 2004), pp. 154–5. Churchill Archives Centre, Godfrey-Faussett Papers, Diary, 24 March 1913. Adrian Tinniswood, *Behind the Throne: A Domestic History of the Royal Household* (Jonathan Cape, 2018), pp. 256–7.

8 Godfrey-Faussett Diary, March 1913. Godfrey-Faussett, *Royal Servant*, p. 193.

9 Edward David, ed., *Inside Asquith's Cabinet: From the Diaries of Charles Hobhouse* (John Murray, 1977), p. 133.

10 RA QM/PRIV/CC26/46, M to Augusta, 13/14 March 1913. RA GV/PRIV/GVD/10 March 1913.

11 Three films of the Davison Derby can be seen on YouTube. Marina Warner, 'Death in plain sight', *London Review of Books*, 4 July 2013. *The Times*, 5 June 1913.

12 Godfrey-Faussett Diary, June 1913.

13 RA GV/PRIV/GVD/4 June 1913.

14 QMD in Michael Tanner, *The Suffragette Derby* (Robson Press, 2013), p. 282.

15 Yale, Beinecke, Gen Mss 614, Box 17, Lascelles to Nicolson, 3 August 1950. Writing in 1950, Harold Nicolson found the Davison Derby incident 'too painful to record' and deliberately left it out (Beinecke, Gen Mss 614, Box 17, Nicolson to Lascelles, 10 August 1950).

16 Anita Anand, *Sophia: Princess, Suffragette, Revolutionary* (Bloomsbury, 2015), p. 290.

17 *Daily Telegraph*, 22 May 1914.

18 *The Times*, 5 June 1914.

19 RA GV/PRIV/GVD/4 June 1914.

20 RA QM/PRIV/CC26/46, M to Augusta, 13/14 March 1913. RA QM/PRIV/CC26/44, M to Augusta, 21 February 1913.

21 RA GV/PRIV/GVD/10 July 1914.

22 RA QM/PRIV/CC26/93, M to Augusta, 15 July 1914.

23 Kenneth Rose, *King George V* (Phoenix Press, 2000), p. 310. Sarah Bradford, *King George VI* (Weidenfeld & Nicolson, 1989), p. 51.

24 RA QM/PRIV/CC26/44, M to Augusta, 21 February 1913.

25 RA QM/PRIV/CC26/54, M to Augusta, 1 June 1913.

26 RA GV/PRIV/GVD/24 May 1913. Sir Frederick Ponsonby, *Recollections of Three Reigns* (Odhams Press, n.d.), pp. 292–3.

27 Ponsonby, *Recollections of Three Reigns*, p. 297.

28 John C. G. Röhl, *Wilhelm II: Into the Abyss of War and Exile 1900–1941* (Cambridge University Press, 2014), pp. 933–4.

29 Ponsonby, *Recollections of Three Reigns*, p. 294.

30 Roderick McLean, *Royalty and Diplomacy in Europe 1890–1914* (Cambridge University Press, 2001), p. 193.

31 RA GV/PRIV/GVD/18 November 1913.

32 RA QM/PRIV/CC26/71, M to Augusta, 20 November 1913.

33 RA QM/PRIV/CC26/72, M to Augusta, 27 November 1913.

34 Godfrey-Faussett Diary, January 1913. Mark Girouard, *Windsor: The Most Romantic Castle* (Hodder & Stoughton, 1993), p. 84.

35 RA QM/PRIV/CC25/80, M to Augusta, 26 November 1910.

36 RA QM/PRIV/CC25/80, M to Augusta, 26 November 1911.

37 RA QM/PRIV/CC25/115, M to Augusta, 15 September 1911.

38 RA QM/PRIV/CC25/119, M to Augusta, 20 October 1911.

39 RA QM/PRIV/CC26/81, M to Augusta, 28 January 1914.

40 RA QM/PRIV/CC26/84, M to Augusta, 6 April 1914.

41 RA QM/PRIV/CC26/33, M to Augusta, 16 November 1912.

42 RA GV/PRIV/CC8/169, M to G, 4 November 1913.

43 Ian Nairn, *Nairn's London* (Penguin, 1966), p. 65.

44 Curzon to Bonar Law, 10 December 1913 in Robert Blake, *The Unknown Prime Minister: The Life and Times of Andrew Bonar Law 1858–1923* (Eyre & Spottiswoode, 1955), pp. 166–7. Rose, *King George V*, pp. 151–2.

45 Godfrey-Faussett Diary, 1 February 1914.

46 Edward, Duke of Windsor, *A King's Story: The Memoirs of HRH the Duke of Windsor* (Cassell, 1951), pp. 86–7. RA GV/PRIV/GVD/18 December 1913.

47 George Dangerfield, *The Strange Death of Liberal England* (Constable, 1936), pp. 119, 324–5. Carolyn White, 'The Strange Death of Liberal England in Its Time,' *Albion*, vol. 17, no. 4 (1985).

48 Lambeth Palace, Davidson Papers, Memo, 'Irish Question', 21 January 1914, pp. 2–3.

49 H. H. Asquith, *Letters to Venetia Stanley*, ed. Michael and Eleanor

Brock (Oxford University Press, 1982), p. 46.

50 RA GV/PRIV/GVD/5 February 1914.

51 RA PS/PSO/GV/C/K/2553(3)/83, Stamfordham's note of Asquith audience, 5 February 1914. Harold Nicolson, *King George the Fifth: His Life and Reign* (Constable, 1952), p. 233 (author italics). Asquith, *Letters to Venetia Stanley*, p. 46n.

52 Balliol College Archive, Nicolson Diary, 17 January 1950.

53 Vernon Bogdanor, *The Monarchy and the Constitution* (Clarendon Press, 1995), pp. 131–2.

54 Nicolson, *King George the Fifth*, p. 234.

55 Davidson Papers, Vol. 12, Memo, 'Irish Question', 21 January 1914, pp. 2–3.

56 RA PS/PSO/GV/C/K/2553(3)/31, Stamfordham's note on G's audience with Asquith, 15 December 1913.

57 RA PS/PSO/GV/C/K/2553(3)/92, Asquith to Stamfordham, 25 February 1914.

58 RA PS/PSO/GV/C/K/2553(3)/100, Stamfordham's note, 28 February 1914.

59 John Gore, *King George V: A Personal Memoir* (John Murray, 1941), p. 285.

60 RA PS/PSO/GV/C/K/2553(3)/87, G to Asquith, 11 February 1914. RA GV/PRIV/GVD/10 February 1914.

61 Stamfordham's note, 19 March 1914 in Nicolson, *King George the Fifth*, pp. 236–7.

62 Asquith, *Letters to Venetia Stanley*, p. 56.

63 RA GV/PRIV/GVD/19 March 1914.

64 Sir James Fergusson of Kilkerran, *The Curragh Incident* (Faber & Faber, 1964), p. 33.

65 RA GV/PRIV/GVD/21 March 1914.

66 RA GV/PRIV/GVD/23 March 1914.

67 Stamfordham to Asquith, 24 March 1914 in Fergusson, *The Curragh Incident*, p. 172.

68 Rose, *King George V*, p. 156.

69 Davidson Papers, Vol. 12, Memo of 25, 26 March 1914.

70 Asquith, *Letters to Venetia Stanley*, p. 61.

71 RA EDW/PRIV/MAIN/A/EW, David to M, 25 March 1914. RA QM/PRIV/CC9, David to QM, 26 March 1914.

72 RA EDW/PRIV/MAIN/A/1256, M to David, 1 April 1914.

73 RA QM/PRIV/CC26/84, M to Augusta, 6 April 1914.

74 RA QM/PRIV/CC26/78, M to Augusta, 9 January 1914. McLean, *Royalty and Diplomacy in Europe*, p. 203.

75 RA QM/PRIV/CC26/84, M to Augusta, 6 April 1914.

76 Ponsonby, *Recollections of Three Reigns*, pp. 301–2.

77 RA QM/PRIV/CC26/87, M to Augusta, 26 April 1914.

78 RA GV/PRIV/GVD/22 April 1914. Richard Davenport-Hines, *Ettie: The Intimate Life and Dauntless Spirit of Lady Desborough* (Weidenfeld & Nicolson, 2008), p. 156.

79 RA QM/PRIV/CC26/93, M to Augusta, 15 July 1914.

80 Asquith, *Letters to Venetia Stanley*, p. 105.

81 RA PS/PSO/GV/C/K/2553(6)/38, Geoffrey Robinson to Stamfordham, 21 July 1914.

82 RA QM/PRIV/CC26/94, M to Augusta, 22 July 1914.

83 Bogdanor, *The Monarchy and the Constitution*, p. 134.

84 RA PS/PSO/GV/C/K/2553(5)/78, Stamfordham to Long, 3 July 1914.

85 David Cannadine, *George V: The Unexpected King* (Allen Lane, 2014), p. 53.

86 RA GV/PRIV/GVD/21, 22 July 1914. Jane Ridley, *Bertie: A Life of Edward VII* (Chatto & Windus, 2012), pp. 488–9.

87 RA GV/PRIV/GVD/25 July 1914.

88 RA GV/PRIV/GVD/28 June 1914.

89 Prince Clary, *A European Past: Memoirs* (St Martin's Press, 1978), p. 158. Sue Woolmans, author email, 10 January 2021.

90 Nicolson Diary, 22 March 1950.

91 RA QM/PRIV/CC26/37, M to Augusta, 12 December 1912.

92 Nicolson, *King George the Fifth*, p. 245.

93 Röhl, *Wilhelm II*, pp.1058–62.

94 Nicolson, *King George the Fifth*, p. 246.

95 Christopher Clark, *The Sleepwalkers: How Europe Went to War in 1914* (Allen Lane, 2012), pp. 528–9.

96 McLean, *Royalty and Diplomacy in Europe*, pp. 191–9. Roderick McLean, 'Kaiser Wilhelm II and the British Royal Family: Anglo-German Dynastic Relations in Political Context 1890–1914', *History*, vol. 86, no. 284 (2002).

97 RA QM/PRIV/CC26/95, M to Augusta, 28 July 1914.

98 RA QM/PRIV/CC26/95, M to Augusta, 28 July 1914.

99 RA GV/PRIV/GVD/3 August 1914.

100 RA GV/PRIV/GVD/4 August 1914.

101 John W. Wheeler-Bennett, *King George VI: His Life and Reign* (Macmillan, 1958), pp. 74–5.

CHAPTER 16

George at War

1 Kathleen Woodward, *Queen Mary: A Life and Intimate Study* (Hutchinson, 1929), p. 176.

2 Frank Prochaska, *Royal Bounty: The Making of a Welfare Monarchy* (Yale University Press, 1995), p. 179. *The Times*, 13 August 1914. Woodward, *Queen Mary*, pp. 206–9.

3 Woodward, *Queen Mary*, p. 181.

4 James Pope-Hennessy, *Queen Mary* (Phoenix Press, 2000), p. 491.

5 Woodward, *Queen Mary*, p. 184.

6 Woodward, *Queen Mary*, p. 195.

7 Woodward, *Queen Mary*, pp. 193, 196.

8 Philip Ziegler, *King Edward VIII: The Official Biography* (Collins, 1990), p. 49.

9 QM to Lady Mountstephen, 5 August 1914 in Prochaska, *Royal Bounty*, p. 179.

10 Sarah Bradford, *King George VI* (Weidenfeld & Nicolson, 1989), p. 60.

11 John Gore, *King George V: A Personal Memoir* (John Murray, 1941), p. 293.

12 Earl of Crawford, *The Crawford Papers: The Journals of David Lindsay, 27th Earl of Crawford and 10th Earl of Balcarres (1871–1940), during the Years 1892 to 1940*, ed. John Vincent (Manchester University Press, 1984), p. 569.

13 Douglas Haig, *War Diaries and Letters 1914–1918*, ed. Gary Sheffield and John Bourne (Weidenfeld & Nicolson, 2005), p. 56, 11 August 1914.

14 Prochaska, *Royal Bounty*, p. 176.

15 Harold Nicolson, *King George the Fifth: His Life and Reign* (Constable, 1952), pp. 248, 252.

16 See Frank Mort, 'Accessible Sovereignty: Popular Attitudes to the British Monarchy during the Great War,' *Social History*, vol. 45, no. 3 (2020), pp. 328–59.

17 Gore, *King George V*, p. 299.

18 Barbara W. Tuchman, *August 1914* (Macmillan, 1980), p. 425.

19 Alexandra Churchill, *In the Eye of the Storm: George V and the Great War* (Helion, 2018), pp. 73–4.

20 RA QM/PRIV/CC4/121, G to M, 30 November 1914.

21 RA PS/PSO/GV/C/Q832/210, Stamfordham to Kitchener, 24 October 1914. RA PS/PSO/GV/C/Q832/209, Major General W. Lambton to G, 23 October 1914.

22 RA QM/PRIV/CC4/121, G to M, 30 November 1914. RA GV/PRIV/GVD/29 November 1914.

23 RA QM/PRIV/CC4/121, G to M, 30 November 1914.

24 RA QM/PRIV/CC4/129, G to M, 3 December 1914.

25 RA GV/PRIV/GVD/4 December 1914.

26 RA QM/PRIV/CC4/129, G to M, 3 December 1914.

27 Mort, 'Accessible Sovereignty', p. 337.

28 Haig, *War Diaries and Letters*, pp. 83–4, 4 December 1914.

29 *The Times*, 24 December 1914.

30 RA QM/PRIV/CC26/98, M to Augusta, 10 December 1914.

31 RA GV/PRIV/GVD/24 December 1914.

32 RA GV/PRIV/GVD/26 December 1914–2 January 1915.

33 RA EDW/PRIV/MAIN/A/1465, M to David, 24 January 1915.

34 RA EDW/PRIV/MAIN/A/1474, M to David, 7 February 1915.

35 Ziegler, *King Edward VIII*, p. 52.

36 RA GV/PRIV/GVD/29 October 1914.

37 H. H. Asquith, *Letters to Venetia Stanley*, ed. Michael and Eleanor Brock (Oxford University Press, 1982), p. 285, 24 October 1914.

38 RA GV/PRIV/GVD/17 December 1914.

39 RA GV/PRIV/GVD/8 May 1915.

40 RA GV/PRIV/GVD/23 December 1914.

41 Kenneth Rose, *King George V* (Phoenix Press, 2000), p. 173, Alix to G, 12 May 1915.

42 *The Times*, 15 May 1915.

43 Bruce Graeme, *A Century of Buckingham Palace 1837–1937* (Hutchinson, 1937), p. 123.

44 Tschumi, *Royal Chef*, pp. 133–6.

45 Bonhams Sale Catalogue, 19 March 2014. Papers of Jean Marie Claude Balerin, Comptroller of Supply at Royal Household.

46 Virginia Woolf, *The Diary of Virginia Woolf, Vol. 1: 1915–1919*, ed. Anne Olivier Bell (Penguin, 1979), p. 14, 10 January 1915. RA GV/PRIV/GVD/5 January, 15 March, 15 June 1915.

47 Tschumi, *Royal Chef*, p. 137.

48 Sir Frederick Ponsonby, *Recollections of Three Reigns* (Odhams Press, n.d.), p. 329.

49 RA GV/PRIV/GVD/29 March 1915.

50 Nicolson, *King George the Fifth*, p. 262.

51 RA GV/PRIV/GVD/6 April 1915. *The Times*, 1 April 1915.

52 Simon Heffer, *Staring at God: Britain in the Great War* (Random House, 2019), pp. 168–71.

53 Ziegler, *King Edward VIII*, p. 64.

54 Frances Stevenson, *Lloyd George: A Diary*, ed. A.J.P. Taylor (Hutchinson, 1971), p. 25, 27 January 1915.

55 Violet Bonham Carter, *Champion Redoubtable: Diaries and Letters of Violet Bonham-Carter 1914–45*, ed. Mark Pottle (Weidenfeld & Nicolson, 1998), p. 35.

56 Margot Asquith, *Margot Asquith's Great War Diary 1914–1916: The View from Downing Street*, ed. Michael and Eleanor Brock (Oxford University Press, 2014), p. 93.

57 RA EDW/PRIV/MAIN/A/1581, M to EDW, 12 June 1915.

58 Edward, Duke of Windsor, *A Family Album* (Cassell, 1960), p. 54. Rose, *King George V*, p. 179.

59 Wigram Papers, Nora to parents, 4, 6, 12 April 1915.

60 Wigram Papers, Nora to parents, 16 April 1915.

61 Wigram Papers, Nora to parents, 8 April 1915.

62 Wigram Papers, Nora to parents, 9, 12 April 1915. The Wedgwood room was completed in January 1914 (CC 26/81, M to Augusta, 28 January 1914).

63 Wigram Papers, Nora to parents, 13 April 1915.

64 Asquith, *Margot Asquith's Great War Diary*, p. 92.

65 Wigram Papers, Nora to parents, 13 April 1915.

66 Wigram Papers, Nora to parents, 16 April 1915. Richard

Davenport-Hines, *Ettie: The Intimate Life and Dauntless Spirit of Lady Desborough* (Weidenfeld & Nicolson, 2008), p. 304. Asquith, *Margot Asquith's Great War Diary*, p. 92.

67 Davenport-Hines. *Ettie*, p. 303, 12 February 1915.

68 Wigram Papers, Nora to parents, 4, 16 April 1915.

69 Edward, Duke of Windsor, *A King's Story: The Memoirs of HRH the Duke of Windsor* (Cassell, 1951), p. 109.

70 Windsor, *A King's Story*, p. 113.

71 Windsor, *A King's Story*, p. 112.

72 Ziegler, *King Edward VIII*, pp. 53–4, 61. Ziegler cut the swear words; but they give a sense of David's attempt to identify with the troops. See Paul Fussell, *The Great War and Modern Memory*, pb ed. (Oxford University Press, 1977), p. 179.

73 RA EDW/PRIV/MAIN/A/1490, M to David, 21 February 1915.

74 RA EDW/PRIV/MAIN/A/1549, M to David, 8 May 1915.

75 RA EDW/PRIV/MAIN/A/1544, M to David, 2 May 1915.

76 Ziegler, *King Edward VIII*, p. 79. Nicolson Diary, 21 July 1948.

77 RA EDW/PRIV/MAIN/A/1581, M to David, 12 June 1915.

78 RA EDW/PRIV/MAIN/A/1490, M to David, 21 February 1915.

79 H. W. Wilson and J. A. Hammerton, eds, *The Great War: The Standard History of the All-Europe Conflict* (Amalgamated Press, 1914–19), vol. 10, p. 21.

80 RA GV/PRIV/GVD/12 January 1915.

81 Roy Jenkins, *Asquith* (Collins, 1964), p. 343.

82 Reginald, Viscount Esher, *Journals and Letters of Reginald, Viscount Esher, Vol. 3: 1910–1915*, ed. Oliver, Viscount Esher (Ivor Nicholson & Watson, 1938), p. 101, 10 May 1915.

83 Wilson and Hammerton, eds, *The Great War*, vol. 10, p. 10.

84 RA GV/PRIV/GVD/7 August 1915.

85 Gore, *King George V*, p. 293n.

86 Mabell, Countess of Airlie, *Thatched with Gold: The Memoirs of Mabell, Countess of Airlie*, ed. Jennifer Ellis (Hutchinson, 1962), p. 132.

87 RA EDW/PRIV/MAIN/A/1490, M to David, 21 February 1915.

88 RA QM/PRIV/CC26/100, M to Augusta, 21 June 1915.

89 RA EDW/PRIV/MAIN/A/1817, M to David, 16 March 1916.

90 RA GV/PRIV/GVD/24/3/15.

91 Sir H. Rider Haggard, *The Private Diaries of Sir H. Rider Haggard 1914–1925*, ed. D. S. Higgins (Cassell, 1980), p. 40, 26 August 1915.

92 Owen Morshead, 'King George V' in *Oxford Dictionary of National Biography 1931–1940* (Oxford University Press, 1949).

93 Nicholas Courtney, *The Queen's Stamps: The Authorised History of the Royal Philatelic Collection* (Methuen, 2004), p. 137.

94 RA EDW/PRIV/MAIN/A/1581, M to David, 12 June 1915.

95 RA EDW/PRIV/MAIN/A/1785, M to David, 13 February 1916.

96 RA GV/PRIV/GVD/10 December 1915.

97 RA QM/PRIV/CC4/131, G to M, 17 May 1915.

98 Churchill, *In the Eye of the Storm*, p. 101.

99 RA GV/PRIV/GVD/22 May 1915.

100 RA QM/PRIV/CC4/132, G to M, 19 May 1915.

101 RA EDW/PRIV/MAIN/A/1574, M to David, 1 June 1915.

102 Esher, *Journals and Letters of Reginald, Viscount Esher, Vol. 3*, p. 247, 10 June 1915.

103 Nicolson, *King George the Fifth*, p. 266.

104 RA GV/PRIV/GVD/1 July 1915.

105 Ponsonby, *Recollections of Three Reigns*, p. 318.

106 RA GV/PRIV/GVD/24 October 1915.

107 RA GV/PRIV/GVD/27 October 1915.

108 Windsor, *A King's Story*, p. 119.

109 Ziegler, *King Edward VIII*, p. 67.

CHAPTER 17

The King and the Generals

1 Kenneth Rose, *King George V* (Phoenix Press, 2000), p. 181. Sir Frederick Ponsonby, *Recollections of Three Reigns* (Odhams Press, n.d.), pp. 324–5. *The Times*, 30 October 1915.

2 RA GV/PRIV/GVD/30 October 1915.

3 Harold Nicolson, *King George the Fifth: His Life and Reign* (Constable, 1952), p. 268.

4 Ponsonby, *Recollections of Three Reigns*, p. 325.

5 H. W. Wilson and J. A. Hammerton, eds, *The Great War: The Standard History of the All-Europe Conflict* (Amalgamated Press, 1914–19), vol. 10, p. 24.

6 Frank Mort, 'Accessible Sovereignty: Popular Attitudes to the British Monarchy during the Great War,' *Social History*, vol. 45, no. 3 (2020), p. 349.

7 Mort, 'Accessible Sovereignty', pp. 330–3.

8 RA GV/PRIV/GVD/1 November 1915.

9 RA GV/PRIV/CC8/195, M to G, 31 October 1915.

10 RA GV/PRIV/GVD/14, 20 November, 8 December 1915.

11 Wilson and Hammerton, eds, *The Great War*, vol. 10, p. 25.

12 RA GV/PRIV/GVD/28 December 1915.

13 RA EDW/PRIV/MAIN/A/1836, M to EDW, 5 April 1916.

14 Winston S. Churchill, *Great Contemporaries* (Thornton Butterworth, 1937), p. 325.

15 John Gore, *King George V: A Personal Memoir* (John Murray, 1941), p. 298. Nicolson, *King George the Fifth*, p. 268. Rose, *King George V*, p. 182.

16 RA EDW/PRIV/MAIN/A/1836, M to EDW, 28 May 1916.

17 Gore, *King George V*, p. 300.

18 G to Stamfordham, 25 October 1915 in Nicolson, *King George the Fifth*, p. 267.

19 Ian Beckett, 'King George V and His Generals' in Matthew Hughes and Matthew Seligman, eds, *Leadership in Conflict 1914–18* (Leo Cooper, 2000), p. 256.

20 RA GV/PRIV/GVD/2–8 November 1915, dictated to QM. Stamfordham to Asquith, 2 December 1915 in Nicolson, *King George the Fifth*, p. 268.

21 Beckett, 'King George V and His Generals', p. 256.

22 David R. Woodward, *Lloyd George and the Generals* (Associated University Presses, 1983), p. 77.

23 Stephen Roskill, *Hankey: Man of Secrets, Vol. 1: 1877–1918* (Collins, 1970), p. 238, 14 December 1915.

24 Nicolson, *King George the Fifth*, p. 254.

25 Douglas Haig, *War Diaries and Letters 1914–1918*, ed. Gary Sheffield and John Bourne (Weidenfeld & Nicolson, 2005), p. 56, 11 August 1914.

26 Countess Haig, *The Man I Knew* (Moray Press, 1936), pp. 120–1. Haig, *War Diaries and Letters*, pp. 3–4.

27 RA PS/PSO/GV/C/Q/832/111, Haig to G, 21 September 1914.

28 Robert Blake, ed., *The Private Papers of Douglas Haig* (Eyre & Spottiswoode, 1952), p. 97, 14 July 1915; p. 118, G to Haig, 17 December 1915.

29 Nicolson, *King George the Fifth*, p. 277.

30 H. H. Asquith, *Letters to Venetia Stanley*, ed. Michael and Eleanor Brock (Oxford University Press, 1982), p. 297.

31 Beckett, 'King George V and His Generals', p. 248.

32 G to Duke of Connaught, 20 December 1915 in Rose, *King George V*, p. 190.

33 C. S. Forester, *The General* (William Collins, 2014), p. 222.

34 Wilson & Hammerton, eds, *The Great War*, vol. 10, p. 25.

35 RA QM/PRIV/CC26/106, M to Augusta, 24 March 1916.

36 RA QM/PRIV/CC26/107, M to Augusta, 31 March 1916.

37 Jennifer Holmes, *A Working Woman: The Remarkable Life of Ray Strachey* (Matador, 2019), p. 149.

38 James Pope-Hennessy, *Queen Mary* (Phoenix Press, 2000), p. 502.

39 Wigram Papers, Nora to parents, 7 January 1916.

40 Princess Mary to David, 19 February 1916 in Philip Ziegler, *King Edward VIII: The Official Biography* (Collins, 1990), p. 80.

41 RA EDW/PRIV/MAIN/A/1939, M to David, 20 October 1916.

42 RA EDW/PRIV/MAIN/A/1847, M to David, 13 April 1916.

43 RA EDW/PRIV/MAIN/A/1978, M to David, 19 November 1916.

44 RA GV/PRIV/GVD/2 June 1916.

45 RA EDW/PRIV/MAIN/A/1900, M to David 1 [4] June 1916.

46 RA EDW/PRIV/MAIN/A/1900, M to EDW, 1 [4] June 1916.

47 RA QM/PRIV/CC4/148, G to M, 16 June 1916.

48 Getty Research Library, Pope 199/7, QMD, 6 June 1916.

49 RA GV/PRIV/GVD/6 June 1916. RA QM/PRIV/CC26/111, M to Augusta, 9 June 1916.

50 RA GV/PRIV/GVD/6 June 1916.

51 RA PS/PSO/GV/C/K/951/14, Stamfordham's memo, 15 June 1916.

52 Roskill, *Hankey*, p. 283, 10 June 1916. Woodward, *Lloyd George and the Generals*, p. 98.

53 RA GV/PRIV/GVD/23 June 1916.

54 Margot Asquith, *Margot Asquith's Great War Diary 1914–1916: The View from Downing Street*, ed. Michael and Eleanor Brock (Oxford University Press, 2014), p. 269.

55 Roy Jenkins, *Asquith* (Collins, 1964), p. 410.

56 Forester, *The General*, p. 240.

57 Ponsonby, *Recollections of Three Reigns*, p. 76.

58 RA EDW/PRIV/MAIN/A/1910, M to David, 9 July 1916.

59 RA GV/PRIV/GVD/7 August 1916.

60 RA EDW/PRIV/MAIN/A/1930, M to David, 5 August 1916.

61 John Jolliffe, ed., *Raymond Asquith: Life and Letters* (Collins, 1980), p. 284, 9 August 1916. Viscount Chandos, *The Memoirs of Lord Chandos* (Bodley Head, 1962), pp. 57–8.

62 RA QM/PRIV/CC4/151, G to M, 9 August 1916.

63 Haig, *War Diaries and Letters*, p. 216. The National Archives CAB 37/153/3, Churchill's Memo, 1 August 1916.

64 Haig, *War Diaries and Letters*, p. 195.

65 RA PS/PSO/GV/C/Q/832/124, Haig to G, 20 August 1916. Haig, *War Diaries and Letters*, p. 219.

66 Rose, *King George V*, p. 180. Geoffrey Madan, *Geoffrey Madan's Notebooks: A Selection*, ed. J. A. Gere and John Sparrow (Oxford University Press, 1981), p. 66.

67 TNA PRO 30/81/1, Lord Carnock Windsor, 25 September 1916.

68 Wigram Papers, Nora to parents, 26 September 1916.

69 TNA PRO 30/81/16, Carnock's note, 25 September 1916.

70 Durham Cathedral Library, Henson Diary, vol. 18, 9 September 1916. Thanks to Richard Davenport-Hines. RA GV/PRIV/GVD/2 September 1916.

71 Forester, *The General*, p. 260.

72 Henson Diary, vol. 18, 9, 10 September 1916.

73 RA GV/PRIV/GVD/17 September 1916. Sarah Bradford, *King George VI* (Weidenfeld & Nicolson, 1989), pp. 70–1.

74 George Slocombe, *The Tumult and the Shouting: The Memoirs of*

George Slocombe (Macmillan (New York), 1936), pp. 218–19. General the Rt Hon. Sir Nevil Macready, *Annals of an Active Life* (Hutchinson, 1924), vol. 1, pp. 257–9.

75 TNA PRO 30/81/16, Carnock's note, 25 September 1916. Carnock advised the King from July to November 1916.

76 TNA PRO 30/81/16, Carnock's note, 25 September 1916.

77 Nicolson, *King George the Fifth*, p. 282, G to Asquith, 4 September 1916.

78 RA EDW/PRIV/MAIN/A/1902, M to David, 25 June 1916.

79 RA EDW/PRIV/MAIN/A/1963, M to David, 14 October 1916.

80 Moritz A. Sorg, 'Of Traitors and Saints: Foreign Consorts between Accusations and Propaganda in the First World War', *Court Historian*, vol. 24, no. 1 (2019), pp. 1–16.

81 RA PS/PSO/GV/C/O/1106/3, Watts-Ditchfield to Stamfordham, 5 April 1917. TNA FO 800/205, Lord Robert Cecil to Buchanan, 13 April 1917.

82 RA GV/PRIV/GVD/3 December 1916.

83 RA GV/PRIV/GVD/5 December 1916.

84 Pope, 199/7, QMD 5 December 1916.

85 Lambeth Palace, Davidson Papers, Vol. 13, Davidson's memorandum, 4 December 1916.

86 Roskill, *Hankey, Vol. 1*, pp. 327–8.

87 RA PS/PSO/GV/C/K/1048 A/1, Fall of Mr Asquith's Administration, December 1916: Diary of Events Recorded by Lord Stamfordham.

88 Vernon Bogdanor, *The Monarchy and the Constitution* (Clarendon Press, 1995), p. 100. Robert Blake, *The Unknown Prime Minister: The Life and Times of Andrew Bonar Law 1858–1923* (Eyre & Spottiswoode, 1955), p. 336.

89 Davidson Papers, Vol. 13, Davidson memorandum, 10 December 1916.

90 RA PS/PSO/GV/C/K/1048 A/1, 'Fall of Mr Asquith's Administration'.

91 RA GV/PRIV/GVD/6 December 1916.

92 British Library, Balfour Papers, Add MS 49692, Balfour's Memo of the Government Crisis, December 1916.

93 Stamfordham's Report of a Conference held at Buckingham Palace on Wednesday December 6th at 3 p.m. in Nicolson, *King George the Fifth*, p. 290.

94 British Library, Balfour Papers. Add MS 49692, Balfour Memo, December 1916.

95 David Gilmour, *Curzon* (John Murray, 1994), pp. 454–5.

96 Davidson Papers, Vol. 13, Davidson memorandum, 10 December 1916.

97 Anne de Courcy, *Margot at War: Love and Betrayal in Downing Street 1912–1916* (Weidenfeld & Nicolson, 2014), p. 340.

98 Churchill, *Great Contemporaries*, p. 249.

99 Blake, *The Unknown Prime Minister*, pp. 339–40.

100 Bogdanor, *The Monarchy and the Constitution*, p. 101.

101 RA GV/PRIV/GVD/6 December 1916.

102 RA EDW/PRIV/MAIN/A/1989, M to David, 9 December 1916.

103 Pope-Hennessy, *Queen Mary*, pp. 101, 502–5.

104 Asquith, *Letters to Venetia Stanley*, p. 395.

105 RA GV/PRIV/GVD/4 December 1916.

106 Lady Cynthia Asquith, *Diaries 1915–18* (Hutchinson, 1968), p. 242.

107 Nicolson, *King George the Fifth*, p. 291.

108 Asquith, *Letters to Venetia Stanley*, pp. 284–5.

109 RA EDW/PRIV/MAIN/A/1978, M to EDW, 19 November 1916.

110 Frances Stevenson, *Lloyd George: A Diary*, ed. A. J. P. Taylor (Hutchinson, 1971), p. 153, 23 April 1917.

111 RA PS/PSO/GV/C/K/1048 A/1, 'Fall of Mr Asquith's Administration'.

112 Parliamentary Archives, Lloyd George Papers, F/29/1/2, Stamfordham to Lloyd George, 14 December 1916.

CHAPTER 18
Unrest in the Country and within the House of Windsor

1 RA GVI/PRIV/RF/11/203, M to Bertie, 5 May 1915. RA EDW/PRIV/MAIN/A/1634, M to David, 17 July 1915.

2 RA EDW/PRIV/MAIN/A/1851, M to David, 19 April 1916.

3 RA GVI/PRIV/RF/11/226, M to Bertie, 28 May 1916.

4 RA GVI/PRIV/RF/11/227, M to Bertie, 4 June 1916.

5 RA GVI/PRIV/RF/11/228, M to Bertie, 10 June 1916.

6 RA EDW/PRIV/MAIN/A/1997, M to David, 17 December 1916.

7 RA EDW/PRIV/MAIN/A/205, M to David, 22 December 1916.

8 RA GVI/PRIV/RF/11/244, M to Bertie, 10 November 1916. Pope 199/7, QMD, 1, 2, 10, 11, 16, 18 January 1917.

9 RA GVI/PRIV/RF/11/249, M to Bertie, 21 January 1917.

10 Getty Research Library, Pope 199/7, QMD, 2 February 1917.

11 Wigram Papers, Nora to parents, 5 January 1917.

12 Wigram Papers, Nora to parents, 14 January 1917.

13 Wigram Papers, Nora to parents, 14 January 1917.

14 Pope 195/15, M to Stamfordham, 6 January 1917.

15 RA PS/PSO/GV/C/M/1067/2, 'Russia 1917 file', G's deciphered Buchanan telegram, 4/5 January 1917.

16 The National Archives, FO 800/205/17–18, Buchanan telegram to Balfour, 7 January 1917.

17 TNA FO 800/200/22, Balfour to Buchanan, 8 January 1917.

18 RA GV/PRIV/AA37/69, G to Alix, 13 January 1917.

19 Pope 195/15, M to Stamfordham, 6 January 1917.

20 Balliol College Archive, Nicolson Diary, 26 July 1950.

21 Parliamentary Archives, Lloyd George Papers, F/29/1/6, Stamfordham to LG, 1 January 1917; F/29/1/7, Stamfordham to Davies, 11 January 1917; F/29/1/8, Davies to Stamfordham, 15 January 1917; F/29/1/11, Stamfordham to LG, 5 February 1917.

22 Robert Rhodes James, ed., Memoirs of a Conservative: J.C.C. Davidson's Memoirs and Papers (Weidenfeld & Nicolson, 1969), p. 67.

23 Haig to G, 28 February 1917 in Robert Blake, ed., The Private Papers of Douglas Haig (Eyre & Spottiswoode, 1952), pp. 203–5.

24 RA GV/PRIV/GVD/2 March 1917.

25 Haig's diary, 11 March 1917 in Blake, ed., The Private Papers of Douglas Haig, p. 209.

26 Rhodes James, ed., Memoirs of a Conservative, p. 67.

27 Stamfordham's memo, 12 March 1917 in David R. Woodward, Lloyd George and the Generals (Associated University Presses, 1983), p. 152.

28 General Rawlinson's diary, 12 March 1917 in Woodward, Lloyd George and the Generals, p. 150.

29 RA GV/PRIV/GVD/13 March 1917.

30 RA GV/PRIV/GVD/15 March 1917.

31 TNA FO 800/205/53, Stamfordham to Hanbury Williams, 19 March 1917.

32 W. Somerset Maugham, 'His Excellency' in Collected Stories (Everyman's Library, 2004), pp. 789–90.

33 TNA FO/371/2998/89, Buchanan telegram, 20 March 1917.

34 TNA FO 371/2998/96, Balfour telegram to Buchanan, 21 March 1917.

35 TNA FO 371/2998/109, Buchanan telegram, 21 March 1917.
36 RA PS/PSO/GV/C/M/1067/29, Stamfordham's note, 22 March 1917.
37 TNA FO 371/2998/111, Hardinge draft telegram to Buchanan, 22 March 1917.
38 See Robert Service, *The Last of the Tsars: Nicholas II and the Russian Revolution* (Macmillan, 2017), pp. 35–53.
39 TNA FO/800/205/50, Stamfordham to Buchanan, 29 March 1917.
40 TNA FO 800/205/63, Stamfordham to Balfour, 30 March 1917.
41 RA PS/PSO/GV/C/M//1067/39, Stamfordham to Balfour, 30 March 1917, draft.
42 Kenneth Rose, *King George V* (Phoenix Press, 2000), pp. 210–18.
43 Sir Henry Channon, *Chips: The Diaries of Sir Henry Channon*, ed. Robert Rhodes James (Weidenfeld & Nicolson, 1967), p. 175, 30 October 1938.
44 Helen Rappaport, *The Race to Save the Romanovs: The Truth behind the Secret Plans to Rescue Russia's Imperial Family* (Hutchinson, 2018), pp. 72–3. This is a very well-researched account of the episode.
45 RA PS/PSO/GV/C/M/1067/51, Stamfordham to Balfour, 6 April 1917.
46 Gore Vidal, *Palimpsest: A Memoir* (André Deutsch, 1995), pp. 207–8. David was at Buckingham Palace until 22 March, when he left for France.
47 RA PS/PSO/GV/C/M/1067/41, Carnock to Stamfordham, 1 April 1917.
48 RA PS/PSO/GV/C/M/1067/41, Stamfordham note, 2 April 1917.
49 RA PS/PSO/GV/C/M/1067/44, Balfour to Stamfordham, 2 April 1917.
50 RA PS/PSO/GV/C/M/1067/43, Stamfordham note, 2 April 1917. Rose, *King George V*, p. 212.
51 RA PS/PSO/GV/C/M/1067/51, Stamfordham to Balfour, 6 April 1917.
52 RA PS/PSO/GV/C/M/1067/51, Stamfordham to Balfour, 6 April 1917.
53 RA PS/PSO/GV/C/O/1106/1, 'Unrest in the Country' file, Hyndman, 'The Need for a British Republic', 5 April 1917.
54 RA PS/PSO/GV/C/M/1067/55, Balfour minute for PM, 6 April 1917. RA PS/PSO/GV/C/M/1067/53, Eric Drummond (Balfour's secretary) to Stamfordham, 6 April 1917.
55 RA PS/PSO/GV/C/M/1067/61, Stamfordham's note, 10 April 1917.
56 TNA FO/800/205, telegram to Buchanan, 13 April 1917.
57 TNA FO/800/205/90, Buchanan telegram, 15 April 1917.
58 Margot Asquith, *Margot Asquith's Great War Diary 1914–1916: The View from Downing Street*, ed. Michael and Eleanor Brock (Oxford University Press, 2014), p. 93.
59 Vidal, *Palimpsest*, p. 208.
60 RA QM/PRIV/GV/CC4/194, G to M, 1 December 1918.
61 Frank Prochaska, 'George V and Republicanism 1917–1919', *Twentieth Century British History*, vol. 10, no. 1 (1999).
62 RA PS/PSO/GV/C/O/1106/40, Stamfordham to Revelstoke, 13 June 1917.
63 Lloyd George Papers, F/29/2/51, Stamfordham to LG, 25 August 1918.
64 RA PS/PSO/GV/C/O/1106/2, Unsworth to Stamfordham, 5 April 1917.
65 TNA CAB 23/2, Minutes of Meeting 118 of War Cabinet, 13 April 1917. Simon Heffer, *Staring at God: Britain in the Great War* (Random House, 2019), pp. 587–90.
66 Churchill Archive Centre, Esher Papers, ESHR 4/8, Derby to Esher, n.d. [1917].
67 RA PS/PSO/GV/C/O/1106/52, H. G. Wells, 'The Future of the

Monarchy', *Penny Pictorial*, 19 May 1917.

68 RA EDW/PRIV/MAIN/A/2042, M to David, 31 March 1917.

69 Harold Nicolson, *King George the Fifth: His Life and Reign* (Constable, 1952), p. 309.

70 Nicolson, *King George the Fifth*, p. 308, told by his father Lord Carnock. H. G. Wells, *Mr Britling Sees it Through* (Cassell, 1916), p. 178.

71 RA PS/PSO/GV/C/O/1106, Watts-Ditchfield to Stamfordham, 5 April 1917.

72 Pope 199/7, Bertha Dawkins, 24 April 1917.

73 Pope 199/7, Bertha Dawkins, 25 April 1917.

74 RA EDW/PRIV/MAIN/A/2059, M to David, 28 April 1917. RA EDW/PRIV/MAIN/A/2042, M to David, 31 March 1917.

75 H. W. Wilson and J. A. Hammerton, eds, *The Great War: The Standard History of the All-Europe Conflict* (Amalgamated Press, 1914–19), vol. 10, p. 32.

76 RA EDW/PRIV/MAIN/A/2026, M to David, 17 February 1917.

77 RA QM/PRIV/CC8/207, M to G, 13 August 1916.

78 Stephen Roskill, *Admiral of the Fleet Earl Beatty: The Last Naval Hero* (Collins, 1980), p. 221. Churchill Archive, BGGF, Godfrey-Faussett Diary, 16 July 1917.

79 Pope 199/7, Bertha Dawkins, 25 April 1917. The digging at Frogmore continued until 4 May.

80 Sissinghurst Papers, Nicolson to Vita, 10 August 1950.

81 RA PS/PSO/GV/C/O/1153/346a, Stamfordham to Rosebery, 20 May 1917.

82 RA PS/PSO/GV/C/O/1153/345a, Stamfordham to Rosebery, 15 May 1917.

83 RA PS/PSO/GV/C/O/1153/346a, Stamfordham to Rosebery, 20

May 1917. RA PS/PSO/GV/C/O/1153/302, Stamfordham note, 23 May 1917.

84 RA PS/PSO/GV/C/O/1153/347, note by Rosebery and Asquith, 22 May 1917.

85 RA PS/PSO/GV/C/O/1153/348a, Stamfordham to Rosebery, 23 May 1917. RA PS/PSO/GV/C/O/1153/346a, Stamfordham to Rosebery, 20 May 1917.

86 RA PS/PSO/GV/C/O/1153/361, G to Stamfordham, 15 June 1917.

87 RA PS/PSO/GV/C/O/1153/354, Rosebery to Stamfordham, 26 June 1917.

88 RA GV/PRIV/GVD/17 July 1917.

89 Churchill Archive Centre, Godfrey-Faussett Diary, 17 July 1917.

90 RA GV/PRIV/GVD/17 July 1917.

91 Sir Almeric FitzRoy, *Memoirs* (Hutchinson, 1925), vol. 2, p. 656. Godfrey Faussett Diary, 17 July 1917.

92 Rose, *King George V*, p. 174.

93 RA QM/PRIV/CC8/2010, M to G, 24 June 1917.

94 RA GV/PRIV/GVD/17 July 1917.

95 Nicolson, *King George the Fifth*, p. 401.

96 RA PS/PSO/GV/C/O/1153/358, Rosebery to Stamfordham, 26 June 1917.

97 RA PS/PSO/GV/C/O/1106/49, Watts-Ditchfield to Stamfordham, 6 July 1917.

98 RA EDW/PRIV/MAIN/A/2047, M to David, 6 April 1917.

99 RA GV/PRIV/GVD/10 April 1917.

100 Esher Papers, ESHR 4/8, Derby to Esher, n.d. [April 1917].

101 Sir H. Rider Haggard, *The Private Diaries of Sir H. Rider Haggard 1914–1925*, ed. D. S. Higgins (Cassell, 1980), p. 105.

102 Frances Stevenson, *Lloyd George: A Diary*, ed. A.J.P. Taylor (Hutchinson, 1971), p. 153, 22 April 1917.

CHAPTER 19

The Nonentity King

1 Richard Davenport-Hines, *Ettie: The Intimate Life and Dauntless Spirit of Lady Desborough* (Weidenfeld & Nicolson, 2008), p. 304.

2 RA EDW/PRIV/MAIN/A/2073, M to David, 20 June 1917.

3 Getty Research Library, Pope 199/7, Bertha Dawkins, 14 June 1917.

4 RA GV/PRIV/CC8/211, M to G, 5 July 1917.

5 Pope 199/7, QMD, 4 July 1917.

6 Mabell, Countess of Airlie, *Thatched with Gold: The Memoirs of Mabell, Countess of Airlie*, ed. Jennifer Ellis (Hutchinson, 1962), pp. 136–7.

7 Airlie, *Thatched with Gold*, p. 139.

8 Pope 199/7, QMD, 8 July 1917.

9 Pope 199/7, M to Dolly, 10 August 1917.

10 RA QM/PRIV/CC8/197, M to G, 30 May 1916. Airlie, *Thatched with Gold*, p. 135. Harold Nicolson, *King George the Fifth: His Life and Reign* (Constable, 1952), p. 316.

11 Pope 199/7, QMD, 10, 16 October 1917. Lady Bertha, 3–15 October 1917.

12 RA GV/PRIV/AA37/71, G to Alix, 4 November 1917.

13 G to Alix, 18 November 1917 in Nicolson, *King George the Fifth*, p. 316.

14 RA QM/PRIV/CC4/151, G to M, 22 June 1917.

15 RA EDW/PRIV/MAIN/A/2095, M to David, 13 October 1917.

16 RA EDW/PRIV/MAIN/A/2095, M to David, 13 October 1917.

17 RA EDW/PRIV/MAIN/A/2097, M to David, 20 October 1917.

18 RA EDW/PRIV/MAIN/A/2075, M to David, 28 June 1917.

19 RA EDW/PRIV/MAIN/A/2086, M to David, 8 June 1917.

20 RA GV/PRIV/CC8/213, M to G, 28 March 1918.

21 RA GV/PRIV/GVD/21, 23 March 1918.

22 Churchill Archive Centre, Esher Papers, ESHR 4/9, Sassoon to Esher, 28 March 1918.

23 Esher to Sassoon, n.d. in James Lees-Milne, *The Enigmatic Edwardian: The Life of Reginald, 2nd Viscount Esher* (Sidgwick & Jackson, 1986), pp. 310–11.

24 Esher Papers, ESHR 2/21, Journal, 15 October 1918.

25 Esher Journal, 17 February 1918 in Lees-Milne, *The Enigmatic Edwardian*, p. 309.

26 Lambeth Palace, Davidson Papers, Vol. 13, 17 February 1918.

27 Charles Sebag-Montefiore Papers, Owen Morshead to Philip Magnus, 7 April 1964.

28 Davidson Papers, Vol. 13, 12 May 1918.

29 Davidson Papers, Vol. 12, QM to Davidson, n.d. [4 May 1918].

30 Davidson Papers, Vol. 13, 12 May 1918.

31 RA EDW/PRIV/MAIN/A/2153, M to David, 22 June 1918. RA GV/PRIV/GVD/22 May/4 June 1918.

32 RA GV/PRIV/GVD/6 May 1918.

33 RA GV/PRIV/GVD/25, 28 July 1918.

34 Pope 199/7, QMD, 24 July 1918.

35 British Library, Balfour Papers, Add Mss 49686, Stamfordham to Balfour, 22 July 1918.

36 TNA FO 800/205/304, Balfour to Stamfordham, 23 July 1918.

37 RA EDW/PRIV/MAIN/A/2164, M to David, 29 July 1918.

38 RA GV/PRIV/GVD/25 July 1918.

39 Helen Rappaport, *The Race to Save the Romanovs: The Truth behind the Secret Plans to Rescue Russia's Imperial Family* (Hutchinson, 2018), pp. 94–5.

40 Yale, Beinecke, Harold Nicolson Papers, Gen Mss 614, Box 17, Nicolson to Lascelles, 10 August 1950.

41 Esher Papers, ESHR 4/9, Stamfordham to Esher, 25 July 1918.

42 RA PS/PSO/GV/C/M/1067/89, Hardinge to Stephen Gaselee, 19 July 1932.

43 TNA FO 800/205/73, Arthur Davidson to Balfour, 6 April 1917; Davidson to Balfour, 18 October 1917.

44 TNA FO 800/205/358, telegram, Archangel, 28/31 August 1918.

45 RA GV/PRIV/GVD/31 August 1918.

46 Princess Marie Louise, *My Memories of Six Reigns* (Evans Brothers, 1956), p. 186.

47 Edward, Duke of Windsor, *A King's Story: The Memoirs of HRH the Duke of Windsor* (Cassell, 1951), p. 129.

48 James Lees-Milne, *Diaries 1984–97*, ed. Michael Bloch (John Murray, 2008), p. 422.

49 RA GV/PRIV/GVD/8 August 1918.

50 RA GV/PRIV/GVD/14 November 1918.

51 Nicolson, *King George the Fifth*, p. 326.

52 Esher Papers, ESHR 2/21, War Journal 1917–22, 18 November 1918.

53 Wigram Papers, Clive to Nora, 11 November 1918.

54 Wigram Papers, Clive to Nora, 12 November 1918.

55 RA GV/PRIV/GVD/9 November 1918.

56 Wigram Papers, Clive to Nora, 11 November 1918.

57 Esher Papers, ESHR 4/10, Esher to Stamfordham, 4 November 1918.

58 RA GV/PRIV/GVD/5 November 1918. Stamfordham's memo, 5 November 1918 in Nicolson, *King George the Fifth*, pp. 328–9.

59 RA EDW/PRIV/MAIN/A/2204, M to David, 6 December 1918.

60 Frank Prochaska, 'George V and Republicanism 1917–1919',

61 *Twentieth Century British History*, vol. 10, no. 1 (1999), p. 46.

61 Wigram to Cosmo Lang, January 1919 in Kenneth Rose, *King George V* (Phoenix Press, 2000), p. 227.

62 Wigram Papers, Clive to Nora, 22 November 1918.

63 Esher Papers, ESHR 4/10, Esher to Stamfordham, 15 December 1918.

64 Prochaska 'George V and Republicanism', p. 48, Stamfordham to Watts-Ditchfield, 25 November 1918.

65 Basil Thomson memo, n.d. in Templewood Papers 2/37, Cambridge University Library. Thanks to Richard Davenport-Hines.

66 RA GV/PRIV/GVD/3 May 1919, 18 December 1919.

67 David Cannadine, *George V: The Unexpected King* (Allen Lane, 2014), p. 61. RA GV/PRIV/GVD/27 September 1917.

68 Wigram Papers, Clive to Nora, 5 November 1918.

69 Wigram to Nora, 15 November 1918.

70 RA EDW/PRIV/MAIN/A/2207, M to David, 14 December 1918.

71 Wigram Papers, Clive to Nora, 15 June 1916.

72 RA EDW/PRIV/MAIN/A/2207, M to David, 14 December 1918.

73 RA GV/PRIV/AA38/1, G to Alix, 3 November 1918.

74 Earl of Crawford, *The Crawford Papers: The Journals of David Lindsay, 27th Earl of Crawford and 10th Earl of Balcarres (1871–1940), during the Years 1892 to 1940*, ed. John Vincent (Manchester University Press, 1984), p. 398, 8 November 1918.

75 David to Freda Dudley Ward, 9 December 1918 in Rupert Godfrey, ed., *Letters from a Prince: Edward, Prince of Wales to Mrs Freda Dudley Ward March 1918–January 1921* (Little, Brown, 1998), p. 143.

76 RA EDW/PRIV/MAIN/A/2207, M to David, 14 December 1918.

77 Stephen Roskill, *Hankey: Man of Secrets, Vol. II: 1919–1931* (Collins, 1972), p. 36.
78 RA GV/PRIV/GVD/18 December 1918. Rose, *King George V*, p. 232.
79 RA EDW/PRIV/MAIN/A/2211, M to David, 29 December 1918. RA GV/PRIV/GVD/26 December 1918.
80 Airlie, *Thatched with Gold*, p. 141.
81 Nora Wigram, 13 April 1926 in Rose, *King George V*, p. 232.
82 RA EDW/PRIV/MAIN/A/2213, M to David, 4 January 1919.
83 RA QM/PRIV/CC4/197, G to M, 3 December 1918.
84 RA GVI/PRIV/RF/11/305, M to Bertie, 18 January 1919.
85 RA GV/PRIV/GVD/18 January 1919.
86 RA GVI/PRIV/RF/11/306, M to Bertie, 24 January 1919.
87 Godfrey, ed., *Letters from a Prince*, p. 158, 20 January 1919.
88 David to M, 27 January 1919 in Philip Ziegler, *King Edward VIII: The Official Biography* (Collins, 1990), p. 80.
89 RA GV/PRIV/CC11/4, Bertie to M, 22 January 1919.
90 RA GV/PRIV/CC11/4, Bertie to M, 22 January 1919.
91 RA GVI/PRIV/RF/11/306, M to Bertie, 24 January 1919.
92 RA GVI/PRIV/RF/11/306, M to Bertie, 24 January 1919.
93 Pope 199/7, Note on QMD 1918.
94 Pope 199/7, Note on QMD 1918. Godfrey, ed., *Letters from a Prince*, p. 158.
95 RA GV/PRIV/CC42/127, Alix to M, 8 August 1917.

CHAPTER 20

The Divine Right of Kings

1 RA GV/PRIV/GVD/28 June 1919.
2 RA GV/PRIV/GVD/19 August 1919.
3 Violet Bonham Carter, *Champion Redoubtable: The Diaries and Letters of Violet Bonham Carter 1914–45*, ed. Mark Pottle (Weidenfeld & Nicolson, 1998), pp. 106–7.
4 Robert Rhodes James, ed., *Memoirs of a Conservative: J.C.C. Davidson's Memoirs and Papers* (Weidenfeld & Nicolson, 1969), p. 107.
5 RA EDW/PRIV/MAIN/A/2249, M to David, 30 September 1919.
6 Getty Research Library, Pope 199/7, Lady Bertha Dawkins, 27 September 1919.
7 Pope 199/7, QMD, 3, 4 October 1919. RA GV/PRIV/GVD/3, 4 October 1919.
8 Mabell, Countess of Airlie, *Thatched with Gold: The Memoirs of Mabell, Countess of Airlie*, ed. Jennifer Ellis (Hutchinson, 1962), p. 145.
9 RA EDW/PRIV/MAIN/A/2218, M to David, 31 January 1919.
10 Stamfordham to David, 22 December 1918 in Edward, Duke of Windsor, *A King's Story: The Memoirs of HRH the Duke of Windsor* (Cassell, 1951), p. 133.
11 Airlie, *Thatched with Gold*, pp. 144–5.
12 Rupert Godfrey, ed., *Letters from a Prince: Edward, Prince of Wales to Mrs Freda Dudley Ward March 1918–January 1921* (Little, Brown, 1998), p. 345.
13 Frances Donaldson, *Edward VIII* (Weidenfeld & Nicolson, 1974), p. 58.
14 Mountbatten to mother, 15 July 1920 in Philip Ziegler, *Mountbatten: The Official Biography* (Fontana, 1986), p. 55.
15 RA EDW/PRIV/MAIN/A/2245, M to D, 21 September 1919.
16 M to David, 7 September 1919 in Windsor, *A King's Story*, p. 143.
17 M to David, 7 September 1919 in Windsor, *A King's Story*, p. 143.
18 Windsor, *A King's Story*, p. 132.
19 Windsor, *A King's Story*, p. 133.
20 RA GV/PRIV/GVD/7 February 1919.
21 Godfrey, ed., *Letters from a Prince*, pp. 281, 283, 284.

22 Godfrey, ed., *Letters from a Prince*, pp. 346, 351.

23 Godfrey, ed., *Letters from a Prince*, p. 359.

24 Andrew Lownie, *The Mountbattens: Their Lives and Loves* (Blink, 2019), p. 33.

25 Mountbatten to mother, 15 July 1920, in Ziegler, *Mountbatten*, pp. 54–5.

26 Airlie, *Thatched with Gold*, p. 146.

27 RA GV/PRIV/GVD/15 February 1921. Right Hon. Viscount Sandhurst, *From Day to Day, Vol. 2: 1916–1921* (Edward Arnold, 1929), p. 332.

28 RA GV/PRIV/GVD/10 June 1920.

29 RA QM/PRIV/CC58/162, Queen Mary's Gowns and Jewels, 10, 24 June 1920.

30 RA GV/PRIV/GVD/22 March 1920.

31 Sandhurst, *From Day to Day*, p. 316.

32 Parliamentary Archives, Lloyd George Papers, F/29/4/25, Stamfordham to LG, 10 September 1920.

33 RA PS/PSO/GV/C/K/1740/4, Stamfordham to Shortt, 20 September 1921.

34 RA GV/PRIV/AA38/20, G to Alix, 10 April 1921. RA GV/PRIV/AA38/21, G to Alix, 17 April 1921.

35 Harold Nicolson, *King George the Fifth: His Life and Reign* (Constable, 1952), p. 342.

36 John Gore, *King George V: A Personal Memoir* (John Murray, 1941), p. 337.

37 RA GV/PRIV/GVD/23 April 1921.

38 RA GV/PRIV/AA38/22, G to Alix, 24 April 1921. There is a silent film of the match and the King's reception: https://www.youtube.com/watch?v=bpiwGLoM51k (accessed 25 June 2021).

39 Whether the King actually used these words was disputed at the time, but they have the ring of authentic George V: see Nicolson, *King George the Fifth*, pp. 347–8;

40 Airlie, *Thatched with Gold*, pp. 148–9.

41 Airlie, *Thatched with Gold*, p. 150.

42 Lloyd George Papers, F/29/4/55, Stamfordham to LG, 24 June 1921.

43 Nicolson, *King George the Fifth*, p. 361.

44 Nicolson, *King George the Fifth*, p. 360.

45 RA GV/PRIV/37692, Marsh to Stamfordham, 20 November 1922.

46 RA GV/PRIV/GVD/19 August 1921. The total bag over the period was 3,731 head.

47 RA GV/PRIV/GVD/18 August 1921. Deborah Devonshire, *Wait for Me! Memoirs of the Youngest Mitford Sister* (John Murray, 2010), pp. 202–3.

48 Rose, *King George V*, p. 322.

49 Ponsonby to Hunloke, 2 August 1920 in Christina Dykes, 'Sir Philip Hunloke: The Sailing King's Sailor' (unpublished MA dissertation, University of Buckingham, 2014), p. 96.

50 Gore, *King George V*, p. 327.

51 RA GV/PRIV/GVD/15 July 1921.

52 RA GV/PRIV/GVD/8 August 1921.

53 Sissinghurst Papers, Nicolson to Vita, 8 November 1949.

54 RA EDW/PRIV/MAIN/A/2295, M to David, 13 July 1920.

55 Rose, *King George V*, p. 322.

56 G to Hunloke, 1 September 1925 in Dykes, 'Sir Philip Hunloke', p. 89.

57 Ponsonby to Hunloke, 19 August 1925 in Dykes, 'Sir Philip Hunloke', p. 97.

58 RA QM/PRIV/CC4/255, G to M, 13 August 1926.

59 RA GV/PRIV/CC8/301, M to G, 21 August 1926.

60 Windsor, *A King's Story*, p. 183.

61 James Pope-Hennessy, *The Quest for Queen Mary*, ed. Hugo Vickers (Zuleika, 2018), p. 94.

62 Philip Hall, *Royal Fortune: Tax, Money and the Monarchy*

(Bloomsbury, 1992), pp. 37–8. Kenneth Rose denies that the King pocketed the savings he made during the war (Rose, *King George V*, p. 243).

63 Earl of Crawford, *The Crawford Papers: The Journals of David Lindsay, 27th Earl of Crawford and 10th Earl of Balcarres (1871–1940), during the Years 1892 to 1940*, ed. John Vincent (Manchester University Press, 1984), p. 406.

64 Lambeth Palace, Davidson Papers, Vol. 14, 3 July 1921.

65 Davidson Papers, Vol. 14, 26 June 1921.

66 Ponsonby to LG, 20 November 1920 in Hall, *Royal Fortune*, pp. 40–1.

67 Hall, *Royal Fortune*, p. 38.

68 Crawford, *The Crawford Papers*, p. 406. Rose, *King George V*, p. 242.

69 Wigram Papers, Clive to Nora, 25 November 1918; Stamfordham to Wigram, 2 June 1910.

70 Hall, *Royal Fortune*, p. 36.

71 David Reynolds, *The Long Shadow: The Great War and the Twentieth Century* (Simon & Schuster, 2014), pp. 74–5.

72 RA GV/PRIV/GVD/11 November 1920.

73 RA GV/PRIV/GVD/11 November 1924.

74 Philip Williamson, 'Royalty, Religion and Remembrance', paper read at Cambridge Conference, 'Monarchy and Modernity since 1500', 8 January 2019. Philip Williamson, 'National Days of Prayer: The Churches, the State and Public Worship in Britain 1899–1957', *English Historical Review*, vol. 128, no. 531 (2013), pp. 342–5.

75 Stamfordham's note quoted in Michael Aidin, 'Kipling and the Commemoration of the War Dead', *Kipling Journal*, vol. 81, no. 324 (2007).

76 King George V, *The King to His People: Being the Speeches and*

Messages of HM King George the Fifth (Williams & Norgate, 1935), p. 123.

77 Balliol College Archive, Nicolson Diary, 23 October 1951 (Owen Morshead). Philip Williamson, 'The Monarchy and Public Values, 1900–1953' in Andrzej Olechnowicz, ed., *The Monarchy and the British Nation, 1790 to the Present* (Cambridge University Press, 2007).

78 Wigram Papers, Clive to Nora, 15 November 1918. Nora to Sir Neville and Lady Chamberlain, 21 January 1922.

79 John Wheeler-Bennett, *King George VI: His Life and Reign* (Macmillan, 1958), p. 159.

80 Steve Nicholson, *The Censorship of British Drama 1900–1968, Vol. 1: 1900–1932* (University of Exeter Press, 2003), pp. 77, 152, 241.

81 Nicholson, *The Censorship of British Drama*, p. 241.

82 Nicholson, *The Censorship of British Drama*, p. 242.

83 Frances Stevenson, *Lloyd George: A Diary*, ed. A.J.P. Taylor (Hutchinson, 1971), p. 208.

84 Nicolson, *King George the Fifth*, p. 342.

85 Stephen Roskill, *Admiral of the Fleet Earl Beatty: The Last Naval Hero* (Collins, 1980), pp. 43–7.

86 Lloyd George Papers, F/29/4/109, Stamfordham to Davies, 9 September 1922.

87 RA GV/PRIV/GVD/18 March 1913.

88 G to Bendor, March 1913 in Christina Dykes, 'Hugh Richard Arthur Grosvenor, 2nd Duke of Westminster (1879–1953), known as "Bend'Or": A Reappraisal' (unpublished PhD thesis, University of Buckingham, 2021), p. 214.

89 Dykes, 'Hugh Richard Grosvenor', p. 217.

90 Loelia, Duchess of Westminster, *Grace and Favour: The Memoirs of*

Loelia, Duchess of Westminster
(Weidenfeld & Nicolson, 1961),
p. 196.

91 Lloyd George Papers, F/29/3/1,
Stamfordham to LG, 9 January 1919.

92 Earl of Birkenhead, *The Life of F. E.
Smith, First Earl of Birkenhead*
(Eyre & Spottiswoode, 1959),
pp. 394–7.

93 Nicolson Diary, 30 June 1948,
quoting Lord Gage.

CHAPTER 21

Grasping the Nasty Nettle

1 Yale Beinecke, Harold Nicolson
Papers, GEN MSS 614, Box 17,
Nicolson to Alan Lascelles, 22
January 1951.

2 Beinecke, Harold Nicolson Papers,
GEN MSS 614, Box 17, Nicolson
to Alan Lascelles, 29 December
1950.

3 Harold Nicolson, *King George the
Fifth: His Life and Reign*
(Constable, 1952), p. 365.

4 National Library of Scotland, John
Murray Archive, Ac13328/171/
EE6, Murray to Gore, 20
November 1939.

5 Charles Gore Papers, Note by John
Gore for George VI, 14 March
1940. John Gore, *King George V: A
Personal Memoir* (John Murray,
1941), p. 367.

6 Balliol College Archive, Nicolson
Diary, 18 January 1949.

7 Beinecke, Harold Nicolson Papers,
GEN MSS 614, Box 17, Lascelles
to Nicolson, 27 January 1951.

8 Beinecke, Harold Nicolson Papers,
GEN MSS 614, Box 17, Godfrey
Thomas to Lascelles [January 1951].

9 Nicolson Diary, 27 April 1949.

10 Nicolson Diary, 6 January 1949.

11 Nicolson Diary, 21 July 1948.

12 Nicolson Diary, 18 December 1948.
The story appeared in print ten
years later, in Randolph Churchill's
biography of Lord Derby, where
Harold Nicolson is named as the
source.

13 Philip Ziegler, *King Edward VIII:
The Official Biography* (Collins,
1990), p. 8.

14 Wigram Papers, Clive to Nora, 2
December 1923.

15 John Wheeler-Bennett, *King George
VI: His Life and Reign* (Macmillan,
1958), p. 140. Rupert Godfrey, ed.,
*Letters from a Prince: Edward,
Prince of Wales to Mrs Freda
Dudley Ward March 1918–January
1921* (Little, Brown, 1998),
pp. 378–9.

16 G to David, 4 May 1920 in Ziegler,
Edward VIII, p. 132.

17 Edward, Duke of Windsor, *A King's
Story: The Memoirs of HRH the
Duke of Windsor* (Cassell, 1951),
pp. 191–2.

18 David to Philip Sassoon, 9
September 1920 in Ziegler, *Edward
VIII*, p. 170.

19 Stamfordham to Godfrey Thomas,
23 September 1920 in Ziegler,
Edward VIII, p. 169.

20 Bertie to David, 13 August 1920 in
Ziegler, *Edward VIII*, p. 169.

21 Lambeth Palace, Davidson Papers,
Vol. 14, 26 June 1921.

22 Windsor, *A King's Story*, p. 164.

23 Wigram Papers, Nora to parents, 24
October 1920.

24 Wigram Papers, Nora to parents, 6
January 1921.

25 Wigram Papers, Nora to parents, 16
October 1921.

26 David to Freda Dudley Ward, 18
October 1921 in Ziegler, *Edward
VIII*, pp. 134–5.

27 Godfrey, ed., *Letters from a Prince*,
p. 91.

28 Ziegler, *Edward VIII*, p. 98.

29 Godfrey, ed., *Letters from a Prince*,
p. 287. Mabell, Countess of Airlie,
*Thatched with Gold: The Memoirs
of Mabell, Countess of Airlie*, ed.
Jennifer Ellis (Hutchinson, 1962),
p. 145.

30 Godfrey, ed., *Letters from a Prince*,
p. 99.

31 Wigram Papers, Nora to parents, 17
October 1920.

32 Lady Cynthia Asquith, *Diaries 1915–1918* (Hutchinson, 1968), pp. 420, 459.

33 David to Freda Dudley Ward, 23 November 1921 in Ziegler, *Edward VIII*, p. 171.

34 Duff to Diana Cooper, 22 May 1918 in Artemis Cooper, ed., *A Durable Fire: The Letters of Duff and Diana Cooper 1913–1950* (Collins, 1983), p. 60.

35 Edward, Duke of Windsor, *A Family Album* (Cassell, 1960), p. 112.

36 Wigram Papers, Nora to parents, 21 January 1922, 22 October 1922.

37 Osbert Sitwell, *Queen Mary and Others* (Michael Joseph, 1974), p. 56.

38 Virginia Woolf, *Orlando: A Biography* (Penguin, 1942), p. 126.

39 David to Freda Dudley Ward, 23 November 1921 in Ziegler, *Edward VIII*, p. 171.

40 RA EDW/PRIV/MAIN/A/2367, M to David, 30 November 1921.

41 RA EDW/PRIV/MAIN/A/2365, M to David, 24 November 1921.

42 RA EDW/PRIV/MAIN/A/2367, M to David, 30 November 1921.

43 Getty Research Library, Pope 195/15, M to Bertha Dawkins, 28 November 1921.

44 RA GV/PRIV/GVD/20 November 1921.

45 David to Freda Dudley Ward, 23 November 1921 in Ziegler, *Edward VIII*, p. 171.

46 James Pope-Hennessy, *Queen Mary* (Phoenix Press, 2000), p. 520.

47 Sir Alan Lascelles, *In Royal Service: The Letters and Journals of Sir Alan Lascelles, Vol. 2*, ed. Duff Hart-Davis (Hamish Hamilton, 1989), p. 9. Airlie, *Thatched with Gold*, p. 164.

48 Edward Owens, 'All the World Loves a Lover: The 1934 Royal Wedding of Prince George and Princess Marina' in *The Family Firm: Monarchy, Mass Media and the British Public 1932–53* (University of London Press, 2019), p. 69.

49 RA GV/PRIV/GVD/28 February 1922.

50 RA EDW/PRIV/MAIN/A/2422, M to David, 2 March 1922.

51 RA GV/PRIV/GVD/1 March 1922.

52 Bertie to David, 25 May 1920 in William Shawcross, *Queen Elizabeth the Queen Mother: The Official Biography* (Macmillan, 2009), p. 115.

53 Airlie, *Thatched with Gold*, p. 166.

54 Airlie, *Thatched with Gold*, p. 166.

55 Lady Strathmore to Lady Airlie, 5 March 1921 in Shawcross, *Queen Elizabeth the Queen Mother*, p. 127.

56 Sir Henry Channon, *The Diaries 1918–38*, ed. Simon Heffer (Hutchinson, 2021), p. 80.

57 BL, Airlie Papers, Add MSS 82748, M to Lady Airlie, 4 August 1921.

58 BL, Airlie Papers, Add MSS 82748, M to Lady Airlie, 28 August 1921.

59 Airlie, *Thatched with Gold*, p. 167.

60 Airlie, *Thatched with Gold*, p. 167.

61 Hugo Vickers, *Elizabeth the Queen Mother* (Hutchinson, 2005), p. 47.

62 M to Lady Strathmore, 6 May 1922 in Shawcross, *Queen Elizabeth the Queen Mother*, p. 140.

63 M to Bertie, 4 October 1922 in Shawcross, *Queen Elizabeth the Queen Mother*, p. 145.

64 Robert Rhodes James, ed., *Memoirs of a Conservative: J.C.C. Davidson's Memoirs and Papers* (Weidenfeld & Nicolson, 1969), pp. 109–10.

65 Elizabeth Bowes Lyon to Bertie, 20 December 1922 in Shawcross, *Queen Elizabeth the Queen Mother*, p. 146.

66 BL, Airlie Papers, Add MSS 82748, M to Lady Airlie, 9 January 1923.

67 Vickers, *Elizabeth the Queen Mother*, p. 59.

68 RA GV/PRIV/GVD/20 January 1923.

69 Shawcross, *Queen Elizabeth the Queen Mother*, p. 175.

70 Nicolson, *King George the Fifth*, p. 366.

71 Nicolson Diary, 3 November 1948. George VI said this to John Gore, who told Harold Nicolson.

72 Beinecke, Harold Nicolson Papers, GEN MSS 614, Box 17, Nicolson to Lascelles, 22 January 1951.

73 Pope 199/8, M to G, 29 June 1922. RA GV/PRIV/CC4/220, G to M, 29 June 1922.

74 RA QM/PRIV/CC4/213, G to M, 17 July 1921.

75 Kenneth Rose, *King George V* (Phoenix Press, 2000), p. 308.

76 Gore, *King George V*, p. 368.

77 Queen Elizabeth the Queen Mother, *Counting One's Blessings: The Selected Letters of Queen Elizabeth the Queen Mother*, ed. William Shawcross (Macmillan, 2012), p. 200.

78 Ziegler, *Edward VIII*, p.170.

79 David to Freda Dudley Ward, 18 October 1921 in Ziegler, *Edward VIII*, p.99.

80 RA GV/PRIV/CC4/225, G to M, 17 August 1922.

81 RA GV/PRIV/CC8/262, M to G, 18 August 1922.

82 Pope-Hennessy, *Queen Mary*, p. 522.

83 Lady Cynthia Colville, *Crowded Life* (Evans Brothers, 1963), p. 123. Windsor, *Family Album*, p. 56.

84 Rose, *King George V*, p. 287.

85 Suzy Menkes, *The Royal Jewels* (Grafton, 1985), p. 75.

86 Airlie, *Thatched with Gold*, p. 162.

87 RA GV/PRIV/AA38/46, G to Alix, 21 May 1922.

88 Pope-Hennessy, *The Quest for Queen Mary*, p. 301. Gore, *King George V*, p. 366.

89 Airlie, *Thatched with Gold*, pp. 128–9.

90 Airlie, *Thatched with Gold*, pp. 146–7. The Prince of Wales taught the song to Lady Airlie (BL Airlie, Add MSS 82749, David to Lady Airlie, 23 August 1923).

91 Pope-Hennessy, *Queen Mary*, p. 525.

92 RA GV/PRIV/CC4/234, G to M, 2 December 1923.

93 RA GV/PRIV/GVD/8 May 1922.

94 James Lees-Milne, *Harold Nicolson: A Biography, Vol. 2: 1930–1968* (Chatto & Windus, 1981), pp. 233, 367. Rose, *King George V*, p. 467.

95 Pope-Hennessy, *Queen Mary*, p. 523.

96 Pope-Hennessy, *Queen Mary*, pp. 522, 524.

CHAPTER 22

The Influence of the Crown

1 RA GV/PRIV/GVD/18 October 1922.

2 Getty Research Library, Pope 199/8, Lady Bertha Dawkins, 1 October 1922.

3 RA PS/PSO/GV/C/K/1814/4, Stamfordham memo, 'Resignation of Lloyd George', 25 October 1922.

4 Kenneth Rose, *Who's In, Who's Out: The Journals of Kenneth Rose, Vol. 1*, ed. D. R. Thorpe (Weidenfeld & Nicolson, 2018), p. 549.

5 Parliamentary Archives, Lloyd George Papers, F 29/4/40, Stamfordham to LG, 19 March 1921.

6 Lloyd George Papers, F 29/3/35, Stamfordham to Davies, 10 November 1919.

7 Lloyd George Papers, F 29/4/103, GV to LG, 3 July 1922. See Kenneth Rose, *King George V* (Phoenix Press, 2000), pp. 250–1. Richard Davenport-Hines, 'Gregory, Arthur John Peter Michael Maundy (1877–1941)', *Oxford Dictionary of National Biography* (2004).

8 Wigram Papers, Nora to parents, [20] October 1922.

9 RA GV/PRIV/GVD/19 October 1924.

10 RA GV/PRIV/GVD/20 May 1923.

11 The best account of the Curzon/Baldwin leadership drama is in David Gilmour, *Curzon* (John Murray, 1994), pp 579–86. See also Rose, *King George V*, pp. 266–73.

12 RA PS/PSO/GV/C/K/1853/10, Stamfordham memo, interview with Balfour, 21 May 1923.

13 RA PS/PSO/GV/C/K/1853/6, Stamfordham to Balfour, telegram

addressed to the Grand Hotel, Sheringham, 20 May 1923.

14 RA PS/PSO/GV/C/K/1853/10, Stamfordham memo, interview with Balfour, 21 May 1923.

15 Rose, *King George V*, p. 269.

16 Vernon Bogdanor, *The Monarchy and the Constitution* (Clarendon Press, 1995), p. 91.

17 RA PS/PSO/GV/C/K/1853/11, Stamfordham memo re Geoffrey Dawson, 21 May 1923.

18 The Devonshire Collections, Chatsworth, J10, Duchess Evie to Duke Victor, 30 December 1911.

19 Winston S. Churchill, *Great Contemporaries* (Thornton Butterworth, 1937), p. 287. Rose, *King George V*, p. 269. Richard Davenport-Hines, *Ettie: The Intimate Life and Dauntless Spirit of Lady Desborough* (Weidenfeld & Nicolson, 2008), p. 251. Max Egremont, *Balfour: A Life of Arthur James Balfour* (Collins, 1980), pp. 326–7.

20 RA PS/PSO/GV/C/K/2223/14, Stamfordham to Geoffrey Dawson, 30 April 1929.

21 RA PS/PSO/GV/C/K/1853/20, Stamfordham memo, 22 May 1923. RA PS/PSO/GV/C/K/1853/12, Stamfordham to Curzon telegram, 21 May 1923.

22 RA PS/PSO/GV/C/K/1853, Stamfordham's memo of Curzon interview, 22 May 1923 in Harold Nicolson, *King George the Fifth: His Life and Reign* (Constable, 1952), p. 377.

23 Gilmour, *Curzon*, p. 584.

24 Nicolson, *King George the Fifth*, p. 377.

25 RA PS/PSO/GV/C/K/1853/38, Stamfordham to Lord Ronaldshay, 30 March 1928.

26 Earl of Crawford, *The Crawford Papers: The Journals of David Lindsay, 27th Earl of Crawford and 10th Earl of Balcarres (1871–1940), during the Years 1892 to 1940*, ed. John Vincent

27 RA PS/PSO/GV/C/K/1853/38, Stamfordham to Lord Ronaldshay, 30 March 1928.

28 Gilmour, *Curzon*, p. 580.

29 Crawford, *The Crawford Papers*, p. 483.

30 RA PS/PSO/GV/C/K/1853/19, Stamfordham memo, 22 May 1923, note of meeting with Colonel Jackson.

31 RA GV/PRIV/GVD/22 May 1923.

32 RA PS/PSO/GV/C/K/1853/35, Stamfordham memo, 29 May 1923.

33 Rose, *King George V*, pp 272–3.

34 Rose, *King George V*, p. 314.

35 Crawford, *The Crawford Papers*, p. 482.

36 Nicolson, *King George the Fifth*, p. 380, G's memo, 12 November 1923.

37 RA GV/PRIV/GVD/16 November 1923.

38 Crawford, *The Crawford Papers*, p. 488.

39 RA QM/PRIV/CC4/238, G to M, 6 December 1923.

40 Churchill Archive Centre, Godfrey-Faussett Papers, 2/15, 'Notes on Pheasant Shooting', Godfrey-Faussett to Fritz Ponsonby, 24 November 1920.

41 Wigram Papers, Clive to Nora, 2, 3 December 1923.

42 RA GV/PRIV/GVD/8 December 1923.

43 RA PS/PSO/GV/C/K/1918/14, Memo by Stamfordham, 8 December 1923.

44 RA GV/PRIV/GVD/8 December 1923.

45 Nicolson, *King George the Fifth*, p. 380.

46 Thomas Jones, *Whitehall Diary, Vol. 1: 1916–1925*, ed. Keith Middlemass (Oxford University Press, 1969), pp. 259–60, 9 December 1923.

47 RA PS/PSO/GV/C/K/1918/23, [Balfour] to Stamfordham, 9 December 1923.

48 RA GV/PRIV/GVD/10 December 1923.

49 RA PS/PSO/GV/C/K/1918/65, Esher to Stamfordham, 17 December 1923.

50 RA PS/PSO/GV/C/K/1918/34, Stamfordham memo, 10 December 1923.

51 RA PS/PSO/GV/C/K/1918/60, Stamfordham to Strachey, 14 December 1923.

52 RA GV/PRIV/GVD/14 December 1923.

53 RA GV/PRIV/GVD/13, 17, 28 December 1923. Dr Woods of the London Hospital gave him electrical treatment every day between 14 and 25 January 1924 (RA GV/PRIV/GVD/14, 25 January 1924).

54 RA PS/PSO/GV/C/K/1918/84, Stamfordham memo to G, 28 December 1923.

55 RA PS/PSO/GV/C/K/1918/97, Stamfordham to G, 1 January 1924.

56 RA PS/PSO/GV/C/K/1918/113, 114, G's note, 5 January 1924.

57 RA PS/PSO/GV/C/K/1918/85, Stamfordham to G, 28 December 1923.

58 David Marquand, *Ramsay MacDonald* (Jonathan Cape, 1977), p. 304, MacDonald diary, 22 January 1924.

59 Marquand, *Ramsay MacDonald*, p. 305.

60 RA GV/PRIV/GVD/22 January 1924.

61 Robert Rhodes James, ed., *Memoirs of a Conservative: J.C.C. Davidson's Memoirs and Papers* (Weidenfeld & Nicolson, 1969), pp. 177–8.

62 Rhodes James, ed., *Memoirs of a Conservative*, p. 191.

63 Neville Chamberlain, *The Neville Chamberlain Diary Letters, Vol. 2: The Reform Years 1921–27*, ed. Robert Self (Ashgate, 2000), pp. 167, 205.

64 RA GV/PRIV/AA38/65, G to Alix, 17 February 1924.

65 Lady Cynthia Colville, *Crowded Life* (Evans Brothers, 1963), p. 135.

66 RA PS/PSO/GV/C/K/1918/188, Memo by Stamfordham, 25 January 1924.

67 Rose, *King George V*, pp. 233–4. Colville, *Crowded Life*, p. 123.

68 Beatrice Webb, *The Diary of Beatrice Webb, Vol. 4, 1924–1943: The Wheel of Life*, ed. Norman and Jeanne MacKenzie (Virago, 1985), p. 10, January 1924.

69 RA GV/PRIV/GVD/22 February 1924.

70 RA PS/PSO/GV/C/K/1918/226, Stamfordham to MacDonald, 1 February 1924.

71 *Daily Express*, 1 February 1924.

72 RA PS/PSO/GV/C/K/1918/207, G's note for Ben Spoor, 28 January 1924.

73 TNA CAB 23/47, 6 February 1924.

74 RA PS/PSO/GV/C/K/1918/207, G's note for Ben Spoor, 28 January 1924.

75 Nicolson, *King George the Fifth*, pp. 391–2.

76 RA GV/PRIV/GVD/11 March 1924. E. S. Turner, *The Court of St. James's* (Michael Joseph, 1959), pp. 354–7.

77 RA PS/PSO/GV/C/K/1918/97, Stamfordham to G, 1 January 1924.

78 RA PS/PSO/GV/C/K/1918/116, Fritz Ponsonby memo, 5 January 1924.

79 RA PS/PSO/GV/C/K/1918/97, Stamfordham to G, 1 January 1924.

80 TNA CAB 23/47, 4 February 1924.

81 Webb, *The Diary of Beatrice Webb, Vol. 4*, p. 16.

82 RA PS/PSO/GV/C/K/1918/239, M to Stamfordham, February 1924.

83 Webb, *The Diary of Beatrice Webb, Vol. 4*, p. 11.

84 Nicolson, *King George the Fifth*, p. 388. Marquand, *Ramsay MacDonald*, p. 308.

85 Marquand, *Ramsay MacDonald*, p. 314.

CHAPTER 23

The Dolls' House

1   RA GV/PRIV/CC4/238, G to M, 6
    December 1923.
2   Lucinda Lambton, *The Queen's
    Dolls' House* (Royal Collection
    Trust, 2010), p. 51.
3   Princess Marie Louise, *My
    Memories of Six Reigns* (Evans
    Brothers, 1956), p. 202.
4   Christopher Hussey, *The Life of Sir
    Edwin Lutyens* (Country Life,
    1950), p. 452. Jane Ridley, *The
    Architect and his Wife: A Life of
    Edwin Lutyens* (Chatto & Windus,
    2002), pp. 303–5, 319.
5   Suzy Menkes, *The Royal Jewels*
    (Grafton, 1985), p. 76.
6   Lambton, *The Queen's Dolls'
    House*, p. 110.
7   Virginia Woolf, *Mrs Dalloway*
    (Everyman's Library, 1993),
    pp. 15–16.
8   Edward, Duke of Windsor, *A Family
    Album* (Cassell, 1960), p. 102.
    Richard Davenport-Hines, *Ettie: The
    Intimate Life and Dauntless Spirit of
    Lady Desborough* (Weidenfeld &
    Nicolson, 2008), p. 309. James
    Pope-Hennessy, *Queen Mary*
    (Phoenix Press, 2000), p. 526.
9   Kathryn Jones, 'Queen Mary as
    Collector', unpublished paper
    (2014). Lady Cynthia Colville,
    Crowded Life (Evans Brothers,
    1963), p. 118. Pope 200/1, M to G,
    13 November 1926.
10 Menkes, *The Royal Jewels*,
    p. 76.
11 Arthur Hamilton Lee, 'A Good
    Innings': The Private Papers of
    Viscount Lee of Fareham*, ed. Alan
    Clark (John Murray, 1974), p. 171,
    18 July 1917.
12 RA GV/PRIV/CC8/273, M to G, 5
    November 1923.
13 Lord Harewood, *The Tongs and the
    Bones: The Memoirs of Lord
    Harewood* (Weidenfeld & Nicolson,
    1981), p. 26.
14 Lee, *A Good Innings*, p. 282.

15 Frank Herrmann, *Sotheby's:
    Portrait of an Auction House*
    (Chatto & Windus, 1980), pp. 156,
    239, 242. Author emails Caroline
    Behr, 24 November 2017; Georgina
    Eliot, 31 March 2020; Marcus
    Linnell, 1 April 2020.
16 Lady Pamela Berry in Kenneth
    Rose, *King George V* (Phoenix
    Press, 2000), p. 301.
17 Balliol College Archive, Nicolson
    Diary, 9 September 1948.
18 James Pope-Hennessy, *The Quest
    for Queen Mary*, ed. Hugo Vickers
    (Zuleika, 2018), p. 143.
19 Jones, 'Queen Mary as Collector',
    p. 12.
20 Pope-Hennessy, *Queen Mary*, p. 413.
21 Pope-Hennessy, *Queen Mary*, p.
    524. QM used the phrase 'one great
    hobby' in a letter to Lady Mount
    Stephen, 10 February 1910, p. 410.
    Jones, 'Queen Mary as Collector',
    p. 13.
22 Colville, *Crowded Life*, p. 125.
23 Jones, 'Queen Mary as Collector'.
24 Pope-Hennessy, *Queen Mary*, pp.
    524–5.
25 Menkes, *The Royal Jewels*, p. 77.
26 Getty Research Library, Pope
    200/12, M's annotations on
    Cavendish biography, 1930.
27 Colville, *Crowded Life*, p. 125.
28 Liverpool Library, Diaries of Sir
    Richard Molyneux, 920 SEF 6/9,
    1925: 19, 21 August.
29 Pope 199/8, M to G, 23 August
    1925.
30 Pope 199/8, M to G, 10 August
    1922.
31 RA GV/PRIV/CC4/247, G to M,
    26 August 1924.
32 Pope 199/8, M to G, 19 August 1924.
33 Kate Bradley, 'Saving the Children
    of Shoreditch: Lady Cynthia
    Colville and Needy Families in East
    London c.1900–1960', *Law, Crime
    and History*, vol. 7, no. 1 (2017),
    pp. 145–63.
34 Pope-Hennessy, *The Quest for
    Queen Mary*, pp. 229–30, Cynthia
    Colville.

35 *The Times*, 31 October 1919.

36 Pope 195/15, M to Lady Bertha, 19 June 1919.

37 Pope 195/15, M to Lady Bertha, 29 April 1919.

38 Neville Chamberlain, *The Neville Chamberlain Diary Letters, Vol. 2: The Reform Years 1921–27*, ed. Robert Self (Ashgate, 2000), p. 303.

39 *British Medical Journal*, 4 April 1953.

40 *British Medical Journal*, 19 February 1936.

41 RA PS/PSO/GV/C/K/1958/1, Note on Dissolution of 9 October 1924, 10 October 1924.

42 *The Times*, 15 October 1924.

43 Helen Hardinge diary Hugo Vickers, *Elizabeth the Queen Mother* (Hutchinson, 2005), p. 89.

44 RA GV/PRIV/GVD/14 October 1924.

45 Pope 195/15, M to Lady Bertha, 18 October 1924.

46 Pope 200/1, Lady Bertha, 5 December 1927.

47 RA PS/PSO/GV/C/K/1958/13, Stamfordham to G, 7 October 1924.

48 RA PS/PSO/GV/C/K/1958/12, Stamfordham to Hardinge, 7 October 1924.

49 RA GV/PRIV/GVD/9 October 1924.

50 RA PS/PSO/GV/C/K/1958/13, Stamfordham to G, 7 October 1924.

51 Ramsay MacDonald Diary, 9 October 1924 in David Marquand, *Ramsay MacDonald* (Jonathan Cape, 1977), p. 378.

52 Harold Nicolson, *King George the Fifth: His Life and Reign* (Constable, 1952), p. 402.

53 RA GV/PRIV/GVD/4 November 1924.

54 RA PS/PSO/GV/C/K/1958/42, Stamfordham's memo, 4 November 1924. RA PS/PSO/GV/C/K/1958/43, Cutting of Churchill's speech, *Daily News*, 13 October 1924.

55 RA PS/PSO/GV/C/K/1958/65, Stamfordham's note, 8 November 1924.

56 Stamfordham memorandum, 4 November 1924 in Philip Williamson and Edward Baldwin, eds, *Baldwin Papers* (Cambridge University Press, 2004), p. 163.

57 RA GV/PRIV/GVD/30 October 1924.

58 Nicolson, *King George the Fifth*, p. 404.

59 Kathleen Hilton Young Diary, 18 November 1924 in Williamson and Baldwin, eds, *Baldwin Papers*, p. 166.

60 Reginald, Viscount Esher, *Journals & Letters of Viscount Esher, Vol. 4: 1915–1930*, ed. Oliver, Viscount Esher (Ivor Nicholson & Watson, 1938), p. 297, 5 November 1924.

61 Sir Henry Channon, *The Diaries 1918–38*, ed. Simon Heffer (Hutchinson, 2021), p. 183.

62 Edward, Duke of Windsor, *A King's Story: The Memoirs of HRH the Duke of Windsor* (Cassell, 1951), p. 200.

63 RA EDW/PRIV/MAIN/A/2504, M to David, 30 September 1924.

64 Sir Alan Lascelles, *In Royal Service: Letters and Journals of Sir Alan Lascelles, Vol. 2*, ed. Duff Hart-Davis (Hamish Hamilton, 1989), p. 36. Ted Powell, *King Edward VIII: An American Life* (Oxford University Press, 2018), pp. 98–111.

65 Windsor, *A King's Story*, p. 201.

66 Windsor, *A Family Album*, pp. 50, 54–9. Simon Heffer, *The Age of Decadence: Britain 1880 to 1914* (Random House, 2017), pp. 22–25.

67 Helen Hardinge, *Loyal to Three Kings* (William Kinder, 1967), p. 67.

68 Windsor, *A Family Album*, pp. 13, 25.

69 Anne de Courcy, *The Viceroy's Daughters: The Lives of the Curzon Sisters* (Phoenix, 2001), p. 80.

70 Windsor, *A Family Album*, p. 62.

71 RA GV/PRIV/AA38/66, G to Alix, 16 March 1924.

72 G to David, 31 March 1924 in Windsor, *A King's Story*, p. 196.
73 RA GV/PRIV/GVD/9 November 1924.
74 de Courcy, *The Viceroy's Daughters*, pp. 97–102, 111–15.
75 Channon, *The Diaries 1918–38*, p. 159.
76 Windsor, *A Family Album*, p. 93.
77 Windsor, *A Family Album*, p. 92.
78 Windsor, *A King's Story*, p. 202.
79 Channon, *The Diaries 1918–38*, p. 183.
80 RA GV/PRIV/GVD/22 February 1925.
81 RA GV/PRIV/GVD/24 March 1925.
82 Pope 199/8, Harry Lascelles to David, n.d. [1925].
83 Pope-Hennessy, *The Quest for Queen Mary*, p. 284 (Duke of Windsor).
84 Pope 199/8, Harry Lascelles to David, n.d. [1925].
85 Windsor, *A Family Album*, p. 78.
86 Pope 199/8, Lady Bertha Dawkins, 22, 23 December 1924.
87 Channon, *The Diaries 1918–38*, p. 91.
88 Pope 199/8, Lady Bertha Dawkins, 22, 23, 25 December 1924.
89 Pope 194/7, Fritz Ponsonby to wife, 29 January 1924.
90 Wigram Papers, Clive to Nora, 2 December 1923.
91 Colville, *Crowded Life*, p. 111.
92 RA GV/PRIV/CC8/279, M to G, 7 May 1924.
93 Pope 194/7, Note on lunch with Lady Cynthia Colville, 31 January 1958.
94 Pope-Hennessy, *Queen Mary*, p. 537.
95 RA GV/PRIV/CC8/289, M to G, 29 July 1925.
96 Pope 199/8, QMD, 19 November 1925.
97 Pope 199/8, QMD, 19 November 1925.
98 RA GV/PRIV/GVD/20 November 1925.
99 Wigram Papers, Nora to parents, 10 December 1925.
100 RA GV/PRIV/GVD/27 November 1925.
101 Pope 199/8, QMD, 28 November 1925.
102 RA GV/PRIV/GVD/2 January 1926.
103 Pope-Hennessy, *Queen Mary*, p. 540. See RA GV/PRIV/GVD/9 January 1926.

CHAPTER 24

Safe Haven

1 Loelia, Duchess of Westminster, *Grace and Favour: The Memoirs of Loelia, Duchess of Westminster* (Weidenfeld & Nicolson, 1961), p. 106. *The Times*, 26 June 1925. Lady Cynthia Colville, *Crowded Life* (Evans Brothers, 1963), p. 115.
2 Ross McKibbin, *Classes and Cultures: England 1918–1951* (Oxford University Press, 1998), pp. 4–8.
3 Anne Glenconner, *Lady in Waiting: My Extraordinary Life in the Shadow of the Crown* (Hodder & Stoughton, 2019), p. 11. Kenneth Rose, *King George V* (Phoenix Press, 2000), p. 101.
4 Westminster, *Grace and Favour*, p. 104.
5 D. J. Taylor, *Bright Young People: The Rise and Fall of a Generation 1918–1940* (Vintage, 2008), p. 37. *The Times*, 6 May 1925.
6 Evelyn Waugh, *Vile Bodies* (Penguin, 1938), p. 127.
7 Arthur Hamilton Lee, 'A Good Innings': The Private Papers of Viscount Lee of Fareham*, ed. Alan Clark (John Murray, 1974), pp. 240–1, September 1923.
8 McKibbin, *Classes and Cultures*, p. 7.
9 RA PS/PSO/GV/C/K/2011/1, Baldwin to G, 2 July 1925. *Hansard*, 1 July 1925.
10 RA PS/PSO/GV/C/K/2011/3, Stamfordham to Baldwin, 3 July 1925.

11 RA PS/PSO/GV/C/K/2011/3, Stamfordham to Baldwin, 3 July 1925.

12 RA PS/PSO/GV/C/K/2011/3, Stamfordham memo, 11 July 1925. Harold Nicolson, *King George the Fifth: His Life and Reign* (Constable, 1952), p. 428. Rose, *King George V*, pp. 338–9.

13 Robert Gray, 'FitzRoy, Sir Almeric (1851–1935)', *Oxford Dictionary of National Biography* (2004). Sir Almeric FitzRoy, *Memoirs* (Hutchinson, 1925), vol. 2, pp. 211, 530.

14 Stamfordham to Birkenhead, 15 July 1922 in Bevis Hillier, *The Virgin's Baby: The Battle of the Ampthill Succession* (Hopcyn Press, 2013), p. 70.

15 Stamfordham to Birkenhead, 15 July 1922 in Hillier, *The Virgin's Baby*, p. 70.

16 Stamfordham to Cave, 6 March 1925 in Gail Savage, 'Erotic Stories and Public Decency: Newspaper Reporting of Divorce Proceedings in England', *Historical Journal*, vol. 41, no. 2 (1998), p. 520.

17 *The Times*, 13 December 1957.

18 A. A. Milne, 'Buckingham Palace' in *When We Were Very Young* (Methuen, 1924).

19 Colville, *Crowded Life*, p. 114.

20 John Wheeler-Bennett, *King George VI: His Life and Reign* (Macmillan, 1958), pp. 164, 168.

21 RA GV/PRIV/GVD/29, 30 July 1925. Rose, *King George V*, p. 322.

22 RA GV/PRIV/CC8/289, M to G, 29 July 1925.

23 RA GV/PRIV/CC4/248, G to M, 29 July 1925.

24 RA GV/PRIV/CC8/289, M to G, 29 July 1925.

25 *Daily Express*, 14 August 1925 in RA GV/PRIV/CC4/249, G to M, August 1925.

26 E.g. RA GV/PRIV/GVD/7 November 1924. John Gore, *King George V: A Personal Memoir* (John Murray, 1941), p. 382.

27 Mabell, Countess of Airlie, *Thatched with Gold: The Memoirs of Mabell, Countess of Airlie*, ed. Jennifer Ellis (Hutchinson, 1962), p. 178.

28 RA GV/PRIV/CC4/251, G to M, 28 April 1926.

29 RA GV/PRIV/GVD/30 April 1926.

30 RA GV/PRIV/GVD/5 May 1926.

31 RA GV/PRIV/GVD/6 May 1926. Nicolson, *King George the Fifth*, p. 418.

32 RA PS/PSO/GV/C/B/2052/13, Stamfordham to Waterhouse, 7 May 1926.

33 H. Hearder, 'King George V, the General Strike, and the 1931 Crisis' in H. Hearder and H. R. Loyn, eds, *British Government and Administration: Studies Presented to S. B. Chrimes* (University of Wales Press, 1974), pp. 234–41.

34 Earl of Crawford, *The Crawford Papers: The Journals of David Lindsay, 27th Earl of Crawford and 10th Earl of Balcarres (1871–1940), during the Years 1892 to 1940*, ed. John Vincent (Manchester University Press, 1984), p. 514.

35 RA PS/PSO/GV/C/B/2052/23, Stamfordham to General Milne, 10 May 1926.

36 RA PS/PSO/GV/C/B/2052/24, Stamfordham memo, 11 May 1926.

37 Hearder, 'King George V, the General Strike, and the 1931 Crisis', p. 239.

38 Hearder, 'King George V, the General Strike, and the 1931 Crisis', p. 241.

39 RA GV/PRIV/GVD/12 May 1926.

40 Liverpool Library, Molyneux Diary, 920 SEF 6/10, 21 April 1926.

41 QMD, 21 April 1926 in William Shawcross, *Queen Elizabeth the Queen Mother: The Official Biography* (Macmillan, 2009), p. 252.

42 M to Duke of York, 17 April 1926 in Shawcross, *Queen Elizabeth the Queen Mother*, p. 251.

43 Shawcross, *Queen Elizabeth the Queen Mother*, p. 252.

44 RA GV/PRIV/GVD/21 April 1926.

45 Shawcross, *Queen Elizabeth the Queen Mother*, p. 253. RA GV/PRIV/CC8/292, M to G, 28 April 1926. RA GV/PRIV/CC4/251, G to M, 28 April 1926.

46 Lord Harewood, *The Tongs and the Bones: The Memoirs of Lord Harewood* (Weidenfeld & Nicolson, 1981), p. 2.

47 James Pope-Hennessy, *The Quest for Queen Mary*, ed. Hugo Vickers (Zuleika, 2018), p. 182.

48 RA GV/PRIV/GVD/17 August 1923.

49 Airlie, *Thatched with Gold*, p. 179.

50 RA GV/PRIV/GVD/6 February 1927.

51 RA GV/PRIV/GVD/21 April 1927.

52 Wigram Papers, Nora to parents, 14 October 1917, 10 December 1925.

53 Pope-Hennessy, *The Quest for Queen Mary*, p. 144.

54 Getty Research Library, Pope 200/1, M to Dolly, 2 September 1926.

55 RA GV/PRIV/CC4/256, G to M, 16 August 1926.

56 Pope 200/1, M to G, 24 August 1926.

57 Pope 200/1, Lady Bertha Dawkins, 6 September 1926.

58 Pope 200/1, M to G, 24 August 1926.

59 Wigram Papers, Nora to parents, 14 October 1917. Pope-Hennessy, *The Quest for Queen Mary*, p. 186. Rose, *King George V*, p. 291.

60 Pope 200/1, Lady Bertha Dawkins, 5 December 1926.

61 Rose, *King George V*, p. 291.

62 Pope 200/1, Lady Bertha Dawkins, 5 December 1926.

63 Queen Elizabeth the Queen Mother, *Counting One's Blessings: The Selected Letters of Queen Elizabeth the Queen Mother*, ed. William Shawcross (Macmillan, 2012), p. 149.

64 RA AEC/GG/012, Owen Morshead Diary, 5 June 1926. Thanks to Jane Roberts.

65 Brian Bond, 'Fortescue, Sir John William (1859–1933)', *Oxford Dictionary of National Biography* (2004).

66 RA AEC/GG/012, Morshead Diary, 5 June 1926. Rose, *King George V*, pp. 299–300.

67 RA AEC/GG/012, Morshead Diary, 5 June 1926.

68 James Stourton, *Kenneth Clark: Life, Art and 'Civilisation'* (William Collins, 2017 edn), pp. 75–6.

69 Kathryn Jones, 'Queen Mary', lecture to Gilbert Collection, 2014, p. 5.

70 Balliol College Archive, Nicolson Diary, 3 November 1948.

71 Sissinghurst Papers, Morshead's note for Nicolson, n.d.

72 Nicolson Diary, 21 July 1948.

73 Pope-Hennessy, *The Quest for Queen Mary*, p. 234.

74 Pope 202/6, Princess Alice interview, 29 April 1957.

75 Sir Henry Channon, *The Diaries 1918–38*, ed. Simon Heffer (Hutchinson, 2021), p. 157, 19 May 1925.

76 Pope-Hennessy, *The Quest for Queen Mary*, p. 234.

77 Gore, *King George V*, p. 436.

78 RA GV/PRIV/AA37/71, G to Alix, 4 November 1917. Rose, *King George V*, p. 290.

79 Nicolson Diary, 14 April 1949 (Duke of Windsor). See e.g. RA GV/PRIV/GVD/25 June, 23 July, 22 October, 5 November 1922; 4, 11, 18 March, 27 May, 10 June 1923.

80 Pope 199/8, Lady Bertha Dawkins to her daughter, 3 September 1923. Nicolson Diary, 27 April 1949 (Alec Hardinge); 19 October 1949 (Cromer).

81 Nicolson Diary, 21 March 1949.

82 Nicolson Diary, 3 November 1948.

83 Pope-Hennessy, *The Quest for Queen Mary*, p. 234.

84 Nicolson Diary, 19 October 1949.

85 Pope-Hennessy, *The Quest for Queen Mary*, p. 235.

86 Pope-Hennessy, *The Quest for Queen Mary*, p. 141.

87 Pope-Hennessy, *The Quest for Queen Mary*, p. 182. Giles St Aubyn, 'Henry, Prince, Duke of Gloucester (1900–1974)', *Oxford Dictionary of National Biography* (2004).

88 RA GVI/PRIV/RF/1/316, M to Bertie and Henry, 3 August 1922.

89 Pope 199/8, M to G, 21 August 1923. George told his father: 'I have been sight-seeing with Mama and seen various cathedrals and abbeys and old houses, but I don't think that it would have amused you' (Prince George to GV, 24 August 1923 in Philip Ziegler, 'George, Prince, First Duke of Kent (1902–1942)', *Oxford Dictionary of National Biography* (2004)).

90 Edward, Duke of Windsor, *A King's Story: The Memoirs of HRH the Duke of Windsor* (Cassell, 1951), p. 239.

91 RA GV/PRIV/GVD/28 January 1927.

92 RA GV/PRIV/GVD/5 February 1927.

93 Susan Williams, *The People's King: The True Story of the Abdication* (Penguin, 2004), pp. 38–9.

94 Duff Cooper, *The Duff Cooper Diaries*, ed. John Julius Norwich (Weidenfeld & Nicolson, 2005), pp. 185–8.

95 Pope-Hennessy, *The Quest for Queen Mary*, p. 213.

96 RA GV/PRIV/GVD/6 February 1927.

97 Duff to Diana Cooper, 8 January 1927 in Artemis Cooper, ed., *A Durable Fire: The Letters of Duff and Diana Cooper 1913–1950* (Collins, 1983), p. 245.

98 Duff to Diana Cooper, 14 January 1927 in Cooper, ed., *A Durable Fire*, p. 246.

99 RA GV/PRIV/GVD/2 April 1927. RA GV/PRIV/CC4/265, G to M, 25 March 1927.

100 Duff to Diana Cooper, 8 February 1927 in Cooper, ed., *A Durable Fire*, p. 252.

101 RA GV/PRIV/CC4/265, G to M, 25 March 1927.

102 RA GV/PRIV/CC8/308, M to G, 25 March 1927.

103 RA GV/PRIV/CC8/311, M to G, 29 June 1927.

104 RA GV/PRIV/CC4/226, G to M, 27 April 1927.

105 Channon, *The Diaries 1918–1938*, p. 332, 6 November 1928.

106 RA GV/PRIV/CC4/266, G to M, 27 April 1927.

107 RA GV/PRIV/CC4/269, G to M, 17 July 1927.

108 Sir Alan Lascelles, *In Royal Service: Letters and Journals of Sir Alan Lascelles, Vol. 2*, ed. Duff Hart-Davis (Hamish Hamilton, 1989), p. 50.

CHAPTER 25

'Sir, the King of England is Dying'

1 RA GV/PRIV/CC4/250, G to M, 3 May 1928.

2 Lady Cynthia Colville, *Crowded Life* (Evans Brothers, 1963), p. 120. John Gore, *King George V: A Personal Memoir* (John Murray, 1941), p. 378.

3 Kenneth Rose, *Who's In, Who's Out: The Journals of Kenneth Rose, Vol. 1*, ed. D. R. Thorpe (Weidenfeld & Nicolson, 2018), p. 527.

4 Colville, *Crowded Life*, p. 119.

5 Ross McKibbin, *Classes and Cultures: England 1918–1951* (Oxford University Press, 1998), p. 5.

6 Leo Amery, *The Leo Amery Diaries, Vol. 1: 1896–1929*, ed. John Barnes and David Nicholson (Hutchinson, 1980), p. 453.

7 William Shawcross, *Queen Elizabeth the Queen Mother: The Official Biography* (Macmillan, 2009), p. 272.

8 RA PS/PSO/GV/C/K/20997/2, Stamfordham to Baldwin, 21

February 1927 in Harold Nicolson, *King George the Fifth: His Life and Reign* (Constable, 1952), pp. 427–8.

9   RA PS/PSO/GV/C/K/2097/3, Stamfordham memo, 23 February 1927.

10 Shawcross, *Queen Elizabeth the Queen Mother*, p. 295.

11 RA GV/PRIV/CC4/227, G to M, 29 August 1927.

12 John Wheeler-Bennett, *King George VI: His Life and Reign* (Macmillan, 1958), p. 151.

13 Wheeler-Bennett, *King George VI*, p. 151.

14 Francis Watson, *Dawson of Penn* (Chatto & Windus, 1950), p. 285, Duchess of York to Dawson, 9 March 1936.

15 James Pope-Hennessy, *The Quest for Queen Mary*, ed. Hugo Vickers (Zuleika, 2018), p. 132.

16 RA GV/PRIV/CC8/328, M to G, 17 August 1928. RA GV/PRIV/CC8/330, M to G, 21 August 1928.

17 Rose, *Who's In, Who's Out*, p. 524.

18 RA GV/PRIV/CC4/286, G to M, 21 August 1928.

19 RA EDW/PRIV/MAIN/A/2599, M to David, 18 November 1928.

20 RA GV/PRIV/CC4/288, G to M, 26 August 1928.

21 RA GV/PRIV/CC4/259, G to M, 28 August 1928.

22 RA GV/PRIV/CC8/311, M to G, 29 June 1927.

23 Peter Millar, 'The other prince', *Sunday Times*, 26 January 2003.

24 Pope-Hennessy, *The Quest for Queen Mary*, p. 199.

25 Philip Ziegler, *King Edward VIII: The Official Biography* (Collins, 1990), p. 193.

26 Philip Williamson and Edward Baldwin, eds, *Baldwin Papers* (Cambridge University Press, 2004), p. 213.

27 Sir Alan Lascelles, *In Royal Service: Letters and Journals of Sir Alan Lascelles, Vol. 2*, ed. Duff

Hart-Davis (Hamish Hamilton, 1989), p. 109.

28 RA GV/PRIV/GVD/21 November 1928.

29 RA GV/PRIV/GVD/14 March 1928.

30 Neville Chamberlain, *The Neville Chamberlain Diary Letters, Vol. 3: The Heir Apparent 1928–33*, ed. Robert Self (Ashgate, 2002), p. 77, 24 March 1928.

31 Mary Soames, ed., *Speaking for Themselves: The Personal Letters of Winston and Clementine Churchill* (Black Swan, 1999), p. 328, 25 September 1928.

32 Watson, *Dawson of Penn*, p. 205.

33 Arthur Hamilton Lee, 'A Good Innings': The Private Papers of Viscount Lee of Fareham*, ed. Alan Clark (John Murray, 1974), p. 287, 27 November 1928.

34 *The Times*, 24 November 1928.

35 *The Times*, 10 December 1928. Gore, *King George V*, p. 387n.

36 *The Times*, 27 November 1928.

37 Getty Research Library, Pope 200/1, Joan Lascelles note on King's illness, n.d. *The Times*, 27 November 1928.

38 Sister Catherine Black, *King's Nurse, Beggar's Nurse* (Hurst & Blackett, 1939), p. 151. *The Times*, 28 November 1928.

39 Black, *King's Nurse, Beggar's Nurse*, pp. 152–3.

40 Pope-Hennessy, *The Quest for Queen Mary*, p. 235.

41 Edward, Duke of Windsor, *A King's Story: The Memoirs of HRH the Duke of Windsor* (Cassell, 1951), p. 224.

42 Pope 200/1, QMD, 2 December 1928.

43 *The Times*, 3, 4 December 1928.

44 Dawson to Balfour, 4 December 1928 in Kenneth Rose, *King George V* (Phoenix Press, 2000), p. 356.

45 Bertie to David, 6 December 1928 in Windsor, *A King's Story*, p. 223.

46 George Godfrey-Faussett, *Royal Servant, Family Friend: The Life*

and Times of Sir Bryan Godfrey-Faussett (Bernard Durnford, 2004), p. 301.

47 The Times, 5 December 1928. Lascelles, In Royal Service, p. 111.

48 Lascelles, In Royal Service, p. 111.

49 Mabell, Countess of Airlie, Thatched with Gold: The Memoirs of Mabell, Countess of Airlie, ed. Jennifer Ellis (Hutchinson, 1962), p. 180.

50 Pope 200/1, QMD, 5 December 1928.

51 The Times, 7, 10 December 1928.

52 The Times, 11 December 1928.

53 Pope 200/1, QMD, 10 December 1928.

54 Pope 200/1, QMD, 11 December 1928.

55 Ziegler, King Edward VIII, p. 197.

56 Black, King's Nurse, Beggar's Nurse, p. 153.

57 Pope 200/1, QMD, 12 December 1928.

58 Pope 200/1, QMD, 6 January 1929.

59 Lee, 'A Good Innings', p. 289, 23 January 1929.

60 Black, King's Nurse, Beggar's Nurse, p. 162. Pope 200/1, QMD, 7 January 1929.

61 Godfrey-Faussett, Royal Servant, Family Friend, p. 302.

62 Pope 200/1, Bertha Dawkins, p. 10, February 1929.

63 RA GV/PRIV/GVD/13 February 1929.

64 Godfrey-Faussett, Royal Servant, Family Friend, p. 303.

65 Lambeth Palace, Davidson Papers, Vol. 20, G to Davidson, 1 January 1930 (sic, really 1931).

66 Davidson Papers, Davidson memo, 16 March 1929.

67 Rose, Who's In, Who's Out, p. 575.

68 Rose, King George V, p. 361.

69 Lady Diana Cooper, The Light of Common Day (Vintage, 2018), p. 76.

70 The Times, 16 May 1929.

71 RA GV/PRIV/GVD/27 May 1929.

72 RA GV/PRIV/GVD/31 May 1929.

73 Liverpool Library, Molyneux Diary, 30 May 1929.

74 RA PS/PSO/GV/C/K/2223/8, 10. Note signed M.O.B., 29 September 1966.

75 RA PS/PSO/GV/C/K/2223/31, 32, note by Mackworth-Young, n.d.

76 RA PS/PSO/GV/C/K/2223/31, 32.

77 RA GV/PRIV/GVD/4 June 1929.

78 Rose, King George V, p. 361.

79 RA PS/PSO/GV/C/K/2223/45, Stamfordham memo, 5 June 1929.

80 RA GV/PRIV/GVD/7 June 1929.

81 Wigram Papers, Nora to parents, 8 June 1929.

82 Wigram Papers, Nora to parents, 8 June 1929. Gore, King George V, p. 394.

83 RA GV/PRIV/GVD/7 July 1929.

84 RA GV/PRIV/GVD/15 July 1929. Rose, King George V, p. 361.

85 Lee, 'A Good Innings', p. 292, 8 July 1929.

86 RA GV/PRIV/GVD/25 July 1929.

87 Chamberlain, The Neville Chamberlain Diary Letters, Vol. 3, p. 200.

88 RA GV/PRIV/GVD/9 August 1929.

89 National Library of Scotland, John Murray Archive, Acc. 13328/171 EE6, John Murray to Gore, 23 May 1940.

90 Murray Archive, Acc. 13328/171 EE6, John Murray to Gore, 9 September 1940.

91 RA PS/PSO/GV/C/K/2223/1, Stamfordham to G, 16 April 1929. RA PS/PSO/GV/C/K/2333/2, Hardinge to Stamfordham, 17 April 1929. RA PS/PSO/GV/C/K/2223/5, Stamfordham to Hardinge, 18 April 1929.

92 Watson, Dawson of Penn, p. 202.

93 Ivan Maisky, The Maisky Diaries: Red Ambassador to the Court of St James's 1932–1943, ed. Gabriel Gorodetsky (Yale University Press, 2015), pp. 57–8.

94 Bertie to David, 6 December 1928 in Windsor, A King's Story, p. 223.

CHAPTER 26

Queen Mary Takes Control

1   See above, p. 319.
2   RA PS/PSO/GV/C/K/2223/151, Stamfordham memo, 26 June 1929.
3   RA GV/PRIV/GVD/27 March 1930. RA EDW/PRIV/MAIN/A/2629, M to David, 27 March 1930. Kenneth Rose, *King George V* (Phoenix Press, 2000), p. 369. Harold Nicolson, *King George the Fifth: His Life and Reign* (Constable, 1952), p. 441.
4   RA GV/PRIV/GVD/9 May 1919.
5   Frances Welch, *The Russian Court at Sea: The Last Days of a Great Dynasty – the Romanovs' Voyage into Exile* (Short, 2011), p. 197.
6   RA EDW/PRIV/MAIN/A/2232, M to David, 16 August 1919.
7   Sir Frederick Ponsonby, *Recollections of Three Reigns* (Odhams Press, n.d.), p. 337.
8   Ponsonby, *Recollections of Three Reigns*, p. 336.
9   RA GV/PRIV/GVD/5 October 1919. RA PS/PSO/GV/C/M/1067/89, Davidson to G, 8 June 1920. John Van der Kiste and Coryne Hall, *Once a Grand Duchess: Xenia, Sister of Nicholas II* (Sutton, 2002), p. 160.
10   *The Times*, 18 April 1923.
11   RA GV/PRIV/GVD/10 February 1925.
12   RA GV/PRIV/AA43/234, Xenia to George, 18 February 1925 in Van der Kiste and Hall, *Once a Grand Duchess*, p. 171.
13   Van der Kiste and Hall, *Once a Grand Duchess*, pp. 189–90.
14   Welch, *The Russian Court at Sea*, p. 203.
15   Van der Kiste and Hall, *Once a Grand Duchess*, p. 159.
16   Ponsonby, *Recollections of Three Reigns*, pp. 337–9.
17   RA GV/PRIV/GVD/22 May 1929.
18   Ian Shapiro phone call and email, 27 July 2020. Copy of Hennells' valuation, 22 May 1929.
19   Ian Vorres, *The Last Grand-Duchess: Her Imperial Highness Grand-Duchess Olga Alexandrovna* (Hutchinson, 1964), pp. 183–5.
20   Patricia Phenix, *Olga Romanov: Russia's last Grand Duchess* (Viking, 1999), pp. 251–5.
21   Suzy Menkes, *The Royal Jewels* (Grafton, 1985), p. 52. The italics are hers.
22   William Clarke, 'How the Dowager Empress's Jewels Survived a Revolution' in Ole Villumsen Krog, ed., *Maria Feodorovna, Empress of Russia: An Exhibition* (Copenhagen: Christianborg Palace, 1997), pp. 334–41. In 1929 Queen Mary bought a pearl and diamond collar with sapphire and diamond clasp valued at £5,678–£6,000 for £6,000 and a pearl and diamond twist brooch valued at £550 for £555. In 1930, when jewellery prices had fallen because of the slump, she bought a cabochon sapphire and diamond brooch valued at £25 to £30 for £26 12s and an oval cabochon sapphire and diamond oval cluster brooch valued at £1,400–£1,900 for £2,375.
23   Ponsonby, *Recollections of Three Reigns*, p. 340.
24   James Pope-Hennessy, *Queen Mary* (Phoenix Press, 2000), p. 548.
25   James Pope-Hennessy, *The Quest for Queen Mary*, ed. Hugo Vickers (Zuleika, 2018), p. 163.
26   Edward, Duke of Windsor, *A King's Story: The Memoirs of HRH the Duke of Windsor* (Cassell, 1951), p. 224.
27   Rose, *King George V*, pp. 300–1.
28   Windsor, *A King's Story*, p. 226.
29   Lambeth Palace, Davidson Papers, Vol. XV, Davidson memo, 16 August 1929.
30   RA GV/PRIV/GV/CC8/335, M to G, 8 May 1929.
31   *The Times*, 11 May, 27 June 1929.
32   Windsor, *A King's Story*, p. 234. *The Times*, 27 June 1929.

33 Errol Trzebinski, *The Lives of Beryl Markham* (Heinemann, 1993), pp. 122–36.

34 Stamfordham to FO (Selby), 21 January 1929 in Noble Frankland, *Prince Henry Duke of Gloucester* (Weidenfeld & Nicolson, 1980), pp. 86–7.

35 Mary S. Lovell, *Straight on Till Morning: The Biography of Beryl Markham* (Hutchinson, 1987), p. 88, citing interviews with Sir Charles Markham and Mrs Cookie Hoogterp, sister of Ulick Alexander, comptroller of Prince George's household.

36 Lovell, *Straight on Till Morning*, pp. 89–91.

37 Ted Powell, *King Edward VIII: An American Life* (Oxford University Press, 2018), pp. 180–1.

38 Arthur Hamilton Lee, 'A Good Innings': The Private Papers of Viscount Lee of Fareham*, ed. Alan Clark (John Murray, 1974), p. 290, 23 April 1929.

39 Godfrey Thomas Papers, February 1929 in Piers Brendon and Philip Whitehead, *The Windsors: A Dynasty Revealed*, rev. ed. (Pimlico, 2000), p. 53.

40 RA GV/PRIV/CC4/293, G to M, 6 May 1930.

41 Lee, 'A Good Innings', p. 289, 2 January 1929.

42 RA GV/PRIV/GVD/10 March, 14, 15 June 1929. Pope 200/1, Lady Bertha Dawkins, 1 April 1930.

43 RA GV/PRIV/GVD/24 May 1930.

44 Pope 200/1, Lady Bertha Dawkins, 24 August 1930.

45 E.g. RA GV/PRIV/GVD/26–30 January, 22 March 1930.

46 RA GV/PRIV/GVD/22 February 1930.

47 RA EDW/PRIV/MAIN/A/2626, M to David, 10 February 1930.

48 RA GV/PRIV/GVD/19 September 1929.

49 Christie's catalogue, 21 March 2001, p. 147. Interview with

Alistair Ferguson. Rose, *King George V*, p. 360.

50 RA GV/PRIV/GVD/24 October 1929.

51 RA GV/PRIV/GVD/6 December 1929.

52 Philip Ziegler, *King Edward VIII: The Official Biography* (Collins, 1990), p. 200.

53 Ziegler, *King Edward VIII*, p., 201.

54 RA GV/PRIV/GVD/4 November 1929.

55 Sarah Bradford, *King George VI* (Weidenfeld & Nicolson, 1989), pp. 140–1. Peter Millar, 'The other prince', *Sunday Times*, 26 January 2003.

56 Sir Alan Lascelles, *King's Counsellor: Abdication and War – The Diaries of Sir Alan Lascelles*, ed. Duff Hart-Davis (Phoenix, 2007), p. 51, 25 August 1942.

57 Wigram Papers, Wigram to Nora, 28 August 1930. William Shawcross, *Queen Elizabeth the Queen Mother: The Official Biography* (Macmillan, 2009), p. 316.

58 Mary Soames, ed., *Speaking for Themselves: The Personal Letters of Winston and Clementine Churchill* (Black Swan, 1999), p. 328, 25 September 1928.

59 Bradford, *King George VI*, p. 132.

60 RA GV/PRIV/GVD/4 January 1931.

61 RA GV/PRIV/GVD/19 January 1931.

62 RA GV/PRIV/GVD/19 January 1931. RA GV/PRIV/CC4/287, G to M, 23 August 1928.

63 Nicolson Diary, 14 April 1949.

64 RA GV/PRIV/GVD/9 March 1931.

65 John Gore, *King George V: A Personal Memoir* (John Murray, 1941), p. 404.

66 RA EDW/PRIV/MAIN/A/2647, M to David, 3 April 1931.

67 Gore, *King George V*, p. 404.

68 Loelia, Duchess of Westminster, *Grace and Favour: The Memoirs of Loelia, Duchess of Westminster* (Weidenfeld & Nicolson, 1961), p. 183. See Richard Davenport-Hines, 'Lygon, William, Seventh Earl Beauchamp (1872–1938)', *Oxford Dictionary of National Biography* (2004).

69 Paula Byrne, *Mad World: Evelyn Waugh and the Secrets of Brideshead* (HarperPress, 2009), pp. 143–5.

70 Peter Raina, *The Seventh Earl Beauchamp: A Victim of his Times* (Oxford: Peter Lang, 2016), p. 418.

71 Byrne, *Mad World*, p. 136.

72 Byrne, *Mad World*, pp. 137–40. Robin Rhoderick-Jones in *The Times*, 19 November 2005.

73 Jane Mulvagh, *Madresfield: The Real Brideshead – One House, One Family, One Thousand Years* (Doubleday, 2008), p. 313.

74 Sir Henry Channon, *The Diaries 1918–38*, ed. Simon Heffer (Hutchinson, 2021), p. 377.

75 RA EDW/PRIV/MAIN/A/2627, M to David, 19 February 1930.

76 Rose, *King George V*, p. 366.

77 Raina, *The Seventh Earl Beauchamp*, p. 108.

78 RA GV/PRIV/GVD/28 May 1931.

79 RA GV/PRIV/GVD/2 June 1931. Westminster, *Grace and Favour*, p. 157.

80 These men were the three friends of her husband whom Lady Beauchamp referred to in a letter to Dorothy Lygon, 21 April 1933 in Mulvagh, *Madresfield*, p. 299.

81 This story first appeared in Mulvagh, *Madresfield*, pp. 277–9, but as Raina points out (*The Seventh Earl Beauchamp*, p. 423), no source is given. However, a comparison with Lady Beauchamp's letter to her daughter Dorothy of 21 April 1933 (Mulvagh, *Madresfield*, p. 299) suggests that the source is Lygon family lore. Byrne, *Mad World*, pp. 146–7.

82 Robin Rhoderick-Jones, *The Times*, 19 November 2005. Michael Bloch, *Closet Queens: Some 20th-Century British Politicians* (Abacus, 2016), pp. 56–7.

83 Dalton's diary, 17 July 1931 quoted in Raina, *The Seventh Earl Beauchamp*, p. 423. The prime minister and the King kept in contact with the banished peer. MacDonald's private secretary asked Wigram in September: 'The Prime Minister wrote to Beauchamp about ten days ago to an hotel in Bad Nauheim, we have had no reply, and I am wondering if Beauchamp is still at his original address' (RA PS/PSO/GV/C/K/2331(1)/2, C. P. Duff (PM's private secretary) to Wigram, 14 September 1931).

CHAPTER 27

King George's Last Stand

1 RAPS/PSO/GC/C/K/2330(1)/4,Alec Hardinge note, 20 August 1931.

2 Vernon Bogdanor, '1931 Revisited: The Constitutional Aspects,' *Twentieth Century British History*, vol. 2, no. 1 (1991), p. 8.

3 Wigram to G, 11 July 1931 in Harold Nicolson, *King George the Fifth: His Life and Reign* (Constable, 1952), p. 449.

4 Edward, Duke of Windsor, *A Family Album* (Cassell, 1960), p. 75. *The Times*, 3 October 1930.

5 RA GV/PRIV/GVD/21 July 1931. More research is needed on the Number 4 account, which is only mentioned in the King's diary in connection with Peacock, who looked after the King's investments. See RA GV/PRIV/GVD/20 July, 19 December 1932.

6 RA PD/PSO/GV/C/K/2330(1)/7, Wigram memo, 22 August 1931.

7 RA GV/PRIV/GVD/22 August 1931. Pope 200/2, Lady Bertha Dawkins, 23 August 1931.

8 Getty Research Library, Pope 200/2, M to G, 23 August 1931.

9 Pope 200/2, Lady Bertha Dawkins, 22 August 1931.

10 RA PS/PSO/GV/C/K/2330(1)/7, Wigram memo, 23 August 1931.

11 RA PS/PSO/GV/C/K/2330(1)/7, Wigram memo, 23 August 1931.

12 David Marquand, *Ramsay MacDonald* (Jonathan Cape, 1977), p. 630.

13 Bogdanor, '1931 Revisited', p. 13.

14 RA PS/PSO/GV/C/K/2330(1)/7, Wigram memo, 23 August 1931.

15 RA PS/PSO/GV/C/K/2330(1)/7, Wigram memo, 23 August 1931. Bogdanor, '1931 Revisited' p. 14.

16 RA GV/PRIV/GVD/23 August 1931.

17 Philip Hall, *Royal Fortune: Tax, Money and the Monarchy* (Bloomsbury, 1992), pp. 68–9.

18 Nicolson, *King George the Fifth*, p. 464.

19 Wigram memo, 23 August 1931 in Nicolson, *King George the Fifth*, p. 464.

20 RA GV/PRIV/GVD/23 August 1931.

21 Nicolson Diary, 1 July 1949, Rosa Rosenberg, MacDonald's secretary.

22 Wigram memo, 24 August 1931 in Nicolson, *King George the Fifth*, p. 466.

23 George Godfrey-Faussett, *Royal Servant, Family Friend: The Life and Times of Sir Bryan Godfrey-Faussett* (Bernard Durnford, 2004), p. 309.

24 Bogdanor, '1931 Revisited', p. 16.

25 Pope 202/2, M to G, 24 August 1931.

26 Pope 200/2, Lady Bertha Dawkins, 25 August 1931.

27 Pope 200/2, Lady Bertha Dawkins, 18, 19, 25 August 1931.

28 Nicolson, *King George the Fifth*, p. 468.

29 RA GV/PRIV/GVD/26 August 1931.

30 Pope 200/2, Lady Bertha Dawkins, 28 August 1931.

31 RA PS/PSO/GV/C/K/2331(4)/2, Ethel Snowden to M, 28 August 1931.

32 Wigram to Archbishop Cosmo Lang, 27 August 1931 in John Gore, *King George V: A Personal Memoir* (John Murray, 1941), pp. 409–10.

33 John Reith, *The Reith Diaries*, ed. Charles Stewart (Collins, 1975), p. 182, 17 November 1932.

34 RA PS/PSO/GV/C/K/2330(1)/18, Wigram memo, 27 August 1931.

35 G to Lang, 2 September 1931 in Gore, *King George V*, p. 409.

36 RA PS/PSO/GV/C/K/2330(2)/169, Laski, 'How the coalition was born', *Daily Herald*, 14 March 1932. Note that this cutting was preserved in Wigram's file.

37 Yale, Beinecke, GEN. MSS. 614, Box 17, Nicolson to Alan Lascelles, 6 July 1949.

38 TNA CAB 21/3754, Correspondence between Nicolson and Brook, May-June 1949.

39 Balliol College Archive, Nicolson Diary, 18 January 1949.

40 RA PS/PSO/GV/C/K/2330(2)/27, annotation on note from royal librarian Robin Mackworth Young, n.d. [1965].

41 Vernon Bogdanor, *The Monarchy and the Constitution* (Clarendon Press, 1995), p. 110. In this book Bogdanor takes a more critical view than in his 1991 article on 1931.

42 RA GV/PRIV/CC4/298, G to M, 16 September 1931.

43 Kenneth Rose, *King George V* (Phoenix Press, 2000), p. 92.

44 Pope 200/2, Lady Bertha Dawkins, 28, 29 August 1931.

45 RA GV/PRIV/CC4/298, G to M, 16 September 1931.

46 Pope 200/2, Lady Bertha Dawkins, 2 September 1931.

47 Queen Elizabeth the Queen Mother, *Counting One's Blessings: The Selected Letters of Queen Elizabeth the Queen Mother*, ed. William Shawcross (Macmillan, 2012), p. 190.

48 Elizabeth the Queen Mother, *Counting One's Blessings*, p. 190.

49 RA PS/PSO/GV/C/K/2330(27)/76, Peacock to Wigram, 4 September 1931. RA GV/PRIV/GVD/22 August 1931. Hall, *Royal Fortune*, pp. 66–7.

50 John Wheeler-Bennett, *King George VI: His Life and Reign* (Macmillan, 1958), p. 258.

51 RA PS/PSO/GV/C/K/2331(4)/4, Ethel Snowden to QM, 12 September 1931.

52 RA PS/PSO/GV/C/K/2330(2)/41, Godfrey-Faussett to Wigram, 4 September 1931.

53 RA PS/PSO/GV/C/K/2330(2)/46, Wigram to Godfrey-Faussett, 5 September 1931. See Chapter 24, p. 340.

54 RA PS/PSO/GV/C/K/2330(2)/52, Godfrey-Faussett to Wigram, 8 September 1931.

55 RA PS/PSO/GV/C/K/2330(2)/77, Wigram to Peacock, 12 September 1931.

56 RA GV/PRIV/CC4/299, G to M, 17 September1931.

57 RA GV/PRIV/GVD/20 September 1931. RA GV/PRIV/CC 4/300, G to M, 19 September 1931.

58 RA PS/PSO/GV/C/K/2330(2)/100, Peacock to Wigram, 21 September 1931.

59 RA GV/PRIV/GVD/29 September 1931.

60 Wigram memo, 24 August 1931 in Nicolson, *King George the Fifth*, p. 466.

61 Bogdanor, '1931 Revisited', pp. 21–2.

62 RA PS/PSO/GV/C/K/2331(1)/20, Wigram memo, 29 September 1931.

63 RA PS/PSO/GV/C/K/2331(1)/23, Wigram memo, 1 October 1931.

64 RA GV/PRIV/GVD/2 October 1931.

65 RA PS/PSO/GV/C/K/2331(1)/29, Wigram memo, 3 October 1931.

66 RA PS/PSO/GV/C/K/2331(1)/31, Wigram memo, 6 October 1931.

67 RA GV/PRIV/GVD/6 October 1931.

68 Nicolson Diary, 1 July 1949, Rosa Rosenberg.

69 Hester Barron, 'Labour Identities of the Coalfield: The General Election of 1931 in County Durham', *History*, vol. 97, no. 326 (2012).

70 RA GV/PRIV/GVD/27 October 1931.

71 RA GV/PRIV/GVD/28 October 1931.

72 RA GV/PRIV/GVD/28 October 1931. *The Times*, 28 October 1931.

73 Leo Amery, *The Leo Amery Diaries, Vol. 1: 1896–1929*, ed. John Barnes and David Nicholson (Hutchinson, 1980), p. 536, 16 February 1928.

74 RA GV/PRIV/GVD/29 November 1930.

75 Nicolson Diary, 23 December 1948.

76 Nicolson, *King George the Fifth*, p. 507.

77 Viscount Templewood, *Nine Troubled Years* (Collins, 1954), pp. 59–60.

78 Templewood, *Nine Troubled Years*, pp. 59–60. RA GV/PRIV/GVD/5 November 1931.

79 Nicolson Diary, 5 July 1949.

80 Godfrey-Faussett, *Royal Servant, Family Friend*, pp. 307–8.

81 Sir Henry Channon, *The Diaries 1918–38*, ed. Simon Heffer (Hutchinson, 2021), p. 331.

82 Lord Harewood, *The Tongs and the Bones: The Memoirs of Lord Harewood* (Weidenfeld & Nicolson, 1981), p. 15.

83 RA GV/PRIV/GVD/26 December 1931.

84 RA GV/PRIV/GVD/5 January 1932.

85 RA GV/PRIV/GVD/1 February 1932.

86 RA GV/PRIV/GVD/24 March 1932.

87 *The Times*, 24 March 1932.

88 James Pope-Hennessy, *Queen Mary* (Phoenix Press, 2000), p. 551.

89 Frank Prochaska, *Royal Bounty: The Making of a Welfare*

Monarchy (Yale University Press, 1995), pp. 203–4.

90 Edward, Duke of Windsor, *A King's Story: The Memoirs of HRH the Duke of Windsor* (Cassell, 1951), p. 248.

91 RA GV/PRIV/GVD/1932: 25 December.

92 Nicolson, *King George the Fifth*, p. 525.

93 Reith, *The Reith Diaries*, p. 182.

94 Reith, *The Reith Diaries*, p. 183.

95 A. C. Benson in Rose, *King George V*, p. 298.

96 Nicolson Diary, 29 August 1951.

97 King George V, *The King to His People: Being the Speeches and Messages of HM King George the Fifth* (Williams & Norgate, 1935), p. 295.

98 David Gilmour, *The Long Recessional: The Imperial Life of Rudyard Kipling* (John Murray, 2002), p. 308.

99 Edward Owens, 'A Man We Understand: King George V's Radio Broadcasts' in *The Family Firm: Monarchy, Mass Media and the British Public 1932–53* (University of London Press, 2019), pp. 94–103.

100 Philip Ziegler, *King Edward VIII: The Official Biography* (Collins, 1990), p. 198.

CHAPTER 28

That Woman!

1 RA GV/PRIV/GVD/6 March 1933. Earl of Crawford, *The Crawford Papers: The Journals of David Lindsay, 27th Earl of Crawford and 10th Earl of Balcarres (1871–1940), during the Years 1892 to 1940*, ed. John Vincent (Manchester University Press, 1984), p. 568. Harold Nicolson, *King George the Fifth: His Life and Reign* (Constable, 1952), p. 516.

2 RA GV/PRIV/GVD/28 January 1933.

3 RA GV/PRIV/GVD/30 January 1933.

4 John Gore, *King George V: A Personal Memoir* (John Murray, 1941), p. 422.

5 James Pope-Hennessy, *Queen Mary* (Phoenix Press, 2000), p. 551.

6 Kenneth Rose, *Who's In, Who's Out: The Journals of Kenneth Rose, Vol. 1*, ed. D. R. Thorpe (Weidenfeld & Nicolson, 2018), p. 576.

7 Rose, *Who's In, Who's Out*, p. 546 (Queen Mother).

8 Rose, *Who's In, Who's Out*, p. 529 (Lord Gage).

9 Neville Chamberlain, *The Neville Chamberlain Diary Letters, Vol. 3: The Heir Apparent 1928–33*, ed. Robert Self (Ashgate, 2002), p. 347.

10 Gore, *King George V*, p. 416. Helen Hardinge, *Loyal to Three Kings* (William Kimber, 1967), p. 51.

11 Crawford, *The Crawford Papers*, pp. 544–5.

12 James Stourton, *Kenneth Clark: Life, Art and 'Civilisation'* (William Collins, 2016), pp. 1–2.

13 Stourton, *Kenneth Clark*, pp. 99–100.

14 Rose, *Who's In, Who's Out*, p. 529.

15 RA GV/PRIV/GVD/17 May 1931.

16 Arthur Hamilton Lee, 'A Good Innings': The Private Papers of Viscount Lee of Fareham*, ed. Alan Clark (John Murray, 1974), p. 281.

17 Kenneth Rose, *King George V* (Phoenix Press, 2000), p. 313.

18 See above, p. 293.

19 Gore, *King George V*, pp. 447–50. See above, p. 87.

20 John Colville, *Footprints in Time*, new ed. (Michael Russell, 1984), pp. 40–1. Gore, *King George V*, p. 448.

21 Owen Morshead note in Gore, *King George V*, pp. 397–99.

22 Rose, *King George V*, p. 385. A. J. Sylvester, *Life with Lloyd George: The Diary of A. J. Sylvester*, ed. Colin Cross (Macmillan, 1975), pp. 93–4.

23 Helen Rappaport, *The Race to Save the Romanovs: The Truth behind the Secret Plans to Rescue Russia's*

Imperial Family (Hutchinson, 2018), p. 277.

24 Rose, *King George V*, p. 218. Sylvester, *Life with Lloyd George*, pp. 106–7.

25 Rappaport, *The Race to Save the Romanovs*, pp. 276–8.

26 Gore, *King George V*, p. 397.

27 Churchill Archive Centre, Godfrey-Faussett Papers, G to Godfrey-Faussett, 12 January 1925.

28 Gary Sheffield, ed., *In Haig's Shadow: The Letters of Major-General Hugo De Pree and Field Marshal Sir Douglas Haig* (Greenhill, 2019), p. 133, Wigram to De Pree (Haig's trustee), 22 February 1932.

29 Sheffield, ed., *In Haig's Shadow*, p. 138.

30 Wigram to De Pree, 22 September 1934 in Sheffield, ed., *In Haig's Shadow*, p. 139.

31 Sheffield, ed., *In Haig's Shadow*, p. 147.

32 RA GV/PRIV/GVD/24, 25, 26 April 1933.

33 RA AEC/GG/012, Morshead draft to Berenson, February 1936.

34 Balliol College Archive, Nicolson Diary, 10 May 1951.

35 Gore, *King George V*, p. 415.

36 Liverpool Library, Diaries of Sir Richard Molyneux, 920 SEF 6/10, 19, 20 April 1926. 920 SEF 6/11, 15 April 1927. Thanks to Bev Kelly.

37 Molyneux Diary, 14, 15 April 1933.

38 Rose, *Who's In, Who's Out*, p. 576.

39 Molyneux Diary, 920 SEF 6/17, 17–23 April 1933.

40 Queen Elizabeth the Queen Mother, *Counting One's Blessings: The Selected Letters of Queen Elizabeth the Queen Mother*, ed. William Shawcross (Macmillan, 2012), p. 187.

41 Edward, Duke of Windsor, *A King's Story: The Memoirs of HRH the Duke of Windsor* (Cassell, 1951), p. 235.

42 Lady Diana Cooper, *The Light of Common Day* (Vintage, 2018), pp. 148–9.

43 Sir Henry Channon, *Chips: The Diaries of Sir Henry Channon*, ed. Robert Rhodes James (Weidenfeld & Nicolson, 1967), p. 50.

44 RA GV/PRIV/CC4/300, G to M, 19 September 1931.

45 RA GV/PRIV/CC4/300, G to M, 19 September 1931.

46 Philip Ziegler, *King Edward VIII: The Official Biography* (Collins, 1990), p. 198.

47 Channon, *Chips*, p. 50.

48 Rose, *Who's In, Who's Out*, p. 546.

49 Duchess of York to M, 1 August 1933 in Elizabeth the Queen Mother, *Counting One's Blessings*, pp. 198–9.

50 M to Duchess of York, 20 August 1933 in Elizabeth the Queen Mother, *Counting One's Blessings*, p. 198.

51 J. Bryan III and Charles J. V. Murphy, *The Windsor Story* (Granada, 1979), p. 37. The flat sold for £5.3 million in 2015.

52 Bryan and Murphy, *The Windsor Story*, p. 39.

53 Michael Bloch, ed., *Wallis & Edward: Letters 1931–1937* (Weidenfeld & Nicolson, 1986), pp. 49–50.

54 Chamberlain, *The Neville Chamberlain Diary Letters*, Vol. 3, p. 402.

55 John Reith, *The Reith Diaries*, ed. Charles Stewart (Collins, 1975), pp. 183, 205.

56 Bloch, ed., *Wallis & Edward*, p. 89.

57 *Times* obituary, Lady Aitken, 9 February 2005. Information from Jonathan Aitken and Simon Jenkins. See Rose, *King George V*, pp. 55–6.

58 Getty Research Library, Pope 200/2, M to G, 24 August 1934.

59 Mabell, Countess of Airlie, *Thatched with Gold: The Memoirs of Mabell, Countess of Airlie*, ed. Jennifer Ellis (Hutchinson, 1962), p. 195.

60 Crawford, *The Crawford Papers*, pp. 555–6.

61 RA GV/PRIV/AA38/48, G to Alix, 1 October 1922.
62 Philip Eade, *Young Prince Philip: His Turbulent Early Life* (HarperPress, 2011), pp. 35–40.
63 Edward Owens, 'All the World Loves a Lover: The 1934 Royal Wedding of Prince George and Princess Marina' in *The Family Firm: Monarchy, Mass Media and the British Public 1932–53* (University of London Press, 2019).
64 Nicolson Diary, 12 August 1949.
65 Bloch, ed., *Wallis & Edward*, p. 105.
66 Rose, *King George V*, p. 392. Ziegler, *King Edward VIII*, p. 231.
67 Ivan Maisky, *The Maisky Diaries: Red Ambassador to the Court of St James's 1932–1943*, ed. Gabriel Gorodetsky (Yale University Press, 2015), p. 20.
68 G to Lang, 1 December 1934 in Owens, 'All the World Loves a Lover', pp. 83–4.
69 Maisky, *The Maisky Diaries*, p. 22.
70 Rose, *King George V*, p. 388.
71 Sir Henry Channon, *The Diaries 1918–38*, ed. Simon Heffer (Hutchinson, 2021), p. 365.
72 Rose, *King George V*, pp. 229–30.
73 Rose, *King George V*, p. 388.
74 Nicolson, *King George the Fifth*, pp. 521–2.
75 Nicolson, *King George the Fifth*, p. 522.
76 See Jonathan Petropoulos, *Royals and the Reich: The Princes von Hessen in Nazi Germany* (Oxford University Press, 2006), pp. 199–201. Tim Bouverie, *Appeasing Hitler: Chamberlain, Churchill and the Road to War* (Vintage, 2020), pp. 42–71.
77 The Devonshire Collections, Chatsworth, QM to Duchess Evie, 14 August 1934.
78 Pope, QMD, 27 February 1935.
79 Chatsworth, QM to Duchess Evie, 2 March 1935.
80 Pope 200/2, QMD, 3–5 April 1935.
81 Ziegler, *King Edward VIII*, pp. 232–3.
82 Richard Aldrich and Rory Cormac, *Spying on the Royals*, Channel 4, April 2017.
83 Ziegler, *King Edward VIII*, p. 231.
84 Ziegler, *King Edward VIII*, p. 233.
85 Pope-Hennessy, *Queen Mary*, p. 544.
86 'Royal Hanoverian Creams', The Regency Redingote blog, 30 April 2010 https://regencyredingote.wordpress.com/2010/04/30/royal-hanoverian-creams (accessed 28 June 2021).
87 Nancy Mitford, *Love from Nancy: The Letters of Nancy Mitford*, ed. Charlotte Mosley (Sceptre, 1994), p. 98.
88 Channon, *The Diaries 1918–38*, p. 424.
89 RA GV/PRIV/GVD/6 May 1935 in Nicolson, *King George the Fifth*, p. 524.
90 *The Times*, 7 May 1935.
91 Crawford, *The Crawford Papers*, p. 563.
92 *The Times*, 7 May 1935.
93 King George V, *The King to His People: Being the Speeches and Messages of HM King George the Fifth* (Williams & Norgate, 1935), p. 299.
94 Mitford, *Love from Nancy*, p. 99.
95 RA GV/PRIV/GVD/9 May 1935 in Nicolson, *King George the Fifth*, p. 524.
96 Gore, *King George V*, p. 431.
97 *The Times*, 10 May 1935.
98 Robert Bernays, *The Diaries and Letters of Robert Bernays*, ed. Nick Smart (Edwin Mellen Press, 1996), p.195.
99 Nicolson, *King George the Fifth*, p. 526.
100 Bloch, ed., *Wallis & Edward*, p. 120.
101 Ziegler, *King Edward VIII*, p. 233.
102 Channon, *The Diaries 1918–38*, pp. 381, 427.
103 Channon, *The Diaries 1918–38*, pp. 437, 469.
104 G to Hitler, 8 May 1935 in *The Times*, 9 May 1935.

CHAPTER 29

Lord Dawson's Syringe

1 Sir Henry Channon, *The Diaries 1918–38*, ed. Simon Heffer (Hutchinson, 2021), p. 431, 3 June 1935.

2 Wigram Papers, Nora to father, 17 May 1935.

3 Channon, *The Diaries 1918–38*, pp. 482–3.

4 Frances Stevenson, *Lloyd George: A Diary*, ed. A.J.P. Taylor (Hutchinson, 1971), p. 309.

5 Viscount Templewood, *Nine Troubled Years* (Collins, 1954), p. 160.

6 Arthur Hamilton Lee, 'A Good Innings': The Private Papers of Viscount Lee of Fareham*, ed. Alan Clark (John Murray, 1974), p. 321.

7 Robert Bernays, *The Diaries and Letters of Robert Bernays*, ed. Nick Smart (Edwin Mellen Press, 1996), p. 123, 23 March 1934.

8 Nancy Mitford, *Love from Nancy: The Letters of Nancy Mitford*, ed. Charlotte Mosley (Sceptre, 1994), p. 98.

9 Getty Research Library, Pope 200/2, QMD, 11, 25 June 1935.

10 Francis Watson, *Dawson of Penn* (Chatto & Windus, 1950), p. 273.

11 Queen Elizabeth the Queen Mother, *Counting One's Blessings: The Selected Letters of Queen Elizabeth the Queen Mother*, ed. William Shawcross (Macmillan, 2012), p. 2–4. RA EDW/PRIV/MAIN/A/2720, M to David, 13 August 1935.

12 Channon, *The Diaries 1918–38*, p. 464.

13 RA GV/PRIV/CC4/304, G to M, 26 August 1935.

14 RA EDW/PRIV/MAIN/A2723, M to David, 10 September 1935.

15 Princess Alice, Duchess of Gloucester, *The Memoirs of Princess Alice, Duchess of Gloucester* (Collins, 1983), p. 107.

16 Lee, 'A Good Innings', pp. 328–9.

17 Robert Beaken, *Cosmo Lang: Archbishop in War and Crisis* (I. B. Tauris, 2012), p. 80.

18 Mabell, Countess of Airlie, *Thatched with Gold: The Memoirs of Mabell, Countess of Airlie*, ed. Jennifer Ellis (Hutchinson, 1962), p. 197.

19 Leo Amery, *The Leo Amery Diaries, Vol. 2: 1929–1945 – The Empire at Bay*, ed. by John Barnes and David Nicholson (Hutchinson, 1988), p. 446, 4 July 1937. Amery was told this by Lang.

20 RA GV/PRIV/CC4/304, G to M, 26 August 1935.

21 RA GV/PRIV/GVD/6 November 1935 in John Gore, *King George V: A Personal Memoir* (John Murray, 1941), p. 435.

22 Keith Middlemas and John Barnes, *Baldwin: A Biography* (Weidenfeld & Nicolson, 1969), p. 976. Philip Ziegler, *King Edward VIII: The Official Biography* (Collins, 1990), p. 199.

23 Sir Alan Lascelles, *King's Counsellor: Abdication and War – The Diaries of Sir Alan Lascelles*, ed. Duff Hart-Davis (Phoenix, 2007), p. 107.

24 Airlie, *Thatched with Gold*, p. 197.

25 Templewood, *Nine Troubled Years*, p. 199.

26 Earl of Avon, *The Eden Memoirs, Vol. 1: Facing the Dictators* (Cassell, 1962), p. 317.

27 RA PRIV/GVD/3 December 1935 in Gore, *King George V*, p. 436.

28 Pope 200/2, QMD, 3 December 1935.

29 Pope 200/2, QMD, 4 January 1936.

30 *Hail and Farewell: The Passing of King George V* (The Times, 1936), p. 2.

31 Michael Bloch, ed., *Wallis & Edward: Letters 1931–1937* (Weidenfeld & Nicolson, 1986), p. 145.

32 Edward, Duke of Windsor, *A King's Story: The Memoirs of HRH the*

Duke of Windsor (Cassell, 1951), p. 260.

33 Bloch, ed., *Wallis & Edward*, p. 137.
34 Windsor, *A King's Story*, p. 260.
35 Pope 200/2, QMD, 21 January 1936.
36 Watson, *Dawson of Penn*, p. 275.
37 Pope 200/2, QMD, 15 January 1936.
38 Pope 200/2, QMD, 16 January 1936. Sir Alan Lascelles, *In Royal Service: The Letters and Journals of Sir Alan Lascelles, Vol. 2*, ed. Duff Hart-Davis (Hamish Hamilton, 1989), p. 196.
39 Lascelles, *In Royal Service*, pp. 193, 196.
40 Windsor, *A King's Story*, p. 261.
41 Bloch, ed., *Wallis & Edward*, p. 147.
42 Pope 202/2, QMD, 17 January 1936.
43 Lascelles, *In Royal Service*, p. 194.
44 Pope 202/2, QMD, 17 January 1936.
45 Watson, *Dawson of Penn*, p. 276.
46 RA GV/PRIV/GVD/17 January 1936 in Gore, *King George V*, p. 440.
47 RA GV/PRIV/GVD/14 February 1936 in Gore, *King George V*, p. 440.
48 *Hail and Farewell*, p. 4.
49 Pope 200/2, QMD, 18 January 1936.
50 Francis Watson, 'The Death of George V', *History Today*, December 1986, p. 27. Pope 200/2, QMD, 18 January 1936. Windsor, *A King's Story*, p. 262.
51 Pope 200/2, QMD, 18 January 1936.
52 *Hail and Farewell*, p. 7. Channon, *The Diaries 1918–38*, p. 494.
53 Bloch, ed., *Wallis & Edward*, p. 148.
54 Pope 200/2, QMD, 19 January 1936.
55 Duff Cooper, *The Duff Cooper Diaries*, ed. John Julius Norwich (Weidenfeld & Nicolson, 2005), p. 226.
56 Windsor, *A King's Story*, pp. 263–4.
57 Lambeth Palace, Cosmo Lang Papers, Vol. 223, Lang's Memo, 'The Death of King George V, 20 January 1936, f. 217.

58 Pope 200/2, QMD, 20 January 1936.
59 Watson, *Dawson of Penn*, p. 278.
60 Pope 200/2, QMD, 20 January 1936.
61 Pope 200/2, QMD, 20 January 1936.
62 *Hail and Farewell*, p. 13.
63 Watson, 'The Death of George V', p. 27.
64 Watson, 'The Death of George V', p. 28.
65 Lambeth Palace, Cosmo Lang Papers, Vol. 223, Lang's Memo, 'The Death of King George V, 20 January 1936, f. 221.
66 Watson, 'The Death of George V', p. 28.
67 Pope 200/2, QMD, 20 January 1936.
68 John Evelyn Wrench, *Geoffrey Dawson and Our Times* (Hutchinson, 1955), p. 328.
69 Watson, 'The Death of George V', p. 28.
70 See J.H.R. Ramsay, 'A King, a Doctor, and a Convenient Death', *British Medical Journal*, vol. 308, no. 6941 (1994), p. 1445.
71 Kenneth Rose, *Who Loses, Who Wins: The Journals of Kenneth Rose, Vol. 2*, ed. D. R. Thorpe (Weidenfeld & Nicolson, 2019), p. 422.
72 Windsor, *A King's Story*, p. 263.
73 Virginia Woolf, *The Diary of Virginia Woolf, Vol. 5: 1936–1941*, ed. by Anne Olivier Bell (Penguin, 1985), p. 10.
74 Bernays, *The Diaries and Letters of Robert Bernays*, p. 234.
75 Ivan Maisky, *The Maisky Diaries: Red Ambassador to the Court of St James's 1932–1943*, ed. Gabriel Gorodetsky (Yale University Press, 2015), p. 58–9.
76 Lord Grantley, *Silver Spoon: Being Extracts from the Random Reminiscences of Lord Grantley*, ed. Mary and Alan Wood (Hutchinson, 1954), pp. 171–2.
77 Watson, 'The Death of George V', p. 27. Lascelles, *In Royal Service*, p. 198.

78 Woolf, *The Diary of Virginia Woolf,
    Vol. 5*, p. 11. Bernays, *The Diaries
    and Letters of Robert Bernays*, p. 234.
79 Avon, *The Eden Memoirs, Vol. 1*,
    p. 52.
80 Watson, 'The Death of George V',
    p. 28.
81 Kenneth Rose, *King George V*
    (Phoenix Press, 2000), p. 297.
82 Ziegler, *King Edward VIII*, p. 241.
    Windsor, *A King's Story*, p. 264.
83 Ziegler, *King Edward VIII*, pp.
    241–2. Frances Donaldson, *Edward
    VIII* (Weidenfeld & Nicolson,
    1974), pp. 177–8.
84 Pope 200/2, QMD, 20 January 1936.
85 Windsor, *A King's Story*, p. 265.
86 Lascelles, *In Royal Service*, p. 198.
    Ettie Desborough in Watson,
    Dawson of Penn, p. 281.
87 Pope 200/2, QMD, 21 January 1936.
88 Lascelles, *In Royal Service*, p. 199.
    Windsor, *A King's Story*, pp. 266–7.
89 Channon, *The Diaries 1918–38*,
    p. 497. Bernays, *The Diaries and
    Letters of Robert Bernays*, p. 234.
90 Pope 200/2, QMD, 28 January
    1936.
91 Bernays, *The Diaries and Letters of
    Robert Bernays*, p. 236.
92 Bernays, *The Diaries and Letters of
    Robert Bernays*, p. 236. Channon,
    The Diaries 1918–38, p. 501.
93 Channon, *The Diaries 1918–38*,
    p. 501.
94 James Pope-Hennessy, *Queen Mary*
    (Phoenix Press, 2000), p. 562.
95 Pope 200/2, QMD, 28 January 1936.
96 Pope 200/2, QMD, 24 January 1936.
97 Pope 200/2, QMD, 24 January
    1936. George Godfrey-Faussett,
    *Royal Servant, Family Friend: The
    Life and Times of Sir Bryan
    Godfrey-Faussett* (Bernard
    Durnford, 2004), p. 317.

CONCLUSION

1   Frances Donaldson, *Edward VIII*
    (Weidenfeld & Nicolson, 1974), p.
    181. Edward, Duke of Windsor, *A
    King's Story: The Memoirs of HRH
    the Duke of Windsor* (Cassell,
    1951), p. 267. Sir Henry Channon,
    The Diaries 1918–38, ed. Simon
    Heffer (Hutchinson, 2021), p. 497.
    Kenneth Rose, *King George V*
    (Phoenix Press, 2000), p. 403.
2   Anna Keay, *The Crown Jewels*
    (Thames & Hudson, 2011) p. 174.
3   Rose, *King George V*, p. 406. This
    is the first version of the poem; in
    the later version the penultimate
    line was changed to 'At the new
    suburb stretching beyond the
    runway'. Kenneth Rose, *Who's In,
    Who's Out: The Journals of
    Kenneth Rose, Vol. 1*, ed. D. R.
    Thorpe (Weidenfeld & Nicolson,
    2018), p. 557. Kenneth Rose, *Who
    Loses, Who Wins: The Journals of
    Kenneth Rose, Vol. 2*, ed. D. R.
    Thorpe (Weidenfeld & Nicolson,
    2019), p. 415. Jonathan Bate,
    'Death of King George V', *The
    Poetry of History*, Series 2, BBC
    Radio 4, 16 December 2007.
    Betjeman was a friend of the
    Maffey family, and this gave him a
    glimpse into the Sandringham
    world of George V.
4   Kingsley Martin, *The Crown and
    the Establishment* (Penguin 1963),
    pp. 18–19.
5   Virginia Woolf, *The Diary of
    Virginia Woolf, Vol. 5: 1936–1941*,
    ed. by Anne Olivier Bell (Penguin,
    1985), p. 42.
6   Channon, *The Diaries 1918–38*,
    pp. 939–40.
7   Sir Alan Lascelles, *King's
    Counsellor: Abdication and
    War – The Diaries of Sir Alan
    Lascelles*, ed. Duff Hart-Davis
    (Phoenix, 2007), p. 107.
8   Windsor, *A King's Story*, pp. 258–60.
9   Donaldson, *Edward VIII*, p. 173.
10 James Pope-Hennessy, *Queen Mary*
    (Phoenix Press, 2000), p. 572.
11 RA EDW/PRIV/MAIN/A/3101, M
    to David, 16 December 1936.
12 George Godfrey-Faussett, *Royal
    Servant, Family Friend: The Life
    and Times of Sir Bryan*

Godfrey-Faussett (Bernard Durnford, 2004), p. 316. Channon, *The Diaries 1918–38*, p. 494.

13 Ross McKibbin, *Classes and Cultures: England 1918–1951* (Oxford University Press, 1998), pp. 3–4.

14 King George V, *The King to His People: Being the Speeches and Messages of HM King George the Fifth* (Williams & Norgate, 1935), p. 308.

15 *Hail and Farewell: The Passing of King George V* (The Times, 1936), pp. 153–4.

16 Windsor, *A King's Story*, pp. 278–9.

17 Lascelles, *King's Counsellor*, p. 433.

18 The Devonshire Collections, Chatsworth, DF 15/3/3/1/3, Ettie Desborough to Evie, Duchess of Devonshire, n.d. [1936].

19 Getty Research Library, Pope 195/3, Owen Morshead note for Pope-Hennessy on Queen Mary, n.d., p. 4.

20 Pope 200/2, QMD, 1 October 1936.

21 Pope 200/2, QMD, 13 July 1936.

22 Channon, *The Diaries 1918–38*, p. 604.

23 Pope 200/2, Note from Morshead re G. M. Young.

24 James Pope-Hennessy, *The Quest for Queen Mary*, ed. Hugo Vickers (Zuleika, 2018), p. 121 (Maggie Wyndham).

25 Pope 200/2, Lady Bertha Dawkins, 27 March 1937.

26 Pope-Hennessy, *Queen Mary*, p. 575.

27 Mabell, Countess of Airlie, *Thatched with Gold: The Memoirs of Mabell, Countess of Airlie*, ed. Jennifer Ellis (Hutchinson, 1962), p. 200.

28 Airlie, *Thatched with Gold*, p. 201.

29 Author information from Iain Scott, 11 March 2021. Pope-Hennessy, *The Quest for Queen Mary*, p. 128 (Lady Shaftesbury).

30 Pope-Hennessy, *The Quest for Queen Mary*, pp. 119, 128.

31 Pope 194/5, Interview with Princess Alice, 29 April 1957.

32 Airlie, *Thatched with Gold*, p. 208.

33 John Wheeler-Bennett, *King George VI: His Life and Reign* (Macmillan, 1958), p. 283. Queen Elizabeth the Queen Mother, *Counting One's Blessings: The Selected Letters of Queen Elizabeth the Queen Mother*, ed. William Shawcross (Macmillan, 2012), p. 229.

34 Balliol College Archive, Nicolson Diary, 27 July 1949 (Lord Carisbrooke).

35 Pope-Hennessy, *The Quest for Queen Mary*, p. 115 (Maggie Wyndham).

36 Osbert Sitwell, *Queen Mary and Others* (Michael Joseph, 1974), p. 40.

37 RA QM/PRIV/CC24/49, M to Augusta, 7 April 1906.

38 Pope-Hennessy, *The Quest for Queen Mary*, p. 119 (Margaret Wyndham).

39 Airlie, *Thatched with Gold*, p. 207. Pope-Hennessy, *The Quest for Queen Mary*, p. 144 (Lord Claud Hamilton).

40 Chatsworth, DF15/3/3/1/3, Lady Airlie to Duchess of Devonshire, 6 February 1936; QM to Duchess of Devonshire, 17 February 1936; QM, 'Household of Queen Mary', n.d.

41 Chatsworth, DF15/3/3/1/3, Lady Constance Milnes Gaskell to Duchess of Devonshire, 26 May 1939.

42 Pope-Hennessy, *The Quest for Queen Mary*, p. 235.

43 Sitwell, *Queen Mary and Others*, p. 38.

44 Pope-Hennessy, *The Quest for Queen Mary*, p.142 (Lord Claud Hamilton).

45 Pope-Hennessy, *The Quest for Queen Mary*, pp. 300–1 (Duchess of Beaufort).

46 Pope-Hennessy, *The Quest for Queen Mary*, p. 307.

47 Pope-Hennessy, *Queen Mary*, pp. 612, 614.

48 Pope-Hennessy, *The Quest for Queen Mary*, p. 144 (Lord Claud Hamilton).

49 Pope-Hennessy, *The Quest for Queen Mary*, p. 234 (Daisy Bigge).

50 Chatsworth, DF15/3/3/1/3, Cynthia Colville to Duchess of Devonshire, 1 December 1945. QM to Duchess of Devonshire, 2 February 1946. Cynthia Colville to Duchess of Devonshire, 16 February 1946.

51 Rose, *Who's In, Who's Out*, p. 321.

52 Rose, *King George V*, p. 284.

53 James Lees-Milne, *The Milk of Paradise: Diaries 1993–97*, ed. Michael Bloch (John Murray, 2005), 19 June 1993.

54 Patsy Grigg Papers, Mark Gambier-Parry, 'Queen Mary's Visit to Highnam', 14 September 1939.

55 Airlie, *Thatched with Gold*, p. 304.

Bibliography

Aidin, Michael, 'Kipling and the Commemoration of the Dead of the Great War', *Kipling Journal*, vol. 81, no. 324 (2007)

Airlie, Mabell, Countess of, *Thatched with Gold: The Memoirs of Mabell, Countess of Airlie*, ed. Jennifer Ellis (Hutchinson, 1962)

Albert Victor, Prince, Duke of Clarence and Avondale, and Prince George of Wales, *The Cruise of Her Majesty's Ship 'Bacchante' 1879–82*, 2 vols (Macmillan, 1886)

Amery, Leo, *The Leo Amery Diaries*, ed. John Barnes and David Nicholson, 2 vols (Hutchinson, 1980, 1988)

Anand, Anita, *Sophia: Princess, Suffragette, Revolutionary* (Bloomsbury, 2015)

Aronson, Theo, *Prince Eddy and the Homosexual Underworld* (John Murray, 1994)

Arthur, Sir George, *Queen Mary* (Thornton Butterworth, 1935)

Asquith, Lady Cynthia, *Diaries 1915–1918* (Hutchinson, 1968)

Asquith, H. H., *Letters to Venetia Stanley*, ed. Michael and Eleanor Brock (Oxford University Press, 1982)

Asquith, Margot, *Margot Asquith's Great War Diary 1914–1916: The View from Downing Street*, ed. Michael and Eleanor Brock (Oxford University Press, 2014)

Avon, Earl of, *The Eden Memoirs, Vol. 1: Facing the Dictators* (Cassell, 1962)

Bagehot, Walter, *The English Constitution* (Chapman & Hall, 1867)

Bailey, Catherine, *Black Diamonds: The Rise and Fall of an English Dynasty* (Penguin, 2008)

Barron, Hester, 'Labour Identities of the Coalfield: The General Election of 1931 in County Durham', *History*, vol. 97, no. 326 (2012)

Basu, Shrabani, *Victoria & Abdul: The True Story of the Queen's Closest Confidant* (History Press, 2010)

Battiscombe, Georgina, *Queen Alexandra* (Constable, 1969)

Beaken, Robert, *Cosmo Lang: Archbishop in War and Crisis* (I. B. Tauris, 2012)

Beckett, Ian, 'King George V and His Generals' in Matthew Hughes and Matthew Seligman, eds, *Leadership in Conflict 1914–1918* (Leo Cooper, 2000)

Bennett, Alan, *The Uncommon Reader* (Faber, 2006)

Bernays, Robert, *The Diaries and Letters of Robert Bernays 1932–1939*, ed. Nick Smart (Edwin Mellen Press, 1996)

Birkenhead, Earl of, *The Life of F. E. Smith, First Earl of Birkenhead* (Eyre & Spottiswoode, 1959)

Black, Sister Catherine, *King's Nurse, Beggar's Nurse* (Hurst & Blackett, 1939)

Blake, Robert, *The Unknown Prime Minister: The Life and Times of Andrew Bonar Law, 1858–1923* (Eyre & Spottiswoode, 1955)

Blake, Robert, ed., *The Private Papers of Douglas Haig* (Eyre & Spottiswoode, 1952)

Bloch, Michael, *Closet Queens: Some 20th-Century British Politicians* (Abacus, 2016)

Bloch, Michael, ed., *Wallis & Edward: Letters 1931–1937* (Weidenfeld & Nicolson, 1986)

Bogdanor, Vernon, '1931 Revisited: The Constitutional Aspects', *Twentieth Century British History*, vol. 2, no. 1 (1991); *The Monarchy and the Constitution* (Clarendon Press, 1995)

Bond, Brian, 'Fortescue, Sir John William (1859–1933)', *Oxford Dictionary of National Biography* (2004)

Bonham Carter, Violet, *Lantern Slides: The Diaries and Letters of Violet Bonham Carter 1904–1914*, ed. Mark Bonham Carter and Mark Pottle (Weidenfeld & Nicolson, 1996); *Champion Redoubtable: The Diaries and Letters of Violet Bonham Carter 1914–1945*, ed. Mark Pottle (Weidenfeld & Nicolson, 1998)

Bouverie, Tim, *Appeasing Hitler: Chamberlain, Churchill and the Road to War* (Vintage, 2020)

Bradford, Sarah, *King George VI* (Weidenfeld & Nicolson, 1989)

Bradley, Kate, 'Saving the Children of Shoreditch: Lady Cynthia Colville and Needy Families in East London c.1900–1960', *Law, Crime and History*, vol. 7, no. 1 (2017)

Brendon, Piers and Philip Whitehead, *The Windsors: A Dynasty Revealed*, rev. ed. (Pimlico, 2000)

Brindle, Stephen, 'Buckingham Palace and the Victoria Memorial 1901–14', *Court Historian*, vol. 11, no. 1 (2006)

Bryan, J., III, and Charles J. V. Murphy, *The Windsor Story* (Granada, 1979)

Byrne, Paula, *Mad World: Evelyn Waugh and the Secrets of Brideshead* (HarperPress, 2009)

Cadbury, Deborah, *Queen Victoria's Matchmaking: The Royal Marriages That Shaped Europe* (Bloomsbury, 2017)

Callendar Smith, Robin, 'The Missing Witness? George V, Competence, Compellability and the Criminal Trial of Edward Frederick Mylius', *Journal of Legal History*, vol. 33, no. 2 (2012)

Cannadine, David, *Ornamentalism: How the British Saw Their Empire* (Allen Lane, 2001); *George V: The Unexpected King* (Allen Lane, 2014)

Carter, Miranda, *The Three Emperors: Three Cousins, Three Empires and the Road to World War One* (Fig Tree, 2009)

Chamberlain, Neville, *The Neville Chamberlain Diary Letters*, ed. Robert Self, 4 vols (Ashgate, 2000–5)

Chandos, Viscount, *The Memoirs of Lord Chandos* (Bodley Head, 1962)

Channon, Sir Henry, *Chips: The Diaries of Sir Henry Channon*, ed. Robert Rhodes James (Weidenfeld & Nicolson, 1967); *The Diaries 1918–38*, ed. Simon Heffer (Hutchinson, 2021)

Churchill, Alexandra, *In the Eye of the Storm: George V and the Great War* (Helion, 2018)

Churchill, Randolph S., *Winston S. Churchill, Vol. 2: Young Statesman 1901–1914* (Heinemann, 1967)

Churchill, Winston S., *Great Contemporaries* (Thornton Butterworth, 1937)

Clark, Christopher, *The Sleepwalkers: How Europe Went to War in 1914* (Allen Lane, 2012)

Clark, Ronald W., *Balmoral: Queen Victoria's Highland Home* (Thames & Hudson, 1981)

Clarke, William, 'How the Dowager Empress's Jewels Survived a Revolution' in Ole Villumsen Krog, ed., *Maria Feodorovna, Empress of Russia: An Exhibition* (Copenhagen: Christiansborg Palace, 1997)

Clary, Prince, *A European Past: Memoirs* (St Martin's Press, 1978)

Colville, Lady Cynthia, *Crowded Life* (Evans Brothers, 1963)

Colville, John, *Footprints in Time*, new ed. (Michael Russell, 1984)

Cook, Andrew, *Prince Eddy: The King Britain Never Had* (History Press, 2008)

Cooke, C. Kinloch, *A Memoir of HRH Mary Adelaide Duchess of Teck*, 2 vols (John Murray, 1900)

Cooper, Artemis, ed., *A Durable Fire: The Letters of Duff and Diana Cooper 1913–1950* (Collins, 1983)

Cooper, Lady Diana, *The Light of Common Day* (Vintage, [1959] 2018)

Cooper, Duff, *The Duff Cooper Diaries*, ed. John Julius Norwich (Weidenfeld & Nicolson, 2005)

Cornwell, Patricia, *Portrait of a Killer: Jack the Ripper – Case Closed* (Sphere, 2003)

Courtney, Nicholas, *The Queen's Stamps: The Authorised History of the Royal Philatelic Collection* (Methuen, 2004)

Crawford, Earl of, *The Crawford Papers: The Journals of David Lindsay, 27th Earl of Crawford and 10th Earl of Balcarres (1871–1940), during the Years 1892 to 1940*, ed. John Vincent (Manchester University Press, 1984)

Crawford, Marion, *The Little Princesses* (Orion, [1950] 2003)

Dalton, Hugh, *The Political Diary of Hugh Dalton 1918–40, 1945–60*, ed. Ben Pimlott (Jonathan Cape, 1981)

Dangerfield, George, *The Strange Death of Liberal England* (Constable, 1936)

Davenport-Hines, Richard, 'Gregory, Arthur John Peter Michael Maundy (1877–1941), *Oxford Dictionary of National Biography* (2004); 'Lygon, William, Seventh Earl Beauchamp (1872–1938)', *Oxford Dictionary of National Biography* (2004); *Ettie: The Intimate Life and Dauntless Spirit of Lady Desborough* (Weidenfeld & Nicolson, 2008); *Edward VII: The Cosmopolitan King* (Allen Lane, 2016); *Enemies Within: Communists and the Making of Modern Britain* (William Collins, 2018)

David, Edward, ed., *Inside Asquith's Cabinet: From the Diaries of Charles Hobhouse* (John Murray, 1977)

Day, J. Wentworth, *King George V as a Sportsman* (Cassell, 1935)

de Courcy, Anne, *The Viceroy's Daughters: The Lives of the Curzon Sisters* (Phoenix, 2001); *Margot at War: Love and Betrayal in Downing Street 1912–1916* (Weidenfeld & Nicolson, 2014)

Devonshire, Deborah, *Wait for Me! Memoirs of the Youngest Mitford Sister* (John Murray, 2010)

Donaldson, Frances, *Edward VIII* (Weidenfeld & Nicolson, 1974)

Dorment, Richard, *Alfred Gilbert* (Yale University Press, 1985); 'Gilbert, Sir Alfred (1954–1934)', *Oxford Dictionary of National Biography* (2004)

Douglas-Home, Jessica, *A Glimpse of Empire* (Michael Russell, 2011)

Duff, David, *Queen Mary* (Collins, 1985)

Dykes, Christina, 'Sir Philip Hunloke: The Sailing King's Sailor' (unpublished MA dissertation, University of Buckingham, 2014); 'Hugh Richard Arthur Grosvenor, 2nd Duke of Westminster (1879–1953), known as "Bend'Or": A Reappraisal' (PhD thesis, University of Buckingham, 2021)

Eade, Philip, *Young Prince Philip: His Turbulent Early Life* (HarperPress, 2011)

Egremont, Max, *Balfour: A Life of Arthur James Balfour* (Collins, 1980)

Elizabeth, Queen, the Queen Mother, *Counting One's Blessings: The Selected Letters of Queen Elizabeth the Queen Mother*, ed. William Shawcross (Macmillan, 2012)

Esher, Reginald, Viscount, *Journals and Letters of Reginald, Viscount Esher*, ed. Maurice V. Brett (vols 1 & 2) and Oliver, Viscount Esher (vols 3 & 4) (Ivor Nicholson & Watson, 1934–8)

Fergusson of Kilkerran, Sir James, *The Curragh Incident* (Faber & Faber, 1964)

Field, Leslie, *The Queen's Jewels: The Personal Collection of Elizabeth II* (Harry N. Abrams, 1987)

FitzRoy, Sir Almeric, *Memoirs*, 2 vols (Hutchinson, 1925)

Forester, C. S., *The General* (William Collins, [1936] 2014)

Fortescue, Sir John, *Narrative of the Visit to India of Their Majesties King George V and Queen Mary* (Macmillan, 1912)

Frankland, Noble, *Prince Henry, Duke of Gloucester* (Weidenfeld & Nicolson, 1980)

Frederick, Empress, *The Empress Frederick Writes to Sophie: Letters 1889–1901*, ed. Arthur Gould Lee (Faber & Faber, 1955)

Friedman, Dennis, *Darling Georgie: The Enigma of King George V* (Peter Owen, 1998)

Fulford, Roger, *Hanover to Windsor* (Fontana, 1966)

Fulford, Roger, ed., *Your Dear Letter: Private Correspondence of Queen Victoria and the Crown Princess of Prussia 1865–1871* (Evans Brothers, 1971); *Darling Child: Private Correspondence of Queen Victoria and the Crown Princess of Prussia 1871–1878* (Evans Brothers, 1976)

Fussell, Paul, *The Great War and Modern Memory*, pb ed. (Oxford University Press, 1977)

Gelardi, Julia, *Born to Rule: Granddaughters of Victoria, Queens of Europe* (Headline, 2004)

George V, King, *The King to His People: Being the Speeches and Messages of HM King George the Fifth* (Williams & Norgate, 1935)

Gilbert, Martin, ed., *Servant of India: A Study of Imperial Rule from 1905 to 1910 as Told through the Correspondence and Diaries of Sir James Dunlop Smith* (Longmans, 1966)

Gilmour, David, *Curzon* (John Murray, 1994); *The Long Recessional: The Imperial Life of Rudyard Kipling* (John Murray, 2002)

Girouard, Mark, *Windsor: The Most Romantic Castle* (Hodder & Stoughton, 1993)

Glenconner, Anne, *Lady in Waiting: My Extraordinary Life in the Shadow of the Crown* (Hodder & Stoughton, 2019)

Gloucester, Princess Alice, Duchess of, *The Memoirs of Princess Alice, Duchess of Gloucester* (Collins, 1983)

Godfrey, Rupert, ed., *Letters from a Prince: Edward, Prince of Wales to Mrs Freda Dudley Ward, March 1918–January 1921* (Little, Brown, 1998)

Godfrey-Faussett, George, *Royal Servant, Family Friend: The Life and Times of Naval Equerry Captain Sir Bryan Godfrey-Faussett RN* (Bernard Durnford, 2004)

Gordon, Andrew, *The Rules of the Game: Jutland and British Naval Command* (Penguin, 2015)

Gore, John, *King George V: A Personal Memoir* (John Murray, 1941)

Graeme, Bruce, *A Century of Buckingham Palace 1837–1937* (Hutchinson, 1937)

Grantley, Lord, *Silver Spoon: Being Extracts from the Random Reminiscences of Lord Grantley*, ed. Mary and Alan Wood (Hutchinson, 1954)

Gray, Robert, 'FitzRoy, Sir Almeric (1851–1935)', *Oxford Dictionary of National Biography* (2004)

Grossmith, George, and Weedon Grossmith, *The Diary of a Nobody* (Penguin, [1892] 1965)

Haggard, Sir H. Rider, *The Private Diaries of Sir H. Rider Haggard 1914–1925*, ed. D. S. Higgins (Cassell, 1980)

Haig, Countess, *The Man I Knew* (Moray Press, 1936)

Haig, Douglas, *War Diaries and Letters 1914–1918*, ed. Gary Sheffield and John Bourne (Weidenfeld & Nicolson, 2005)

Hail and Farewell: The Passing of King George V (The Times, 1936)

Hall, Philip, *Royal Fortune: Tax, Money and the Monarchy* (Bloomsbury, 1992)

Hamilton, Sir Edward Walter, *The Diary of Sir Edward Walter Hamilton 1885–1906*, ed. Dudley W. R. Bahlman (University of Hull Press, 1993)

Hardinge, Helen, *Loyal to Three Kings* (William Kimber, 1967)

Harewood, Lord, *The Tongs and the Bones: The Memoirs of Lord Harewood* (Weidenfeld & Nicolson, 1981)

Harris, Steve, *The Prince and the Assassin: Australia's First Royal Tour and Portent of World Terror* (Melbourne Books, 2017)

Hearder, H., 'King George V, the General Strike, and the 1931 Crisis' in H. Hearder and H. R. Loyn (eds), *British Government and Administration: Studies Presented to S. B. Chrimes* (University of Wales Press, 1974)

Heffer, Simon, *The Age of Decadence: Britain 1880 to 1914* (Random House, 2017); *Staring at God: Britain in the Great War* (Random House, 2019)

Herrmann, Frank, *Sotheby's: Portrait of an Auction House* (Chatto & Windus, 1980)

Hillier, Bevis, *The Virgin's Baby: The Battle of the Ampthill Succession* (Hopcyn Press, 2013)

Holmes, Jennifer, *A Working Woman: The Remarkable Life of Ray Strachey* (Matador, 2019)

Holmes, Richard, *Edward VII: His Life and Times*, 2 vols (Amalgamated Press, 1911)

Holroyd, Michael, *A Book of Secrets: Illegitimate Daughters, Absent Fathers* (Chatto & Windus, 2010)

Hussey, Christopher, *The Life of Sir Edwin Lutyens* (Country Life, 1950)

Hyam, Ronald, *Empire and Sexuality: The British Experience* (Manchester University Press, 1990)

Jenkins, Roy, *Asquith* (Collins, 1964)

Jolliffe, John, ed., *Raymond Asquith: Life and Letters* (Collins, 1980)

Jones, Kathryn, 'Queen Mary as Collector', unpublished paper (2014)

Jones, Thomas, *Whitehall Diary*, ed. Keith Middlemas, 2 vols (Oxford University Press, 1969–71)

Judd, Alan, *Ford Madox Ford* (Collins, 1990); *The Kaiser's Last Kiss* (HarperPerennial, 2004)

Keay, Anna, *The Crown Jewels* (Thames & Hudson, 2011); *Landmark: A History of Britain in 50 Buildings* (Frances Lincoln, 2015)

Knight, Sam, '"London Bridge is down": the secret plan for the days after the Queen's death', *Guardian*, 17 March 2017.

Lambton, Lucinda, *The Queen's Dolls' House* (Royal Collection Trust, 2010)

Lascelles, Sir Alan, *In Royal Service: The Letters and Journals of Sir Alan Lascelles, Vol. 2*, ed. Duff Hart-Davis (Hamish Hamilton, 1989); *King's Counsellor: Abdication and War – The Diaries of Sir Alan Lascelles*, ed. Duff Hart-Davis (Phoenix, 2007)

Lavery, Sir John, *The Life of a Painter* (Cassell, 1940)

Lee, Arthur Hamilton, *'A Good Innings': The Private Papers of Viscount Lee of Fareham*, ed. Alan Clark (John Murray, 1974)

Lee, Sir Sidney, *King Edward VII: A Biography*, 2 vols (Macmillan, 1925–7)

Lees-Milne, James, *Harold Nicolson: A Biography*, 2 vols (Chatto & Windus, 1980–1); *The Enigmatic Edwardian: The Life of Reginald, 2nd Viscount Esher* (Sidgwick & Jackson, 1986); *Ceaseless Turmoil: Diaries 1988–1992*, ed. Michael Bloch (John Murray, 2004); *The Milk of Paradise: Diaries 1993–1997*, ed. Michael Bloch (John Murray, 2005); *Diaries 1984–1997*, ed. Michael Bloch (John Murray, 2008)

Lovell, Mary S., *Straight on till Morning: The Biography of Beryl Markham* (Hutchinson, 1987)

Lownie, Andrew, *The Mountbattens: Their Lives and Loves* (Blink, 2019)

McKibbin, Ross, *Classes and Cultures: England 1918–1951* (Oxford University Press, 1998)

McLean, Roderick, *Royalty and Diplomacy in Europe 1890–1914* (Cambridge University Press, 2001); 'Kaiser Wilhelm II and the British Royal Family: Anglo-German Dynastic Relations in Political Context 1890–1914', *History*, vol. 86, no. 284 (2002)

Macready, General the Rt Hon. Sir Nevil, *Annals of an Active Life*, 2 vols (Hutchinson, 1924)

Madan, Geoffrey, *Geoffrey Madan's Notebooks: A Selection*, ed. J. A. Gere and John Sparrow (Oxford University Press, 1981)

Magnus, Philip, *King Edward the Seventh* (John Murray, 1964)

Maisky, Ivan, *The Maisky Diaries: Red Ambassador to the Court of St James's 1932–1943*, ed. Gabriel Gorodetsky (Yale University Press, 2015)

Mallet, Marie, *Life with Queen Victoria: Marie Mallet's Letters from Court 1887–1901*, ed. Victor Mallet (John Murray, 1968)

Marie, Queen of Roumania, *The Story of My Life*, 3 vols (Cassell, 1934)

Marie Louise, Princess, *My Memories of Six Reigns* (Evans Brothers, 1956)

Marquand, David, *Ramsay MacDonald* (Jonathan Cape, 1977)

Martin, Kingsley, *The Crown and the Establishment* (Penguin, 1963)

Matthew, H.C.G., 'King George V (1865–1936)', *Oxford Dictionary of National Biography* (2004)

Maugham, W. Somerset, 'His Excellency' in *Collected Stories* (Everyman's Library, 2004)

Maylunas, Andrei and Sergei Mironenko (eds), *A Lifelong Passion: Nicholas and Alexandra – Their Own Story* (Weidenfeld & Nicolson, 1996)

Menkes, Suzy, *The Royal Jewels* (Grafton, 1985)

Michael, Prince, of Greece, *Eddy and Hélène: . . . An Impossible Match* (Rosvall Royal Books, 2013)

Middlemas, Keith and John Barnes, *Baldwin: A Biography* (Weidenfeld & Nicolson, 1969)

Midleton, Earl of, *Records & Reactions 1856–1939* (John Murray, 1939)

Millar, Peter, 'The other prince', *Sunday Times*, 26 January 2003

Milne, A. A., *When We Were Very Young* (Methuen, 1924)

Mitford, Nancy, *Love from Nancy: The Letters of Nancy Mitford*, ed. Charlotte Mosley (Sceptre, 1994); *The Pursuit of Love* (Penguin, [1945] 2010)

Montefiore, Simon Sebag, *The Romanovs 1613–1918* (Weidenfeld & Nicolson, 2016)

Morgan, Helen, *Blue Mauritius: The Hunt for the World's Most Valuable Stamps* (Atlantic, 2006)

Morshead, Owen, 'King George V' in *Oxford Dictionary of National Biography 1931–1940* (Oxford University Press, 1949)

Mort, Frank, 'Safe for Democracy: Constitutional Politics, Popular Spectacle, and the British Monarchy 1910–1914', *Journal of British Studies*, vol. 58, no. 1 (2019); 'Accessible Sovereignty: Popular Attitudes to the British Monarchy during the Great War', *Social History*, vol. 45, no. 3 (2020)

Mulvagh, Jane, *Madresfield: The Real Brideshead – One House, One Family, One Thousand Years* (Doubleday, 2008)

Nairn, Ian, *Nairn's London* (Penguin, 1966)

Nash, Michael N., *Royal Wills in Britain from 1509 to 2008* (Palgrave Macmillan, 2017)

Nicholson, Steve, *The Censorship of British Drama 1900–1968, Vol. 1: 1900–1932* (University of Exeter Press, 2003)

Nicolson, Harold, *King George the Fifth: His Life and Reign* (Constable, 1952); *Diaries and Letters of Sir Harold Nicolson 1930–62*, ed. Nigel Nicolson, 3 vols (Collins, 1966–8); *Diaries and Letters 1930–64*, ed. Stanley Olson (Collins, 1980); *Some People* (Oxford University Press, [1927] 1983)

Olechnowicz, Andrzej, ed., *The Monarchy and the British Nation, 1790 to the Present* (Cambridge University Press, 2007)

Orwell, George, 'The Lion and the Unicorn' in *Essays* (Everyman's Library, 2002)

Owens, Edward, *The Family Firm: Monarchy, Mass Media and the British Public 1932–53* (University of London Press, 2019), http://humanities-digital-library.org/index.php/hdl/catalog/book/family-firm

Pack, Captain S.W.C., *Britannia at Dartmouth* (Alvin Redman, 1966)

Pakula, Hannah, *The Last Romantic: A Biography of Queen Marie of Roumania* (Weidenfeld & Nicolson, 1985); *An Uncommon Woman: The Empress Frederick – Daughter of Queen Victoria, Wife of the Crown Prince of Prussia, Mother of Kaiser Wilhelm* (Weidenfeld & Nicolson, 1996)

Paulley, Sarah, 'Earl and Countess Beauchamp: A Queer Marriage', unpublished MA thesis, University of Buckingham (2019)

Petropoulos, Jonathan, *Royals and the Reich: The Princes von Hessen in Nazi Germany* (Oxford University Press, 2006)

Phenix, Patricia, *Olga Romanov: Russia's Last Grand Duchess* (Viking, 1999)

Pimlott, Ben, *Hugh Dalton* (Jonathan Cape, 1985)

Ponsonby, Sir Frederick, *Recollections of Three Reigns* (Odhams Press, n.d.)

Pope-Hennessy, James, *Queen Mary* (Phoenix Press, [1959] 2000); *The Quest for Queen Mary*, ed. Hugo Vickers (Zuleika, 2018)

Powell, Ted, *King Edward VIII: An American Life* (Oxford University Press, 2018).

Prochaska, Frank, *Royal Bounty: The Making of a Welfare Monarchy* (Yale University Press, 1995); 'George V and Republicanism 1917–1919', *Twentieth Century British History*, vol. 10, no. 1 (1999); 'Mary Adelaide, Princess [Princess Mary Adelaide of Cambridge], Duchess of Teck (1833–1897)', *Oxford Dictionary of National Biography* (2004)

The Queen's Gift Book: In Aid of Queen Mary's Convalescent Auxiliary Hospitals for Soldiers and Sailors Who Have Lost Their Limbs in the War (Hodder & Stoughton, 1915)

Quennell, Peter, ed., *A Lonely Business: A Self-Portrait of James Pope-Hennessy* (Weidenfeld & Nicolson, 1981)

Raina, Peter, *The Seventh Earl Beauchamp: A Victim of His Times* (Peter Lang, 2016)

Ramsay, J.H.R, 'A King, a Doctor, and a Convenient Death', *British Medical Journal*, vol. 308, no. 6941 (1994)

Rappaport, Helen, *The Race to Save the Romanovs: The Truth behind the Secret Plans to Rescue Russia's Imperial Family* (Hutchinson, 2018)

Reith, John, *The Reith Diaries*, ed. Charles Stewart (Collins, 1975)

Reynolds, David, *The Long Shadow: The Great War and the Twentieth Century* (Simon & Schuster, 2013)

Rhodes James, Robert, ed., *Memoirs of a Conservative: J.C.C. Davidson's Memoirs and Papers* (Weidenfeld & Nicolson, 1969)

Riddell, Lord, *More Pages from My Diary* (Country Life, 1934)

Ridley, Jane, *The Architect and his Wife: A Life of Edwin Lutyens* (Chatto & Windus, 2002); *Bertie: A Life of Edward VII* (Chatto & Windus, 2012); '"The Sport of Kings": Shooting and the Court of Edward VII', *Court Historian*, vol. 18, no. 2 (2013); *Victoria: Queen, Matriarch, Empress* (Allen Lane, 2015); 'The British Monarchy and the Tsar' in Wm Roger Louis, ed., *Resplendent Adventures with Britannia: Personalities, Politics and Culture in Britain* (I. B. Tauris / Harry Ransom Center, University of Texas at Austin, 2015); 'Harold Nicolson and Royal Biography' in Wm Roger Louis, ed., *Effervescent Adventures with Britannia: Personalities, Politics and Culture in Britain* (I. B. Tauris / Harry Ransom Center, University of Texas at Austin, 2017)

Roberts, Andrew, *Churchill* (Penguin, 2019)

Röhl, John C. G., *Wilhelm II: Into the Abyss of War and Exile 1900–1941* (Cambridge University Press, 2014)

Rose, Kenneth, *King George V* (Phoenix Press, [1983] 2000); *Who's In, Who's Out: The Journals of Kenneth Rose, Vol. 1*, ed. D. R. Thorpe (Weidenfeld & Nicolson, 2018); *Who Wins, Who Loses: The Journals of Kenneth Rose, Vol. 2*, ed. D. R. Thorpe (Weidenfeld & Nicolson, 2019).

Roskill, Stephen, *Hankey: Man of Secrets*, 3 vols (Collins, 1970–4); *Admiral of the Fleet Earl Beatty: The Last Naval Hero* (Collins, 1980)

Ruffer, Jonathan Garnier, *The Big Shots: Edwardian Shooting Parties* (Debrett's Peerage, 1977)

Sacks, Benjamin, 'The Prince of Wales's Children Act 1889', *Albion*, vol. 5, no. 4 (1973)

Sackville-West, V., *The Edwardians* (Hogarth Press, 1930)

St Aubyn, Giles, 'Henry, Prince, First Duke of Gloucester (1900–1974)', *Oxford Dictionary of National Biography* (2004)

Sandhurst, Right Hon. Viscount, *From Day to Day, Vol. 2: 1916–1921* (Edward Arnold, 1929)

Savage, Gail, 'Erotic Stories and Public Decency: Newspaper Reporting of Divorce Proceedings in England', *Historical Journal*, vol. 41, no. 2 (1998)

Service, Robert, *The Last of the Tsars: Nicholas II and the Russian Revolution* (Macmillan, 2017)

Shawcross, William, *Queen Elizabeth the Queen Mother: The Official Biography* (Macmillan, 2009)

Sheffield, Gary, ed., *In Haig's Shadow: The Letters of Major-General Hugo De Pree and Field Marshal Sir Douglas Haig* (Greenhill, 2019)

Sitwell, Osbert, *Queen Mary and Others* (Michael Joseph, 1974)

Slocombe, George, *The Tumult and the Shouting: The Memoirs of George Slocombe* (Macmillan (New York), 1936)

Soames, Mary, ed., *Speaking for Themselves: The Personal Letters of Winston and Clementine Churchill* (Black Swan, 1999)

Sorg, Moritz A., 'Of Traitors and Saints: Foreign Consorts between Accusations and Propaganda in the First World War', *Court Historian*, vol. 24, no. 1 (2019)

Statham, Commander E. P., *The Story of the 'Britannia': The Training Ship for Naval Cadets* (Cassell, 1904)

Stephenson, John, ed., *A Royal Correspondence: Letters of King Edward VII and King George V to Admiral Sir Henry F. Stephenson* (Macmillan, 1938)

Stevenson, Frances, *Lloyd George: A Diary*, ed. A.J.P. Taylor (Hutchinson, 1971)

Stourton, James, *Kenneth Clark: Life, Art and 'Civilisation'* (William Collins, 2017)

Strachey, Lytton, *Queen Victoria* (Collins, [1921] 1958)

Summers, Anthony and Tom Mangold, *The File on the Tsar* (Orion, [1976] 2002)

Sylvester, A. J., *Life with Lloyd George: The Diary of A. J. Sylvester*, ed. Colin Cross (Macmillan, 1975)

Tanner, Michael, *The Suffragette Derby* (Robson Press, 2013)

Taylor, D. J., *Bright Young People: The Rise and Fall of a Generation 1918–1940* (Vintage, 2008)

Templewood, Viscount, *Nine Troubled Years* (Collins, 1954)

Tinniswood, Adrian, *Behind the Throne: A Domestic History of the Royal Household* (Jonathan Cape, 2018)

Trzebinski, Errol, *The Lives of Beryl Markham* (Heinemann, 1993)

Tschumi, Gabriel, *Royal Chef: Recollections of Life in Royal Households from Queen Victoria to Queen Mary* (William Kimber, 1954)

Tuchman, Barbara W., *August 1914* (Macmillan, 1980)

Turner, E. S., *The Court of St. James's* (Michael Joseph, 1959)

Van der Kiste, John, *Edward VII's Children* (Alan Sutton, 1989)

Van der Kiste, John and Coryne Hall, *Once a Grand Duchess: Xenia, Sister of Nicholas II* (Sutton, 2002)

Vickers, Hugo, *Elizabeth the Queen Mother* (Hutchinson, 2005)

Victoria, Queen, *The Letters of Queen Victoria, Second Series: A Selection from Her Majesty's Correspondence and Journal Between the Years 1862 and 1878*, ed. George Earle Buckle, 2 vols (John Murray, 1926); *Advice to a Grand-Daughter: Letters from Queen Victoria to Princess Victoria of Hesse*, ed. Richard Hough (Readers Union, 1976)

Vidal, Gore, *Palimpsest: A Memoir* (André Deutsch, 1995)

Villiers, John, 'Sir Francis Villiers and the Fall of the Portuguese Monarchy', http://www.mod-langs.ox.ac.uk/files/windsor/7_villiers.pdf

Vincent, James Edmund, *His Royal Highness Duke of Clarence and Avondale: A Memoir* (John Murray, 1893)

Vincent, Vin, *Olga; or, Wrong on Both Sides* (Griffith Farran Browne, [1885])

Vorres, Ian, *The Last Grand-Duchess: Her Imperial Highness Grand-Duchess Olga Alexandrovna* (Hutchinson, 1964)

Warner, Marina, 'Death in plain sight', *London Review of Books*, 4 July 2013

Watson, Francis, *Dawson of Penn* (Chatto & Windus, 1950); 'The Death of George V', *History Today*, December 1986

Waugh, Evelyn, *Vile Bodies* (Penguin, [1930] 1938); *Brideshead Revisited* (Everyman's Library, [1945] 1993)

Webb, Beatrice, *The Diary of Beatrice Webb*, ed. Norman and Jeanne MacKenzie, 4 vols (Virago, 1982–5)

Welch, Frances, *The Russian Court at Sea: The Last Days of a Great Dynasty – the Romanovs' Voyage into Exile* (Short, 2011); *The Imperial Tea Party: Family, Politics and Betrayal – the Ill-Fated British and Russian Royal Alliance* (Short, 2018)

Wells, H. G., *Mr Britling Sees It Through* (Cassell, 1916)

Westminster, Loelia, Duchess of, *Grace and Favour: The Memoirs of Loelia, Duchess of Westminster* (Weidenfeld & Nicolson, 1961)

Wheeler-Bennett, John, *King George VI: His Life and Reign* (Macmillan, 1958)

White, Carolyn W., 'The Strange Death of Liberal England in Its Time', *Albion*, vol. 17, no. 4 (1985)

Wilde, Oscar, *The Picture of Dorian Gray* (Penguin [1891] 2012)

Williams, Robin Harcourt, ed., *The Salisbury–Balfour Correspondence: Letters Exchanged between the Third Marquess of Salisbury and His Nephew Arthur James Balfour 1869–1892* (Hertfordshire Record Society, 1988)

Williams, Susan, *The People's King: The True Story of the Abdication* (Penguin, 2004)

Williamson, Philip, 'The Monarchy and Public Values 1900–1953' in Andrzej Olechno-
wicz, ed., *The Monarchy and the British Nation, 1790 to the Present* (Cambridge
University Press, 2007); 'National Days of Prayer: The Churches, the State and Public
Worship in Britain 1899–1957', *English Historical Review*, vol. 128, no. 531 (2013)

Williamson, Philip and Edward Baldwin, eds, *Baldwin Papers: A Conservative Statesman, 1908–1947* (Cambridge University Press, 2004)

Wilson, H. W. and J. A. Hammerton, eds., *The Great War: The Standard History of the
All-Europe Conflict*, 13 vols (Amalgamated Press, 1914–19)

Windsor, Edward, Duke of, *A King's Story: The Memoirs of HRH the Duke of Windsor* (Cassell, 1951); *A Family Album* (Cassell, 1960)

Woodward, David R., *Lloyd George and the Generals* (Associated University Presses,
1983)

Woodward, Kathleen, *Queen Mary: A Life and Intimate Study* (Hutchinson, 1929)

Woolf, Virginia, *Orlando: A Biography* (Penguin, [1928] 1942); *The Diary of Virginia
Woolf*, ed. Anne Olivier Bell, 5 vols (Penguin, 1979–85); *Mrs Dalloway* (Everyman's
Library, [1925] 1993)

Wrench, John Evelyn, *Geoffrey Dawson and Our Times* (Hutchinson, 1955)

'X' (Herbert Vivian), *Myself Not Least: Being the Personal Reminiscences of 'X'*
(Thornton Butterworth, 1925)

Ziegler, Philip, *Mountbatten: The Official Biography* (Fontana, 1986); *King Edward
VIII: The Official Biography* (Collins, 1990); 'George, Prince, First Duke of Kent
(1902–1942)', *Oxford Dictionary of National Biography* (2004)

Index